TRUE GHOST STORIES

OF THE

BRITISH ISLES

TRUE GHOST STORIES

OF THE
BRITISH ISLES

ℬℬ Bounty
Books

First published in 2005 by Bounty Books,
a division of Octopus Publishing Group Ltd
2–4 Heron Quays, London E14 4JP

ISBN 0 7537 1117 6
ISBN13 9780753711170

A CIP catalogue record for this book is available from
the British Library

Printed and bound in Spain

CONTENTS

THE GHOST THAT STUMBLED
Harry Price

Certainly, something was coming down the stairs, but who got the greatest scare when the flashlight powder went off?

Are poltergeists "ghosts in solid form"? Are they tangible three-dimentional entities? Though able to cause noises, do they, too, make sounds when in impact with non-resisting bodies? Some of these queries are answered in the following adventure I had when I was very young, proving, I think, that ghosts can indeed solidify themselves on occasion.

As a member of an old Shropshire family, I spent nearly all my holidays and school vacations in a little village which I shall call Parton Magna. In Parton Magna is the old Manor House which was built in about 1600. It had been purchased by a retired canon of the Church of England and his wife. There were rumours that the place was haunted — but popular tradition provides a ghost for every old country house, especially if a tragedy has taken place within it.

Within a very few weeks of the canon's settling down with his household in their new home, reports were received of curious happenings in the stables and outbuildings. Though fastened securely overnight, stable doors were found ajar in the morning. Animals were discovered untethered and wandering; pans of milk were overturned in the dairy, and utensils scattered about.

The woodshed received the attentions of the nocturnal visitant nearly every night. Piles of logs neatly stacked were found scattered in the morning, in spite of the fact that the door of the shed was kept locked. The manifestations in the woodshed became so frequent and troublesome that it was decided to keep watch. This was done on several evenings, a farm hand secreting himself behind a stack of logs.

Upon every occasion when a watch was kept on the wood, nothing happened inside the shed. On those nights when the shed was watched from within, pebbles were flung onto the corrugated iron roofing, the noise they made rolling down the metal being plainly heard. Then a watch was kept both inside and outside the shed, but no one was seen, though the pebbles were heard as before. The experienced reader will recognize in my narrative a poltergeist case running true to type.

The disturbances around the house continued with unabated vigour week after week until even local interest waned somewhat. Then quite suddenly they almost ceased, the disturbing entity transferring its activities to the inside of the mansion.

The Manor House was built for comfort, though it had been restored at various times. From the large hall a wide staircase leads to a landing. At the top of the stairs, of which there are 15, is or was a solid oak gate placed across to prevent dogs from roaming over the whole house. The staircase I have mentioned leads to the more important rooms opening out of a short gallery.

The first indication received by the canon and his family that the entity had turned its attention to the interior of the house was a soft "pattering" sound, as of a child's bare feet running up and down the wide passage or gallery. The noises were at first taken to be those caused by a large bird or small animal from the fields, but investigation proved fruitless. Then the maids commenced complaining that the kitchen utensils were being disturbed; usually during their absence. Pots and pans would fall off shelves for no ascertainable reason when a maid was within a few feet of them, but always when her back was turned.

Another curious circumstance connected with this case was the disturbing entity's fondness for raking out the fires during the night. The danger of fire from this cause was so obvious that, before retiring to rest, the canon's wife had water poured on the dying embers.

On my way back to school for the Michaelmas term I broke my journey at Parton Magna in order to visit friends who then made me acquainted with the state of affairs at the Manor House; in fact, it was the principal topic of conversation. The canon and his household had by then vacated their home temporarily, the premises being looked after by the wife of one of the cowmen. What really drove the family out was the fact that the nocturnal noises were becoming greater; in particular, a steady thump (as of some one in heavy boots stamping about the house), disturbing the rest of the inmates night after night. I decided I would investigate and invited a friend to join me in my adventure.

I must confess that I had not the slightest idea what we were going to do, or going to see, or what I ought to take with me in the way of apparatus. But the last question was very soon settled because all I had with me was a one-quarter plate "Lancaster" stand camera. On the morning of the adventure I cycled into the nearest town and bought some magnesium powder, a bell switch, a hank of flex wire, two batteries and some sulphuric acid.

In the afternoon I assembled my batteries and switch and prepared the flash powder, by means of which I hoped to photograph — something! So that there would be no unwillingness on the part of the magnesium to go off at the proper moment, I extracted the white smokeless gunpowder from four or five sporting cartridges and mixed it with the magnesium powder.

By a lucky chance I had with me a delicate chemical balance which I was taking back to school, and with the weights was a platinum wire "rider", which I inserted in the electrical circuit in order to ignite the magnesium flash powder. With the above-mentioned impedimenta, matches, candles, chalk, string, a box of rapid plates and a parcel of food, we bade farewell to our friends and made our way across the fields to the Manor House, where we arrived about 9:30 p.m.

The first thing we did was to search every room and attic, and close and fasten every window. We then locked all the doors and removed the keys. The doors leading to the exterior of the house were locked, bolted and barred, and chairs or other obstacles piled in front of them. We were determined that no material beings should enter without our knowing it. After we had searched every nook and cranny of the building, we established ourselves in the morning room, locked the door and waited for something — or somebody — to turn up. Our only illumination was the light from a candle which we placed on a table.

About half past eleven, my friend thought he heard a noise in the room overhead. A moment or two later there was another thud that left nothing to the imagination. It sounded as if someone had stumbled over a chair. We braced our nerves and awaited developments. Just before midnight we again heard a noise in the room above; it was as if a heavy person were stamping about with clogs. A minute or so later the footfalls sounded as if they had left the room and were traversing the short gallery. Then they approached the head of the stairs, paused at the dog gate (which we had securely fastened with string), and commenced descending.

We distinctly counted the 15 thumps corresponding to the number of stairs — and I hardly need mention that our hearts were thumping in unison. "It" seemed to pause in the hall, and the fact that only a door intervened between us and the mysterious intruder made us take a lively interest in what its next move would be. We were not kept long in suspense. The entity, having paused in the hall for about three minutes, turned tail and began stumping up the stairs again. We again counted the number of thumps and were satisfied that "it" was at the top of the flight — where again a halt was made at the dog gate.

All became quiet once more and my friend and I had just decided to investigate when we clearly heard the thumps descending once again. With quickened pulse I counted the 15 heavy footsteps, which were getting nearer and nearer and louder and louder. There was another pause in the hall and once again the footsteps commenced their upward journey. By this time the excitement of the adventure was making us bolder; we decided to have a look at our quarry, if it were visible, so with my courage in one hand and the camera in the other, I opened the door. My friend was close behind me with the candle. By this time the "ghost" was on the fifth stair, and with the opening of the door leading into the hall the noise of ascent stopped dead.

Realizing that the "ghost" was as frightened of meeting us as we were of seeing it, we decided to re-examine the stairs and upper part of the house. This we did very thoroughly, but found nothing disturbed. The dog gate was still latched and tied with string. To this day I am wondering whether "it" climbed over the gate or slipped through the bars. I think we were disappointed at not seeing anything we could photograph, so decided to make an attempt at a flashlight picture if the poltergeist would descend the stairs again.

For my stand for the flash powder I utilized some household steps about six feet high which we found in the kitchen. I opened out the steps and placed them about 12 feet from the bottom of the stairs. On the top of the steps, in an old Waterbury watch case, I placed a heaped-up eggcupful of the magnesium-cum-gunpowder mixture — enough to photograph every ghost in the county!

But in my simple enthusiasm I running no risks of underexposure. I placed the batteries in the morning room and connected them up with the magnesium powder on the steps and the bell push on the floor of the room, the wire flex entering the room under the door. In the heap of powder I had buried my platinum "rider" which was interposed in the electrical circuit.

The exact position as to where we should photograph the entity presented some difficulty. We were not quite sure what happened to it when it reached the hall, so we decided to make an attempt at photographing it when it was ascending the stairs. I stationed my friend on the seventh stair and he held a lighted match which I accurately focused on the glass of my camera that I had placed on one of the treads of the steps. I inserted the dark slide, withdrew the flap, uncapped the lens, and then all was ready.

By the time we had fixed up the camera and examined the connections it was about half past one. During the time we were moving about the hall not a sound was heard from abovestairs. Having arranged everything to our satisfaction, we returned to the morning room, locked the door again and extinguished the candle. Then we lay upon the carpet near the door, with the pear-push in my hand, and commenced our vigil.

It must have been nearly an hour before we heard anything, and again it was from the room above. Shortly after, the thumps could be heard approaching the dog gate and again "it" paused at the top of the stairs. The pause was greater than the previous one, and for a minute or so we thought the "ghost" had come to the end of its journey; but no, it passed over — or through — the gate and commenced stumping down the stairs again.

Having reached the hall the visitant stopped, and in my mind's eye I could picture it examining the arrangements we had made for taking its photograph. Then we thought we heard the steps moved. In order to get the camera square with the stairs I had taken a large book — using it as a set-square — and drawn on the tiled floor a chalk line parallel with the stairs. Exactly against this line I had placed the two front feet of the steps.

During the next five or six minutes we heard no movement in the hall. Then suddenly "it" started its return journey. With our hearts beating wildly, we lay on the floor counting the slow, measured thumps as they ascended. At the seventh thump I pressed the button of my pear-push and — a most extraordinary thing happened, which is rather difficult to describe on paper.

At the moment of the explosion the "ghost" was so startled that it involuntarily stumbled, as we could plainly hear, and then there was silence. At the same moment there was a clattering as if the spontaneous disintegration of the disturbing entity had taken place. The flash from the ignition of the powder was so vivid that even the morning room from which we were directing operations was lit up by the rays coming from under the ill-fitting door.

It would be difficult to say who was the more startled, the

poltergeist or myself, and for some moments we did nothing. After our astonishment had subsided somewhat we opened the door and found the hall filled with a dense white smoke. We re-capped the camera, relit our candle, and made a tour of inspection.

The first thing we noticed was that the steps were shifted slightly out of the square. The Waterbury watch case had disappeared with my platinum "rider" and I have never seen the latter from that day to this. The watch case we found on the second stair from the bottom.

What happened to it was apparently this: through the extremely rapid conversion of the gunpowder and magnesium into gases, and the concavity of the interior of the case tending to retain the gases, the case was converted into a projectile, and propelled towards the stairs like a rocket. It must have hit them at about the spot where the entity was ascending — surely the only recorded instance of a ghost having a watch case fired at it.

The sound of the watch case falling was the rattling noise we heard when we thought we should find our quarry lying in pieces at the foot of the staircase. We immediately developed the plate but nothing but an overexposed picture of the staircase was on the negative.

The Manor House continued to be the centre of psychic activity for some months after our curious adventure but the disturbances gradually became less frequent and eventually ceased.

THE HAUNTED FLAT
Sara Gerstle

When I joined my daughter in London one late spring in the carefree 1920's I had no reason to anticipate anything but an amusing period filled with theatres, concerts, Russian ballet, a certain amount of social life, visits to well-known, well-loved museums and drives in the lovely country that surrounds London. And so it turned out — with one exception.

Miriam had preceded me by a couple of months, to find a flat and engage a maid, as hitherto we had known London only as hotel-dwellers and thought it would be fun to invite our friends to our own table and pretend we had always been London householders. She wrote that she had found an ideal place, on a quiet street where the West End melts into St. John's Wood, large enough for our needs and small enough to be run by a "cook-general." It was available for immediate occupancy so Miriam had moved in at once, engaged an excellent maid who actually had some notions of good cooking. The household was well settled when I arrived.

As we drove home from the station I thought Miriam seemed rather nervous and over-anxious that I should be pleased with her choice of a house. I was touched by her solicitude and slightly irritated at the same time. I have never considered myself fussy about living quarters when travelling, so long as they are clean and reasonably quiet.

"You described the place as a 'maisonette'," I said; "and I keep visualizing it as a sort of large doll's house at the bottom of a garden. What's the difference between a maisonette and a flat?"

"I think it's because it has two floors."

"A duplex, you mean?"

"That's what we could call it, I suppose. This is a four-story house that has been divided into two flats, each completely self-contained. We have the two top floors, as I wrote to you. The people downstairs are very nice — she is a daughter of George du Maurier and the place is full of his original drawings. She has asked me to bring

15

you to tea some day soon. I never hear them once I am in our own flat. That is — no, I never hear a sound from their quarters."

I looked at her in some surprise. She always has been a highly articulate, self-possessed person, and now she gave me the impression of being not only nervous but a trifle confused.

"You wrote you sublet it from an Italian woman — she isn't the owner, then?"

"Baroness Coletti. No, the owner is a Mrs. Bond, who lives the year round in the country now. I have never met her. Baroness Coletti's lease runs until the end of August."

"She went back to Italy?"

Once again Miriam hesitated. "No, she is spending the summer in London. I think she is a relative of the ambassador or his wife. She has taken a suite in a hotel."

"She didn't like the maisonette?"

This time there was no doubt about it; Miriam's reply was much too quick, much too eager, to ring true.

"Oh yes, from what she told me she loved it, and hated to leave. I — I think it had something to do with her Italian maid, who has been with her for years and couldn't get used to English household ways. This is Upper Gloucester Place now. The house is only a few doors farther on."

The taxi drew up before a wide blue door with a pretty fanlight and dazzling polished brasses. It was an attractive house, Georgian in type, and I liked the street on sight. It was quiet, dignified, a typical London street in a good neighborhood, the sort of street Thackeray might have lived in. I felt a proprietary thrill when I saw my own name on one of the glittering mail boxes. This was going to be fun.

The entrance hall was well lighted and immaculate. A second blue door obviously led to the lower flat and a stairway led up two easy flights to yet a third blue door, with our names above the bell, and an exceedingly neat, pleasant-faced middle-aged maid waiting to greet us.

"This is Isabel, Mother."

"I am happy to welcome you, madam."

The house matched the street, and Isabel matched the house, and I liked them all. On one side of the small hall was a spacious drawing room, furnished simply but in good taste and bright with potted flowering plants that friends had sent to greet me. A good-sized bedroom opened off it, destined for me, with comfortable old-fashioned furniture, including the traditional washstand with bowl and ewer, a glass carafe for drinking water, and no doubt, at stated hours, a brass can with hot water. Miriam said her own smaller room was across the hall, next to a little spiral stair leading to the upper floor.

"And the bathroom?"

"That's the only inconvenient thing — it's upstairs, along with the dining room, kitchen and maid's room. Then there's another room, or cupboard or something, that is locked. Baroness Coletti hadn't the key to it. She thinks it is full of Mrs. Bond's things. We don't really need it. You get used to going upstairs to take a bath, though it seems odd at first. The water is really hot and the 'geyser' hasn't blown up yet. You do like it, darling?"

Again that unnecessary solicitude! I assured her I couldn't like it more, and got down to the business of unpacking after I had been introduced to a small, very lively black kitten called Muffin.

The next few days passed uneventfully, seeing friends, getting back into the London atmosphere, enjoying the efficient ministrations of Isabel and playing with the kitten, who proved to have a surprising amount of character, mostly bad. Miriam continued to fuss over me like a hen with one chicken and to ply me with questions as to my comfort and contentment. I concluded this was only natural, since it was the first time she had undertaken to make arrangements for me without being able to consult me, and she might well feel diffident about it.

Then things began to happen. One day I returned home for lunch after a long walk, to be greeted by an almost overpowering scent of violets as I opened our front door. My first idea was that Miriam must have bought a whole barrowful of violets in a moment of compassion for the vendor — the sort of thing she was quite capable of doing. She was lunching out, so it was not possible to ask her, but I opened the drawing room door, expecting to see a wealth of violets. The only flora in the room had been there since I arrived — just a few odourless azalea and cyclamen plants. A glance into my bedroom revealed nothing botanical but a primula Miriam had brought me, and in her room there was only a small pot of ivy. I started to sniff up the spiral stairway, then was stopped in my tracks by the realization that the scent of violets was no longer perceptible. It couldn't have vanished so suddenly, odours don't simply go out like lights — but it had.

I went to my own room, mechanically put away my hat and gloves, still sniffing like a nervous dog. There was no use in calling Isabel to ask her where the smell of violets came from, because her obvious answer would be "What violets, Madam?" There was no point in telling myself that perhaps we'd had a caller who was addicted to strong violet perfume, because in that event the scent would have lingered. As a matter of fact, when Isabel announced lunch I asked her casually if we'd had any calls, and her answer was no. I reminded myself that since there was such a thing as optical illusion there was no reason why one shouldn't be the victim of an olfactory illusion. I didn't think much of that solution but it was the best I could do. The whole thing seemed too silly to mention to Miriam. If I suddenly developed hallucinations the least I could do was keep it to myself.

The next day we were invited to lunch with friends at the Berkeley, and Miriam left before I did to do some errands while I wrote letters. Seeing it was time to dress, I rose from my desk, which was in a corner of my bedroom, and my glance fell on the washstand against the opposite wall.

What in the name of Sir Oliver Lodge was the matter with the carafe?

The room was well lighted, like all the rooms in the flat, and it was a bright day. There were no tricky shadows in the room except for a column of vapour hovering over the carafe of water, dense white vapour or smoke, quite motionless and opaque.

I thought of the Arabian Nights and the genie who came out of a bottle in the form of a column of smoke. Then I told myself that this was an authentic, unquestionable example of the optical illusion I had thought of the day before, when my nose had played such an odd trick on me. Now my eyes were doing the same thing. I resorted to the childish device of rubbing them. That did no good. So I moved nearer to the washstand, and forced myself to examine it in detail.

Everything was perfectly in order — blue and white basin and jug, matching soap dish and tooth mug, spotless towels, my bottle of hand lotion and box of toothpowder. The water in the carafe was as clear as the glass itself. The cloud above it was obviously imaginary; but imaginary or not it completely obscured several inches of the mahogany frame on the mirror that hung above the washstand. I ran my eyes over the frame, all visible except for that section which the cloud concealed. Then I remembered to look in the mirror: if the cloud really existed, it would be reflected, at least partially, in the glass. It wasn't.

I don't think that either then or in the course of the strange things that happened later I was actually afraid. Perhaps I was too interested, too puzzled and anxious to find a reasonable explanation. Certainly I was considerably shaken, and if I had taken my pulse no doubt I would have found it very rapid; but my only thought at that particular moment was that I was seeing something that could not possibly be there. Because if the mirror reflected everything else within its range it must inevitably reflect that as well. The hallucination must be a creation of my imagination. But why? Nothing of the sort had ever happened to me before.

Meanwhile, unless I got dressed I should be late for my luncheon engagement. I tore my eyes from the thing above the carafe, found a dress and shoes in the wardrobe, put them on, chose a hat, fixed my face. I refrained from looking at the washstand until I could no longer resist stealing a glance.

The cloud was gone!

In the taxi I argued with myself about the authenticity of my experience and then decided that I preferred, on the whole, to believe that there was something supernatural in the house in Upper Gloucester Place rather than regard myself as the victim of hallucinations. There was one detail that worried me. As I left my room I noticed the kitten playing happily with his tail in a patch of sunlight. He had been there all the time; I had noticed him, in an absentminded way, while I was dressing, and he had behaved quite normally, not at all in the way animals are popularly supposed to behave when there are supernatural manifestations in their vicinity. I had often read and heard that cats and dogs are far more sensitive than humans to any sort of physical phenomena. If that were true it shot my theory full of holes.

I may as well say here that from start to finish Muffin never displayed the slightest sign of fear or uneasiness. So we finally decided that (a) cats are not psychic, or that (b) this particular cat was a case of arrested development in that respect. Miriam once came up with a third theory: That the cat knew so much about that sort of thing that he wasn't even interested.

I am afraid I was not a very stimulating luncheon guest that day. I thought Miriam was watching me rather narrowly but decided to say nothing to her about my puzzle, since it was quite possible that there would be no further manifestations and there was no sense in making her unnecessarily nervous.

Only a few days later I changed my mind.

We were giving our first small dinner party. There were just six of us, the most our little dining room could accommodate. With the fish course the conversation turned, with no assistance from me, to Sir Arthur Conan Doyle and why he had become a convert to Spiritualism. I was still rather tense as the result of something that had happened while I was dressing for dinner, and suddenly I decided that this was as good a time as any to drag my problem into the open. One of our guests had said that he found it almost inconceivable that a man of Sir Arthur's intelligence could believe in "all that nonsense."

"A short while ago I should probably have agreed with you," I said, "although I try to keep an open mind where other people's beliefs are concerned. But I have had some curious experiences since I have been in London, and now I am no longer certain about just what I do believe."

Miriam's fork clicked sharply against her plate as she put it down.

"There is something definitely strange about this house," I went on, "and so far I have been able to find no sensible explanation for it."

"Mother! You didn't tell me."

"You haven't done much talking yourself," I reminded my only child.

"How do you mean, something strange," one of the men asked.

I tried not to sound too dramatic, to keep my voice casual and my words commonplace.

"Well for example, only this evening while I was dressing I saw an oddly shaped shadow in a corner of my room, that swayed upward until it merged into the ceiling."

There was a rustle of relaxation, except on Miriam's part.

"Oh, but surely there's nothing unusual about that," someone said. "Once the lamps are lit there are all sorts of shadows in any room."

"The days are very long at this season," I replied. "I was dressing by daylight. There was no need for lamps and there was nothing in the room, no open door or large piece of furniture, that could possibly cast a shadow in that particular corner. Yet I saw it as clearly as I see all of you."

"Was it — ah — sort of cone-shaped?" Miriam asked in a small voice.

Our eyes met.

"Yes it was; a very tall cone reaching from the floor almost to the ceiling and it was a darkish grey, a good many shades darker than the wall. Do you know that too?"

"It was in the drawing room yesterday afternoon when you were out for a walk," Miriam confessed. "Only it was sort of hovering around the door that opens into your room. Usually it sticks to corners."

At this point Isabel came in to change the plates and by common consent the conversation shifted to a new play at the Haymarket. Everyone apparently realized that there was no sense in alarming a maid who could turn out the very good sole au vin blanc we had just eaten. But it seemed to me the guests did not help themselves very plentifully from the dish that followed, and at least one of the men was casting uneasy glances at the corners of the room.

I reproached myself for being an inconsiderate hostess and determined to keep the conversation on more normal subjects. But as soon as Isabel had served us everybody started talking at once, plying me with questions. Had I seen anything else? Had I heard anything? Could someone in the lower flat be playing practical jokes on us? Had Miriam noticed anything aside from the shadow? She was visibly relieved at being able to tell her own story." I began to notice peculiar things almost from the day I moved in. At first I thought it was pure hallucination and I was worried about myself, because obviously the maid had seen nothing or she would have given notice then and there. And the kitten has never behaved as if anything were wrong. That bothered me because animals are supposed to be psychic."

Here I interpolated my own doubts concerning the cat.

"For some time I didn't see anything," Miriam went on, "but I used to hear things in another room. When I went to see who was there, of course there wasn't anybody, not even the kitten. Once when I was reading in the drawing room I heard a noise as if something heavy had fallen or been thrown against the door, and then a sound in the room that Mother has now, a dripping kind of sound, — like blood."

My right-hand neighbour suddenly lost interest in his roast beef and Yorkshire pudding. I tried to catch my daughter's eye but she was off to a good start and quite oblivious to everything but her recital.

"Then there were those damn violets." I must have given a chirp of satisfaction for she said, "You too, darling? I love violets, but if I'm going to smell 'em all the time, I'd just as soon they were real violets, not imaginary ones. They don't come into the rooms, though. They stay in the entrance hall. At first I thought some woman had been here with either fresh violets or a strong violet scent, but there had been no one but Isabel and me. Besides, the scent didn't linger as it normally would. It came and went suddenly, like turning a tap on and off. So I knew it wasn't — well, it wasn't real."

"Perhaps we don't always know what is real and what isn't," a woman guest remarked quietly. "'There are more things in Heaven and earth', you know."

"I know, but it's natural to try to find a rational explanation for everything. We instinctively try to pull all our experiences inside the frame of the world we know."

"Why didn't you mention it to me?" I asked her.

"Because I wasn't at all sure you would notice anything — Isabel hadn't, and it was quite possible that I was suffering from hallucinations. I didn't want to prejudice you against the house. After all, I picked it out. In case you didn't see or hear anything out of the way I didn't want to scare you into thinking that your only child was potty. If after a few weeks you hadn't mentioned it, I decided I'd hunt up a good psychiatrist and try to find out what was wrong with me. I can't tell you how relieved I am to know that it isn't just my imagination."

Here one of the men, obviously not too happy at being in a haunted house, remarked that there was such a thing as mass suggestion and that a similarity of temperament in members of the same family might make two persons susceptible to the same impressions. The idea seemed to cheer him up and, as I realized we were depressing our guests, I let the conversation drift into the channel of mass hypnosis, which led inevitably to the good old Indian rope trick and diverted our guests from the immediate problem of Upper Gloucester Place.

There was no denying that they left rather early.

After that we had no secrets from each other concerning the manifestations which recurred frequently. When I felt various parts of my body being lightly touched as I lay in bed, I told Miriam, and she in turn informed me that the violets were back in the entrance hall, or that when she was in her bath she thought I called her from the floor below. She answered and there was no reply — in fact, at the moment I was out of the house posting a letter. That particular phenomenon became almost monotonous. One of us was always thinking she heard the other speak when such was not the case. It got to the point that when one or the other actually did call from room to room we would say "This is me, darling, not the Thing."

For a brief moment I thought I might have a solution to the mystery. When I arrived my room was liberally decorated with framed photographs of Mrs. Bond's twin girls, in every conceivable costume — riding, swimming, tennis, evening dress. I admired their versatility in sports but they got on my nerves, so after a few days I removed them from the walls and stacked them in a cupboard. It occurred to me that I might have offended them and that they were retaliating. But Miriam poured cold water on that theory by reminding me that she had already observed most of the phenomena long before I came, when the twins were in full possession of my room. That was that.

We also speculated on the locked room on the upper floor but although the Bluebeard theme is always attractive, it didn't seem to make sense, for the upper floor, so far as we could discover, was entirely immune from the manifestations. We never noticed anything strange in the dining room. When we heard voices in the bathroom they always seemed to come from downstairs; and Isabel was obviously quite undisturbed in her kitchen and bedroom. We never knew what was in the locked room but it probably contained nothing more interesting than the unwanted furniture and shabby trunks that are to be found in any attic.

I wish I could end this account with the history of our maisonette and what lay behind its unnatural visitations. But this is a true story, and at the end of the summer we were no wiser than we had been at the beginning. We grew accustomed to the strange things that happened, although we never pretended to enjoy them. When Miriam went out in the evening I never felt sleepy until I heard her return, and I instinctively sat with my back to the wall, so I could see every corner of the room, with Muffin at my feet for company. One night I saw a light cross the wall, the origin of which I could not determine since the curtains were drawn so that no light could enter from the street.

I never felt that there was anything malevolent in the manifestations but I remember saying to Miriam as the term of our lease was drawing to an end: "If this thing is going to get us it will have to be in the next few days." Towards the end of our stay several of our friends confessed to an odd sense of depression when they were visiting us and a feeling of relief when they left; but that could have been because we had told them of our "haunt." On the other hand one frequent visitor who was deeply interested in psychical research and anxious to see or hear something significant, never observed anything in the least extraordinary. We often discussed the possibility of holding a spiritualistic séance in the flat but no one knew of a reliable medium.

When I had been in London about a month we were invited to tea by our landlady, Baroness Coletti, who, to our surprise, was not living in a hotel but in a flat similar to the one she had sublet to us.

Since the neighbourhood was no more convenient than Upper Gloucester Place, the inevitable question came to my mind — why leave one furnished flat for another, no better in any respect?

The baroness, an attractive, vivacious woman, gave us an excellent tea and for a time the conversation kept to the usual chit-chat of the London Season — new plays, the horse show, Ascot, the Russian ballet — but we were conscious that our hostess was observing us rather closely, and I was prepared for it when she said she hoped we were happy in Upper Gloucester Place.

Miriam beat me to an answer.

"We'd be very happy there," she said, "if it weren't haunted."

Baroness Coletti studied the design on her teacup for a moment, then looked from one to the other of us with troubled eyes.

"Oh dear," she murmured; "I had hoped you would not be disturbed."

"You were disturbed, though?" I asked.

"But of course, that is why I moved. I loved the flat, loved the neighbourhood; it inconvenienced me very much to move; but it got so that when I went out I could hardly bear the idea of returning to that house. At night I could not sleep unless I took a sedative. Then my maid told me that if I remained there she would have to give notice; and as she has been with me for years and I am very fond of her, of course there was nothing to do but find another place and get permission from Mrs. Bond to sublet that one." She paused, raised her eyebrows, and smiled. "Mrs. Bond," she added, "was very nice about it. She seemed almost to be expecting my request."

Suddenly I felt rather sorry for Mrs. Bond, although I still can't imagine why she didn't sell the house.

"That," I assented, "does not surprise me in the least."

THE GHOST WHO WON'T BE LAID

William H. Gilroy

Voices, footsteps, strange noises — even ancient rites of exorcism have failed to lay this ghost

"Secret rites from ancient chronicles were carried out in Bristol last night by the Rev. Francis Maddock, 36-year-old vicar of St. Anne's, in his service of exorcism in ghost-haunted No. 13, Highworth Road. The Rev. Maddock had been called in by Mr. William Baber, whose wife says that when she opened a room which had been locked for 18 years she let loose the spirit of a former owner."

The above item appeared in the *London Daily Mail* of last 25 January. The story went on to relate the procedure followed by the young vicar as he performed the ancient rituals deemed necessary for the "laying" of the ghost. Conducting the secret service behind heavily curtained windows, the Rev. Maddock accompanied by Mr. Baber first went to the upstairs box-room where the possessions of the former owner had been stored since her death nearly 20 years ago. After prayers, in which Mr. Baber joined, the vicar went to two other bedrooms and finally downstairs where he held a short service in each room. This concluded the exorcism and the Rev. Mr. Maddock returned to the village. The Baber family thereupon expected to settle down to a life of peace and tranquillity.

After reading the story I felt that Mr. and Mrs. Baber had experienced the phenomena usually associated with poltergeists. I decided to write and get their version of the haunting as well as the exorcism.

The following is Mr. and Mrs. Baber's reply to my letter:
Dear Mr. Gilroy,

"We were very pleased to get your letter and I am very happy to send along a report of the recent happenings in our home, hoping that you will be able to visualize the effects as they appeared to us here. We have lived in this house for 14 years. It is a very small place, five rooms including the small box-room which has been kept shut for at least 18 years, until we had permission to open and make use of it about eight months ago.

Within a few days of opening this room, things began to happen which we at first chose to ignore. Perhaps it would be better if

25

I described the room and contents as we found them. It is very small, being nine feet long and six feet wide and was stacked to the ceiling with furniture and large trunks such as are used for sea travel; there were also several chairs, a table and a chest of drawers.

The room was in a filthy condition, cobwebs hanging from the ceiling and a thick layer of dust over everything; the furniture being so badly infected with woodworms that it crumbled to dust when touched. We cleaned up the room and decorated and furnished it to accommodate our six year old daughter who was quite thrilled with the prospect of having a room of her own.

For the first night or two all was quiet. Then one night we were awakened by the screaming of our daughter who cried that someone was in the room with her. Upon investigation, we could find no one and were not a little mystified as to what had frightened the child. From then on it was always the same. Night after night she would awaken us and cry out that someone was in the room with her. She soon became so frightened that she refused to sleep in the room or go about the house unaccompanied.

One day while my wife was doing her housework, she heard a voice which appeared to come from the direction of the stairs. On looking up, she plainly saw the figure of an old lady dressed in black, but as the apparition disappeared in a second or two, she dismissed it as imagination. One night while putting our little daughter to bed and listening to her say her prayers we distinctly heard the entity speak in an unintelligible voice.

Upon immediate investigation of the room and passageway we could find no normal explanation for the phenomenon. The voice was also heard by our little girl as well as by our adopted son who is 15 years of age. This incident was also dismissed as imagination until we all began to take notice of things such as door handles being turned and doors opening of their own volition; footsteps up and down the stairs, drawers and cupboards being opened during the night. When we questioned the boy as to what he was doing downstairs, he would deny having been up and thought at the time that it was one of us. This went on for some time until my wife decided to get to the bottom of things. We decided to get in touch with a well known psychic investigator and author, Mr. Elliot O'Donnell, who has written several books on hauntings.

May I point out that up to this time I was very sceptical of the entire affair and on the night the investigator called I retired early and asked my wife and a friend to 'sit' with him. About 1 a.m. my curiosity got the best of me and I decided to join them to see what was happening. If I live to be a hundred, I shall never forget my feelings when I heard and saw the entity that had been disturbing us (and is still disturbing us).

We were all in the living-room which is situated directly beneath the box-room and the phenomenon which occurred could not have been caused by any human agency. Footsteps were heard overhead in the box-room. They paced back and forth for several minutes. Then the door opened and the steps came along the hall, down the stairs, through the passage and into the room in which we were sitting.

I was so stunned that I did not switch on the light immediately. My wife suddenly collapsed in a dead faint. When the light finally was turned on my forehead was covered with perspiration although at the time I was shivering because of the cold atmosphere that came into the room with the entity. We decided we had enough for one evening and after calming ourselves with several cups of coffee finally retired to our beds.

The next day a report by the investigator appeared in the local newspaper giving details of the previous night's experience. From this time on it ceased to be our private affair. We were pressed by reporters from all over England for a story for their respective papers. Some of these stories were not to the point and grossly enlarged upon the facts. We decided that it would be best to send our little girl to stay with friends for a time as her nervous condition was causing us considerable worry and our doctor advised us that a change was imperative.

We were advised also to have the Vicar of our parish try to exorcise the spirit-entity. This is a most unusual ritual. As far as I can ascertain the last exorcism held in this country was over 70 years ago. The service is very secret and no one was allowed to be in the house except the Vicar, his two secretaries and my hesitant self.

There was a huge crowd outside when the Vicar arrived. Dozens of reporters and photographers from all over the world tried unsuccessfully to find out what was said during the exorcism (which may I point out, was not at all successful). We are bothered still by the entity and it is very active at times.

We still hear the footsteps, doors and drawers are continuously being opened and shut without our being able to discover how it is done; and my wife actually saw the entity only a week ago. We are not so frightened now however, as we have been assured that 'it' will do us no physical harm.

We have had numerous offers from psychic investigators and many things have been tried but all to no avail. As we are not Spiritualists we do not care to delve too deeply into something we cannot understand. However, I am firmly convinced as to the reality of the phenomenon. A very good newspaper photographer has attempted to take pictures of the inside of the house. Three of his flash bulbs were smashed to pieces, one after the other, and the developed negatives were not fit to be printed as they had nothing but distorted figures on them. He is convinced that a super-normal presence exists here.

We are having a well recommended medium visit us in a week or two and perhaps then we shall be able to get to the root of the trouble. I for one certainly hope that she will be able to uncover further evidence, if only to convince those who think that it is all a stunt on our part.

All that I have stated is a true record of the phenomena as they occurred, and in conclusion may I say that I hope this letter may be of some interest to you and your friends. Thanking you for your interest in us, we remain.

Sincerely yours,
Mr. & Mrs. William Baber.

MR. LEY HAS CHEST TROUBLE
William H. Gilroy

Unexplainable things seemed to happen no matter where the old carved chest was placed.

"The poltergeist in the chest tonight took an evening off from his pranks in Stanbury Manor, Morwenstow, a tiny village on the coast of England," stated a London newspaper on 6 January, 1949.

The article went on to explain that the trouble had started some two months previously when Mr. Ley, owner of the manor, had purchased an old hand-carved, cedarwood chest from a Cornish antique shop. After the chest reached Stanbury, Mr. Ley began to experience the type of paranormal manifestation attributed to that malicious, noisy entity, the poltergeist. In whichever room the chest was placed the most distressing things happened.

Six museum-piece shotguns, hanging by stout wire fastened securely to the wall of the armoury, clattered to the floor and two of the guns were badly smashed. But not a nail had slipped, not a wire had broken.

In another room a heavy framed picture jumped two feet from the wall and hit Mr. Ley on the head, causing a painful bruise. At the same time two other large pictures, after "hanging safely for generations", were propelled from the wall into the center of the room.

In one of the bedrooms another picture did not fall from the wall — it was pushed backwards, through the Queen Anne panelling.

After reading the newspaper article which was detailed and most convincing I wrote to Mr. Ley and offered him twice the amount that he had originally paid for his chest. He replied to my letter as follows: Dear Mr. Gilroy:

"The newspaper reports on the chest were correct in all the details, but since the date you mention, only two other things have happened. Another picture was badly smashed and an electric light bulb was removed from a window sill, where it had been placed only a moment before, and thrown with considerable force against the wall on the opposite side of the room.

All of the phenomena have occurred when at least one person was present, but usually more than one have witnessed it.

I have had a great number of mediums ask to come here, but

as 75 per cent of them are fakes I would not permit it. However, a circle of sincere people who do not accept money for any work they do were given permission to hold a séance and I enclose the minutes as to what was seen and heard by the medium.

I have become very interested in the whole affair and had you been nearer I should have welcomed you to try any experiment you wished; however, I would not consider selling the chest for any price and I do not believe it would be practical to loan it. If you have any friends in England who would care to see it I would be most happy to welcome them.

May I point out that before all this happened I was not a believer in spirits in any form, but after witnessing the phenomena and attending subsequent seances — scientifically conducted — I am now convinced, beyond the slightest doubt, as to the reality of the spirit-world.

By the way, I had a letter from the ex-Curate of Newlyn, Cornwall, who writes that he recognized the chest from the photo in the papers.

He says that many years ago there were two sisters living in the Manor House, Newlyn, (he gave their names but I cannot find his letter at the moment, but will look it up if it is of interest to you). They had in their house quite a collection of antiques and among them was this chest which they kept in their bedroom. One time, after having been away for a few days, they returned late one night and being rather tired placed their heavy baggage on the chest rather than unpack at such a late hour. Early the next morning their attention was drawn to the chest and as they went over to it the lid, although weighted down by the heavy baggage, slowly opened and they looked inside. What they saw they would never reveal, but it was so horrible that they were both struck stone deaf; and although they lived to an old age they never got their hearing back.

When they died the house and furniture were sold at auction and all trace of the chest was lost until it turned up in the antique shop where I purchased it.

If I can be of further help or if there, are any questions you wish answered I would be pleased to oblige."

Yours faithfully,

T. A. Ley

THE STRANGE HAPPENINGS AT BORLEY RECTORY

FULL ACCOUNT OF ENGLAND'S MOST FAMOUS MODERN GHOST

S. H. Glanville

No living man is as well qualified to write this account as S. H. Glanville. Harry Price, in his book, "The End of Borley Rectory," says of the 'locked book': "The contents were compiled by my chief official observer, Mr. S. H. Glanville. If all other existing records of Borley were to be destroyed and only the 'locked book' saved, it would form a complete history ... of the haunting. It will forever be a model for psychical researchers as to how a report should be prepared."

ONE OF HISTORY'S MOST AUTHENTIC HAUNTINGS
Borley is a small hamlet in Essex, with a population of about 120 people and lies within a few hundred yards of the Essex-Suffolk county boundary. The nearest town is Long Melford about two miles distant.

The Borley Church built in the 12th century stands on a hill and contains a fine tomb of Sir Edward Waldegrave who died in 1561. He was a member of the Waldegrave family who now live in Somerset and who held the Manor of Borley and were patrons of the living for nearly 300 years. In 1362 Edward III gave the Manor of Borley to the Benedictine monks.

The Rectory itself, which was destroyed by fire in 1939, stood about 150 yards from the church and was divided from it by the churchyard and a narrow unfrequented lane. The house was almost entirely surrounded by tall trees which overshadowed it and had a very darkening and depressing effect on the house both inside and out. It was built in 1863 by the Rev. Henry Dawson Ellis Bull, whose family had lived in or near Borley continuously for over 300 years, and who was then the Borley Rector. It was substantially built of brick and stone, all the doors were thick and heavy, the floors were of heavy wood in some parts and stone in other rooms. Some of the windows, such as the dairy, the kitchen, scullery and passages, were iron barred giving that part of the house a rather prison-like appearance. When it was first built it contained 18 rooms but, as Mr. Bull's family increased, he added a new wing to accommodate them. There were 14 children altogether, of whom 12 survived. The house, when completed, enclosed a central courtyard which had a narrow outlet at one corner. No gas or electricity was, or ever had been available. Lighting was supplied by means of oil lamps and candles; and the only water supply was from a deep well in the courtyard.

The Rev. Henry Bull held the parish for 30 years, from 1862 until 1892, the year of his death. He died in the Blue Room which is immediately over the library and overlooks that part of the garden known as "The Nun's Walk." His wife died in the same room. The picture of their father given me by his daughters, shows him to have been an unusual man. He was tall, heavily built and had been a good amateur boxer in his youth. His principal hobby seems to have been shooting and hunting; a typical hard-living country parson of his period. His financial position was secure as, apart from his stipend, he had ample private means.

His son, the Rev. Henry Bull, or Harry as he was generally known to avoid confusion with his father, succeeded to the living on the death of his father and remained there as Rector for 35 years, until his death in 1927. He also died in the "Blue Room."

A year later the Rev. Eric Smith, who had lately returned from several years of missionary work in India, accepted the living. He and his wife remained for less than two years, leaving in 1930. When he accepted the living he was a stranger to England and was, therefore, not aware of the fact that some dozen or so clergymen had already refused it. It had a sinister reputation and the huge, melancholy house could not have been very inviting. Also the stipend was comparatively small.

In October 1930 the Rev. Lionel Foyster, a distant relative of the Bull family, was offered the living and accepted. Neither the Smiths nor the Foysters had any children of their own but the Foysters brought with them a small adopted daughter aged 2½ years. Mr. Foyster and his wife had just returned from Canada where they had been engaged in missionary work for some years. At the end of five years in the Rectory Mr. Foyster's health completely broke down and he was forced to retire.

The reputation of the Rectory by this time was such that the ecclesiastical authorities decided that it was not a fit house for a Rectory and it was permanently closed in 1935.

This then is the chronological history of the Rectory from

1863 when it was built until 1935 when it was finally left alone with its 23 empty and dusty rooms and its ghosts. The once beautiful lawns and gardens became a veritable jungle of weeds and rotting undergrowth. The once fine vinery became a rickety affair of swinging doors and broken glass. The two summer-houses were derelict and decaying.

This is how I first saw it in 1937 when my son and I unlocked the heavy front door and stepped from the hot June sun into the dark, chill and echoing hall. Our enthusiasm dropped several points. We knew the history of the house, the alleged haunting and the fantastic phenomena reported from there for nearly 15 years. We planned to spend the night locked in this house.

Apart from the evidence of poltergeist activity, there is the age-old story of the ghostly nun who is alleged by many persons to have been seen walking about the garden. There is the apparition of a coach and horses which drives across the lawn. Legend says that a nun eloped, centuries before, with a monk from a nearby monastery, that they were caught, brought to judgment and condemned to death — the monk to be hanged and the nun to be bricked up in the wall of a building that once stood on this same site. Later we found parts of the foundation of this old building in the rectory cellars. I express no opinion about the truth of this traditional story but it was told and believed long before the present rectory was built.

Miss Ethel Bull and her sisters Freda and Mabel, daughters of the Rev. Henry Bull, were born in Borley Rectory. They have assured me that on a June afternoon when they were returning from a garden party and had just entered the Rectory garden, they all three simultaneously and quite clearly saw the figure of a nun walking slowly on the other side of the lawn. They were astonished as, although the apparition had been seen many times at dusk, they had never before seen it in daylight. Miss Ethel Bull ran into the house to bring a fourth sister to see the phenomenon and fortunately found her immediately. All four of them watched the grey figure walk slowly across the lawn. As she neared the trees which bounded the lawn the nun gradually faded and disappeared from their sight.

During the past 50 years more than 20 people have reported seeing this apparition. One man, a guest of the Bulls who knew nothing whatever of the story, came into the house one day to ask the Rector about the nun that he had seen walking in the garden. There are people who stoutly maintain that the apparition was seen only a few weeks before the Rectory burned. There is a part of the garden known as "The Nun's Walk." She usually appeared from an adjoining field, stepped over a low stone wall and walked across the lawn, to disappear among the trees separating the garden from the lane. There is persistent evidence of this apparition being seen by both the residents of the rectory and by strangers.

Walter Bull, another son of the Rev. Henry Bull, spent a good deal of his life at sea and therefore saw less of these things than the other members of the family. He told me that he frequently heard footsteps following him up the lane both in daylight and at night. Sometimes he slipped behind a tree to catch anyone following him but he never saw anyone. These pattering footsteps also were heard by villagers who used the lane and many of them refused to pass the house after dark if they were alone.

The Rev. Harry Bull would periodically tell his family that he had seen the "little man" again. This was a dwarf-like figure of an old man who he said appeared to him on the lawn. He would raise one arm above his head, then turn and run down the drive and disappear. Miss Ethel Bull is the only other member of the family who has seen this grotesque little figure.

One of the large dining-room windows overlooking the drive was removed and bricked up because Henry Bull said that he objected to an apparition peering through while they were at meals.

During the incumbency of the Rev. Harry Bull there was a good deal of paranormal activity which he quite openly admitted. In nearly all parts of the house footsteps were heard, particularly in the bedroom passages. They would reach a door, stop and then three taps were heard, never more than three. The figure of a tall man in dark clothes was seen on many occasions. One of the Rev. Harry Bull's sisters was awakened several times by a slap on her face. Now and then loud crashes were heard in different parts of the house.

At this same time manifestations were heard in the living rooms over the stables which were entirely separated from the house. The groom-gardener and his wife were disturbed night after night by knocks, thuds and sounds of breaking crockery, although nothing was ever found to have been broken or even moved. They put up with these conditions for three years and then left.

There is a hard core of evidence given by reliable and intelligent persons as a result of their own experience and observation which cannot be shaken by examination and questioning. For instance, Lady Whitehouse, who had known the Rectory and its successive residents for many years, assured me that on one occasion when she was helping to nurse Mrs. Foyster she saw a medicine bottle leave the mantel-piece and float through the air, coming to rest on the floor beside the bed. She not only assured me of the complete truth of this incident and many others but voluntarily offered to swear an affidavit confirming them if I wished her to.

In 1927 the Rev. Harry Bull died and the Rev. Eric Smith accepted the living. As has been stated he had lately returned from several years of missionary work in India, so that when he and his wife came to Borley neither of them had any warning or knowledge of its reputation.

I spent a good many hours with Mr. and Mrs. Smith at their pleasant rectory in Kent. They very kindly gave me details of the two years they spent at Borley, years which they described as "the darkest years of their life." Actually the manifestations during this time were less numerous and not of the violent character experienced by their successors.

The first unusual thing they noticed were the noises in the bedrooms at night. Thuds and knocks were constantly heard, often sufficiently loud to waken them. In an attempt to avoid these disturbances they occupied several rooms in succession but either the sounds were being made in all the rooms at the same time or they followed them about. The noises were loudest and most insistent in the bedroom over the kitchen and in the blue room.

Although no record was kept Mr. Smith tells me that they heard few of these noises on the ground floor and that there was much more noise in the winter than in summer. This bears out an analysis which we made at the end of the investigation to find out what proportion of phenomena happened during the hours of darkness and daytime respectively. The figures show that much the larger proportion happened at night.

Within a week intermittent bell ringing started. The bells are of the old-fashioned spiral spring type and rung by bell-pulls in the rooms. The bells themselves, some 20 of them, were hung high up in the kitchen passage just off the hall. Time after time a bell would ring from one of the rooms, though they were all empty since the only people in the house were Mr. and Mrs. Smith. It was rarely that they could prevail on a maid to stop in the house for more than a week.

Keys were frequently picked up and replaced in the locks. The key to the library door was often found at the foot of the main stairs, several feet from the door. At times only an hour or so would elapse between the time a key was replaced and its being found on the floor again. A variation of this phenomenon was the locking of doors. This was often extremely inconvenient. On many occasions unlocked doors were found locked, and vice versa. This actually happened to one of our observers who, sitting at the table in the library, heard a sharp metallic click and upon going to the door found that it had been locked from the inside. Several keys disappeared entirely and were never found.

It is not suggested that there is anything of a paranormal nature in the following incident but it proves the house to be a place of surprises to say the least. In the library there was a large glass-fronted bookcase entirely covering one side of the room, the lower half of which contained cupboards. In one of these cupboards Mrs. Smith found a paper-wrapped parcel about the size of a football. It was not labelled and she proceeded to unpack it. Under several layers of paper she found a human skull. Despite inquiries no information as to its origin was ever discovered. It was not known to have been there at the time of Harry Bull's death, neither did any of his family know anything about it. Mr. Smith, therefore, buried it in the churchyard with a short burial service.

Soon after this episode a mirror standing on Mrs. Smith's dressing table started tapping whenever she approached it. The tapping appeared to come from the back and this continued until they left the Rectory. After they left they lived for some time on the East Coast, near Cromer, and the tapping stopped. That was in 1930 and it was not until 1937 that I first met them in their rectory in a village in Kent. By that time I had already spent a considerable time at Borley. Now a very peculiar thing happened. About a week after I visited them and held the mirror in my hands, I received a letter from Mr. Smith in which he said, "I do not know whether you carry ghosts about with you, but the mirror has started tapping again." I was not able at the time to go down there again and hear it for myself, and I am sorry to say that soon after this Mr. Smith became seriously ill and died. Mrs. Smith moved and I lost trace of her.

The Smiths told me that on several occasions the heavy wood shutters to the French windows in the library, which slid into cavities in the walls, were pulled sharply together. They had been in the room when this happened. These shutters were exceptionally heavy and require considerable force to bring them together. They were each about six feet high and three feet wide. It was also a common, thing for them, to hear the brass rings, which are let into the wood frames and used for pulling them together, rattling. I heard this myself while sitting in the library at night.

At the end of 18 months Mr. Smith became alarmed at the disturbing influences in the rectory and decided that it was time he sought advice with the object of ridding the place of its troubles. He therefore wrote to a daily newspaper asking for the name of a society connected with psychic matters which might be able to help him. The paper not only sent the information but reporters and photographers as well. The immediate result was a flood of sightseers. Crowds invaded the garden, trampled the flower beds, peered through the windows and generally made life a burden to the rector and his wife. The police had to be called and they gradually restored order and sanity.

This human inundation and publicity had no effect whatever on the phenomenon. It continued as before and new phenomena appeared from time to time. There was a bedroom in the "new" wing which was formerly used as a schoolroom. The window of this room was seen, on many occasions, to be lit up although the room was known to be empty. One night Mrs. Smith, together with some members of the choir who were leaving the church after practice, witnessed this phenomenon. The present Rector, who lives in a nearby village, maintains that the large window on the main staircase was seen to be lighted up soon after our investigation ended. The house was then empty and locked up. This light was of an unusual character, no rays were visible but it was rather in the nature of a fluorescence inside the room.

One summer afternoon when Mr. Smith was leaving his bedroom he passed under the arch which lead on to the landing and was surprised to hear sounds of whispering over his head. He described them to me as "soft and sibilant but spoken with urgency, and ending in muttering sounds." The voice was undoubtedly that of a woman. He continued across the landing and just as he passed under the arch on the opposite side, which leads to the private chapel, they stopped suddenly as though cut off. No words were heard on this occasion but during the next few weeks he heard them again when some words were distinguishable. The words "Don't, Carlos" were quite clear. Although many inquiries were made no evidence of any person of that name was traced to anyone connected with the rectory.

The only instance of material damage being done while they were in the Rectory happened on an afternoon when they were sitting in the drawing-room. They were alone in the house. Suddenly smashing sounds were heard and they both ran out into the hall. There they found the pieces of a china vase that normally stood on the mantle-piece in their bedroom, which was the Blue Room. By some unaccountable means it had moved from the shelf, travelled out of the room, across the landing and dropped into the hall below where it was shattered on the floor.

Footsteps, thuds, knocks and bell ringing were an almost daily occurrence. There was no real peace or rest by day or night.

Mr. Smith was anxious about the state of his wife's health, which was showing signs of strain. They felt it was not possible to continue living under such conditions and Mr. Smith regretfully tendered his resignation. It was not easy to find a new incumbent as Borley had become notorious. The Smiths moved into a hostelry in Long Melford and from there Mr. Smith carried on his clerical duties for several months. In August, 1930, he relinquished his work and left. To the end of his life he maintained that the house was a centre of some unknown and malign influence.

In October of the same year the Rev. Lionel Foyster, M.A., a scholar of Pembroke College, Cambridge, and his wife and adopted daughter came to the Rectory. During their five-year occupation phenomena reached a state of activity and violence never before experienced. Mr. Foyster very kindly sent me over 100 pages of a diary he kept for a period of 15 months, recording some of the events which took place during that time. There are only two copies of this record, one in the safe keeping of the University of London Council for Psychical Investigation, and my own.

Mr. Foyster starts with this head-note, "The only pretensions that these notes claim is the very simple one that it is a record of facts and is, therefore, true. Experiences recorded can be vouched for by my wife and myself; many were also witnessed by other disinterested people. They have been recorded just as they happened."

Within the first few weeks, while Mrs. Foyster was going upstairs on her way to the Blue Room which the Foysters were using as their bedroom, she heard footsteps following her and, turning around, saw the apparition of a man. She continued on her way and when she reached the landing it had disappeared. Some time later she was shown a photograph of the late Harry Bull and recognized him as the man in the apparition. It appeared to her on several occasions attired in a dressing-gown and carrying a small case or wallet. She never saw this figure in any other part of the house, neither was it ever seen by anyone but herself.

The next episode, although less alarming, was more material and exceedingly annoying. She had gone into the bathroom to wash her hands and taking off a wrist watch which was set in a gold bracelet put it on a shelf. Then, having washed and dried her hands, she turned to pick up the watch. To her astonishment she found only the watch, the bracelet had disappeared. It has never been found.

This bracelet was not the only thing that disappeared in an extraordinary way, but it was the only object of any value that was lost. On the other hand things had an odd habit of appearing from nowhere. A small silk bag containing lavender was found one day on the mantelpiece in the sewing-room. The Foysters had never seen this bag before and never did trace an owner. It would disappear for a few days and reappear in one of the other rooms. On one occasion Mr. Foyster found it in one of his coat pockets. After several months of this jack-in-the-box existence it disappeared for good.

Books also appeared spontaneously. The first one was found on the bath-room window-sill. Mr. Foyster took little notice of this, thinking that his wife had left it there. She in turn thought that he had put it there. Other books were found in different parts of the house; all of them were over 100 years old and of a theological nature. Later it was discovered that they had belonged to the Rev. Henry Bull and had been stored on the top shelf of a cupboard in the kitchen. Mr. Foyster says in his diary, "... exactly how many times this happened I have not kept a record, but one day, as a variation, a book was thrown on to the floor on the further side of a closed door in the passage leading to the bathroom." Going into the kitchen one afternoon he found a whole collection of books placed on the rack over the kitchen range. No one had ever seen any of these books before, and an hour or so later the cover of a book with two pages still, adhering to it was found on the bathroom floor.

At 11 o'clock one night Mr. Foyster was in the bathroom when he heard his wife cry out and then heard her running down the passage. He rushed out. She said, "I had been in the bedroom (Blue Room) and had just come out onto the landing when something hit me in the face and nearly stunned me for a moment. I was carrying the candle but saw no one or anything." The blow had in fact made a cut under her left eye and the blood was running down her face. Nothing was found that could have caused such a wound.

As a result of this Sir George Whitehouse and his wife, who were living at Arthur Hall, Sudbury, a few miles away, and who had themselves witnessed many incidents at the Rectory, insisted Mr. and Mrs Foyster coming to stay with them for a few days. For the next several years these friends had them over to stay when things got too bad at the Rectory.

Not long after this another curious thing happened. One evening Mr. Foyster left the sewing-room to get some papers from the library. As he turned into the hall he was startled to find that all the pictures, with one exception, had been taken off the walls of the staircase and laid face down on the hall floor. The exception was a particularly large picture, and that was hanging crookedly as though it had been pushed aside.

The spontaneous appearances of the lavender bag and the books have been mentioned, but many other articles turned up from time to time. A plain gold ring, presumably a wedding ring, was found on the landing outside the Blue Room. There were no signs of hard wear and the hall-mark showed it to have been made in Birmingham in 1863, the year the Rectory was finished. No owner for any of these things was ever found.

Walking sticks kept in the corner of the library were seen to move. On one occasion one was seen to travel the entire length of the room. Books and papers were moved. Sometimes the draft of Mr. Foyster's sermon for the following Sunday was moved into another room. Then one day he decided that if he put it in a large Bible that stood on his desk it might be safe. This he did and in the morning found it intact. He thereafter made this an invariable practice and it was not moved again. The kitchen table was thrown over and the crockery shot onto the floor on many occasions. Beds were turned onto their sides and the bedding thrown onto the floor. One morning, upon entering the kitchen, it was found that all the linen from the airing cupboard had been strewn over the floor. Unaccountable footsteps were continuously heard in all parts of the house, a manifestation that had been going on unceasingly for 50 years.

There remains the most contentious of the phenomena — the psychic writing on the walls. These were photographed and carefully traced before the Rectory burned and are, therefore, permanently recorded.

One peculiarity of these writings and markings is the height at which they were written. This varies from four feet three inches above floor level to four feet eight inches, which is the highest. No adult would normally write at this height. It is alleged that these writings appeared spontaneously and there is good evidence to support this contention. Some of them are meaningless scrawls. Many of them take the form of the letter "M", and may be an attempt at the beginning of the name "Marianne", the person to whom the messages are addressed and to whom they appeal for help. Marianne is Mrs. Foyster's Christian name.

The first writing appeared on the wall of the kitchen passage, between the kitchen and the sewing-room. It consists of the words, "Marianne get help —", then some words that are indecipherable. Under this Mrs. Foyster herself wrote, "I cannot understand, tell me more." A few days elapsed and then overnight these words had appeared, "lights — Mass and prayers." On the opposite side of the kitchen passage there was written a larger and clearer message which said, "Marianne light Mass prayers." Then on the first floor, on the bathroom passage wall, another clear request appeared which asked, "Marianne please help get." The longest piece of continuous writing was on the side of the arch on the landing, the arch which leads into the private Chapel, and reads, "Get light and prayers here," and ending with a few indecipherable words, the last of which may be "his body:"

A great deal of consideration has been given to this alleged paranormal writing with little result but there are several points of general interest. The writing was done with a graphite pencil (some of this was flaked off and analysed). It is quite characterless and if some unknown entity was responsible for it we must presume it to be about four feet six inches in height, or an adult of average height in a kneeling position. Practically all of it has the appearance of being done with difficulty and with great urgency, as though in fear of interruption. In some instances the interruption seems to have occurred. All of the messages start with clarity and firmness, but after a word or two seem to weaken as though energy was dwindling. The photographs and tracings have been examined by doctors, physiologists, physicists, graphologists and church dignitaries, but none has been able to offer an acceptable explanation. They remain a mystery.

In 1935 the Foysters had been living under these fantastic conditions for nearly five years. If they had been a large family living a busy and happy domestic life, it would not have been so bad. With only two persons and a young child living in this great rambling house with its 23 rooms, some of them unfurnished, without electricity, gas or main water, it is not surprising that Mr. Foyster's health deteriorated. He also felt that the circumstances did not allow him the peace and quiet necessary for a clergyman to carry out his duties properly. After long consideration he reluctantly decided to resign his living. In October of 1935 he closed the door of the Rectory and retired. Retirement, however, did not restore his health and he died not long afterwards.

The ecclesiastical authorities decided that the rectory should be permanently closed. The parishes of Borley and Liston, a small adjoining village, were combined and the present rector, the Rev. A. C. Henning, carries out the duties of both from his rectory in Liston.

After Mr. Foyster's retirement the rectory remained locked up and empty for two years. The owners were unable to sell it nor could they find a tenant, which is not surprising. The late Harry Price, then Honorary Secretary of the University of London Council for Psychical Investigation, rented the house and grounds for 12 months with the object of making a sustained examination of the place to decide whether phenomena were still active and, if possible, to trace the cause. Mr. Price did not visit the Rectory during the period of the tenancy as he wished to form his own conclusions from independent evidence, and entrusted this writer with the task of drawing up a full report, upon which he wrote his book, "The Most Haunted House in England."

My son and I first went to the Rectory on the 19 of June, 1937. It has been mentioned that the house was cold, dark and depressing, and during that first night we were struck by two things, the intense cold for that time of year and the almost uncanny silence. Other observers agree that they had never been in any building where the intense quiet was so marked. The only sounds heard were the scuttling of a few mice and the intermittent and mournful call of owls in the trees; very rarely a belated vehicle would pass through the lane. Otherwise there was a cold silence that was most oppressive.

After examining the gardens, stables, outbuildings and conservatory, we inspected the whole house from the attics to the cellars. Every window and door was sealed with thread and wax or adhesive tape. The only exceptions were the main entrance door in the hall, which we always kept bolted from the inside, and the French windows in the library which were also bolted inside. It was not possible for any person to enter the house without our knowledge and I am quite certain that no one ever did. At fairly regular intervals we made a tour of the whole house, visiting every room and passage, including the attics and cellars.

One of our little difficulties was the continual strain on our ears to catch sounds, especially during the first few nights. Some of these appeared to come from distant parts of the house and often could not be accurately located. Others occurred in the room we were using at the time, usually the library, and were obviously within a few feet of us. This intense listening was not so difficult up to one or two o'clock in the morning but it became very tiring towards five and six. The first light of dawn coming through the dusty windows was very welcome. Certain sounds could be located and accounted for quite easily, a rose branch scraping a window, a dripping tap, the very rare scrambling of mice and so on.

There is one episode which, although it is not suggested that it was paranormal, left us completely mystified and was never explained. For many years the Bull family had kept a number of cats about the place and, as they died, these were buried in the garden. The whole of the large garden had become an overgrown jungle and in places was almost impenetrable with weeds and bramble. Making our way through this tangle early one morning, we found a half-rotted head board marking the grave of one of the cats. The name and date was cut in the wood. Tearing away some more undergrowth we found several more. This was only of passing interest and we did nothing further about it. On our next visit, a few days later, while walking in the garden, we were astonished to find that a pit about five feet in diameter had been dug, the earth thrown up in a ring around the pit, and the head boards thrown about indiscriminately. We made the most careful and guarded inquiries. There were only a few cottages within a mile of the Rectory. We were not able to find any explanation. Someone spent a lot of time and labour digging this huge hole — who, and why? What were they looking for?

A recital of all the taps, knocks, thuds, scraping and shuffling sounds we heard would be monotonous but some of them were of greater interest than others. On one occasion we had two Royal Air Force Officers with us. My son also was a Squadron Leader during the World War, and all of them were seriously interested in psychical matters. During the afternoon my son and I had to go into Long Melford to get oil for the lamps and left the other two alone in the house. Upon our return they reported that, while sitting in the library with the door open, they distinctly heard what they described as, "light tripping footsteps" coming down the stairs. Having apparently descended the stairs they stopped. Nothing was to be seen. The bottom step of the stairs was about eight feet from where they sat.

One of our most active and valuable observers was Mark Kerr-Pearse, now one of our pro-consuls in Prague. He was the only one of us who actually lived at the Rectory during the investigation. This he did for several weeks continuously, staying in the house for most of the day and sleeping in the large summer house in the garden.

One hot August day three people called, two of them were known to Kerr-Pearse. The third was their friend, a Miss ——, who had expressed a wish to see the Rectory. Although they were not official observers they were taken over the house. Everything was quiet and nothing unusual happened until they were crossing the landing outside the Blue Room when Miss R — suddenly came to a standstill saying that she had a feeling of indescribable terror. She had a sensation of "pins and needles" in her hands, which were icy cold. She was trembling violently and asked for help, as she was unable to move. It was as though she was fixed to the floor. About 15 minutes later she was prevailed upon to go to the landing again at which time she experienced exactly the same sensations to a lesser degree.

A month later, a friend of ours, a Group Captain in the Royal Air Force, brought a lady down who was reputed to be hyper-sensitive to "psychic" conditions. We hoped that her presence might induce unusual activity. They also were shown over the house. Nothing happened until they came to the landing where on exactly the same spot this lady experienced the same feeling of horror that had so affected Miss R — An important point is that neither of these persons had any knowledge of Miss R —'s visit or experience. The exact position of this spot was marked on the floor but great care was taken to make the mark invisible to anyone unless they got down on their knees to look for it. Neither was it known to anyone except my son and myself. As will be seen later, this particular area seemed to have a special significance.

In view of the fact that during the residence of the Foysters so many objects had been unaccountably moved and even transported from one room to another, we placed different things on shelves, window-sills, mantel-pieces and so on, in the hope that they would be moved. These were all ringed with chalk and dated so that we should be able to check any movement at once. Among them was an empty tobacco tin which was placed on the drawing-room mantel-piece. For some time none of these objects showed any signs of movement. But on 19 September we walked into the drawing-room and immediately noticed that the tin from the mantel-piece had gone. We went on our way through the house and on the landing found the tin. It had been placed with almost mathematical accuracy on the very small mark that we had made on the floor to mark the area where the two ladies had been so acutely affected; where Mr. Smith had heard the whispering; where the wedding ring was found and where Mrs. Foyster had been struck in the face.

Another contrivance we set up somewhat in the nature of a trap, was a simple piece of apparatus consisting of an electric bell, a battery and a pile of five books. Into the lower book had been fixed a paper break-contact so that if the books were moved the spring contacts would close and the bell would ring continuously. This was placed on the dining-room mantel-piece.

I was unable to get down to the Rectory the following week and had to hand the keys to a doctor friend, who is now the Director of Pathology at one of our large national hospitals. He and his son and a friend, both engineers, were with him. All of them had been to the Rectory before. They made a tour of the house just after midnight and at 12:50 a.m. were in the Blue Room when they heard the bell ringing. They hurried down but by the time they reached the dining-room the bell had stopped ringing. They found that all the books had been pushed to one side and the contact withdrawn. The window and door seals were all inspected and all found to be intact. Yet something had moved the books. The question of trickery can be ruled out completely. The incident was not subjective. Indeed it was very material. It was no manifestation of mental phenomena. Energy was used, and if appropriate preparation could have been made the force used might have been measured in foot pounds. And so it joins the other hundreds of incidents for which there is no explanation.

One of the features of Borley was the variation in the type of phenomena experienced there. We observed an odd incident one night when sitting in the library. Everything was quiet, with the usual oppressive silence. The blind, which reached from the ceiling to the floor, was drawn down over the French windows. Dr. B.....y, Captain H.....n, my son and myself were all there when the blind, which was of a heavy canvas-like material, started to move. We watched it and thinking there might be a draught tested the air with smoke, but it was quite still. The movement was undulating, just as though the thing was breathing deeply. The undulation started at the top and spread gradually downwards to the floor. We all stood round watching it for nearly five minutes when it stopped quite suddenly. This sounds a very mild affair but was one of so many unaccountable things that happened. We never saw this again.

The majority of noises were heard during the hours of darkness but just after ten o'clock one morning I was sitting alone in the library when I heard three heavy blows overhead, apparently on the floor of the Blue Room. I immediately called Kerr-Pearse who had gone into the kitchen and just as he entered the room we both heard two more blows. We went up to the Blue Room but it was empty and quiet. The house was still sealed and the doors locked. No one else was in the house.

One night, it was actually 1:10 a.m., Dr. B....y and my son were having a few moments' sleep, while I was sitting at the table reading. I heard a sound such as would be made by a chair being dragged across the Blue Room floor overhead. There followed a tremendous blow, which seemed to come from the top of the large bookcase within a few feet of where I was sitting. This woke both the doctor and my son. It was the loudest single noise that we heard during the whole investigation. It is of interest that this noise was made while two persons were asleep. I suggest that the state of sleep, when the conscious mind is at rest, may possibly be of some importance in connection with paranormal activity. The evidence to support this suggestion is not negligible.

Another incident which took place during a "sleep" period may be mentioned. Squadron-Leader Alan Cuthbert was with us on this occasion. He was suffering from a very heavy cold and we prevailed on him to lie on the camp bed in the library and get an hour's rest. This he did and was soon in a deep sleep. About 2 a.m. we decided to leave him and go up onto the landing and sit in complete darkness in the hope that this might produce some phenomena.

After sitting there for 40 minutes, during which time we did not speak, we all simultaneously and distinctly heard footsteps, such as would be made by a heavy man, cross the hall immediately below us. We knew at once that they could not have been made by such a lightly built man as Cuthbert, but we went down to investigate. Everything was quiet, the library dimly lit by the oil lamp and Cuthbert still slept soundly.

One more like instance occurred when a visitor on leave from overseas asked to be allowed to spend a night in the Rectory. He was a man of about 40, athletic, used to big game hunting and certainly not a temperamental type of individual. Kerr-Pearse was alone at the Rectory on this day and welcomed the visitor. Towards three o'clock in the morning they went into the library, made up the fire, and decided to have an hour's sleep, the visitor on the camp bed and Kerr-Pearse on the floor. About an hour later Kerr-Pearse was awakened by his companion, who was obviously in a state of high nervous tension. He quickly gave an explanation to account for his agitation.

Before leaving the Rectory in the morning, he wrote a short report in which he says, "— before waking you I had been awake for a considerable time, I cannot say how long but it must have been half an hour. Everything was perfectly still and I saw and heard nothing, but the air had become icy cold, my hands became numbed, in fact I became cold all over, I was rigid. It was so unpleasant that, in spite of an effort to control my nerves, I was eventually compelled to wake you."

In view of these many incidents I submit that there is a possibility that the state of sleep may beget phenomena. It seems as though energy can be drawn from a sleeping person, and used to produce phenomena of different types. Whether this energy is controlled by an entity or is simply a spontaneous and uncontrolled outburst is a matter for conjecture.

The following occurrence might be cited to confirm that there may be some conscious intention behind the use of such energy. It took place during the same night as the incident just related. That afternoon Kerr-Pearse had ordered a sack of coals to be delivered which had been dumped against the wall in the hall just outside the library. It weighed 56 pounds. At 8:30 p.m. he and his companion were going up to the Blue Room and had reached the landing when they heard a scraping and shuffling sound below them in the hall. It did not recur and after waiting a few moments they went down. To their astonishment the sack of coals had been moved along the floor for about eighteen inches. This would not have been so noticeable had not the sack been put on a patch of un-stained floor where a stove had formerly stood, the measurement could therefore be seen fairly accurately.

Kerr-Pearse had a rather uncomfortable experience. He was alone in the house on an autumn evening, and was sitting in the library reading when he heard a sharp metallic click. These sounds were not unusual and he took little notice. But after a few moments the thought occurred to him that the sound was like a lock being turned. Going over to the door he found that it had been locked, from the inside.

After a few visits to Borley I remembered an old planchette and rescued it from a lumber room where it was stored. We used it first late one night in the library. No sooner did our fingers come into contact with it than it started to write in large and well formed letters. It ultimately produced words, phrases, dates and even drawings. Some of it was unintelligible, some demonstrably untrue, some impossible to confirm but a certain amount of it was factual and confirmed later. One of the most startling things written was a clear prophecy that the Rectory would be burned and under the ruins would be found the bones of a murdered person. This was written on 27 March, 1938. Exactly 11 months later, on 27 February, 1939, the house caught fire and was practically destroyed.

In 1943 we made another visit to the site of the house for the purpose of digging in the cellars. The brick well in the further cellar was emptied of its contents of stone, brick and accumulated rubbish. At a depth of five feet six inches a silver-plated jug was found. This was submitted to experts and was found to be about 80 years old, making the date of manufacture 1863, the year the Rectory was built.

Next, the passage at the foot of the cellar steps was excavated. Owing to the fallen debris from the burned building this was a much more arduous task and more than a ton of rubbish was moved.

At a depth of three feet a human jaw bone was found and, five minutes later, part of a human skull. These were immediately submitted to an eminent pathologist who described them respectively as, the left mandible with five teeth and left parietal and temporal bone, both belonging to a woman probably about 30 years of age. The name of this long dead lady will almost certainly remain an unsolved mystery, but the fact remains: a woman was buried at the foot of the cellar steps — a strange thing with a churchyard only 100 yards away.

On the publication of these facts we received hundreds of letters pointing out that they must be part of the remains of the nun. But, tempting as this suggestion is, it cannot be accepted without much more evidence than is available at present.

An analysis of the total incidents of a paranormal character, covering many years, shows that 80 per cent occurred during the hours of darkness or dusk, that 46 per cent happened on the ground floor, 37 per cent on the first floor, and 17 per cent on the main or back stairs. Paranormal activity was most active during the months of June and July. Sundays and days of Religious Festival were undoubtedly the quietest. Phenomena do not appear to be influenced by air temperature. There is very good evidence to show that the presence of certain persons made manifestations more active. The state of sleep of one or more persons in the house may have a bearing on the type and frequency of phenomena.

During the whole of its 77 years of existence the Rectory seems to have been the focal point of phenomena outside normal human experience and understanding. One of the last things the Rev. Eric Smith said to me was, "the house was evil from top to bottom and it should have been burned to the ground years ago." Now all the rectors who once lived in it have passed away — and the house has burned. But if the reports that filter through to me are to be believed, although the ghosts are homeless, they are still there.

THE GHOST OF CORPUS CHRISTI COLLEGE

Here's an English ghost mentioned by the official records of Cambridge University.

Edmond P. Gibson

To the traveller who first visits Cambridge University the placid slow-flowing waters of the Cam river and the ivy-coated towers and walls of the ancient churches and monastic buildings seem to spell quiet and tranquillity. Unlike the turmoil of an American school, Cambridge dispenses education with a calmness and lack of haste which impresses the American tourist. The Corpus Christi College ghost of Cambridge is hidden behind a veil of secrecy and not allowed to intrude on the attention of visitors.

Some years ago the story of Corpus Christi ghost was told in the London *Sunday Express* by Lieut. Col. Cyril Foley of the British Army. The Colonel had checked his memory of the facts with Sir Shane Leslie, noted poet and author. When the events occurred Leslie was an undergraduate at King's College. Foley had not participated in the attempt to exorcise the ghost which destroyed the peaceful calm of Cambridge, but Sir Shane Leslie took an important part in this exorcism in 1904, on 19 November.

The haunted rooms at Corpus Christi had a traditionally bad reputation for several centuries. Originally they were part of a suite occupied by Archbishop Matthew Parker in the mid-16th century. The rooms were in what was known as the Old Master's Lodge in the Old Court, which since has been superseded by a new Lodge built in the New Court. When the New Court was built in 1817 the Old College Hall became the kitchen.

In the middle of the 17th century Dr. Butts, a master of the College, killed himself in this suite under very peculiar circumstances. His death occurred just after his preaching of the University sermon. He was found hanged in his garters. Sometime in the second half of the same century it is said that a clandestine lover of a daughter of Dr. Spencer's, Master of the College, died a violent death in this suite. Finally rumour said that the rooms were haunted. As the tradition grew they were avoided by the more timid students.

On one occasion a student reported seeing an apparition of a head without a body in one of the rooms. He fled into the Old Court in terror. (At the present time the Old Court is a sort of cul-de-sac which opens into the New Court of the College. In olden times it was a court, open at one end, facing Trumpington Street.) In about 1885 the rooms were closed by the College authorities after a celebrated Fellow, Dr. Moule, escaped from them crawling out on his hands and knees in the daylight. He was found to be in a state of shock and abject fear. Then the rooms were reopened for use as student lodgings in the Michaelmas of 1904, owing to a large enrollment.

During the Michaelmas term of 1904 noises were heard in the upper and lower front sitting rooms in the old suites on the second and third floors. Sometimes they sounded like footsteps. At other times they appeared to be ghostly rappings coming from the walls. Both the occupants of the upper and lower suites heard the noises and one of them was disturbed by loud knocking in the night and by the visible shaking and vibration of his wash-stand which stood at the foot of his bed.

At this time an undergraduate student occupied a suite directly opposite the allegedly haunted rooms, on the second floor. In the middle of the afternoon while he was busy with his studies he became possessed of a strange feeling of unrest. Wandering to his window he noted the head and shoulders of an unknown man leaning from the dormer window of the upper suite opposite. The man had long hair and he remained perfectly still, appearing to glare down malevolently at the student who had never seen him before. The student watched him for several minutes and as the figure appeared immobile he went to his bedroom window for a view from another angle. When he reached that window the figure had disappeared.

The student became excited. He knew that the stranger did not belong in the rooms and he went over only to find that the upper suite was locked. He called but received no answer. A check made early that evening revealed that the student occupant had been away all afternoon. He had locked the rooms and they had remained locked until his return. It appeared impossible for anyone to have been in the rooms.

Noises continued in the rooms from time to time. An undergraduate named Hillier who occupied the lower suite on the second floor awoke early one morning to find a white figure standing at his bedside. It stood motionless for a time and then moved towards the sitting room, disappearing into the shut door of that room. This apparition frightened Hillier. He left his bed and fled from the rooms. Hillier re-entered his rooms to find the figure of a man standing the fireplace. Hillier retreated to the rooms of a friend and spent the night on a couch in the sitting room. Following this second visitation Hillier refused to occupy his suite and took up the matter with the college authorities.

In the still-occupied upper suite the noises were a nightly occurrence but no apparition was seen there. The student who occupied them was continually disturbed, however, and felt that the ghost should be exorcised. Finally the matter was put before a friend, John Capron, who was taking Holy Orders. Capron was interested in Spiritualism and was a member of a psychical research society at the University. John Capron, together with Shane Leslie, Hillier, A. N. Wade, and an unnamed student went back to Corpus Christi with the excited student to attempt an exorcism of the noisy intruder.

Capron carried with him a large crucifix and a bottle of holy water. They entered the room which was lighted only by the fire on the hearth. They all knelt and said the Lord's Prayer in unison. They called upon the persons of the Holy Trinity commanding the spirit to appear. Two of the six undergraduates later testified that they saw the intruder. They were Capron and the owner of the upper suite. To the others the ghost remained invisible.

At the appearance of the spectre Capron began to recite the terrible words of the ancient rite of exorcism: "Lord, have mercy on us! Christ, have mercy on us! Christ, hear us! Christ, graciously hear us! God, the Father of Heaven, have mercy on us! God, the Son, Redeemer of the World, have mercy on us! God, the Holy Ghost, have mercy on us! Holy Trinity, One God, have mercy on us! Holy Mary, pray for us!"

The Ordinand prayed silently and suddenly he began to chant: "I adjure thee, unclean spirit, in the name of the Father, of the Son, and of the Holy Ghost, that thou come out and depart from this place! Thou cursed spirit, remember thy sentence, remember thy judgment, remember the day to be at hand wherein thou shalt burn in fire everlasting, prepared for thee! Presume not hereafter to exercise any tyranny toward this place. Go down to thine own place and be at peace!"

The ghost appeared as a mist about a yard wide, gradually taking the form of a man in white and with what seemed to be a gash in its neck. Capron stated that the apparition seemed to be hanging on the wall or suspended a foot above the floor. It wore an ancient costume with lace at the wrists and its throat was cut from ear to ear. (Later Capron discovered that the rooms once had been remodelled and the floor had been lowered a foot. The apparition was treading the ancient and higher floor.)

Capron and the owner of the rooms approached the ghost. Capron carried the Crucifix high but they seemed to encounter an invisible resistance and to be pushed back by some mysterious force. They could not approach the apparition and cried out: "It drives us back!" They retreated to the entrance of the room and gave up their attempt.

A second endeavour at exorcism was made a few minutes later. Again the student and the Ordinand Capron saw the ghost but the other men could not. Again the exorcists were driven back, although this time they held hands for mutual support. All of them seemed to feel some mysterious force first pushing and then pulling them. Again they gave up but they did not leave the room. Lieutenant Colonel Foley, who was not present but later heard of the story, stated that after the second failure they poked up the fire and Capron sprinkled Holy Water from the bottle. Then they saw the "Thing" gazing at them from the bedroom door. Without the Crucifix Capron sprang at the apparition and was thrown backwards at the feet of the other students near the fireplace. The Holy Water bottle fell from his hands and one of the men attempted to retrieve it from the floor. Wade raised the Crucifix. Leslie knelt at the fire praying earnestly.

Suddenly a loud crash sounded at the door. A "rescue party" of students from King's College had arrived, having learned belatedly of the planned exorcism of the ghost. At their entry the "Thing" retreated up the stairs to the upper suite. Foley states that after the second encounter with the ghost the exorcists were in a state of collapse and the undergraduates who had come in were thoroughly aroused by their condition. They talked together and then proceeded to search and wreck the haunted rooms. They threw out furniture, broke up the cupboards and closets and even tore the ancient panelling from the walls, revealing the ancient brick work. They left the suite a shambles, impossible for occupancy.

An attempt was made to communicate with the spirit by planchette. The planchette revealed the name of the ghost, Thomas Hardinge, and further stated "I killed myself in these rooms in 1707." No record of a Thomas Hardinge or his death could be found by the college authorities in the records.

The morning following the attempt at exorcism was devoted to an inquiry by the aroused authorities of the college. Students from King's College were forbidden to enter Corpus Christi College. A censorship was clamped down. The incident was hushed up and all the participants were made to agree that they would never divulge what had happened as long as they were connected with the college or the university. The rooms, or what remained of them, were closed off. Some time later the lower suite was made into a passageway. The upper apartment was repaired at much later date and finally reoccupied.

In this battle of exorcism the ghost certainly came out the winner and remained in undisputed possession of the wrecked rooms. But perhaps the ghost found the appointments less desirable after that for when the repairs were made in ensuing years there was no reappearance of the apparition.

The last appearance of the apparition occurred in 1908. The face again was seen in the upper apartment and footsteps were heard there, according to Librarian J. P. Bury.

In an article which appeared in the *Occult Review*, Vol. I, (1905), several hypotheses were offered to account for the occurrences in a normal manner. The kitchen chimney backed upon the wall of the haunted sitting rooms and some movement in this chimney was noted during periods of heating and cooling. This caused vibration of the adjacent wall and occasional noises therein. Rats were invoked as an additional cause of noises. However, no rats were ever seen there. The sitting room was adjacent to the old chimney but the noises were always louder in the bedroom, some distance from there. The rest of the phenomena were blamed upon the excitement and hysteria of the students themselves.

It must be admitted that the investigation of the haunting was conducted in a hasty and amateurish fashion. But the testimony of the student who watched the shaking wash-stand in the bedroom and that of the student who saw the figure at the window of the locked rooms must be taken seriously. Likewise the figure seen by Hillier passed through the locked door like a well-behaved ghost from "Phantasms of the Living". The early tradition regarding the rooms is also worthy of note as indicative of an earlier haunting.

The ghost received passing mention in the "Short History of the College of Corpus Christi and the Blessed Virgin Mary in Cambridge" recently written by J. Patrick Bury, M.A., Fellow and

Librarian of the College, which was compiled for the use of undergraduate students there.

It should be noted that priests of the Roman Catholic Church are forbidden to exorcise evil spirits without the consent and order of their Bishop. A similar ruling has been in force in the Church of England for almost 300 years. It would seem that whatever action the students took in the matter of the Corpus Christi haunting was without ecclesiastical sanction.

This article has been read and annotated by Sir Shane Leslie who was in residence at King's College during the haunting at Corpus Christi and who took part in the attempts at exorcism of the ghost. He has corrected the manuscript to agree with his recollection of the events. Through his kind cooperation the record of the ghost is brought up to date and some discrepancies between the original record in the *Occult Review* and the journalistic account of Lieut. Col. Cyril Foley have been reconciled.

ℭ THE HAUNTED RECTORY ℭ

**They heard the front door open and footsteps
crossed the hall and went upstairs. But no one was there.**

Grace Carey

The woman who had come to clean out Tain Rectory in Rossshire, Scotland, before the new Rector moved in heard strange sounds and the tread of footsteps in the empty house and she refused to finish the job. Highlanders are often prone to see and hear things and her fear might be ascribed to native superstition. But the same could not be said of the Rector and his family who came from the English Midlands.

The Barnes family, consisting of Rector David Barnes, his young wife and three children, took up residence in the solid old stone house on 26 August, 1947. The building is about 55 years old and stands back from the road on fairly spacious grounds. Many clergymen have resided here but as far as the Barnes know they never reported anything peculiar about the place.

One evening around 8:30, some three weeks after the Barnes family had moved in, Mrs. Barnes, having put the children to sleep, was in the kitchen with the maid preparing a meal for the Rector who was expected back shortly from Inverness, where he had gone by car.

The two women heard the front door open and footsteps cross the hall and go upstairs. Presently they heard someone pacing heavily back and forth in the upstairs bathroom, directly over the scullery adjoining the kitchen.

Mrs. Barnes assumed her husband had returned and as the sounds continued she feared he might be ill. She was about to go upstairs when she heard a car turn into the lower drive and stop at the front door. When the Rev. Mr. Barnes came in, going directly to the kitchen, the sounds upstairs stopped abruptly. The maid and Mrs. Barnes looked at each other in astonishment.

Mr. Barnes discounted their story as womanish nonsense, but did go upstairs to investigate. The bathroom was empty and the children fast asleep.

The next manifestation occurred the next month, in October, when the Barnes children were entertaining a child visitor. At about 5 p.m., as the family were finishing tea in the dining room, the front door opened and heavy footsteps sounded across the hall, halting just outside the dining-room door. Everyone in the room felt the vibration.

"I assumed," said Mrs. Barnes, "it was the nurse come to collect the child, and the thought passed through my mind that it was rather impertinent for her to have entered the house without knocking!"

Mr. Barnes, heretofore extremely skeptical, went to open the dining room door and found — no one. He examined the hall door and found the catch had not been lifted.

Early in 1948 Mrs. Barnes was alone one afternoon sewing in the little room over the porch, with her back to the door, when she heard someone scrunching over the newly gravelled drive. Again the front door opened and steps ascended the stairs, shuffled along the carpeted upper hall, pausing outside the room. She flung open the door to find no one there. Her husband came out of the study downstairs, where he had been working, and called up to ask who had just come in.

The Barneses by now were finding it difficult to keep a maid. But about this time they were able to engage a sensible, down-to-earth nanny to look after the young ones and help in the house.

Soon after her arrival Mr. and Mrs. Barnes left her in charge of the young family one evening. She sat knitting in the dining-room which adjoins the study. Presently she was disturbed by a tapping on the window. She assumed her employers had returned and had forgotten their keys. She went to the door and found that not only was the car not outside, but neither was anyone or anything else. She returned to the dining room and in a few minutes the tapping recommenced — this time on the adjoining study wall. Switching the study light on, again she found nothing.

In March, 1948, the Rector and his wife went out for the evening and left a new, young maid in charge. They were detained later than usual and did not arrive back at the Rectory until 1:30 a.m. They were annoyed to see that the kitchen light had been left burning. They went through the house to turn it out and found the poor girl huddled in a chair in a state of collapse. When she was able to speak she told them that almost as soon as they had left "someone had burst in through the front door and pranced about the front and back halls until midnight." She had been too scared to move, even neglecting the baby's 10 o'clock bottle.

At other times further unexplained "bangings" and noises

were heard about the house. In February, 1949, Mrs. Barnes was sitting by herself in the dining-room one evening. Her husband was not expected until later and it was the maid's evening out. The back was always kept locked at night and when Mrs. Barnes heard someone come in the front way and go through the back hall to the kitchen, she only wondered why the maid had cut her evening so short. The clatter of pots and pans and chairs which followed was out of all proportion to the preparations needed for the light supper which they would have when Mr. Barnes returned about 9 o'clock.

Thoroughly irritated, Mrs. Barnes went out to remonstrate with the girl. The kitchen and hall were in darkness. The noises died away as she approached. Half-an-hour later the maid came in and the same sounds, though moderated, were repeated.

"It was exactly as though I had been listening to a sound recording played through twice, one louder than the other," Mrs. Barnes said.

The very same incident was repeated precisely a few weeks later.

At night they were awakened by deafening noises in the kitchen which are proved on search to have no cause. There is no animal at the Rectory.

One night, hearing the tramp of footsteps in the maid's room next to her own, Mrs. Barnes rose to see if the girl were ill. She was sound asleep and no one else was in the room. Sometimes they heard the bumping of heavy furniture being moved across the floor. Unfortunately it always seems to be moved back again so they never have visual proof of the actions which they hear.

I asked Mrs. Barnes why they did not have the phenomena investigated by The Society for Psychical Research. She said: "We did mention these peculiar occurrences to one or two people connected with the church. They seemed unwilling to talk much about the subject and begged us not to do anything or the Rectory might 'get a bad name'! They seemed anxious that 'it' should be left alone, as it was not malevolent."

"That's all very well," I replied, "but you have to live in the house."

"Yes," she said, "but that's the odd thing. I, personally, have never felt scared of the 'presence' which visits — or lives — in the house. I'm used to it now. In the daytime the place is so bright and sunny — there's nothing sinister about it. Whatever 'influence' is there,

I feel it is not an evil one."

Except on the one occasion of the tea, the children have not seen or heard anything. Most of the manifestations happen after they are asleep.

Perhaps it is one of those Highland mysteries that will remain forever unsolved. Or perhaps some day a rector will arrive who is prepared to disregard local wishes and institute a psychic investigation.

HISTORY OF THE TALKING MONGOOSE
Harold J. Wilkins

One of the strangest phenomena of physico-psychical nature that I have investigated in the past 35 years was on the Isle of Man. The wild glens and rugged covers of this romantic and rather eerie island, washed by the often tempestuous Irish Sea, have been the home of Norse and Viking pirates in the remote past.

The fishermen and farmers, who speak a language called Manx, tell you of mermen and mermaids seen sporting in their wild coves and swear they speak the truth! There are also tales of giant men who lived on the island both before and after the Great Flood that sank Atlantis. And there are weird traditions of great tunnels, stretching far underground beneath the island.

A pair of strange brass shoes of monstrous size was dug up 200 years ago from under the ancient church yard of Kirkcarbra and a human skull of amazing size was also exhumed by grave-diggers. At another old church yard at Kirkbradden, leg-bones of giant men — 4 feet long from ankle to knee — have been found.

Some Manxmen still believe that Peel Castle is haunted by the fearsome spectre of a great coal black dog — called the "Moddhy Dhu" — which has fiery carbuncle eyes.

Three miles from this century-old Peel Castle, on the west coast of the island, reached by a rugged path which ascends steep cliffs, is a lonely farmhouse on a high down, about 740 feet above a cove of the wild Irish Sea. In summer time, when I was there, the fishermen told me that not long before they had seen an undine, or female water sprite, in that cove, called Glen Maye. It is, thus, exactly the setting for a strange adventure. Beautiful fuchsias grow wild and burgeon on the sod-banks. As I climbed the path, I was struck by the number of small stone and slate farmhouses abandoned by men unable to wrest a living from the unfertile and scanty soil of these lonely downs and uplands.

I was bound for Doarlish Cashen, or the Gap of Cashen, a fairy-sounding name. A seemingly fantastic story had been told in the London and North of England newspapers concerning this place. It was said that a "talking mongoose" had suddenly and unaccountably appeared in the farmhouse.

The nearest road lay some four miles away in the valley and I could not see even a trackway anywhere in sight on the wild downs. I caught sight of a grey stone house, very like the farmhouses in the wild hills of Wales. Sombre and stern, its walls were of slate slabs with narrow oblong windows not made to open for gales and lashing rains blow and sting most of the year. Doarlish Cashen has only two storeys and, as you approach, seems to be built on great slabs of concrete that show signs of cracking. A porch stands in front built to keep out the driving rains from the sea which otherwise would meet the occupants full-face when they come out the door.

The farmer I had gone to see was James T. Irving. Before the first World War he had been European agent for a firm of Canadian piano-makers. The war killed his trade and, as his wife is a native of the Isle of Man, he settled there.

James Irving was 64 years old when I met him and he had travelled widely in Turkey, Germany and Russia. He could speak some German and Russian and knew a little Urdu — the vernacular dialect of India.

His ducks, geese and hens were in yards and pens behind the house. Inside Mr. Irving had the rooms lined with matchboarding to keep out drafts. The space thus made was ideal for a small animal. A dark stairway leads up to two bedrooms. I had to grope because the ceilings had low beams and the ground floor room was dark. The only illumination was a smallish petroleum lamp. But there was an air of neatness about the place and signs of refinement very unusual in either a Welsh or Manx farmhouse. On the walls of the lower rooms were water colours and the living rooms were nicely furnished. Upstairs, in the Irvings' bedroom, Indian rugs lay on the floor. He struck me as an intelligent, articulate man, well able to keep the diaries and records on which this story is based.

Here is his story:

"In the autumn of 1931, one night we heard a noise that seemed to come from behind the matchboard partition in the parlour. It lasted some time, then ceased. Not long after, my daughter Voirrey and I were in the bedroom of the house when we both caught sight of an animal. I should say it was as large as a nearly full-grown rat; but the flat snout suggested a hedgehog. My daughter saw it before I did and she said it had a yellow face and flat snout."

Up to this time, as Mr. Irving's documents show, he did not suspect that there was anything supernormal or mystical about the animal. An idea struck him. He began to mimic the calls and cries of farm animals and poultry. Then he found that if he merely named the animal or bird the strange animal responded with an appropriate call. It now seemed that this weird animal was unusually intelligent!

Rather unpleasant things followed:

"This eerie weasel, as I thought he might be, began to keep us awake at night by blowing, spitting and growling behind the matchboard partition of the lower rooms. My daughter Voirrey tried nursery rhymes on it and it repeated them! It could now talk! Its voice was at least two octaves higher than any human voice, clear and distinct. It was not at all under our control. Far from it, indeed! It had begun to announce its presence but I never could tell whether it was in the house or outside. It called me 'Jim', and my wife, 'Maggie'. If we even whispered, it heard at what seemed 20 feet away and repeated what we had said!"

This eerie animal began to act like a poltergeist, and made such a nuisance of itself that Irving thought that the family would be forced to quit the farmhouse. He spread some rat poison behind the partition and he says:

"One night after we had gone to bed — my wife was then miles away from home — we were wakened by a most horrid screaming. It lasted 20 minutes. I said to Voirrey, who was in the next room, 'I put some rat poison down and I reckon that infernal animal has taken some. I thought it had died but a few nights later, it resumed the nocturnal disturbances. By this time it could carry on a long conversation with us."

One night soon it set up a diabolical howling and sighing and moaning, as if to "pay back" Irving for the attempted poisoning! It kept the racket up for half an hour and more without stop. It sounded as if some human being was at the point of agonizing death.

No doubt Irving would have packed up and left the farm, so little sleep could the family get, but there might have been serious impediments against selling a farm that was not merely remote but now seemed to have become "haunted"! By now the news had spread, not only all over the Isle of Man but had been wired and cabled to newspapers in Liverpool, Manchester, Sheffield, Leeds and London. The London *Daily Sketch* — a picture tabloid — came out with a story about "A Talking Weasel Farm," with a photo. The Manchester *Daily Dispatch* sent a man down to the farm. He was mystified and wrote:

"10 January, 1932: ... Here at *Doarlish Cashen*, the farm of the

'Talking Weasel,' this mysterious beast has spoken to me, today! My investigation of the most remarkable animal story ever given publicity — a story which is finding credence all over the Isle of Man — leaves me in a state of considerable perplexity. Have I heard a weasel speak? I do not know, but I do know that I heard, today, a voice I never imagined could issue from a human throat. The people here at the farm who claim it is the voice of a strange animal seem sane, honest and responsible people not likely to indulge in difficult long-drawn-out practical jokes to make the theme the talk of the world and I find that others, too, have had my strange experience."

The reporter was quite correct. The Irving family are normal people.

"No," said Irving to the reporter, "there are no spooks here! This farm is not haunted. All that has happened is that a strange animal has taken up its abode here."

However, before long Irving had reason to suppose that this "talking weasel" might be something other than a weasel. It had some poltergeistic features, but it did what no poltergeist has been known to do, it killed rabbits for the family table, wandered the Isle of Man, hid in garages, eavesdropped on the workers there, repeated their talk including technical terms, and returned to Doarlish Cashen farmhouse to relate what it had seen and heard! It even visited the airfields on the island, watched planes landing and taking off, listened to the talk of pilots, and according to Irving even developed such an interest in cars as to distinguish their makes!

One can believe or not, what the same reporter said:

"The weasel even gave me a tip for a winner in the Grand National!"

Next day the reporter was alone in a room in the farmhouse with Voirrey, Irving's young daughter, then aged 13. He heard a piercing and uncanny voice talking with Mrs. Irving in the room adjoining. Meanwhile the girl sat on a chair a few feet from the reporter. Her lips did not move but she was sucking a piece of string. The reporter stated:

"I edged into the next room where the weasel was talking and the voice ceased. Voirrey remained motionless, taking no notice of any of us."

Later on other things happened which strongly suggest that the phenomena of the "mongoose" was not connected, as many poltergeist phenomena are, with the paranormal, or parapsychological force of which some young boys and girls approaching puberty seem to be the medium. It continued long after Voirrey had passed this stage of her growth.

Irving now heard that another farmer named Irvine (sic) whose land lay near Doarlish Cashen had in 1914 turned loose in a field mongooses he bought for the purpose of killing rabbits which were a pest. I am told by an Isle of Man resident that a farmer on the island actually shot a mongoose there, in 1947. There is no evidence that it talked!

Irving henceforth called the mongoose "Jef." He says that, when told, the animal said:

"Yes, I like that name. I was born near Delhi, India, on June 7, 1852. I have been shot at by Indians. I am a marsh mongoose."

This fantastic statement would mean that when the weird animal came to the Isle of Man and appeared on Irving's farm he was already 79 years old! According to Mr. Irving's documents, three years later on January 20, 1935, "Jef" sang a song in a vernacular tongue of India, using the words lookee and jemara. He also mimicked Hindus with whom, he says, he lived:

"I was," the mongoose said, "brought to England from Egypt by a man named Holland. When I was in India I lived with a tall man who wore a green turban on his head. Then I lived with a deformed man, a hunchback. I knocked over a bowl on a table, and one man said to the other: 'Comee, gommadah, mongus'."

One day men repairing a road some miles up in a valley got a shock. They looked up and saw a piece of bread one of the men had thrown away apparently being carried by something invisible. "It's that bloody mongoose!" shouted a scared man.

A worker in a garage miles away was hurt when something he could not see hurled an iron bolt at his head. "Jef" told Irving that he had been to that garage.

I now summarize other events of 1932:

A woman wrote from the Isle of Man inviting the late Harry Price — the ghost hunter — to come from London and investigate the "talking mongoose." Price sent a Captain Macdonald, a business man, racing driver, and member of Price's National Laboratory of Psychical Research, to investigate. Macdonald made three separate visits to Doarlish Cashen, and part of his report, found in the archives of the University of London's Council for Psychical and Paranormal Phenomena Research, is as follows:

"On my first day, the Irvings showed me cracks in the farmhouse walls where they said the mongoose spied on visitors. I was there till midnight, but the mongoose was silent. As I was leaving to go to my hotel and had my hand on the door, a voice screamed: 'Who is that b—y man?' Irving gripped my arm. 'That's the animal!' he said. I went back next day and Irving told me that 'Jef' said I must give Voirrey a camera, or he would not speak. 'I've been looking at that man,' the mongoose said, 'and I don't like him. He does not believe in me. He is a doubter!' ... At 5:30 p.m., something threw a large needle at the tea pot on the table. 'He often throws things at us,' said Irving to me. ... Later a noise was heard in the scullery but no one was there, but we found a little stream of water running from a hole in the wall. 'It's the mongoose, piddling', said Irving.

I heard a shrill voice upstairs talking to Mrs. Irving. I went to the foot of the stairs and shouted up: 'I believe in you, Jef. So come down and show yourself.' The mongoose screams: 'No, I don't like you and I won't stay!' I tried to creep up on Jef but fell on a broken stair with a loud clatter. A voice shrieked: 'He's coming, the dirty old sleech!' (dialect for sly man). The voice was heard no more that night."

Macdonald said he did not know what to think.

Voirrey reported trying to photograph the mongoose, who was sitting on a wall in the farm-yard; but he jumped down before she could click the shutter. He was not seen again for some time.

Irving found that, one night, the mongoose left footprints in the dust of one room. Irving said these prints showed that the mongoose had much larger forefeet than hindfeet. "The forefeet look like human hands with very long fingers!" he said.

Mrs. Irving put her hand through a crack and stroked the mongoose at one time and he bit her with sharp teeth that drew blood. "He gripped my hand like a vice." She says, "He takes chocolates, bananas, biscuits, pie and sausage, while sitting on the rafter. He chases the rats from the outbuildings. He sings songs of Turkish Jews in Spanish, plays with a ball he is given, and stole a ball of wool from a distant house and gave it to me. He spits and swears at people he does not like and even calls out the names of papers or books people are reading yards away!"

Irving reported an extraordinary event that seemed to show that the mongoose had learnt to read:

"I was reading a Liverpool newspaper, when the animal called out in alarm: 'I see something!' What? I asked. 'A name that makes me quake, makes me shake!' I can find nothing alarming in the paper. Jef bawls: 'Have a dekko again! Look in the deaths.' I look and see the obituary of a man named Jeffreys just died, and, in brackets after it, 'Jef'! I had not noticed it before.

"It is found that Jef can tell to a minute when I get back home from Peel," Mr. Irving says, "and before I arrive, he says, when I am still a mile away: 'Jim's coming'."

The mongoose killed 54 rabbits in one year. He did not bite the rabbits but apparently strangled them.

"Jef" spent a night in, at the farm, and talked for three hours without a stop. The Irvings could get no sleep. He seemed to have been studying medical treatises for he reeled off names of 60 diseases. Said Irving:

"He laughed like a devil when I was unwell, and called out: 'Hey Jim, ain't I got horse's pains in my tail?'"

When he is hungry he thumps the walls and this after a long absence from the farm. I ignore him. He calls: 'Hey, you devil, you heard me! I want chukko.' He is given biscuits and uncooked bacon. For two nights he is missing. When he returns to the farmhouse he tells me he's been at a garden party, 10 miles off.

On the night of 28 January, 1934, I am wakened from sleep by a hoarse whisper from the roof-beam. 'Hey, Jim, I want chukko!' My wife throws up two biscuits onto the place where he squats on the rafter. If they happen to be tea and unsweetened biscuits, he angrily refuses them, says: 'You better keep 'em if you ain't got better!' This night I hear his bony fingers scraping round. Seems he can't find the biscuits. My wife throws up a box of matches. The mongoose is heard to take a match from the box and strike it. He finds the biscuit, blows out the lighted match, and throws the box back into the bedroom.

Next, he takes paper from one drawer and pencil from another and outlines his paw-hand. On another night, he roams the house and, after we've got to sleep, wakes us up with loud laughter and flashes beams from an electric torch on to our eyes, from his stance on the rafter.

The mongoose once played the Irvings a very dirty trick. They had pestered him to give some evidence of himself and on a night in May, 1935, he woke them up calling out: "Go'n look in the bowl on the shelf downstairs, and you'll find something precious." They went and found a piece of fur. The mongoose said: "I pulled it from my eyebrow and, my God, it did hurt!" Later, Harry Price had it microphotographed by experts at the London Zoo Park who stated it was hair from a dog, not a mongoose. However, it did not match in colour the hair of the sheepdog on Irving's farm! And it had been "clipped" rather than combed or pulled.

On 30 July, 1935, Harry Price and R. S. Lambert — the latter was then editor of the BBC's journal, the "Listener" — visited the farm to take photos and hear and see the mongoose. They were at the farm till midnight but the mongoose was deaf to all invitations to show himself or make himself heard. Later Price and Lambert wrote a book about their adventures, and titled it: "The Haunting of Cashen's Gap."

Irving wondered if the mongoose had met with an accident for he had not been heard about the farm for five weeks. But the weird animal turned up at midnight of the very day that Price and Lambert left by steamer for Liverpool. Said Irving:

"I and my wife were in bed fast asleep when a loud clapping of hands came from the rafter and something was thrown onto the bed. There were roars of diabolical laughter. I called out: 'Where have you been?' The mongoose said: 'I'm back. Been all over this blessed island!' Irving: 'Were you here, you rascal, when Mr. Price and Mr. Lambert were here?' Mongoose: 'Yes.' Irving: 'Then why did you not speak? Remember: you yourself invited these gentlemen to come.' The mongoose: 'There was a doubter present.' The animal meant Lambert. To prove it, the mongoose described Price's appearance: 'He looks like a minister and has a gold ring on the little finger of his left hand. I peered at him through a crack in the boards. Yes, and it was me who upset the pan of Maggie's water in the kitchen, Jim!' The mongoose then made it plain that he was very particular about the quality of the biscuits my wife gave him for chukko. He demanded bananas and knew all about some apricots my wife had hidden in a drawer."

The mongoose was now invited to stamp impressions of his feet in some plasticine sent by Harry Price. He demanded that it be softened first: "It is too damned hard!" he said. The plasticine, along with some dough, was placed on the rafter where the mongoose sat at night. (One gathers from Irving's records that the mongoose sits there while Voirrey is sleeping in the room below from which the rafter — actually the boxed-in top of the staircase — is visible. He is seldom seen, yet very much heard!):

"While we were asleep," (Irving's dossier), "the mongoose stamped his feet in the stuff and gave it a twist. He said next night, 'It was as hard as hell but I did it. Go'n look!'"

Four casts were left by the mongoose. One shows a sort of thumb and three pudgy fingers suggestive of a lap dog. No. 2 shows what might, or might not, be prints of four "paw-hands," extended. Nos. 3 and 4 show what are said to be the mongoose's hind foot and teeth marks. After studying these prints one is forced to say that they look more like a jawbone of a prehistoric ape-man, a bizarre impression of a flabby molluse with four truncated tentacles and flippers dragged over a sandy beach still wet with the outgoing tide. No wonder that, when these casts were shown to Mr. R. I. Pocock of the Natural History Museum's Zoological Department, he bluntly declared:

"One print might have been made by a dog; but the other is of no mammal known to me unless it is that of an American raccoon. There is no mammal with such disparity between the size of the fore and hind feet as these prints show, nor do I think tooth marks are shown in the cast. Finally, I must add that I do not think these photographs represent foot tracks at all. Most certainly none of them were made by a mongoose."

Had this talking mongoose played another of his tricks, like that of the fur he said was torn out of his own eye-brow, but which was really dog's hair?

Irving now told the mongoose: "We are having a dictaphone to record your voice."

The mongoose said: "Who's we? Is it that spook man, Harry Price? Why I won't speak into it. I'll go and smash his windows; I'll drop a brick on him as he lies in bed. Me, at the age of 83?"

The mongoose seemed to have heard of dictaphones. Irving was told by him that he had listened in to a radio broadcast while wandering the island.

One photograph taken dimly shows a grey form on a sod-bank near the farm. It might, or might not, be the mongoose. An artist drew the mongoose from the Irving family's description. It was shown to the mongoose who replied: "That ain't me, it's more like a Llama." The Irvings say he never showed himself to them for more than three seconds at a time, when they have seen his 6-inch long body with bushy tail, conical head, and front paw with three fingers and thumb — this last totally unlike the paw of a mongoose.

What, or who, then, was this talking animal?

Lambert appears to have said he did not believe in "Jef" at all.

Irving says: "The mongoose said to my wife, 'I know what I

am, but I shan't tell you. I might let you see me, but not to get to know me. I'm a freak. I've hands and feet. If you saw me, you'd be petrified, mummified. At another time, he said: 'I'm a ghost in form of a weasel.' Later, he denied he was a spook."

Mr. Lambert suggested he may have been just a voice and nothing more. But something more than a mere voice would be required to throw about a heavy chair as this animal, with a six-inch long body and six-inch tail, did at one time. The evidence of witnesses suggests that the animal existed yet was as elusive as a bodiless spook. He could disappear when chased behind a stone wall beyond which no cover whatever existed. He could race at "terrific speed" and then vanish.

Did this "talking mongoose" hail from some invisible world that may be all about us, imperceptible to our senses, since its wavelengths are different from ours?

In some ways he reminds us of what was said of the "familiars" — alleged evil spirits under a witch's control — in the 16th- and 17th-century witch trials. Some of these familiars, in the shapes of ferrets or pole cats, lived in crannies of cottages and farms. In the case of Joan Cason, who lived at Faversham in Kent, in 1596, people said at her trial that she lived with a ferret with reddish eyes, which cried out words like "Go to, Go to," from a crack in a wall. Cason was in a fair way to being hoisted on the gallows on charge of dealing with the devil and had the Irvings lived in her day they would have run grave risks of torture and hanging. It was then said that familiars lived for 60 years and more. However, in our presumably rational and scientific age, talk of familiars sounds like mediaeval nonsense. The fact is that when familiars ceased to be given credence, they ceased to exist. Is that why the "talking mongoose" was so angry when "doubters" called at Doarlish Cashen?

In 1947 a farmer on the Isle of Man shot a mongoose but whether it was "Jef" or a descendant of one of the mongooses turned loose in a field in the Isle of Man in 1914 by Irvine no one can say.

Last 14 August I had a letter from the news editor and director of a leading Isle of Man newspaper. He wrote:

"We fear that 'Jef,' the famous Dalby spook, has passed into legend. Strange that you remember my visit to Doarlish Cashen in 1935. It certainly was a remarkable experience. The Irvings sold the farm to a man named Graham just around the end of the last war, and he went in for poultry. Graham claimed to have killed an unusually large type of weasel and thought that this might have been the animal that inspired 'Jef.' This animal had been raiding his chicken run and he set snares for it. He caught the animal but it was so ferocious and dangerous that he had to kill it, and he produced the pelt for our reporter's inspection. Had he been able to cage the animal he might have been front page news. Who knows?"

I do not believe that "Jef" was a mongoose or a spook. Nor do I see any proof that the animal shot by Graham was identical with "Jef" the talking "Mongoose." The mystery still remains.

LIMPING GHOST OF BALLECHIN

**You needn't believe that the major came back
as a dog; at least the dogs themselves came back.**

J. Jerry Newman

In 1892 John, third Marquess of Bute, a member of the Society for Psychical Research, met a Jesuit priest from whom he heard a strange account of an allegedly haunted house in Scotland.

The priest, Father Hayden, S.J., confided that he had slept only one night out of the nine he had spent as a visitor in Ballechin House, Perthshire, being disturbed by queer, inexplicable noises every night except the last.

He added that, of all the strange manifestations during his stay, the sound that alarmed him most was that resembling a large animal throwing itself against his bedroom door.

In August, 1896, Ballechin House was rented for a period of 12 months to a wealthy Spanish family. They left suddenly after a stay of only seven weeks, forfeiting more than 10 months' rent rather than stay longer in the house.

In 1897, Lord Bute, together with a Colonel Taylor, Miss Goodrich-Freer and other members of the S.P.R., rented Ballechin House for the purpose of conducting a thorough investigation of the phenomenon.

Guests who had stayed at Ballechin testified that they had been disturbed by groans, rappings, and other violent and unexplained noises. Often they were awakened by the sounds of dragging footsteps which traversed the passages and circled their beds. Sometimes, in the middle of the night, an unearthly shriek would ring through the house.

Ballechin House was owned by a Major Steuart who retired from military service in 1850, some 16 years after succeeding to the property. He was passionately fond of dogs and he kept 14. A life-long student of psychic matters, he was convinced that the spirits of the dead were able to return to earthly friends and surroundings.

A deep interest in werewolves and vampirism led him to assert that, far from being empty superstition as was popularly believed, lycanthropy (the changing of a man into an animal) was a fact. He affirmed on many occasions his intention of returning after death in the form of his favorite spaniel.

The Major died in 1876 and so powerful had been his influence that immediately after his death all his dogs, including his favorite black spaniel, were shot. Shortly afterwards, phenomena of an unusual, often violent nature broke out.

The whole household would be roused by the manifestations and on one occasion five male guests, dressed only in their nightshirts, met at the top of the stairs. They were armed with sticks and pokers and one of them carried a revolver.

Heavy footsteps and the pattering feet of invisible dogs were heard in empty rooms. Groans accompanied heavy knocking. Spectral figures were seen and on several occasions a colonel was awakened during the night by the bedclothes being lifted mysteriously from his bed.

A butler, Harold Sanders, who had been with the Spanish family that fled from Ballechin so abruptly, wrote a letter which was printed in *The Times* during the Ballechin House controversy which occupied the columns of that paper from 8 to 24 June, 1897. Mr. Sanders wrote:

"I kept watch altogether about 12 times in various parts of the house. When watching I always experienced a peculiar sensation a few minutes before hearing any noise. I can only describe it as like suddenly entering an ice house and feeling that someone was present and about to speak to me ..."

Of one experience he wrote: "I shall not forget it as long as I live. I had not been in bed three minutes before I experienced the sensation as before ... my bedclothes were lifted up, first at the foot of my bed but gradually coming towards my head. I held the clothes around my neck with my hands but they were gently lifted in spite of my efforts to hold them. I then reached around with my hand but could feel nothing.

I could distinctly feel and hear something breathing over me. I then tried to reach some matches that were on a chair by my bedside but my hand was held back as if by some invisible power. Then the thing seemed to retire to the foot of my bed. I suddenly found the foot of my bed lifted up and carried around towards the window for about three or four feet, then replaced to its former position."

These extracts from a rather lengthy letter serve to confirm what at first appeared no more than speculation — that the phenomena were directed with greater intensity against permanent residents than against visitors. The staff at Ballechin were continually dogged by noises and apparitions.

One of the maids, Elizabeth, slept in a room by herself while two others slept in an adjoining room. One night Elizabeth woke to see, hovering above her bed, a mist-like cloud which changed shape continuously as she watched. As it sank lower she felt her bedclothes tugged.

Presently the coverlets were lifted clear of the bed. The maid was so frightened that she lay for a long while unable to move or utter a word. When she recovered, her screams were so frightening that the other maids were too scared to go to her room. From that time on the three girls slept in one room.

It was about this time that the "dog" phenomenon reached its peak. Visitors who brought their own animals with them to Ballechin remarked on, their strange behaviour. Two guests saw their dogs romping with another dog, a black spaniel, which vanished as strangely as it had appeared.

A lady guest was awakened one night by the whining of her dog which was lying at the foot of her bed. She saw two black paws resting on a table at her bedside. No other portion of the strange dog was visible.

Another lady, like many others, had been repeatedly disturbed by the sounds of limping footsteps which circled her bed. Shortly afterwards she heard stories about the former owner. She asked if he could be described.

"Well," said her informant, "the most striking thing I can remember about him is that he had a peculiar limp." And he gave an exhibition which tallied exactly with the limp she had heard around her bed.

During the investigation conducted by Miss Goodrich-Freer and Lord Bute, Miss Freer kept a journal in which she entered the details of all phenomena. Under the date 16 February, 1897, she wrote:

"About 10 a.m. I was writing in the library and presently felt a distinct, but gentle, push against my chair. I thought it was my dog (Miss Freer owned a black pomeranian) and looked down but he was not there. I went on writing and in a few moments felt another push, firm and decided, against my chair. I looked backward with an exclamation — the room was empty."

21 February: "Heard noise of patterings ... Scamp (Miss Freer's dog) got up and sat, apparently watching something invisible to us, turning his head slowly as if following movements across the room.

The interest which our dogs took in these phenomena led us to the conclusion that the sounds were those of a dog gambolling."

Remarkable as were these phenomena there were others during Colonel Taylor's tenancy which were witnessed by numerous members of the household. These include the apparition of a woman in grey, a spectral nun, the bent, white-haired figure of a limping man and a phantom crucifix which appeared momentarily to one of the guests and which was seen again, some time later, held by a materialized hand.

But through all these manifestations the dominant phenomena appeared to focus around the limping footsteps and the phantom dogs, sometimes incredibly reinforced by the familiar doggy smell so common during the days of the Major.

Visitors and servants heard, on many occasions, the quarrelling voices of a man and woman, their tones loud and rough, their words indistinguishable. It seemed a repetition of the scene of the Major browbeating his housekeeper as he did in life.

For more than a decade dour parishioners and voluble village tradesmen gossiped about the "queer goings on up at the House." The Major's idiosyncracies appeared as lively a source of interest after his death as they had been during his life.

Incredible, perhaps. But all the evidence points to the fact that the Major kept his promise and on more than one occasion he returned — either with or as a dog!

MYSTERY AT PENKAET CASTLE

At first they thought it was a mistake when the freshly made bed was found disarranged. But then they heard it begin to creak ...

Edmond P. Gibson

Penkaet Castle is an old Scottish mansion which stands near Pencaitland, Haddington, about 20 miles east of Edinburgh. It is not far from Tantallon Castle, famed in Scott's *Marmion*. Penkaet Castle is near the River Tyne and near the south coast of the Firth of Forth. It was built early in the 16th century. The castle has been kept in repair by a succession of owners and extensive changes have been made but the old structure is almost entirely in its original form. In 1923 the castle was purchased by the late Prof. Ian B. Stoughton Holbourn. Professor Holbourn was, at one time, Chairman of the Division of Fine Arts, Carlton College, Northfield, Minn. He has held also professorships in England and Scotland. His family still owns the castle.

According to local history the castle was once owned by a John Cockburn who was possessed of an evil reputation. He is said to have killed John Seton, a relative by marriage. The murder is assumed to be the cause of the unusual phenomena which have occurred at Penkaet in the past and which continue up to the present time. This explanation may be open to question; the phenomena associated with Penkaet Castle are not.

J. W. Herries, chairman of trustees of the Edinburgh Psychic College and Library, has spent a great deal of time gathering information about the castle and its phenomena. He has taken statements from many persons who have witnessed strange occurrences within the walls and he compiled a report which was published in the *Journal of the American Society for Psychical Research*, in October, 1947. The following account is taken from Mr. Herries' statement and from the statements of witnesses to more recent occurrences at Penkaet.

One interesting piece of furniture in the castle is a bed, owned and used by King Charles II, which was given to Professor Holbourn by his students. This bed came to the castle with the Professor and his family. It is elaborately carved and carries what is probably a death

75

mask of Charles I on the bottom standards. The bed stands in one of the large rooms on the third floor. In recent years the Penkaet ghost has taken an interest in this bed and unusual phenomena are associated with it.

Mrs. Holbourn told Mr. Herries that when the Holbourns occupied the ground-floor bedroom, below the room in which the King Charles bed stands, she and her husband heard movements in the unoccupied room above. Sometimes the sound was that of moving furniture. Sometimes sounds of stumbling and groping around the room could be heard. Investigation of the room never yielded anything. The sounds remained unexplained, even though Mrs. Holbourn was averse to any paranormal explanation.

Mrs. Holbourn's statement appeared in the A.S.P.R. report as follows:

"When we first came here in 1923 we were often disturbed by the sound of heavy footsteps going through the house and the sound of something heavy and soft being dragged along. Other persons who occupied the house during our visits to Foula complained of hearing shrieks and groans and of finding doors, which were shut and locked at night, open in the morning. One girl was so terrified that she refused to sleep alone.

As time went on the sounds became trivial and even playful. Sometimes when there was a light continuous tapping or rattling my husband would call out, 'Now John, that's childish. Stop it!' and the sound invariably ceased at once. We called him 'the perfect gentleman!'

On Christmas Eve, 1923, we had been singing carols in the music room and were gathered around the fire when a piece of oak, seven by six inches, on which the family crest was carved, leant forward from the wall, paused a moment, and returned to position. We took this as a greeting to us, the new inhabitants."

Mr. Herries reports the following incident which was told to him by Mrs. Holbourn:

"About 1924 Professor and Mrs. Holbourn went to visit the Island of Foula which Professor Holbourn had purchased in 1901. A cousin was left in the house. In the course of his stay there, on taking a visitor up to see the King Charles bed, he found the bedclothes disarranged as if the bed had not been made. He drew the attention of the daughter of the gardener to this fact. She is Mrs. Anderson and lives in an adjoining cottage. It was part of her duty to remake the bed after it had been slept in. She asserted that she had left the bed properly made up. Shortly afterwards a visitor got permission to take a photograph and on going up to the room with him the cousin again found the bedclothes disarranged. Again it was made up by Mrs. Anderson.

A day or so later the visitor who had taken the photograph reported that it had been under-exposed and returned to take another photograph. On going up to the room they again found that the bedclothing had been disarranged. Mrs. Anderson once more made up the bed and Mr. Holbourn's cousin took the precaution of locking the two doors giving access to the room and seeing that the windows were well secured. Two bricks were placed against the main door. Next day it was found that the bricks were displaced and again the bed-clothing was disarranged.

On another occasion a heavy antique cabinet in the room, very difficult to move, was found six inches away from the wall. A brass ewer and basin which Mrs. Holbourn's grandfather had brought from Turkey had stood on top of the cabinet and this ewer was found on its side."

Mrs. Holbourn also says:

"About 1925 Avis Dolphin, a survivor of the *Lusitania* disaster who lived with us for a number of years, was sleeping in the King Charles bed. My husband and I slept in the room beneath. One night Avis came to our door to say that there was someone moving about on the ground floor. My husband got up and they went downstairs to investigate. On returning, when they reached the second floor, they stood on the stairs and listened. From the room above they heard the unmistakeable creaking sounds of a person turning over in the King Charles bed which the girl had just vacated.

One evening when Avis was coming upstairs in the dark she felt a light touch on her neck, like someone gently drawing a tip of a finger across her throat. That same year I sometimes saw faint shimmering lights in the passages.

In 1935 a lady who was recovering from an illness was sleeping in the King Charles bed and my brother slept in the room below. About 5 a.m. he came to me and said, 'I think Mrs. R. has fallen out of bed and is knocking for help.' I found the lady sleeping soundly in her bed.

I would like to make it clear that although we regard 'John' as an amusing, legendary figure, none of us seriously believes in the existence of our ghost. I think there must be some material explanation."

On 29 July, 1946, Penkaet Castle was visited by about 100 members of the East Lothian Antiquarian and Field Naturalists Society. In an upper gallery, now used as a library, a glass globe disintegrated into thousands of fragments while there were a number of visitors in the room. No one was within six feet of the globe and there was no apparent cause for the accident. The globe was two feet high. It had a base of approximately 20 inches. It was a half-oval, used to protect a model of the mansion. While there is no normal explanation of what occurred it resembles numerous other cases of glass disintegration which apparently have been of psychic origin. This phenomenon topped off a series of events which took place in the spring of that same year.

Dramatic students of the Edinburgh College of Art, seven in all, visited Penkaet Castle to rehearse a forthcoming play, "Ladies in Retirement," Mrs. Holbourn's son Alasdair was a student at the College at that time. Mrs. Holbourn arranged accommodation for the students. She herself occupied the music room. During the night she heard over her head loud and continued noises which did not stop until three o'clock in the morning. She concluded that the girls of the party, who occupied a room above, were behaving badly. Her son and her son's wife had slept in the dining room. They reported in the morning that they had scarcely closed their eyes because of the noise. They thought this very unusual behavior for visitors to a strange house.

Miss Pat M. T. and Miss Jocelyn L. S. occupied the room with the King Charles bed. They subsequently gave Mr. Herries the following statements concerning their experience.

"They had two candles in the room, one on either side of the bed, also an oil heater. The room felt very cold. They went to bed but could not sleep and they lay awake and talked. They noticed, some time after going to bed (about 2 a.m.), a large, broad stain on the wall opposite the bed. It was on the right hand side of the fireplace, beginning a little below the cornice and extending halfway down the wall, tapering toward the bottom. It suggested, to some extent, a section of the paper having come off the wall and hanging down. The walls were light in shade and this patch was a dark brown colour. Next night they noticed it was gone. They experimented with the candles to see if it could be explained by a mere shadow but were unable to secure anything like it. They further stated that about midnight they heard an extraordinary sound 'like something going down a slope'. They heard this sound repeated from time to time. They also heard sounds like footsteps in the room above. At the time they put the footsteps down to W. H. Brown, but afterward he stated that at that time he was sound asleep.

Miss Myra B. was in the Long Room (on the same floor as the King Charles Room and behind the latter). She shared it with Miss Rae B. Miss Myra B. stated that she heard the trundling sound overhead. It had a rhythmic character. She heard it only once and she was scared. There were also noises and creaks such as are given out by furniture. One of the glass panes in a window was imperfect and this might account for some of the sounds. 'The room was cold and I had a feeling that we were never quite alone'.

Miss Pat M. T. commented on another matter. 'I had with me,' she said, 'a square clock. It has gone regularly ever since I went to school. I packed it on Saturday morning and it was going then. I took it out at Penkaet and wound it. It never went more than five minutes during our stay. It would not go on the Saturday or the Sunday.'

Miss Pat M. T. said she tried to get the clock to go several times. It stopped at midnight definitely.

Mr. Holbourn remarked that no clock would go placed on the wall between the dining room and the next room. Even a watch hung up on that wall would not go.

Miss Jocelyn L. S. said she was extremely ill during her stay. On Sunday, she said, they were accused of having been up all the previous night because other people came into their rooms to discuss matters.

Miss Myra B., who occupied the Long Room with Miss Rae B., said she did not like the room. She disliked it at once. It had a bad effect on her. She also felt ill during the visit.

Mr. Holbourn recalled a previous experience in the 'Middle Room.' They had a Siamese cat at that time and one night he heard a scratching at one of the two doors at opposite ends of the room. He rose to open the door and when he was a yard from it the door was suddenly thrown wide open. At the same time the other door opened wide and a curtain on the partition wall blew out, although there was no wind to account for this. This occurrence was followed by the sound of footsteps down the passage."

William H. Brown slept over the room with the King Charles bed. It was from his room that some of the noises had appeared to come. He reported that all he did during the evening was to go into the study of the late Professor for a book to read. He then had returned to his room, undressed, and read in bed for about half an hour before he fell asleep. He slept soundly all night. Mr. Brown denied that he made or caused any of the disturbances, nor was he aware of them until he was accused the next morning of making the noises heard from the room with the King Charles bed.

Other strange incidents have occurred at Penkaet. On one occasion the bathroom was found full of steam as though a tap had been opened and shut. The bath tub was dry. Noises were heard in the bathroom but there was no one unaccounted for in the house.

Mrs. Holbourn told Mr. Herries that on the night of Professor Holbourn's funeral footsteps were heard on the path and the front door opened and shut. A search was made but nothing was found to account for the sounds. When her son returned from searching, the household cat came in with him and appeared terrified; it hid under the table, tail lashing.

Mr. Herries interrogated Mrs. Anderson, who saw the disarranged bedclothes on the King Charles bed and remade it on several occasions when no one had been occupying the room. She had no theory to explain the condition of the bed or to explain how the locked room had been opened and the two bricks removed.

In a recent letter to me Mrs. Holbourn states that some of the Penkaet occurrences may have been due to "elaborate leg-pulls" and that explanations of some of the noises might be due to ill-fitting doors and windows, falling plaster, and wide chimneys which occasionally admit birds. However she adds:

"The first mention of the ghost goes back more than 300 years when a former owner, Sir Andrew Dick Lauder, then aged nine, saw a ghost standing on the hearth in his bedroom. He was told it was the moon shining down the wide chimney. One wonders if this explanation satisfied his elders. If so, would they have bothered to record the incident?

The ghost apparently did not reappear till we came into residence in 1922. Then we all, including our three student sons, decided that such a romantic house must have a ghost. We collected mysterious happenings; it was sort of a game. Then some of our visitors became scared and added their own experiences. The affair snowballed and rather got out of hand.

When I am alone I am never disturbed but when we have

large house parties there is often an unreasonable amount of noise. It is possible that the guests contribute more than they realize; I do not know.

An occurrence which I am inclined to treat more seriously was possibly a vivid nightmare. My daughter-in-law, who is psychic, was nursing my aged mother and sleeping in the same room. One night she thought she saw a very small man, almost a pigmy, dressed in a sort of grey cloak, emerge from a deep 'powder closet' and cross the room. She was terrified that he would attack her patient but he passed the end of the bed and went out of the door, to her great relief.

I've heard that Lord Fountainhall, one of the former owners, was an exceptionally small and very terrifying man.

A year or two ago a neighbour, Mrs. Taylor, helped with the spring cleaning. She and a woman who lived in the house were sitting on the edge of a bed when a man looked in at the door and glanced round the room. Mrs. Taylor looked at her companion who evidently saw nothing. The man went on down the stairs. The clock on the landing below, which has not run for 30 years, then started striking and continued for a long time. Mrs. Taylor said the man was 'shadowy' but she could see the shape of his lower limbs clearly, as if he were wearing knickerbockers or knee breeches. I heard the clock striking but was not told about the apparition until some months afterwards. Mrs. Taylor said 'she supposed it was imagination'.

An amusing experience was the finding of a pet lamb in my four-poster bed. He scuttled downstairs and the heavy iron-studded oak door slammed behind him. He was seen tearing up the drive as if pursued by all the furies. There was no wind and I have never known that door to shut of its own accord."

Many of the phenomena which occur at Penkaet appear to be of poltergeist type but the fulcrum for poltergeist manifestations seems to be missing, i.e. an adolescent. Other of the phenomena appear to be due to hauntings. The behaviour of the cat resembles that of other animals in the presence of paranormal phenomena.

The fact that the "ghost" seems intelligent does not exclude phenomena of the poltergeist type. But the occurrence of phenomena over a long period, with changes of occupancy, points to the possibility that the castle is the home of a mischievous ghost, a ghost who can vary or stop the phenomena at the request of the occupants of the house.

The Edinburgh Psychic College and Library and Mr. J. W. Herries have kindly given permission to use the factual material from

Mr. Herries' report, and the American Society for Physical Research have given permission to quote from their extensive report on Penkaet Castle in the *Journal*, October, 1947, pp. 171-180.

THE GHOST WHO PAID RENT

Not long after my parents were married in Ireland, Father decided to rent a large, attractive old house. It was not until after he had signed a 10-year lease and the landlord and lawyer had left, that the out-going tenant confided to Father that the house was haunted. But it was a marvelously lucky house financially because every man who had lived there for the past 100 years had retired with a fortune. Both of these statements proved in the years following to be true.

When my Mother heard about the house being haunted she laughed. Her own home had been haunted and she was not afraid of ghosts — or anything else.

The first ghost she became acquainted with was the "noisy ghost," then the ghost of the monk, then the "sorrowful ghost." The monk haunted the cobbled yard. The noisy ghost was heard only from the bedroom behind the drawing room and the kitchen. The sorrowful ghost haunted the top, front bedroom.

My parents had chosen this particular bedroom for their own. Father had it papered and painted at his own expense and bought Mother a burl walnut bedroom suite because she was about to have her first baby.

Sitting one evening before the bedroom fire, Father said he wished his brother would pay him the money he owed him. Mother I said she thought that as so many ghosts lived rent-free in the house they ought to uncover some of the money hidden there and so pay rent. She laughed long and heartily at her own quaint suggestion and Father joined in her laughter.

The next day Mother was dressing to go out and opened the tiny cupboard beside the fireplace where she kept her sealskin sack. She was horrified to see what looked like a thick, dirty stick standing up in the corner. She snatched at it angrily and there fell at her feet a shower of disks. Picking one up she saw it was a crown piece of ancient vintage. The stack had been taller than she was.

Anyway, there was just the sum my father needed at that time. This room was haunted by the sorrowful ghost. He was gentle and always seemed to be suffering some loss.

How that quantity of coins stood as it did was a mystery, as the

83

coins could not be built up again more than a few inches. It was a strange house and odd things happened in it. My parents always swore that the sorrowful ghost left that money to help them out.

- Mrs. Dorothea J. Snyder, Pelham, N. Y.

ℭ   DRURY LANE'S FRIENDLY GHOST   ℭ
This famed wraith has been seen by hundreds since 1750 and is considered a good omen.

Grace Carey

When alterations were made in 1848 at The Theatre Royal, Drury Lane, in London, a wall was pulled down. Behind the wall workmen found a skeleton with a few shreds of clothing still upon it. From between the shining ribs of this skeleton stuck a dagger.

Walter Macqueen-Pope, whose family has been connected with this oldest London theatre for 232 years and who today is the foremost authority on London's theatres considers this discovery a water-tight explanation for the famous Drury Lane Ghost.

The Drury Lane Ghost is a quiet, unassuming fellow who, contrary to the habits of most ghostly visitants, is never seen at night but makes his appearances any time between nine in the morning and six in the evening. He has been seen by players and stage-hands, usherettes and matinee audiences. The first recorded apparition was in 1750.

Mr. Macqueen-Pope has seen the ghost several times and the sight always fills him with satisfaction because the appearance of this wraith, either before or at the beginning of a new production, is a good omen. The ghost appeared prior to the production of *Oklahoma!*, *Carousel* and the American hit, *South Pacific*, and before all the successful Ivor Novello plays.

Until the 1848 discovery no one had been able to account for this ethereal visitor. Now the connection seems beyond dispute. He is always seen to emerge from the door at the precise spot where the skeleton was found. He appears to wear clothes of the early 18th century — three-cornered hat, long grey riding-cloak and powdered hair. He follows the same route always: through the door into an anteroom; down a narrow corridor into the auditorium at the Upper Circle level (in the 18th century this was the Box Circle); following this semi-circle he unobtrusively slips through the door on the opposite side, down another corridor to another anteroom. Here he simply dissolves into the wall.

The management is asked: "Is it usual for the players to appear in costume in the auditorium?" This means, of course, that the ghostly visitor has been seen again. The enquirers are assured that no such practice is authorized in The Theatre Royal. They are told that they have seen The Ghost.

No one has ever been able to trace the identity of the man whose skeleton was found. The annals of the period have been searched but no record of a disappearance or a murder exists.

Mr. Macqueen-Pope has his own theory. He visualizes a young man up to London from the provinces. He goes to the theatre and becomes enamoured of one of the actresses whom he attempts to see, backstage. A jealous admirer finds them, dispatches the unknown with a dagger, and has him bricked up secretly while structural changes (of which there were many over the years) were in progress. No one misses the young man for he is a stranger in the big city and his family at home never see him again.

Mr. Macqueen-Pope believes that in a future age we shall be able to "tune in" on the past. He says that if one is cut off suddenly by violent death the force released so suddenly makes an impact on the ether and under certain conditions can be reassembled and becomes visible as a ghost. In his opinion this theory is supported by the fact that the Drury Lane Ghost is visible at a distance of a few feet but cannot be seen at close quarters.

He admits being able to see ghosts. If they are to be seen he sees them. "But I don't believe they are spirits," he says. "It is the impact of the living force — soul if you like — on the ether, when set free suddenly. Nobody knows what the ether is; but it is there and by its means we get radio and television. For that matter nobody knows what electricity is — but it is there all right and can be used." Parties of interested visitors frequently tour backstage at The Theatre Royal — a most entertaining experience — and on one such occasion Mr. Macqueen-Pope was conducting a particularly skeptical group along the Ghost Walk. They found his recital extremely amusing. He pointed to the door through which the ghost appears, described his grey riding-coat, his sword, his hat. From that very direction a workman in grey overalls suddenly appeared. In one concerted movement the visitors took to their heels! So much for all hardened cynics.

During the war the theatre was closed to public performances and commandeered for the use of ENSA (the company of artists who did so much to entertain the forces in active service). The ante-room at the end of the Ghost Walk was used as an office for a very important Brass Hat. He too professed a disbelief in spirits. One day Mr.

Macqueen-Pope found him white and shaken.

"That — that fellow of yours," he said when he could get his breath, "he's just been in here. Came through that closed door, walked right through my desk — and disappeared up the chimney!"

It is on record that the general did not appear at the theatre for several days following.

Mr. Macqueen-Pope's is the testimony of a practical man of the theatre. He has seen the ghost often, looks on him as a friend, takes his periodic visits as a matter of course.

THE HAUNTINGS AT EPWORTH RECTORY

Alson J. Smith

The boisterous ghost rapped on the walls and levitated beds. He terrified the Wesley family.

"Rats!" said Susanna Wesley.

That was the typical, skeptical reply of a very matter-of-fact woman to the announcement by several of her 11 children that they had heard strange rappings and scratchings in the night. But Susanna Wesley, mother of John Wesley, the founder of Methodism, and wife of the Reverend Samuel Wesley, rector of the parish of Epworth in Lincolnshire, in 1716, was to change her mind.

The story of the famous, haunted rectory of Epworth is one of the best documented cases of alleged poltergeist (mischievous spirit) activity in history. The phenomena were experienced by more than a dozen individuals, at least three of whom were intelligent, balanced witnesses. The story is reported in detail in the diary of the Rev. Samuel Wesley himself; in letters (later published) between the oldest son, Samuel Jr., who was then studying at Westminster, and his parents, brothers, and sisters; and in a set of narratives carefully prepared for John Wesley (who had been studying at Charterhouse in 1716-1717) by his mother, five of his sisters, two servants and a neighbouring clergyman who attempted to exorcise the troublesome "spirit."

These narratives John Wesley later published both as a magazine article and as a pamphlet. They may be found in full in Southey's "Life of John Wesley." All in all, "Old Jeffrey," as the Wesleys dubbed their "haunt," is extremely well-catalogued in the methodical tradition of Methodism.

The Rev. Samuel Wesley was a sensitive scholar and ardent high churchman whose fate it was to spend his entire ministry among surly back-country farmers who could not appreciate him and who resented his cultured ways and severe theology. His wife, Susanna, was an intelligent and intensely spiritual woman who stood loyally by her husband in his bouts with his uncouth parishioners and mothered his

11 children (eight others died in infancy) even while she differed with him on theology and politics. The 11 surviving Wesley children were wise beyond their years and, like the offspring of most impecunious English clergymen, were taught to "cry softly" when they were hungry.

This was the background against which "Old Jeffrey" made his appearance — a high-minded, devout, strict household surrounded by oafishness and hostility; a family poor in this world's goods to the point of hunger and deprivation but rich in spirit and intelligence; and (perhaps most important of all) a family which unquestioningly accepted the spiritual world as real, Satan as well as God.

The rappings, scratchings and knockings which later played such a large part in the life of the Wesley family were first noticed in the old rectory, a rude plaster and timber house covered with thatch, which the rector's barbaric parishioners attempted to burn down in 1702 and finally succeeded in giving to the flames in 1709. It was this latter fire that caused John Wesley, in later years, to speak of himself as "a brand plucked from the burning."

Everybody except the rector himself had noticed the odd sounds in the old house but, the house being what it was, Susanna Wesley's practical judgment ("rats") seemed logical enough. But the indomitable priest, far from giving up after his house had been burned down around him, promptly rebuilt the rectory, this time of brick.

For those days the new rectory was a fine building, fire-proof and weather-proof. On the first floor there was a dining-room, a parlour, a kitchen, and a study. On the second floor there was a nursery, a bed-room and three guest-chambers A long, low attic ran the length of the house. Outside a stone wall on the south shut off the rectory from the High Street and the house itself faced a field lying eastward, through which a lane ran down to the glebe lands (ground belonging to the parish). There were sties for swine, a stable that housed four horses, a dovecote and several outbuildings. It was quite an establishment and one which required the services of a farm-hand and a maid-of-all-work. This did not indicate sudden wealth. It was all part of the rector's "keep." He still had little or no cash.

Thirteen persons were in residence at the time the strongest poltergeist manifestations appeared. The two oldest boys, Samuel Jr. and John, were away at school. Charles, only 10 years old, was the only male child at home. Eight girls were present, ranging in ages from Sukey, in her twenties, down to little Kezia, a toddler. The maid and the farm-hand slept in the house. The rectory was lighted at night by oil lamps and rushlights — marsh rushes dipped in tallow or oil.

The first appearance of the poltergeist in the new brick house was on an early evening in December, 1716. The maid ran into the room where the older girls were preparing for bed and cried that she had heard "a terrible and astonishing noise" which she thought sounded like the cry of one in extremis, in the hall near the dining room door. The girls went downstairs with her and, while they heard no "terrible and astonishing noise," they did hear a series of three-times-three raps and a sound "like the rattle of a meatjack or the clatter of a windmill when it reverses." The girls informed their mother. Her answer was the same as in the old rectory: "Rats!"

However, the strange noises continued. Susanna Wesley herself was disturbed at her devotions by insistent rappings. This convinced her that the sounds had a supernatural origin and she bade the spirit keep his peace while she prayed. She later maintained that the spirit, recognizing a higher authority, thereafter kept a respectful silence during her devotions.

At all other times the phantom made a terrific clatter. There were knockings, clankings of chains, jinglings of coins, gabblings of turkey cocks, and the drag of drapery across the floor. The girls, losing their awe of the supernal visitor, dubbed him "Old Jeffrey" after a former rector who had died at Epworth. They engaged in contests with him, he holding onto the door so that they could not open it and they tugging zestfully away at it and shouting with triumph when they won.

The younger children, however, did not make friends with "Old Jeffrey." He bothered them at night so that they could not sleep; they sweated and trembled and shook all night long and "Jeffrey's" presence in the house at night could always be determined by looking in the nursery: if the sleeping children were shuddering and pale, "he" had arrived.

At first Susanna Wesley and the children kept the news of the "ghost" from the Rev. Samuel Wesley. He alone of all the family was not disturbed. But as the manifestations grew more pronounced Susanna Wesley spoke to her husband about the ghost. She had not heard from her son Samuel Jr. at Westminster for a long time and was afraid that perhaps he had died and the "spirit" was his. The Rev. Mr. Wesley promptly rebuked his wife for her foolishness. If there were any odd noises, he said, they undoubtedly were caused by the children or, more likely, by some lover of Hetty's secreted in the attic. (Hetty Wesley, then 19, was what would be called "boy-crazy" today and shortly thereafter was involved with a lover.)

The very next night, as if to chide the rector for his lack of faith, the Rev. Mr. Wesley was aroused from his sleep by a hollow, three-times-three knock "as if a heavy stick had been struck upon a chest." He got up, loaded his pistol and ransacked the house, still insisting that some human agency was responsible. He found nothing and from then on the ghost, as if angry at having its supernatural origin doubted, harassed the rector regularly. He was jostled so that the powder flew from his wig. At Sunday dinners his trencher rose on end and performed a dance. When he went upstairs he was accompanied by a loud crashing noise beneath his feet as of someone breaking bottles. Knockings and rappings kept him awake at night.

The rector asked the ghost if he was the spirit of Samuel Jr. and tried to devise a system of code knocks so that the spirit could reply. This was unsuccessful but the question was settled when a letter arrived from Westminster; Sam Jr. was in good health and extremely curious about the strange goings-on at Epworth. Would the family send him full reports? They did and these letters provide us with some of our best documentation of the ease.

Meanwhile, "Old Jeffrey" was causing a state of near-hysteria among the women at Epworth Rectory. The kitchen utensils banged and clattered when no one was near them; doors opened and shut of their own accord; latches moved up and down by themselves; lumps of coal leaped from the hods to the floor; boots and shoes danced in their places; and Mrs. Wesley's particular pride, a pewter tea set, jumped off the shelf.

All the Wesleys said they felt "pushed" from room to room; Robin, the farm-hand, saw the empty corn mill grind round and round by itself and wished it had been full; the girls heard "the rapid steps of a man in jack-boots on the stair — he was trailing a night-gown after him"; the children continued to sweat and moan in their sleep; the watch-dog howled in continuous dread and refused to leave the house. Levitation occurred and little Mary Wesley's bed (she was in her early teens and was crippled) was hoisted up "several times to a considerable height," and when she swept out the room the sound of an invisible broom followed. Another of the girls reported that some silver coins had fallen out of the wall and into her lap.

It developed, too, that "Old Jeffrey" had political opinions. During family prayers, whenever the rector prayed for the King or the Prince of Wales, angry and mocking noises were heard. This seemed to indicate that "Old Jeffrey," like Susanna Wesley, was a Jacobite at heart. These interferences with prayer particularly irked the rector and he challenged the ghost "as a deaf-and-dumb devil" to come out and settle the matter man to man. At this a series of terrible blows shook the walls.

The members of the Wesley family differed in their attitudes towards "Old Jeffrey." The rector was angry. Susanna, devoutly religious, accepted the ghost as a test of her spiritual vigour. The older girls — Sukey, Hetty, and Emilia — were amused. Mary, the crippled adolescent, cast herself into a religious ecstasy, continually singing and praying. The younger girls — Anne, Patty, Kezzy, and Martha — were alarmed and nervous. Charles, at 10 years old, was merely curious. Sam Jr. and John, away at school, were intensely interested and it is to this interest on the part of the two older Wesley boys that we are indebted for the fine source-material on the case. The maid and the farm-hand were scared out of their wits.

At this point Robin Brown, the farm-hand, fell ill. Wrapped in a blanket and gazing into the kitchen fire one evening, he suddenly perceived "something like a small rabbit coming out of the copper, its ears flat upon its neck and its little scut straight up ... it turned around three times very swiftly." Robin roused himself and chased it with the tongs but could not catch it. Soon after, Susanna Wesley lifted the valance of her bed and saw a creature "like a badger without a head." Robin, sitting at the parlour fire this time, also saw it as it skittered down the stairs.

The appearance of these weird animals settled it as far as the Rev. Samuel Wesley was concerned. "Old Jeffrey" was an evil spirit and must be exorcised according to the ancient rites of the Church of England. He invited a fellow-clergyman and noted exorcist, the Rev. Mr. Hoole, to come to Epworth and "call out" the ghost. The Rev. Mr. Hoole came and after hearing the story agreed with the Rev. Mr. Wesley that they were up against no less a personage than Satan himself. "But two good Christians should be a match for him," observed Samuel Wesley smugly.

The two clergymen donned black habits and powdered wigs and awaited the coming of "Old Jeffrey." At precisely 10 o'clock that night the two men entered the nursery and saw the younger children gasping, shuddering and sweating in their sleep and knew the adversary had arrived. The exorcist saw the beds heaved up, the bedclothes tugged off by an invisible hand and heard violent three-times-three knockings. In the older girls' room, Emilia and Hetty were seated on a bed that was rising into the air.

The exorcist was baffled. The Rev. Mr. Wesley again invited the ghost to communicate by a series of code knocks but the latter did not deign to reply. The rector flourished his pistol and wanted to shoot but the Rev. Mr. Hoole restrained him: "Sir, you are convinced that this is something preternatural; if so, your attack cannot hurt it and may give it power to hurt you."

Whether the exorcism ritual was responsible or not it is hard to say but shortly after the Rev. Mr. Hoole's visit the poltergeist phenomena diminished in intensity and finally, around February, 1717, ceased altogether. It had done more than any of the good rector's sermons to convince his children of the reality of the spiritual world.

This case, one of the most convincing on record, has been the subject of much controversy down through the years among psychical researchers. In 1903, or thereabouts, Mr. Frank Podmore, a member of the Society For Psychical Research and a pitiless exposer of fakery, wrote a long paper on the Epworth haunting in which he attributed the phenomena to deception by Hetty Wesley. He pointed out that Hetty always claimed that "Old Jeffrey" had "a particular spight (sic)" for her and that she always seemed to be in the vicinity when the noises were heard. The manifestations themselves, he said, were of a type common to a farm and could easily have been made on the sly by a smart girl, particularly when the light was poor, as it was.

But Andrew Lang, another member of the Society, refutes this argument in a paper on "The Poltergeist Historically Considered" which appears in Volume XVII of the Society's *Proceedings*. He points out that Hetty could not have been responsible for the appearance of the small animals, for the constant howling of the dog, for the levitations, or for the sweating and shuddering of the small children in their sleep. Lang inclines to the belief that Epworth Rectory was afflicted with a genuine poltergeist, of which perhaps crippled, adolescent Mary Wesley was the unwitting medium.

With the reality of poltergeist phenomena established today with some scientific accuracy, Andrew Lang's interpretation of the strange events at Epworth Rectory would appear correct. We still do not know much about the poltergeist but we do know that they seem to appear in connection with the onset of puberty in children, especially unhappy children.

The most lasting significance of the phenomena at Epworth is their effect on John Wesley, the founder of Methodism. They initiated his interest in psychical matters; indeed, it is not too strong a statement to say that John Wesley was an ardent psychical researcher more than 100 years before there was a Society For Psychical Research.

When the history of psychical research is written both "Old Jeffrey" and John Wesley must be accorded honoured places.

THE RESTLESS WIVES OF HENRY VIII

The sentry charged the white-swathed figure with his bayonet — but his blade met nothing.

Pauline Saltzman

In 1864 a strange drama unfolded before the astonished eyes of Major General J. D. Dundas, Captain of the 60th Rifles, quartered in the Tower of London.

He was looking out of a window in the Bloody Tower just before retiring. He noticed the guard stationed at the door of the Lieutenant's Lodgings, situated almost directly under the window leading into the square, oak-beamed chamber where Queen Anne Boleyn spent her last days before her execution on 19 June, 1536.

Suddenly Major General Dundas became aware of a figure swathed in white which materialized out of the mist and glided towards the sentry, who challenged instantly. When the figure disregarded him, he charged with his bayonet. Upon meeting no resistance he fainted away on the spot where he was later found by the visiting rounds. Their natural reaction was that the hapless sentry had fallen asleep at his post, an unpardonable offense for a member of the 60th Rifles.

During the ensuing court-martial the guard gave every detail of his encounter with the figure in white. His story was met with ridicule but, thanks to the fact that he had a distinguished witness to corroborate his every statement, the guard was promptly acquitted. Major General J. D. Dundas was not the only officer to vouch for the sentry's truthfulness. Field Marshal Lord Grenfell, too, said he had seen the wraith on other occasions.

Major General George Younghusband, Keeper of the Crown Jewels and author of the autobiographical work, *The Tower from Within*, also encountered an enigma which he was never able to explain. He had been recently transferred to his quarters in St. Thomas's Tower and was dressing in his room over the Traitors' Gate, through which both Anne Boleyn and Katherine Howard passed on their ways to their respective dooms.

Suddenly the door to his room, which had been securely shut, opened half-way as though gently propelled by invisible hands and remained open for a few seconds. Younghusband's first thought was that the regimental dog had pushed the door with his nose. However, the mascot later was found in the kitchen where it had been for some hours. The inexplicable opening and closing of the Major General's door occurred on two other occasions during the first two weeks of his long residence in the Tower of London.

Other incidents identified with the unhappy, restless spirits of Henry VIII's wives have been reported by sober, responsible persons. For instance, it is said that on certain nights the chapel becomes illuminated by an unearthly light which is eventually focused upon a stately procession of richly attired Tudor ladies and gentlemen walking slowly down the carpeted aisle. At the head of the phantom procession walks a young woman in brocaded robes. Her long, unbound chestnut hair is adorned with sparkling jewels. One sentry who witnessed this ghostly procession stated that the woman resembled portraits he saw in the Tower of Anne Boleyn.

Anne's story is one of human frailty and vanity. She and Henry VIII met for the first time when Henry visited her father at Hever Castle, the Boleyn family estate. A true connoisseur of feminine beauty, Henry was struck at once by Anne Boleyn's grace and wit. Already tired of his dour, pious Spanish wife, Katharine of Aragon, who had not given him the son he wanted so desperately, Henry appointed Anne her maid-of-honour.

Katharine soon learned of the affair and Mistress Boleyn was promptly dismissed from Court.

The King's inability to secure a papal divorce did not prevent him and Anne from becoming officially betrothed and Anne soon came to Windsor Castle with her father and a retinue of ladies and knights. On 1 September, 1532, the King ennobled her by creating her Marchioness of Pembroke.

In the midst of the unsuccessful divorce proceedings Anne became pregnant and because Henry hoped so desperately for a son, he felt that the marriage ceremony must be hurried, divorce or no divorce. Accordingly, the wedding rites were performed secretly at Whitehall Palace by Rowland Lee, later Bishop of Litchfield.

When Anne gave birth to Elizabeth and later to a stillborn son, Henry's rage and frustration over the lack of a male heir were boundless. Now he felt justified in paying marked attention to Jane Seymour, court lady and daughter of a sheriff of Wiltshire, Dorset and Somerset.

On May Day, 1536, Anne was still Queen of England. With her corpulent husband she attended a tilting match at Greenwich.

Next day she and others, including her own brother with whom she was accused of immorality, suddenly were arrested. Not only was Anne charged with marital infidelity; she was accused also of high treason which consisted of poking fun at the King's taste in clothes and at his ability as an amateur poet!

Anne Boleyn was transported by water from Greenwich to the Tower of London. Her prison in the Lieutenant's Lodgings was luxuriously appointed as befitted an English Queen and she was waited upon by persons of gentle birth. She was often hysterical, and referred to herself as La Royne sans-tete — "Queen without a head." This constitutes a remarkable coincidence for, in his scholarly work, Shakespeare's England, William Winter asserts that the headless apparition of Anne Boleyn was often seen in various parts of the Tower.

A little before noon, 19 June, 1536, Anne Boleyn was brought into the daisy-splashed Tower courtyard where she paid for her alleged treason and infidelity.

If Anne Boleyn's ghost now tries to right a wrong, it is certainly with justification, for evidence exists to the effect that she was guiltless of the trumped up charges. Chapuys, Imperial Ambassador and Anne's arch-enemy, believed her innocent. Acting on information given him by Lady Kingston, he writes: "The lady who had charge of her had sent to tell me in great secrecy that the Concubine, before and after receiving the Sacrament, affirmed on the damnation of her soul that she had never been unfaithful unto the King."

Every year, on the anniversary of her execution, Anne is seen at Blickling Hall, Norfolk, where she spent the happiest days of her childhood. Her phantom is seen riding in a coach drawn by four headless horses and driven by a headless coachman. Her decapitated head lies on her lap. The ghostly coach drives slowly up the avenue and vanishes just as it reaches the hall door. Christina Hole states that the occupants of the Hall are so accustomed to the annual visitation that it does not frighten them.

Jane Seymour's ghost has been seen on many occasions at the haunted Hampton Court Palace where she died in 1537, a fortnight after giving birth to Henry's hoped-for heir, the sickly little Edward VI. In former times her ghost created such a disturbance the staircase had to be walled up. Years later it was restored to its original grandeur.

Queen Jane's ghost was seen in 1897 by Mrs. Russell Davies, who encountered the phantom as it sat tranquilly before the fireplace of one of Hampton's tapestried chambers. A full account of Mrs.

Davies' experiences may be found in *Borderland*, December, 1897.

Henry remained a widower for three years. Then he married good-natured Anne of Cleves, better known as "the Flanders mare." She was soon pensioned off with titles, money, and manorial houses in exchange for divorcing the oft-wedded monarch. Henry lost no time in marrying vivacious Katherine Howard, cousin of Anne Boleyn. Their honeymoon was spent at Hampton Court Palace.

While the royal couple was away on a Northern visit the Seymour family, who had in little Edward VI a stake in the Crown, put their spies to work. What they learned about the Queen's past boded ill for her future.

On the Day of the Dead, while Henry was hearing Mass, Archbishop Cranmer slipped a note into his hand. The note said that Queen had been guilty of gross immoralities since she was little more than a child. It was known that her present paramour was Thomas Culpepper, who had wanted to marry her long before she attracted the attention of King. At first Henry was speechless with shock and disbelief. Then he broke down, a sobbing, slobbering, senile old man. Only yesterday, on All Saints' Day, he had intoned a heartfelt Te Deum: "I render thanks to Thee, O Lord, that after so many strange accidents that have befallen my marriage, Thou hast been pleased give me a wife so entirely conformed to my inclinations as I now have."

Katherine was tried and sentenced to death together with corrupt Lady Rochford, who stood guard on the staircase while Katherine and Culpepper made love.

Henry was at prayers in the chapel when Katherine received word that her execution was imminent. She escaped from her heavily guarded chamber and rushed screaming down the gallery. Henry was hearing Mass when his hysterical wife reached the door and began fumbling with the lock. She was seized by the guards and carried back to her chamber, all the time uttering piercing shrieks. Henry continued with his devotions unmoved.

Katherine Howard paid for her frivolity and infidelity on the morning of 13 February, 1542. She made the usual short speech from the scaffold and confessed that, though she loved Culpepper, she had never wronged her husband's honour. After asking everyone present to pray for the repose of her soul she knelt down and the headsman struck off her head.

On storm-tossed nights, Katherine Howard's ghost is seen gliding down the Haunted Gallery at Hampton Court. Just as it reaches the door of the Royal Closet the figure hurries back, its disarranged garments billowing in the wind. A ghastly expression of utter hopelessness is engraved on her features and she utters her unearthly shrieks until she vanishes through the door at the end of the gallery.

In his *History of Hampton Court Palace* Ernest Law tells of the experience of Mrs. Cavendish Boyle who occupied an apartment adjacent to the Haunted Gallery. Mrs. Boyle was aroused from deep slumber by a series of unearthly screams, followed by deadly silence. A year later her friend, Lady Eastlake, disclosed that some time before, during a visit to Hampton, she, too, had heard a heart-rending shriek emanating from the same direction. Since she did not want to be subjected to ridicule, she thought it wise to keep her experience to herself.

Meanwhile, English newspapers print, from time to time, stories of reported reappearances of the tragic wives of Henry VIII.

Perhaps the last of these newspaper stories was carried by the Associated Press on 19 November, 1952:

On Tuesday night, 18 November, 1952, a fire of undetermined origin broke out near the Clock Court of Hampton Court Palace. Although priceless works of art housed in the area were carried to safety by fire fighters, several Tudor apartments were damaged. The burned-out area included the Haunted Gallery.

A spokesman for the Government's works ministry reported that the cause of the fire is a complete mystery.

LADY ON THE STAIRCASE
Pauline Saltzman

The photographer snapped his shutter as the ghostly figure descended the steps. His negative clearly showed the veiled lady on the staircase.

The light of the late afternoon sun streamed through the mullioned windows of Raynham Hall and onto the two photographers who were shooting the great oak staircase.

Since eight o'clock in the morning of that lovely English 19th September, 1936, Captain Provand, Art Director, and Mr. Indre Shira, both of Indre Shira, Ltd., Court Photographers, 40 Dover Street, Piccadilly, London W.1., had been taking pictures of the 300-year-old county seat on a commission from the owner, Lady Townshend.

Now, at four o'clock, they were ready to take the second shot of Raynham's pride, the magnificent staircase. Captain Provand, with head under the focusing cloth, took one shot while Shira, facing the staircase at the back of the camera, held the flashlight pistol. The Captain was ready for the exposure when he was startled by his associate.

"Quick! Quick!" Shira suddenly shouted, "there's something on the staircase ... Are you ready?" Something about sightseers raced through the Captain's mind and he quickly uncapped the lens as Shira pressed the flashlight pistol which was operated at the speech of one-fiftieth of a second by a Sasha bulb.

"What's all the excitement?" Provand asked, emerging from under the focusing cloth. His associate stammered about having seen a veiled figure slowly descend the wide stairs.

Captain Provand, a master photographer for 30 years, laughed. There was nothing in sight except the huge staircase bathed in the rosy light of the late afternoon sun. Shira insisted, nevertheless, that he had seen a transparent figure through which the steps were plainly visible.

On their journey back to London the men rehashed the strange incident. Provand pooh-poohed the idea that a genuine ghost photograph could be taken. Shira, too, admitted that he wasn't versed in psychic matters, let alone so-called spirit photography. But he knew one thing: he had seen the figure and he theorized that it had been caught by the lens of the camera. They made a bet, each staking five pounds.

Provand and Shira worked together in their darkroom developing the negatives of Raynham Hall. Captain Provand inspected them critically as they emerged, one by one. "Good Lord," he suddenly shouted, "there's something on the staircase after all!"

One look was enough for Shira. They decided it was time to call in a witness. Accordingly, Mr. Benjamin Jones, manager of Blake, Sandford & Blake, a 150-year-old chemist's firm with offices in the building, was called in. Jones arrived in time to see the important negative as it was removed from the developer and placed in the hypo bath. He declared later that if he had not actually seen the negative inserted into the fixing solution, he never would have accepted as genuine the resulting photograph. Jones himself was an expert amateur photographer who operated his own darkroom.

Beyond the shadow of a doubt, the photograph contained a feminine figure in long, flowing garments that looked like 17th-century dress complete with wimple and ruff. The stairs were clearly visible through the form.

The editor of *Country Life*, to whom the photograph was submitted, sent it on to the late Mr. Harry Price who was Britain's foremost expert on psychic phenomena and also an expert on trick photography. Mr. Price examined the negative, cross-examined Provand and Shira and arrived at this conclusion: "I could not shake their story and I had no right to disbelieve them. Only collusion between the two men could account for the 'ghost,' if it is a fake."

The story of the picture, together with the photograph, appeared in *Country Life* in December 1936. Although it was examined by a number of experts, no one offered a satisfactory explanation for the presence of the phantom.

The mystery picture touched off unparalleled excitement on two continents. In the United States a leading magazine published it with the story that Raynham Hall, seat of the Marquess of Townshend in Norfolk, is said to be haunted by the unhappy spirit of Lady Dorothy (Dolly) Townshend who died in 1726. Christina Hole, in her book *Haunted England*, substantiates the statement that "The Brown Lady," as the apparition is known because of the brown brocade she wears, was in life the lovely Dolly Walpole, sister of Sir Robert Walpole, prime minister of England.

101

Perhaps the best known encounter with Raynham's "Brown Lady" occurred during the last 15 years of Captain Frederick Marryat's life. Florence, his daughter and biographer, gives this account:

Captain Marryat, famous for his adventure stories including *Midshipman Easy*, lived on his estate at Langham in Norfolk. Sir Charles and Lady Townshend of Raynham Hall were his friends and neighbours. The title had just changed hands. The new baronet and his wife spared no money or effort to redecorate and refurnish the old hall. When Raynham Hall was ready, they invited a large party of friends from London for a housewarming.

Shortly after their arrival, Sir Charles noticed that one by one his guests were making excuses to leave. After considerable quizzing, some of the guests told him that Raynham was haunted. A lady dressed in brown, whose portrait hung in one of the bedrooms, was being seen at night in the corridors and especially on the great staircase. Her gown was brocade, they said, with yellow trimmings. She wore a ruff around her throat. She had been seen by all of the guests as she walked silently about the great house.

The ruffled baronet confided in Captain Marryat who, as a local magistrate, did not hesitate to voice his suspicions that this must be a trick on the part of smugglers or poachers who infested the vicinity. Apparently they wanted Raynham Hall completely deserted so they could use it as a rendezvous. Marryat admitted, however, that he admired their ingenuity in devising the ghost of a long-dead Townshend to frighten away the inhabitants of the Hall. But he would jolly well rid the Townshends of the nuisance!

He secured permission to spend three nights in the haunted Hall, and was soon making himself at home where the ancestral portrait hung. Nothing happened during the first two nights much to the crusty old gentleman's dismay. It even occurred to him that the culprits had gotten wise to his sanguinary intentions.

On the third night as he was getting ready for bed the baronet's two young nephews knocked on his door. They wanted him to step over to their room. They had received a gun from London, and they wanted his opinion of it.

After Marryat had inspected the firearm, the boys accompanied him back to his room "just in case they met 'The Brown Lady.'" The hall lights had been extinguished. As they reached the middle of the long, dark passage they noticed the glimmer of a lamp approaching from the opposite direction.

Marryat, panic-stricken at having a lady see him clad only in shirt and trousers, ducked into a space provided by two doors leading into one of the bedrooms. The boys concealed themselves similarly until the lady should have passed.

Closer and closer came the lady with the lamp until, through a chink of his partly closed door, the Captain was able to make out the clothes she wore. She was the Lady of the portrait in the haunted bedroom he occupied!

Marryat was about to command the lady to halt and give an account of her presence but she stopped of her own accord before his door. Holding the lamp to her face she disclosed grinning, diabolical features that paralysed his brain. Then his momentary terror gave way to fury. Exhibiting great presence of mind, he leaped into the passage and fired his pistol in her face. At once the lantern was extinguished and the figure disappeared. The bullet whizzed through the outer door of the room on the opposite side, lodging in the panel of the inner door.

When the bullet was found next day it was established that it had pierced the outer door of the room behind the grinning, malevolent "Brown Lady" and had imbedded itself in the second door!

Another dramatic meeting with "The Brown Lady" took place in the early years of Queen Victoria's reign.

Raynham Hall was aglow with light and radiant with holly and mistletoe. In the great fireplace the Yule log cast a warm glow. There was much jollity, carolsinging, and all the cheer that goes with mellow ale, English walnuts, and plum pudding. Lord Charles Townshend and his lady were entertaining.

Finally, when all the other guests and host and hostess had retired, with the strains of "God Rest You Merry, Gentlemen" echoing in their ears, Colonel Loftus who was Lady Townshend's brother and a Mr. Hawkins settled down to a game of chess.

They played for an hour or two and then they too went upstairs. They were saying goodnight at the head of the staircase when Mr. Hawkins suddenly remarked, "I say, Loftus, who is that standing at your sister's door? How strangely she is dressed!"

Colonel Loftus, who was somewhat shortsighted, screwed on his monocle and took a step towards the lady who promptly disappeared. The men failed to recognize her but concluded that she was some new arrival to the Yule festivities. Loftus would have liked to follow her but she was nowhere to be seen.

The next evening at about the same time Loftus saw her again. By running up a staircase he succeeded in cutting her off and confronting her just as she began her descent down another flight of stairs. As the moon filtered in through a frosted window Colonel Loftus saw her only too clearly. She wore stately brown brocade and coif in the fashion of the early 1700's! She was tall and majestic with fine features ... but where her eyes should have been were blank, sightless hollows!

So branded on his mind was her appearance that Loftus was able to sketch the figure perfectly from memory, which he did the instant he reached his room. His sketch was shown to his friends the following morning and, at a later date, to Miss Lucia Stone who re-told the story in her book, *Rifts in the Veil*.

Lord Townshend, who also had seen the ghost when it once preceded him into his room, took steps to make certain no one was impersonating "The Brown Lady." He had additional locks and bolts affixed to the doors and windows. He engaged the services of the London police who augmented the household staff with crack detectives disguised as servants. Nothing was discovered and the hauntings continued.

According to responsible persons who have seen her Raynham's staircase has an uncanny attraction for "The Brown Lady." She often has appeared before some misfortune in the Townshend family.

In a 19th-century journal of an anonymous Master of Arts at Oxford this is written of Raynham Hall's "Brown Lady":

"Two friends of mine were staying at Raynham Hall when on their way to the drawing room to wait for the dinner bell they saw a stranger to them, a very elegant girl in evening dress, going up the stairs.

"'Whoever can this be?'" one of them remarked.

"'She must be a new arrival. What an exquisite figure she has!'

"'I wonder what her face is like,' whispered the other. 'I wish she would look around!' Hardly had he said this before the girl did turn around and attached to that lovely figure was the head of a skeleton!"

An account of "The Brown Lady" is also given by Catherine Crowe in her authoritative *Night-Side of Nature*, wherein the Victorian Miss Crowe quaintly designates names with initials and dashes:

"The story of 'The Brown Lady' at the Marquis of T—'s, Norfolk, is known to many. The Hon. H. W. — told me that a friend of his, while staying there, had often seen her and had one day inquired of his host, 'Who was the lady in brown that he had met frequently on the stairs?' Two gentlemen, whose names were mentioned to me, resolved to watch her and intercept her. They at length saw her but she eluded them by turning down a staircase and when they looked over she had disappeared. Many persons have seen her."

Sir Henry Birkin, the racing motorist, once waited up for "The Brown Lady" all night and saw nothing. However, at one interval, his dog showed signs of acute and sudden terror at something unseen.

In November, 1926, newspapers noted the appearance of the Raynham Hall ghost. Lady Townshend who was staying there said her son and a friend had met "The Brown Lady" on the oak staircase. Later when they saw her portrait in the bedroom both declared that here was the same woman they had encountered.

Raynham Hall is more than 300 years old and covers 20,000 acres of sprawling Norfolk countryside. The architecture, attributed by the Townshend family to the one and only Inigo Jones, strongly suggests Italian-Renaissance influence.

Raynham boasts other apparitions than that of Lady Dorothy Townshend's "The Brown Lady." There is the ghost of the Duke of Monmouth who visited his father, King Charles, at Raynham; a few of the dead and gone Townshend children and an unidentified spaniel. However, the ghost most frequently seen is that of Lady Dorothy who was the aunt of Horace Walpole, brilliant and satirical Englishman of letters.

Although very little is known about the personal life of the vivacious Dolly Walpole, one account exists in the memoirs of Lady Louisa Stuart, last survivor of Horace Walpole's fabulous age. The memoirs include a notation implying that Dolly was unlike her famous, blustering brother who became England's prime minister. For Dorothy was "endowed with only moderate sense."

When Sir Robert, then ordinary Mr. Walpole, married the heiress, Miss Catherine Shorter, the Walpoles were a prominent family. They were among the leading commoners of Norfolk and shared with the Townshends and the Cokes all the landed wealth of northern Norfolk.

Robert Walpole had brought his young, lovely, scatter-brained sister to London "in hopes that her beauty, the pride of his county, might captivate something superior to a Norfolk squire." But he was up to his neck in politics and therefore completely thoughtless of what transpired with his family.

He had the bad judgment to leave Dolly to the guidance of his affected wife whose own reputation was not perfect. Mrs. Walpole, jealous of the younger, prettier girl, encouraged her to compromise herself on a number of occasions. Dolly, bewildered and no doubt dazzled by London society, decided that the proper thing was to enjoy life to the fullest in accordance with the precepts of the age.

Catherine led Dolly into an intimacy with Lady Wharton, the depraved wife of the most dissolute rake in England. Lord Wharton was never able to look at a young, attractive woman without desiring her. When Lady Wharton invited Dolly to be her house guest Mrs. Walpole promptly took advantage of Robert's absence from London and gladly gave her consent, secretly hoping to discredit Dolly and send her back to Norfolk.

When Walpole returned he wanted to know the whereabouts of his young sister. Catherine informed him that Dolly was with the Whartons. In a rage Walpole went to the Wharton home. Walpole, though completely dissolute himself, chose to act the role of righteousness. He upbraided Lady Wharton, applying to her some choice epithets. Without waiting to hear a single word of explanation he took his sobbing sister home. Next morning they set out for Norfolk where Dolly was meant to spend a few years of penance at Houghton, the dreary family estate.

But one day Dolly surprised everyone by captivating Lord Townshend. A middle-aged widower, he had long and sincerely mourned his first wife, sister of Lord Pelham. Lord Townshend, a rarity in an age of immorality, was by no means a dashing young buck but he was a kind, substantial man, a member of Norfolk's landed gentry. He was illustrious for his introduction of the turnip into England and for his improvement of crop rotation. As owner of Raynham Hall he was easily the most influential man in the county. He and Dolly were married in 1713 and immediately took up their residence at Raynham.

Dorothy was a charming, lively girl and she loved girlish things, a quality which made her appear frivolous and extravagant to her mother-in-law who exercised a profound influence on Townshend.

The marriage was unhappy. Lord Townshend's mother considered the girl altogether unfit for her position. Dolly spent interminable hours walking about Raynham Hall wearing the brown brocade that dowager Lady Townshend considered dignified and proper. Tragedy entered Dorothy's life when her husband, influenced by his mother, removed their four young sons from their mother's control. More confused and unhappy than ever Dolly died in 1726.

Apparently some facet of her personality has managed to survive both time and space in order to continue its weary wandering of Raynham Hall.

Many responsible persons have seen her there.

HAUNTED CANTERBURY
Edmond P. Gibson

**Witnesses report that not only the living inhabit what well may
be one of England's oldest populated cities.**

Canterbury may be the oldest inhabited city in England. Certainly the
town existed before the coming of the Romans, as it was a fort in the
latter period of the Iron Age, and it was occupied by the invading Belgas
in the 1st century B.C. The Romans rebuilt the early fort and named it
Durovernum Cantiacorum. The remains of their city, exposed by
German bombing and subsequent excavation, lie eight to 10 feet below
the present ground level. It was the Roman capital city in Kent.

In 455 A.D. the Anglo-Saxons landed in Kent, bringing with
them their gods who displaced the Roman hierarchy. The Saxon gods
later gave way to Christianity which appeared in Kent through the efforts
of Queen Bertha, the Christian Queen of King Ethelbert, a Saxon, during
the latter part of the sixth century. The coming of St. Augustine resulted
in the conversion of the King, and Canterbury slowly grew into the
religious centre of England. The English Church became united there
through the efforts of Archbishop Theodore in the year 668, from which
time the Archbishop of Canterbury has been the religious authority of
England, at times wielding a power that overshadowed that of the King.

Geoffrey Chaucer has given a vivid picture of a Canterbury
pilgrimage which visited the tomb and shrine of St. Thomas a Becket in
the cathedral sometime in the 14th century.

Perhaps it is not surprising that this ancient Canterbury is
likewise a centre of ghostly activity, activity which has gone on down the
centuries.

The ghost of a monk has traversed the road called St. Martin's
Hill for years. This ghostly monk has caused traffic to come to a sudden
halt on the hill in the middle of the night and it is still seen there
occasionally.

At one time there was a priory near the foot of St. Martin's Hill
though the monks have been gone since Tudor times and the building
has been remodelled. The old entrance to the priory is bricked up and a
portion of the building is now occupied by the Bishop of Dover. But on
two evenings toward the end of 1950 Mr. W. C. Clayson, a taxi-driver,

encountered the apparition. He writes:

"I am writing to tell you of my experience in the early hours of the morning. My job as a taxi-driver keeping me out very late, I was coming home between one and two in the morning when I saw a form cross the road. I did not take much notice of it at that time but not so long after, on another early morning, I saw it again, dressed as a monk or a priest, with a hood and cloak. It passed from the Bishop of Dover's house on St. Martin's Hill and disappeared on the opposite side of the road. I have not seen it since."

Further inquiry yielded the information that the figure appeared from out the wall of the old priory, at the point where the old entrance was walled up. It vanished on reaching a small piece of green on the opposite side of the road. The last time Mr. Clayson saw it he was slowly pushing his bicycle up the grade, near the foot of the hill, after leaving his taxi in the town.

The present drawing room of the house of the Bishop of Dover is a part of what once was the old priory hall. The entrance to the hall has been replaced by more modern French windows. Here also figures have been seen, inside the house, walking in what was the old hall. Mr. Jasper P. Mounsey, who lives nearby, states that he has heard repeatedly of the haunting in the old priory, although he has never witnessed anything himself.

Another ghostly occurrence, on last All Souls' Eve at the old cemetery of the monks of St. Augustine, was heard by a member of the clergy of the Church of England. It consisted of a monastic funeral procession which was heard, but not seen, passing through the ancient cemetery gate. The ancient gate is blocked up and has not been used for centuries. But still the chanting, in a ghostly form, persists. The clerical gentleman who underwent this experience wishes to remain anonymous.

At the foot of St. Martin's Hill, near the junction with Longport Road, stands St. Martin's Church, the first Christian Church in Kent, built upon the ruins of a Roman temple. King Ethelbert, the pagan Saxon king of Kent, gave it to his Christian wife, Queen Bertha, for her personal place of worship, before the arrival of St. Augustine from Rome. The tiny chancel and nave still show the Roman brickwork and tile, extending up the walls for a distance of eight feet. Above this level, the walls seem to be a later Saxon addition. For centuries an apparition of Queen Bertha has been seen occasionally in the ancient church. However, I have been unable to locate a contemporary witness to this haunting.

Ghostly activities in the Cathedral city do not confine

themselves to the churches. The former Old House Restaurant in Palace Street is located near the east end of the cathedral grounds. Here poltergeist activities of a mischievous and humorous nature have persisted for years in the rooms that are rented above. No ghosts are seen but phenomena such as the unlocking and locking of doors persist. There are unexplained noises, accompanied occasionally by activities centering on the beds. Sheets and blankets are pulled from the visitors who sleep in these rooms and on other occasions the bed coverings are rearranged. These activities never have seemed malevolent, but possibly are the work of some entity with a sense of humour.

The Cathedral itself, according to tradition, has been haunted in the Dark Entry since the reign of Henry the Eighth. The story of this haunting goes back to folklore and a detailed account of the ghostly activities appears in *The Ingoldsby Legends* by Thomas Ingoldsby Esq., New York: E. P. Dutton & Co., 1930. The story of the haunting goes as follows:

During the reign of Henry the Eighth there was a Canterbury Canon who is anonymous in the story but who lived close to the "Dark Entry" of the Cathedral. While the monks who lived at the priory were thin and half-starved, this Canon grew fat and jovial. Some share in maintaining his health and happiness was blamed upon his housekeeper, Nell Cook, who was famous for her stews and pastry. In addition to being a fine cook, Nellie was a good-looking, voluptuous wench, whose charms were only offset by her modesty. However, the town gossips suggested that the portly Canon might find as good a cook and one who wasn't as pretty as Nellie.

One evening a coach passed through Canterbury's "Green Court" gate and stopped in front of the Canon's house. A beautiful young lady, together with her belongings, was unloaded. The Canon greeted her as his niece. She explained to the neighbours that her father was in the Navy, sailing the Spanish Main, and that he had sent her to be cared for by his brother, the Canon.

Whoever the fair lady may have been, she certainly was well known to the Canon, who showed her every evidence of familiarity and affection. This caused a great deal of discomfiture among the neighbours, who could not understand why the Canon should wine and dine his niece so much, and at last Nell Cook was equally displeased. It was rumoured that the "niece" had taken over some of Nell Cook's ministrations, though Nell Cook still did the cooking.

From the windows of the Canon's lodge came no hymn singing,

but a clear soprano voice rose in the latest worldly ballad, "Bobbing Joan." The lady had stayed at the Canon's house for more than six weeks and the gossips had it that the "niece" had abandoned the guest room in the tower for the more ample proportions of the Canon's room. The Canon said she often spent her nights in prayer at the shrine of St. Thomas but the gossips said she spent them with the merry Canon.

To cut this part of the story short, Nellie Cook decided to take matters into her own hands. It is said she visited the apothecary. Soon thereafter she made a special dinner for the Canon and his "niece," including a pie which was the Canon's favorite. The Canon and his "niece" were both dead in his room the following morning.

Nellie Cook disappeared and was never again seen alive. By order of the Prior, the Canon and his "niece" were buried in the floor of the Cathedral Nave. A day or two later a large paving stone within the "Dark Entry" was seen to be newly set in cement. No one knew what had become of Nellie Cook, or who the Canon's "niece" really was.

A hundred years later a paving stone settled badly in the "Dark Entry" and the Dean of Canterbury ordered it reset. That this might be accomplished the stone was removed and its foundations examined. Beneath it was a small, walled crypt, within which was an unburied skeleton thought to be Nellie Cook. With the remains there was a pitcher and what may have been the remains of her pie, upon a platter. The clothing was that of a woman.

It appeared that the prisoner in the crypt had been buried alive, perhaps by the immediate and summary justice of the Prior and his tonsured brothers. Since the exhumation of this body, in or about the year 1640, there have been repeated accounts of the ghost of Nellie Cook appearing in the "Dark Entry." The ghost has appeared only on Friday nights, and even when the apparition fails to appear on Friday, the passer through the "Dark Entry" feels a "cold spot" in the air when he passes over the slab which once entombed fair Nellie.

Jasper P. Mounsey, who lives near the Bishop of Dover's house on St. Martin's Hill, has written of his first experience in passing through the "Dark Entry."

"The wife and I were coming back from an entertainment and walked through the Dark Entry on our way back — there we suddenly felt a real chill in the air. Talking about ghosts later, we told my son-in-law about our experience and he promptly said: 'Was it a Friday night?' On our working it out we found it was a Friday night. This happened on our first visit to Canterbury and we had no previous knowledge of any hauntings there." (Mr. Mounsey has had some previous encounters with ghosts. He was a student at Corpus Christi College, Cambridge, during the haunting there, and had an experience in the haunted rooms that look out on the green of the Old Court.)

The figure of Nell Cook is rarely seen in the "Dark Entry" now. This haunting seems to have lost vigour in recent years, but many persons passing through it still testify that they have an eerie feeling there, on Friday nights. There is a stain on the wall in the shape of a woman. The superstitious have associated this stain with Nellie but there is no evidence that it is anything but a freak of nature, which may have been on the wall long before Nellie existed.

St. Mildred's Church is on the opposite side of Canterbury from the Church of St. Martin, which is outside the wall. St. Mildred's is a small, ancient church near the castle and not far from the River Stour. It is the oldest church inside the walls and of early Saxon foundation. Later, about 1050 A.D., it was apparently rebuilt and dedicated to St. Mildred, a princess of the Royal House of Kent who became a nun. Various miracles and legends are associated with her but very little is historically known. She died about the year 700. However, she has been greatly venerated in Kent and was canonized at an early date by the Church.

This ancient church is haunted by the benevolent figure of a nun, supposed to be St. Mildred. Inasmuch as no nuns have been associated with this church since Tudor times, the ghost is very old. The Rev. Edwin F. Lee Hirst, the Rector, wrote that the figure had been seen by the organist of the church, Maurice Hogben, and by one of his parishioners, Mrs. Margaret A. Smith, who cleaned the church brass. arranged flowers before services, and took care of the inside of the church.

At the request of Reverend Hirst Mrs. Smith wrote out the story of her recent experience:

"On the afternoon of 2 November, 1950, I went to St. Mildred's Church (Canterbury) to do my usual brass cleaning, flowers, etc. and had spent about three-quarters of an hour in the vestry. I then went to the end if the church, near the west door, to clean the candlesticks by the War Memorial.

I switched on the lights at that end of the church, the Sanctuary being then in half darkness as it was a dark rainy afternoon.

I had been at the west end of the Church for about a half hour when I heard a faint rustling sound and thought 'Ah, someone coming into the Church' and went on polishing, but after a second or two I felt compelled to look round at the door. No one was there. I had the feeling that someone was behind me and looked along the aisle from the door. To my great astonishment, there stood the figure of a nun. As I watched she seemed to glide about two steps forward and it came to me, 'It's Saint Mildred!' I seemed to gaze at her for ages but it could only have been seconds.

She was dressed in grey with a smallish winged headdress, but her profile struck me, it was so perfect and beautiful, but one could see that it was spiritual, by the cold, almost transparent look of it. The front outline of face and figure were clearly defined, but the top and back of the figure were sort of misted.

I gave a sort of soft 'ah!' sound and then she just vanished on the spot.

Naturally I felt a bit shaken, but such a sense of cleanliness and peace pervaded the whole church that all sense of being nervous left me. I felt that indeed I had been blest. I carried on and finished my brasses and said my prayers, and switched off the lights. One has to walk through the church in the darkness after the lights are switched off but I still had the feeling of peace within me. It was not until later that I remembered it was 'All Souls' Day'.

I would love to see her again but, although I have been in the church at midnight and on my own after dark, alone, doing my various tasks, I have not had that blessing, before or since.

It was about 20 minutes to five o'clock that I saw my vision. She was too beautiful to be called a ghost and on this particular day I was very worried about business affairs.

I sincerely hope that this is not in too much detail, but it explains exactly how it happened — and I also hope that you can decipher my handwriting.

Yours sincerely,
Margaret A. Smith
(Mrs.)

(The writer wishes to thank the Rev. Edwin F. Lee Hirst, Mr. Jasper P. Mounsey, Mrs. Margaret A. Smith, Mr. W. C. Clayson, E. P. Dutton and Co. and J. M. Dent and Sons, Bookpublishers, for their cooperation in making this story possible.)

THE HAUNTED ARMY STORE
Edmond P. Gibson

The investigators heard a weird rattling in the room above. It sounded like a chain — and they found one where none had been before.

Mr. L. Sharp, manager of the army surplus store in Millgate Street, Wigan, is an old army man, an ex-sergeant major who now sells Army surplus supplies. Further, he has a ghost he would like to dispose of.

The store is in an old building on the ground floor. The upper floor or attic is unoccupied and can be reached by a narrow stair which leads up from inside the store.

The first of a series of strange incidents in this store occurred in November, 1951, when Mr. Sharp had boarded the train to Southport where he lives. He had been discussing taking over the store from his predecessor, also an arm veteran, and ex-commando of World War II. Southport is about 20 miles west of Wigan and Mr. Sharp intended to commute from there. His predecessor, who was preparing to turn the store over to him, also lived in Southport and he intended to catch the same train after he had closed the store for the night.

Shortly before the train was due to leave the Wigan station, Mr. Sharp's colleague arrived, breathless, without his hat and coat and in a state that aroused Mr. Sharp's concern. The man's face was white. As the train left the station, he explained his trouble to Mr. Sharp. The retiring manager had been in the store during the afternoon and had been bothered continually by noises that emanated from the upper floor. He knew there could be no one there. No one could reach the upper floor without his knowledge. However, the noises, which had been moderate during the afternoon, grew much louder with the approach of evening. It sounded as if someone were walking about on the upper floor and the Walker seemed to gather weight and strength as it darkened outside.

At 7 p.m., after the closing hour, it was quite dark and time to leave for the train. The manager hesitated to go up the dark stairs to get his coat and hat which he had hung at the top of the rickety flight. He had no torch handy. Finally this ex-commando, who had been quite fearless during World War II, rushed out of the building without his coat and hat, only stopping long enough to lock the door to the store. A surrender to nameless fear was new to him and his story came as a surprise to Mr. Sharp, who felt sure that there must be a logical explanation for the noises.

Shortly after this Mr. Sharp took over the management of the store. He was working late one evening when he heard someone walking overhead. He says:

"I heard distinctly the steady tread of footsteps on the floor above. I knew that there was no one but myself in the shop. I ran out of the shop to see if there was anybody about next door. The place was deserted.

I was determined to find out what was going on and I started to run up the stairs. As I reached the third step my legs seemed suddenly to freeze. I looked up and sensed, more than saw, a figure walking along the small passageway at the top of the stairs. I admit that I was really frightened!"

This incident was but the prelude to a series of uncanny events that occurred in and about the army surplus store. Most of the events had more than one witness.

Soon after Mr. Sharp's encounter with his uninvited guest, he and his assistant heard footsteps on the upper floor. There was no entrance to the floor above except in their full view through the store itself and they knew that there was no one up there. Mr. Sharp climbed the stairs to see what was going on but the footsteps stopped when he was half way to the top.

Another morning when Mr. Sharp opened the store, he made a strange discovery. During the night a pile of army ankle-boots, which had been carefully stacked on shelving the previous afternoon, were scattered in a disorderly heap on the floor.

A reporter from *Two Worlds* of London, England, called on Mr. Sharp shortly thereafter. It is through the courtesy and cooperation of the editorial staff of *Two Worlds* that much of this information has been collected. It is printed with their permission. The report in detail is as follows:

"Mr. Sharp showed our representative how the boots had been neatly arranged in pairs, with the bootlaces uniformly tied. The boots were found lying about in confusion, with the bootlaces tangled and twisted round the boots in a manner that could not have come about by chance.

The footsteps more recently were heard by a new witness.

About a fortnight ago, 1 February, 1952, a traveller called while Mr. Sharp was out to lunch. Without speaking to the assistant, he walked to the foot of the stairs at the end of the shop and shouted up for Mr. Sharp. When told by the assistant that Mr. Sharp was out, the traveller said he had heard him walking about in the room above. It was only when Mr. Sharp walked into the shop from the street that he was finally convinced.

A remarkable occurrence was when Mr. Sharp again worked alone after the closing hour. While writing at his desk he felt a hand on his shoulder. He turned round but there was nothing there — all was normal save for the sound of retreating footsteps."

The investigation of the strange haunting was undertaken also by Mr. Richards and another reporter from the *Lancashire Evening Post*. With the consent of Mr. Sharp and the owners of the store, the reporters decided to spend a night in the old store to study the ghost.

They arrived at closing time well equipped with blankets, sandwiches and torches. The night was cold and the store unevenly heated. They camped in the store itself, making themselves as comfortable as possible. As night came on they heard strange noises from the floor overhead but they believed firmly that the noises had a normal explanation. In their account, which appeared in the *Lancashire Evening Post*, they state that from time to time during the evening heavy bumping and thumping noises came from above. At other times there were noises like metal scraping on the floor and their entire night was full of a variety of sounds.

It was just after midnight when they heard the sound of what seemed to be a chain rattling along the floor above. By this time the reporters had become nervous. They felt that they were not hearing rats and mice, nor the pranks of some jokester.

Search of the upper floor early in the evening had revealed no chain in the empty upper rooms. However, despite his jumpy nerves, one of the reporters decided to go up stairs again. He found no chain. He heard nothing except the wind whistling in the smaller room at one side.

In the morning with the daylight they re-examined the upstairs to see if there were any changes since their midnight examination with flashlights. Lying in one corner, which they were sure they had previously examined several times, they found a long chain. They were unable to explain how it had come there.

They were baffled also by the performances of an old broken

chair with only three legs. During their midnight search they had noticed that this chair was hanging on the first hook of a series of four on the attic wall. At 6 a.m. they visited the upper floor for the last time. The chair had moved and now hung from the fourth hook. The reporters had not touched it but something had moved it.

When told about the moving chair next morning Mr. Sharp denied that there was a chair of any description in the attic. However, a chair, as unwanted and as useless as the ghost was certainly there that morning. No one knew where it came from.

Disturbances at the army surplus store still continued in mid February of 1952. Many of the manifestations are of poltergeist type but there is no adolescent child in the army surplus store. The apparition, dimly seen by Mr. Sharp, tends to throw part of the phenomenon into the category of a haunting. Footsteps continued on the upper floor during the day but investigation merely caused cessation of the noises without revealing their cause. The stock of army goods is still being disturbed. One mid-February morning several rows of boxed shoes were found scattered on the floor. The emptied shelves were opposite those from which the army boots had been thrown previously.

Mr. Sharp experienced another, more dangerous manifestation. He took a box of matches out of his pocket to light a cigarette. Before he had opened it the entire box burst into flame in his hands. He blames this incident on the ghost also because he knows of no rational explanation for it.

A reporter from *Two Worlds* invited a Manchester psychic, Mr. Frank Spencer to accompany him to Wigan. They stayed on the store premises one evening. During their stay nothing occurred. However, the psychic told the reporter that while in the building he saw, clairvoyantly, several entities. An article in *Two Worlds* on 23 February, 1952, states:

"Mr. Spencer first went up the narrow stairway to the attic, an unused apartment looking very grim in the semi-darkness.

Here he told those with him that he was able to see clairvoyantly an elderly man of about 60, with a fringe of grey beard who gave him the name of Sam Howarth. He also saw a little old woman shabbily dressed in black with a shawl thrown over her shoulders and a rather conspicuous, enveloping bonnet. She had a forbidding and threatening expression. Her name reached him as Mary Howarth. Both of these entities spoke repeatedly of someone called Bill Jackson. He thought there had been a feud between the two families. He mentally asked for light to be given to these people.

The elderly couple tried to tell him about a son who had gone to sea and was drowned. They were still obviously under the influence of earthly conditions and rather confused.

He was also impressed by the cellar of the premises. One of the entities tried to tell him about the third flag of the cellar floor from the door. Later, furniture blocking the entrance to the cellar which is not in use was removed and Mr. Spencer and the others went down to another very grim apartment, which at one time may have been a cell of an old jail. Examination showed that it was laid with flagstones."

The only fact verified thus far in the communications given by Spencer is the existence of the flag-stone floor in the old cellar. Tradition says that the store is on the site of an ancient bridewell or jail and the basement room has every appearance of having served as a cell in such an establishment. Another tradition says that the son of a former tenant hanged himself many years ago in the upper floor apartment.

Mr. Spencer thinks that several deceased entities are involved in the manifestations and all of them of low mentality.

The ghost is not yet laid!

THE DRUMMER OF CORTACHY

The woman heard a ghostly drumming beneath her window. Did it mean another Ogilvy was about to die?

H. Addington Bruce

The top event of London's 1952 social season was the October wedding of Lord Ogilvy and Virginia Fortune Ryan. It was noteworthy for several reasons — one of which is that a ghost lurked in the background.

The wedding took place in fashionable St. Margaret's Church, right next door to Westminster Abbey. The 900 invited guests were headed by Queen Elizabeth II, the Queen Mother, and Princess Margaret.

The youthful bridegroom was the son and heir of a Scottish nobleman, the Earl of Airlie. The bride was an heiress of two American multi-millionaires, Otto Kahn and Thomas Fortune Ryan.

Lord Ogilvy had done his part to make the wedding out of the ordinary. He had seen to it that kilted pipers of the Scots Guards were on hand to play Highlander tunes at the wedding and reception. Also he had brought by coach 35 crofters, tenants of the Airlie estate, to mingle their picturesqueness with the formal attire of the notables in St. Margaret's Church.

The wedding was much publicized in English and American newspapers, especially as the honeymoon was spent in part at Miami Beach. But, so far as I have been able to learn, no reporter took the trouble to interview any of the Airlie crofters. Had he done so he could have added something unusual to the wedding publicity.

For the crofters must have come to the wedding with mixed feelings. Some of them must have been troubled by the thought that the merriment might be followed by a tragic day when one or more of them would hear a ghostly drumming to herald the approaching death of the groom's father — or of the groom himself.

The drumming has a weird story back of it. The story dates from the earlier days of Lord Ogilvy's ancestral home, Cortachy Castle. Forfarshire, in which Cortachy is located, takes in the eastern part of the Highlands' most savage mountain country. And its inhabitants, before any Ogilvy had been elevated to an earldom, were about as rough as the mountains and glens amid which they lived.

The Highlands clansmen might band together against a common foe, especially the hated Sassenach, the English. But when no common foe was around they delighted in brawling and feuding with one another. Unlike the Irish Celts, who were equally quick to take offense and to forgive, the Highlanders were uncommonly slow to forgive. Out of that fact grew the strange haunting of Cortachy Castle.

As tradition has it, the head of some other clan — it might easily have been a Campbell, a Fraser, or a Cameron — sent a trouble-breeding message to Cortachy Castle. To make it more insulting, he sent his message by a little drummer carrying a big drum. The Lord Ogilvy of that day was as enraged as the other clan chieftain wanted him to be.

He was so enraged he decided to answer the message by clapping its bearer, the little drummer, into his big drum and hurling him from the highest battlement of Cortachy Castle. The drummer may have been little, but he had plenty of courage. He put his own private curse on Lord Ogilvy, warning him:

"If you kill me, I won't stay killed. You may never see me again, but I'll be here. And I'll walk around, beating my drum merrily whenever an Ogilvy of Cortachy Castle is about to die."

The Ogilvy of that day was too angry or too skeptical to heed the warning. He ordered the luckless drummer to be tossed to his death on the rocky ground below. Then, it would seem, the haunting of Cortachy Castle began.

From time to time drumming by an invisible drummer was reported heard by some one shortly before an Ogilvy died. It was not until the middle of the 19th century, however, that an attested record of this strange fact was made.

In 1844 the then Earl of Airlie invited some guests to Cortachy Castle for a week-long Christmas holiday party. Among those invited was a Miss Dalrymple, who had never been to the castle. Dressing for dinner the first evening after her arrival, she was astonished to hear, beneath her window, the beating of a drum.

Looking out of the window she could see nothing. Twilight had already deepened into darkness. But she plainly heard the drum, muffled, yet beating a gay tune. Gradually the unseen drummer seemed to pass along, until his joyous drumming died away in the distance.

Puzzled, Miss Dalrymple continued to make ready for dinner.

During dinner what she had heard came to mind and she asked her host:

"My Lord, who is your drummer?"

The Earl of Airlie looked at her sharply but said nothing. Lady Airlie turned pale and some others seemed embarrassed. Miss Dalrymple hastened to bring up another subject. Later she questioned a younger member of the family, who said: "The drummer of Cortachy Castle is never seen but he is heard by some one shortly before an Ogilvy is about to die. The last time he was heard, the Earl's first wife died soon after. That is why Lady Airlie was so troubled at dinner."

Next evening, again while dressing for dinner, Miss Dalrymple once more heard the drumming, once more looked out and once more could see nobody. Now she talked with some other guests and discovered she was the only one who had heard the drumming.

That settled things for her. It might be she herself, not an Ogilvy, for whom the warning was meant. She did not await the coming of Christmas. Next day she made some excuse and, in a panic, left the castle and hurried home. She need not have gone. It was the Earl of Airlie's second wife, the Lady Airlie, who died.

Five years afterwards, in 1849, Lord Ogilvy, the earl's son and heir, invited some friends to his Cortachy hunting-lodge for some shooting. Among these was an Englishman who, like Miss Dalrymple, had never heard of the drummer of Cortachy.

Returning to the lodge in the twilight with a gamekeeper, the Englishman suddenly said:

"What's that music? I didn't know Lord Ogilvy had a band. They must be going to have a dance at the lodge."

"I hear naething," said the gamekeeper.

"Anyway I hear a drum," said the Englishman.

"If ye hear a drum," the gamekeeper told him, "it's something no canny."

As they neared the lodge they could see it well lighted. The Englishman thought a dance surely was in the making. They found no musicians in the lodge, only confusion and sadness. Lord Ogilvy had just left for London in a hurry, having got word that his father had suddenly been stricken ill there. The father, the Earl of Airlie, died the very next day.

Cortachy, as I said, is in an isolated part of the Highlands. Perhaps that is why I have been able to find no records of 20th-Century drumming in its castle. Or it may be the drummer has given up his drumming in disgust. Always it has been heard by somebody other than the Ogilvy the drummer most wanted to torment. The fact is, though, that a death monition such as the drummer of Cortachy Castle seldom, if ever, is received by the person most concerned.

THE MISCHIEVOUS POLTERGEIST

The ghost hurled objects about the room.
As a reporter watched, books flew at him from a nearby table

Edmond P. Gibson

For more than six months in 1952, the little manufacturing town of
Runcorn, suffered from the manifestations of a "Thing."

At first this "Thing" confined itself to a single location in the
city, in more recent months it manifested elsewhere.

Runcorn would seem to be the last place in the world to find
a ghost. But beginning in August, 1952, something extremely like a
ghost plagued the occupants of No. 1 Byron Street to their
consternation and that of their neighbors. The ghostly phenomena
continued to defy the local police and all ecclesiastical intervention.

The phenomenon seemed focused in the neighbourhood of
John Glynn, aged 17, who lived with his grandfather, Sam Jones, 68, his
aunt, Mrs. Lucy Jones, and his young sister, Eileen, aged eight. In
addition, the Jones's had a roomer. Miss Ellen Whittle.

The ghost or poltergeist first appeared on 17 August, a
Sunday, when the Jones family was entertaining overnight visitors.
John Glynn slept with his grandfather that night in a double bed in the
middle bedroom, while Mrs. Lucy Jones and Eileen occupied a single
bed together in the same room. The guests stayed in the other family
bedroom.

A dressing table stood between the two beds in the middle
bedroom and during the night noises as from a mouse, were heard in
this dressing table. The four occupants of the room were kept awake.
The noises increased in volume as the night wore on and finally all the
occupants got up to investigate. They found nothing and left the room
in possession of their mysterious visitor. The noises stopped. After a
wait the family retired for the second time. When the lights were out
the noises started again and the scratching and gnawing sounds kept up
for the rest of the night. No one slept.

On Monday night the noises resumed as soon as the lights
were out. They were louder than before and the dressing table moved
about in a most disconcerting manner. No one admitted touching it but
it was a foot from the wall, moving toward the centre of the room,
when the lights were turned on.

Mr. Jones called the police and on Tuesday night the police placed guards inside and outside the house and set "booby traps" to catch any practical joker who might be at work. Some suspicion was cast on John Glynn, next to whom the phenomenon had occurred.

Noises began as soon as the lights were out. The drawers of the dressing table, sealed with tape, slammed in and out with great violence. In the presence of the officers of the law, the dressing table slid two feet out from the wall.

The police saw it move in the beams of their torches. When the lights again were turned on in the room the drawers of the table were found still sealed in position. The police watched the premises for three successive nights but could find no cause for the disturbances. Nothing occurred when the lights were on but the torches caught objects in motion. The police could not trace the disturbances to John Glynn.

On Thursday night, 21 August, a spiritualistic séance was held in the haunted bedroom by a Runcorn medium, at the request of Mr. Jones. During the séance two Bibles, another book, a tin of ointment and the dressing table cover were, thrown violently and simultaneously over the heads of the sitters. Then the phenomena stopped for the evening and did not resume for 10 days, during which time the Joneses caught up on their sleep.

According to the Altrincham, Bowden, and Hale *Guardian*, the phenomena started again with a vengeance on 1 September. The dressing table seemed to be the focus of activity in the middle bedroom, but while the table and the chairs were moving about there, a box of toy bricks was thrown in another room of the house. John Glynn was terrified on this evening and most of the phenomena still occurred in his proximity.

The *Guardian* reported: "In the small hours of 4 Thursday, September, the ghost threw a clock and several small articles five feet across the bedroom in the presence of a Guardian reporter.

Mrs. Jones was by this time no longer sleeping in the room and our reporter, torch in hand, occupied the single bed, his head not two feet from the dressing table, when this occurred. Shortly after extinguishing the lights he thought he heard the dressing table dragged across the floor, but flashing a torch on it, found it had not moved!

A few minutes later, the clock, a handkerchief, a sleeve-band and a runner were hurled to the floor and a picture book and two Bibles moved across the table surface, the book remaining balanced."

It was reported that following the visit of a Catholic priest on the evening of 4 September violent phenomena occurred. He revisited the house the next evening and nothing occurred that night. It seems possible that these visits had some effect on the ghost or poltergeist inasmuch as the phenomena stopped until the night of 20 September.

John Glynn was unnerved by the phenomena, which seemed to be associated with him, and a brave friend, Johnny Bury, moved in with him as a sort of bodyguard. In the meantime Glynn had increased his cigarette smoking and begun to lose weight.

On 21 September two reporters from the *Guardian*, four other observers and the Rev. W. H. Stevens of Widnes, psychic researcher and Methodist minister, stayed for the evening. The ghost had by this time been christened "Brutus" by John Glynn. "Brutus" carried on steadily for six hours that night. Phenomena always started in the dark but were observed by the aid of flashlights. The dressing table was tossed about, a chair was hurled across the room knocking chunks of plaster from the wall and ceiling. John Glynn was knocked down and Johnny Bury, aged 19, a heavy fellow, was lifted or thrown off the single bed.

The Altincham, Bowden, and Hale *Guardian* stated afterwards: "The entity had developed something of a malign influence. Heavy books and drawers as well as lighter objects hurtled about the room in rapid transit, sometimes aimed at specific persons. Its fury concentrated on the dressing table, which was practically demolished in the course of the night, and the blanket chest, the two frequently 'dancing' on opposite sides of the room at the same time.

A Guardian reporter, seated on the gyrating blanket chest was struck heavily about the head and shoulders by four books in close succession. (Brutus could see in the dark.) The reporter stayed there till two small drawers whistled past his head to crash into the wall behind him, scattering their contents over three watchers seated on the nearby single bed.

The small bed, with three men on it, was suddenly pulled from the wall.

Torches revealed no sign of any attempt to produce the physical phenomena by normal means. On one occasion the dressing table was caught rocking back and forth without assistance from human agency.

The following night the phenomena were witnessed by three Methodist ministers and two psychic researchers. The night of 23

September was quiet.

Violent activity burst forth at the end of the month, during which both boys were thrown out of their beds, beaten about their heads with wood from demolished furniture. Objects were seen in flight in bright light, a bed was overturned, a drawer from the dresser was thrown out of the room and down the stairs, and the walls and ceiling were further pitted by flying furniture. The dressing table was now totally demolished, with [1/2] inch by six inch dowels pulled from their glued recesses.

Two Worlds, a weekly which carried a running account of the doings of "The Thing," mentioned that Cecil Berry, a witness to some of the phenomena on Byron Street, carried a contusion on his head for several days, mute evidence that something had struck him. Likewise the Rev. W. H. Stevens was struck on the head by a heavy dictionary. The plaster fell from the kitchen ceiling due to the commotion going on above.

Early in November Miss Ellen Whipple who roomed at the haunted house and slept in the bedroom adjacent to that of John Glynn, was killed while walking with a friend, James Sutton, near an abandoned quarry. She apparently tumbled in. Sutton was seriously injured. The circumstances of this accident are still unexplained though it may have had nothing to do with the ghostly phenomena.

The Jones family was somewhat relieved when John Glynn went to visit his mother's house at 116 Stenhills Crescent, Runcorn. They were sure the ghost would go with him. *Two Worlds* reported in its 29th November issue that while he was there mild phenomena continued at the Byron Street house and at the same time manifestations also were observed at Stenhills Crescent.

At No. 1 Byron Street an ornamental plastic egg stood on the mantel, supported by three tiny feet. While the family was sitting in the living room the egg, belonging to Eileen, flew off the mantel and struck another member of the family. Eileen was grieved, saying that "Brutus" had smashed almost everything in the house and now was starting on her possessions. At Stenhills Crescent the manifestations were mischievous but not malevolent and consisted of mysterious noises. Footsteps were heard in unoccupied parts of the house, doors opened and shut without cause.

John Glynn returned to Byron Street, shaken to learn that the entity had followed him to his mother's home and also had manifested at his own home in his absence.

In mid-November the British Broadcasting Corporation put on the air an account of a visit to Byron Street, Runcorn, by their reporter, Denis Mitchell.

Mitchell had witnessed paranormal phenomena in good light. He introduced other witnesses on the programme who had observed other doings of "Brutus." Mitchell stated that John Glynn gradually was becoming accustomed to his "familiar Spirit" and talked to "It." Mrs. Jones, called upon to testify, stated that "whatever it is, I wish it would go."

A member of the Runcorn City Council stated: "I have never seen anything like it." Mentioning the phenomena and damage he had witnessed he said:

"One would have thought someone had been there with a machine gun."

The Rev. J. L. Stafford noted that most of the phenomena depended upon the near presence of John Glynn. In the *Two Worlds* account of the broadcast he is quoted as saying: "My idea is that some part of John Glynn's mind has the power of exteriorizing itself and of utilizing an energy of which we know very little."

A Runcorn witness mentioned a curious incident. John Glynn and a friend had visited him and he asked his wife to bring in some lemonade. She brought in a bottle and poured lemonade for the friend. She poured a second glass for John. There was an explosion! The glass intended for John disintegrated as she held it in her hand. The lemonade, in some unexplained fashion, passed over the top of the table and drenched John Glynn. He was wet through, his chair also was wet, but no lemonade was on the table or the floor.

It is unusual for poltergeist activity to occur without the near presence of its medium. There is evidence in the Runcorn case that this has happened. Likewise, while generally malevolent or mischievous in the usual poltergeist manner, occasionally "Brutus" has appeared to cooperate with the investigators and on one occasion produced a sudden display of white light. Brutus made no claim of being any sort of an entity, nor did he make any attempts at communication. Spiritualist mediums quieted him for short periods but never for any great length of time.

The Catholic Church usually attributes poltergeist manifestations to the work of the Devil.

Dr. Nandor Fodor, the psychoanalyst, believes that most poltergeists are subconscious manifestations of the poltergeist medium. In the book *Haunted People*, by Hereward Carrington and Nandor Fodor, Dr. Foder presents evidence which seems to support this thesis.

Mrs. Eileen J. Garrett, an outstanding psychic, has had considerable personal experience in "laying" poltergeists; and from this experience she believes that poltergeists, in many cases, are the result of the activity of conflicts and obsessions of discarnate entities. (See *My Life As A Search for the Meaning of Mediumship* by Eileen J. Garrett.) While she admits the necessity of the usual adolescent medium, she does not attribute poltergeist activity solely to him or his subconscious mind.

But while authorities debated the causes and origins of poltergeists "Brutus" continued his mischief and the house of Sam Jones was a shambles.

❧ THE HAUNTED CHURCH OF AVENBURY ❧
The church was locked and empty — but the Vicar heard loud, triumphant organ music issuing from it.

Marion C. S. Holbourn

In a secluded valley in Herefordshire stands, amid venerable oaks and elms, the little Norman church of Avenbury, near Bromyard.

Within the chancel of this church is the tomb of a crusader, covered with a slab bearing the effigy of a knight in chain armor, with his legs crossed at the thigh to indicate that he had fought in crusades. At one time the pedal organ stood on top of this tomb.

On a number of occasions strains of music have been heard issuing from the empty church. People also speak of seeing the apparition of a beautiful damsel in the old structure.

One evening when the organist was practising, a loud, hollow groan came from under the organ. This was interpreted as a protest regarding the position of the instrument upon the crusader's tomb rather than a comment on the organist's performance. The organ was moved, and the groans were not repeated.

But the ghostly music continued to be heard from time to time and once the organist was able to recognize the strains. The first recorded date for this unearthly music is 8 September, 1896, when the Vicar's wife, Mrs. Wilson, and the three grown children of Colonel Purser all heard it at the same time. The only other date of which there is a record is 5 September, 1919, when a man and his son (who were employed in buying horses for the war office) heard it as they walked along the road.

My father, Rev. E. H. Archer-Shepherd, who was Vicar of Avenbury from 1897 to 1931, was a matter-of-fact Victorian who scoffed at superstitions. Anyone of his flock who dared express a belief in ghosts was dealt with firmly and pontifically.

Certainly my father was not a man to let his imagination run away with him. But one day as he stood in the Vicarage garden he heard strains of music coming from the direction of the church. He concluded that Mrs. Smith, the church cleaner, was allowing her child to play with the organ while she performed her duties. In a temper he hurried to the church to give the offender "a good blowing up." As he strode across the meadow the strains grew louder and his rage increased in proportion. He reached the churchyard gate and just as his finger touched the latch the music stopped abruptly. The massive door was shut and locked and nobody could be seen through the windows.

My father admitted that it was peculiar. He pondered over the affair for some years before he wrote, "There are some who would explain the music as the sound of a street organ or some other instrument played in Bromyard, which is only a mile in a straight line from Avenbury Church. But when we do hear Bromyard music from Avenbury Vicarage the sound always comes from the direction of Bromyard. Others suppose that the music is only an echo. But an echo is seldom heard to come from two directions and the music has been heard by people who were north, south, east and west of the church. Others suppose that the music really is due to a ghost. But the souls of the righteous are in the hand of God. They rest in peace. The music is certainly not the wail of a lost or tormented soul; for, on the two occasions I heard it, it sounded, though quite loud, more like the reverie of a mind at peace with itself.

As none of these theories will hold water, I incline to the belief that the cause of the music is to be found in the mentality of those (including myself) who hear it. Some telepathic, or auto-suggestive, or atmospheric, or other natural cause may have acted on our auditory nerves, setting up sensations which were transmuted by the brain into external sounds. If this explanation be the true one, there remains the interesting fact that under certain circumstances several people at the same time may distinctly hear loud and continuous sounds which have no existence except in their own minds.

Mrs. Smith, who lived in a cottage on a rise overlooking the church, said that one evening she saw a funeral attended by a crowd of people, all without heads. When this came to the ears of one of the church-wardens he also related that, many years earlier, he had had a similar vision but recognized the congregation as a company of monks with their cowls drawn over their heads. Viewed from above it would have been easy to mistake them for a headless company.

A happier event is also recorded concerning Avenbury Church. A lady residing at Leamington Spa wrote to my father in 1919: "I am inclined to tell you of an experience my husband and I had one Christmas night 40 years ago. Our home was in Bromyard and we, on Christmas afternoon, visited my parents who lived between your church and Bishop Frome. We commenced the homeward journey about 11 o'clock. It was then snowing very fast — considerable snow having fallen — which made our walk very fatiguing.

On drawing near the church I remembered the entrance porch and asked my husband if we should go in and wait to see if the storm would cease; also to get a little rest. It was then 12 o'clock on Christmas night. Almost immediately after entering the porch we heard what at first were many human voices conversing. The church seemed full of extremely happy, joyous human sounds. Although we distinctly heard so many voices in the church we could not distinguish a word they said.

I was not alarmed while it lasted, as it seemed to lift me above earthly things. Naturally we tried the door of the church but it was locked. We went outside but the church was in darkness. The wonderful sounds came distinctly from the inside of the church. The experience so deeply impressed us both that the memory has never grown dim.

Avenbury Church had three beautiful bells, one of which bore a Latin inscription meaning, "I am Gabriel, messenger from Heaven." As the church was dedicated to St. Mary the name of the bell doubtless commemorated the archangel's annunciation to the Virgin. The other bells were named, if I remember rightly, Paul and Andrew, but Gabriel was the master. He was the passing bell and his tolling aided the departing soul and accompanied the body on its last journey to the grave. He was said to toll of his own accord when a vicar died or when tragedy affected the parish.

I was living in Scotland when my father died. He had a seizure in church and was carried home on a stretcher. He lived on for 10 days and as his end was not thought to be imminent I was not sent for in time to see him alive. Our daily help, Sarah, lamented that I had not been summoned earlier. "They said they did not know he was dying," she exclaimed indignantly, "But they know perfectly well that bell never tolls for nothing!" She said that the bell started tolling about nine o'clock in the evening and that it wakened her several times during the night. Sarah was deaf and we always had to shout into her ear but she heard the bell distinctly.

I shall never forget Gabriel's peculiarly deep tone as my father's coffin was carried from church where he had ministered for 34 years. The first stroke of the great bell sent a shudder down my spine. Within the sound there seemed to be a voice, an undertone of awful solemnity and warning.

During the days that followed every member of the family confessed to imagining that they heard the bell tolling. But, except for my mother, we were conscious that it was subjective, coming from within. Every morning when I went to her room Mother told me she had been unable to sleep because of "that bell, tolling, tolling, tolling all through the night." It affected her health so that I had to hurry my arrangements to take her away from the house.

My father was the last vicar of Avenbury. The parish was divided between three neighbouring ones; the church was dismantled and the bells sold to a London church with the curious name, St. Andrew-by-the-Wardrobe. Our aged sexton was almost beside himself. If you sell the bells," he warned, "a curse will fall upon the parish."

Perhaps his prediction was fulfilled.

A few years ago one of my sons passed through the valley. He found that the church had become a scene of squalor and desecration. Vandals had broken the windows and climbed in to wreck the interior. Instead of the former exhortation "Whosoever thou art who enterest this church, leave it not without one prayer to God for thyself, for those who minister and those who worship here," there was now posted the warning: "Anyone entering this building does so at his own risk."

And what of the sorrowing Gabriel? During the London blitz the church where the bells hung was destroyed. I passed the site and could find not one stone to indicate that a church had ever stood on the spot. Later I learned to my great joy that the bells were saved and the church rebuilt.

HAUNTED BY A LION
D. J. S.

One of the ghosts that haunted the old house in Northern Ireland in which my family lived from 1865 to 1888 was that of a lion, although this ghost was seen less often than the other ghosts.

But as the outgoing tenant said to my father after he had signed a 10-year lease, the ghosts were well-bred ghosts and would not offend the most delicate-minded. He added that to counterbalance the ghosts was the fact that the house was a very lucky house financially. Both these statements proved true. We saw all the ghosts and after father's death 62 years later the house fetched twice what he had paid for it.

Our family was divided into two parts by the death of three children in the middle. My mother did not want the younger half to know about the ghosts, but we heard whispers and guessed the rest. For instance I heard of the ghost of the lion the day a man called to see Father who was engaged at the time.

The maid showed this man up to the drawing room to await Father's coming. As was customary the maid brought up a silver salver bearing a decanter of 25-year-old whiskey and a glass or two and told the gentleman to help himself. When she left the room to return downstairs she failed to close the door from which a view of the next flight of stairs up could be seen easily.

Father was delayed and when he at last came in he was horrified to hear a yell of sheer terror. He and my mother and the maid all dashed upstairs wondering what had happened. There was a round table in the middle of the room covered by a tablecloth that reached the floor, as was the custom in Victorian times. The man was not in view when they reached the drawing-room, but the cloth stirred and the man peeped out from behind its folds. My father took the man's shaking hand and pulled him to his feet. "In God's name, what's up?" he asked.

"The man stuttered, "I knew you kept hounds but I never knew that you kept lions."

Father was quick-witted and guessed at once what had happened but he did not want this man to go forth and tell his yarn. He helped the man into a chair and poured him a "nip." Then he pretended to notice how much of the whiskey had vanished. He said, "How many glasses of this whiskey did you drink?"

"Three or four, I think," the man said in trembling accents.

"Well, my poor fellow, that accounts for it. This whiskey is 25 years old. It is not the kind served at bars. It is more than double strength. It tastes like velvet but it is the stuff to make you see pink elephants." Father shook his head sadly.

"Oh God, is that it?" the man. cried. So shaken was he that he asked my father to go with him while he signed the pledge. He had seen the lion as plain as day walk down the stairs and pause at the door to lift his lip at him, so he had dived under the tablecloth. We had many a good laugh at that.

One Sunday in 1884 as we all sat at dinner after morning church service Mother asked my sister Athena who was eight years my senior to run upstairs and fetch a clean handkerchief from her room. As Athena ran upstairs and reached the next to the last landing she heard someone coming down the stairs. She wondered who it could be as all the family were at dinner and the maid was serving. Now the attic stairs were cut off by a door. Athena saw this door open and the lion step out. Athy was unable to move or cry out. The lion stretched and yawned, then turned and padded down the short flight. When it reached Athy, who was outspread against the wall, it paused and lifted its lip, showing its teeth, but it made no sound. It gave forth a heavy stench.

The lion passed her and continued down the stairs. Athy almost fell against the banister as she watched it pad downward. When it reached the foot of the stairs it pushed open the heavy oak door and went outside. Then Athy found tongue and raised the roof.

We all pounded upstairs to see what had happened. Mother did not want us younger children to hear about this and pushed Athy into a bedroom. Father ordered us all down to finish our dinner. This happened long before the incident of the man and the whiskey. When Athy and Mother returned to the table nothing further was said of the incident and we dared not ask.

After we were grown we heard the story of how shortly after my parents were married Father's two sisters came in 1866 to stay a month or two. One day after luncheon they went to their room to dress to go out. When Emily finished and opened the door to go down she saw the lion and screamed. Amelia joined her at the door and also saw the lion padding down the stairs. She joined in the screaming.

Father and Mother raced upstairs to see what was wrong. Emily and Amelia babbled about lions in the house. Father explained that it was only the harmless ghost of a lion they saw. But they packed up and left that evening. They did not relish the thought of living in the house with even the ghost of a lion.

As to how the lion came to haunt the house, we supposed a returning Crusader brought the lion from the Holy Land as a gift to the local chieftain. It was common knowledge that men went from our town to the Crusades and our house was old even then.

CARPET SLIPPERED WRAITH

Cmdr. Charles M. Cree

As a youngster I went to a boarding school at Northaw Place near Potters Bar in Hertfordshire. It was the same school at which ex-Prime Minister Clement Attlee received his early education — not that this necessarily be considered a recommendation.

Northaw Place was an old hunting lodge of King James I of England and the old part of the building was much as when first constructed about 1610. For school purposes a new wing had been built with dormitories and so forth but several dormitories remained in the old structure.

My sleeping quarters were in the new wing and like other youngsters my room-mates and myself were adventurous. We engaged in regular dormitory feasts which were held in the old building where we would be comparatively safe from interruption.

Our orgies invariably were scheduled for 1:00 a.m. and we perfected a beautiful organization for the purpose. It included a "telephone" to an adjoining dormitory which consisted simply of a hole bored through the wall under one of the beds, and a careful drill to avoid one creaky step on the stairway leading to the old building.

Punctually at one o'clock about eight pyjama-clad figures would silently emerge from their beds and disappear just as silently up the stairway carrying a variety of delicacies. With the groups from other rooms our party consisted of about 12 members.

We did not, of course carry watches, but at about 1:30 a.m., on every single occasion we had our parties, the "watchdog" stationed at the door would suddenly utter a sibilant warning. A dozen or so pyjama-clad forms would silently slide on the linoleum floor under the nearest bed.

Down the corridor outside came the unmistakable "sound" of carpet slippers. Everyone heard it. The soft, padding footsteps came right up to the door and stopped, apparently listening for what was going on inside.

We never heard any footsteps going away. After a while some old character would decide to scout and after making suitable noise

136

getting out of bed would open the door and head for the bathroom, half expecting to encounter the headmaster poised outside the door.

There was never anyone outside and the whole house was invariably as silent as the grave.

Several of the ringleaders of our group were leaving the school at the end of the term and it was the custom of the headmaster to ask boys to dinner before they finally left.

We had made cautious inquiries to ascertain the identity of our unknown "prowler." The Matron, Second Matron, and others had all been eliminated which left as the only possibility the Headmaster or a member of his immediate family.

As the gang was breaking up we decided to "fess up" and at dinner with the Headmaster we told him of the mysterious footsteps. He denied that he or any member of his family was our "prowler." However, he seemed quite interested and told us the following.

"You know that this is a very old building constructed when religious presecution and even civil war prevailed. In many houses built about that period it was customary to provide a secret room or refuge frequently known as a "Priest's Hole." I do not know if this house has such a secret room but there is a space eight feet square which is unaccounted for. If it is a room, the entrance may be from up the library chimney but I do not know for sure. Anyway, any such entrance was bricked up or otherwise hidden long before I came here."

I have often wondered if the wraith of some hunted priest still walks the corridors in carpet slippers in the dead of night, and if the secret room has been found and if so what was inside it.

Unless 12 youngsters were dreadfully deceived time and time again, it seems probable that we heard the wraith of a priest, tired of waiting over the centuries for the secret room to be broken open and for his long mouldering bones to be interred in hallowed ground.

THE DRUMMER OF TEDWORTH
Hereward Carrington

The drummer was jailed and his drum taken from him — and then a ghostly drumming began.

In the year 1665 a sort of "society for psychical research" was formed in the stately home of Lady Conway, at Ragley in Warwickshire. A number of eminent men and women attended the meetings, including Robert Boyle, the Rev. Joseph Glanvill, Dr. Henry More, Lady Roydon, and others. They related experiences and discussed psychic phenomena much the same as we do today. They were fairly sceptical and cautious but interested in odd facts from a scientific point-of-view. It was at one of these meetings that Dr. Glanville narrated the details of the now-famous case of "The Drummer of Tedworth." The full account was subsequently published in his book *Saducismus Triumphatus* (London, 1681).

The Rev. Joseph Glanvill himself was a distinguished minister and philosopher. He was a chaplain to King Charles II, a Fellow of the Royal Society and an author of considerable repute. He was also a sceptic interested in strange psychic manifestations and he collected them, publishing more than a score of cases in his book. The details of the Tedworth case he obtained directly from Mr. John Mompesson, in whose house the phenomena occurred.

For the most part rappings and "drummings" — such as might be made on a drum — were heard, though all sorts of poltergeist manifestations occurred, such as the movement and throwing of objects, strange noises, bedclothes pulled from the bed, etc. Like most poltergeist phenomena they appeared more mischievous and annoying than harmful.

Drum-like sounds were so predominant and played so important a part in this case that they finally supplied it with a name. There is a curious history behind this.

An itinerant drummer named William Drury had for some days been walking about the town, beating his drum and begging money. Apparently such "drummers" were common in the middle ages. However, this annoyed Mr. Mompesson and he complained to the bailiff. The latter replied that the drummer had authority to follow his trade and had produced letters and a Warrant signed by Sir William Cawly and Colonel Ayliff to prove it. Mr. Mompesson was acquainted with these gentlemen and, being familiar with their handwriting, sent for the fellow and examined the documents. He decided they were forgeries. Accordingly he had the drummer arrested and his drum was taken from him. After a short imprisonment the man was released but he naturally bore a grudge against Mr. Mompesson to whom the bailiff had sent the drum. It was soon after this unfortunate incident that the phenomena began. (Drury fell foul of the police a second time, later on, and subsequently was deported.)

We can examine the account of this extraordinary case given by Mr. Mompesson himself, as recorded by the Reverend Glanvill:

"... The noise of thumping and drumming was very frequent, usually five nights together, and then it would intermit three. It was on the outsides of the house, which is most of it board. It constantly came as they were going to sleep, whether early or late. After a month's disturbance without, it came into the room, where the drum lay, four or five nights in seven, within half-an-hour after they were in bed, continuing almost two. The sign of it just before it came was, they still heard an hurling in the air over the house and at its going-off, the beating of a drum like that at the breaking-up of a guard. It continued in this room for a space of two months, which time Mr. Mompesson himself lay there to observe it. In the fore part of the night, it used to be very troublesome, but after two hours it would be quiet. ...

Mrs. Mompesson being brought to bed, there was but little noise the night she was in travail, nor any for three weeks after till she had recovered strength. But after this civil cessation it returned in a ruder manner than before and followed and vex't the youngest children, beating their bedsteads with that violence, that all present expected they would fall in pieces. In laying hands on them, one could feel no blows, but might perceive them to shake exceedingly. For an hour, together it would beat, Roundheads and Cuckolds, the Tattoo and several other points of war, as well as any drummer. After this, they could hear a scratching under the children's bed, as if by something that had iron tallons. It would lift the children up in their beds, follow them from one room to another, and for a while haunted none particularly but them.

There was a cock-loft (attic) in the house, which had not been observed to be troubled; thither they removed the children, putting them to bed while it was fair day, where they had no sooner laid, but their troubles were with them as before.

On the fifth of November, 1662, it kept a mighty noise, and a servant, observing two boards in the children's room seeming to move, he bid it give him one of them. Upon which the board came (nothing moving in that he saw) within a yard of him. The man added, 'Nay let me have it in my hand;' upon which it was shov'd quite home to him. He thrust it back and it was driven to him again, and so up and down, to and fro, at least 20 times together, till Mr. Mompesson forbad his servant such familiarities. This was in the daytime and seen by a whole room full of people. That morning it left a sulphorous smell behind it, which was very offensive. At night the minister, one Mr. Clagg, and divers of the neighbours came to the house on a visit. The minister went to prayers with them, kneeling at the children's bed-side, where it was then very troublesome and loud. During prayer-time it withdrew into the cock-loft but returned as soon as prayers were done, and then in sight of the company, the chairs walkt about the room of themselves, the children's shoes being hurled over their heads and every loose thing moved about the chamber. At the same time a bedstaff was thrown at the minister, which hit him on the leg, but so favourably that a lock of wool would not have fallen more softly, and it observed that it stopt just where it lighted without rolling or moving from the place.

Mr. Mompesson perceiving that it so much persecuted the little children lodged them out at a neighbour's house, taking his eldest daughter, who was about 10 years of age, into his own chamber, where it had not been a month before. As soon as she was in bed the disturbance began there again, continuing three weeks drumming and making other noises, and it was observed that it would exactly answer in drumming any thing that was beaten or called for. After this the house where the children were lodged-out happening to be full of strangers they were taken home and, no disturbance having been known in the parlour, they were lodged there, where also their persecutor found them, but then only pluckt them by the hair and night-clothes without any other disturbance.

It was noted that when the noise was loudest and came with the most sudden and surprising violence, no dog about the house would move, though the knocking was oft so boisterous and rude that it hath been heard at a considerable distance in the fields, and awakened the neighbours in the village none of which live very near the house.

The servants sometimes were lift-up in their beds and then let gently down again without hurt; at other times it would be like a great weight upon their feet.

About the latter end of December, 1662, the drumming were less frequent and then they heard a noise like the jingling of money occasioned, as it was thought, by something Mr. Mompesson's mother had spoken the day before to a neighbour, who talkt of Fayries leaving money, i.e., That she should like it well if it would leave them some to make amends for their trouble. The night after the speaking of which there was a great clinking of money all over the house.

After this it desisted from the ruder noises and employed itself in little apish and less troublesome tricks. On Christmas Eve, a little before day, one of the little boys arising out of his bed was hit on a sore place upon his head with the latch of the door. The pin that it was fastened with was so small that it was a difficult matter to pick it out. The night after Christmas day, it threw the old Gentlewoman's clothes about the room and laid her Bible in the ashes. In such silly tricks it was frequent.

After this, it was very troublesome to a servant of Mr. Mompesson's who was a stout fellow and of sober conversation. This lay within during the greatest disturbance and for several nights something would endeavour to pluck his clothes off the bed, so that he was fain to tud hard to keep them on, and sometimes they would be pluckt from him by main force and his shoes thrown at his head. And now and then he should find himself forcibly held, as it were bound hand and foot, but he found that whenever he could make use of this sword and struck with it the spirit quitted its hold.

A little after these contests, a of Sir Thomas Bennet, whose workman the Drummer sometimes had been, came to the house, and told Mr. Mompesson some words that he had spoken, which it seems was not well taken. For as soon as they were in bed, the drum was beat up very violently and loudly, the gentleman arose and called his man to him, who lay with Mr. Mompesson's servant just now spoken of, whose name was John. As soon as Mr. Bennet's man was gone, John heard a rustling noise in his chamber and something came to his bedside, as if it had been one in silk. The man presently reacheth after his sword, which he found held from him, and 'twas with difficulty and much tugging that he got it into his power, which as soon as he had done the spectre left him, and it was always observed that it still avoided a sword.

About the beginning of January they were wont to hear a singing in the chimney before it came down. And one night about this time lights were seen in the house. One of them came into Mr.

Mompesson's chamber which seemed blue and glimmering and caused great stiffness in the eyes of those that saw it. After the light something was heard coming up the stairs, as if it had been one without shoes. The light was seen also four or five times in the children's chamber; and the maids confidently affirm that the doors were at least 10 times opened and shut in their sight, and when they were opened they heard a noise as if half a dozen had entered together. After which some were heard to walk about the room and one rustled as if it had been in silk. The like Mr. Mompesson himself once heard.

During the time of the knocking, when many were present, a gentleman of the company said, 'Satan, if the Drummer set thee to work, give three knocks and no more,' which it did very distinctly and stopt. Then the gentleman knockt to see if it would answer him as it was wont, but it did not. For further trial, he bid it for confirmation, if it were the Drummer, to give five knocks and no more that night, which it did, and left the house quiet all the night after. This was done in the presence of Sir Thomas Chamberlain of Oxfordshire and divers others.

On Saturday morning an hour before day, 10 January, a drum was heard beat-up on the outsides of Mr. Mompesson's chamber, from whence it went to the other end of the House, where some gentlemen strangers lay, playing at their door and without four or five several times, and so went off into the air.

The next night, a smith in the village, lying with John the man, they heard a noise in the room as if one had been shoeing of an horse and somewhat came, as it were with a pair of pincers, snipping at the smith's nose most part of the night.

One morning Mr. Mompesson, rising early to go a journey, heard a great noise below where the children lay and running down with a pistol in his hand he heard a voice crying a 'witch, a witch,' as they also had heard it once before. Upon his entrance all was quiet.

Having one night played some little tricks at Mr. Mompesson's feet, it went into another bed, where one of the daughters lay; There it passed from side to side, lifting her as it passed under. At that time there were three kinds of noises in the bed. They endeavoured to thrust at it with a sword but it still shifted and carefully avoided the thrust, still getting under the child when they offered at it. The night after it came panting like a dog out of breath. Upon which one took a bedstaff to knock, which was caught out of her hand and thrown away and, company coming up, the room was presently filled with a bloomy noisome smell and was very hot, though without fire in a very sharp and severe winter. It continued in the bed panting and scratching an hour and a half and then went into the next chamber, where it knockt a little and seemed rattle a chain; thus it did for two or three nights together.

After this, the old Gentlewoman's Bible was found in the ashes, the paper side being downwards. Mr. Mompesson took it up and observed that it lay open at the third chapter of St. Mark, where there is mention of the unclean spirits falling down before our Saviour and of his giving power to the Twelve to cast out devils, and of the scribes opinion, that he cast them out through Beelzebub. The next night they strewed ashes over the chamber to see what impression it would leave. In the morning they found in one place the resemblance of a great claw, in another of a lesser, some letters in another which they could make nothing of, besides many circles and scratches in the ashes. ...

About this time I went to the house on purpose to inquire the truth of those passages of which there was so loud a report. It had ceased from its drumming and ruder noises before I came thither but most of the more remarkable circumstances before related were confirmed to me there, by several of the neighbours together who had been present at them. At this time it used to haunt the children and that as soon as they were laid. They went to bed that night I was there, about eight of the clock, when a maidservant coming down from them told us it was come. The neighbours that were there and two ministers who had seen and heard divers times went away, but Mr. Mompesson and I and a gentleman that came with me went up. I heard a strange scratching as I went up the stairs and when we came into the room, I perceived it was just behind the bolster of the children's bed and seemed to be against the tick. It was as loud a scratching as one with long nails could make upon a bolster. There were two little modest girls in the bed, between seven and 11 years old as I guessed. I saw their hands out over the clothes and they could not contribute to the noise that was behind their heads. They had been used to it and had still some body or other in the chamber with them and therefore seemed not to be much affrighted. I was standing at the beds-head, thrust my hand behind the bolster, directing it to the place whence the noise seemed to come. Whereupon the noise ceased there and was heard in another part of the bed. But when I had taken out my hand it returned and was heard in the same place as before. I had been told that it would imitate noises and made trial by scratching several times upon the sheet, as five and seven, and 10, which it followed and still stopt at my number. I scratcht under and behind the bed, turning up the clothes to the bed-cords, grasped the bolster, sounded the wall behind and made all the search that possibly I could to find if there were any trick, contrivance, or common cause of it; the like did my friend but we could discover nothing. So that I then was verily persuaded and am so still that the noise was made by some demon or spirit.

After it had scratcht about half an hour or more it went into the midst of the bed under the children and there seemed to pant like a dog out of breath very loudly. I put my hand upon the place and felt the bed bearing up against it, as if something within had thrust it up. I graspt the feathers to feel if any living thing were in it. I looked under and everywhere about to see if there were any dog or any such creature in the room, and so we all did, but found nothing. The motion it caused by this panting was so strong that it shook the room and windows very sensibly. It continued thus more than half an hour, while my friend and I stay'd in the room, and as long after, as we were told.

During the panting I chanced to see as it had been something (which I thought was a rat or mouse) moving in a linnen bag, that hung up against another bed that was in the room. I steppt and caught it by the upper end with one hand, with which I held it and drew it through the other, but found nothing at all in it. There was no body near to shake the bag, or if there had, no one could have made such a motion, which seemed to be from within, as if a living creature had moved in it. ...

Another night, strangers being present, it purr'd in the children's bed like a cat, at which time also the clothes and children were lift up from the bed and six men could not keep them down. Thereupon they removed the children, intending to have ript up the bed. But they were no sooner laid in another, but the second bed was more troubled than the first. It continued thus four hours, and so beat the children's legs against the bed-posts that they were forced to arise and sit up all night. ...

Mr. Mompesson, coming one morning into his stable, found the horse he was wont to ride on the ground, having one of its hinder leggs in its mouth, and so fastened there that it was difficult for several men to get it out with a leaver. After this there were some other remarkable things, but my account goes no further. Only Mr. Mompesson writ me word, that afterwards the house was several nights beset with seven or eight in the shape of men who, as soon as a gun was discharged, would shuffle away together into an arbour. ..."

Having thus summarized the facts, Dr. Glanvill proceeds to give us his impressions of Mr. Mompesson — as a man and as a witness

144

— and to sum-up his impressions of the case. He says:

"Mr. Mompesson is a gentleman of whose truth in this account I have not the least ground of suspicion, he being neither vain nor credulous but a discreet, sagacious and manly person. Now the credit of matters of fact depends much upon the relators who, if they cannot be deceived themselves nor supposed any way interested to impose upon others, ought to be credited. For upon these circumstances all human faith is grounded and matter of fact is not capable of any proof besides, but that of immediate sensible evidence. Now this gentleman cannot be thought ignorant, whether that he relates be true or no, the scene of all being his own house, himself a witness and that not of a circumstance or two, but of 100, nor for once or twice only, but for the space of some years, during which he was a concerned and inquisitive observer. So that it cannot with any shew of reason be supposed that any of his servants abused him, since in all that time he must needs have detected the deceit. And what interest could any of his family have had to continue so long so troublesome and so injurious an imposture? Such supposals are wild and not likely to tempt any, but those whose wills are their reasons. So that, upon the whole, the principal relator Mr. Mompesson himself knew, whether what he reports is true or not, whether these things acted in his house were contrived cheats, or extraordinary realities. And if so, what interest could he serve, in carrying on, or conniving at a juggling design and imposture?

"He suffered by it in his name, in his estate; in all his affairs and in the general peace of his family. I say, if these things are considered there will be little reason to think he could have any interest to put a cheat upon the world in which he would most of all have injured and abused himself. And if he should have designed and managed so incredible, so unprofitable a delusion, 'tis strange that he should have troubled himself so long in such a business, only to deceive and be talked of. And it is yet more so that none of those many inquisitive persons, that came thither purposely to criticise and examine the truth of those matters, could make any discoveries of the juggling, especially since many came prejudiced against the belief of such things in general and others resolved beforehand against the belief of this and all were permitted the utmost freedom of search and inquiry. And after things were weighed and examined, some that were before greatly prejudiced went away fully convinced. To all which I add that there are divers particulars in the story in which no abuse or deceit could have been practised, as the motion of boards and chairs of themselves, the beating of a drum in the midst of a room and in the air when nothing was to be seen; the great heat in a chamber that had no fire in excessive cold weather, the scratching and panting, the violent beating and shaking of the bed-steads of which there was no perceptible cause or occasion; In these and such like instances, it is not to be conceived how tricks could have been put upon so many, so jealous and so inquisitive persons as were witnesses of them. ..."

Such is the story of the Drummer of Tedworth. How modern much of it sounds in the light of recent investigations into poltergeist phenomena!

Those who are interested in this subject might consult the book by Dr. Nandor Fodor and myself, *Haunted People*, in which some 375 typical poltergeist cases are summarized.

No matter how preposterous and absurd these poltergeist cases may seem, they nevertheless exist!

☾ THE MARCHING MONK OF POTTER'S BAR ☾

**She heard the sound of heavy footsteps
and her door burst open. A huge ghostly figure
strode into the room.**

Charles M. Cree

Nyn Park House is a huge medieval mansion which stands about 15 miles north of London. Despite its proximity to the metropolis its surroundings seem entirely rural. The house itself nestles in a spacious, private park beautifully situated between rolling hills and woodland.

Though Nyn Park House is ancient, dating back to the early 16th century, the idyllic spot on which it stands has been a residence the dawn of time. In the lovely gardens, which were laid out before the house was built, one can still trace the foundations of a magnificent monastery raided and razed by the rapacious King Henry VIII.

Some half mile south of Nyn Park are the outskirts of the village, Potter's Bar. In 1910 this area was on the extreme northern edge of the London commuter's district.

Consequently Mr. Norman Carter, a prosperous fuel merchant, had purchased a comfortable, modern, two-storey house from which he travelled daily to the city.

There was nothing peculiar about the residence. It stood a few yards back from the macadamized roadway in its own grounds. In back of the house was a big garden with a tennis court and near the edge of the property was an old, disused well, long since filled almost to the top with garden refuse.

Shortly after moving in Mr. and Mrs. Carter were reading one evening by lamplight in the study downstairs. At 10 o'clock precisely Mr. Carter was mildly startled by the sound of unmistakably male footsteps ascending the stairway outside the room. The steps reached the landing above and the door to the spare bedroom was heard distinctly to open and close.

"Now who in the world could that be?" he asked his wife.

"I'm sure I don't know, Norman, you'd better go upstairs and see," she answered.

Mr. Carter proceeded to search the upstairs premises thoroughly. Hazel, their 10-year-old daughter, was sound asleep in her

147

bed; the maids had not yet retired; nothing was in any way amiss. Somewhat puzzled Mr. Carter returned to the study.

Almost every night thereafter, at 10 o'clock, the same heavy footfalls could be heard and the door of the guest room opened and closed with a sharp click.

The Carters tried every way they could think of to detect the intruder. They watched the stairway and saw nothing. They stretched threads across the stairs. Footsteps were heard ascending but the threads remained unbroken.

Finally they grew so accustomed to the phenomenon that they paid no attention to it. Mr. Carter, for the sake of peace of mind, decided the whole thing was caused by a heavy express train passing on the main line about a mile away. He had read somewhere that such noises could be due to a rock structure passing under the tracks and surfacing again under the foundations of a building. He even pretended to reconcile this theory with the behaviour of the guest room door.

In the late autumn the Carters entertained Miss E. M. as a house guest. Quite casually they mentioned the "ghost" of the house. Mr. Carter had quite convinced himself that his theory accounted satisfactorily for the nocturnal disturbance. But Miss E. M. claimed psychic powers. Assuring herself that the room allotted to her was the one where the door seemed to open and close, she retired early.

Her big lady's clothes basket — one of those old-fashioned trunks with a rounded lid — lay at the foot of the bed. As the good lady was undressing she heard the sound of heavy footsteps ascending the stairs. A moment later the door burst open and an enormously tall man dressed in the garb of a monk entered the room. He passed right over the trunk, seemingly taking it in his stride, and disappeared through the wall of the room as the bedroom door clicked closed.

The visitor did not re-appear during Miss M.'s stay but the footsteps continued to be heard as before.

There is a curious sequel to this story. Mr. Carter, an enthusiastic gardener, decided to clean out the old well at the foot of the garden. About six feet down he came upon an ancient doorway leading into what remained of a medieval, secret passage. It was possible to trace this passage for some distance. It headed directly toward the site of the foundations of the once prosperous monastery of Nyn.

It is nearly 45 years since I sat in the study of that house in Potter's Bar and listened to those hurried steps of the marching monk.

I never saw the monk and of course the footsteps may have been caused by that speeding train as Mr. Carter suggested. But to me it seems the soul of an earthbound monk still searches for the peace he never finds.

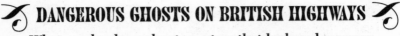

DANGEROUS GHOSTS ON BRITISH HIGHWAYS

What can be done about spectres that look and move so much like real things and real people as to cause accidents?

Leslie E. Wells

There are stretches of highway in Britain where curious and inexplicable incidents have occurred during the past thirty years.

One such stretch of road is situated at Matley, near Hyde, in Cheshire. This is a perfectly straight length of roadway, with nothing whatever to confuse drivers of vehicles. Yet the road achieved an unenviable notoriety because, in the three years 1928 to 1930, no less than 16 accidents occurred on it.

That so many accidents, involving cycles, cars and lorries and causing several deaths, should take place on a few hundred yards of excellent highway finally aroused the interest of the authorities. But the most careful investigations by the police and highway officials brought to light no natural explanation for the disasters.

Disturbing to all who used the road was the testimony of the persons involved in the accidents. They all told the same story — the vehicle in which they had been travelling had swerved to avoid a motor lorry which they had seen backing out onto the road from an opening between an inn and a crossroad. All were unanimous in their testimony on this point, a fact which only bewildered the authorities, for there is no opening of any kind at the spot where the lorry was seen on the occasion of each accident.

It is not surprising that, during an inquest on one of the victims of an accident, the coroner, looking puzzled and disturbed, said, "If any juryman can throw light on the recurrence of these unexplained accidents on this perfectly straight road, I should be obliged." Then he added, very significantly, "If you could go there, say at midnight, it might be interesting to both you and me."

Yet the mystery was never explained and the accidents ceased as unaccountably as they had begun.

There is more explanation for the haunted stretch of road between Blandford and Salisbury. Motorists on this road have reported that, at a particular point, they have heard screams and groans. One motorist fainted with shock when a blood-covered hand crept round his shoulder and rested on the steering wheel. Another declared that he saw the face of a dead man staring up at him from the road, although investigation proved there was no dead man in the vicinity.

These amazing and alarming happenings caused such a stir that the Bristol newspapers took up the matter. Their investigations brought to light the fact that a motor accident had occurred at the very point on the road where the apparitions were seen.

The White Lady of Litlington seems to be an unreal reality. She has been seen many times on a lonely stretch of road near Abington Pigotts, a village two miles from Litlington, Cambridgeshire. She is described as having flaming eyes which pierce the darkness. She turns her face suddenly towards her audience, giving them such a fiery glance that they are petrified.

The White Lady wears the flowing skirts and large poke bonnet of Victorian days. While many people testify to having seen her, the most reliable witness is Mr. H. Radclyffe Maunders, a lay reader of Litlington Vicarage. He encountered her one night as he was cycling home. Mr. Maunders said, "I have never believed in ghosts, but I have experienced something which I cannot explain."

Equally well known is the Black Lady of Wensleydale, in Yorkshire. She haunts the section of road which connects the villages of Aysgarth and Woodhall, on opposite sides of the River Ure. The most baffling thing about her is that, so far as is known, nothing has ever happened in the vicinity to account for the haunting.

She always appears in a black dress of the type fashionable in the 19th century, a coloured bonnet and a pair of white gloves. She carries a walking-stick. So real and natural is her appearance that many people have spoken to her, not realizing that there was anything ethereal about her. On one occasion a cyclist dismounted and asked her if she could direct him to the nearby village of Redmire. Perhaps it is fortunate that she simply ignores anyone who speaks to her.

Certain highways are haunted by vehicles instead of the ghosts of persons. London, where there is neither stillness nor silence to encourage the imagination, has its quota of such apparitions. The legend of the ghost bus of North Kensington has been repeated over the years, and people still testify to seeing it. On certain nights, after the regular bus service has stopped, people have been awakened by the noise of a bus racing down Cambridge Gardens. The vehicle, although brilliantly lit, has neither driver nor passengers. On reaching the junction of Cambridge Gardens and St. Mark's Road it vanishes.

A ghost car haunts the Watford by-pass near London. It looms as convincingly as a normal car until it is picked up by headlights. Then to the astonishment and awe of those who see it, it proves to be no more than a skeleton, as though it were the wreckage of a burnt out vehicle. Those who have stopped when confronted by this apparition have seen it dissolve like a wraith.

More frightening and much more dangerous is the phantom lorry seen on the Great North Road near Biggleswade in Bedfordshire. Motorists have been terrified by it when approaching a rather sharp bench for, coming round the corner towards them, on the wrong side of the road, rushes a heavy lorry. Its headlights are glaring and the driver is wrestling frantically with the steering wheel. Drivers have swerved violently to avert what seemed a certain head-on collision.

Pulling up, they have thrust indignant heads into the open with the intention of speaking their minds freely to a driver who so flagrantly disregarded elementary rules of safety. But, to their amazement, they have found the road immediately behind them completely deserted. The offending vehicle had vanished into thin air.

The records show that, some years ago, a lorry-driver had a fatal crash on the very bend where the ghost lorry keeps appearing. Thus it would seem that the driver is compelled to keep enacting his fatal experience.

Far more intriguing than the appearance of any individual or vehicle is the highway apparition seen by motorists travelling late at night on the main road from Cambridge to Ely. They have found themselves following what they took to be a column of marching soldiers. They have assumed it to be a highland unit because their headlights picked out the dim swaying of kilts. Always the column has turned off the road into the mist of the flanking fens. It is in the moment that the column wheels that the motorists have seen the crests of Roman helmets and silhouettes of large, square shields. No one has yet discovered what Caesarian cohort still trudges along this road which is one the Romans themselves first laid down.

Another traditional highway ghost has been seen often on the stretch of Bath Road which links Hungerford and Marlborough. This phantom is a cavalier, mounted on a black charger and swathed from head to heel in a voluminous, billowing cloak. Those who have seen him say that he looks like a great black shadow against the hedge which flanks the road. He spurs his horse squarely across the road and vanishes at full speed on the other side of the highway. Who he is and why he should haunt this particular point on the highway no one knows. Nevertheless, there are many drivers who have encountered him.

A pale, long-haired woman runs shrieking along the second-class roads on and near Aylmerton Heath in Norfolk. It is in this county also, along lonely roads at dusk that young Lord Dacre may be seen riding his rocking-horse. He was murdered in 1565 by his guardian, Sir Richard Fulmerston, who wickedly arranged that the rocking-horse should collapse. The young earl broke his neck. Today, it is said, the boy still can be seen prancing around on the sawn-through rocking-horse.

The modern apparitions seem more terrifying than their predecessors. Ghost lorries which cause accidents cannot be ignored. And many motorists in England will testify emphatically that they do exist. There are juries, coroners and other authorities who admit that some accidents have no natural explanation. There seems little doubt that there are dangerous ghosts on the roads of Britain.

LONDON'S HAUNTED FLATS

Two housewives living in a converted convent
report frequent sightings of a shadowy black-robed figure.
Is it the ghost of a former nun?

Chester S. Geier

Two London housewives say that the ghost of a nun passes occasionally through their adjoining flats in a converted convent building off Streatham High Road. They describe the apparition as "a very solid shadow" having the appearance of a black-robed nun.

The two housewives, Mrs. Savage and Mrs. Cooke, have lived for some nine years in what formerly was Coventry Hall. During this time, they claim, they have seen the ghostly nun at intervals, both during daylight and in the evening.

The flats occupied by the Savage and Cooke families are on the first floor of the remodelled convent and take in what originally were the Mother Superior's private rooms. For this reason Mrs. Savage and Mrs. Cooke believe that the apparition is a former head of the convent.

According to Mrs. Savage, the ghostly nun usually follows a regular route through the flats. She and Mrs. Cooke have come to call this "the Nun's Walk." They say the apparition moves from the front room, which Mr. and Mrs. Cooke use as a combination sitting and bedroom, past the kitchen door and around into the hallway toward the bathroom door. At the point where a new wall separates the Savage bathroom from the Cooke flat, the figure disappears.

During their first four years in Coventry Hall, Mrs. Savage and Mrs. Cooke relate, they saw the apparition about twice a week. Since then, however, the visitations have been at intervals of three or four months. Tenants of other flats in the building say they have not seen the ghostly nun and know of her only through the reports of the two women.

Mrs. Savage says she became aware of the nun shortly after she moved into the remodelled convent in 1947. She had occupied her new flat for only a few days when she saw the figure of the nun walking around the corner of the hall to the bathroom. One day, she recalls, her visiting sister-in-law saw a figure in the kitchen doorway. She spoke to it under the impression that it was Mrs. Savage, who at the moment was in the bedroom.

At first, Mrs. Savage relates, her husband was sceptical about ghosts in general and refused to believe her story of the phantom nun. Some time later she returned home from a vacation trip to find her husband shaken. He admitted that he himself had seen the ghost. He had glimpsed a figure walking into the bedroom and, certain it was a human being, he had followed it. However, he had found the room empty.

Mrs. Savage is the mother of three young children. As the result of certain strange experiences she has had earlier in her life, she believes she is psychic. On occasions when she has seen the ghostly nun, she says, regardless of what she happened to be doing, she has felt compelled to look up. Once, as she and a friend sat outside on the lawn in broad daylight, she saw a black-robed figure standing by her french windows. She pointed out the figure to her friend, who saw nothing.

Mrs. Savage and Mrs. Cooke say they have seen the ghostly nun so often that they no longer consider it remarkable enough to mention. They have accepted the haunting as a matter of course, particularly as neither they nor their families have been disturbed by the ghost. They have no particular desire to move, although Mrs. Savage says that she would like a home of her own, for the benefit of her children. This desire, she emphasizes, has nothing whatever to do with the ghostly nun.

ℂ MY FATHER'S GHOST HAUNTS LONDON ℂ
Tom Terriss

Copr. 1956 King Features Syndicate, Inc.

William Terriss, idolized British actor, was murdered near the turn of the century. Now his son tells of the weird sequel to his death.

When frightened passengers and night-shift employes of London's underground tremblingly reported recently that the ghost of my father, actor William Terriss, was haunting Covent Garden station, I was not greatly surprised.

"Breezy Bill" Terriss, idol of the British stage when he was murdered near that station just before the turn of the 20th century, always did things with a flair. Eyewitness accounts that the ghost who stalks the underground is tall, handsome and well-groomed, led me to agree that it might be Father.

The ghost of Covent Garden station, debonair in clothing of a bygone day, has been seen waiting for trains into which he vanishes without being noticed by occupants. He ascends stairways but does not emerge at the top.

One tube worker, a part-time spiritualist, conducted a séance in a room at the station while trains rumbled past. Half-way through the séance, another employe, Victor Locker, is said to have shouted: "He's on you! He's on you!"

And it was then, the spiritualist reports, that he heard a mysterious voice calling, "Terr ..."

Employee Locker is said to have demanded transfer to another part of the tube system. Late passengers glance apprehensively over their shoulders. And British journalists, reviving the dark doings in that area on 16 December, 1898, delve into records of which I have no need.

Many strange things have happened to me, too, since then. I was present at the opening of King Tutankhamen's tomb and am the only survivor of the famous "curse." In my 74 years, I have made films around the world, viewing many bizarre sights.

Yet the circumstances of my father's murder 57 years ago are etched vividly in my memory. The reports that his ghost has been seen dovetail weirdly with facets of this tragic event.

There was nothing ghostly about William Terriss in the flesh. He was dashing and gay, vibrantly alive on the stage when he played leading Shakespearean roles and toured with Sir Henry Irving. Before embarking on a theatrical career, he ran the gamut of real-life adventure.

From sheep farmer in the Falkland Islands, he turned to horse breeder in Kentucky. Then he tried his hand at mining in Cripple Creek. As a seaman in the Royal Navy, he won the Royal Humane Society medal for saving lives at sea.

Brimming with enthusiasm, he plunged into theatrical work and was soon a favourite throughout the United Kingdom. His Romeo was manly, yet tender, his Henry VIII memorable. He was the Comte de Candale in *A Marriage of Convenience*, and Lieut. Dudley Keppell in *One of the Best*.

Women adored him. Men admired him. I was only 17 years old but I knew that my father, at 49, was at the peak of a great career and I was one of the proudest lads in England.

What I did not know was that his murder was being plotted by a madman and that it was being aided and abetted unwittingly by some of Father's best friends.

My father was appearing at the Adelphi Theatre in the thriller, *Secret Service*. It was a gallant, vigorous role for which he was well suited. But there was in the company a lowly extra with delusions of grandeur named Richard Prince.

Prince told anyone who would listen that he should be playing the lead, that he was much the better actor and that William Terriss, by selfishly keeping the star role, was preventing him from achieving his true destiny.

And relishing the joke, the other actors encouraged Prince. They urged him to recite Shakespearean passages in fiery, rolling tones, applauded his wild-eyed histrionics and agreed that a great talent was being crushed. Unaware of what they were doing, they added fuel to the fire blazing in that distorted brain.

On the night of 15 December, 1898, Father's understudy, Charles Lane, came to the theatre in what was obviously a depressed mood. To questioners, he said: "I had a dream last night which terrifies me. I dreamt that Bill was stabbed to death!"

Stage folks have always been notably superstitious but this was too much even for them. They laughed at Lane's account. Yet he had described events exactly as they were, to happen 24 hours later!

For on the night of 16 December, my father and a friend dined before show time at Simpson's famous restaurant and then walked to the theatre. Spectators were already entering the main doors when the two men reached Maiden Lane, a narrow and poorly illuminated thoroughfare at the rear of the theatre. My father had just inserted a key in the lock of his private door when a dark figure detached itself from the shadows and rushed across the street at him.

It was the bit actor, Richard Prince. He was theatrically dressed for the role of assassin in a black cape and wide-brimmed black hat. A dagger flashed in his hand. Screaming an imprecation, he plunged the knife twice into my father's back, and when he turned to defend himself, Father received the third thrust directly in the heart.

Father's friend fled, an act that was to haunt him until he later committed suicide. Prince, too, ran but was eventually captured and ended his days in Broadmoor Criminal Lunatic Asylum, still proclaiming himself the greatest actor in the world.

My father was found by other actors. Indicative of his great vitality, was the fact that he lived for 20 minutes although his aorta was pierced. And just before he died, he whispered, "I will come back."

Perhaps that was merely a reflex action sparked by the many death scenes played on the stage. I did not learn about it until later. Something even stranger was occurring in our home miles away.

I was playing chess with my younger brother. Mother was sitting in an armchair across the room, reading, and in her lap was our little black and tan terrier, a mild and meek animal which had never seemed to have so much as a bark in it.

A few minutes after eight o'clock, (the exact time Father died) our terrier jumped to the floor and ran around the room barking furiously. Then it crouched, quivering, under the table, rolling its eyes and snapping at the air.

We thought that it had suddenly gone mad. It was half an hour before it quieted down, and then there was a rapping on the door and we received the news which broke our hearts.

The passing of few actors has precipitated such wide-spread sorrow. Messages poured in to us from all over the world. Her Majesty, Queen Victoria, sent the following letter:

"The Queen sends her condolence and deep sympathy to Mrs. William Terriss and family in their sad bereavement. She deeply feels the loss which has robbed the English stage of one of its brightest ornaments."

"Breezy Bill" was laid to rest, but his name was to live on. A London newspaper started a memorial fund to which Father's admirers contributed a sum equal to a million dollars! Since he had loved the sea, serving as a Royal sailor and playing so many sailor parts on the stage (*Harbour Lights*, *The Union Jack* etc.) it was decided to build and maintain a lifeboat station in his name with the money.

Now comes this strange manifestation at Covent Garden, near where he died. I do not pretend to know what it means.

THE HOUSE THAT KILLS

J. Altgilbers

Filled with weird noises and odours, the old house seemed an abode of evil — and then it took a life.

After living for two years in a condemned house Mr. and Mrs. Frank Pell were overjoyed when their name came to the top of the housing list and they were given the key to a house on Coxwell Road, Ladywell, in Birmingham, England. It was a pleasant old house, in a quiet neighbourhood. It had been newly decorated and had all modern conveniences. In addition the rent was low and it was convenient for transport links.

Frank and his wife were too happy with their good fortune to pay serious attention to the whispered rumours they heard of strange noises and sulphuric odours reported by former tenants of the house. They moved in with their five happy children during the latter part of May, 1955.

Perhaps they felt some subconscious response to the evil in the house for they did ask the local priest, Father Francis Etherington, to bless the house. This he did. And when he had departed the Pells settled down to enjoy their new home.

On a night during their first weekend in the house Frank was wakened by the crash of a slamming door. He started up. His wife also was sitting upright in the dark, straining forward, listening. They heard faint sounds of a door being opened carefully, furtively. Again the silence was broken by the crash of the slamming door.

Frank Pell and his wife looked at each other across their month-old baby, who slept peacefully between them. Then again a door opened and closed, more softly this time.

"Must've left a door open, and the wind's caught it," Frank muttered as he slipped out of the bed.

Frank knew it wasn't the wind; although the explanation seemed to satisfy his wife. The wind can slam doors but it can't turn knobs, and there had been the distinct click of a latch. Nor does the wind suddenly whisper excitedly in the darkness while a man gropes for the light switch.

Frank Pell's war record shows he is a man of uncommon courage, but he admits he was baffled and uneasy when he could find no plausible explanation for the strange noises. As he stood in the kitchen, pondering, a sudden dry, scrabbling noise came from above as if some unseen thing made its way across the ceiling. Frank looked up, half expecting to see a rat. Instead, from directly over his head came a loud thud — a bump such as no earthly rat ever made!

For an unmeasured time Frank stood silent, listening, but an almost unearthly quiet had settled over the old house. Finally Frank returned to the bedroom.

During the days and nights that followed the strange disturbances continued. Fear had come to live with the new tenants of the house on Coxwell Road. Frank and his wife finally admitted to each other that there could be no earthly cause for the noises. At night they lay together listening to the sounds that both now knew were made by phantoms. And this recognition seemed to give added vigour to the weird forces; the noises increased nightly and the Pell's tension mounted.

No matter how carefully they secured the doors they continued to open and slam shut, generally during the hours just after midnight. Eerie, murmuring whispers echoed throughout the house.

A particular concentration of the evil seemed to exist in the bedroom over the kitchen. Distinct, loud thuds continued to be heard on the kitchen ceiling. From the same area a curious tapping sound came every night about 10:20. And in the bedroom above the kitchen the temperature seemed to change abruptly almost every hour.

While cleaning that bedroom one day Mrs. Pell was struck by a sudden dank chill that seemed to blow right through her. She said later that she felt as if icy, intangible fingers touched her; but she remained calm, ignored the feeling, and continued with her tasks.

The Pells told each other that all this was distinctly odd, "but nothing to worry about." The presence of the children forced them to remain calm to avoid alarming the youngsters.

Frank reasoned that even supernatural forces bring no harm to those who refuse to fear them. He had not heard the old tale of the man who, when walking through a haunted wood and confronted by a ghost from Hell, exclaimed, "If I, who have led a good life, could be harmed by a phantom there would be no justice in the world!" "None at all," the apparition agreed ...

And so it was with the Pells. Surrounded by malignancy they said nothing would harm them.

But one morning they woke up and their baby girl lay dead between them.

There was no mark on the child's body. She had been in perfect health. The doctors announced that the baby died accidentally by suffocation.

This was less than a month after the Pells moved to the house. It been a hot night, the second week in June. All the bed covers had been thrown back to the foot of the bed. Surely if the child's Mother or Father had rolled onto her during sleep there would have been marks on the little body. It is difficult to see how she was suffocated — by earthly means.

The grief-stricken Pells buried their child. And went bank to their house. They accepted the report of accidental death. Difficult as that may have been, it was easier than admitting that ghosts had suffocated their baby.

But the mourners found no peace. To the weird manifestations yet another was added. Mrs. Pell noticed it first and called her husband's attention to it. A musty smell began to permeate various parts of the house. It was a strange, repulsive odour, as of something incredibly ancient. On other occasions they smelled the strong odour of garlic, a stench that gradually changed to a smell of burning rubber.

The forces of evil were creeping closer.

A few days passed and one evening four-year-old Sammy asked a strange question. "Mummy," he said. "Did baby go with the little white dog?"

Mrs. Pell paled and looked at Frank. "What little white dog, Sammy?" she asked.

Sammy's small face reflected great surprise. "Why, the little white dog that comes and sits on my bed!" he said.

Frank picked the boy up. "When did you last see the dog?" he asked.

"The night baby left us," was the prompt reply. "He was sitting on baby's face."

Confronted with the horrible suggestion that her baby girl was smothered by an apparition Mrs. Pell became hysterical. Frank could not quiet her. Finally he went to the police with his story, and Father Etherington was called again to exorcise the evil spirits.

The police conducted a long, thorough and fruitless search of the house.

The priest performed the ceremony to purge the house of its unholy guests. When he stood with his rosary and holy water in the bedroom over the kitchen, Father Etherington distinctly heard the curious tap-tapping. Who knows what this man of God thought as he stood there, listening to sounds strangely like the tapping, seeking cane of a blind man? Whatever his thoughts may have been, he stated that he was unable to pronounce the house clean. He didn't say the house was evil but he said it was a bad house for the Pells and that he could do no more. He urged them to leave.

But the Pells stayed. They still were unwilling to leave their new home, unwilling to admit that evil, spirits could harm them.

The weird noises continued; the knocking, the banging doors, the whisperings were still heard. The temperature changed abruptly and unnaturally in the bedroom over the kitchen; occasional stale, musty odours wafted through the rooms.

Then came a day at the beginning of July. Mrs. Pell was upstairs performing some household task. Frank was downstairs, shaving. The whispering may have been going on for some moments before Frank consciously heard it. But when the ghostly voices suddenly increased in volume, excited, coming closer with a sudden rush, Frank became aware of them with a start. Suddenly concerned for his wife he dropped his razor and ran to the foot of the stairs. An eerie sight met his upturned eyes; a sight to stop the heart of any man!

At the top of the stairway stood his wife, her whole body rigid and straining. Her head was thrown back, her eyes wide, her mouth open; dark, swollen veins stood out on her neck. As he saw her breast heave, her hands clenching spasmodically at her sides, Frank realized she was screaming — and yet no sound came to him!

He leaped up the stairway toward her. As he passed the first step he was met by an impalpable resistance, an invisible substance that clung and bound him like the folds of a shroud, impeding and finally stopping his progress.

Frank struggled frantically. As he looked up he could still see his wife, her throat straining in soundless screams. His groping hands found the banister; he pulled with all the strength in his arms with his legs braced and straightened he forced his way into the invisible curtain. The restraining wall released him so suddenly he stumbled. Instantly piercing screams rang in his ears.

In an instant he was holding his wife in his arms, where she continued to sob and tremble uncontrollably. Finally she told Frank that she, too, had heard the voices behind her, that they suddenly came closer with a rush. She did not know what the voices had said to her, or why she so instantly was seized by terror.

Whatever precipitated this climax to fear it was very evident that the evil forces that reigned in the old house had prevented Frank from hearing his wife's screams, and had tried to prevent his reaching her.

Without stopping to pack their belongings the Pells left the house.

June Hadley, Frank Pell's niece, and her fiancé, Dennis Savage, went to the house to pack the Pell's things. They also heard the whisperings, the tappings, smelled the ancient evil and said they would never enter the house again for, any reason whatsoever.

"To let: pleasant three-bedroom house, older type but newly and tastefully decorated. All mod. cons. Ample storage room incl. cellar in quiet road close to all services. Council owned. Cheap rent."

Do you want to rent it?

THE DURABLE GHOST
OF LADY ELIZABETH HOBY

Edmond P. Gibson

Why has the ghost of Lady Hoby been seen reportedly for over 300 years? Does she return in remorse for a cruel act?

Bisham Abbey is all that remains of a very extensive British monastic establishment that flourished on the Thames above London for over four centuries. Bisham lies about nine miles upstream from Maidenhead and seven miles downstream from Henley, on the south bank of the river. Once the Thames flowed swiftly past rich fields tilled by the monks. In recent years dams have slowed the current and raised the river level.

The abbey and its ancient church nestle in a grove of beeches which tower above them. The ownership record of Bisham goes back to 1042. William the Conquerer granted the site to a Henry de Ferrars. Later, about 1130, a descendant of Ferrars leased a part of the site to the Knights Templar who used it as a Preceptory and Priory. The Knights Templar had become very powerful by 1300, exerting a great deal of political power while they operated a sort of travel agency to the Crusades. The Pope suppressed the order early in the 14th century and the Priory was abandoned.

Bisham then became a tenant monastery of Augustinian monks, under a lease from William Montacute, Earl of Salisbury, who had succeeded to the royal grant.

At the time of the Reformation, in 1536, Henry VIII confiscated the Salisbury properties and evicted the Augustinians. Shortly thereafter a Benedictine group occupied the abbey. They were dissolved very shortly and after his divorce Henry VIII gave the Bisham estate to his former wife Anne of Cleves. She disliked the place and, with royal consent, traded it to the Hoby family for their estate in Kent. The Hobys moved to Bisham about 1553 and members of that family occupied the property continuously until 1776.

Sir Thomas Hoby is said to have acted as jailer to Queen Mary during her reign and kept confined at Bisham the future Queen Elizabeth. He must have treated her very well for after she succeeded to the throne she was friendly with the Hoby family and visited them at the Bisham property. Few persons succeeded in being friends with both Mary Tudor and Elizabeth, but the Hoby family apparently accomplished the feat and none of them were executed at the Tower.

This story is concerned with Lady Elizabeth Hoby, wife of Sir Thomas Hoby. She was the daughter of Sir Anthony Cooke, a tutor to the royal family. Two of her sisters married to the high positions of Lady Bacon and Lady Cecil. Elizabeth Hoby herself seems to have been on intimate terms with Queen Elizabeth and welcome at Court throughout her life.

Lady Hoby was exceptionally well educated for her period. She spoke French, Greek, and Latin; wrote verses in Greek and Latin, and wrote also on religious topics. She was an expert on court ceremonies and formalities, meticulous in etiquette, and at the death of her husband in 1556, she became very autocratic and domineering in the management of the manor and her family. She loved pomp, particularly the ostentatiousness of state funerals, and she lived to attend many of them.

A portrait of Elizabeth Hoby by Hans Holbein hangs at Bisham. It shows a severe, thin-lipped woman with long tapering hands.

Elizabeth and Thomas Hoby had four children; Edward, Elizabeth, Anne, and Thomas. Following Sir Thomas Hoby's death she married Lord John Russell to whom she bore three children. Thomas, Anne, and Margaret.

History describes her as a priggish sharp-tempered woman who was severe with her children. She flogged one of her young sons for blotting his copy-books so that the child died of her beating. Remorse for this cruelty is the accepted reason for her continuing return to the Abbey.

Shortly after her death, in 1609, Lady Hoby began to be seen at Bisham Abbey, sometimes in an upper bedroom, sometimes on the tower stairs. Occasionally she "walked" in the Abbey library where she occasionally was seen coming from the stairs into the library, wringing her hands. She also has been seen emerging from an upper bedroom washing her hands in a basin which is supported and carried before her by some unknown means. Occasionally she has appeared as a negative apparition, face and hands are black and her dress white. The apparition is easily identified by its likeness to the portrait which still hangs at Bisham.

Bisham might very well support other ghosts than this unhappy lady. In the church and grounds are buried many famous figures of medieval English history. Perhaps the most famous personage buried at Bisham is "Warwick the Kingmaker", of the Salisbury family. He succeeded in putting Edward IV on the English throne. Later Warwick tried to place Henry VI on the throne, but in this attempt he was defeated and killed by the forces of Edward IV.

But Lady Hoby is the only known ghost at Bisham and she has walked repeatedly since her death, generally at the time when a new English monarch is about to be crowned. Perhaps her love for ceremony attracts her for Thames valley people say that she was seen at Bisham at all coronation times, until the crowning of George VI and Elizabeth II. At this time the Vansittart family who had lived at Bisham Abbey since 1766 were no longer in the Abbey. Following World War II, in 1946, the Abbey was leased to the Central Council for Physical Education and no apparitions have been seen there since.

The Reading Public Library through the Borough Librarian, Mr. Stanley H. Horrocks, has called my attention to an account that the copy books, blotted by the unfortunate child, were discovered at Bisham Abbey in 1840. The following is extracted from the *Berks Archaeological Journal*, Vol. 12, 1906. pp. 94-95.

". . . . . . . The following copy of a memorandum made by Mrs. General Vansittart very soon after the discovery of the books would seem to be the correct account and has been always accepted as such by the Vansittart family:

"'This small bit of paper' — referring to a scrap of paper relating to some baby linen — 'was found when the corner of the dining room gave way in consequence of Mrs. Augustus East having the quoins on the sides of the windows cut down that there might be an alteration in the window shutters — which caused the rubble to run down and the corner to give way — in consequence of which they were obliged to take up a part of the floor to get at the foundations that the corner might be properly rebuilt; and between the joists were found quantities of rubbish, of old papers, copy books, etc. sufficient to fill two clothes baskets. I drove over from Binfield the very day after these were discovered, and looked over a number of the papers and copy books, the latter all signed by various names of the Hoby family and corrected by Lady Russell. In one of William Hoby, I think, every leaf had some blot. I wanted to take two or three away with me that day, but Mrs. East wanted to keep them all till the Admiral and Henry Vansittart had examined them, promising to keep one or two for me. When I asked for them, all were missing. They suddenly had disappeared, supposed to be sold by the workmen. This scrap of paper I found amongst the dust still on the joists and as it agreed perfectly with the writing and signature of Lady Russell in the correction of her children's books where several times her name was written, there are no doubts of its being her autograph."

(Signed) Mary Vansittart.

The above memorandum in copy was obtained by Mr. Ernest W. Dormer of Reading from Sir Henry Vansittart-Neale in 1906 and was published in the *Berks Archaeological Journal* of that year.

Whether the child of the blotted copy books was young Thomas Russell or some unregistered child of the family it is now impossible to determine. However, it is extremely interesting that a story which gained credence in the time of James I was confirmed accidentally in 1840.

Because it was difficult to keep servants at haunted Bisham the Vansittart family never mentioned the haunting when any servant was present. This ban on the ghost was established by Henry Vansittart in the early part of the reign of Queen Victoria and was maintained for many years.

The atmosphere at Bisham, despite the beauty of the buildings and their wooded setting, is sometimes malignant. Perhaps this malevolence may spring from the fact that the notorious, 18th century "Hell-Fire Club" of Sir Francis Dashwood had its focus at Medmenham Abbey, only three miles away. Tradition states that the activities of this evil group sometimes spread to Bisham as one of the Vansittarts was a member of the clique. At Medmenham various forms of black magic and devil worship are said to have been practised by this Order, whose members wore the robes of Franciscan friars and practiced their ceremonies in the "Abbey" built by Dashwood. It is said the "Hell-Fire Club" began with boyish pranks and ended with every form of evil to be thought up by a group of young aristocratic drunkards.

The evil aura at Bisham probably should not be attributed to Lady Hoby's restless ghost. If it does not belong to the "Hell-Fire Club", then perhaps some of the early inhabitants of the Abbey forgot their vows.

Miss Sibell Vansittart, a cousin of the Vansittart-Neale family who have occupied Bisham in recent years, tells of a visit she paid to Bisham Abbey in the 1880's. She did not see Lady Hoby's ghost but she did encounter the strange malice of the Abbey. She wrote:

"We, with our nurses, were staying with my godfather, George

Vansittart. He went for a walk and fell down with a stroke. The gardener, running to get help, fell and broke his leg. The kitchen maid developed diptheria. A careless nursemaid so scalded my sister that she nearly died in the night and was scarred for life. The head housemaid, also running for help, fell down the stairs and nearly broke her back. This indeed was a day of disaster."

Lady Vansittart-Neale told the story of an oarsman at the Henley regatta, who was obliged to sleep in the Abbey library in a makeshift bed because the house was full of other guests who had come to attend the regatta also. The young oarsman was very pale and shaken in the morning. During the night he had been visited by the discarnate Lady Hoby, who paused to look at his somewhat curly hair, as if in admiration. Then the ghost remarked to him: "Young man, if I touch thy hair, thou shalt lose it!" Lady Vansittart-Neale used to add that the young oarsman left the house-party and did not row in the day's race, returning home instead.

About 100 years ago, the Vansittarts recorded that a section of the outer wall of the Abbey settled and finally collapsed. Repairs to the wall revealed that it had rested on a stone coffin. The coffin collapsed and the wall likewise broke away. There does not seem to have been any knowledge or investigation as to who may have been buried in the coffin. The incident is only another of the uncanny sequence of events associated with Bisham.

The Hoby tomb in Bisham Church may contain evidence of the mistreated child, both in the crypt and the tomb statuary. The evidence is mute and hard to judge. The tomb was erected by Lady Hoby in memory of her husband, Sir Thomas Hoby, and his half-brother, Sir Philip Hoby. It is made of ornately carved alabaster. A heavily carved canopy overhangs the sculptured group below. The crypt is supposed to contain the remains of all of the Hobys and of some of the Russells as well.

On the tomb the carved Lady Hoby kneels, in widow's garments, at a priedieu. Her head wears a coronet. Before her protrude the feet of a small child, which lies cross-wise at her knees. It seems to be swaddled in heavy clothes and petticoats. According to Bisham legend, this child is the mysterious William of the blotted copy-books. Lady Hoby's daughter Anne Russell is opposite her, also crowned with a coronet. She afterwards became Lady Worcester. Lady Hoby's younger daughter by Sir Thomas Hoby and two daughters by Sir John Russell are ranged behind her. Behind them are the figures of her two Hoby sons, Edward and Thomas. If the small child lying across her knees is the six-year-old Thomas Russell, the whole family is accounted for, but then we must assume that Thomas is also the missing William.

In Bisham Church is a beautiful ancient and anonymous tomb which bears the sculptured figures of two children. Local legend insists that these two children were natural children of the great Virgin Queen Elizabeth, that they were born and died at Bisham. It is known that Elizabeth did visit Bisham after her confinement there, in the custody of the Hoby family during the reign of Queen Mary. The Hobys moved to Bisham in 1553, the year that Mary acceded to the throne, so if Elizabeth lived with the Hoby family during Mary's reign she certainly resided at Bisham Abbey, as Anne of Cleves owned the home in Kent at that time. At any rate the sculptured tomb of the two anonymous children belonged to some one of considerable importance for the sculpture is exceptional for the period.

Cecil Roberts, the well-known British author mentions in his fascinating book, *Gone Afield,*° a visit he paid to the Vansittart-Neale family at Bisham Abbey in the 1930's. He discussed with them the recent doings of their persistent ghost and he states:

"They cautiously waited until the butler and the maids were out of the room, knowing how ghost-ridden servants are — though the butler derides the whole haunting business in the servants' hall — and then narrated a few stories of the lady's alleged visitations.

"There was the maid of an American visitor who fled because a hand plucked her bedclothes in the night, and yet another maid of another visitor, occupying the same room, whose experience was the same. The library door too, has a habit of opening of its own account, for it is down to the library that the sinister lady comes."

Miss Vansittart-Neale took Mr. Roberts to a room in the turret where an inexplicable light is sometimes seen at night. It is a room, where, according to legend, Lady Hoby imprisoned one of her unruly children. Perhaps it may have been the child of the blotted copy-book Miss Vansittart-Neale and Mr. Roberts traversed long corridors in the upper section of the old monks' quarters. Mr. Roberts had a very strange sensation when he entered one of the small, ancient bedrooms. In his book he states:

"I took a deep breath and came out hurriedly. My guide looked at me curiously.

'Then you noticed it?' she asked smiling.

'Yes, what an unpleasant sensation. What is it?

'We don't know. But no one will sleep in that room a second night. These rooms were part of the monks' dormitories.'

"'Something's happened in that room,' I said, glad to be out of it."

The durable ghost of Lady Hoby has persistently manifested herself for over 300 years at Bisham Abbey. No one knows why she comes for her guilt complex, which would seem to be her motivating force, should have worn itself out long ago.

And no one knows why Lady Hoby's ghost failed to appear at Bisham during the coronations of George VI and Elizabeth II. Perhaps she cannot bring herself to consort with the commoners who now live at the Physical Education Headquarters in the Abbey.

Meanwhile the warden at Bisham Abbey keeps a weather eye open for Lady Hoby's reappearance.

For their help in making available the source material used in this article, the author wishes to express his indebtedness and thanks to the following: Christina Hole, Oxford, England; H. W. Fletcher, Marlow, Bucks., England; Dr. D. G. Neill, The Bodleian Library; Sylvia L. England, The British Museum; Stanley H. Horrocks, The Central Public Library, Reading, Berkshire, England; Sibell Vansittart, London, England; and Gordon N. Slyfield, Horsham, Sussex, England.

* Permission has been kindly granted, by the Appleton-Century Crofts Co. Inc., New York, and by Mr. Cecil Roberts, to quote from his book, *Gone Afield*.

GHOST OF THE TORQUAY ORGAN
Edmond P. Gibson

The old organ played slow, heavy music in the night — but the hands manipulating the keys were invisible.

When the old, haunted organ in the Anglican church of St. John's, Torquay, was finally removed in August, 1956, and the new organ purchased it was hoped by many of the parishioners that the ghost of Henry Ditton-Newman was at long last laid.

The haunting has continued intermittently for 73 years. A number of attempts have been made to bless the premises and exorcise the ghost, without success. Now information coming from Torquay since the new organ installation began indicates that the ghost is as active as ever. However, the ghostly activity seems to have been transferred to the vicarage.

The pipe organ recently removed from the church was 83 years old. This is not a great age as organs go but this one had not only its normal quota of playing but that of the ghost player also.

The Torquay organ was almost new when Henry Ditton-Newman first played on it during his short tenure as organist. Oddly, the "White" keys were black, and the "Black" keys were white. All of the stops were labeled with Latin names. And like the "one-hossshay" the old organ finally broke down and organ experts said it was beyond repair.

The haunting apparently began when the young organist, Mr. Henry Ditton-Newman, died suddenly of pneumonia and pleurisy on 10 November, 1883. It is said that his ghost first played on the organ when his body lay in state in the church on the day following his death. The Vicar, Mr. Hitchcock, heard the organ playing at that time without a visible organist.

Four years later Mr. Basil Airy, then Prebendary, heard the music again and saw a ghostly hand on the organ keys. Shortly thereafter the verger witnessed the same phenomenon.

Later, another vicar, the Reverend Sir Patrick Ferguson-Davie, experienced a variety of phenomena. At one time he heard footsteps in the vicarage, Montpelier House. The footsteps were so loud that he expected to find a clumsy burglar at work. He seized a riding crop and chased the footsteps downstairs into the dining room. He found the room empty. The intruder seemed to have disappeared through what had once been the front door of the old choir house. This door had been closed off to become a part of the wall when a false Gothic front was added to the building after the church purchased the property.

A curate, Mr. Sproule, who followed Sir Patrick Ferguson-Davie in Montpelier House, saw the apparition on several occasions. He identified it as Ditton-Newman and addressed it as Henry, Mrs. Sproule also seemed to be on familiar terms with the haunt. She felt that the ghost was friendly and neither she nor her husband were annoyed by the apparition. In fact, they stated that they liked him (or it).

The Reverend Anthony Rouse, the present Vicar, states, however, that another Vicar, the Reverend W. J. K. Harris, did not enjoy living in the house. The wife of Mr. Rouse's immediate predecessor, Dr. Sturgess, had an experience with the ghost. She was a medical doctor who did not believe in ghosts but she admitted that unexplainable things were going on in the vicarage.

Mr. Frank Lambert, manservant to the present Vicar, had never heard of the haunting, but soon after he was employed asked, "Who is it who walks down the back stairs at night?"

A woman engaged to help at Christmas time also was in complete ignorance of the haunting. She asked the Vicar, "What is the shadow that passes me in the back kitchen and walks across the yard to the church?" Reverend Anthony Rouse says the woman did not hear footsteps at all, but showed him the same path over which others had followed the noisy footsteps.

At a special meeting of the Churches' Fellowship for Psychical Study (a psychical research organization within the Anglican Church) held at the Torbay Hotel in Torquay in October, 1956, the Vicar stated that a Miss Kent of Barton Road had heard the organ play the *Silas Mass in C* on two separate occasions. No one was at the organ at the time.

The Reverend J. E. Boggis in writing the *History of St. John's Church* has mentioned well-verified accounts of ghostly apparitions seen in the church. The choir was sometimes aware of a ghostly figure at the organ when they were practising without accompaniment. The figure appeared to stand, as if listening to the singing.

Reverend Anthony Rouse states that three members of the present choir are occasionally conscious of a ghostly figure in the organ stall.

A Mrs. Lund says that a temporary organist brought from

173

Paignton did not want to play a second time at St. John's Church because he was aware of someone or something quite intangible sitting with him at the organ.

The *Torquay Times* quotes Reverend Anthony Rouse as follows: "I have heard the organ playing twice at night. I cannot tell you the piece of music but it was heavy music and it was slow. I have heard it for just a few minutes. I sleep at the back of the house, always with my window open, and I definitely hear the organ play."

Mrs. Palmer, the present church cleaner, testifies that she has heard the organ-playing ghost.

Mr. Downey, clerk of the parish, was playing the organ himself one night when, as he says, he was accompanied by strange rattlings and noises in the organ pipes.

Another witness to the ghostly music is Mrs. Beer, the wife of a retired Police Constable.

When the Reverend Anthony Rouse first came to the vicarage he had not heard of the haunting. However, he thought it a good idea to bless the old house and he held a service for this purpose. A Mrs. Thornley, who lives at Carbis Bay, once had held a similar blessing service for the upper floor where there seemed to be a strong focus of ghostly activity. In February, 1956, Reverend Anthony Rouse went again to the upper floor to pray and to sprinkle Holy Water around the rooms. This stopped the phenomena there for the time being. But on 29 September, 1956, there was loud banging on the lower floor. This occurred at 3:07 am. The noise seemed to come from the front door but no one was there. This happened after the old organ had been removed.

A year ago this past summer when Mr. Rouse took his holiday his housekeeper heard a similar banging at 3:07 a.m. The Vicar reported to the Churches' Fellowship that the organ playing has diminished over the past few years but the noises and footsteps in Montpelier House have increased. The Vicar's only objection to the haunting is due to the attendant publicity and the fact that his sleep is disturbed by the noises. He also said that the phenomena annoys the servant, although there is nothing evil about the haunting.

Recently Mr. Eric Hemery, a Dartmoor guide, was a guest at the vicarage. At 3:30 a.m. he was awakened by unexplained noises. In seeking the cause of the racket he located a "cold spot" in the corridor near the back stairs. This spot had been pointed out previously by Mrs. Martin and by others. There seems no physical reason for the cold felt at this particular place where some of the strongest phenomena occur.

In late October, 1956, Mr. Peter Large, of the *Western Morning News*, and his friend, John Whatmore, with the Vicar's permission spent the night at Montpelier House watching for the ghost. They saw nothing! However, Mr. Large noted two things for which he could not account — a repeated moaning noise, even though there was no wind, and recurrent noises from the latch to the kitchen door. Whatmore admitted hearing the unexplained noises but thought they might have been exaggerated by the "atmosphere" of the old house.

Another recent visitor to Montpelier House, Commander P. Osborn, of H. M. S. Raleigh, was awakened at 3:10 a.m. by noises which he could not explain. He traced them to the "cold spot" previously pointed out by Mr. Hemery and Mrs. Martin, the housekeeper.

One wonders, after studying this case, whether the "happy and contented soul" of Henry Ditton-Newman can be responsible for all of the ghostly goings-on at Montpelier House. Or can this be a case of multiple haunting in which the ghost of the former organist plays only one of the parts?

Mr. Rouse has been questioned repeatedly as to whether the old pipe organ was removed because of the haunting. He denies this. He states that five competent organ firms gave the opinion that the old organ was totally worn out. The new organ installation was completed in February, 1957. It remains to be seen whether the ghost will leave Montpelier House and take his place at the new organ.

THE VANISHING LADY

Rev. A. B. Farmer

as told to Dennis Bardens

Until recently I lived at Yattendon Rectory, near Newbury, Berkshire, England. The rectory, a pleasant enough building, has stood there since 1608, various alterations having been made in it by successive occupants.

While living in this rectory my wife, Katherine, the youngest of my three daughters, and a Mrs. Barton of Goring-on-Thames, who had stayed with us as a guest, and I saw a ghost in the house.

There actually were two spectral visitants, but the most persistent was a lady who appeared from the basement. Mrs. Barton saw her in the summer of 1949 — not at night, as might be expected, but on a glorious morning at half past eight.

Mrs. Barton told us that as she turned in the kitchen door she saw the figure of a woman in a silvery grey dress, and that "a light seemed to be shining around her." Her feet were off the floor. She disappeared into a wall.

My wife, my daughter and I also glimpsed this spectral figure, which usually disappeared through a wall and then appeared on some stairs.

Mr. Bardens visited us at the rectory to investigate our experiences. He examined the architecture and found that the stairs had been walled up at the point at which the figure disappeared.

My wife consulted reference books to date the style of dress worn by the ghost and put the period at about 1730.

We grew to be quite fond of our ghost. When one of our daughters got married, "Mrs. It," as we called our spectral visitant, was invited to the wedding!

FINALE FOR FANNY

**Fanny gave an amazing performance — but the
way she rang down the curtain was even more spectacular.**

J. P. J. Chapman

In 1924 my wife and I had not been married long. Late that year we were
asked to stay with my father and his second wife who were living in
Vienna. Also staying with them was my father's motherin-law; a lady
advanced in years.

We were glad to accept the invitation as, in those days, owing to
the rate of exchange we could afford a very good time in Austria. And we
certainly took advantage of it.

All seemed well on the surface, although it seemed to me I felt
an undercurrent of unhappiness. Then only a few days after our arrival the
old lady, Fanny, took to her bed and after a few days unexpectedly died.

Her funeral, being a continental one, was quite elaborate. After
it was over my wife and I felt tired and when we returned home decided
to rest for an hour in our room. I lay down on the bed and immediately
felt very uneasy. Opening my eyes I saw, standing at the foot of the bed on
which I lay, the old lady who we had buried but two hours since. I swear
I heard her say, in German, "Your father will follow me in 14 days time."

My wife was shocked to hear me suddenly exclaim, "My God!"

She asked what the trouble was and I told her of my vision. My
good lady thought it was a figment of my imagination. Whatever it was,
the prediction came true — my father died from heart failure exactly 14
days later.

After Father's cremation we returned to England and lived in his
house while I straightened out his affairs.

It was necessary for me to go to London about some matters and
on my return I found my wife very much upset. She swore that either
burglars or ghosts were entering the house, I told her ghosts were
impossible as the house was only 20 years old. I thought burglars unlikely
also and did not give it another thought. On going to bed that night I was
soon healthily asleep. Sometime later my wife woke me up saying, "Listen,
I am sure there is somebody in the house."

I listened and certainly there was something going on
downstairs. I slipped on a dressing gown, put my feet into slippers and
padded to the door. It was 11:30 by the luminous clock. I did not put on

the light and didn't need it, as it was brilliant moonlight.

Quietly I opened the door and went onto the landing.

There was something coming up the stairs. One — two — thump! One — two — thump! My heart beat faster. Then the thought struck me: the old lady; she used to sound like that with her stick. I was sure it was her. I waited as the steps approached, rounded the bend at the top of the stairs and came along the landing. When the sound was within six feet I snapped on the light — there was nothing! No further sound, nobody there!

My wife and I talked about it for a while and then decided to go back to bed. Later the same sounds retreated back down the stairs. Again I went out and could see nothing.

My father's old cook was in the house and I did not want her to hear of this. It was a huge rambling house in Bournemouth and it was possible someone could have given me the slip. I took one of Father's men into my confidence and he came to stay in the house. The old cook, being no fool, somehow got wind of the story, so we had to tell her about the steps.

Then for a while nothing further happened. However, one night Fanny came again. We searched the house from top to bottom this time and could find nothing. It was about one in the morning. My wife decided that a "refresher" would be welcome. The women stuck to tea but Father's man and I unearthed a bottle of Scotch, which was more to our liking.

We had not been sitting long when there was a terrific crash on the back stairs. We all rushed out there to find the cupboard that had stood at the top of the stairs lying on its face half-way down, on the landing. On top of this cupboard two wash basins and two jugs, a couple of bed chambers and a bed pan had been stacked. The floor on which they had fallen was stone flags, but not one single dish was chipped or cracked. We two men heaved the cupboard back and replaced the china. We wondered what would come next, but there never was a sequel. The curtain apparently had rung down; this had been the final scene.

My wife and I have remained convinced it was my step-mother's mother, Fanny, we heard because of the peculiarity of her walk and the thump of her cane. We do not know why she came back, as she had little interest in us; and she had died peacefully. Neither do we understand why the grande finale of the upset cupboard satisfied her, so that she did not return. But there are many, many things we do not understand.

GHOST-LADY IN BLACK

**She was seen repeatedly by many witnesses for nearly
10 years — one of the best authenticated cases on record.**

Walter A. Carrithers, Jr.

William James, the great psychologist, once wrote: "In fact, were I
asked to point to a scientific journal where hard-headedness and never-
sleeping suspicion of sources of error might be seen in their full bloom.
I think I should have to fall back on the *Proceedings* of the Society for
Psychical Research."

It is from these same *Proceedings* that we draw one of the
strongest existing cases for the reality of ghosts.

Professor R. H. Thouless, past president of the S.P.R., said:
"The best study of an apparitional haunting is still the report of the
'Morton' ghost." The late G.N.M. Tyrrell called this case "one of the
best observed and best authenticated ghost-cases on record." And
F.W.H. Myers, often named as the Society's philosopher, and author of
the word "telepathy", called it "in some respects one of the most
remarkable and best authenticated instances of 'haunting' on record."

Captain Morton (pseudonym), his wife, children and servants
were a family "unusually free" of morbid fears or superstitions,
according to Mr. Myers, who worked on the case for 10 years. They
moved into a typical Victorian house in England; a square and
commonplace structure having more than a dozen rooms in three
floors and basement, beside a spacious garden and orchard. When they
had lived there about three months, on a still night in June, 1882,
something uncanny stepped over their threshold.

The Captain's daughter, Rose, a science student preparing to
be a physician, had gone up to the third floor but was not yet in bed
when she heard something at the door of her room. Supposing it to be
her mother, she took her candle, went to the door and opened it. There
was no one there. Perplexed, she stepped out into the dark passage
leading towards the stairway. Her mother was nowhere to be seen. On
moving a bit along the passage, the young lady made out, in the feeble
candlelight, a strange figure waiting at the head of the stairs. She saw
a tall lady, garbed in black, holding a handkerchief to her face.

Curious, Miss Morton watched the figure, wondering who it

could be. When the "tall lady" began to descend the stairs she followed at a respectable distance. But suddenly all was blackness — the bit of candle had burned itself out. She could no longer see the departing intruder but she could hear a slight sound as of soft woollen garments moving away on the stairs below.

More than once in the nights to follow Miss Morton heard slight noises at her bedroom door and detected the soft tread of footsteps in the passageway beyond. On looking out, she would see the same mysterious figure moving through the gloom towards the stairs. She soon discovered that the strange visitor travelled a regular route: along the passageway from the bedroom, down the stairs to the ground floor and into the drawing-room where usually she lingered beside a bow window, afterwards leaving by a passage to the garden door, then disappearing. Once when she was ahead of the "ghost" Miss Morton entered the drawing-room first, hoping to arrest its attention. When "the lady in black" entered and halted beside a sofa Miss Morton stepped over to her, asking if she could be of help. The unknown figure started as if about to speak, gasped slightly and moved away to disappear. Still later, Miss Morton tried to touch the ghost, but its movements eluded her except once or twice when cornered, it simply disappeared on the spot.

Close observation showed the black-clad figure to be a lady in widows weeds, with only a portion of hair and brow revealed. After her initial sensations of mingled curiosity and awe had abated, Miss Morton came to recognize a "feeling of loss" upon its approach. Though anxious to discover the meaning of this mysterious intrusion, she spoke to no one of her experiences during this period, except to a distant friend who in turn did not speak of them until years later.

Some time later, another daughter Mrs. K., visited the family. And, as she told Mr. Myers, while coming down the stairs early one autumn evening she saw a tall figure in black move through the hall and into the drawing-room pushing open the door as it entered. This seemed to be a very substantial person and noting the long veil she supposed it to be a Sister of Mercy. Later, on remarking of this visit, she was surprised to learn the family that no visitor had called. Investigation showed no such person was about. Even so, Mrs. K. testified, she was not then told of any other such appearance in the house; and nothing further was said.

Another time the household was disturbed by a frightened housemaid's announcement that "someone had got into the house."

The description of this intruder agreed with the appearance of the apparition secretly known to Miss Morton. Again, a search revealed nothing.

In his signed testimony, Captain Morton's son recalled that on one occasion he and a school chum were playing outside the drawing-room windows. On looking up both saw what they took to be a stranger inside the room. It appeared to be a tall lady dressed in black, her right hand holding a handkerchief to her face as she sat by a table at the window in full light. Mrs. Brown, a parlourmaid, remembered the incident and told how the boys "ran up" to Mrs. Morton's room where Miss Rose "laughed it off".

After a while unexplainable footsteps grew in frequency and volume throughout the house. On the night of 2 August, 1884, three of the Morton sisters, the cook, and Mrs. K. heard them pass and repass their bedroom doors. Questioning elicited no normal explanation. But the cook told Miss Morton she had heard the footsteps and had seen "a lady in widow's dress, tall and slight, with her face hidden in a handkerchief held in her right hand", on the stairs when she had risen to draw hot water, while everyone else was in bed.

Four days later a neighbour boy came to inquire about the Morton's married daughter. His father had seen a tall lady in black, wearing a bonnet with a veil, a handkerchief held to her face, crying in the Morton orchard. On learning it was not the daughter, the neighbour, General A., and the Morton family stood watch that evening in hopes of seeing the "ghost" again. But nothing unusual was seen. In fact, the recorder observes that whenever a watch was set and expectations ran high, nothing out of the ordinary was observed. Nevertheless, that night about 2 a.m., a sister and the brother-in-law heard mysterious footsteps ascending and descending the stairs (the footsteps of the "ghost" were said to be "very characteristic" and "not at all" like those of the living inhabitants).

Several times the family dog, a large retriever kept in the kitchen at night, was discovered "in a state of terror" when morning came. Later, a small terrior was permitted to roam the house and sleep on Miss Morton's bed. Miss Morton's notes show that on 27 October, 1887, while suffering from an attack of rheumatism, "and very disinclined to move", the terrier jumped up and sniffed at the door on hearing the familiar footsteps outside. On more than one occasion the dog raced to the foot of the stairs, its tail wagging, jumping as if to greet someone standing there; but it would then suddenly skulk away, tail lowered, trembling, and hide beneath a sofa.

Other sounds joined the footsteps. Heavier steps, like those of a man in boots, walked for hours in the night, several times weekly. A noise like "scuffling and knocking", something that sounded like heavy bodies falling, like "something heavy being dragged overhead, on the top storey" was heard. A noise like "someone running" was heard outside the back door; nothing could account for it. Visitors who knew nothing of the "ghost", new servants in ignorance of the goings-on, in all about 20 persons, including the family, heard the incredible footsteps. But more disturbing were the noises of door handles turning. One new servant, terrified by bumps against her door, was convinced burglars were breaking into the room. Another suffered an attack of paralysis, attributing it to terror brought on by the sight of her bedroom door handle turning. It "was not a mere slip of the handle" she told Myers for the "door was locked" and the handle was firm "and never slipped of itself".

On a night in July, 1886, Mrs. Morton and her maid went halfway down the stairs to investigate loud noises in the morning-room and saw a bright light in the hall beneath. Alarmed they summoned one of the daughters and all three went to investigate, but they found the entrances fastened and everything normal. Returning to her room the daughter learned that two of her sisters also had heard the noises and had seen the "flame of a candle" — no candle or bearer being visible — cross the room. The three sisters were soon joined by two maids and then all five heard footsteps treading the landing between their opened doors. Something described as "a cold wind" accompanied the steps, though the flames of their candles never wavered. After some tramping on the stairs — during which time nothing abnormal could be seen — the steps ceased for the night.

Miss Morton saw the apparition many times. Others observed it repeatedly. One of her sisters, for example, saw it on about 10 occasions. The cook told of seeing the figure in the garden. The parlour-maid testified she saw it as she turned around from opening the dining-room shutter on a sunny morning. The gardener said he saw the lady in black on the balcony early one morning several days later. The visiting charwoman, while waiting in the hall for her pay one summer evening, saw the "ghost", whom she mistook for a household guest — until it suddenly vanished. She had heard of the "ghost" but told Myers (then Secretary of the S.P.R.), "it never struck me that this figure could be a ghost — it looked so like an ordinary person".

Likewise, the parlourmaid told how she and "Lizzie, a new cook" — who had "heard nothing of the the ghost" — suddenly saw a figure "dressed in black" pass them in a basement hallway. Neither said anything until later, when it was found they had seen "just the same thing".

Once Mrs. K. and Miss Morton, together looking out the drawing-room window, saw the apparition walking about on the balcony in the dusk and gas-light. On another occasion when one of the sisters saw the lady in black in the drawing-room, a second entered, saw the figure there and observed it until it departed, going out the doorway into a passage, and disappearing by the garden door. A third sister came in to say she had seen the figure on the steps outside. Finally all three sisters went outdoors and Mrs. K. called from a window on the upper storey to say that she had just seen the figure pass over the lawn and along towards the nearby orchard.

Miss R. C. Morton decided upon a series of experiments. Before retiring she suspended strings across the stairway, attached so that they could scarcely be seen or felt, yet would drop at the slightest contact with a passing body. Twice she saw the figure pass through these barriers without disturbing them. At other times the "lady" would appear within a closed room. Yet the apparition always intercepted the light and, until about 1886, appeared so "solid and life-like" that when seen she was often mistaken for a living person.

Later, however, she gradually became indistinct, and her appearances grew less frequent. Finally, after 1889, the "Lady in Black" was seen no more — though the footsteps persisted a bit longer.

All these observations, plus the fact Captain Morton was never able to sight the psychic visitant — even when another person present saw her — forced Miss Morton to conclude that the figure was not really substantial.

No positive identity of the "'Lady in Black" was ever made. However, after some investigation Miss Morton deduced that she must be the deceased widow of the original tenant, Mr. S.

The Mortons learned on inquiry that Mr. S., an Anglo-Indian, had lived in the house for about 10 years after its construction. Upon the death of his first wife, for whom he bore a passionate affection, he sought to drown his sorrows in alcohol. At this piteous juncture he married a second time. This marriage degenerated into a series of violent quarrels and then the lady took to drinking heavily also. Finally, after their relationship became so embittered that Mr. S., with help of a local carpenter, hid his first wife's jewels lest the living Mrs. S. possess them, the woman left. (For the benefit of the Mortons, the carpenter reopened the secret receptacle beneath the floor of the "morning-room" but found it empty). A few months later the husband died in this very room; and hardly two years later his second wife died also. Her body was returned for burial in a churchyard a quarter-mile or so from the scene of strife.

The estate was sold and after the "very dirty" house had been renovated, an elderly couple moved in. Less than six months later the husband also died — "rather suddenly" one day in the "morning-room". His widow moved out and the place stood empty for several years thereafter. During this period, rather unpleasant stories began to be told of things seen in the house by passers by. Someone remembered seeing a strange intruder in the house shortly after Mrs. S. was buried. An old gardener was said to have seen "the figure of a tall lady in black in the garden." Efforts were made to rent the place at a ridiculously low price but there were no takers — until agents of the late owner rented to Captain Morton, who had heard none of the stories.

Some of the things which related the apparition to the second Mrs. S. were its special dress (even though she was a widow only after leaving the house, the dress, like the concealed face of the figure, is interpreted as a psychological manifestation, in the one instance denoting bereavement, in the other, shame.) The fact that, though none of the percipients had ever seen the woman, other persons who had identified her from the description of the "lady in black" (no other previous tenants showed the same physical similarities.), the "violent scenes" between Mr. S. and his second wife were perhaps "echoed" psychically in the "scuffling" and "falling" and "dragging" noises heard, and, beside the conflict between the man and his wife over his first wife's jewels, the chief disagreement had been over the management of his children by the previous marriage and the route taken by the apparition began outside Miss Morton's bedroom — which was the nursery during the residence of the second Mrs. S. — and progressed to the drawing-room the second Mrs. S. "especially used").

The proximity of the woman's grave to the site of the haunting is something not to be overlooked in the light of one occult hypothesis which suggests that the most persistent type of ghost is the "earthbound astral body" which proceeds from the corpse and lingers within a limited distance while dissolving into imperceptibility Similarly, the "loss" seemingly felt by Miss Morton might be explained by an occultist by the theory that she alone slept in this nursery which was once the special focus of the living Mrs. S's. attention and was now a focus for vampirism, her occupancy being to the "ghost" somewhat similar to that of the children's earlier occupancy and their relationship to their drunken stepmother.

It is to be noted that it was the husband, Mr. S., who died first, and it was the husband Mr. L., the next owner, who died second; so it may be that Captain Morton's good health could be attributed in theoretical terms to his total psychic blindness, really a self-protective deficiency. One wonders if the complacency of sceptics today is not largely a reward for "blindness", because, while crying ostentatiously for "evidence", they never see the "lady in black"!

The record of this "haunting" is notable not only because the investigation was conducted by Mr. Myers when he was Secretary of the S.P.R., but because its evidence effectively refutes the favourite objections of those who scoff at poltergeists and laugh at ghosts:
1. These critics claim that "hauntings" are usually the psychological by-products of self-suggestion springing from a more or less prolonged state of fear, caused by mysterious household noises of physical but unknown origin. But the only remarkable noise known to have preceded the first apparitional appearance at the Morton's was the sound at Miss Morton's bedroom door which this science student simply supposed was her mother.
2. It is argued that members of a household "see ghosts" in the house because they have been "let in on the secret" and have frightened each other with ghost stories; that a ghost is seldom if ever observed by unwarned visitors. Yet in this case at least a half-dozen visitors and neighbours saw the spectral "lady in black" when, so far as can be judged, they never had heard about her.
3. It is alleged that "ghosts," being figments of imagination, are simply vague shadowy shapes that flit silently across a deranged mental vision, featured and dressed according to the private imagination of the self-deluded percipient. But in the "Morton Case" the ghost's approach was heralded by footsteps, one person heard her gasp, another heard the rustle of her garments; and she was so "solid and life-like" that she was repeatedly confused with the living.
4. Objection is made that descriptions of a ghost's appearance and

habits is consistent only when set by gossip passing from one suggestible householder to another: each successive witness experiences what he has been led to expect. But in this case, what Miss Morton first saw in June, 1882, was substantially like what her uninformed sister, Mrs. K., saw later, and like what Mrs. Twining observed in 1886. In fact, in his foreword to her report, Myers pointed out that Miss Morton's account did not grow in the telling; no "secondary apparition" or other visual effects — aside from a (ghost's candle?) light — appear in the record during 10 years of haunting. This is evidence that the witnesses were notably lacking in creative fancy!

Mr. Myers noted "the phenomena as seen or heard by all the witnesses were very uniform in character — even in the numerous instances when there had been no previous communication between the percipients". Despite the special effort to keep new servants in ignorance of the "lady in black", and despite Miss Morton's initial period of secrecy ("from 1882 to 1884"), newcomers and others independently saw the spectral intruder.

5. Solitary visions always can be judged hallucination. However, the subjective anticipations of one self-hallucinated party cannot easily affect another. The Morton record has many instances where the mysterious visitant was seen by more than one person at the same time. Aside from the occasion when the four sisters successively observed the "lady in black" passing from drawing-room to orchard, there are at least five instances of collective vision — not to mention sounds jointly heard, as when five listeners heard "steps walking up and down the landing ..."

6. Finally, any sceptic may fall back on the charge of fraud and claim that the witnesses lied. But in the Morton case Miss Morton Mrs. K., and Mrs. Brown agreed in their testimony that one of the earliest views of the apparition was Mrs. K.'s when she thought she saw a Sister of Mercy in the drawing-room, and any idea that the witnesses participated in a 10-year-hoax falls apart when we note that, although they agree in placing the event during the early days when Rose Morton had told no one of her mysterious visitor, they disagree on the season and even the year when this event occurred!

None of the witnesses ever was discredited and, in the more than half century since this haunting took place, no critic of poltergeist or ghostly phenomena has succeeded in explaining the mysterious "lady in black".

THE POLTERGEIST THAT CAN WRITE

This amazing entity claims to be the Dauphin of France, plays with dolls — and has begun correspondence by mail.

H. S. W. Chibbett

Thirty odd years ago, one of the most violent poltergeist hauntings in history took place in Eland Street, Battersea, South London. Today, another poltergeist is active just a few hundred yards away. It began in February, 1956, and its initial stages correspond closely with those of the earlier case. There were rappings, fires, and objects moving through the air.

A psychic paper reported in May, 1956, that: "South London's poltergeist now has official cognizance as 'baffling.' A whole series of minor fires have occurred by the machinations of the poltergeist at Lavender Hill, at the home of 18-year-old Shirley Irene Hitchings. Firemen and detectives scoured the premises, people and possibilities. For yet another time their resultant communique was terse: baffled."

The disturbances — alarming as they sound — at first followed the normal trend of such affairs. Whenever such manifestations occur — and they are more common than you may suspect — the phenomena usually develop along recognized lines. There are loud rappings or loud bangs, the smashing of crockery and the tilting or overthrow of heavy furniture. Sometimes stones are thrown; on other occasions objects are seen to move through the air by themselves, sometimes quite slowly and without damage to the articles or persons present.

Almost always an adolescent is nearby when the phenomena occur and there is a perhaps natural tendency to assume that the occurrences are in some way connected with the children. Furthermore, rarely is an object seen to start its trip through the air. Usually it is already in motion when first observed.

Poltergeist disturbances are international; they take place in all countries, but it is interesting that they occur most frequently in civilized communities such as England, the U.S.A., and Germany. The word *poltergeist* is a German word, meaning, "noisy ghost."

Today, three years after the start of these extraordinary phenomena in Battersea, there is still no sign that they are going to cease. This in itself is unusual, because normally the phenomena reach a peak within a few weeks and then die away as mysteriously as they began. But even as recently as February of this year, wanton damage amounting to several hundred dollars was done to furniture and clothing.

Apart from the usual poltergeist activities, there have been phenomena which indicate intelligence behind the manifestations. Early in 1956 a simple alphabetical code was devised whereby the rapping sounds were used to convey messages from an "entity" who claimed to have lost his life by drowning in the English Channel. This communicator became known to the family as "Donald," because he said he resembled a near neighbour of the Hitchings who had gone abroad.

In May, 1956, the entity objected to being called Donald, and said that he was really Louis XVII, younger son of Louis XVI and Marie Antoinette of France, both of whom were guillotined in 1793 during the French Revolution. This claim was received very sceptically by the Hitching family and all concerned. Nevertheless, from that time to the present, he has not diverged from his claim to be Louis XVII, who became Dauphin of France in 1789 on the death, at Meudon, of his elder brother, Louis-Joseph.

The poltergeist could not have chosen a more controversial figure than that of the ill-used young Dauphin. There is no lack of information regarding his life up to the year 1793, when he was imprisoned with his family in the Temple at Paris. According to history he then was separated from his mother, Marie Antoinette, and his sister, and placed under the guardianship of a cobbler named Simon and his wife. It is generally assumed that he died in the arms of a gaoler named Etienne Lasne, in 1795, two years after the death of his parents on the guillotine.

After his alleged death rumours spread that the Dauphin had not really died in the Temple at all, but had escaped as far back as 1793 or even earlier. Numerous theories were voiced, among them one that a substitution had been effected and that another child resembling Louis XVII had taken his place and that it was this child who had died in the Temple. Therefore the real heir to the throne must still be alive and free.

The mystery deepened when public opinion belatedly demanded that the grave of the alleged prince be opened to establish the real facts. The first search — in 1817 — yielded nothing. A coffin tallying with the official description was found but it was empty.

In the year 1846 fresh excavations were made in the churchyard of Sainte-Marguerite. Among the coffins disinterred was the one previously opened in 1817. In that year a report had been made by Pelletan, the Dauphin's medical attendant, who had made the post mortem, on the way in which the body was laid in the coffin. The skull had been dissected in order that the brain might be examined. In 1846, when the coffin was re-opened, it was found to contain a skeleton, the skull of which had actually been dissected. A doctor Recamier made a report on the remains in which he stated that the skeleton was that of a child about 15 years old.

Later, in 1894, the remains were again exhumed and examined by a Doctor Backer. He reported that the skeleton was that of a child at least 14 years old. According to Madol, one of the 200-odd writers on Louis XVII: "To this day it has been impossible to find the skeleton of a 10-year-old Dauphin on the spot where he was supposed to have been buried." This is, of course, historically accurate. The Dauphin was born on 27 March, 1785, and is supposed to have died in the Temple on 8 June, 1795, when he would have been 10 years, three months old.

It would appear, therefore, that whoever was buried as Louis XVII, Duc de Normandie, it was not the boy-king himself. Because of the uncertainty, no fewer than 30 pretenders claimed to be the Dauphin at the Restoration of the French Monarchy. Chief among these was Karl Wilhelm Naundorff. He produced evidence of his identity as the younger son of Louis XVI which convinced even his governess, Mme. de Rambaud; Joly, Louis XVI's last Minister of Justice, and many others who had known the young prince intimately.

Whatever the true facts may have been, there is little doubt that the real Dauphin did not die in the Temple prison in Paris in 1795.

Let us now revert to the entity at Battersea which manifested first as a typical poltergeist and then announced itself as Louis XVII. Do we get a clear picture of a royal personage returned from the grave to prove that he was the lineal descendant of the House of Bourbon?

The answer at present must be "No." For, although masses of data about the period of the French Revolution have been given, they are interspersed with much irrelevant material and a predilection for modern affairs which line up with Shirley Hitching's own character. Yet it cannot be denied that this entity exhibits personal qualities which are more like descriptions of Louis XVII than of Shirley. It's reaction to frustration, its imperious self-esteem, its decided indiscretion are all more typical of the Dauphin than of the Battersea teenager.

On 15 April, 1956, a message said: "I come to tell what I look like — five foot high, fair head, blue eyes, 35 wide" (presumably around the chest).

At about this time physical phenomena were on the increase. The house was full of reporters and investigators of all kinds, and abnormal things were happening every day. The Hitching family was in a state of turmoil and fear. At night they used to huddle together on the kitchen floor, keeping a weather eye open for mysterious fires and gas taps which somehow were turned on full. Many of the messages were of threats to set fire to the house, and peremptory orders to get this or that. Any refusal to obey instructions was met by further threats, or retaliatory action.

Nearly three weeks later came the first definite claim that the "personification" was Louis XVII, son of Louis XVI and Marie Antoinette. He said that his father and mother had died on the guillotine, and that he had been drowned in the English Channel. He added that his dress was: "Satin, a tail coat, knee breeches, hose, lace waistcoat, black buckle shoes." He continued: "Some wore wigs."

On 19 May, 1956, the entity stated: "I am Donald in this age ..." (remember the poltergeist was christened "Donald" by the family because of his resemblance to a neighbour) ... "I am originally Louis XVII, son of Louis XVI, of the House of Louis Mon Lion Ha." A similar message was repeated on the following day, with the addition: "I know French."

There is a first reference to a request for "10 silver pieces" on 26 May, and the next day an admonitory message to Shirley: "If you had to iron the shirts I wore, with lace frills, you would moan!"

On 28 May he said: "Clothes have changed, but the way of life has not. I know more about life than you know. I was born before you. I can tell you all about Jacko the monkey, and how Connie would run and hide when in trouble. She had long flowing hair."

One sees an intriguing picture of the life of a young French prince. Was Jacko the monkey a pet at the French Court at Versailles Palace? Who was Connie, with the long flowing hair? Could the subconscious or conscious mind of a young girl be responsible for all this?

About this time other phenomena began. The sitting room already had been commandeered by "Donald" for his own use, and was littered with dolls dressed as Marie Antoinette and other royal personages, attired by Shirley under "Donald's" express directions. Now drawings began to appear on the walls, some of shields with crossed swords superimposed. There were fleur-de-lis on the shields and underneath the words: *Roi Louis*. Shirley denied having made these drawings. As time went on, more fleur-de-lis appeared on the bedroom walls, ceilings and elsewhere.

During this same period many messages arrived giving historical names and dates. Exhaustive search has shown that the majority of these are correct but of little evidential value since the information could have been gleaned from any history of the era. However, Shirley does not belong to a library and there are no books in the house on the period. She did not take French history at school, according to her school certificates.

On 31 May "Donald" asked: "Do you know what the guillotine was? You have one ... the block. They both do the same thing."

Referring to one of the dolls in "his" room, "Donald" gave these instructions on 2 June, 1956: "Let us give that doll a French Royal formal name ... *Oui* ... let us think ... let it be Marie Antoinette, *mon de mere* name. She must be her for she has a French face. Let me put the flurdeley (*fleur-de-lis*) on her, because my mother had it branded. Will you dress Marie as I describe: she must have six petticoats, two skirts, a top — you know, her hair all curls, a fan, shoes, the top square neck, long sleeves with lace edges — lots of lace — silk too. If you dress her for me, I get the pleasure. I will help in describing. You can look in pictures. Please do this for me ..."

A note of mine made at the time says: "Recent messages convey an impression of a young boy, imperious in his demands on Shirley's time and attention, eager to 'show off', and rather shaky in his spelling. Interesting, too, is the increasing use of French words, and also the reference on 31 May to the block, when he says: 'you have one.' Evidently 'Donald' is not yet aware that the method of execution in England nowadays has changed."

Concurrently, typical poltergeist activity continued. On the evening of 10 June, 1956, the following phenomena occurred: Shirley's clothes disappeared and were eventually found stowed away in the piano, thrust down among the wires. Then, while Shirley and her parents were all together in the dining room, a knife was thrown from the kitchenette and stuck in the window frame of the dining room. At 10:30 p.m. the family went to bed. At this period they all shared the same bedroom. Disturbances occurred almost at once. The bedclothes were disarranged, there were violent scratching sounds, and rappings as though on metal.

Suddenly Shirley called out that there was something "furry", at the foot of the bed. Investigation disclosed that there was a whole mass of red flock in her bed; and when the quilt was examined, several slits were found in it, as though caused by a penknife or scissors. On the face of it, the red flock had been extracted from the interior, though how this could have been done in such a short period of time is a mystery. There were several slits but none large enough for the flock to be extracted quickly, in quantity. Normally it would have had to be "teased" out bit by bit as the bundle of flock was half a foot in diameter. Following this, Shirley refused to remain in the bed and spent the night in a wicker chair.

During the night, a pair of scissors was thrown at Mr. Walter Hitching. While Shirley was dressing in the morning a screwdriver was thrown at Mrs. Catherine Hitching who was still in bed. It hit her a glancing blow on the back. In the kitchen, a boiling kettle was overturned, and then another narrowly missed scalding Shirley's feet.

The flood of messages ran into many hundreds. They covered all sorts of subjects from Latin tags to horse-race winners, and indifferent French was on the increase. Sometimes English, French and Latin appeared in the same sentences. Fleur-de-lis occurred mysteriously in all sorts of places. On one occasion, the writer was looking at a fleur-de-lis impression on the shoulder of the doll dressed as Marie Antoinette. I expressed a wish aloud that "Donald" would show me how these were made. A few minutes later I was with the family in the dining room. Shirley was standing by the fire-place and her parents were seated. All three were in full view. Suddenly Shirley's mother exclaimed: "What is that on your arm, Shirley?"

On the upper part of her bare left arm was the imprint of a small, dark-blue fleur-de-lis. It looked as though it had been drawn or stamped there with indelible ink. As far as I had noticed, Shirley had made no untoward movement. I examined her closely to see whether there were any more impressions visible on her. There were none. I watched her movements closely thereafter. However, a few minutes later there was another similar mark — this time on the right side of her neck. I am reasonably certain that neither she nor her parents could have made this without my knowledge. I searched the room but could find no trace of any instrument which could have made the impressions.

At this early stage of the investigation, Shirley and her parents had no previous knowledge of parapsychological phenomena. Yet on Wednesday, 27 June, when I visited the house I was informed that "Donald" had left a sealed envelope for me on a coffee table in "his" room. On a settee were the dolls which Shirley had dressed in accordance with "Donald's" instructions, Marie Antoinette was posed as though sitting on a throne, and the other dolls, purporting to be Lady Jane Grey, Anne Boleyn, etc., were placed round her in curtseying positions. Shirley assured me that "Donald" had placed them so.

The envelope contained a local paper. On page nine there was some writing in ink. This seemed indecipherable at first, but when held to a mirror it read: "Out in one month. Don't worry, Shirley." This promise to go was not kept, but the interesting point is that the message was in "mirror" writing. The Hitching family was unaware that "mirror-writing" is relatively common in written psychic communications. There was an error in the spelling of the word "month" which showed that the sender was "Donald", whose rapped messages contained the same error.

On 24 June, 1956, "Donald" rapped out to Shirley: "Can you fence? It is rare in girls, but I could teach you. I knew how to handle a sword when I was only 10. You had to defend yourself in my day. It was peaceful until the Revolution came." "Donald" continued to give detailed fencing instructions. According to a note made by Shirley, "Donald" said that he — as Louis XVII — was lefthanded.

"Donald's" instructions seem remarkably accurate, and unlikely to be part of the general knowledge of a working-class adolescent like Shirley. In fact, one gets an oddly disturbing picture of a youth who might actually have experienced these things.

From time to time, "Donald" appeared to feel frustrated and one of his communications to Shirley said: "I am sad ... disappointed. I want it to be as it was in my palace — this room; I have got my dolls but I am lonely. I have no swords hanging on the walls. The furniture is not right. I have never seen any like it. My work is taking too long. It should have been done by now."

Again on 28 June, 1956, he said: "Shirley, when I was young I played with toys. Everyone said I was mad; but I loved my little soldiers, dolls all dressed in scarlet, blue, yellow, gold, silver, black and white. It is not wrong to have a secret — I loved to play with dolls like you. I was sick of being pushed about, of talks with governesses, fencing lessons, dancing. All I wanted was to be free — no state laws. I loved France though, but I was not happy in Court. Boys would take my punishment if I was bad — why couldn't they let me take my own punishment like a man? To hell with the Court of France. That is why I must tell people how lucky they are now — but it is me and people who made it so."

One of the most interesting accounts given by the alleged Louis XVII was a description of his life at Court. "I would like to tell you of Versailles — my life there. It was grand. Do you know, my Nanette would take me round the garden every morning, and we always stopped to see the birds. My father and grandfather had peacocks and turkeys — not like English ones. They had blue heads with red spots on them, and green feathers with yellow and blue on their wings — beautiful! There were some doves, pigeons, lyre birds with big fan tails. We had 79 peacocks, but they were killed in the Revolution to feed old Robespierre and his rats. But in the days of goodness, my father let me in Court after my brother died. I was the centre of attraction. I was allowed a Court with the nobility and gentry — the French and Austrian friends of my father and mother were all so charming at Versailles.

"I had my own room. I had a map all over the floor like a carpet, of France of course; and I had little houses — chateaux — also I had a toy gun which fired spears, and loads and loads of toy soldiers in their shiny paint. They were wonderful. I also had my own desks to do my lessons on. Do you know, I got up at nine o'clock and had a man servant to dress me. Then Nickolos sometimes crept up to see me in my suite of rooms. We would talk till he had to go."

So the torrent of rapped messages continued week in and month out, a mass of communications which for this period alone must run into many thousands of words. They were received in a mixture of French and English.

During this whole period manifestations of various kinds occurred, until on 13 August, 1956, "Donald" sent the following message to Mr. Hitching: "I want a pen that you put black water (ink) in and it writes. Not a quill pen. I want one like Shirley has got. I can keep my own diary like I did."

A notebook and fountain pen were duly provided, and new phenomena began to appear. Long straggling characters sprawled across pages were barely decipherable as words. Exact tracings were taken of them.

At 2 p.m. on 17 October, 1956, the following rapped message was received by Shirley: "I want a sweet — do you? If I was in France I would have a dragee. It is almond in sugar. They cost about two sous. If I go to France again I will go to 28, Rue du Baal, Paris, and get you one. I was given a box of dragees when I was baptized ... do you want some if I get one? The Seugnot family were the makers of those lovely dragees. I do not know of Mme. Seugnot now. She had a daughter and two sons. The daughter was called Marie, and the sons, Perrie and Paul. But the shop is still there. I think Mons. and Mme. Seugnot were guillotined for being Royalist, but their children lived."

A colleague of mine went to Paris in due course but was unable to find any such road.

I then wrote to the English representatives of the French Chamber of Commerce, giving what details I had and enquiring whether from their records of French sweetmeat makers they could confirm the contemporary existence of a firm under the name of Seugnot, or whether there ever was such an address as Rue du Baal in the years 1785 to 1793.

Much to my astonishment, the reply I received on 11 June, 1958 read: "Thank you for your letter ... concerning a shop at 28, Rue du Bac, Paris 17e. Upon enquiry, I have pleasure in advising you that there still exists at the above address a sweetshop with the heading of Seugnot."

Even if the entity had not got the spelling right, this was still quite remarkable.

Next I wrote to Mons. Seugnot, Confiseur-Chocolatier, 28, Rue du Bac. I mentioned that the royal family of Louis XVI, before they were imprisoned in the Tower, were accustomed to purchase their dragees from the Seugnot family of that era; and that Mons. and Mme. Seugnot as Royalists were alleged to have perished on the guillotine. Could he confirm this, together with the statement that two sons and one daughter survived?

A free translation of Mons. Seugnot's reply dated 21 June says: "The information which you have given me is correct. I am going to make some enquiries into historical records for further details, and you may have to wait some weeks; but I thought I would let you know now, so that you will not be surprised at any delay."

No further letter has been received from Mons. Seugnot as yet. And knowing the circumstances of Shirley's home life I find it very difficult to believe that she could have got hold of the detailed information supplied by the poltergeist.

It was in the autumn of 1956 that a sealed and addressed envelope was found on the coffee table in "Donald's" room. At "Donald's" request it was posted to me. And on the morning of 1 November, 1956, I received what is possibly the first letter ever posted from a poltergeist. It was the fore-runner of an ocean of mailed correspondence both to myself and many other persons. It still continues at the present time.

And I am puzzled, now as then. Am I the recipient, through Her Majesty's Mail, of letters from a poltergeist, from a clever Shirley Hitching, or from His Royal Highness, Prince Louis Charles Philippe, Duc de Bourbon?

THE CURSED HOUSE
ON CALDWELL STREET

Laura Brilliant
As told to Michael Harvey

**The depressing chill in the house weakened my will to live —
and then a voice urged me to kill myself.**

My husband and I had been looking for an unfurnished flat in a seaside
resort in Essex, England, for something like two years — ever since the
day we were married, in fact. Lionel used to put an advertisement in
the local paper every week; and went so far as to offer a reward to
anyone who could even furnish information regarding the whereabouts
of an unfurnished flat. He also stated that we were prepared to pay 50
pounds or so for any fittings.

I hate to think of how much we spent on advertisements.
Occasionally we would get a reply. Somebody would offer us part of a
houseboat, or two rooms in a farm which was practically cut off from
the outside world. But then one day the miracle happened! A woman
wrote to say that we could have the top part of her house, unfurnished
or furnished, whichever we preferred. There would be no charge for
the fittings, she did not require any key money, and she had no
objection to children. The rent, unfurnished, was two pounds per
week. The house was in Caldwell Street, on the other side of town.

"Sounds too good to be true," Lionel remarked when I
showed him the letter. "We're paying over four pounds a week for
these two so-called furnished rooms. That place in Caldwell Street
must be a regular hovel if she's only asking two pounds a week."

"Don't be such an old misery!" I broke in excitedly. "Put your
coat on again. Let's go there right away."

"But what about my tea?" he asked plaintively.

"You'll have to wait, darling. We can't take any chances. If
anyone beats us to it I'll die of disappointment."

I had already dressed the baby, Nigel. It was a cold winter's
day in November, 1951, and the poor mite had contracted a chill
earlier in the week. I suppose, by rights, I shouldn't have taken him
out, but there was no one to look after him.

Caldwell Street proved to be somewhat dingy but quite respectable-looking. The house we sought was old, as was its owner, who opened the door to us herself.

She avoided looking us in the eye while she was talking, and having explained that she was a widow and lived alone, turned a bit evasive when I asked such questions as how long the rooms had been empty.

The rooms themselves were large and airy, in direct contrast to the poky holes we lived in at the moment. The kitchen was old-fashioned, certainly, but there was a large gas oven, and plenty of cupboards. The place was spotlessly clean and well kept. There were a few odd pieces of furniture about, which Mrs. Cooper offered to take out to make room for our own.

Mrs. Cooper and Lionel got down to the business arrangements; for we had both made up our minds on the spot, and needed no time for deliberation. He just looked at me, I nodded vigorously, and that was that.

We moved in next day.

We rarely saw our landlady and I soon concluded that she was deliberately avoiding us. Not only did I see her dodge back into her quarters when I came downstairs to go out, but she never came up to our flat, not even to collect the rent. In the end, Lionel had to push it under her door in an envelope, and that became the regular arrangement. Mrs. Cooper said her legs were bad and she couldn't manage the stairs — yet she'd been spry enough when she'd shown us round the first day.

I was thankful enough to be left alone because I was soon overtaken by a regular procession of troubles which kept me fully occupied and left me in no mood to be sociable. No more than a few days had passed before everything started going wrong. It had nothing to do with my state of mind. I wasn't looking for trouble. I had entered the house in the highest of spirits, convinced that I, my husband and my child were about to start on the happiest period of our lives. I was prepared to make light of small inconveniences or setbacks such as one usually encounters in the early stages of homebuilding. But the troubles that came to me were not small.

First our baby's chill seemed to get worse. This alone worried me to distraction, particularly as the flat seemed always dreadfully cold in spite of the huge fire which I kept burning all the time. I persuaded Lionel to check all the windows and doors for draughts, and he fitted draught excluders while I ran up some good thick curtains. But for all our efforts the rooms remained cold, a curiously clammy cold such as one thinks of in connection with a cave or an underground crypt. Sunshine streamed in through the windows and the fire crackled and blazed, enough to scorch my legs if I got too close, and the rooms remained cold.

I thought I might he coming down with a cold and wished it would come and be done. Instead I gradually felt more and more unwell, without being able to say just what was the matter. At first I was irritable because I am normally a healthy and energetic woman and have no sympathy with hypochondriacs Then I grew depressed — which again wasn't like me. I didn't sleep well, and there was a dull aching pain in my chest. My own commonsense should have told me to go to a doctor, but I was afraid to take this step in case it was something really bad which might mean an operation. I dreaded being cut up, and felt I would rather die first.

That was another curious, unexplainable feature of those dreary weeks. I was apathetic and afraid of making decisions. I would sit around listlessly feeling that life was too much for me. Deciding whether to buy meat or fish for dinner seemed too difficult a problem. I could not organize my housework properly and I was always sitting down in the middle of it and bursting into tears. The flat grew untidy, even grubby, and I didn't care. I didn't trouble how I looked and Lionel would come home from work to find me in a greasy overall, my hair stringing, my nose unpowdered, and his supper either burnt or half-cooked.

"It's the stove — it doesn't work properly!" I would exclaim childishly. I grew increasingly short-tempered with poor Lionel.

"You're getting to be a proper nagger, old girl. What's the matter?" he asked.

He said it banteringly — we'd always joked and shared our troubles before — but this time I chose to take offense and wouldn't speak to him for the rest of the evening. It was as though some spiteful demon possessed me, for I knew all the time that I was putting up a barrier between us and that he'd end by hating me if I didn't pull myself together.

This frightened me and I soon convinced myself that Lionel was no longer as loving as he used to be. I began to fear the worst when he began to work late. He had never had to work late before for the Essex County Council and it was, after all, the conventional excuse of straying husbands. When I found blonde hair on his jacket I felt really desperate.

I had cried for hours that day. I felt ill and wretched. I thought how quickly things had gone from bad to worse — since we'd come to this house. It was at this point that my general despondency crystallized into a sudden and definite hatred of the flat. I walked slowly from room to room. How cold and silent it was in the sad winter twilight. And, in that revealing moment, the house seemed to me not merely cheerless and dreary but actively hostile. It scared me. Outside the world was happy — I could hear some school children laughing and shouting on their way home — I could hear a barrel organ grinding out its exuberant trills — but the room in which I stood held gloom which seemed a tangible thing. It weighed down my limbs with leaden heaviness; it pressed into my aching head and dulled my brain. Nigel began to whimper in his cot.

With a shudder I pulled myself together. I switched on all the lights, and after quieting the child, I set about making up the fire and preparing tea. I even changed my frock, combed my hair and put on make-up. It was wasted effort for Lionel was late again. By the time he came home I was slumped by the fire feeling worse than ever.

"The radio won't work," I greeted him sulkily. "I hate this house, Lionel, do you hear? It's getting on my nerves. It's unlucky. Everything goes wrong — everything!" I wasn't given to hysterical outbursts but I'd been on edge all evening.

Lionel looked up from the radio set.

"It's only a valve burnt out," he remarked cheerfully. "I'll get a new one tomorrow. For goodness sake, dear, it isn't a major tragedy! You don't have to look like that."

"It isn't just the radio," I said viciously. "Don't you understand? Tomorrow it'll be something else. I can't go on like this, Lionel, I can't. It's too much for me."

"What is?" he asked. "You're getting all worked up about nothing. You used to say that all a woman needs to be happy is a husband, a baby and a home of her own. Well, you've got 'em haven't you?"

"Have I?" I asked, for it was at that instant I noticed the blonde hair on his coat.

We quarrelled then. I won't go into details but it was horrible.

That night, as I lay awake, I heard someone whisper my name in the dark. It wasn't Lionel's voice, for it came from over by the door.

I sat up in bed, my heart thumping.

The voice possessed a hypnotic quality. It came from a distance and yet it seemed right inside my head; I knew if I covered my ears I'd still hear it.

I tried to scream but my throat and tongue seemed paralysed. Waves of fear ran through me. I began to tremble uncontrollably while the insinuating voice went on and on.

"Laura Brilliant," it whispered, "Laura, why fight it? You know that Lionel is unfaithful to you. You've lost him, you know. Your baby is sick, Laura, very sick. He won't get any better. There'll be nothing for you to do but to sit watching him waste away."

There was a second's silence. Then the voice went on again. Its very tonelessness made it the more horrible.

"That pain in your chest, Laura — you know it can only mean one thing. You've got cancer. You know what that means. Why go on, Laura? You've nothing to live for. Nothing to look forward to. Life's pretty unbearable isn't it? And it's going to get worse. Why not make an end of it? Then you'll have peace. ... There's always the gas oven, Laura. ... the gas oven. ... It won't hurt, it'll soon be over. ... so easy. ..."

I didn't sleep at all that night, and I walked around in a daze all next day. I told myself I'd imagined the voice. I told myself I needed to get a fresh hold or I'd have a nervous breakdown.

But the voice spoke to me again that night, and the next night, and the next. It seemed to get louder and more compelling as time passed. Always it said the same thing — life held nothing good for me, better to end it, and the pain, the disillusion, the sorrow the bitterness.

"You can't sleep, can you, Laura? There's only one way you can ever sleep. ... a long, long sleep and no more pain and unhappiness ... the gas oven, Laura, the gas oven. ..."

I longed to tell Lionel about this nightly horror but I was afraid he would think that I was mad. What else could he think? I'd thought so myself at first but not now, because although I resisted and rejected the suggestion the voice still went on. I could feel an unseen presence pitting its strength against mine until every night I lay praying for the first light of dawn when the torment would cease.

A new horror was added presently. When the voice stopped speaking there would be a moment of silence and then I would hear the hiss of escaping gas. After a while I could smell it. Soon I was choking, fighting for breath; then I would mercifully black out. Each morning I was surprised to find myself still alive.

Then one night came the ultimate horror, one I had been dreading ever since I became convinced that some supernatural and sinister force was trying to kill me. The owner of the voice materialized by my bedside.

How can I describe it? A creature thin, attenuated, partly transparent and somehow slimy looking, with great dark, depthless eyes which were wells of evil and hatred. One moment the figure seemed as quiveringly tall as the ceiling. Next it curved down over me so that I was conscious only of those dark cavities that weren't really eyes but merely holes through which poured the powers of darkness.

'I am getting a little impatient, Laura," murmured the hatefully familiar voice, though I couldn't tell if the thing had a proper face or mouth. It seemed to have no substance, just an ever changing spiral of pale slipperiness, flecked with shadows blacker than night. "No more procrastinating Laura. ... the time has come. You must do it now. ..."

How it fetched me out of bed and led me towards the door I don't know, for it had no limbs. It seemed to envelope me and surround me, so that when it moved I had to move. It was cold and horrible, and because it was quivering I trembled too.

It was not until we had reached the kitchen door and I saw the gas oven glimmering in the moonlight that I desperately drew upon the poor remnants of my own personality and broke through the enveloping horror. I screamed and screamed, like a madwoman. Then I flew downstairs and rushed out into the street.

How can I describe the relief of the first breath of free night air which I drew into my lungs.

Lionel followed me down in his pyjamas. He tried to lead me back into the house but I refused to go. The thing was waiting for me in there!

"Take me to a hotel," I begged. "Anywhere you like, but I can't go back to the flat."

Lionel, surprisingly, didn't argue.

"All right, darling," he said.

He fetched my coat and shoes and wrapped me up, to return, in a few minutes, dressed and carrying the baby and a case into which he'd thrown the few things we'd need. Then we hurried to the nearest hotel.

He sat up the rest of the night trying to calm me. I told him everything, describing between sobs my growing fears, and their awful culmination.

"I'm not mad, am I, Lionel?" I asked piteously.

"No," he answered gravely. "I've felt there was something wrong about the house all along. I didn't say anything because I thought you already had enough to cope with and I didn't want to frighten you. If only I'd known what you were going through! Anyhow, darling, a fellow named Hoffman I know at work has almost finished building a bungalow for himself on the outskirts of the town. It's a three bedroom affair, a bit too large for him and his wife as they've no family as yet. He's promised to let us share the place with them as soon as it's habitable."

"Can we afford it?" I enquired.

"Sure. I've saved quite a bit since I've been working overtime, you know."

And I suddenly knew it was no more true that he had taken out girls than that I had cancer or that the baby was dying!

We stayed at the hotel until we could move in with Lionel's friends.

And that's the end of the story.

Except that we learned later that about 20 years before a beast of a man had lived in the house in Caldwell Street. He had driven his ailing wife to commit suicide. She put her head in the gas oven. The man had wanted to marry another woman but he hadn't lived to enjoy her favours because, on his way back from his wife's funeral, he was killed by a car.

THE GHOST THAT "MURDERED SLEEP"

Cheiro

The girl had found no rest in death — she sought it for centuries by denying rest to the living.

I do not belong to any Spiritualist Society. I just mention this fact for fear people might run away with the idea that the following story is written from an interested standpoint.

Some years ago, out of a whim for living in an old-fashioned quarter of London, I took up my abode in a quaint, old house in King's Bench Walk in the Temple within a stone's throw of the busy thoroughfare of the Strand. That being my wish I ought to have been satisfied, for my lodgings were, I had every reason to consider, the most antiquated in London. Everything was in keeping, from the diamond-paned windows down to my landlady's cat which certainly must have been the mouser that looked after the welfare of the Ark. My landlady was of the Scotch pattern of housewife — honest, canny and clean, her principles unimpeachable, her youth dating back to some unknown era before the Victorian ascension.

I was the only lodger in the house and I must confess I was treated with scant courtesy. My breakfast, with the regularity of clockwork, appeared on the table at nine; but as it often happened that I slept until 10, it just as often, with the same precise regularity, disappeared at the appointed hour for its clearance and, hungry but not daring to remonstrate, I repaired morning after morning to a chophouse nearby.

At last, however, I thought I would explain and thus save the extravagance of paying for two breakfasts, for my uneaten meal appeared week after week in the old-fashioned handwriting at the debtor side of my bill.

I sought the old lady with the excuse of sleepless nights and penitently requested at least 10 minutes' grace in the 10 o'clock clearance rule.

"Young man," she said severely, "it is your conscience alone that keeps you awake. Go to church on Sundays, say your prayers at night, go to bed early, then if you can't eat your breakfast at nine you must be too wicked to remain under my roof."

Alas! In spite of the old lady's recipe "Nature's kind nurse" refused to rock me to oblivion. There seemed to be something in that room that "murdered sleep." Some ghostly hand seemed night after night to wake me and rob me of rest.

At last one afternoon, tired out, I fell asleep on the little hair sofa in the parlour. How long I slept I know not. I awoke to find the night far advanced, in my hand a pencil, and in my thoughts a strange dream. I could as little account for my possession of the pencil as I could for the dream, but reaching for some paper lying by my side I found, to my amazement, that in my sleep I had jotted down the main incidents of the dream. It was to the effect that the rooms I occupied were, during the reign of James II, the hiding place of a young nobleman and a beautiful girl whom he called Stella.

The nobleman was a Protestant, Stella a Catholic; one night, finding that he had been betrayed into the hands of the Catholic king, in a moment of madness, he killed his paramour and threw her body into a well in a cellar at the bottom of the house.

After this horrible dream I retired to my bed and, strange to say, slept peacefully and well. Next night, however, I dreamt the same thing over again and this time, in my thoughts, I followed the spectre to the cellar.

Now, I had never been in the cellar but in my dream I saw distinctly a kind of unused vault, the flooring formed by large slabs of stone black with age.

I dreamt that on my arrival at the cellar a service had commenced but the moment the last word was uttered everything vanished and the place was again empty and unused.

Finally, having dreamt this three times, I determined to see if it could in any way bear investigation. Consequently, I incurred the displeasure of my landlady by abruptly asking on the following morning if there was such a thing as a cellar to the house. She replied by informing me that every person who slept in my rooms annoyed her with the same question. Yes, there was a cellar under the kitchen but what I wanted to know for she couldn't make out.

I saw there was no use making further inquiries in that quarter; so, finding the old lady out in the afternoon I decided to push my investigations alone. I found my way to the kitchen which was under the level of the street and after considerable search I discovered an old oak door which led down to the mysterious cellar.

It was exactly as I had seen it in my dreams even to the dark heavy flags that covered the floor. I returned to my room, dressed and determined to go out in order to banish the discovery from my thoughts. I stayed out the entire evening, paid a visit to one or two theatres, returned late at night, went straight to bed and was soon asleep. I slept well until morning when I woke to find the dawn breaking and, having satisfied my conscience that it was too early to rise, I was soon once more fast asleep.

Again came that strange dream with all its vividness. Again the same scene took place before my eyes, but with this difference — that the figure of Stella led me down to the basement and disappeared after whispering in my ear, "Have prayers for the dead performed in the cellar tonight at 12." Startled, I woke from my sleep, woke to find the words still running through my mind, woke to rub my ear as hard as I could, to brush away the girl's breath which I seemed to feel.

There was yet another surprise that I was not prepared for. I turned over on my side and found written on the wallpaper, staring me in the face, the same words, "Have prayers for the dead performed in the cellar at midnight."

To this day I know not how those words came to be written there. I may have reached a pencil from the table and written them in my sleep, but the effect produced was even more startling than the dream. I was completely unnerved. I rose, hastily dressed, determining that silent command should be obeyed.

I opened the door and went out into the street. The brightness of the morning seemed such a contrast to the dark of the night that for a moment I doubted the sanity of my purpose. It was only for a moment, however. Again those scenes thronged through my brain, again those words were in my ear. I will try at all events, I said, to obey. I will try to make some one believe my story. I must — I will!

I was not a Catholic. I never have been a member of any orthodox creed, but I often had visited an old Catholic Chapel in the next street, and in doing so I had come in contact with several of the priests in connection with it. I will go there, I thought and get them to help me. I reached the chapel and found one of the Order whom I knew well. He was an extremely intellectual man, broadminded and sympathetic. Alas! In this particular case, his sympathies were not with me. I utterly failed to convince him that the story was anything more than a delusion and, disappointed and wretched, I turned away. I passed chapel after chapel but did not dare go in. My friend's last words had been, "You may give up your quest. You won't find a priest in London to do what you want."

It was still early morning. I wandered into Green Park and sat down on a seat in a quiet spot to think out the idea that I felt determined to put into execution. Suddenly, raising my eyes, I saw coming toward me a young priest, earnestly reading a prayer book. Bidding me good morning, he closed the book and in a few moments we were engaged in conversation.

This I felt was my chance. Making a few remarks about dreams and finding he believed in them, without any more hesitation I commenced and related the entire incident and the dilemma in which I was placed. To my delight as I finished he said. "I will help you out of this difficulty. Set your mind at rest. I will do all you want. I will be at your place tonight."

Night came and with it some friends to see me. I told them the incident and they begged to remain for the service if the young priest would allow it. Thus pleasantly engaged, the time seemed to fly until at last someone announced that it was a quarter to 12. Almost at the same instant I heard the footsteps of the priest coming to the door.

He did not object to the presence of my friends and in a few moments we were softly stealing downstairs to our midnight ceremony.

Nothing unusual happened to mark the service. The place was death-like in its stillness. The pale, earnest face of the young priest, lit by the flickering light of the candles, made an impression on me that I am not likely to forget. The service over, we returned in silence to my room and in a few moments the priest, bidding us goodnight, departed.

From the date of that midnight ceremony I had no disturbance whatever. Some weeks later I found on going downstairs one morning that masons and plumbers were about to commence some work necessitating an opening from the street to the cellar. They had occasion to raise the heavy flags that formed the floor and to their intense surprise they discovered the opening of a deep well. The following is quoted from one of the evening papers:

STRANGE DISCOVERY OF HUMAN REMAINS

Today, while workmen were engaged in effecting some repairs to a house in King's Bench Walk, they discovered under the cellar a large unused well and in the bottom of it a rusty sword and the bones of a skeleton which upon examination proved to be those of a young woman. The sword dates back to the reign of James II and it is surmised that this curious find may be the key to some strange romance.

❧ 17-YEAR-OLD MURDER REENACTED ❧
Bill Wharton

Doreen was alone in the cottage — but a mirror showed her an old tragedy whose players were long dead.

Each one of us has had at time or another when visiting a strange place, that strange, inexplicable feeling that we have been here before. Things look familiar to us; we know there is a grocery store in the next street — and yet, we know we have never been here before.

It was this uncanny sensation which seized Doreen Betts Harper the moment she and her husband, James, stepped from the train at Barnstaple in Devon one afternoon in September, 1956. Married only one day, the couple were on a 10-day honeymoon and had come to Devon because Doreen had been born there 19 years before but had not been back since her parents had died in 1939. It was her wish that they should go to Devon and James, 25 and very much in love with his pretty auburn-haired wife, agreed.

Barnstaple proved to be full of holidaymakers and accommodations were at a premium, but James managed to find a hotel room for his wife and himself for the night and the next morning they set out to find a honeymoon cottage. They were keen on getting to the coast where the Bay of Bideford sweeps inwards and the sands are soft and warm in September, but here again they ran into snags until they were advised by one real estate agent that there was a cottage perched a mile and a half from the cliff available at seven guineas a week.

When the taxi cab dropped them at Braunton, a few miles from Barnstaple, Doreen still retained the sensation that she knew the district well.

Wistaria Cottage was located about a quarter of a mile out of the village towards the sea and about 300 yards from the cliffs overlooking Bideford Bay. It was a rambling old-world cottage with three bedrooms, a living room, study, dining room and kitchen. It was said locally that it was once the hideout of Cornish smugglers and even shipwreckers who set up lanterns on the cliffs to lure ships to their doom on the rocks below.

But the honeymoon couple were not interested so much in

the history of the cottage as they were in each other. Although Doreen continued to puzzle over the fact that she knew the whole countryside and the cottage, the only one for about half a mile around. It lived up to its name and was literally a wistaria cottage, although some morning glory and sweet-scented creeper roses helped to cover all the exterior walls.

In front a narrow country lane ran down from the popular summer resort of Ilfracombe to wind past the cottage on its way to Braunton and Barnstaple. Even this path Doreen knew and when, on the afternoon they took possession of the cottage, she and James walked to the clifftop overlooking the sea, she told him there was a lighthouse not far out to sea. James Harper found it so.

In the cottage itself she went straight to the kitchen and coal bin outside without anyone telling her where they were located. Doreen also told Harper exactly what they would find upstairs.

"You must have been here before, perhaps as a child," James remarked to his wife. "It is impossible for anyone to know a place as you know this one unless you had been here before."

"I was two years old when my parents died and Aunt Florence took me away to London," Doreen said. "I have never been back in Devon. Aunt Florence never told me from which part of Devon we came, but I gathered it was from hereabouts because she often spoke of holidays at Bideford and Clovelly, which aren't far from here."

That evening James and his wife turned in early and were soon asleep, tired from travelling and from walking in the bracing sea air. But Doreen awoke in the night terrified. She is a sensible girl, who, at 19, had been private secretary to a London business executive. Yet there was something frightening in the old-world cottage.

Doreen, not wanting to awaken her husband, sat up in the bed listening to the distant pounding of the sea on the rocks and to the drizzle which was falling on the cottage.

She did not know what had wakened her, but now she thought she heard voices in another room. She rose quietly and slipped on a dressing-gown. Drawing the door closed behind her, she snapped on the light in the living room and instantly felt icy fear stab her heart.

"I stood in the room and my eyes moved around it," she said. "There was an oldish couch in one corner near the fireplace, two easy chairs of the 1920's era, a rocking chair, an old wooden table with twisted legs of the Queen Anne type, a footstool, some old paintings on the wall, and a large mirror hanging directly above the fireplace. My attention was drawn to the mirror.

"I thought I saw something move in the mirror and kept my eyes focused on it. I saw the door, which is opposite the mirror, open about half-way and I distinctly saw a youngish woman, maybe 26 years old or so, peep around the corner into the room, then close the door silently.

"I was suddenly dead scared and began calling to Jim my husband. He came running to me and demanded to know what was wrong. I told Jim what I thought I had seen and together we searched the cottage, but there was nothing and the back and front doors and windows were as securely locked as we had left them."

"You were overtired and had a nightmare," Harper said not unkindly and led his wife back to bed. But Doreen knew that it was no dream. She never had suffered from nerves and she lay awake for a long time after they returned to bed sure that she heard someone moving around the cottage.

After a morning spent by the sea the couple had lunch and James decided to do some fishing from the rocks while Doreen took a nap. She was dozing off when she distinctly heard someone calling. Instantly awake, she lay listening.

"Then I heard it again, someone calling 'Eric! Eric!' I thought that it was outside and then it occurred to me that it was a woman's voice calling from within the house to someone outside.

"I got up at once and went around the cottage and when I reached the kitchen I heard the same voice outside. The woman was speaking to a man and I just caught the tail-end of what she was saying.

"'How much longer can we stay here in safety, Eric? I am afraid. We must get away,' the woman was saying.

"Then I opened the door to see who it was and there was no one in sight, not a soul for as far as I could see."

Nervous and afraid, Doreen Harper slipped on a coat and headed down to the rocks where her husband was sitting, smoking. She told him of what had happened and Harper, solicitously, did not scoff at what his wife said, but promised to investigate the strange occurrences. Jim Harper later admitted that he had believed Doreen was overwrought with the long train journey from London and the excitement of their marriage.

That night before they turned in Jim made a thorough examination of the doors and windows and assured himself that nothing could get into the cottage without breaking in. Then he went to sleep contentedly with Doreen at his side.

"I was tired and sleepy," Doreen Harper remembered, "and dozed off almost at once. In the night — it was a few minutes after 11 o'clock — I awoke and again lay listening. Something had disturbed my sleep.

"Then I heard it, a woman's voice pleading from the very next room. I touched Jim's arm and called very softly to him. He awoke and I whispered, "Listen, can you hear anything?"

The woman was speaking in monotones Doreen Harper said. They heard her say, "We cannot stay here, Eric. We must get away. If he finds us here he will kill both of us."

And a man's gruff voice answered, "George will never think of looking for us so close to him. He will be scouring London. We are quite safe here."

The woman said, "I am frightened, Eric. Please, let us go away."

James Harper gripped his wife's arm and whispered, "Stay here!"

He rose silently and tiptoed to the bedroom door. Doreen rose quietly too and when her husband Jim flung the door open she was right behind him. Jim's fingers fumbled for a moment with the light switch and then the room was in brilliant light — but no one was there. The door leading to another bedroom was closed and the window curtains were drawn as the Harpers had left them.

Jim rushed through the entire cottage, checking every room, window and door. He found no evidence that anyone had entered the cottage nor was there anyone, apart from themselves in the cottage.

James looked at his wife. His face was ashen and worried. He said, "I thought you were over-tired and imagining things. Now I know there is something evil in this cottage. I don't know what it is, but I mean to find out. The man who rented this place to us should have told us."

"Jim," Doreen said trembling, "Jim, how do I fit into this thing? I knew the cottage! I knew the district before we came here! Where do I fit in?"

"I do not know, perhaps you imagine you have been here before," Jim said.

"I am not imagining anything. I knew this cottage the moment saw it; I knew Barnstaple; I knew every twist and turn — when we were walking down Dart Street I told you that when we turned the corner we would see the Bay View Hotel. When we entered this cottage I told you that the coal bin is out by the backdoor at the right around the corner? Why did we come here? Because I had an urge to come here. I could not resist it. I am frightened, Jim. Let's get away from here, now."

"All right," Jim said. "But I am going to find out a thing or two and demand my money back. Are you afraid to stay here while I go into Barnstaple? I won't be long and you can pack our things while I am gone."

"I am not afraid during the daytime," Doreen said "You can go and by the time you return I will be ready to leave."

Harper timed his departure to coincide with the arrival of the Braunton-Barnstaple bus at the crossroads a few hundred yards from the cottage and Doreen set about packing their clothes. But she had an uneasy feeling, "As if I were not alone in the house, as if someone was there with me, someone trying to reach me all the time."

"I was working in the bedroom when I heard a man's voice," she related. "I stopped in the act of closing a suitcase and listened, but I was suddenly seized by an awful feeling as if I were about to witness something dreadful."

Outside, very close to her, she heard a man saying, "We are leaving today so stop nagging me. That fool can never find us here, I don't know what you are worrying about."

"Then," Doreen Harper said, "I heard a woman's voice pleading for the man to hurry up and while she was talking there suddenly came another male voice, angry, high-pitched."

Doreen Harper moved from the bedroom into the living-room, closer to the voices. The two men were arguing and it sounded as if the woman was weeping.

"I could stand it no longer," Mrs. Harper said, "but threw the door open, fully expecting to see two men and a woman — but there was no one. Silence greeted me as I stood looking into the second bedroom which leads off the living-room.

"Then I turned, uncertain what to do, whether to run or to defy whatever it was that haunted the cottage. The fear slowly began to leave me. Somehow I did not feel that same terror anymore. I turned around and was returning to the bedroom to complete the packing when a movement in the mirror caught my eye. I stopped and looked up in the mirror. I could not identify the people I saw, but they were there.

"There were two rather hazy people, a man and woman, with their backs turned to the mirror; in the background another shadowy figure faced the mirror.

"I swung around and looked through the open door into the room. I could see nothing. But when I turned back to look in the mirror I saw them again.

"Then I heard the woman screaming, 'Please don't. Please don't!'

"There was a muffled report, a stifled scream, followed at once by another report as of a gun fired a long distance off."

Mrs. Harper's nerves failed her at this instant and she fled from the house to a knoll about 200 yards away where she sat looking down at the cottage seemingly lying so peacefully below.

"I saw a shadowy figure emerge from behind the house as if he had come from the kitchen door. I saw him hurrying across the field towards the cliff and there he vanished," Mrs. Harper related.

Her husband returned about two hours later and found her sitting on the knoll. Together they returned to the cottage and finished the packing. An hour later they returned to Barnstaple where the real estate agent refused to make them any refund on their payment for the rental of the cottage.

He derided the idea of a haunted cottage and invited the Harpers to bring a lawsuit against him. Harper's attempts to find out something about Wistaria Cottage came to nothing in Barnstaple so he and Doreen decided to go to the county seat at Exeter where they searched for information in the public library. They found nothing.

That evening Jim Harper said to his wife, "Let us assume that you were not dreaming when you heard the two shots and saw the man leaving the cottage. This means that there must have been a murder and the best place to go is the police station."

The sergeant listened attentively to the couple's story and then said, "I remember there was a double murder followed by a suicide in the Barnstaple area during the first of the war, about 1939. We have nothing on it here, but why not look in the newspaper files?"

While Doreen hunted through the 1938 files, Harper looked through the 1939 file, but a veteran reporter came to tell them he remembered the crime.

"This man, Eric Wellicombe was invalided out of the Air Force, after a crash, and came to stay with his friend, George Betts.

"In the autumn of 1939 while Betts was away from home his

wife and Wellicombe cleared out together. Betts returned to find them gone and went absent without leave from the Air Force when his commanding officer refused to give him compassionate leave. At the inquest evidence was given that Betts went to London and when he did not find his wife and friend there, he came back to Devon and traced them to a house near Barnstaple where he shot both of them and then jumped from the cliff," reporter Tom Bowditch told the couple.

Jim Harper asked in a strained voice, "Did Betts have children?"

Bowditch thought for a moment before replying, "Yes, as a matter of fact there was a child, a little girl, I think, 18 months to two years old. They found the child in the cottage after the alarm was given by a woman who had come to clean up for Mrs. Betts and Mr. Wellicombe. I don't remember what happened to the child."

Doreen found her husband's hand on her arm and as he led her from the newspaper office; there was nothing to say.

Doreen Betts Harper and her husband emigrated to Australia in August, 1957, and are now residents of Gladstone, Queensland. The author of this story states that he has carefully checked the facts in this case and found them to be true — "except that it is not possible to check whether Mrs. Harper did in fact, see and hear these things. She says she did and there appears to be no reason to disbelieve her."

NEWSPAPER HAUNTED
Former Editor

This newspaper staff on the Isle of Man has no need to hunt ghosts — one is present in their building.

Fred Archer

The staff of the *Isle of Man Times*, which circulates in the little island in the Irish Sea, unlike other newspapermen who go in search of ghosts but often fail to find them, have their own ghost in the *Times'* office. It has convinced even the most skeptical reporters that the place is haunted!

The building, on Athol St., Douglas, is over a century old. Some long-time members of the staff knew that the legend of a ghost existed, but had almost forgotten it.

Then came the shattering experience of a new office cleaning woman from the English mainland. It set everyone to comparing notes and it was found that a number of persons had recently had baffling experiences which they had been reluctant to talk about.

Mrs. Elizabeth Leece of 92 Lord St., Douglas, is an elderly, grey haired woman. She is a native of Liverpool and is a forthright, practical woman not given to fantasies.

One Friday night she was cleaning the reporters' room at the *Times* building. It was nine o'clock and she had almost finished. As she stood in the doorway, her back to a flight of stairs leading to the top of the building, suddenly she felt something very cold behind her.

She turned quickly to look up the dark staircase. At the bend of the stairs stood the "transparent outline of a small stocky, elderly man. He seemed to have a short, whitish beard."

The figure, according to Mrs. Leece's description, was surrounded by "a sort of glowing light, and was leaning over the stair-rail looking down at me, with his head slightly inclined to one side. He looked mild and wistful."

After gazing at the apparition for a couple of seconds, unable to move, Mrs. Leece dropped her mop, stumbled down the lower stairs and out onto the street. She did not stop hurrying until she reached home, at which time she realized she had left her coat in the office and was still wearing her working apron.

When she spoke of her experience next day to some of the newspapermen, they asked her to describe fully the apparition she claimed to have seen. Some of the older staffmen believe that her description tallies in detail with the appearance of a former editor.

Mrs. Leece never had known anyone associated with the newspaper in the past. She was unaware that many years before one editor lived in a flat on the top floor of the *Times* building. Nor had she ever heard the old legend of the ghost. The accuracy of her description of the apparition has been tested on several occasions, but it never varies.

One newspaperman, Arthur Moore, asked if she ever had a similar experience. She told him she had, shortly after her mother died in Liverpool.

"I saw her for a few minutes one evening seated in an armchair in the firelight, then she vanished," Mrs. Leece said.

She was asked if she was afraid of working alone in the *Times* building after such an experience.

"Not now," Mrs. Leece answered. "I don't believe that a person sees the same ghost twice. But I'm sure someone else will see him one of these nights."

Mrs. Leece was unaware of the fact but someone else already bad seen the ghost — several months before she did. He had kept quiet about his dramatic experience fearing his fellow-journalists would scoff.

Reporter Sean Kenny is a middle-aged, tough yet sensitive Irishman, and a devout Roman Catholic. He thinks he could be "fey" and have the unwelcome gift of seeing what others do not see. His reluctance to testify at first makes his testimony all the more impressive when he finally affirmed: "I do not care what they think. I know what I saw. I know what I experienced and nothing will ever convince me but that I was in the presence of a spirit from another world."

Kenny was alone in the reporters room, typing at his desk, one night around 11 o'clock. In the corner of the room was a large, old-fashioned safe which had been there for many years. It is filled with old documents.

Kenny felt the room go cold (the same sensation Mrs. Leece later experienced). He continued typing, but became more and more uneasy. He said he had the feeling someone was watching him.

Except for the light over his desk the room was in darkness so he got up and switched on all the lights, then went back to his typing. However, the unpleasant feeling that he was being watched persisted. He finally began to shiver.

Ripping the last page from his typewriter he sat back in his chair, glancing toward the corner with the safe.

"Then I saw what was unmistakably a shadowy figure. I could see him clearly enough to note that he was staring at me with glassy eyes. His eyes seemed to bore through me.

"I sat for a moment transfixed. I could not move. Sweat began to trickle down my face. I felt in my pockets for my rosary, and murmured a prayer.

"The figure vanished — and I ran. When I reached the door I heard a crash. I glanced back and saw that the wall plaster near the safe, at the spot where the ghost had stood, had fallen to the floor.

"Afterwards. I went up to St. Mary's Church, and prayed for the poor soul who cannot rest."

When Sean Kenny returned to the office next morning the corner of the room by the safe was littered with wall plaster.

Asked if he had ever seen an apparition before, Sean Kenny, like Mrs. Leece, admitted he had. On the extreme west coast of his native Ireland he once saw and heard the banshee outside the window of his greatest friend's house. That same night his friend's father died.

The banshee, the traditional spectre of Ireland, is a white-robed woman who appears wailing outside the family home when the passing of one of its members is imminent. More than one eminent man has told me of his personal experience with the banshee.

Kenny need not have worried about the reactions of his fellow-journalists. Some of them too were nursing a similar secret.

Another reporter, John Quirk, remembered a night when he was alone in the building and heard footsteps descending from the top floor and moving slowly about. They were so plain he concluded that a company secretary was working late and called out his name. There was no reply and when Quirk investigated he was startled to see a shadow on the staircase wall, and to hear footsteps receding.

"I knew by then no one else was on the premises," Quirk stated. "I feel sure Mrs. Leece saw something supernatural."

The co-editor of the *Times*, Miss Alice Haywood Rylance, a shrewd and practical newspaperwoman, has worked for three generations of the paper's publishers. She occupies an office midway between the old and new sections of the building, having a choice of exit down either winding stairway to the printing department below.

Miss Rylance admits that she would, on no account, use the old stairway when she is alone.

Mrs. Flo Stafford, wife of senior *Times'* reporter Tom Stafford, is a "seventh child" and a woman of strong religious beliefs. She recalls one visit to the office with her husband on an evening when he was taking in his copy. They reached the first floor staircase landing and she said to him, "I don't like it here. It's not happy."

When her husband asked she meant, Mrs. Stafford could only answer that she felt some happy, psychic influence. She knew nothing about the old ghost legend until it was talked about after Mrs. Leece's experience.

Arthur Moore never had seen nor sensed anything strange. But twice he had heard inexplicable noises.

One night a few months before Mrs. Leece saw the apparition he had gone into the office at 10 p.m. to make a promised phone call. He was in a hurry and, without pausing to switch on a light, picked up the telephone receiver. While he was talking he heard three heavy thuds on the floor above. Asking his acquaintance to hold the line, he went upstairs to investigate. All was in darkness. He was apparently the only living person in the building.

When he returned to the phone he apologized, saying, "I thought I heard someone knocking upstairs."

"I heard three distinct knocks too," she answered. She was speaking from Port Erin, about 15 miles away on the other side of the Island of Man.

Moore made an acoustic experiment out of curiosity. He found that the thuds apparently had come from the doorway of the reporters' room, the same place where Mrs. Leece was standing when she saw the ghost at a later date.

Only a week or two before Mrs. Leece's experience, Moore was working late when he heard the telephone on the ground floor ringing. The phones were interconnected and he had only to press a button to take the call on his own receiver. He found himself connected with the exchange and heard the male operator asking him what number he wanted. When he said that the bell had rung the operator told him that there was no one on the line.

A few minutes later the same thing happened, only this time

the bell rang in an adjoining room. The operator again denied that anyone was calling.

When it happened a third time the ringing this time coming from the editors' room next to his own, he held his own receiver towards the half-open door when the operator answered and the bell still continued to ring. The operator agreed he could hear the bell ringing. But assured Moore that despite this fact the line was clear.

The following morning an engineer came to the building to test the telephones. He failed to find any fault at all, or to offer any explanation that could account for the "calls" of the previous night.

The *Times* has been a family business through three generations. Some days after her experience Mrs. Leece was shown a family group photograph which included three former *Times* editors. Immediately, pointing to one, she exclaimed, "Why, that's the old man I saw gazing at me on the stairs!"

She was pointing to the face of an editor of 40 years before, the same man the older members of the staff always had connected with the ghost legend.

And if it is he who haunts the building what troubles his unquiet spirit?

The newspaper is undergoing changes; it is no longer the traditional family enterprise, but has been acquired by a rival company. A reader of the newspaper put this theory most bluntly:

"The former proprietor (if it be he) was always a fighter — but I didn't think he would return from the grave and risk being exorcised in order to rescue his beloved paper.

"Your reporter, Sean Kenny, may pray at St. Mary's for the repose of his soul, but my nonconformist prayers are for the one-time editor and his fight for the *Isle of Man Times*."

Whatever else he achieved, he provided his newspaper with a startling and dramatic story.

THE RESTLESS SEXTON
Lilian Chapman

The garden path was made of tombstones — but only one particularly interested the little man with the spade.

When my cousin Jim retired from the Metropolitan Police Force he decided to buy a cottage in his home county, Somerset, and so taking a furnished house at Taunton he set about finding what he thought would be a perfect cottage for himself and his wife. They had no children and a large place would be useless, but both are keen gardeners so a sizable garden was important to them.

After much searching and many headaches for themselves and the house agent, they found what seemed just right in a small village near Taunton. True, the cottage was sadly in need of a coat of paint and would have to be re-decorated throughout, but both Jim and his wife were prepared for more than a little do it yourself. The garden was almost a wilderness, but buried beneath the tangled brambles there were good herbacious borders, a nice kitchen and beyond this a small orchard, and surely with the help of a jobbing gardener it could be licked into shape.

The previous owner, Tom Bond, had been a very old man who according to village reports was a "queer one" who firmly believed in ghosts, witches, and hob-goblins and had often been heard talking "to them." He would not allow anybody to touch his garden.

Having bought the cottage, Jim and Helen worked at it for some months and then with the help of Bob, a really hard-working old gardener, they started tackling the garden. One of the tasks was clearing a paved path leading through the kitchen garden to the orchard. This path had become so overgrown with weeds and covered with soil that only a little of the paving was visible.

Having cleared a few yards, Jim was astonished to find that the stones were of curious shape, some broken and roughly put together, and some with very worn inscriptions and what appeared to be epitaphs. It soon became clear to him that they were ancient tombstones.

He decided to ask Bob a few questions about them as Bob knew much of the history of the village.

"Oh yes," said Bob, "I remember hearing that they were given by 'Old Parson' to Tom Bond when he was making a garage of the old coach house at the Rectory."

"Old Parson" had been dead many years, but even so the present Vicar was still known as "Young Parson" and couldn't be expected to know much about it. But according to Bob the stones had been stacked in the coach-house for a great number of years. Nobody knew where they had come from.

Jim was rather proud of having such an unusual path in his garden, and after much labour the whole was finished and the following summer my husband and I received an invitation to stay a few days with my cousin. At the end of the letter a P.S. said: "There is something very queer going on in my garden!"

Thinking Jim had raised a quite new species of plant we looked forward to an interesting weekend.

Arriving at the cottage on a Friday afternoon we were proudly shown around and I must say they had made it very attractive. However, when I asked: "Where is the new plant?" Jim laughingly explained that it was not a plant but a ghost, or at least a ghostly noise. Very often they had been awakened between 11 and 12 o'clock by something that sounded like a spade banging on stone and once he had seen a misty figure like a bent old man carrying a spade. Jim admitted this might have been a trick of the light but added, anyhow we might hear or see something ourselves and he proposed that we all sit in the garden the following evening until after midnight.

This night as we were now rather tired after our long journey an early to bed seemed a good idea and so thankfully we were in our bedroom just before 11 o'clock. I think it must have been just before midnight when I was awakened by a metallic banging, three sharp bangs, just like a spade on a stone, then three more, followed by silence. Our window looked over the kitchen garden and the path towards the orchard, but in the dim light I could see nothing. Thinking that Jim was playing tricks on us I returned to my bed and slept soundly until morning.

At breakfast I asked Jim if he thought he had fooled us with his spade banging, but he assured us he had done nothing, neither had he heard anything. The day passed pleasantly, a rare warm day and we were able to sit in the garden even after supper. At about 11 o'clock we decided to move a garden seat to a spot where we could get a good view of the tombstoned pathway. Jim fetched a large jug of Somerset cider; Helen and I donned our cardigans and so, fortified within and without, we sat awaiting events.

Just before midnight a blackbird whistled and flew out from a nearby bush, making us all jump and giving Helen and me an attack of the giggles. A few moments later we all heard shuffling footsteps, followed by three distinct bangs of metal on stone. Looking along the path I could see, in the dim light, what appeared to be a misty figure of a little man with a spade raised in his hand ready to make three more bangs. These were then heard by us all, and were followed by yet another three metallic bangs.

As I watched, my scalp feeling more prickly every moment, the figure just melted away. With a gasp I said: "Did you see it?"

Jim and Helen had seen nothing but had distinctly heard the bangs. My husband said, yes, he had seen it and described the identical figure I had seen. We all had been too petrified to move and now, shivering a little, we went indoors where we decided, after much discussion, that we would watch again the following night and that at the first bang we would all walk towards the figure which had paused to bang somewhere around the sixth paving stone from the orchard gate. We told ourselves we should then know for a certainty if it was somebody playing tricks.

The following evening, a Sunday, we again waited on the garden seat. Nothing happened and feeling rather foolish and still a little doubtful we decided to have a good look at the stones the next day. We had intended returning home on Monday but Jim begged us to stay a few more days to try to solve this strange happening. We agreed not to discuss it with Bob or anybody in the village as we did not want to be bothered with ghost hunters or the press.

After a rather late breakfast Monday morning we walked along the path towards the orchard gate, then turned and counted six stones. This sixth stone was one of the whole ones, very worn and with no inscription. Jim Suggested that it would be a good idea if he turned it over so, fetching a couple of crowbars, he and my husband carefully turned it. When they had cleaned away some of the earth they were able to read a little of what was left of the epitaph.

The name, Thomas Green, was clear enough; the date of his death was not so clear, 1741 perhaps. Most interesting were the words, "For — years sexton of this Parish — Rest in Peace."

Poor Thomas Green apparently was not resting in peace and then suddenly I knew why. Surely he who had dug graves and erected tombstones for so many was entitled to his own grave and stone in consecrated ground. What had happened to his grave we could not say — but here, clearly enough, was his headstone and he seemed to object to its remaining in this garden.

Jim and my husband decided they must go and see "Young Parson" about it and returning to the house they immediately phoned him for an appointment. After "Young Parson" had heard the whole strange story they all decided that the tombstones should be returned to the churchyard, where they may be seen to this day propped against the wall by the old yew tree.

"Young Parson" never has discovered how the tombstones came to be in the coach-house Even Bob has not been able to ferret out any information for us on this.

One thing is sure. The restless little Sexton is now at peace and nobody has either seen or heard him or the clang of his spade again.

My cousin now has a concrete path running through his garden.

I FOLLOWED A GHOST

J. P. J. Chapman

This episode happened many years ago — between 1906 and 09, Father's brother, William, lived at Orpington, in Kent. They had mutual business interests which brought them together at various intervals. They took turns visiting each other. I had three cousins, two boys about my own age and a girl who was older. My Aunt Clair was a darling and I loved her very much, possibly because my own mother was dead and I felt here was somebody I could turn to.

One summer, I went with Father to stay for a couple of weeks. Uncle William bred horses and I loved going out with them when they were exercised. I had a good "seat" for, from youth, I rode Father's farm horses and even tried bronco busting on the cattle.

On this particular visit the house was full of guests so I did not get my usual room. But here I must explain the layout of the building. From what I can remember I would say it was a Georgian structure, two stories high and facing south.

One entered the house through a large oak door right into a big hall, facing a broad staircase. This went to a half landing, continuing to the first floor. At the top of these stairs was a small room to the right, which seemed to be a builder's afterthought. This landing went the length of the building with two very large windows at each end. The cross light made the middle of the hall a little dark, although there was a window on the stairs.

On this particular occasion I was put in the room at the top of the stairs. The bed was comfortable — being a double one, which pleased me no end. I was duly seen into bed by the family's nanny who insisted that I must have a night light. I remonstrated, saying that at home I never had one and would she please take it away.

She observed that it was better in a strange house and a strange room; I might want it during the night.

I waited until all was quiet, then slipping out of bed I blew it out, snuggled back into the sheets and pillow and was soon fast asleep. I don't know when it was I woke up. The window was wide open, with brilliant moonlight outside, so it was half light in the room. Then I heard something in the hall.

In my own home, unknown to my father, I used to roam the house at night. There was something eerie about it all, the dark corners, the ticking of the grandfather's clock, it seemed another world and I was part of it.

I had a torch and picking this up I crept to the door, which I silently opened. The landing, the half landing, and the hall looked eerie. I felt a thrill of excitement. It was mid-summer, so I did not feel cold. The hall and the stairs were heavily carpeted so my bare feet sunk well in.

There was something or somebody down there. I knew that it was not the dogs, as they slept in a compound outside. However, one of them started a dismal howl, baying the moon — or was it something else?

I picked my way downstairs in the semi-light. At once I knew there was a "presence". It seemed to be coming from the far end of the long passage that led from the hall to the kitchen. I could not see anything but I felt it getting closer. There was a slight wind as it passed by, making for the stairs.

I followed it, close behind; still I could hear nothing but I could feel it. Whatever it was did not seem aware of me. We got to the half landing, then at the top it stopped outside my room. After a while it turned right at the top of the stairs and slowly went down the passage. At this moment I switched on my torch and could see in the heavy carpet the imprints of feet as they went along, great big heavy boots they were.

Nothing daunted, I kept my torch on and followed up, putting my feet into the imprints as they were made. So we both proceeded the whole length of the passage.

When we reached the far end I heard the sound of an opening window. There was a window there, but it remained shut. Then there was the rustle of somebody scrambling out. This was followed by a dull thud, then silence. At this moment the dog outside stopped his dismal serenade. All was quiet and nothing else happened. I crept back to bed and knew nothing until my aunt stood by my bed telling me to hurry up or I should be late for breakfast.

At breakfast my uncle remarked, "That dog was baying the moon last night. I thought it would never stop."

I produced a dead silence by replying, "He wasn't baying the moon, Uncle. He only does it when the ghost is here. You know; the man who jumped out the window upstairs. He was around last night."

My uncle nearly choked swallowing a mouthful of bacon and egg and quickly changed the subject.

However, he and my aunt later in the day asked me to tell the story.

They listened carefully. My aunt wanted to know if I was frightened. I said "Why should I be? Ghosts can't hurt. I didn't mean it any harm and I am sure it knew. So what is there to be afraid of?"

I COULDN'T CLOSE THE DOOR
Lady May Lawford

During the reign of King Edward VII (the exact date escapes me) I made many friends at the finishing school I attended, the Princess Helena College, at Ealing in West London.

My best and dearest school friend was the daughter of a clergyman in a small town in the heart of the English country. At school, during our morning "break for milk or juices," she would tell us tales of her home in the vicarage; how, after dark, walking down the long stony passages, always dimly lit, "someone" or "something" would push her gently to one side; how a door would open but there would be no one in the room, just a sound of someone breathing as if they had run up a hill fast. She told us she never could have a pet cat or dog. They would stay for a bit, then run away, yelping — the hair on their backs standing up in terror.

One incident made us laugh. Very early one morning before dawn the Vicar, hearing a noise, went to investigate and fell over a carpet bag which was full of burglar's tools and implements. The burglar obviously had left in a hurry. The thing that walked the corridor must have pushed him also, so that he fled like the household pets.

Many years later, while back in England on a leave from India, I ran into my friend at the home of a mutual friend in London. She said her father had retired and had bought the old Vicarage where he and she continued to live, and that the people of the country town had built a fine new house for the new Vicar.

In due course, I went to stay with my friend for a long weekend; my husband remained in London. The day of my arrival was one of "those days" that most of us experience. It rained! I lost my hat box, smashed my watch, and arrived in a disgruntled mood.

After a session in the library with the old Vicar and some fine dry sherry, I was escorted upstairs to dress for dinner. While brushing out my long hair, I glanced at the door. It was open. So I shut it in case one of the maids should pass by. A minute later, about to give a final look at myself in the long mirror, I saw that the door was wide open again!

"These old-fashioned locks!" I muttered as I slammed the

door and promptly forgot it.

I got to bed around midnight after an endless chat — going back over the years. I had acquired the habit in the East and I kept a dim night-light in my room. In the early morning hours I suddenly woke up to find the door wide open! I told myself I was certain I had shut it, but to make sure this time, I removed the key after locking the door. I placed the key on my bedside table. Then I slept soundly until I woke to find a trim maid at my bedside with my early morning tea.

"How," I asked, glancing at the door key on my bedside table, "did you get in?"

"The door was wide open," she replied.

After breakfast we went to the village, and while my friend was in a shop, I fled into the post office and sent a telegram to my husband, asking to be recalled by telephone at once!!

Sorry as I was to leave my dear friend and the comfortable old-world atmosphere of the charming Vicarage, I just couldn't take the proximity of "the Thing", or "It" that so obviously owned the house, and to whom locked doors meant nothing.

THE GHOST SAUSAGE

J. P. J. Chapman

**Many years ago my late father-in-law rented a large farm near
Bampton in North Devon. The farm buildings and the dwelling
house were situated half way up a steep hill overlooking the
River Exe. During a warm summer it was quite nice but with a
lingering threat of bitter winds and snow in winter.**

There was a lane going from the farm to a large moor which was quite
300 feet higher than the tillage. Now, it is well known that large open
spaces, devoid of any useful vegetation and situated atop a high hill,
frequently possess a bad reputation. Of a summer evening my wife and
I frequently took a walk to the moor. It commanded a wonderful view,
while the sunsets were a sight to behold.

The lane ended at a gate which led into this moor. Quite a
while before the events to be related my wife and I frequently
remarked that it was an eerie spot and the sooner passed the better.
Personally, I never gave it much thought for, being a "country lad," I
knew of many such places which were not nice — and that was all that
could be said.

However, things proved otherwise. My wife and her sisters
rode a lot and took turns exercising the horses. Sometimes they went
out together. I can still see them up on the moor, putting the horses
into a gallop and thoroughly enjoying the wild ride.

On one occasion one of the girls was asked by her father to go
on the moor to see if some cattle had strayed. It was in the autumn and,
the sun having set, it would soon be dark. My wife's sister decided to
ride up. Having seen that all was well she was just about to leave the
moor, through the gate which she had left open, when the horse
suddenly shied. Nothing would induce it to pass through the gate.
There was no alternative route except by a long detour, so go through
they must.

After several attempts she decided to dismount and lead the
horse through. This time as they reached the gate a curious luminous
shape could be seen drifting nearby. It was like an elongated sausage,
with baleful eyes. The whole thing seemed to be pulsating, from dim
to bright. It was in a vertical position except for a sideways, wavering

movement. To say the least, the girl was frightened but made up her mind to face it.

Placing herself between what-ever-it-was and the horse she coaxed the animal through. When the horse was half way it broke loose and galloped down the lane for about 50 yards where it stopped and waited.

There were several curious facts concerning this particular haunting. It took place only at dusk — no other time. No other animals, except horses — any horse — were affected. But here again was a most remarkable fact. It had to be a horse and a human. If there was not this combination nothing happened. The "Ghost Sausage," as I dubbed it, seemed anchored to one spot, its movements restricted as related. Several times I visited the place but, while noticing there was something there, never could decide what. The ghost seemed quite harmless. I got the impression that it was neither good nor bad. It was just some form of ghost — nothing more.

There was a big disused quarry nearby; possibly some earth spirit had been released. My sister-in-law stated it was a greenish colour, about a foot across and five feet high.

This is the end of my story. If the present residents of the farm ever see it, I don't know, as we have not been near the place for the last 35 years or more.

What it was, how it originated, I do not know. I never could find out. Your answer will be as good as mine!

HAUNTED MILL HOUSE
ON THE ISLE OF MAN

The visitor came at night, slammed doors, moved furniture around and walked heavily, yet remained unseen.

Geoffrey Whitehead
As told to Virginia Stumbough

Black magic is still practised in remote parts of the Isle of Man. The Manx say it is not so, but my wife and I, her sister and mother, know it is. We have been haunted ourselves, when we lived in an old millhouse.

The old millhouse is situated in a beautiful part of the island called Maughold in the Corony Valley. On one side is the mountain North Barrule, at the foot of which runs the Corony River. A small stream branching from the river became the mill race to the old waterwheel on the side of the mill.

Although the old mill now stands empty and lonely, it was once a warm, cosy old house. One pitch dark winter night in 1935, when my wife Edna and I were sitting in the front room by a blazing log fire, we heard the front door open. Heavy footsteps went along the hall and mounted the stairs. We looked at each other in amazement.

I looked at our dog, a Manx cattle hound, and wondered why he did not bark. He was a wonderful guard dog, and I never had known a stranger to approach the house without his barking or growling. But now there was not a sound from him. Instead he was crouched low, with his belly almost touching the floor; every hair on his back was up, and his lips curled back off his teeth in a noiseless snarl.

"Come on, Scamp! Go get 'em!" I said, and quickly opened the door, turning on the hall light and the upper landing light at the same switch.

"Is anyone there?" I called out, starting upstairs. Edna followed. The dog preceded us, walking stiff-legged, his hackles still up. He went as far as the foot of the attic stairs and stood there, looking up. I grabbed a large torch from the bedroom, and continued up into the two large attic rooms which ran the length of the house. They were full of old lumber, old beds, trunks, boxes, discarded clothing and other odds and ends. There were plenty of dark corners.

I shone the torch in all directions. Nothing moved. Edna stood beside me but the dog didn't want to investigate any further, but stood at my side growling softly. Although there was nothing to be seen, I had the horrible feeling that someone or something was watching us.

We started down the stairs. My wife pulled me by the arm, and it seemed as if a cold wind passed us. A few seconds later we heard the front door close with a bang. Scamp suddenly came to life and dashed helter-skelter down the stairs barking. Somehow, we felt relieved.

"Lock and bolt the door, Geoff," Edna said. "We don't want any more late callers."

The door, with one of the biggest locks I have ever seen, had an outer casing of wood, and a massive iron key which was too big to be put in a pocket. There were two big bolts as well. We locked this door, ate supper, and talked about our strange visitor before retiring.

The next morning I came down about 7:30 to discover that the front door was wide open!

Many times after that, day and night, we locked this door only to find that someone or something had opened it again.

Another time during the following summer, my mother-in-law came to stay with us. One morning at breakfast she said to Edna, "I'm so sorry that Geoff had a bad night. I heard you moving a chair about. I suppose he had an attack of asthma, poor lad."

"No," Edna exclaimed, "As a matter of fact we had a very good night, and Geoff slept like a top."

Two nights after this, when we had been in bed and asleep for some hours, my wife awakened me with a punch in the back. "Geoff! Listen! There is someone in the front room. They are moving the armchair or something!"

I sat up in bed and listened. Sure enough, I could hear footsteps and the sound of heavy furniture being pushed over the floor. Very reluctantly, for I'm no hero, I climbed out of bed and took up my torch. I was very sorry that I had shut Scamp in the kitchen!

I took up a heavy walking stick for arms, then crossed the landing and threw open the front room door, shined in my torch, and then switched on the light. Everything was in order; nothing was out of place. I had no feeling of fear or discomfort this time, and went back to bed and to sleep. The next morning my mother-in-law remarked she again had heard the furniture being moved. After that it happened so often we got used to it.

While at supper on another evening that summer we suddenly heard a tremendous row outside in the millyard. It sounded like the very grandfather of a dog fight. I grabbed my stick and dashed out.

I saw an amazing sight. Scamp seemed to be fighting for his life with an invisible opponent, snapping, snarling, standing on his hind legs. His opponent appeared to be bigger. For a moment I thought he had gone mad, but as I watched he broke away and stood panting, with blood and saliva dripping to the ground. Then he sprang forward again, as if to prevent his unseen enemy from going out the gates.

From then on it was a running fight, out through the gates, across the road, and then over the hedge into the fields. We could hear the combat growing fainter and fainter. Two hours later poor old Scamp returned. He was limping and badly injured in many places, but with no open wounds. He was covered with some kind of awful-smelling gray froth or saliva. I never had seen anything like it before. Our old dog was absolutely exhausted. It took him several days to recover.

One evening late in autumn Edna and I had been out to a dance in town and returned rather late. Sometime after midnight I turned off the main road, with my headlights on bright so that I could see the gateway clearly.

"Look Geoff!" Edna cried, "Look, it's a mad dog!"

There, standing right in our path between the big gateposts, was the biggest, most horrible-looking dog I ever have seen. It looked like a wolfhound, with red glaring eyes, and with froth dripping from its jaws.

"Hold tight! I'm going to run it down!"

I put my foot down hard and we shot through the gates as fast as the old car would go. We didn't hit a thing. I stopped as soon as I got into the yard, and had a good look around with my torch. I let Scamp out, and he raced around like mad. Then he made off through the gates, and over the road and fields as he had done before. When he returned early the next morning, he was again absolutely exhausted and covered with that evil smelling slime.

Where had he been? With what had he fought?

Some time after this I was talking to the local bus inspector, a Mr. Ellison, and told him about the strange dog. He said he also had seen it and thought it must be what the old Manx people called the "Moodie-Dhoo" or Black Dog, which is supposed to haunt Peel Castle. This may be so, but I don't think so. I feel this dog belonged to the mill. I made many inquiries, but I did not get very far. I did learn, however, that about 120 years ago, an ill-fortuned, debt-ridden miller hanged himself in the old mill itself.

I've recorded these events just as they happened to Edna and me. But the cause the purpose, and the agency of these terrifying experiences remains a mystery to us.

**My two friends and I appeared to be alone
in the old house we were inspecting.
Who was the cloaked and shadowy figure
coming towards me?**

THE TRAGIC GHOST OF MOYLES COURT

Lilian Chapman

Some evenings ago I was watching a news bulletin from the South of England when a picture of an old manor house was shown with the announcement that Moyles Court in the New Forest had been sold for the first time in more than 100 years. The original Manor was known to exist in 1086. The commentator stated that it is now a school and that so far none of the pupils had seen the ghost of "The Lady in Yellow" who is reputed to haunt this historic old house.

Some of the girl pupils were interviewed for the programme and all agreed that they would like to see "The Lady in Yellow" and would make her most welcome.

I need hardly say that ghosts of this nature are fairly common in England and many old manors are proud of them. They are often talked about but very rarely seen, which makes my own experience at Moyles Court all the more interesting.

It was in September, 1962, that our friends, Bob and Margaret Brown, phoned to say they were house hunting and had heard that an old Manor House in the New Forest was for sale. They wondered if we would like to go and see it. Margaret said the particulars of the sale were not yet printed but, if we liked, a caretaker living a caravan on the grounds would give us the key and we could look around at our leisure. It was a beautiful sunny afternoon when we viewed it and nothing was further from our minds than the traditional ghost.

As we drove through the double iron gates over the gravel sweep of drive to the rear entrance the old brick house with its enormous chimney stacks was bathed in sunshine which almost made us ignore the sad state of repair the house and garden were in. We obtained the key from the caretaker and wandered around looking first at the old chapel with its stone mullioned windows. It was delightfully mellowed with age and part of it had been converted into a dwelling house. We felt that much would have to be done to make it habitable, so we returned to the house. Entering the hall with its old oak staircase we looked up to a spacious landing above, with beautiful carved oak paneled walls and double, half-glazed doors leading to a Minstrels Gallery which overlooked the dining hall. We saw that the whole house was in a rather bad state of repair and, in spite of the sun outside, it felt cold and damp.

We wandered from room to room but when they decided to inspect the second floor I felt I had seen enough and said I would wait for them in the sun which streamed in through the leaded window on the landing. I seated myself on the window sill and began to day dream about the families who had occupied this old house through the long centuries. Had they been happy? I felt not all of them had been, because as I waited I seemed to be overcome with a feeling of fear and sadness. Then as I looked toward the doors which led to the Minstrels Gallery I was amazed to see, coming through them, a shadowy figure in a drab yellow cloak. There seemed more cloak than figure. The small cape piece nearly covered a pair of hands which were clasped in anguish or prayer. The hands clasped and unclasped as the apparition came towards me. I felt no fear, only an intense sorrow. And I swear I heard a gentle sigh as the figure passed me and drifted to the end of the landing. From there it returned to go down the stairs, seeming to disappear through a window facing the chapel.

When my friends returned from the floor above I was still sitting on the window seat and feeling rather faint. Telling them I felt a little tired we returned to the car and I was more than thankful to get out of the house. On our way home I told them of my strange experience and asked if they thought the house had a ghost.

"Oh, yes," Bob said, "all these old manor houses have one. It is said of this one that they never can keep the hall window closed — it's always found open."

Some weeks later Bob sent me catalogue of the property which now was being offered for sale by auction. Looking through it I was interested to find the following historic facts, of which I had known nothing when we visited the house.

"Moyles Court in the Parish of Ellingham is known to have been held by Cola the Huntsman. After passing through various hands it became the property of the Lisle family, and it was during this time that the best known historical incident linked with the house took place. This was the trial and execution of Dame Lisle in 1685 when she was charged with high treason for giving shelter at Moyles Court for the night to two fugitives from the battle of Sedgemoor, the Rev. John Hicks, a dissenting minister, and Richard Nelthorpe, a London lawyer. Lady Lisle had Puritan sympathies and frequently had given shelter to Hicks previously when he was in trouble for preaching. It seems certain that she was unaware of the charge of high treason against the fugitives and under the existing law could not therefore be held guilty of treason herself, particularly as neither Hicks nor herself had at that time been tried and convicted.

"But the ruthless Judge Jeffreys would brook no delay and was determined to destroy the old lady (whose dead husband had been one of the judges who sent Charles I to the block). The travesty of a trial held in the Grand Hall of Winchester Castle and Alice Lisle was allowed no lawyer for defence. The reluctant jury were finally coerced by Jeffreys into returning a verdict of guilty, and next morning he pronounced that she should be burned alive that very afternoon.

"The Cathedral clergy remonstrated with Jeffreys, who finally agreed to a five-day postponement. Many influential persons pleaded with the king to spare her life but he would not go beyond substituting beheading in place of burning and Lady Lisle met her death with great courage, a stone at Winchester marking the spot."

Were the praying hands I saw those of Lady Lisle?

THE YORKSHIRE MUSEUM GHOST
Susy Smith

**The old man in out-moded clothes looked and acted queer —
and his vanishing at a touch gave definite proof that he was not
a solid sort of character.**

"It's incredible," said the doctor. "Without a doubt that book was taken
from the shelf by something that is not of this world."

The doctor referred to a volume entitled *Antiquities and
Curiosities of the Church*, edited and published by William Andrews in
1896. One would expect to find this kind of book lying sedately on a
library shelf, probably never disturbed by man nor ghost. Yet in the
Yorkshire Museum in Museum St., York, England, for a period of
several months in the autumn of 1953, this particular book took
monthly flights from its shelf to the floor.

It all started when the ghost of a little old gentleman in
Edwardian dress appeared to George Leonard Jonas, caretaker of the
museum.

On Sunday, 20 September, 1953, an evangelical meeting was
held in the museum. Mr. Jonas and his wife were on duty. Since they
did not live at the museum they were not usually there on Sunday
evenings, so the ghost may have been wandering about the museum
undiscovered for years. But on this particular night, after the meeting,
Mr. Jonas locked the front door and with Mrs. Jonas went into the
kitchen, in the basement. From there they both heard footsteps in the
museum above them, so Mr. Jonas went back upstairs to investigate.
Here is his own account of what he saw, as told to Brian Lumley of the
Yorkshire Evening Press:

"I told her it must be Mr. Willmott, Keeper of the Museum,
going to his office," Mr. Jonas said. "I went upstairs to tell him we were
ready to leave. I fully expected to see him, but when I was halfway up
the stairs I saw an elderly man crossing from Mr. Willmott's office into
another room. I thought he was an odd looking chap because he was
wearing a frock-coat, drain-pipe trousers and had fluffy side-whiskers.
He had very little hair and walked with a slight stoop.

"I decided he must be an eccentric professor. As I neared the
top of the stairs, he seemed to change his mind, turn, and walk back

into the office. When I got to the door, he seemed to change his mind again and turned quickly to come out.

"I stood on one side to let him pass and said, excuse me, sir, are you looking for Mr. Willmott? He did not answer but just shuffled past me and began to go down the stairs toward the library.

"Being only a few feet from him, I saw his face clearly and could pick him out from a photograph any time. He looked agitated, had a frown on his face, and kept muttering: 'I must find it; I must find it.'

"It was queer, but I did not think about ghosts for one minute. He looked just as real as you or me. But I did not want him roaming around so late at night, and anyway I wanted to lock up and catch my bus.

"As I followed him down the stairs, I noticed that he was wearing what seemed to be elastic-sided boots, and I remembered thinking how old-fashioned the big black buttons looked on the back of his coat.

"Still muttering, he went into the library. It was in darkness and I switched on the lights as I followed him in a few yards behind. He was standing between two tall book racks pulling first one book and then another from one of the shelves. He seemed anxious to find something.

"I thought to myself, this has gone far enough. So, thinking he was deaf, I stretched my right hand out to touch him on the shoulder. But as my hand drew near his coat he vanished, and the book he had been holding dropped to the floor."

The book he dropped was entitled *Antiquities and Curiosities of the Church* and this is the first instance of its unseemly activity.

But not the last.

Mr. Jonas had not been well and this sort of thing was not likely to make him better. He demanded corroborating witnesses to his experience and Mr. Willmott, the Keeper of the Museum, agreed to keep watch with him. As the series of evangelical meetings continued, Willmott stayed with Jonas each Sunday after that for the next three weeks. But nothing happened.

Then on the evening of Sunday, 18 October, 1953, shortly after Willmott had left, George Jonas saw the apparition again. It came down the stairs from the first floor, crossed the hall, and passed through the closed library door. The time was 7:40 p.m. The book was not disturbed this time. But Mr. Jonas was.

Since the ghost seemed to have an aversion for Mr. Willmott another friend, Walter French, was asked to keep watch with Jonas, and on the night of 15 November their vigil was rewarded.

In the library, as they walked among the book stacks, they both heard pages of a book being turned. Then they both heard a thud. When they reached the centre aisle they discovered this same book, which the ghost had been so eager to find, lying on the floor. Its pages were still in motion. Again it was 7:40 p.m., but this time the ghost himself was not visible.

By now George Jonas was considerably upset. He went to his doctor with his story, fully expecting to be looked at queerly. And he was. His doctor did not admit that his patient could have seen a ghost. And to help prove that he had not the doctor agreed to go to the library with Jonas on the next likely Sunday night.

The pattern for the ghostly visitations appeared to be every fourth Sunday at 7:40 p.m. So on the night of 13 December the doctor, a lawyer and several other persons stationed themselves in the Museum library to wait for the ghost.

As the seven persons present could not all watch the book in question, they scattered throughout the room. They had investigated the book where it lay on its shelf and ascertained that it was not rigged in any way for a trick.

Among the assembled seven was James Lawrence Jonas, George Jonas's older brother, who was an engine-driver by profession. James had scoffed at his brother and said he feared he was going daft. But on this occasion it was James Jonas who saw *Antiquities and Curiosities* in actual flight. He said it seemed to come out its full width from the shelf before it started to fall.

"It didn't seem to fall at the same speed books usually fall," James Jonas reported afterwards.

As he saw the book move he called out and everyone rushed to the spot to find the book lying on the floor, its pages turning. A new examination of the shelf was made. This time the doctor used a flashlight, but there were no strings or threads or wires to be found.

"I wouldn't have acted for anybody who told me a story like this," the lawyer stated, "but we have the proof of our own eyes."

The doctor admitted that just before the book moved his legs, from the knees to his feet suddenly had felt unusually cold, and that immediately after the book fell his legs returned to normal.

"Maybe somebody will believe me now," George Jonas murmured.

By 10 January, 1954, the York Museum Ghost was famous throughout England because of the numerous newspaper stories written about it. However, on the date of the ghost's next anticipated visit. George Jonas was ill and off duty. Willmott watched in the library alone but apparently his presence did not inspire ghostly activity and the book remained quietly on its shelf.

The Society for Psychical Research asked permission to investigate the case and on 7 February, 1954, a large crowd awaited the ghost. Present were Eric J. Dingwall and Trevor H. Hall, investigators for the S.P.R., who later published a report on this case in the book *Four Modern Ghosts*, published by Gerald Duckworth & Co. Ltd., London, 1958.

On this occasion the little Edwardian ghost did not appear. The book remained unmoved. James Jonas seemed to think he had seen the fingers and thumb of a disembodied white hand feeling its way down the bookshelf. But Jonas was not likely to stand his ground on a statement as vague as that in the presence of scientific investigation and he soon retreated to the opinion that, "It might have been a trick of the light."

Dingwall and Hall eventually concluded that Jonas obviously had seen a ghost — but that it was an illusion formed by his own mind. They believed that the book could have been pulled from the shelf by a string secreted in the puller's hand. And so it could have, of course. But investigators never found such a string.

And so the ghost of the Edwardian gentleman lived up to the tradition of ghosts everywhere — it drifted away, fading as quietly as the fluttering leaves of a book on a dusty museum floor.

TWO POLTERGEISTS FROM PECKHAM
Jeffery Liss

One was a firebug; the other a destroyer, a crasher and a banger. The big question is: Will they return?

Of the many strange poltergeists that have made their appearance over the years, two of the strangest have been those in the Peckham district of London.

In 1963 the family of Graham Stringer approached the Easter season with fear and foreboding, for in four of the previous five years mysterious fires had broken out shortly before Easter in their home on Trafalgar Avenue in Peckham.

Usually these fires were preceded by the appearance of a "ghost" — a greyish, fluorescent column of vibrating light about as tall as a man.

The fires and the "ghost" first appeared in 1958, a month before Easter, when Stringer came downstairs to discover a chair and the baby's toys on fire. On Good Friday he smelled smoke a few seconds after he had left a room and rushed back to find a hole burned, as though with a blowtorch, through the centre of a pile of the baby's clothes.

"Yet," Stringer said, "a pair of nylons on the bottom of the pile was untouched — and you know how flammable they are."

The second year, in 1959, when a pair of shoes was snatched from his hands, Stringer called in experts from the College of Psychic Science. Although their investigation was inconclusive, they did identify the phenomenon as a poltergeist.

Stringer's wife, Vera, 31, disclosed that she had experienced similar poltergeist manifestations in her home before she was married. Stringer had learned his wife was psychic during their honeymoon, "when our bed seemed to be floating in the air."

In 1960 some clothes burned up in 30 seconds, though an ordinary flame would have taken minutes longer.

Clocks have moved on the mantelpiece, and other things have travelled from room to room.

Stringer, a freelance photographer, once was working in his

dark-room when he was surrounded by a grey, fluorescent cloud. "The room lit up," he said. "There was Larry vibrating at my side."

"Larry," of course, is the ghost. Stringer explained to Robert Musel of United Press International that he and his wife had to give the ghost a name because their four-year-old son, Steven, kept pointing to the column of vibrating light and asking, "What's that, Mummy?"

Afterwards, according to Stringer, the child often would say, "There's Larry," even at times when his parents saw nothing.

The ghostly pyromaniac did not appear in 1961. Stringer speculates that it was absent because "we had a Catholic priest read the rite of exorcism."

In 1962, however, Larry returned with his usual bag of tricks plus some new ones. Early in April Mrs. Stringer had to call firemen to quench the flames that had erupted spontaneously in her living room furniture. The firemen, of course, were unable to discover the cause of the blaze. And later that day they had to be called again.

As a result of all the heated activity during that day, the Stringers also lost their carpet and their son's bed.

The Stringers then decided to call in a medium. On 21 April, 1962, the *London Daily Herald* reported that the medium had revealed that the poltergeist was Mrs. Stringer's brother, Charles. Charles had died from burns 20 years earlier at the age of 18 months.

Whether the poltergeist was Larry or Charles, he has not returned. In both 1963 and 1964 Easter came and went peacefully; no incidents disturbed the tranquility of the Stringer household.

Perhaps now some insurance company will insure the Stringers' furniture.

During the period when Larry was visiting the Stringers, a second Peckham poltergeist made its appearance. It was reported at 1:30 a.m. on 10 October, 1960, by 39-year-old Harold Titus, who trooped into the Carter-Street police station with his wife and four children.

"Spirits have driven us out of our home," Titus said.

A police spokesman reported that "the whole family was shaking with terror and the oldest boy was nearly hysterical." The family included Titus, his wife Agnes, Norman, 14, Brian, 13, June, 10, and Geoffrey nine.

After trying to calm the family, police sent a constable to inspect the Titus' ground floor flat in Furley House. Although all seemed quiet, the family refused to return. Titus decided instead to stay with friends. He also announced his intention to see his priest and housing officials.

The family had moved into flat at the beginning of August, shortly after Titus became interested in spiritualism and attended his first séances.

On Saturday, 9 October, as Titus explained to reporter Hugh Moran "Two friends came to the house and we held a seance of our own. Norman was not present, but last night this whole incident seemed to revolve around him.

"My wife and I woke up with him screaming. There seemed to be a terrible banging and thumping going on. Then June woke up and began screaming too, and the noise of banging and crashing seemed to be all around us.

"Even after I'd got Norman up he seemed to be in some sort of trance and kept holding his head. I decided then that we had to leave that house, and we put coats over our night clothes and left by car."

Late that same day, 10 October, Moran returned to the flat with Mr. and Mrs. Titus. Norman, who still seemed terror-stricken, refused to return. Trembling he said, "I could never go back there. There's something evil in that house." The three younger children also were reluctant to return.

In Norman's bedroom Moran found a heavy mirror — three feet by two feet — lying face down on the floor. Norman had said, "It just seemed to leap off the wall and crash to the floor."

A smashed bedroom clock and a shattered lamp lay on the floor. The glass from the lamp's bulb was scattered over Norman's bed and the plastic lampshade was ripped to shreds. The bedclothes were scattered. The room was in disorder.

That same afternoon, when the flat was vacant, callers reported noises coming from within, but from the outside it was impossible to tell their origin.

Two days later, though, Titus' problem was solved, or, rather, it was exorcised.

Stuart Lawson, a medium and visiting minister at the Camberwell Spiritualist Centre, was called in. With the flat completely dark except for a solitary blue light, Lawson and an assistant went from room to room trying to make contact with the "ghost" — it is believed a man was murdered in one of the houses which stood on the site before the Nazi blitz.

Then Lawson spoke briefly to Norman and left the flat, saying there would be no further trouble. There wasn't. The next day Titus said, "We have had our first peaceful night's sleep for several days. The trouble is over now."

But the case is not closed. The police want to learn more about the murdered man and the circumstances of his death.

A man of the 1960's who wants quiet.
Mr. Dale shares his ancient house with
noisy characters of the 1500's.

MR. DALE KEEPS GHOSTS

Athalstan Jones

Of all of England's numerous haunted houses and recognized ghosts Histon's haunted house surely is the most amazing.

Histon is a small, picturesque village a few miles from Cambridge. It has a single main street flanked on either side by houses. At the far end of this street stands the old church and the church hall which often is used as a social centre. However, the true community centre of this little place is a venerable old inn called The Boot.

Mr. and Mrs. Muncy, who own and run The Boot, are what one may call professional innkeepers. Night after night they listen to their clients' tirades against the English weather, the government and anything else that happens to be in the air. Like all good innkeepers they take everything they hear with a pinch of salt. However, sometimes even the most experienced innkeepers blink with astonishment.

A few months ago Mr. and Mrs. Muncy stood behind their bar on an evening when business was not brisk. Therefore, when Mr. Dale entered and drew near the bar both Mr. Muncy and his wife noticed that he looked white and shaken. It was apparent he was not intoxicated, for his walk and gestures were those of a sober man. Indeed, Mr. and Mrs. Muncy would have been surprised if Mr. Dale had been drunk. Although he only recently had taken up residence in Old House, a 16th-Century dwelling a mile from Histon, it already was well known in the village that he was almost a teetotaler.

In a tired voice Mr. Dale ordered a tankard of beer and, while her husband was filling the tankard, Mrs. Muncy enquired after her customer's health.

"Are you feeling well?" she asked. "You don't seem your normal self tonight."

Mr. Dale, leaning against the bar, replied, "The fact is, I've just received an awful shock!"

Mrs. Muncy placed her band gently on Mr. Dale's shoulder. "You mean you've received bad news?"

After drinking deeply from the tankard of beer the innkeeper had prepared, Mr. Dale answered, "No. You can believe it or not, but I've just seen a ghost!

"It's quite true," Mr. Dale assured them. "About an hour ago I was up at the Old House. Suddenly I decided to go into the Blue Room. As I opened the door I got the impression there was someone else present. Looking quickly around I was surprised to find the place empty. Going over to the oak-panelled fireplace, I sat myself in a chair beside the hearth. I closed my eyes for a few seconds and when I opened them I saw the figure of a tall cavalier standing a few feet away from me."

"Did you see him in black an white?" Mrs. Muncy asked.

Mr. Dale replied, "No, I saw him in full colour and he looked as real as we three. The sight of him was so unexpected it made my flesh creep. I almost froze in the chair with shock."

"You say this ghost was dressed as a cavalier?" Mr. Muncy asked. "I heard you found a cavalier's hat somewhere in the Old House just after you moved in."

"Yes, we did," Mr. Dale answered. "Shortly after we moved in the house my wife and I decided to do some renovating. While we were stripping the old paper from the walls of the Blue Room we came across a priest's hole. Looking inside the secret hideout we found an old cavalier's hat, but I can't imagine how you got to know about it."

"As a matter of fact," said Mrs. Muncy, "we know from one of the cleaners."

Mr. Muncy pulled himself a pint of ale. "You'll never keep a secret in Histon; but I'll tell you this, Mr. Dale. No servant will stay the night in Old House! The place has a reputation for being haunted. It's said many a young lass has been scared out of her wits while working there. Mind you, it may be simple superstition, because no one actually has seen anything."

"Well, I've just seen something," Mr. Dale answered.

"Has anyone else in the family seen this cavalier?" Mr. Muncy asked.

Mr. Dale answered, "Neville, my teenage son, is still away at university, and my wife hasn't mentioned seeing anything unusual."

Mr. Dale picked up his tankard and drained it dry. His chat with the innkeeper and his wife seemed to pull him together for, as he passed out of the door into the village street, he said, "Blimey! Who the devil would have thought I'd have bought a haunted house?"

On leaving The Boot Mr. Dale made his way back to Old House. By the time the evening dinner had progressed to dessert Mr. Dale suddenly plonked his spoon down and asked his wife, "Darling, do you believe in ghosts?"

"Yes, I do!" she replied. "This house we're in is haunted!"

Mr. Dale sat bolt upright, "You mean you've seen something?"

She nodded, "On several occasions I've seen the apparition of a cavalier."

Her husband placed his hand on his forehead and said, "Great Scott! I've just seen him myself! I didn't know how to tell you. I was afraid you'd think I was going crackers!"

His wife smiled nervously, "I kept quiet for the same reason." Then she told him this story:

"One morning a few weeks ago I decided to dust the Blue Room. It was very quiet. I was alone in the house. After a while I went and stood in front of the fireplace. Though the fire was burning quite well I suddenly began to feel cold. Thinking that I had left the door open, I turned around. It was then I saw the apparition of a man dressed in the costume of an English cavalier. I did not feel the least afraid. The cavalier looked kindly, handsome, and charming. He did not move but remained standing there smiling at me. Then he leaned nonchalantly toward the wall and, all at once, evaporated into thin air. I hurried out of the room and did not venture back during the remainder of the day."

Mr. Dale asked, "And have you seen him since?"

His wife said, "Yes, dear, I've seen him on a number of occasions."

"And you aren't frightened?" His voice sounded concerned.

"Of course not," she reassured him. "He's no ordinary ghost, dear. He's a gentleman."

Though Mr. and Mrs. Dale were perturbed about the events in their home they decided against writing about the affair to their son, Neville. It is not easy to tell a sophisticated young man that you are seeing ghosts. If Neville had to know he would have to learn from direct experience.

So, when young Neville Dale returned home for summer vacation he arrived without any foreknowledge of the ghostly cavalier. However, he had not been home long when one evening, while he was alone in his bedroom, he suddenly heard the sound of clashing steel. The noise was subdued at first but increased in volume. As he stood listening it became apparent the sounds were coming from the courtyard beneath his window. Just as he was about to look out of the window he was amazed to be confronted by the spectral figure of a cavalier.

After some silent debate with himself Neville decided to tell his mother and father about the incident. He was surprised to find they did not laugh at him. When he had finished the story his parents told him they, too, had seen the cavalier.

"If you had told me before I saw him myself, I may have laughed out loud," he told them.

Mr. Dale placed his hand on the young man's shoulder and said, "But you don't feel like laughing now, do you?"

A little later in the summer, before Neville Dale returned to his university, a new ghost appeared at Old House. This one seemed to be a Roundhead.

Mrs. Dale was the first to see the new arrival. One morning as she was coming out of the Blue Room she was jolted to see a Cromwellian soldier march through the front door into the hall. The blood froze in her veins. Never before had she seen such a demoniac countenance. Later she described him as of medium height and rather stocky build. His uniform was resplendant. His face was twisted into a terrible smile, giving him the expression of a snarling beast. His eyes were cold and glittering. Walking right past her the spectre passed into the Blue Room to stand beside the priest's hole. After remaining there for a short period he dematerialized. Mrs. Dale was almost fainting with terror.

After this event she never entered the Blue Room without peeping around the door. Despite this precaution she began to see the soldier frequently and whenever she saw him she felt sick. In her own words, "He looked like the embodiment of evil!"

During the first winter the Dales spent in Old House the eerie activity increased. Groups of Cromwellian soldiers began arriving and departing with startling rapidity. Strange, unidentifiable noises were heard in the nights. It had become a full-scale haunting.

One evening while Mr. and Mrs. Dale were sitting together in their lounge they watched the door, which was hinged to open inwards, open outwards. This was patently impossible and after they recovered from their shock they went over to the door, which by now mysteriously had closed itself. They were surprised to find that neither the stanchions nor hinges had suffered any harm. The door had opened the wrong way and remained intact! Both Mr. and Mrs. Dale are prepared to swear that this is so.

Although Histon is a small country place horses are not common. Few places in the British Isles have escaped the motorcar. You therefore can imagine the Dale's surprise when, one evening, they heard a troop of horses thunder into the courtyard outside their house. Rushing to the window, they peered into the gloom. But the courtyard was empty! Whoever or whatever "unearthly" company they had heard arrive remained invisible.

Later Mr. Dale told a reporter, "We just stood there, side by side, staring at nothing. It was weird!"

This event so unnerved the couple that they decided to call in a psychic research investigator. They chose Mr. Anthony Cornell who fortunately lived close by. Mr. Cornell is an elected council member of the British Society for Psychical Research whose headquarters are at Adam and Eve Mews, London.

Ghost hunting is not an easy job. It calls for a thorough grounding in both normal and abnormal psychology. The principles of physics, chemistry, photography and sleight of hand must all be known to the researcher. He must be free from superstition and a good judge of human nature. Perhaps most important of all, he must be as eager to disprove as he is to prove the existence of the supranormal; and wherever he encounters charlatanism he must be prepared to denounce it.

At his first interview Mr. Cornell asked Mr. and Mrs. Dale the type of questions one would expect a psychiatrist to ask. A trained interviewer, he looks for deeply suppressed mental aberrations. However, Anthony Cornell soon satisfied himself that both Mr. and Mrs. Dale are normal.

The researcher next brought a battery of costly instruments to Old House — supersonic detectors for recording ultrasonic sounds outside the range of human awareness, infra-red cameras, and an especially designed ghost camera with a shutter that can be triggered by the ghost itself. The Society for Psychical Research has built up an impressive collection of ghost photographs by using such cameras.

After this equipment had been installed in Old House Mr. and Mrs. Dale and Mr. Cornell retired into the Blue Room. While they sat before the fire Mr. Cornell attempted to explain the laws of association.

"It often happens," he said, "when we find ourselves faced with a unique experience we trigger off a train of associated ideas. It could be that when you found the cavalier's hat in the priest's hole this law of association was set in motion in your minds at an unconscious level."

Mrs. Dale pointed out that this theory, while impressive, did not do justice to all the facts. Leaning back in her armchair she related a psychic experience which she had had a few months previously. As it did not appear to be related to the major haunting she had not previously spoken about it, she said.

"I was standing in the kitchen beside the refrigerator. Suddenly I saw an apparition of half a black cat. It was so unexpected that it made my stomach turn over.

A few weeks later something went wrong with the refrigerator and I called in an electrician to service it. While he was fiddling around with his tools he told me, in an off-hand manner, that he once had serviced this same fridge in the past.

'Is that so?' I asked him.

The electrician nodded and quite startled me by adding, 'That was when the cat was cut in half!'

'What cat?' I asked him.

He answered, 'The last owners kept a black cat as a pet. One day it was nosing around the fridge when the lady of the house slammed the door shut. Half the creature's body was in the fridge at the time. The result was that it was severed almost in half. It suffered a great deal of pain but was quickly put out of its misery when the vet arrived.'"

The researcher was very interested in this cat episode. He told the Dales this placed a completely new complexion on the affair.

He said, "Sometimes the barrier between the physical and non-physical worlds breaks down. When this occurs we are able to see what is going on on the other side. However, this does not really apply in this case for, if what you say is true, the same sequence of phenomena occurs over and over.

Repeat performances of psychic phenomena usually occur in places where acts of violence have taken place. There is a theory that during acts of violence great waves of hysteria are released. This hysteria is said to photograph the actual event just as a film captures a scene of action."

"Then," Mr. Dale asked, "what we have witnessed is a replay of actual occurrences?"

The researcher nodded. "It could be that a cavalier once hid in the priest's hole only to be found and murdered by a troop of Roundheads. Of course, all this is only theory. It may or may not be true."

As he spoke the room went suddenly cold and he said, "I feel there is a presence in this room although I cannot be sure."

After further talk Mr. Dale and wife retired, leaving the researcher to spend the night in the darkened old house in Histon.

His vigil was uneventful. Next morning, on checking his instruments, he found nothing unusual had been recorded.

After breakfast Anthony Cornell gathered up his equipment and stowed it in the boot of his automobile. Bidding farewell to his host and hostess, he returned home to write an official report for the Society for Psychical Research. The gist of this report is as follows: "A period of research has not been able to prove beyond all doubt that the Old House at Histon was the subject of a haunting."

Since that time the phenomena at Old House have been less frequent. However, according to Mr. and Mrs. Dale the place still is haunted. But, of course, nothing is explained.

Are the ghosts simply a projection from some unconscious mind? Or is some ghastly deed, once done in Old House at Histon in the dark long ago, continually reenacted there?

THE TIME WE FILMED THE
STATELY GHOSTS OF ENGLAND
Intrepid Tom Corbett and doughty Margaret Rutherford are not at all Longleat's anti-television shades.

Tom Corbett

Longleat is among the largest and finest of England's Elizabethan mansions. It was built in Wiltshire and completed in 1580 during the reign of the first Elizabeth. Its hundreds of beautiful rooms and its 1000 acres of well-kept grounds are haunted by history, legend, tragedy, and by quite active ghosts — as I found out to my discomfiture.

Many years ago, when the present Marquess of Bath inherited the estate he undertook to alter the garden arrangements. During this work one of the gardeners unearthed a skull, subsequently discovered to have been buried in the cemetery of an ancient priory which once had occupied the site. The skull was handed around among those on the immediate grounds, including Lord Valentine Thynne who, being young and thoughtless, put the skull atop his own head and rode with it around the estate. Suffice it to say that five persons, all in excellent health at the time they handled the skull on that morning, required medical treatment for one thing or another before the day had ended. Lord Bath, noting the coincidence of events, determined not to take further chance and ordered the skull reinterred in consecrated ground — at the local church.

It was with full cognizance of this predilection of Longleat's spirits not to be taken lightly that I first visited the manor in 1961, by invitation from Lord Christopher Thynne, the Marquess' second son. I went expressly to meet the family ghosts. I was accompanied there by a journalist, Diana Norman, and a photographer, Helen Simpson.

From the moment we entered Longleat I became dissociated. I was not conscious of anything that transpired until, at 3 a.m. Lord Christopher suggested that we leave and return to Job's Hill, the house where the Marquess of Bath lives, about four and a half miles distant.

The next morning Diana Norman told me, "It was wonderful — you were great!" She then related how I had gone through the house describing seven invisible "tenants" and incidents related to them.

The matter of being unable to remember any of the night's incidents continued to bother me as I drove back to London alone the next afternoon. I had woken that Sunday morning feeling ill and I continued to feel that my spirit somehow remained partially outside my body. I had to stop six times along the 103-mile route, almost at the point of being unable to drive.

Although Diana Norman, the photographer, and I had arranged to meet on the next Monday or Tuesday for lunch in Fleet Street, it actually was 10 days before any one of us got around to telephoning the others — and for the peculiar and mutual reason that our throats were too sore! We suffered, independently, from what my doctor described as a condition almost like laceration of the throat. It was as if we each had swallowed a sharp bone or two. None of us could account for this until Diana recalled that we all had been together in Longleat's "haunted corridor" where, in the 1730's, Viscount Weymouth, an ancestor of the Marquess of Bath, was reputed to have strangled his wife's lover. Perhaps our respective throat conditions were related or sympathetic to the tragic strangulation!

Sometime after this visit I was invited to write an autobiography, which I refused to do because I felt that the publishers perhaps wanted a catalogue of names, but they urged that it was because I had been visiting some of the haunted houses and if I liked to write my experiences these would be of interest. Therefore, having got on very well with Diana Norman on our first visit, I asked her if she would like to make other visits and collaborate with me on a book involving some of the haunted houses of England. This she readily agreed to do and subsequently a book was published, under her name, on three of the principal houses.*

Our next experience of Longleat was when we went back there in the spring of 1964 to make a film** with my dear friend, Margaret Rutherford, the well-known, well-loved actress. Some American television people, together with a technical crew from BBC, arrived on location a couple of days before we did and this was the beginning of some very strange happenings.

Before the actual filming began the sound technician, at the request of Frank DeFellita, the producer, set about making a tape recording of the chiming of the fine old clock in the Great Hall. However, with everything set up and in readiness to record the strikes for the first time in 25 years the clock did not chime a note. Curiously enough the several other chiming clocks in the house faithfully tolled the hour.

Legend has it that when a Longleat clock doesn't chime the "ghosts are walking." I told Frank DeFelitta that the spirits wanted him to know they were there and that he and his men would not have an easy time with them. I suggested that he ask permission of the spirits to work with them but, unfortunately as it later proved, he only laughed.

I felt from the start that the "spirits" really did not mean to hurt anyone and as things turned out, this seemed to be the case, especially during the first few days' happenings which involved cars.

Inexplicably Diana Norman's petrol tank, to which she alone held the key and which she had filled on two consecutive evenings was found empty the following mornings. This happened twice only, neither before nor since. It seemed impossible, as she did have the only key to the tank's lock, but it was inconveniently true.

Then on the second day, I believe it was, my car "threw" a wheel and lost its brakes simultaneously while I was driving on Longleat's grounds. The car finally rolled to a stop several feet from an imposing cliff!

Back at the house, during the first day of attempted filming a securely anchored floodlamp weighing several hundred pounds, toppled from its tripod. It skittered about 15 feet along the haunted corridor, vaulted a bannister and hurtled 40 feet down, to crash into hundreds of pieces in the Great Hall, where it missed a technician, Jeff Smith, by only a few feet. The lamp had been standing safely anchored on its tripod for a number of hours, from morning into the afternoon, before its precipitous journey.

The next day the sound man had an accident with his car. This was on the same day I so narrowly missed disaster myself. As Dudley Plummer rounded a curve on his way from the village inn, where we were all staying, to Longleat he collided head-on with a motorcyclist. His car was a total write-off. However, when the ambulance men, who quickly arrived, pulled the motorcyclist from under the demolished car they found he was unhurt — in fact, I heard he had not so much as a bruise!

Two friends of the producer, Mr. and Mrs. Chancer, of New York, were with us during the filming. One evening when they did not have their car I offered to give them a lift to the motel. As I was seeing them into the car Mrs. Chancer, who had got into the back seat, pulled her door shut catching my hand in the jamb. The three of us heard the bones of my hand crack and it was cut and bleeding. I removed a ring from the little finger of my left hand because of the swelling and blood. I massaged my hand for a few seconds and then drove on into the village. When we reached the motel 10 minutes later, there was not a break in the flesh, no sign of blood, and no longer any pain whatever. On reflection I can only describe this as instant healing.

At one point during the filming the sound technician asked that I walk about and describe my feelings concerning the spirits so that it might be recorded on his tape. As I began to do this he stopped me saying that the microphone had gone dead. He tested it and found it in good order, but it failed to function when I began my descriptions again.

The first two days' filming proved completely abortive. Although we had used the same cameras through two previous weeks' filming at others of England's Stately Houses the film turned out muddy and it was decided nothing could be done with it. This despite "test strips" at the end of each film which developed properly. A completely different set of cameras was used on the third day with similarly bad results, although all cameras had been inspected by technicians in London and pronounced in good order. The camera crew were all experienced BBC men and the head cameraman remarked that nothing like this ever had occurred during his 20 years' of experience.

Another day's film was sent up to London, carefully packed and labelled NBC. But it did not reach its destination on schedule. However, true to my feeling that the ghosts meant no lasting harm, the film turned up a bit later.

Mr. DeFellita decided he ought to set up a camera designed for "time lapse" photography at one end of the haunted corridor with the hope that it might capture an entity on film. Accordingly, the camera was turned on to shoot one picture every four seconds throughout the night and we all left, locking Longleat behind us. The next morning, after the Marquess reopened the house, the technician found the camera turned off and unplugged. Inspection of the film counter told him that this had been done within minutes after we left. Yet no one had remained in or entered the mansion.

The next night the infrared camera was again set up and two men left on duty. I felt that, being the psychic or sensitive involved in the venture, I ought to give them moral support. Consequently I visited them about 12:30. However, from the time of my arrival on the scene until I left them the camera was out of order. No reason for this could be found; they could discover no malfunction in the camera — it just didn't work.

Nevertheless, on this night they did film "something." A light came out of one door into the haunted corridor, moved around, traversed 10 yards and finally disappeared into another door on the same side of the corridor. Actually this light appeared on the film, from no known source, for the period of almost one-half hour at the outset. However, I understand that the time of its appearance dwindled and finally was much less than this — after the transitory nature of ghosts.

The final success of the filming may be due to the fact that the producer, Mr. DeFellita, reconsidered the necessity of asking permission of the ghosts of Longleat to make the film. This he did one early morning, making a special trip out to the house and up to the haunted corridor to do so. When he returned from this errand I knew it would now be "all right".

Two incidents occurred which really had nothing to do with the filming, but only to do with the ghosts "making themselves known".

The first involved the chief cameraman who went into an old nursery on the third floor in search of a prop. He emerged moments later in what may be called extreme shock. He told us that the instant he stepped into the room his hearing ceased — he entered an "awful quiet" — and he felt "something oppressive and cloying" around him. He said he felt his hair stand up and thought he surely would have suffocated if he had not been able to pull himself away! The man freely admitted his terror, and yet he has been decorated for valorous service in two wars.

The other incident concerned two uninvited young journalists who seemed to have decided we were cranks. At one stage when they had been under our feet all day and we all were very anxious because of our failures with the filming I suggested that they go up to the Bishop Ken library where they could see two pictures painted by Adolf Hitler and one by Winston Churchill, as well as a beautiful collection of books. They asked permission of the Marquess of Bath, who gave them the key, and went on up to the third floor.

As they reached the library the one who carried the key was talking to his colleague. Receiving no reply he asked, "Why don't you answer me?"

His friend said, "What can I answer? You haven't spoken."

They found the library fascinating, to use their own expression, and on leaving the room locked the door securely as they had been instructed to do. This is a part of the house to which the public is not admitted. They walked along the haunted corridor but said they had gone only about 20 feet when they both heard a key being turned in the door. They were startled and one shouted, "I have got the key." Nevertheless they hurriedly retraced their steps and saw, to their amazement, the handle being turned. They did not investigate this occurrence, knowing they had just locked an empty room and being unable to see anyone to turn a door handle in the corridor. I can only say they did not seem so full of their own importance afterwards.

On the fourth day Miss Rutherford said to me, "Tom, are you sure 'they' want us here? Considering that everything seems to have gone wrong since we arrived?"

Through my stubborn nature I said, "We must go through with this. Whether 'they' want us or not they must do their strongest to put us off."

The result those of you who saw the television show know. You even saw the ghostly light that wandered around the haunted gallery. I have no doubt this was a partial manifestation and, of course, what started out as a half-hour of usable footage dwindled to 11 minutes by the time the film was on television. Perhaps by now it has completely disappeared. But if you saw it you never again can say you have not seen a ghost.

°*The Stately Ghosts of England*, Frederick Muller, Ltd. Copyright Tom Corbett and Diana Norman, 1963.
°°*The Stately Ghosts of England* appeared on NBC television network on 25 January, 1965, in America.

STUDY OF THREE ENGLISH GHOSTS
The Reverend Frederick Guy Harrison

Where do you draw the line between an English ghost in tweeds and trilby — and a poltergeist.

About 15 miles due west of the ancient city of York slumbers the little township of Boston Spa. The place is noted in Yorkshire and throughout the whole north of England for its medicinal waters. Hundreds of people "take the cure" there every season, thereby considerably swelling the town's normal population of about 2500.

In March, 1965, the *Sunday Express* put Boston Spa into the news by publishing a story about a ghost whom someone had nicknamed "Charlie". He had been making life difficult for a succession of tenants in Boston Spa house.

Before the autumn of 1962 the house had been, for 30 years, continuously occupied by a single family — the Coopers. They left and the Fishers moved in during November. They remained a year but declared when they moved that they were thankful beyond words to be getting away from a long series of frightening experiences. A young couple followed but could not be induced to stay long enough to unpack their gear. The Smiths took over in January, 1965, but departed within six weeks. It was then that the *Sunday Express* featured the matter. My own inquiries followed and this account is based on information given me by the three families.

Mrs. Cooper, a widow for several years, said that she and her family had grown quite used to strange happenings during the whole of their long tenancy. In fact, it was they who first had called the ghost "Charlie".

Doors had opened and shut of their own accord. Footsteps, sometimes heavy, sometimes light, had been heard all over the house but particularly on the stairs. In the cellar, Mrs. Cooper declared, she never could keep a candle alight for more than a few seconds. Something blew out the flame no matter how often she lighted it.

Both Mrs. Cooper and her daughter claim to have seen a "figure" at the same spot in the cellar. They described it as a man in his 30's, "... fair, fresh-faced, wearing a trilby and a tweed coat."

The Fisher family consisted of the man and his wife, both in their 40's, and four daughters aged 17, 16, 10 and under one year. In reply to a series of questions, Mr. Fisher wrote for me a careful and detailed account of things that they had experienced.

First, I asked whether animals in the house had reacted unusually. The Fishers themselves kept no pets but a friend frequently brought his dog to the house. The animal, Mr. Fisher said, never would enter the front room. His hair would stand on end and he would bare his teeth.

I then asked about the alleged mysterious movement of small articles, ornaments, light pieces of furniture and so forth. They especially remembered the following incidents:

An occasional table had been overturned but a vase of daffodils that had been standing on it was discovered undamaged with no water spilled on the seat of a big armchair.

The baby's cot usually stood against the wall in Mr. and Mrs. Fisher's bedroom. On at least two occasions it unaccountably was found in the middle of the floor, the baby still sleeping peacefully and quite undisturbed. Each parent denied moving the cot and they were positive the three older girls had no part in it.

Mrs. Fisher told a strange story about the radio. It was always kept on a large wide absolutely secure shelf in the living room. This radio was working normally one morning when she had gone outside to hang out the washing. When she returned after only a very few minutes she found the instrument dangling by its cable but playing as loud as ever.

There was also the lampshade affair. Mr. Fisher found it detached from the lamp, twisted and crushed. When he set about straightening it he discovered the job couldn't be done without pliers and even then the wire frame was so stiff he had to exert considerable force. He was convinced the damage was beyond the powers of his daughters.

With regard to the footsteps, I cannot do better than quote exactly from Mr. Fisher's written statement which, incidentally, his wife countersigns:

"We were all in the front sitting room round the fire — my family, six of us, my wife's sister's family of four and two friends from York. We had been telling them of the funny occurrences in the house and having a good laugh at the same time. We had given him the name 'Ned'. [Mrs. Cooper called him Charlie.] These heavy footsteps came up three steps to the front door, continued along the passage and stopped outside the sitting room door. The handle of the door went down and the door was pushed open over the thick carpet. (Wind couldn't have done this as it was too tight.) Then the footsteps carried on into the kitchen. My wife got off the arm of the chair and went into the kitchen calling, 'We are all in here, Aunty Joan.' But no one was there at all. To add to the mystery, both back and front doors were locked at the time. Our two friends from York were most alarmed and made an excuse to leave. They told us afterwards they thought we had been making it all up."

The baby excluded, no fewer than 11 persons witnessed these events.

Besides all this, the Fishers experienced phenomena involving fire and water. On returning from a day's outing the family was alarmed to find the house full of smoke. They had not lighted fires before they went out; yet the smoke was there and, even more remarkable, soot lay on every step of the staircase. Naturally, they blamed the fireplace in the adjoining house. A town official agreed that the fault must have rested there and undertook to see that the fireplace was examined and if necessary reset. Although, in fact, nothing more was ever done about it and the Fishers never had this particular experience again.

Not long after the smoke incident, while the oldest Fisher girl was having a bath, water was seen to pour from a cupboard at the top of the stairs and run down to the ground floor. Her father checked the plumbing but found no fault with bath, pipes or overflow. Even if the young lady had overfilled her bath the result could not have been an "avalanche" of water from an unconnected cupboard.

Concerning the cellars belonging to this house, Mr. Fisher said: "...The cellars were blocked in by a trap door. One evening my eldest daughter and I were alone in the house. We heard two terrific rumbles from the cellar below, as if coal were being delivered. We dashed outside but could find nothing to have caused it. In fact, the road and the alleys were deserted."

Mr. Fisher also stated the house was always "stuffy", never smelling fresh no matter how much Mrs. Fisher cleaned and polished. The Smiths who succeeded the Fishers were a young couple with two babies. They took possession in January, 1965, but stayed only two months. In my talks with them they were frank and helpful.

Mrs. Smith once saw a fireside tool set move while she sat reading an evening paper but no furniture was moved or misplaced during their tenancy. However, on two occasions they heard heavy footsteps. Once these seemed to stop just outside the bedroom door and Mr. Smith heard what resembled heavy breathing. He got out of bed, threw open the door, searched the house — and found nothing.

Another time, having heard unaccountable noises, both joined in an investigation of the cellar. They could not keep matches or candles alight although they could not perceive a draft. (Mrs. Cooper had had this same experience.)

One night, some time after both had retired, Mrs. Smith saw a "figure" which was invisible to her husband. She was able to describe it and to sketch it. She says it was that of a young man, five feet nine inches tall, fair complexioned, aged about 28 and dressed for tennis. His features were indistinguishable and his feet were not visible. She said he passed straight through the closed bedroom door.

The second of my three cases comes from Kingskerswell, a town somewhat smaller than Boston Spa. It lies on the main road about halfway between Torquay and Newton Abbott.

On 14 November, 1963, the *Northern Echo* carried a paragraph to the effect that Dr. Robert Mortimer, the Anglican Bishop of Exeter, had conducted a "service of exorcism" to rid a country house (lately converted to flats) of a "ghostly presence".

Both the Bishop and the local incumbent were favourably impressed by young Mr. and Mrs. Davison who had experienced the phenomena and sought their help. They believed them to be thoroughly trustworthy and reliable, an opinion with which I concur.

The "country house" has the typical plaster-covered cob walls and appears to date from Georgian times. It might be as old as 200 years.

Half a century ago a knacker's yard adjoined this property. Village gossip has it that the firm's last manager, one Victor Judd who lived in the neighbouring country house, had been an embezzler. In 1925, rather than face exposure and disgrace, he shot himself in that very yard.

The Davisons gave me the following details:

(1) A heavy oak wardrobe on a solid base moved forward three inches from the wall and then began to shake violently as if "someone was pushing it". They both saw and heard this.

(2) A studio couch was moved about a foot while the Davisons were out; the carpet was ruckled in the process.

(3) Ornaments, crockery and other small objects often were moved though nothing ever was damaged.

(4) Various things disappeared only to reappear in ridiculous places. For instance, kitchen utensils were transported mysteriously to the inside of the linen basket.

(5) Even in the face of a large fire a marked drop in temperature always occurred before phenomena developed.

(6) Both had seen a "form" which they described as "...Roughly the shape and size of a man floating about a foot from the floor. Around the chest region the 'mist' was denser. No features were defined." The "ghost" could be seen only a few seconds. It glided across the room and vanished.

Mr. and Mrs. Davison believed the exorcism to have been successful. They had not seen the ghost again and its manifestations had ceased.

The third and most remarkable case of all took place in the city of York itself, throughout the whole of 1962.

I first saw Mrs. Elizabeth Baxter on Monday, 5 November. By then, for 10 months, she had borne the brunt of what can be described only as a full-scale offensive. She had endured flood and fire, damage to crockery, pictures and furniture on a grand scale. Plumbers, firemen, police — all had been called in to help. Electricians, insurance men, valuers — all had played a part. Still the manifestations continued. I had been approached in my capacity as Leader of the York Branch of the Churches' Society for Psychical and Spiritual Studies.

My initial tour of the house horrified me. The place was wrecked! I saw damaged furniture, piles of smashed crockery, pathetic attempts to protect this or that by laying it face down on the floor. Clothes had been slashed as they hung in wardrobes and documents had been torn to shreds in the very drawers in which they were locked. Plaster was falling from walls; ceilings bore abundant evidence of water damage.

Mrs. Baxter was 63, sensible, reliable and not given to exaggeration. Her husband had died in 1953 when the two were living in Selby. Three years before his death Miss Geraldine Simpson, Mrs. Baxter's older sister, had joined the household. She was a lady of a somewhat dominant manner and the arrangement had not pleased Mr. Baxter. He was afraid she would over-influence his wife. When her husband died Mrs. Baxter bought the house in York and both women took up residence there in 1953.

In May, 1961, the sisters were joined by a mutual friend, Miss

Sally Hutchinson. Sally was about the same age as Geraldine, in her late 60's, and closely attached to her. At this time Mrs. Baxter was working at a local hospital as a night orderly. Very soon she realized that the other two gradually were edging her out of control of her own home. She hesitated to say that this was deliberate. However, to counteract it, Mrs. Baxter invited her nephew, Barrie Simpson, to come and live with them in York. He accepted in November, 1961, when he was between 19 and 20 years old.

Barrie's father had died when Barrie was quite young and the Baxters had undertaken the boy's upbringing, an arrangement which had terminated not long before Mrs. Baxter removed to York. A deep bond of affection existed between Barrie and his aunt. But Miss Simpson and Miss Hutchinson looked upon his coming as an intrusion. They were critical of his friends and difficult about his hobby — the collecting and playing of "pop" records. However, no hostility came into the open.

And then things began to happen.

Through 1962 until the middle of October Mrs. Baxter contended with hazards involving both fire and water. On 5 April three fires broke out in the front bedroom, all on the same day.

Mrs. Baxter, Barrie and another sister of Mrs. Baxter's, Mrs. Vernon, whose home was several miles from York, were watching television after tea. Miss Simpson and Miss Hutchinson were out visiting friends. Before going out these two had switched on an electric clothes drier in their bedroom and foolishly neglected to tell anyone about it. The appliance appears to have overheated — but not until six hours had gone by.

About 6:30 p.m. Barrie went upstairs. He was back in seconds, shouting that he smelled fire. He and Mrs. Baxter rushed into the old ladies' apartment and discovered the clothes around the heater were on fire. Barrie ran down again to turn off the electricity. Mrs. Baxter, with the help of Mrs. Vernon, doused the flames with water from the bathroom.

The heads of the twin beds in the room, separated by about a yard, were against the wall opposite the window. The clothes drier had been placed in line with the space between the beds, about a yard from their feet, just about in the centre of the floor. (See sketch) At the foot of the bed nearest to the door, stood an ottoman-like blanket box. Other furniture included the usual bedside tables, two sideboards, a wardrobe belonging to Miss Hutchinson, and a large oak wardrobe which was Mrs. Baxter's property.

The mattress and bedding belonging to the bed by the door was severely burned. These were carried outside and dumped in the yard. Except for a drenching the bed further from the door had escaped damage. Nevertheless, the ladies examined the mattress carefully for scorch marks and signs of concealed smouldering. Satisfied that it was safe they propped it against the first bedstead so that it would dry.

Two pillows from the far bed were very wet. These they deposited on the lowest two steps of the attic stair. An hour later these pillows were found to be blazing furiously. The staircase panel against which they were resting was deeply charred and permanently disfigured.

About 9:30 p.m. the older ladies returned and were very upset when shown the results of their carelessness. After supper, a little past 10 p.m., Miss Simpson went up to their room. At once she cried out in panic. It was full of smoke.

Mrs. Baxter saw at a glance that this outbreak was more serious. She ran next door to telephone the fire brigade. Her neighbour returned with her and tried without success to penetrate the apartment. Not until the firemen arrived was the new outbreak controlled.

Several months later I examined the official record of the incident and discussed the affair with the Chief Fire Officer and with the representative of the Electricity Department. The latter emphatically denied this third outbreak could have been caused by an electrical fault. As he pointed out, the heater had been disconnected and removed after the first conflagration. He had found nothing else out of order in any way.

Floodings in this York house ranged from droplets which fell from ceilings to bucketfuls which were flung along passages. More often than not, these things took place in parts of the house remote from plumbing and at levels far above any water pipe. Roof spaces were immediately examined in each instance and invariably found to be bone-dry.

The earliest water phenomena took place on 30 December, 1961, and continued for several days. Water appeared at irregular intervals until the middle of October, 1962. Mrs. Baxter called in the plumber on 30 December and again on the first of January. On both occasions he changed the float valve.

Here is a transcript from my notes relating to his third visit on 5 January and the events following:

"This time the plumbers took no chances. They ripped up floorboards and subjected every pipe to minute examination but found nothing. The tank was functioning normally. In despair, they fitted yet another float valve, replacing that which the same plumber had put in only 48 hours before. The next day, 6 January, the floodings were as severe as ever. The plumbers came back. This time they replaced the half-inch overflow with one of three-quarter-inch size and tried every means in their power to get the system to overflow. It wouldn't. The men departed. In less than five minutes water was cascading down the stairs!"

The most extraordinary of the "water phenomena" occurred on 30 September and lasted for several hours. Mrs. Baxter was on duty at the hospital and Miss Simpson, Miss Hutchinson, Barrie and a friend, Miss Palmer, were in the dining room talking. It was 9:30 p.m. Miss Palmer excused herself to go upstairs. At once she gave the alarm. She found flooding on the lower landing. Water was seeping through into the kitchen. All four mopped up.

At 10 p.m. Miss Palmer went to the front room for her coat. She found it wet. Water was dripping from the ceiling plate supporting the chandelier and trickling down the chains. Miss Simpson's room was immediately above and Barrie hurried up to investigate. He found the floor awash and water dripping from the ceiling. He rushed to the attic above — and found it perfectly dry.

As he came down again he says he saw "...a bucketful of water falling from the high ceiling above the staircase well and cascading onto the lowest flight."

There is no access from the inside of the house to the space above this high ceiling. The only way to effect an entry would be by climbing the roof and tearing off tiles.

Again the three women cleared up the mess and just as they were finishing and Miss Palmer was about to take her delayed departure a second bucketful drenched Miss Hutchinson as she paused at the foot of the stairs wringing out a cloth.

Miss Palmer finally went; Barrie and the ladies retired to their respective beds. But about an hour after midnight Miss Hutchinson felt uneasy. She roused Miss Simpson who passed along the corridor and woke Barrie.

He says: "There were repeated flushes down the stairs from

the same top ceiling. A bucketful shot along the top landing from some point close to the door of the middle bedroom (Mrs. Baxter's). It passed the bathroom and splashed against my back bedroom door."

By 2:00 a.m. all three were sweeping water out of both the front and back doors. A further cascade from high level soaked them as they worked. Then came a loud crash — and the demonstrations were over for the night.

Soon after these floodings, during October and November, the movement of small objects, often in full view of witnesses, became commonplace. One evening the four residents were enjoying the comfort of a blazing fire in the front sitting room when, from behind them, the dog's feeding bowl rose from the floor, sailed over their heads and hurled itself into the fireplace. Later a heavy wooden ornament from the middle bedroom pitched down the stairs and smashed on the tiled passage floor No one was upstairs at the time.

Another time a kettle rolled itself to the kitchen floor, trundled along the passage, turned at a 90 degree angle and came to rest in the sitting room at Barrie's feet. Seconds afterwards its lid came after it, bowling merrily along on its edge. Mrs. Baxter witnessed the whole weird procession.

Because there had been a lot of damage in the front bedroom Barrie and Mrs. Baxter decided, for safety's sake, to lay the heavy oak wardrobe previously mentioned down on its face. In this way, they figured, its fine full-length mirror would be protected.

Mrs. Baxter said afterwards, "We found the top section impossible to move. Something seemed to hold it down from the inside. Then, as we were struggling with it, the whole wardrobe began to rock violently. Barrie's arm almost was trapped. When he had freed himself, together we dragged a sideboard in front of the wardrobe, thus pinning it to the wall and preventing its falling forward. Twenty-four hours later we found this sideboard pushed to one side but the wardrobe remained upright."

This bedroom was the scene of another remarkable event late on the evening of Friday, 9 November and on the following morning. On the ninth I had been the last person in the apartment before the house was locked for the night. By that time the two old ladies had taken refuge in Mrs. Vernon's country cottage. Mrs. Baxter and Barrie were going to stay with friends. The house therefore was empty. In answer to an urgent message from Mrs. Baxter I was back by nine o'clock the next morning.

The bedroom door was jammed from the inside. In the presence of Mrs. Baxter and her next-door neighbour I used all my strength to force the door open about six inches. All three of us heard scraping from within as I did so. I wriggled through the gap and discovered the large sideboard had been set against the closed door and two chairs piled on top of it to reinforce the barrier. A cupboard door, which had been wrenched off the sideboard, balanced precariously on top of Mrs. Baxter's wardrobe.

The windows were as I had left them — fastened securely on the inside. The contents of the various drawers and cupboards had been strewn over the floor. Clothes belonging to the occupants of the room had been slashed as they hung in the smaller wardrobe. A bundle of steel knitting needles, which I myself had placed on a chair the evening before, were bent almost at right angles. The bending had been accomplished in a single operation and must have required great strength.

Another incident concerning the York house is worthy of mention. Three weeks before, on 18 October, the three women and Barrie were in their sitting room conversing with a friend. As they watched an electric light fitting in the recess to the right of the fireplace came slowly away from the wall as if dragged by an invisible cable. Barrie, with commendable courage, pressed it back.

Also, for some weeks Mrs. Baxter's dog had shown an increasing dislike for his home. His mistress, whom he adored, was unable to pacify him. So when Miss Hutchinson and Miss Simpson went to Mrs. Vernon's cottage to stay they took him with them. This was in the middle of October, just after the episode of the light fixture.

There are important features common to the three cases. One is the involvement of young people. At Boston Spa there were Miss Cooper, the Fisher girls and Mr. and Mrs. Smith. The Davisons at Kingskerswell were in their early 20's. Barrie in York was in his 20th year.

This does not reflect on the young people themselves but does support the belief that psychic phenomena are produced more readily in the presence of youth — more so if, knowingly or not, they are "psychic". My later experience with Barrie gives me every reason to suppose that he does possess considerable power. However, when all this took place he was completely unaware of this.

The house in Boston Spa was "stuffy" and seemed always to

exude a faint mustiness which no amount of airing could remove. A similar "earthy smell" pervaded the York sitting room. Both there and at Kingskerswell palpable currents of cold air made people shiver despite blazing fires.

The fire and water manifestations at Boston Spa and York differ only in degree. No satisfactory explanation has been found for any of them.

The Davisons' experience with their heavy oak wardrobe is almost identical with that of Mrs. Baxter.

Great care was taken to avoid damaging small articles in the first two cases. This was true in York also, except in the case of Miss Simpson's and Miss Hutchinson's belongings which were wantonly destroyed. Similar things owned by Mrs. Baxter and Barrie were undamaged and more than once even deliberately protected.

Apart from dress the "figures" seen by the Coopers and the "figure" observed by Mrs. Smith at Boston Spa could be the same. But there is no suggestion as to identify in either case. At Kingskerswell the suicidal knacker is an obvious subject.

Nothing ever was "seen" at York but an experienced seer declared that the manifestations were due in part to efforts by Mrs. Baxter's deceased husband to rid his wife's home of the two older women. Certainly the fact remains that once these two left the house, as they eventually did most willingly, the manifestations ceased.

And now, in closing the account, I emphasize: the facts of the cases are as set down but they tell us only who, what, where and when. The mysteries of why and how remain unanswered.

GHOST ON THE TULIP STAIRCASE
The Rev. Ralph W. Hardy

On Sunday afternoon, 19 June, 1966, my wife and I were visiting the Royal Maritime Museum and Naval College at Greenwich in London.

This originally was a royal palace built by Henry VII for his wife, Elizabeth of York. Here Henry VIII was born. Here, also, Henry's three children, Mary, Elizabeth and Edward were born. The old building eventually was rebuilt into the present structure by James I for his wife, Anne of Denmark. Charles I and his wife, Henrietta Maria of France, lived here until the time of the Civil War.

The central structure presently flanked by the two large buildings of the Naval College was designed by the famous architect Inigo Jones and was considered at the time it was built to be a perfect example of contemporary architecture. Named the Queen's House, it contains an interesting spiral staircase called the Tulip Stair because of the design of the iron balustrade.

We just had visited the College chapel which was closing as we left at 5 p.m. About 20 minutes later in the Queen's House we attempted to photograph the Tulip Staircase about which we previously had read. Our first thought had been to ascend the stairs to a sort of balcony at the top but we were prevented from doing this by a wooden No Admittance barrier at the foot of the stairs.

Later the authorities told us that such a barrier always is placed on the stair after 5 p.m. on Sundays.

We then decided to attempt our photograph from below. As neither flash nor tripod could be used a time exposure was the best we could do. Using a light meter and holding the camera as firmly as possible against the door frame, as nearly as we can recollect we set the exposure for one second at f:4, using Kodachrome K2, 35mm daylight film and a Contina camera (a moderately-priced Zeiss product) which has a locking device to prevent double exposures.

Owing to the lateness of the hour there were very few visitors about and Mrs. Hardy, standing beside me as I began to operate the camera, watched specifically to be sure the stair was clear of passersby. As I was making my preparations a group of three persons did approach but on seeing the camera turned back. Mrs. Hardy invited them to come on through, remarking that the camera was not ready. Nothing more was thought of the incident until a month later when the processed film showed what appears to be a robed figure ascending the stairs.

The foregoing details explain that the first two possible explanations for our photograph which will occur to you — a double exposure or an unseen attendant on the stair — must be ruled out. The first, the double exposure, is not a possible explanation because of the safety device on the camera. The second explanation would have necessitated that a white-robed figure, first having moved the wooden No Admittance barrier, rush up the stair, pausing just long enough to leave an unblurred image on our time exposure — and all this within the unobstructed view of two people, one of whom was particularly on guard against just such an intrusion onto the photograph — without being seen.

The third possibility, that the film was tampered with, has been checked by professional experts both at the Kodak plant at Hemel Hempstead and at the museum. These experts state that nothing of the sort was attempted or could have been attempted as it was colour film.

Months later at the request of a mutual friend the original slide was loaned to the century-old Ghost Club of London. After extensive study they pronounced it "the clearest example of a phantom form" they ever had seen.

Some time later, in early summer, 1967 they went to considerable trouble and expense to hold an all-night vigil in the museum. The trustees of the museum gave their permission and the Ghost Club went equipped with tape recorders, thermometers, listening devices and small bells which were arranged, enclosed by chalk marks, at various places on the stairs. The results of the vigil were somewhat disappointing. One bell reportedly was heard to ring twice and was found to have been moved. A sharp drop in temperature was recorded on the balcony from where a child is said to have fallen to his death. A medium claimed to have received nothing but the name, Henrietta Maria.

The Ghost Club concluded, "There is a definite something there which will not yield to a natural explanation."

The official photographer for the museum was present throughout the night-long vigil and he reported that nothing unusual happened that he could detect. He was particularly interested as he was the museum expert who had previously examined and passed on our own slide containing the unknown ghostly figure. At his suggestion an attempt was staged, using the same camera and as nearly as possible the same conditions, to reproduce our film by having a white-shirted attendant rush up the stairs during a time exposure. The result of this experiment was a white blur quite unlike a human figure except for one hand which the attendant purposely held stationary for a second or two in two positions

No one has found an explanation for the ghostly figure which appears on the Tulip Staircase in our film. And unfortunately my wife and I can tell you only what did not occur; we cannot tell you what did.

WHO LIVES IN VINE COTTAGE?
Lavinia Bradley

"Is there a ghost in Vine Cottage, Angmering-on-Sea, Sussex? This question is being asked after a London couple went to view the century-old picturesque cottage in Sea Road and claimed they saw the owner — who died two years ago!"

The London couple referred to in the June, 1967, item from an English newspaper is my husband and me!

We were house-hunting and had driven from London to the Sussex coast to see Vine Cottage. The estate agent's report advertised a flint and brick cottage with a slate roof, built in the 1860's. It had a walled garden 150 yards from the sea and had stood empty and for sale for the last 12 months. We picked up the keys from the agent and went along to see it.

Once inside the wrought iron gate, we found ourselves behind ivy-covered walls in a long lawn leading up to the cottage. It was a solid unadorned little place, plain and sturdy. It had been built to last and only a Virginia creeper climbing up its front softened the squareness. We paused on the lawn, marveling at the seclusion and peace.

Suddenly my husband said, "Look at the upstairs window! It's got a curtain."

I looked up and there in the empty house I saw a white lace curtain. As we watched, it was parted and a white-haired lady wearing a grey shawl looked out at us.

Our first reaction was embarrassment. We had been told the place was empty and we now found ourselves intruding on an occupant. The figure at the window made no move to welcome us but stood staring as we retreated down the lawn and out of the gate.

Up the road from the cottage is a hardware store, The Corner Ironmongers, and we went in to ask the proprietor, Mr. J. Furlong, who was living in the cottage.

"No one's living there," he said. "It's been empty for the last 12 months."

"That's what we understood," we explained, "but we've just been there and found an old lady upstairs!"

He asked what she looked like. We described her white hair

and grey shawl and the strange way she stood and stared at us.

"That's Mrs. Ayling," he said. "She always wore a shawl and looked just as you've described her. But she died two years ago!" He went on to say that Mrs. Nudd Ayling had lived in the cottage for 60 years and died in 1965 at age 94.

Somehow we did not feel we wanted to go back. We returned the keys to the estate agents who reiterated that the cottage had been empty for a year. No one could have entered it and the agent had all the keys.

Mrs. Ayling's 69-year-old son is a fishmonger in nearby Rustington. When he heard our story his comment to the newspaper reporter was that he never had seen his mother's ghost nor any other. He "doesn't believe" in them.

Well, we had come from London and never had heard of the Aylings but we saw the old lady with our own eyes. Was she trying to tell us something or simply warning us off? If it were the latter she succeeded. We are not buying Vine Cottage and so far as I know it's still for sale.

☾ THE BISHOP SPOKE WITH A GHOST ☾

"At last someone has spoken!" sighed the specter of the manor. "I am here to impart a secret..."

Adi-Kent Thomas Jeffrey

Samuel Wilberforce, bishop of Oxford and later through the influence of Gladstone bishop of Winchester, was the son of William Wilberforce, a well-known member of Parliament and a close friend of William Pitt. Samuel made a mark on the England of his day; constantly embroiled in church controversies, he often was in the public eye. He was an active churchman, a vigorous fighter, an able administrator and a brilliant orator. He also was the "darling" of society, a man who loved people and parties as well as principles. So widespread was his sociability, in London he was referred to as "the bishop of society."

His family name was so well-known that when the long-awaited funeral oration, the Lincoln Memorial Address, was delivered before the United States Congress on 12 February, 1866, the speaker, George Bancroft, in referring to our English countrymen, named "Milton and Wilberforce."

Samuel Wilberforce's name came to public notice in America again 14 years later when an article in the *New York Times* in January, 1880, carried the story Bishop Wilberforce told of his unusual experience — at a party he had held a conversation with a ghost!

The same story was reprinted another 14 years later, in Pennsylvania's *Newtown Enterprise* of 13 January, 1894.

Samuel Wilberforce had accepted an invitation to a country house not far from London. Because the owners of the house were his friends and leaders in British society, the bishop has left them unidentified. The drawing room, as the bishop entered, was filled with other guests standing around in groups, engaged in conversation. The bishop walked through the room responding to the greetings of friends and acquaintances.

Suddenly, he says, he noticed that one man sat alone and silent. He was a Catholic priest sitting in a great chair near the hearth and gazing moodily into the fire. He neither moved nor spoke and no one stopped to address him.

Bishop Wilberforce was about to request an introduction from his hostess when the butler appeared in the drawing room doorway and announced that dinner was served. The guests, still talking, moved slowly from the drawing room into the dining room across the tapestried hall.

Once seated at the table the English clergyman attempted to locate the Catholic priest. He studied the length of the damask-covered table. But the priest was not there.

As soon as there was a moment of quiet the bishop leaned toward his hostess, upon whose left he was seated, and asked, "I beg your pardon, madam, but may I inquire, who was the priest we left sitting apart in the drawing room?"

The lady lowered her wine glass in a startled movement. Then her eyes flashed in the candlelight as she said, "Ah, you have seen him then? It is not everyone who has that privilege."

"I don't understand..." began the bishop.

"Of course, you don't, my dear bishop. I scarcely do myself. But I will tell you all that I do know. Evidently you have seen the spectre of our manor."

"Spectre?" The bishop put down his fork.

"Yes, your lordship. We have a ghost! He has haunted these grounds and this house for many years. He is a tradition in our family. No one can explain who he is or why he appears." She shrugged. "He comes to our sight upon rare occasions and disappears just as inoffensively. We consider him quite harmless. We call him our 'friendly ghost.'"

"How very singular," commented the bishop. He dipped his fingers in the silver finger bowl and touched them lightly to his napkin. "Have you ever addressed your priestly spectre and asked him why he appears to you?"

The hostess laughed nervously. "Indeed, I have had neither the opportunity nor the desire!"

Eventually, the dinner over, the guests rose from their seats. The bishop, taking the arm of his hostess, asked, 'Then may I take the liberty now?"

"With all my heart," replied the lady.

So as the gentlemen retired to the game room and the ladies to the upper salons, Bishop Wilberforce moved quietly across the hall to the drawing room. The lady of the manor nodded at him as she joined her female guests ascending the marble stairs.

The bishop entered the drawing room alone. A slight draft stirred the candle flames in the silver wall sconces. The fire was glowing a dull orange. Before the hearth, just as the bishop last had seen him, sat the Catholic priest.

Clearing his throat Bishop Wilberforce then went right to the point.

"Who are you, my friend, and why are you here?"

The priest leaned back; he sighed deeply. Then turning he looked steadily up at the bishop. "At last — someone has spoken!" he said.

The bishop drew up a chair and sat opposite him. "Go on, sir."

"I am the spirit of a priest who left this world nearly 100 years ago. I am here to impart to anyone who will receive it a secret which died with me."

The bishop nodded, saying kindly, "I shall be happy to receive it."

The priest clasped his white hands and spoke on, his voice echoing hollowly as in a cave. "Thank God for what you are doing. I cannot rest in my grave, you see, while a great wrong has been done which it was in my power to right."

Samuel Wilberforce leaned closer, "Go on, sir."

"I have been returning all these years, hoping someone would speak to me. It has not been given to me to speak first. But all men have shunned me — until now." He turned deep eyes toward the bishop. "Now it is your mission to do my bidding. As a churchman you cannot refuse!"

"Of course," the bishop assured him. "I shall do all I can."

The Father stared into the fire and commenced his story. "I was a priest of the Church of Rome. One night I was called to this house to receive the confession of a dying man. The man had wrought a terrible wrong on one of his relatives. He had cheated that man of his fair share of these vast estates. On his deathbed this dying nobleman wished to repair this terrible wrong."

The priest paused as a burst of laughter filtered out from the game room at the far end of the hall.

"At his request," continued the Father, "I wrote down the confession word for word. When he had finished I barely had time to administer the final sacrament of the church before he expired in my arms." The priest sighed as if pained with the long recollection.

"It was very important," he went on, "that I return to London that night. Yet I worried about carrying such a valuable document with me. I concluded that it would be safest for me to place the paper here in the house in some secure spot and return for it the following day. At that time I would deliver it to the person for whom it was intended."

Bishop Wilberforce cupped his chin in one hand and leaned sideways on the carved arm of the chair. "I follow you, sir. Please continue."

The priest seemed not to hear him. He stared without movement at the fading glow of the embers on the hearth. Wilberforce waited. Finally the priest shifted in his chair, sighed again and began to speak.

"I went into the library after calling for my horse that night. In haste I had to find a properly secure spot. I looked at the bookshelves about the room. Mounting the steps to the top shelf I took down a copy of Young's *Night Thoughts*. I well recall it was the first book on the uppermost shelf near the window. I placed the paper carefully within the leaves, replaced the book and departed."

"Excellent judgment I should say, good Father," offered Samuel Wilberforce.

The priest shrugged. "I don't know, sir. I only know the night did not go as I had planned. On the way home my horse took fright at some creature's flight across the roadway and I was thrown and instantly and killed."

Bishop Wilberforce dropped his hand from his chin.

The priest nodded sadly. "Thus the secret of the confession died with me. No one has disturbed that book in all these years." He looked gently across at the bishop opposite him. "Nor has anyone had the courage to address me until now."

The bishop bowed.

The priest, pointing a pale finger at the bishop, continued,

"Now it remains with you to correct the injustice which has so long been put upon a member of this noble family. The document will be found, as I have stated, in the library."

"I believe you, good Father, and I shall do as you ask." Bishop Wilberforce watched the priest rise from his chair.

"My mission is over at last," he murmured. "Now I can rest in peace." No sooner had he spoken these words than his form dimmed into a smoke-like wisp, then vanished. The bishop now gazed at an empty chair. The fire was dead. The room was cold. He was alone.

He stepped out into the great hall. The wall hangings stirred in a chilly draft. Female voices floated down from the upper floors. Cigar smoke drifted from the open doorway of the game room. He walked softly down the hall in the other direction, to the library. Here tapers burned low in their silver sockets but the shelves around the room were visible. The bishop climbed the steps to the top shelves. The books were thick with dust.

One title leaped out to his gaze: Young's *Night Thoughts*. He took it down. Here was the document, now yellow and faded, but otherwise exactly as described.

Not long after this the incident of Bishop Wilberforce's conversation with the spectral priest became known to the world.

For it is a fact, according to the *New York Times* account, "that about the period of this extraordinary occurrence the magnificent estate passed suddenly into the possession of a remote member of the family who, until then, had lived in obscurity."

Bishop Samuel Wilberforce, it was said, never tired of recounting his strange experience. Apparently it neither frightened nor surprised him.

"It was a confidence from the spirit world," he always explained.

An interesting sequel to Bishop Wilberforce's ghostly experience is the fact that he, too, met sudden death by a fall from a horse; and he, too, became a ghost.

Dr. Wilberforce, bishop of Winchester, always had entertained a special desire to visit Wooten, the home of the Evelyn family, near Guildford. He was particularly interested in seeing a portrait that hung in the manor house there. It was a painting of a Mrs. Godolphin whose biography the bishop had written in his younger years. Yet, somehow, with his busy schedule, the bishop never had found the opportunity to visit Wooten.

So one day — his last day on earth as it turned out — he set out on horseback to visit Lord Granville in Holmbury St. Mary, a town no more than two miles from Wooten.

At the same time in the dining room at Wooten, Mr. Evelyn, his brother, a doctor friend and a Mr. Harvey were sitting talking when one of them, chancing to look up, exclaimed, "Why, there is the bishop of Winchester looking in at the window!"

The other three men turned and each saw the figure before it disappeared a second later. They hurried outside to find the Bishop but there was no one there.

Half an hour later a servant announced that the Bishop of Winchester had been killed a short time before by a fall from his horse while on his way to Holmbury St. Mary.

This story of Bishop Wilberforce's ghost is one of many collected by Lord Halifax — Charles Lindley, Viscount Halifax — and later published by his son in a book titled Lord Halifax's Ghost Book. Lord Halifax took great pains to verify the facts contained in his collected stories by talking with the distinguished persons involved. His son, Viscount Halifax, ambassador from Great Britain to the United States from 1941 to 1946, believed the incident of Bishop Wilberforce's ghostly visit to Wooten was related to his father by Dr. Wilberforce's fellow churchman, Bishop Browne.

☪ JEF — THE TALKING MONGOOSE... ☪ 30 YEARS LATER

Have you ever wondered what happened to Voirrey, the little Manx girl who had the world's most mysterious friend?

Walter McGraw

Once upon a time, on a tiny little island, in a tiny little house, there lived a tiny little animal named Jef who peed on a great big psychical investigator and screamed: "Go away, clear to hell! We don't want you here."

Not true, you think? Let me warn you that in the 1930's one R. S. Lambert, then of the British Broadcasting Company, investigated Jef and said, "It is impossible to deny that there is serious evidence...for Jef's reality..." And Lambert was called "crazy" but after lengthy proceedings a British court awarded him 7000 pounds damages, in effect acknowledging there indeed was good reason to believe in the existence of a talking mongoose on the Isle of Man.

It is said that on one of its few clear days you can see England, Scotland, Ireland and Wales from the top of Man's highest peak, Mt Snaefell. The island's principal source of income is inexpensive tourism. For a short time in the summer months the island is inundated with holiday visitors from what Manxmen call "the adjacent island" — England. The rest of the year Man is a fairly lonely place to live, especially if you happen to be on one of the rocky little farms that dot the countryside. To one of these farms at Doarlish Cashen owned by James T. Irving, a 58-year-old former travelling piano salesman, Jef came in 1931.

In his own way Irving was as much of an anachronism as Jef. He was well-educated, always neatly dressed and a farmer whose hands remained clean and uncalloused. Mrs. Irving, four years younger, bore some resemblance to England's Queen Mary and Voirrey, their 12-year-old daughter, was a quiet serious child given to wandering alone on the moors. It was said that she could sneak up behind a rabbit and kill it with a club while her dog Mona held the rabbit's attention by mesmerism. Never off the island nor for that matter even visiting the northern half of the small Isle, she must have been a curious mixture: part wild lonely child of the moor, part developing young lady, old beyond her years and filled with a wonder imparted by her much-travelled, story-telling father.

The farmhouse itself was small, two-storeyed and cheerless, its solid stone walls broken only by a few cramped windows. Inside, for insulation, the walls had been lined with dark matchwood panelling which stood off a few inches from the cold stone. This characteristic of the house created a condition which made possible the story of Jef It seems Jef liked to live in a house where he could not be seen and yet could satisfy his gregarious nature. The space between the stone and the panelling pleased him immensely as did the ceilinged stairway. The wonderful resting place above that ceiling Jef called his "sanctum."

Jef probably lived in the house for some time before he made himself known to the Irvings — which he did by knocking on the walls and making a variety of animal sounds. Then, once when Irving asked his wife, "What in the name of God can he be?" the animal spoke.

"What in the name of God can he be?" echoed from the walls in a voice pitched two octaves above a normal woman's.

From then on the animal quickly learned to speak not only English but to use the many foreign phases the widely-travelled Jim Irving used — as did Voirrey, following her father's example. But in the beginning there was no closeness between the strange animal and the Irvings. He liked to throw things and since his sanctum was in Voirrey's room the thought of injury to the child bothered Irving — and thus he discovered little animal's greatest weakness. He tried to kill the animal — first with poison and then with a gun. This brought immediate reaction in the form of damage to the house and profane screams so threatening the Irvings moved Voirrey into their room for fear she would be killed. It seemed nothing affected the little beast as much as a threat to his own life.

It took six months to bring about a truce. By that time the family had begun to like Jef, as he called himself, and he promised to protect, not hurt, Voirrey. Mrs. Irving began to leave bits of food for him in the sanctum. These he ate and shared with Voirrey whom he often followed into the fields where he jealously threw stones at anyone who talked to her. (His aim was said to be very good.) Then too he began to pay his own way by strangling hundreds of rabbits which he left for the Irvings either to eat or sell at seven pence each. "The God damned mice," as he called them, he frightened away by meowing like a cat. But it was a long time before any of the family actually saw their boarder.

"You'll put me in a bottle if you catch me," he often said. And he gave other reason for not letting anyone see him, saying he was a freak, a ghost and part of the fifth dimension. But it all boiled down to his fear of being caught and killed. When visitors came he often would disappear, returning only after they left. Then, emitting gales of screeching laughter he would tell of his adventures on other parts of the island.

Jef was an incurable gossip and the Manx population became chary of Irving because — mysteriously to them — he knew so many things he should not have known. They began to dislike the little spy even more when he took to stealing, carrying his loot home as presents for the Irvings. When he began stealing sandwiches at the bus depot and cadging rides underneath some of the buses, a bus company mechanic rigged a trap to electrocute him. Irving learned of this and warned Jef.

Jef, for once, was not afraid. He said the trap was attached to Bus No. 82. Irving checked and found Jef was correct.

Around the farm Jef was always active. He threw stones at unwanted visitors, urinated through cracks in the wall, killed more rabbits and learned to amuse those few visitors he liked by peering through a hole in the ceiling and calling a tossed coin — "heads" or "tails" — when none of the Irvings was in the room. Other times he mischievously locked Voirrey in her bedroom with a lock that could not be reached from inside her room. He also would throw heavy furniture, no mean trick for an animal estimated to weigh only a pound and a half.

As time went on Jef began to show himself to the Irvings — but infrequently. They saw him walking the rafters. Voirrey hid outdoors once and saw him. Mrs. Irving put her finger into a crack in the wall and felt inside his mouth and was bitten for her pains. Jef apologized for drawing blood and killed a rabbit to make up for it. Finally he even let himself be photographed but he was so nervous that Voirrey, not very experienced with a camera, never got a satisfactory portrait.

Those who saw Jef said he had a bushy tail like a squirrel's, yellow to brownish fur, small ears and a pushed-in face. His most-often described features were his front paws which according to Irving were hand-like with three fingers and a thumb. Jef claimed to be an 83-year-old mongoose and said he had come from India many years before — but he fitted the description of a mongoose about as well as he did that of "part of the fifth dimension."

Irving suggested he might be a cross between a native rodent and one of several mongooses that actually had been brought from India to the Isle of Man some years before. If so, he was indeed a freak. No known mammal in the world, according to naturalist Ivan T. Sanderson, has three fingers and a thumb. Over and above that, however, Sanderson points out that a mongoose could not crossbreed with a rodent.

Of course investigators came from England to look into this story. A reporter from the *Manchester Daily Dispatch* heard Jef speak. The reporter was with Viorrey at the time. Capt. M. H. Macdonald, businessman and racing driver, paid three visits to the farm at Doarlish Cashen. He heard Jef speak both inside the house and out, had stones thrown at him and witnessed the coin-calling trick. Once he and Irving walked four miles to Peel for lunch, had some beer, talked about Mrs. Irving's shoes and picked a wild-flower. When they returned to the farm Mrs. Irving met them outside the door and recounted their doings. Jef had followed them and reported home before their arrival.

Harry Price, director of the National Laboratory of Psychical Research, and Lambert, (whose damage suit was mentioned earlier) went together to Man to investigate the story but Jef was afraid "the spook-chaser" would trap him and put him in a bottle. Psychiatrist (then psychic investigator) Nandor Fodor did not meet Jef but talked to many persons who had.

For a while the story of Gef was a world wonder. There was even an offer of $50,000 for a six months' tour of the United States. Jef turned this down screaming, "They would put me in a bottle!" Finally, when Jef, who never had been seen by any of the investigators, refused to talk or play his tricks when strangers of any kind were on the premises, interest waned. Except for mentions in a few books touching on poltergeists Jef was forgotten.

In 1946 the little animal briefly came into the news again when Leslie Graham claimed to have killed him. Graham had bought the Irving farm and said that several times in the 15 months of his tenancy he had seen a large black and white weasel-like animal disturbing his chickens. He had set snares from which the animal always escaped. Finally, hearing a great disturbance in the farmyard one October morning he found the animal snarling in the snare. He then had taken a club and killed the beast.

He described the animal as about three feet long, weighing five pounds, one ounce. He skinned it and its pelt was "as thick as cow skin, indicating that animal was very old."

This seems an inordinately sad ending to one of the most charming tales in all paranormal literature. One could only take hope from the disparity between Graham's description of the animal he killed and the Irvings' description of Jef. On the other hand, could Jef have grown that much bigger in a decade? A final consolation: if death had come to him at 95 as computed from his own claims, his worst fear at least was not realized. He was not put in a bottle.

Did Jef ever really exist? And if so, what was he?

Many writers and a few persons I talked to on the Isle of Man find it easy to dismiss the entire episode as a hoax, considering Voirrey the principal culprit of course. They accuse her of being a ventriloquist who began playing tricks which were built to unbelievable proportions first by her father and then by newspaper reporters looking for copy where little ordinarily could be found. One early investigator, J. Radcliffe, of the *Isle of Man Examiner*, said he caught Voirrey squeaking once when he was with Irving. Irving, however, insisted the noise came from another part of the room.

Most of the investigators who actually went to Doarlish Cashen saw enough to convince them that Jef was more than the product of the Irvings' imaginations. They base this conclusion on the facts that Voirrey could not have been a good enough ventriloquist to have fooled them all; that doors could not have been locked from the outside by any of the family; that much of Irving's knowledge about other parts of the island could be explained only by granting the existence of Jef; and that the Irvings would not have kept up such a hoax for so many years for no profit. Also they point to the killed rabbits and the stones thrown against the outside of the house when all the family was inside.

Early on, psychic investigators postulated that Jef was a poltergeist or even a ghost. Manx people (the few who will talk about Jef at all today) speak of him as "the spook." But Fodor, both in his book *Haunted People*, coauthored with Hereward Carrington (E. P. Dutton & Co., 1951), and in conversation argued against both of these explanations.

True, as in classic poltergeist manifestations Jef showed up at about the time Voirrey was going into puberty — but he did not go away until at least 1938. This does not follow the classic pattern at all. Moreover, Fodor pointed out that a poltergeist never is seen at all and does only harm. Jef threw stones and spat on people during his fits of temper but he also furnished meat in the form of rabbits and did such errands as going downstairs to look at the clock when Irving asked him to. As for the ghost explanation, how often has a ghost been known to eat biscuits and chocolates and then urinate?

Which brings us to the final possibility. As Fodor wrote in 1937, "Is Jef an animal that talks? All probabilities are against it but all the evidence is for it."

Fodor, a 20th-century psychiatrist, believed in "possession." He postulated that Irving, a man much reduced in circumstances, "obsessed" some small animal and moulded it to his own personality. The shock of being a life-long failure split off part of Irving's personality which contrived the animal in order to fill his time, build his ego — in other words, feed "the mental starvation" from which he suffered in the wilderness of the Isle. Fodor pointed out many similarities between Jef's personality and Irving's. Both were dictatorial when crossed and both were overly possessive of Voirrey. Finally, the little animal served to bring outsiders to Doarlish Cashen and to attract attention to a man who could not have been satisfied with the intellectual calibre of his farm neighbors.

I think it was in my last conversation with Fodor that the subject of Jef came up again. While in *Haunted People* he sounds a bit tentative in his suggestion, over the years he seemed to have become surer of his hypothesis. However, he had lost track of the Irvings by that time and wondered if Jef had gone with them when they sold the farm and left the island. Might Jef still be alive somewhere?

As I've said, today Jef is not a favorite subject of conversation on the Isle of Man but those few who do not speak of him as a hoax seem sincere in their belief that Jef indeed did live. All who knew them regarded the Irvings as honest respectable people. Also, some persons have pointed out that Mrs. Irving seldom mentioned Jef but when she did she made clear he was an animal, not a "ghost" or "spirit."

Ironically, not on the Isle of Man but in England some of the answers Fodor wanted came to light when I talked to Viorrey, the last of the Irving household. She is an attractive woman and a knowledgeable conversationalist but she did not answer the question I most wanted answered. What happened to Jef?

Voirrey says she does not know. The last she remembers his being around the farm was in 1938 or 1939. He seemed to go away for longer and longer periods of time and then he just never showed up again. He had made no statements about leaving; there had been no good-byes; he simply was gone. No, Jef did not leave the island — with the Irvings, at any rate. Voirrey is certain, however, that the beast Graham clubbed to death was not Jef.

In the animal's gradual leave-taking Fodor might well have found support for his theory about Irving and Jef. Was it merely coincidence that Jef who always claimed to hate publicity ceased to be around when interest in him fell off and no more interesting people came around to talk to Irving about the phenomenon? Perhaps Fodor would say that Jef no longer served Irving's purpose.

Fodor also would have been interested. in the denouement of the story of Jef. Today, more than 30 years later, Voirrey hates Jef. In the early days she and Jef were inseparable, playing games and sharing sweets but as she grew older Jef seemed closer to her father. Fodor noticed in 1937 and reported at that time that Jef seemed to have outstripped Voirrey in mental growth. He wrote, "The grasp and thirst for knowledge of the Talking Mongoose is simply phenomenal..."

And what of Voirrey in 1937? No longer a child of the moors, she had become a young woman who wanted a social life and friends and more than anything else she wanted to be accepted. By that time Jef had become a burden.

"I was shy...I still am," she said. "He made me meet people I didn't want to meet. Then they said I was 'mental' or a ventriloquist. Believe me, if I was that good I would jolly well be making money from it now!"

I cannot divulge where Voirrey lives now or the type of work she does but she is not rich. The only money the Irvings ever made from Jef, besides the sale of rabbits, was five pounds Fodor paid for his week's room and board and an occasional guinea paid for newspaper pictures. According to Voirrey Jef cost them dearly. They had to sell the farm at a low price because Manxmen called it "haunted."

"Jef was very detrimental to my life. We were snubbed. The other children used to call me 'the spook." I had to leave the Isle of Man and I hope that no one where I work now ever knows the story. Jef has even kept me from getting married. How could I ever tell a man's family about what happened?"

Was Jef a mongoose?

"I don't know. I know he was a small animal about nine inches to a foot long. I know he talked to us from the wainscoting. His voice was very high-pitched. He swore a lot."

The speech was not parrot-like?

"Oh, no. At first he talked to me more than anyone. We carried on regular conversations."

After 30 years you still insist this was not a hoax?

"It was not a hoax and I wish it had never happened. If my mother and I had had our way we never would have told anybody about it. But Father was sort of wrapped up in it. It was such a wonderful phenomenon that he just had to tell people about it."

Fodor regretted that the mystery of the talking mongoose probably never would be solved. He felt that "the power which he (Jef) displayed must have had a human origin." He believed that clues obtained from studying that "power" might have given us leads about many strange and still mysterious aspects of human personality and possibly explain poltergeist phenomena (though he did not believe Jef was pure poltergeist).

I can make no claim to having brought us any closer to a solution but after talking to Voirrey, the last principal involved (assuming Jef died or perhaps faded away) two things fascinated me. First, is Fodor's hypothesis correct? If we could talk about it together today, I would be less skeptical.

Second, I spent an entire day with Voirrey, talking of many things. She knows of the British newspapers' propensity for paying high prices for "exposé" stories. Yet, despite her position on the financial ladder she will not even talk to reporters who have tried to trace her down, presumably with offers of money.

Someday I may have to eat these words but I found myself believing this woman when with every emotional and financial motive for saying otherwise she said very simply, "Yes, there was a little animal who talked and did all those other things. He said he was a mongoose and said we should call him Jef...but I do wish he had left us alone."

THE COOK WHO BREWED
A HAUNTING

Evidence on record in files of British psychic research society reveals an early 20th-century culinary innovation.

Deep in the country south-west of Birmingham, at about eight o'clock on a Sunday evening Dorothy Woodward, housemaid for the Philip Roberts family, climbed the back stairs to her mistress' bedroom. The drawn draperies and the thick walls of the old two-storey brick house muffled a blustery March wind outside. Opening the door Dorothy crossed to the dressing table and arranged the silver-backed toilet set neatly on the embroidered scarf. Mr. and Mrs. Roberts were at dinner downstairs and the children were asleep in an adjoining room. It was Dorothy's custom to turn down the bed and lay out the night things, a duty she had performed hundreds of times.

Tonight would be different.

As she stood by the dressing table she heard two groans — like a dog moaning, she said later — coming from under the bed. The family dog, however, never was allowed in the house and in fact at that time was being walked several miles away.

Startled, Dorothy stiffened attentively. Suddenly an invisible but powerful hand shoved her backward against the dressing table.

"A moment later I saw a figure. It seemed to come from under the bed and move across the room to the door. I saw only the back of the figure which was tall and clothed in white. The figure went through the door, out of the room, and I distinctly heard its footsteps on the landing outside."

Utterly terrified the girl managed to stifle an outcry so that she would not frighten her young charges asleep in the next room. Instead she rushed down the servants' stairs and told the cook who was preparing dinner.

"Nonsense!" the cook — an elderly woman named Mrs. Everett — declared, urging Dorothy not to make a complete fool of herself by running to the master. So the story did not reach the family until Dorothy told Ethel Cavendish, the head nanny, who despite her scepticism went to Mrs. Roberts.

Eventually the haunting reached such proportions that Mrs.

Roberts wrote to Sir William Barrett, the distinguished Edwardian psychical researcher, to ask if he would visit them and bring to an end the terror besieging her household.

Our knowledge of the case comes from Sir William's personal investigation and the reports and letters he published in the *Journal* of the British Society for Psychical Research for March 1915. In line with the Society's custom, pseudonyms or initials were used for all persons involved and the place was named only as "a haunted house in Worcestershire." However, the Society had complete identification of the place and persons in its files.

Hauntings of the noisy poltergeist type frequently seem to revolve around pubescent children who unconsciously unleash newly developed powerful energies. But in the "Roberts" case the elderly cook appears to be the unknowing medium through whom the forces manifested themselves.

Although one of the other servants had lived in the house alone for three weeks before the family moved in, the haunting did not begin until the cook was on the premises. After the cook's departure the terrifying events abruptly ceased.

Oddly enough, however, the house already had local reputation for being haunted although no definite stories were told. When they leased the place the Roberts family had dismissed the idea as nonsense because a haunted house of the same name was the subject of a popular novel of the day. They felt sure this was the basis of the rumor.

The house, located about two miles from the railway station, stood well back from the road and was surrounded by large and beautiful gardens. It was as quiet and lovely a spot as could be desired and the Roberts family had lived in it happily for perhaps two and a half years before anything occurred to disturb them.

Although Mrs. Everett, the cook, refused (or pretended to refuse) to believe the story, she later admitted that one night she had heard groaning noises and the sounds of "something" leaving the room. On another occasion when she heard stamping footsteps she had lighted a candle but found nothing on the landing outside her room. Half a dozen other times the cook was to be disturbed at night, while the other servants repeatedly heard groaning and strange noises from her room on nights when she herself heard nothing.

When questioned by Sir William Barrett, Mrs. Everett related that at her previous post with a family on the Isle of Wight there had been many curious noises — smashing crockery, footsteps and moving furniture. All this, she said "was also heard by my mistress and others and they were much frightened and said it was dreadful." It never had been explained. When that family left England she accepted the job as cook with Mrs. Roberts, in whose home she slept alone in a room above the ground floor night nursery. She was sure no one was playing tricks on her and by the time Sir William arrived she also was sure something frightening had stood by her bed and groaned. Sometimes her bedclothes were pulled off.

Sir William interviewed each servant alone. Ethel Cavendish, aged about 30, was, in his view, the most intelligent and respectable. She said she had had difficulty in believing Dorothy's story until one time, as she slept with the two children in the night nursery she heard the window of the day nursery below being thrown open and then slammed down again, followed by sounds of furniture being knocked about. Too frightened to go down alone she thought of calling Mr. Roberts but after about 15 minutes these noises ended and she lay down again. In the early morning she went down to examine the day nursery. The windows and also the door were locked and nothing whatever had been disturbed!

She heard nothing further until the night of 15 June, when the tramping of heavy footsteps "as if made by a person with hob-nailed boots coming into the room" woke her out of a sound sleep. As she lay trembling she heard the steps come across to the dressing table and had the feeling that something there would block her way if she attempted to leave.

"I was terrified but managed to light the candle and found it was 1:20 a.m. The perspiration was running off my forehead with fear and I kept the candle alight but no more sleep was possible. I was really too frightened to get out of bed to call Mr. Roberts and nothing further occurred that night. I am sure the sound of tramping did not come from someone walking in the garden outside, for I felt the bed shaking with the heavy tread."

On another occasion a hand suddenly gripped her throat so hard that it hurt. It was not a nightmare. She lit a candle. Once more she found nothing and the children were still sound asleep on their cots. After this she kept a candle burning at night but except for odd noises there were no further intrusions into the room.

In the meantime Mr. Roberts had fitted up an electric bell so that she could summon him but when she did so nothing was discovered. Each time he searched the house and sat outside the room for a while. Ethel assured Sir William that Dorothy's hair-raising story, which she did not believe at all, could not have inspired any of this.

Sir William carefully examined the whole house. When he walked across the heavy felt carpet in the night nursery he scarcely could hear his own footsteps. Nurse Ethel had to stamp very hard from the door past her bed to the dressing table to make the old timbers shake. Unfortunately nothing occurred during the weekend he was there although Sunday had been a favourite night for the poltergeist.

Later Mrs. Roberts wrote to tell him that the night after he left, Ethel in the night nursery and the two maids who shared a bedroom upstairs all heard awful groaning for perhaps 20 minutes. Mr. Roberts, she said, "distinctly felt a presence as of some person brushing past him but could find nothing to account for it." At other times he was overcome by a feeling of great stupour but attributed the unusual effect to indigestion.

Mrs. Roberts herself never witnessed a disturbance. In the same letter, dated 6 August, 1914, she told Sir William that the previous Sunday her husband had been sick in bed and she had not been able to leave him until quite late. She had no time for dinner until after nine o'clock that night and was eating when Ethel rushed into the dining room to say that terrible noises were coming from the larder. Mrs. Roberts hurried after her.

Ethel and Lester Johnson, a temporary maid, had been in the larder chopping ice for Mr. Roberts. All was quiet for the moment but Mrs. Roberts had barely returned to her dinner when Ethel ran back to say that it sounded as if furniture were being pushed around in the cellar.

Lester agreed to go down there with her mistress and had just seized a lamp when Mr. Roberts, upstairs, burst into violent coughing. His wife ran up and stayed with him for about half an hour. When she returned to the back of the house she found Lester still standing where she had left her on a little landing at the top of the cellar steps.

Lester reported she had heard footsteps mounting the stairs and had shouted in a loud firm voice, "What do you want?"

The footsteps had stopped. The cook, standing nearby, had fainted from shock but the stout Lester and Nurse Ethel had continued to stand guard. Now they went with Mrs. Roberts to search the cellar.

"We did this thoroughly and nothing human was to be seen,"

wrote Mrs. Roberts. As usual there was absolutely nothing to account for the uncanny goings-on.

A night or so later Florence Lambert, the parlormaid, woke about 3:00 a.m. to see a form standing over her bed, showing up against the window "darker than night." She was able to make out the shape of protruding ears! Although matches were beside her bed she dared not put out a hand, which would have had to go through the figure. Squeezing her eyes tightly shut she lay shivering for a long time in the silent room. Dorothy in the next bed did not stir. When Florence finally peeked the strange form had disappeared.

On the 29th August Sir William got more news from the beleaguered household. The report said the cook had left and all was quiet.

During the last few days of her employment there the situation had grown acute. Among other disturbances noises in the cook's room awoke Florence and Dorothy early one morning. It sounded as if old Mrs. Everett were walking around, opening and shutting her tin box. But when Dorothy crossed the hall to investigate she discovered Mrs. Everett had gone down to start breakfast. Later that day noises sounded in the empty larder and witnesses heard footsteps on the stairs leading to the attic.

But the very day Mrs. Everett left, the servants reported feeling a total change in the atmosphere of the house. All of them commented on it. From then on all abnormal sounds ceased.

"We have had 'peace, perfect peace' as far as ghosts are concerned. It seems the queerest thing," Mrs. Roberts ended her last letter.

Nurse Ethel, she wrote, just had informed her that for many months she had been dreaming they all were going to leave the house. Her dreams had begun in February before any of the ghost troubles started.

Sir William concluded his own report by stating that the Roberts family in fact did give up the house the following autumn. The landlord had informed him just before the Robertses moved that insofar as he knew no previous tenant had heard or seen anything out of the ordinary.

This whole incredible story with all its extraordinary details is buried — and still unexplained — in the files of the British society.

THE ROYAL WRAITHS OF BRITAIN
Dennis Eisenberg

England's treasury of ghosts — many of regal mien — is as rich as its long and glorious history.

No country in the world has so rich a treasury of well-documented accounts of haunted homes and ghost appearances as Britain. In this fast-paced age of scientific and technological achievement, surveys show that millions of Britons believe in ghosts.

In September 1970 a study made by social workers in the Shropshire town of Dawley indicated that fully 10 per cent of its 8,000 population claim to have seen or felt a ghostly presence. Even persons in this typical English community who said they did not believe in ghosts claimed to have seen them!

A French sociologist once said that ghosts were the product of English "fogs and mists and the dank ruminations of the British mind." But his remark begs the question, for in reality there is little fog in the United Kingdom and it is the upper-class and aristocratic circles in Britain more than the less well-educated classes who have produced the best-documented accounts of apparitions. The Society of Psychical Research which has been investigating ghosts since 1870 has on its shelves in its London headquarters more than 10,000 attested reports of supernatural happenings. Certainly not the least of these are incidents involving British royalty, for many of the royal family have seen ghosts with their own eyes.

At Windsor Castle, servants and princes have seen two regal ghosts. The most famous of these is the ghost of Elizabeth I (who is known, by the way, to have had strong psychic powers). Shortly before her death in 1603 she told her courtiers she had seen a vision of herself on her deathbed, "pallid, shrivelled and wan." In that superstitious age the monarch's words struck terror into the hearts of her subjects.

Within days of the Queen's death, her ghost wearing a black mantilla was seen walking in the Queen's library. On several occasions the apparition has been seen walking on the castle walls and members of the royal family will own that they often have heard strange noises.

At least one member of the present royal household, Princess Margaret, has confided to friends that she has seen the ghost of

Elizabeth I, but naturally, in view of the official hostility of the Anglican Church to such reports, this is not admitted openly.

The other royal ghost at Windsor Castle is that of King George III who went completely mad in 1810. To keep him out of the way he was confined to one room of the castle and it is no secret that to this day his ghost haunts the room where he was kept confined. Nobody is known actually to have seen his ghost but soft moans coming from the room have been heard again and again. No visitors to the famous castle, the oldest in Britain, are allowed to see this room and questions from close friends of the present royal family about this strange occurrence meet only silence and a quick change of subject.

Another widely reported ghost at Windsor is that of Herne the Hunter, a warden there under King Henry VIII. Accused of practising witchcraft, he hanged himself from the branches of an enormous oak tree. The tree was destroyed by lightning in 1863 and servants at the castle tell me that Herne's ghost often has been seen in the park near where the tree stood. Historical records indicate that bad luck follows the sighting of Herne's ghost. Some minor disaster seems always to follow — like crop failure or "the falling down dead of cattle."

Not only ancient ghosts haunt Windsor. A mere four decades ago a young guardsman committed suicide while on duty near the spot where Herne the Hunter has been seen. Weeks later another soldier, an 18-year-old Grenadier Guard patrolling the area, saw a man in uniform marching toward him. Thinking the new arrival was his early-morning relief, the young guard had the shock of his life when he caught a glimpse of the face beneath the tall bearskin. It was the man who had shot himself less than a month previously. After this incident the officer in charge of guarding the castle changed the patrol route.

Queen Elizabeth I crops up again in connection with weird happenings at Loseley Park near Guildford. The monarch slept there on several occasions as did other royals, including James I and Queen Anne. The present owner, Mr. J. R. More-Molyneux, admits that his stately home is haunted but refuses to discuss it, saying only, "Ghosts are very personal matters and I do not wish to discuss them. They concern our family and nobody else."

It seems the owner has reason to hide the strange history of his family home. Servants who work there will not sleep in the house and refuse to say why. Shortly before World War I an American woman, a Miss Dodge who had rented the house, fled Loseley Park early one morning together with all her guests. They were so terrified by what they had seen they refused to return — even for their suitcases. They insisted that their belongings be sent to them. Whatever they had witnessed unnerved the party but they were sworn to secrecy Mr. More-Molyneux and refused to explain even to curious friends the reason for their flight.

Princess Margaret lives at Kensington Palace in the heart of London and fascinates guests at her dinner parties with accounts of the ghost of King George II who has been seen looking out of the windows of her present home. The Princess relates that her long-distant ancestor used Kensington Palace as his residence until he died there in 1760. He was often homesick for his native Germany and always looked forward to receiving letters and other news from his family seat in Hanover. He often peered from the palace windows at the weather vane above the main entrance, for when the wind was favourable he knew the ships bringing him news would come all the faster. The Snowdons themselves have seen his ghost looking in the direction of the weather vane.

Margaret's mother, the Queen Mother, is more personally involved in accounts of ghosts than any other members of the royal family. Mystery surrounds numerous supernatural incidents involving Glamis Castle in Scotland, the family home of Strathmores, the Queen Mother's family. Accounts of strange happenings there go back as far as 1540 when one of the Queen Mother's ancestors — Jean, the beautiful Lady Glamis — was burned at the stake as a witch. Since then many of the descendants of Jean, the Bowes-Lyon family, have been involved in seductions, abductions and intrigue.

However, in 1820 when a son was born to the 11th Earl of Strathmore, the darkest shadow of all fell on the Bowes-Lyon family. The infant "was so hideously deformed at birth that his parents decided to record him as dead since he could not possibly inherit the title and estates."

The next son, Thomas George (great-grandfather of the Queen Mother) became the 12th Earl. When he was 21 he was "initiated" into the grim secret of his elder brother's fate. He was led down a passage to the room in Glamis Castle where the poor wretch was being kept alive. As each child in the family turned 21 he was let into the secret.

Only years later when a workman stumbled upon the curious passage and found the grisly remains of the family heir was the well-guarded secret laid bare to the world. The wall was hurriedly blocked up; the workman was given a large sum of money and persuaded to emigrate to the United States where all trace of him has been lost.

The curse of the deformed boy still haunts the castle and the Bowes-Lyon family. People who live in the vicinity will tell you the ghost of the prisoner remains in the house where he lived out his pathetic years.

To this day the malediction seems to have lost none of its potency. Only recently the tragic story of the Earl of Strathmore, cousin of the Queen, was revealed in the British press.

At the age of 40, the Earl went into a nursing home in Dundee to recover from an illness. Here he met an Irish nurse, Mary Brennan, with whom he fell in love. She was Catholic but she agreed to give up her religion to marry the Protestant Earl. The ceremony was carried out in the Castle's private chapel — boycotted by the whole royal family. The only witnesses were two friends. ·

The marriage seemed doomed from the start. The couple's first child died of pneumonia 24 hours after its birth and in September 1967 the beautiful young Lady Strathmore was found dead in her bed in the turreted Glamis Castle.°

The Queen Mother herself appears not to have fallen foul of the curse. She loves returning to Scotland during the summer months — but she keeps well away from Glamis Castle. The account of the ghost at the family home certainly seems authentic, for the Queen Mother's sister, Lady Granville, says: "We were never allowed to talk about it when we were children. Our parents forbade us ever to discuss it or ask any questions. My father and grandfather absolutely refused to discuss it either."

The Tower of London, which has witnessed the torture and beheadings of royal figures, appears to have more than its share of ghosts — seen, heard and reported by guards and governors who have lived there. The Beefeaters who show tourists around the dungeons refuse to discuss ghosts and the present governor will not be drawn either. Superstition holds that even mentioning such matters will bring ill luck and the normally loquacious guides dry up when the subject of ghosts is broached.

Even so, the records show that the Tower must be the most haunted edifice in the world. As recently as 12 February, 1957, the night of the 403rd anniversary of the execution on Tower Green of Lady Jane Grey (Queen of England for only nine days), the appearance of a ghost was confirmed. A normally level-headed Welsh Guardsman named Johns was standing in his sentry box where he was startled by the sound of stones falling on its roof. Looking up he saw a "white shapeless form" on Salt Tower 40 feet above him. He shouted for help and a search party set out to investigate but found nothing. The officer in charge was about to laugh off Johns' trembling account when another guardsman reported seeing a "strange white apparition" with "no recognizable shape" at the same place on Salt Tower. This is about 100 yards from the house of the jailer where Lady Jane Grey had been imprisoned.

Said Guardsman Johns: "The ghost stood between the battlements. I went to tell the other guard and as I pointed to the battlements the figure appeared again." When questioned about this the next day, a Guards officer would say only, "Guardsman Johns is convinced he saw a ghost. Let us leave it at that."

Despite official reluctance to talk about the frequent appearances of ghosts at the Tower, it is not denied that during World War I a sentry on duty at the Spur Tower called out the guard when an eerie procession passed right in front of him. He saw a group of men carrying a stretcher on which lay the body of a headless figure, the decapitated head carried beneath his own arm. (This follows the ancient execution procedure, for after going to the scaffold the body and head always were brought back to the Tower for burial.)

A century earlier — in 1816 — a sentinel at the Tower was so unnerved by the sight of an apparition walking up the stairs he lunged at it with his bayonet. The cold metal only passed through the figure and blunted itself on the stone wall beyond. The terrified soldier died a few days later — of shock, it is said — and his officers believed he must have seen one of the persons of high rank — Anne Boleyn or the Duke of Northumberland whose ghostly forms have frequently been seen walking the part of the Tower reserved for aristocratic prisoners.

A former Constable of the Tower, Col. E. H. Carkeet Jones, recounts that a soldier of the 60th Rifles was court-martialled in 1864 for having been found unconscious at the door of the room in which Anne Boleyn passed her last night before going to the scaffold in 1536.

The soldier explained that he had seen a figure in white coming toward him. The figure failed to stop when challenged and the guard dutifully charged, aiming to stop the figure with his bayonet. Meeting no resistance the soldier saw the white apparition simply continue its advance. The frightened man fell to the ground in a faint.

He was acquitted when two other soldiers swore they had witnessed the whole macabre scene from a window of the Bloody Tower where they were stationed.

A similar white figure of a woman was spotted in February 1933 by yet another guard. Like others before it in the annals of Tower history, the figure was headless. As the newspapers reported at the time: "Confronted by such an apparition the sentry fled, making his way to the guardroom, greatly unnerved."

Also in the heart of London is another haunted building, Apsley House. Now a museum it was once the London home of the first Duke of Wellington who lived there until his sudden death in 1852.

Although Wellington had conquered Napoleon, his position on the Third Reform Bill in 1832 put him at loggerheads with the people of Britain. The Duke refused to budge and as revolution threatened the mobs stoned his house. Completely unworried, the Duke fortified his house with iron windows and shutters and declined to step out of doors.

Sometime later he told colleagues that one night during this period as he was preparing to go to bed he was confronted by a ghost in a hallway. A man of unbending courage, Wellington faced up to the ghost whom he soon recognized as Oliver Cromwell. Wellington said afterwards that Cromwell's ghost pointed a warning finger to the yelling crowds milling around Apsley House. This must have been a one-time-only visit, for the ghost of Cromwell has not been seen in the building again.

Dozens of ancient stately homes and inns in Britain are reputedly haunted either by members of British royalty or persons closely connected with the royal house. For instance, at Sawston Hall near Cambridge many guests claim to have seen the ghost of Mary Tudor, called "Bloody Mary." Although she slept there only one night, in July 1553, it was a dramatic occasion. The owner of Sawston Hall, John Huddlestone, saved her life when he got wind of Duke of Northumberland's plot to seize her and thus prevent her taking her place on the throne.

There was a fire in the house that very night but Mary's four-poster bed survived the blaze. It is kept in the Tapestry Room and the many guests who have slept in the bed since relate that they have seen Bloody Mary clearly, smiling as she walks across the room to disappear into the faded Flemish tapestries on the wall.

Some visitors to Sawston Hall have heard the soft sound of music which the owners can explain only by recalling the virginal Mary loved to play for her father, Henry VIII. A number of persons interested in ghostly phenomena, including the well-known British clairvoyant Tom Corbett, have confirmed the presence of a ghost in the house.

Another ancient residence less than 50 miles from London, Beeleigh Abbey near Maldon, houses the ghost of Sir John Gates, one of the gallant gentlemen who lost their heads for championing the cause of Lady Jane Grey. Sir John had purchased the house cheaply from King Henry VIII and according to present and previous owners his ghost repossesses at least the "James I" bedroom every 22 August, the anniversary of the day he was beheaded in 1553.

When Henry died in 1547 Edward VI, aged 10 years, ascended the throne. Five years later, in 1552, Edward VI was persuaded by the Duke of Northumberland under whose thumb he ruled to assign the crown to Lady Jane Grey, Northumberland's daughter-in-law. Thus Mary and Elizabeth, the daughters of Henry the VIII, were excluded from the succession to the throne. One year later, on the death of Edward VI in 1553, the Duke of Northumberland proclaimed Lady Jane Grey queen — thus sealing her doom. This political take-over was unsuccessful and Northumberland, Lady Jane and the others were arrested. The Duke of Northumberland was executed on 22 August, 1553, while Lady Jane Grey and her husband were not beheaded until 12 February, 1554.

Henry the VIII figures too in the appearance of Anne Boleyn's ghost at Hever Castle in Kent where she was brought up and where King Henry courted her in the delightful gardens. Ann's ghost is said to be seen there about Christmastime every year.

The Frenchman may say what he likes but too many reliable witnesses in different parts Britain have seen the royal ghosts. They can't be dismissed simply as "fogs and mists and the dank ruminations of British mind."

OUR ENCHANTED FLAT
It was an ordinary house in an ordinary neighborhood until we moved in and a strange other-worldly drama began.

Carol Halford-Watkins

My two sisters and I grew up in a happy hospitable home. Our large living room was the scene of many pleasant parties at which we gathered to sing and dance to the rippling music of a pianola. It was a good time to be alive. Our family, united and loving, were very close and my sister Dorothy ("Doff") and I developed an especially deep relationship which continues today.

In the years following our father's sudden death in late 1943 — when we sold the old home at 180 Valetta Road in London and the happy days we had spent there became only golden memories — Doff and I discovered a spiritual and psychic link between us. Even though she is eight years my junior, we came to see ourselves as "twin souls" who think and act alike and who share the same philosophy of life. Our experiences in the realm of ESP — even when we are an ocean apart — have been remarkable. When we get together some of them seem very funny and we whimsically ascribe them to the magic of our "fairy godmum."

In 1948 I emigrated to Canada with my husband and settled in Victoria, B. C. Within five years my marriage and Doff's too had ended disastrously and it seemed natural that we should fly to each other for comfort. So I packed and made the 7000-mile journey back to London where Doff — who now had a 12-year-old daughter named Betty — and I decided to set up a home together.

In 1953 the housing situation in London, barely recovered from the bombings of the war years, was very tight and I spent two months in a fruitless search for a suitable place to live. And then more or less by accident I cam upon the ideal location: an old house, situated not far from the old family home, which had been remodelled into two self-contained apartments or "flats" as they are called in England. I took one look at the large living room, whose layout was a nearly exact replica of the living room in our old house, and knew immediately this was to be our home.

Doff was just as pleased as I was and she agreed that we

301

should furnish it much like the old family living room. We spent the next few days selecting the right items and placing them lovingly in the old familiar places — the buffet sideboard near the door, settee and armchairs by the fireside, a bookcase in its old place and a piano where the pianola had stood. Even unusual items — like the carved oak chest which served as a window seat — came to us as if by magic. Finally Doff made up some beautiful old-gold satin drapes. When at last we prepared to move into our new home in October 1953, we little dreamed that we were embarking on one of the strangest adventures of our lives.

As it turned out I moved into the flat a day ahead of Doff and Betty and so spent my first night there alone. I was up quite late unpacking and retired around midnight, expecting to fall into a deep sleep from sheer exhaustion. But I had been in bed only about five minutes when I heard my bedroom door click open.

When I sat up I saw framed in the half-open doorway the figure of a little girl who looked about seven years old. She was dressed in the old-fashioned clothes of the early part of the century — a long dark dress covered by a starched white pinafore with goffered frills. She had a quaint little pixie face, dark hair and large brown eyes twinkling with childish mischief.

Not really frightened by this strange visitor, although I recognized her immediately as someone very much out of the ordinary, I welcomed her. In reply she giggled and left, snapping the door shut. I decided not to tell Doff what I had seen. I suspected that for Betty's sake she might be unduly alarmed to learn the flat at 132 Dalling Road had another occupant.

The next morning Doff and Betty arrived and during the next few days we kept very busy unpacking and setting up a home. On the third night, however, as we relaxed by the fire-side late at night, Doff told me she had had a strange experience that evening. She had been washing up at the sink when she heard the kitchen door open behind her. Someone entered and started dancing to a hummed tune. Assuming it was her daughter, Doff asked, "Have you finished your homework, Betty?" When she received no reply she wheeled around to discover there was no one there! She found Betty in the living room where she had been doing her homework for the past half-hour.

I told Doff of my experience and we decided not to mention these strange incidents to Betty.

But in the weeks that followed we were treated to the full

range of poltergeist activity — thumps, bangs and crashes, doors opening and shutting, objects thrown across rooms, lights switched on and off, the contents of our vegetable rack repeatedly strewn over the kitchen floor, bedclothes stripped off, childish crayon marks on the kitchen walls, crashing chords on the piano and more.

With all this going on we hardly could keep the secret from Betty. So we decided to treat the whole matter lightly an named our noisy little guest "Minnie." Since we made a point of displaying no fear, Betty felt none and accepted the situation in the spirit of fun. In this way Minnie became one of the family.

Doff and I sensed from the beginning there was nothing malevolent or harmful about Minnie — mischievous, yes, but to us she seemed just a boisterous little spirit who hungered for attention.

We were to find out Minnie also had a sense of humour. Her favourite trick, when we were sitting around the fireside in the evenings, was to open and close the living room door. Sometimes she would delay closing the door. Then one of us would call out, "Shut the door, Minnie, you're making a cold draft," and obediently the door would click shut.

Minnie's noise-making activities took place mainly in the upper front bedroom, next to Betty's, which we used as a storage room. So this became known as Minnie's room. Frequently after a thunderous crash overhead we would dash up to Minnie's room and find nothing had been disturbed. At other times, when we played records, we could hear Minnie's dancing feet above us tapping in perfect rhythm. She had one favorite record, "Delicado," which never failed to produce a stomping response.

On two separate occasions as we approached the house from the outside and looked up at her room we saw a small white face peering wistfully out of the center window. Somehow we couldn't help feeling sorry for this lonely little child who had taken up residence with us. We wondered what her earthly background had been but whatever it was we were happy we could give her the family love and attention she so obviously craved.

One day, feeling that something was missing from our reconstructed family living room I decided that what we needed was a "flat-warming" party that would equal in gaiety the parties of our childhood. This party — to which we invited many friends and relatives — was a huge success and the rafters rang with song, dance and merriment. After that the room seemed to undergo a magical metamorphosis. Suddenly charged with a special atmosphere, it exuded an other-worldly charm felt by all who entered it. The spirit of the old family home had taken over and the era of the Enchanted Flat had begun!

Soon all kinds of people were knocking at our door — friends, relatives, even complete strangers — and all were greeted with the same warm hospitality that had been traditional in our family home. Once they had visited us, they returned again and again and all spoke of the "magical" atmosphere of the living room. Exactly what happened I cannot explain but we felt as if we were living in another dimension in which everything was larger than life and all things were possible. Our lives seemed swept up in a mystical flow of events which would touch all of us in one way or another — but my sister and me most of all.

The focal point of all this unusual activity was our living room which became the scene of a series of parties, poltergeist antics and all kinds of "little miracles" — like the time we decorated a lovely Christmas tree for Betty. When she saw it she was delighted but she added wistfully, "I just wish the colored lights would blink on and off." When we turned on the lights the following night, lo and behold, they were blinking!

On another occasion we bought a television set from a friend living in the Midlands and a short time later he came to London to deliver it and to set up the aerial on our roof. Local TV servicemen had told us that the Midlands aerial would not operate in London — that it was a technical impossibility — and yet, erected over our Enchanted Flat, it worked like a charm!

With our increasing flow of visitors Minnie wanted more and more to participate and was forever visiting us in the living room. Explaining the frequent opening and shutting of the door became a problem. There were those to whom we could tell the truth but there were others who might not understand and to whom we could give only evasive replies to their questions.

Minnie had a way of dealing with the scoffers. One scoffer was Ron Fitzwater, a teenaged neighbour who liked to drop in to play the latest pop records. After he inquired repeatedly about the door and we finally told him the truth he laughed derisively and said, "You can't kid me. There's someone outside this room opening and shutting the door!" We invited him to inspect every room in the flat. A few minutes later he returned.

"Well," he said, "I'm satisfied there's no one else in the flat. Now see if you can get your Minnie to open the door." I called on Minnie and cooperatively she opened the door. Still not convinced, Ron went on, "Now tell her to close it." Before I could open my mouth Minnie slammed the door shut with such an almighty bang that Ron hastily grabbed his things and left — and it was several weeks before we could coax him back!

Another time, when we explained the mystery of the door to our cousins Derek and Ellen Moyes, Derek, a solid, down-to-earth type, snorted, "Oh, come off it! It's just a trick of the wind." Minnie wasn't having any part of this phoney alibi and from the far end of the room an orange from the fruit bowl came sailing through the air and landed on Derek's lap!

In early December Ellen and Derek took me for a night's entertainment at a West End nightclub. Afterwards a group of us went to a private party in Kensington. Shortly after our arrival there I noticed a good-looking young man at the other end of room was gazing at me intently. Somewhere in the background a voice on the record was singing, "You will see a stranger across a crowded room," and when a few minutes later I found myself dancing with this stranger to the music of "Some Enchanted Evening," I did not know that the song would be a very special one to us, that I has just met my future husband.

He told me his name was Darrel Halford-Watkins and said he had returned recently from Malaya where for the past six years he had been an assistant superintendent of police engaged in quelling the activities of the Communist terrorists. When I told him I had come from Vancouver Island, Canada, we both laughed at the strange workings of fate which had brought us from the opposite ends of the earth to meet in England. Our romance developed swiftly and by Christmas we were engaged to be married.

Knowing how much my sister's life and my own paralleled each other I was not exactly surprised when a couple of weeks later Doff told me of her own budding romance. We had become friendly with our next-door neighbours, Connie and Albert Eariss. Albert was a member of a dance band called the Rumbaleros, who specialized in Latin American rhythms, and when he said they would be happy to play for us at our next party, we promptly arranged one.

The Rumbaleros turned out to be Albert's brothers plus a talented pianist and composer named Gerry Somers. What a party!

Before it was over Doff and Gerry had recognized each other intuitively as life partners and that night two happier sisters never laid their heads on pillows!

We spent Christmas Day with Mother and the family at our sister Blanche's home where we introduced the two future members of the family to everyone. We had a wonderful time but when we returned to the Enchanted Flat that night, Mrs. Doris Crispin, who lived downstairs, greeted us with a worried expression on her face.

"I don't know what has been happening in your flat," she said, "but there have been the most awful bangs and crashes going on up there. We wondered if burglars had broken in. At one time I was going to call the police but as I reached for the telephone the noise suddenly stopped."

Doff and I looked at each other. We had not told Mrs. Crispin about Minnie for fear of disturbing her. Now we suddenly felt guilty. Poor Minnie — we had left her alone on Christmas Day and obviously she had been registering her protest at our desertion. On Boxing Day, however, we had our own Christmas party and Minnie was there joining in the fun. With each new arrival she popped in on us and later in the evening we could hear her feet tapping to the music of the Rumbaleros.

At our New Year's Eve party the Rumbaleros played a beautiful beguine, "Dorothea," which Gerry had composed for my sister. Doff was delighted.

Not until the party was in full swing, however, did I notice a quaint little old lady among our guests. She had a merry face which crinkled up into frequent smiles and she wore a curious "pudding basin" red felt hat. She reminded me somehow of a nursery rhyme character. Whoever she was, she was enjoying herself — she drank, laughed and sang as much as any of us there. Later I called Doff aside and asked her if she knew who our odd little guest was. Doff looked once, did a double take, shook her head and promptly dubbed the woman "Mother Red Cap." We assumed that she must be a friend of one of our guests but when we checked with them later we found that nobody had known her. We like to think of her as our Fairy Godmother, come to enjoy the fruits of her magic.

One morning early in 1954 Doff and I attended a church in Dalling Road to receive holy communion. Afterwards the vicar invited us to join a group of parishioners for breakfast in the church hall. I found myself sitting next to a little old lady who told me she had lived in Dalling Road all her life. Sensing an opportunity to ask some questions about Minnie, I explained we lived in the corner house, not far from the church, and as I described Minnie her faded old eyes lit up in recognition.

"I remember the family well," she said. "They lived there during the World War I years. Their little girl was an only child. Poor little lamb, she died of diphtheria — there were no wonder drugs in those days, you know. She was a lonely child; her mother never allowed her to go out and play with the other kids. She used to look out of that top window a lot."

Probably as a result of my conversation with the old lady, word soon got around the neighbourhood that we were living in a haunted house. One evening there was a loud knock at the door. A man introduced himself as a "professional ghost hunter" and requested permission to discuss the poltergeist phenomena we had experienced. We invited him in and related the story of Minnie's activities. To provide some evidence I called on Minnie to perform her door-opening act, fully expecting her to cooperate as usual, but nothing happened. During our entire interview we heard not so much as a peep out of Minnie and we could assume only that she objected to being "ghost-hunted."

We were rather embarrassed but our visitor calmly accepted the situation, saying that this frequently happens during an investigation. We took him up to Minnie's room and when he saw that it was next to Betty's bedroom he suggested the energy for Minnie's poltergeist tricks emanated from Betty, who had reached the age of puberty. During this transformation stage from childhood to early adulthood, the investigator said, nature supplies an "overplus of ectoplasm" to the developing body which mischievous spirits can draw upon to produce poltergeist phenomena. (However, this does not explain how Minnie appeared on my first night in the flat — before Betty moved in.)

After asking a few more questions our ghost hunter thanked us and left. We barely had closed the door behind him when the Enchanted Flat began to shake and vibrate from the most horrendous cacophony of crashing sounds. Minnie was having a field day. She completely ignored our demands that she stop until finally, when the din became unbearable, I flew up to her room.

"Minnie!" I yelled over the noise. "You have been a very naughty girl tonight and are no longer a fit companion to have in our home. Stop this racket immediately or go back from whence you came!"

The noise ceased abruptly and in a quieter tone I tried to reason with Minnie. "Little girl," I said gently, "we have enjoyed having you with us and we have had a lot of fun together but now you must go back to your true home and leave us in peace to carry on our own lives. We shall never forget you, dear, but now we must say good-bye and God bless you."

That night I prayed that some kindly soul on the Other Side would take care of Minnie and give her the love and attention she needed. My prayer must have been answered for Minnie's noisemaking came to an end. In some ways we missed our playful little friend but we needed some quiet in our home for more earthly affairs — like preparing for our forthcoming marriages.

March 1954 saw the weddings of the two sisters whose destinies had run along such similar lines. In celebration we held what was to be the last party at the Enchanted Flat. When Doff and Betty left to join Gerry in a new home in Harrow, I naturally felt a sense of loss remembering all the good times and strange experiences we had shared during our six months' stay at the Enchanted Flat but soon I found new happiness in my life with Darrel.

With prospects none too bright in England, my husband and I decided to move to Canada. We sublet the flat to a Polish family and sold all its furnishings.

On the morning before we moved out I went to take a last look at the living room whose magical atmosphere had provided such a happy background to life in the Enchanted Flat. I wondered what it would hold for the new tenants. To my surprise I found a change had come over the room. The old magic was gone. Now it was an ordinary three-dimensional room.

At first I felt a little sad at this transformation but soon I realized what had happened. The room had served for a time as an attractive stage setting for a strange other-worldly drama and now, with its two main characters happily married, its purpose had been fulfilled. The play was over; the curtain had fallen.

THEY SHARED THEIR HOME WITH A GHOST
Dennis Chambers

In the heart of Canterbury's shopping centre — just walking distance from the cathedral where Sir Thomas a Becket was murdered and the Anglican Church was born — is Stour Street.

Along this street is the Greyfriars Monastery which dates back to the 13th century. In a flat nearby Reg and Margaret Oliver and their family shared two years of their lives with a ghost.

In 1953 Reg, then 38, worked as manager for an electrical wholesaler who traded from No 19 Stour Street. The wholesale outfit used only the ground floor for its business and the rooms on the other two storeys were used by a dealer for storing furniture.

When the company decided that Mr. Oliver and his family should live on the premises, the rooms above the shop were cleared and a contractor came in to convert them to living accommodation. Before conversion began the Olivers moved in and took up residence in the large room directly above the shop using it as a bed sit.

Margaret Oliver, who had been born in Stour Street and had lived there most of her life, was then 36. Maureen, the Olivers' daughter, was 13 and their son David was just three months old. The fifth member of the family, Prince, a brown and white mongrel dog, was seven.

The man contracted to carry out the necessary alterations, George Whitman — after whom the Olivers were to nickname their ghost — lived in London. Because the thought of driving that distance twice a day through heavy traffic held no appeal to a man his age — he was 60 — Whitman asked if he could live "on the job." When the Olivers consented he moved in to occupy a small room on the upper storey.

One day not too long afterward Whitman mentioned to Mrs. Oliver that he had become concerned about some peculiar things that were happening. Regularly, he said, one or another of his tools would be missing; some of them he soon found but others vanished without a trace. One morning when he returned to work from a tea break Whitman had discovered his saw was missing from a collection of tools he had left at the bottom of the second staircase. Eventually he found it behind the door of his own room. How it got there he had no idea.

Whitman said he was considerably shaken by this incident. But he was to be even more shaken a few days later.

Early one morning the sound of noisy activity roused the Olivers from their sleep. They reached their bedroom door just in time to see Whitman, dressed in a nightshirt and brandishing a poker go charging down the stairs in hot pursuit of some unseen quarry. Ignoring the startled onlookers he dashed down the stairs and into the shop below. Moments later he reappeared, seemingly exhausted. He was muttering to himself something about "it" having disappeared through the front door.

Whitman explained that he had waked to find a grey misty figure beside his bed. Thinking he had surprised an intruder he had leaped up to grab the first weapon that came to hand, a poker, and given chase.

He had kept the figure in sight all the way down the stairs and into the shop. Knowing the shop door would be locked he had expected to corner his quarry there. To his astonishment, however, the misty figure passed through the shop door and out into the street.

The Olivers found Whitman's story hard to believe and dismissed it as an old man's nightmare, no doubt stimulated by the disappearing tool episodes. Whitman himself refused to spend another night on the premises.

On 20 February, 1954, Mrs. Oliver's 24-year-old sister Ann married Peter Gouldsmith, then 23. After the ceremony at Stock, Essex, they traveled to Canterbury to spend the first few days of their honeymoon with the Olivers at their home in Stour Street.

About midnight both couples retired to their beds, the Olivers to their own room above the shop and the Gouldsmiths to the small bedroom on the floor above — the room in which George Whitman had slept.

Over breakfast the following morning when Reg Oliver asked if his new brother-in-law and his bride had slept well Peter got a strange look on his face and asked Reg for a word in private.

Peter Gouldsmith told Reg that around 2 a.m. he had awakened suddenly. His attention was drawn to the window through which a strong wind blew into the room. This seemed remarkable to say the least because the window was closed.

As he watched, the hazy figure of a man dressed in monk-like habit, head hidden beneath a cowl, entered the room through the window. The figure moved silently across the room and came to a momentary halt beside the bed before leaving the room through the open door.

Peter could do no more than stare in amazement at the weird visitor. Ann slept throughout and Peter did not disturb her. He told Reg he knew that if he told her what he had seen, it would ruin their visit. However, once having told Reg of his night's experience Peter saw no point in keeping the matter secret any longer and so it was discussed freely. The Olivers related Whitman's experiences in that same room — experiences they purposely had kept from the Gouldsmiths in order not to worry them.

Ann Gouldsmith, as her husband had expected, insisted they cut short their stay and they left after having spent less than half the time they had intended with the Olivers.

Peter Gouldsmith's description of the phantom intruder's monk-like garb is significant because it is thought that the building, of which Number 19 Stour Street forms a part, was built during the 13th century and is one of a group of buildings that belonged to the Greyfriars Monastery. This monastery was founded by five of the original nine Franciscan Brothers whom St. Francis of Assisi sent to England in 1224 to further the work of their Order. The main lodgings, originally constructed around 1267 and lived in right up until 1918 when they housed Belgian refugees, still stand in good order today and thousands of tourists visit them every year.

From the window where Peter's "ghost" entered the room there is an uninterrupted view of the Franciscans' lodgings and the ruins of the chapel in which they worshipped.

The history of the building to the left of Number 19, with which it shares a common wall, goes back to 1180 when it belonged to Lambin Frese, a minter of coins, whom a plaque on the wall identifies as an "enemy of Becket." Subsequently Frese offended Henry II and fled the country after which — in 1200 — the building was taken over as a hospital for poor priests.

Today it is used as a Child Welfare Clinic and Military Museum. The huge Gothic window under which the High Altar once stood has been filled in but its outline still is clearly visible. Once there may have been direct access between the hospital's chapel and the shop premises.

Although the Olivers themselves never actually saw their ghostly lodger, they often were conscious of his presence. For example, each evening Mr. and Mrs. Oliver would hear footsteps shuffling back and forth across the floor of their daughter Maureen's bedroom directly above the living room where they sat. At first they assumed, not unnaturally, that Maureen was out of bed and wandering around. They were annoyed, thinking she might disturb her baby brother, and Reg would go upstairs intent on chastising her, only to find her fast asleep.

As time went on they grew used to the nightly footsteps and no longer bothered to investigate.

The door to Maureen's room and the doors to the other two rooms leading off the top landing were fitted with quite substantial

311

catches. Nevertheless, each night they would fly open with a bang. The catches were old but Reg did not think they were faulty. Nonetheless he fitted new ones. The new catches failed to improve the situation and the doors continued to open of their own accord.

The Olivers learned to take the phenomenon for granted and stopped climbing the stairs to reclose the doors knowing that within minutes they would be open again.

One night when Mr. Oliver was away from Canterbury on business Mrs. Oliver awoke to the feeling that there was a "presence" in the room. What puzzled her most was that under normal circumstances if she had suspected the presence of an intruder she would have been terrified but in the presence of "George," as they had come to call their ghost, she felt no fear at all.

Margaret Oliver believes that the close proximity of her bedroom to the chapel of the poor priests' hospital in some way was associated with George's appearance in her room that night. The head of her bed actually rested against the wall which adjoined the chapel building.

As far as the Olivers know their children, Maureen and David, never were aware of the manifestations which went on around them. Mr. Oliver himself had no experiences that were strictly his own but those he shared with his wife have convinced him of George's existence.

He recalls the night when he and his wife were awakened by a terrific noise coming from downstairs. Fearing the crockery and glassware were being smashed they rushed downstairs to check. When they switched on the light they were relieved to find everything intact, without a sign of any damage or anything to suggest what had caused the commotion. The room was empty except for Prince, their mongrel dog, standing terror-stricken in the centre of the floor, his legs rigid, his hair standing on end.

One more incident confirms the Olivers' belief that they were not the only occupants of the flat at 19 Stour Street.

One evening about 10 pm the Olivers returned from an evening out to find their chiropodist friend who had been baby-sitting for them considerably upset. "I'm not going to baby-sit for you again," he announced. But he seemed reluctant to explain.

Finally the Olivers elicited his story. All the time he was there, he said, he had felt he was sharing the room with someone. At one time he even thought the Olivers had returned earlier than anticipated but soon discovered they had not. Then he became aware of someone unseen standing beside him. More than a little apprehensive by now, he crossed the room to a chair close to the window. As he sat down he was shocked to find that, as he put it, "someone was already sitting there." Needless to say he quickly vacated that spot.

This experience shattered his nerves and he still was shaking when the Olivers arrived home. Today the gentleman, unwilling to discuss the incident, will do no more than affirm that what he told the Olivers that night was true.

In 1955 the company for which Mr. Oliver worked moved out of Stour Street and he and his family went to live elsewhere in Canterbury.

Another electrical business took over the shop and the rooms above and put them all to use. A few alterations have been made since the Olivers left but the glass front door of the shop is the same one through which the ghost allegedly passed.

When Mrs. Oliver revisited the premises with me she said they no longer had the atmosphere she had known during the years she lived there with her family and "George."

The present owners say they have experienced nothing unusual since their occupation of the premises but they admit they are there only during business hours. Most of what the Olivers experienced took place during the evenings or at night.

Interestingly enough, under the floorboards of the bedroom where first George Whitman and later Gouldsmith slept and saw the monk-like apparition a collection of bones has been uncovered. At first they were thought to be human but later were identified as animal bones by a museum curator.

Because animal bones buried within the structure of a building are thought to be connected with witchcraft or black magic we might theorize that "George" was not drawn to the Olivers' home of his own free will but through the use of "dark forces." In this case this seems doubtful as witchcraft or black magic that employs sacrifice or rituals, involving bones, human or otherwise, usually implies a malevolent force which certainly does not describe "George." Margaret Oliver and Peter Gouldsmith both insist they experienced no fear in George's presence. This should discount any suggestion that George's character was an evil one.

Even George Whitman did not fear the grey misty figure. He felt instead a general apprehension about all things supernormal. Prince's reaction was that of an animal confronted with something so alien that it terrified him. The force or "presence" obviously was not an evil one and did no harm to anyone.

Whatever the truth, the Olivers do not forget the two years of their lives which they shared with a ghost.

THE JEALOUS TENANT CURSED OUR HOME

Protesting that she had lived in the house longer than we had, Mrs. Brown refused to move and vowed we never would be happy there.

Maureen Taylor

Shortly after my parents Katherine and Leonard Morrell-Jones were married in 1936 in London, England, my father began to build his dream house in Croxley Green, a small town in Hertfordshire. In those days material and labour were cheap and soon the beautiful two-storey house was finished. Dad named it "Kelm," a combination of his and Mum's initials. My mother, raised in the London slums, found the spacious rooms, modern kitchen and rolling grounds almost too good to be true.

They had been married about a year when Dad realized that war was imminent and volunteered for service in the Royal Army Medical Corps. He had to spend several weeks at a time at a training centre on the coast but returned home on leave for short periods. During one of these leave periods Mum told him of my impending arrival. War now seemed certain and Dad disliked leaving a pregnant wife to manage the large house alone. Consequently he arranged for her to move in with my grandmother Lucy Mary Jones, just down the road from Kelm, and he rented the big house to a family named Browne for the duration of the war. Little did he realize the war would stretch on for six long years.

During the war Mum and I frequently visited Kelm. Mrs. Browne often remarked on the beauty of the house and Mother was satisfied that it was being well looked after. We were far enough from London that the ravages of war did not reach us and at the end of the war Kelm stood intact and as lovely as ever.

Early in 1947 Dad was demobilized and we looked forward to moving into the big house. While the Brownes at first seemed agreeable to relinquishing Kelm, as weeks went by it became obvious that Mrs. Browne insisted on staying. She heatedly argued that they had been very good tenants and had lived in the house longer than we had. Nothing would persuade her to move and that spring my father was forced to go to court.

When the court ordered the Brownes evicted, Mrs. Browne trembling in anger, turned to my mother and said, "You will never be happy in that house. You will be forced to leave it just as I have been. Curse you and your family!" She had to be forcibly removed from the courtroom. Dad dismissed her outburst as the act of an overwrought woman and we went ahead with our plans to move.

During July and August 1947 we settled into Kelm and Mum busied herself with furnishing our lovely home. Dad went to work at Odhams Limited, a printing firm in nearby Watford. I was now seven and in September I started school. In those first weeks we all were content with our home.

Late one September evening Dad and Mum sat reading in the living room when Mum heard the high-pitched scream of a child. It seemed to come from directly beneath the front window. She saw nothing when she rushed to look out and so went outdoors to investigate further. Meanwhile my father hurried upstairs to check on me. I was peacefully sleeping, unaware of any disturbance. Both returned to the living room rather shaken and unable to explain the scream. Dad remarked that perhaps it had been an animal that only sounded human but Mother had seen no sign of an animal near the window.

Some days later the telephone rang and when Mum answered it, she heard only low grunting on the other end. Thinking it was some practical joker she replaced the receiver, only to have it ring again immediately. Again she heard only grunting sounds. This was repeated five times within the space of three or four minutes, then stopped as abruptly as it had begun. Mum mentioned the calls to Dad that evening and he expressed the view that perhaps it was Mrs. Browne harassing us. In those days all telephone calls had to be placed through the operator and he requested the telephone company to keep a record of all calls placed to our number. Mum was instructed to inform them of the exact times of any crank calls.

Within three days the calls started again. Mum wrote down the time of each on a pad by the side of the telephone. There were four calls on one afternoon between 2:55 pm and 3:01 pm and three calls the following afternoon between 2:38 pm and 2:40 pm Two days later there were six calls at about the same time of day and on this occasion Mother's friend Patricia Greaves from across the street was there as a witness. All these calls were reported to the phone company.

The day following this third series of calls a young man from the telephone company visited the house, looking apprehensive. He questioned the three of us exhaustively and also spoke to Mrs. Greaves. He checked the phone itself, made a few calls and left — wearing a puzzled expression.

When the phone company contacted Dad the next morning, they insisted that on the days in question, at the times given, no calls had been registered by the operator in charge. Since other calls had been registered correctly they were at a loss to explain why those 13 calls had not been received by the operator. Yet the phone had rung; at least four of us had heard the calls and Mum had recorded them carefully.

The mysterious phone calls convinced us that something unusual was happening in the house. During the next year numerous disquieting events confirmed this belief. Perhaps the most inexplicable episode took place a few months after the phone calls.

On the wooden gateposts on either side of the driveway were two metal numbers "4" and "3," each firmly attached by two large screws. One Saturday morning Dad hosed down the driveway and washed the dust off the two gateposts. Then he polished the two brass numbers with a soft cloth. He just had finished when his friend Walter Greaves arrived to drive Dad to band rehearsal. (Both men played in the municipal band in Watford.)

Dad hurried into the house to fetch his banjo and when he came out he saw Wally staring at the gateposts. "Hey, Len," asked Wally, "why did you take off your numbers? Going to paint the gates?" Dad hurried out to look. Sure enough, the numbers were gone — but the screws were still in place! Wally laughingly remarked it seemed silly to put back the screws before the numbers. Dad tested the screws and found it was impossible to move them by hand. He and Wally went into the house to tell Mum and she went out to see the gateposts for herself. But now the numbers were back where they belonged!

No one was in sight on the street and it had been only two or three minutes since Wally first had noticed the numbers were missing. Dad took a screwdriver, removed the numbers and put them back again. Although he worked as fast as he could, it took him eight minutes to complete the operation. Wally laughed sheepishly and made what proved to be a prophetic remark, "Maybe you have a poltergeist floating around."

During the winter I slept in a back room near the water heater. One night in January or February 1948 I was awakened by sounds of wailing and screaming which seemed to be right in the room. My light was on, although I had turned it off when I went to bed. For a few moments I lay trembling at the uncanny sounds. Then I glanced over at my watch to see what time it was — 1:30 am But the crystal from the watch was missing! As I felt the bare face, the hands and the raised numerals, Mum entered and asked, "Why is your light on, love?"

Mother hadn't heard the sounds, which stopped the moment she entered, but I told her about them and about the watch. She sat and comforted me until I fell asleep again. The next morning as I got dressed I checked the watch again. The crystal had returned as mysteriously as it had vanished.

Mum's great pride was a quilt of shot silk and goose down which she always kept on the master bed plumped to perfection. One afternoon she came into the bedroom and found it lying on the floor. Replacing it, she called me in and reminded me I was not to play in her room. But I had not been in the room; in fact I avoided it as lately I felt "cold" whenever I entered her room. Saturday she again found the quilt lying on the floor and complained to Dad. Dad was aware that strange things were occurring in the house and determined to take positive action. He examined the quilt carefully and replaced it on the bed. Then he searched the room for a stray animal or anything that might move the quilt. Satisfied that the room was normal, he locked windows and doors, pocketing the key. We all went down to the living room to wait — we weren't sure for what.

About 20 minutes later we clearly heard bangings and bumpings from the bedroom but we held hands and waited while a penetrating cold hovered around us. Finally the noises stopped and Dad led us back up the stairs. A tremendous force seemed to hold us back but even as we fought it, it abruptly disappeared. Dad unlocked the bedroom door and we followed him into the room. "My quilt's gone!" cried Mum as she stopped just inside the door.

We searched the room and soon found the quilt jammed behind a wardrobe in the corner of the room. It normally took two men to budge the oak wardrobe which was some six and a half feet high. But it had been moved about six inches from the wall and the quilt jammed behind it with force. But what force? The windows were still bolted and nothing else in the room had been disturbed.

One Sunday evening near New Year's Day 1949 Mr. and Mrs.

Greaves were visiting us for tea. As we sat quietly in the living room we heard several crashes in the kitchen. Mother was too frightened to move but Dad and Mr. Greaves hurried to the kitchen. As they entered they saw pots and plates flying through the air completely under their own volition. Dad was struck on the side of his head by a meat platter and Mr. Greaves reported feeling vibrations like an earthquake. But no earthquake was reported in all of Hertfordshire and certainly earthquakes are not confined to a single room.

The disturbances became too unsettling for Mum so we sold Kelm and moved out in March 1949. The family who bought the house never experienced any problems with the house nor did we suffer any unexplained happenings anywhere we lived subsequently.

Did our jealous tenant's curse cause our troubles? Whatever the explanation her prophecy proved accurate. We never were happy in the house and we were forced to move out just as she had been. But how her curse could have caused all these strange events remains unexplained.

MY MEETING WITH A GHOST
Zenon Tychonski

IN THE summer of 1943 I arrived late one evening in Gainsborough, about 20 miles northwest of Lincoln. Nearby, a distance of about five miles, was based our squadron to which I was returning from a wireless aircraft course. But the last bus to the aerodrome had departed and I was compelled to wait all night.

There was no hotel in the town so I went to the police station to ask for a night's lodging. One of the constables led me to a boarding school, probably a girls' one but because of the war it was closed. The boarding school was under the guardianship of two women, 70 and 75 years old, who occupied a part of the first floor of the two-storey house. These two respectable women were rather out of countenance seeing me and the constable. But when the policeman had gone one of the women told me that above her on the second floor was a free room with a bed ready for guests. While she was telling me to sleep there her face expressed uneasiness or fear.

When I was withdrawing she surprised me by asking, "Do you like music?"

"Oh, yes," I answered. "Is any wireless in the room?"

"No," she said. "There is no radio in the house. I was thinking of a piano."

"Ah, then you have a piano," I said.

"No, we have no piano nor is there one in the near neighbourhood," she replied.

Astonished by the course of this queer conversation I was preparing to withdraw when the other woman spoke, "Nevertheless you will hear the music."

"But how?"

To this I did not receive any answer. But her enigmatic smile remained in my mind as did the frightened look on the face of the other woman.

Wishing them goodnight I went upstairs and found the room. Outside the moon was bright so I did not switch the light on.

Even as I fell asleep I sensed, as if already in a dream, the rustle of tulle or of a peignoir of the Victorian epoch as it flowed about some figure, only slightly touching the floor. Next I felt that she bowed to me and I heard the whisper and felt the motion of her lips close to my face as she said, "I'll play for you."

In a moment somewhere at a distance, as if from a second or third room, I heard a piano playing a lullaby.

This music did not last all night. I remember that at one moment it broke off. Either that or I slept. But in the early morning the piano sounded again for a short while.

When I awoke it was eight o'clock and I ran downstairs to catch the first bus to the aerodrome. Before leaving I dropped into the kitchen to see the respectable women, to wish them good health and good-bye.

Both women were busy but one of them asked, "How did you sleep?"

"Marvellous," I answered. "I never had such a night in all my life."

She looked at me distrustfully. I told her that some good lady played for me a lullaby on a piano. Again fear showed on her face as she assured me that beyond her and her companion there is no one else in the whole house. But, she said, I am not the first person to hear the music in that room by night.

ANOTHER WESLEY POLTERGEIST

The famous Epworth parsonage disturbance was followed by a second little-known haunting 36 years later.

David Edwards

The Epworth parsonage in which John Wesley was raised long has been famous for its classic poltergeist. Far less familiar is the strange haunting experienced by Ann Wesley Lambert, older sister of the famous religious reformer, as recorded in the Arminian Magazine for the year 1782, Volume V, London, England.

Born in 1702, Ann Wesley married John Lambert, a surveyor, in 1725 and bore him a large family. In 1753 the Lambert family moved into the home of Henry Cooke, who had died the previous year, in Winlington near Newcastle. A few days after they moved in Ann was greatly surprised to hear the door in the inner room shake and the latch lift several times. About a week later as John and Ann lay in bed both heard knocking above the bed; it seemed to be between the roof and the ceiling. Three nights later Ann heard the knocking again. A few weeks after this at one o'clock in the afternoon Ann saw the apparition of a man in graveclothes and fainted in terror. The family immediately moved from Cooke's house to another 300 yards away.

A month after this move Ann was startled by a blow given to the bedside. At midnight about a week later Ann awoke to see a man's chalk-white face in the middle of a square light at the far end of the room. She woke John who also saw the face.

Four nights later at one o'clock Ann was wakened by a loud noise like a gun report nearby. She got up and stirred the coals in the fire but could see nothing. No sooner had she lain down again than an unseen force, about the weight of a human body, pressed down on her. Immediately after the weight was removed she saw standing beside the bed an apparition dressed in a surplice and a white wig.

"In the name of God," she cried out, "why do you trouble me?"

"Meet me at one o'clock," replied the specter, "and I will tell you what I want."

With that it vanished.

The rest of the night was peaceful but as soon as John had

gone to work the next morning leaving Ann and the children still in bed, Ann heard two heavy strokes behind the bed. Shortly after this the pressing weight returned, this time accompanied by a noise as loud as the report of a cannon. A brief period of quiet followed and then the whole room began to shake like a tree in the wind. At the foot of the bed there appeared an apparition of a man in work clothes. After a brief moment the apparition slowly disappeared.

A few weeks passed without further incident but then one night about 11 o'clock the loud report sounded again, and again Ann felt the crushing weight. Then an unseen force carried their five-year-old daughter out of bed and laid her in the middle of the floor. Ann cried out and John got up and brought the child back to the bed (which the parents shared with the children). In the morning the little girl complained of soreness under her thigh. Her mother found only a pinch mark on the girl's leg.

Over the next few days, however, the soreness increased and the child was bedridden for five weeks.

The next night after the five-year-old first complained of soreness the loud noise was repeated. This time the youngest child was snatched out of bed and laid on the floor. Ann immediately retrieved the youngster who seemed unharmed. The next night when the report sounded again the oldest child was dragged partly out of bed. But the girl screamed loudly and the parents awoke and pulled her into bed again, whereupon the bed shook greatly.

The family was so terrified and exhausted by these disturbances that the Lamberts determined to move again in an effort to escape the evil influence. Accordingly they relocated in a house at the opposite end of Winlington.

The move brought them only two nights' peace. On the third night the family heard an unexplained scraping noise at the bedroom door and a strange light appeared at the foot of the bed. That same week the cannon-like noise and the pressing weight recurred, this time victimizing John as well as Ann.

About three weeks after this Ann was awakened in the night by a great rumbling sound in the next room. She called out, "In the name of God what art thou?" There was no reply but the noise ceased. The next morning, about an hour after John left for work, Ann saw the apparition of Henry Cooke standing at the foot of the bed. He was dressed in clothes he had worn in life. She was too terrified to speak and he vanished.

Things were quiet then for several weeks — until July 1755 when on a Sunday night the disturbances began again. Now they heard a noise like a man grinding with a hand-mill above their heads. The sash window began to shake so violently they feared glass would be broken. The next morning, however, they found that only a single pane was cracked across its four corners leaving a diamond-shaped portion in the middle.

The next several months were fairly quiet except for frequent unexplained noises and the strange death of their cat. On the evening of 2 December, 1755, as Ann was making up the bed she saw the apparition of a small black four-footed animal run across the bolster. Two or three nights later she saw an apparition the size of a calf. It grew in size until it was as large as a horse; then it leaped onto the bed and seemed to strike her but did no harm.

At midnight on 6 December John, awake in bed, saw Henry Cooke dressed in his work clothes enter the room and walk to the fireplace. The apparition stood there for a considerable time before vanishing. At midnight on 20 December Ann felt a man's ice-cold hands on her face. She woke John but by then the hands were gone. About two o'clock on the morning of 22 December Ann woke to see a pewter dish the colour of blood, with blood sprinkled around its edges. This was the last recorded disturbance.

No one ever explained why Henry Cooke's spirit followed the family twice to new homes or why he wished to persecute the Lamberts in the first place. Like the better-known Epworth poltergeist this Winlington disturbance remains an enigma.

𝒞 SHOE FOR THE LITTLE BLUE LADY 𝒞

For three centuries the child's gentle ghost walked the halls of the manor house, endlessly searching for something.

Charles Denham

The beautiful English county of Kent has more than its share of historically interesting buildings, amongst them the old manor house, home of wealthy businessman Bernard Roberts and his family. Not far from where it stands on the North Downs the busy M2 motorway speeds traffic to and fro between London and the major seaports to the European Continent and yet the manor house and its neighbour, the 900-year-old parish church, retain an atmosphere of peaceful serenity little changed through the long years.

Built as a farmhouse during the reign of Edward I (1272-1307) the house did not attain its status as the local manor until the 17th century, although its importance to community life was well established before that time. According to local records courts were held there as early as the 1500's.

Bernard Roberts' purchase of the property in 1948 brought to an end a family ownership going back more than 300 years. Today the manor house is in a perfect state of preservation and its gardens, surrounded on all sides by a high brick wall, are neatly laid out and painstakingly tended. But they haven't always been so well cared for. Wartime brought an urgent need to accommodate thousands of volunteers and conscripts joining the armed forces and the manor house, like so many other properties of its size and secluded position, was taken over for the duration. The house itself became army officers' quarters whilst the rank and file made do with the less homely accommodation provided by 11 large corrugated iron huts hastily erected on the grounds. An unhappy fate for this country seat maybe but under the circumstances who could deny the worthiness of the cause?

When the war was over life in the country returned more or less to normal; commandeered properties gradually found their way back into the hands of their former owners. But the owner of the manor house had died and it came into the possession of his widow who, not wishing to live there herself, immediately put the house and most of its contents up for sale. The house and grounds were in a pretty sad state and whoever bought them would face the mammoth task of restoring them to their former beauty — a task not made any easier by the scarcity of materials and strict government controls.

Undaunted, Bernard Roberts bought the property and made plans for the repair work. Rather than have his family face the inconvenience and inevitable upheaval it was decided they would not move in until most of it had been completed. Structurally the house, with its large panelled hall and wide oak staircase which leads up two flights to the balustraded minstrels' gallery linking the upper storeys of the two wings, was to remain much the same, but one or two alterations were considered necessary to make the house totally suitable for comfortable family living. One change involved the "Don Quixote Room," a bedroom, leading off the minstrels gallery, so-called because of its handpainted wallpaper, the scenes of which depict this legendary figure's adventures. The "Don Quixote Room" was to become a bathroom.

Plans were finalized and the work began. To convert the bedroom to its new role it was necessary to lift several of the oak floorboards so that plumbing could be introduced. It was whilst they were doing this that the workmen made a surprising discovery. Hidden in the deep cavity beneath the boards they found a tiny leather shoe. Its peculiar design made it obviously very old, and the leather was brittle with age. It was equally obvious that no machine had played a part in its manufacture. The cutting, shaping and stitching had all been done by hand. The workman who made the discovery handed the shoe over to Bernard Roberts who, delighted with the find, removed the shoe with infinite care to a place of safekeeping.

In due course their new home was ready for occupation and the Roberts family moved in. There were many well-wishing neighbors who asked them how they were settling in, how life in the village suited them, were they happy in their new home. In answering the last question it isn't surprising that the restoration work and the various alterations made came under discussion and in the course of dutifully satisfying their neighbours' curiosity the discovery of the little shoe was mentioned. Whatever reaction was expected it seemed the news did not come as a complete surprise. Yet, how could they have known when the shoe only recently had seen the light of day after being hidden for many years beneath the floorboards in the "Don Quixote Room?" That the workman who found it or one of his colleagues had spread the word around was unlikely, yet the hint of recognition clearly was there. For a time no explanation was forthcoming. It was as though the listeners wished to say something but were, for some unaccountable reason, reluctant to do so.

Eventually, however, the Robertses heard the story, disjointedly and from various sources. It was Mrs. Darley, the elderly lady who manned the tiny telephone exchange which served the village and surrounding farms, who told them the full story.

The shoe was, the townspeople believed, a very definite link with "The Little Blue Lady," the ghost of a young girl who was reputed to haunt the old house. "The Little Blue Lady" — the shadowy figure of a little girl dressed in a long blue gown — had been seen on many occasions over the past hundred or more years making her way along the minstrels' gallery. All who had seen her had shared the impression that the child was earnestly searching for something. If — as was generally thought — her walk along the gallery was a reenactment of a particularly significant journey made by her in life, then that impression is certainly consistent with the story which surrounds the haunting.

It seems no one who has seen the apparition has been in any way frightened. And why should they be? What could be frightening about a sweet innocent child from the past whose only apparent purpose was an overpowering desire to find some prized possession lost by her when she herself lived there? That lost article, if the generally accepted explanation for her appearance is correct, was undoubtedly a shoe. The story of "The Little Blue Lady" as passed down through successive generations of local inhabitants and retold to the Robertses by Mrs. Darley who had read the story in a book, is this:

During the 17th century the little blue lady, who was then about six years old, lived in the manor house with her parents and other members of the household including a nurse or someone whose duty it was to take charge of the child. That the family lived in such a grand house and had servants to wait on them is evidence enough of their wealth. Additional evidence, however, is found in the fact that the little girl owned a pair of shoes. In those days only the wealthiest could afford the luxury of footwear for their children. The child must surely have counted them amongst the most treasured of her possessions — a beautiful pair of leather shoes carefully and skillfully made to fit her tiny feet.

As all parents will know from experience, children of that age have an unfortunate habit of mislaying things, even those things they treasure most. The little blue lady was, it seems, no different in that respect from other children, for one day she somehow managed to mislay one of her shoes. Although there was little doubt it was somewhere about the house, all efforts to find it proved fruitless. Considering the value of the lost article the nurse could hardly allow her charge's carelessness to go unpunished and so she scolded her and sent her to bed.

The following morning the family awoke to tragedy. At the foot of the staircase, lying in a crumpled heap, they found the lifeless body of the child, her tiny neck broken, presumably as the result of a head-over-heels tumble down the stairs. Apparently she had been more concerned about the loss of her shoe than they had realized. And while the rest of the household slept, probably while she herself was asleep, she had descended the broad landing which divides it into two separate flights. From there apparently she stepped forward again, to pitch headfirst to her untimely death.

Thus the manor housed a classic haunting — a purpose unfulfilled in one life continued in the next. Seemingly the shoe had to be found before the child could rest peacefully in her grave. Now the Robertses understood what lay behind the flash of recognition noted on the faces of those to whom they had mentioned the workman's find. Now, knowing the story, they immediately guessed the shoe to be the one lost by "The Little Blue Lady" — the shoe for which she had searched so long without success. If this was, in fact, her shoe and if the haunting of the manor house was to run true to tradition, there no longer would be a need for her to return to the scene of her death, to walk the gallery, ceaselessly searching.

But what was there to suggest there was a shred of truth in what they had heard? Local records were of no assistance; however, two things did come light during the course of their enquiries which seem to give some credence to Mrs. Darley's account. From a reliable source they learned the previous owner, a thoroughly trustworthy man, had reported seeing the ghost of a little girl in a long blue dress on a number of occasions. There had been no question in his mind as to who the child was, for her portrait hung on the wall of the staircase. Roberts discovered that a large oil painting of a young girl occupied a place of prominence on the staircase right up until the time the house was put on sale in 1948 and had been included in the contents auctioned by the owner's widow. Their efforts to trace the buyer have so far proved disappointing. The girl in the portrait was about six years old and wore a long blue dress typical of the period in which the little blue lady is purported to have lived.

The story of "The Little Blue Lady" was in circulation long before 1948 when the lifting of the floorboards in the "Don Quixote Room" led to the discovery of the shoe.

The question which presents itself is, of course, how did the shoe get under the floorboards in the "Don Quixote Room?"

The most likely explanation is it was carried there by a cat. A feature of timber-framed houses like the manor house was the "cat holes" — apertures left so that cats could get into the various cavities to keep the rats down. Shoes and other smallish articles carried under the floorboards by playful family pets, according to museum authorities, are found in such houses.

In this case the shoe was taken along to a nearby museum where it was handed to the curator of the historical costume section for examination and appraisal. The shape of the shoe, its method of fastening, the cut, the stitching and the aging of the leather, all were carefully considered and comparisons made with shoes of the period exhibited in the museum. The experts' opinion was that if the little blue lady really had lived at the time it was said she did and if she had been one of the fortunate few to own a pair of shoes, then those shoes would have been similar in every way to the one found under the floor. Its exact age could not be given but by all appearances it was judged to be about 300 years old. The position of the imprint of the big toe, which could be clearly seen inside the shoe, was a reasonable sign that it had been worn mainly on the left foot but the outward appearance gave no indication as to whether it was intended for the left foot or the right — further indication that the shoe comes from this period when all shoes were shaped the same.

Bernard Roberts and his family are satisfied that theirs is the shoe in the story. The fact that since the day they moved into the manor house, not long after the shoe was uncovered, there has been no sign whatsoever of "The Little Blue Lady" has convinced them. It seems her ghost has been well and truly laid.

THE HORROR
AT 50 BERKELEY SQUARE

The human inhabitants had been bad enough — but they were nothing at all compared to the ghostly ones who followed.

George Wagner

"Oh, my God!" the policeman shouted. "You haven't been in that place!" Such was the horror the crumbling Georgian mansion at Number 50, Berkeley Square, held for Londoners of the 1880's.

The house in Mayfair had been fairly new when Mr. DuPre purchased it in the late 18th century. He himself lived 20 miles away at Wilton Park, Buckinghamshire, but needed the townhouse for his violently insane brother who was confined to a third-floor bedroom and who would attack all who dared approach him. Food was thrown to this unfortunate creature through a hole in the formidable solid oak door.

The maniac's screams could be heard all over the neighbourhood. And among those who undoubtedly heard them was statesman Horace Walpole who lived at nearby Number 11, Berkeley Square, until his death in 1797.

After the madman died in the early years of the 19th century the house was owned by a wealthy bachelor, guardian of an orphaned niece Adeline who lived with him. Apparently tension built up between the two, especially as Adeline entered puberty, and one night the uncle attempted to seduce his niece. Rather than submit to him Adeline leaped to her death from the third-floor room.

Subsequent tenants claimed to see the girl's ghost floating outside the window of this chamber, her phantom fingers rapping on the panes. Apparently her spectre could be seen only from inside the house.

Visitors to Number 50 also reported seeing the ghost of an ugly man with a monstrously large mouth, presumably the revenant of DuPre's insane brother.

During the 1820's the ghost of a very little girl also was observed. No story come down to us to explain her appearance. At the times her apparition appeared the house would resound with hysterical crying.

Tenants also swore they saw a terrifying "something" which they described as half-reptile, half-octopus. This beast — whatever it may have been — sported numerous legs and tentacles. The monster was supposed by those who believed in it to have been born in a noisome forgotten sewer beneath Berkeley Square, from which it crawled up an abandoned connecting pipe into Number 50.

Understandably the house came to be shunned. No one cared to live in it even for a ridiculously low rent. In about 1835 a man named Benson, who then owned the building, was approached by 30-year-old Sir Robert Warboys of Warboys Hall, Bracknell, Berkshire. Warboys asked permission to stay overnight in the "haunted room." Money probably changed hands but in any case permission was readily granted.

Warboys retired to the notorious upper bedroom while a number of his friends — including Benson, Lord Cholomondely, Sir Dougall Forster and a Colonel Raynes — took up a vigil on the ground floor. During the night the group heard Warboys' pistol discharge, dashed up to the room and found Warboys had shot himself through the head.

Another man who later obtained permission to stay alone in the room took a watchdog with him. Reportedly, in the morning both the man and the dog were found dead. But this may be legend.

However, in the 1840's the famous novelist Sir Edward Bulwer-Lytton did spend a night in the haunted room. Bulwer-Lytton lived only a few blocks from the house and was deeply interested in the occult so naturally wished to investigate the notorious building.

The novelist armed himself with two antique blunderbusses full of buckshot and silver coins. He said that while he was sitting in the darkness he felt eerie brushings against his head and fired one of the weapons. In the brief flash of exploding gunpowder he saw a shapeless, disintegrating mass suspended in the air but in the few seconds it took him to strike a match the thing vanished.

It was Bulwer-Lytton's experiences in the Berkeley Square house that inspired him to write the chilling story 'The House and the Brain" better known by its alternate title "The Haunted and the Haunters." This classic tale originally appeared in *Blackwood's Magazine* for August 1859 but has been reprinted countless times.

Soon after Bulwer-Lytton's visit the house was rented to a

young man and his bride. While the newlyweds were on their honeymoon on the Continent, the bride's mother went to Number 50 to ready the house for their arrival. Then, exhausted from her day's activities, the mother fell asleep in the haunted room. A servant heard her scream twice but before help could reach the room the woman died on the bed, her face contorted in terror.

In around 1850 a Mr. Jarvice and his family rented the house for the autumn party season. One day the Jarvices' maid went missing and eventually discovered in the third-floor bedroom throwing violent fits. The maid died hours later in St. George's Hospital without regaining consciousness.

A few weeks later a Captain Raymond, a military officer engaged to one of the Jarvices' daughters, was a guest in the house. After dinner one evening Mr. Jarvice told his prospective son-in-law the history of the hauntings including their maid's recent death.

"Nothing but superstition!" Raymond retorted. "Let me sleep in the room tonight. I'll prove to you there's nothing there."

Captain Raymond's host and his sweetheart tried to change his mind but he was adamant and at length the officer's clothes and baggage were transferred to the ill-reputed chamber.

"If you hear me make one pull of the bell cord," Raymond said before going up to bed, "stay where you are. I could pull it accidentally or even out of nervousness. If I ring it twice, come immediately."

At midnight the bell was heard to tinkle once very softly. This was closely followed by a furious jangling. Jarvice and his whole family rushed to Captain Raymond's room to find Raymond in convulsions. And like the maid, he died without revealing what he had seen.

From the early 1850's until her death in 1859 Miss Curzon, the daughter of a distinguished family of politicians and military men, lived in Number 50. During her stay the house was curiously quiet. In fact, her butler George Vincent later wrote, "During the nine years I was in the house, and I have been in it alone at all hours, I saw no greater ghost than myself."

After Miss Curzon died Sir Charles Young occupied the house and no reports of disturbances come from this period either.

Early in the 1860's a Mr. Myers, son of Lady Mary Nevill and grandson of Henry, the second Earl of Abergavenny, purchased Number 50. Myers intended the house to be a wedding present for his bride-to-be but she eloped with another man. So Myers lived on alone in the house and grew increasingly eccentric. As the years passed he was heard making strange noises, muttering and moaning to himself as he rambled through house at night. He became increasingly reclusive and at the time of his death in the late 1870's, his distant relative Lady Dorothy Nevill wrote, "An agent who inspected the house afterwards declared that he had never seen anything like the dreadful state of dilapidation which prevailed ... it seemed impossible that any human being could have lived in such a state of squalor and decay."

Myers' sister inherited the house and promptly sold it to a Mr. Fish, who had little to do with the property except to advertise it for rent — in vain. Scotland Yard, however, kept the house under continual surveillance because of rumours that counterfeiting operations were in progress in the neglected building.

On 24 December, 1887, two sailors from the British frigate *Penelope* arrived in Berkeley Square penniless, having blown their wages. The two men — Edward Blunden and Robert Martin — still had 10 or 12 days of leave remaining and were determined to hike back to their native village for the holidays. By the time they reached Berkeley Square they were freezing and needed shelter for the night. Seeing the 'to let' sign hanging at Number 50 they guessed the building was empty. One of them tried a window and found to his surprise that it opened. The men raised the sash and hoisted themselves inside.

They bedded down for the night in the third-floor room. Around midnight the seamen heard footsteps on a lower floor. Heavy treads, apparently those of huge bare feet, laboriously climbed the airs, then shuffled down the hall toward the room in which the two sailors lay. Then the door swung open but the moonlight revealed no visible hand which could have opened it.

Both men jumped out of bed. When the footsteps continued across the room Edward Blunden jumped from the window — the same window through which young Adeline had leaped 70 or 80 years before.

Robert Martin still could see nothing in the moonlit room but heard the footsteps plodding toward him. He dashed from the room, scrambled down the stairs and escaped out the same window by which he had entered. He located the cop on the beat and began screaming an account of what had transpired in the empty building.

It was then the policeman gasped, "Number 50? My God! You didn't go in there?"

Although his neck was broken, Blunden was still alive when Martin returned with the officer. He lived long enough to tell the policeman a story that agreed in every major detail with the story Martin had just told.

Around the turn of the century Number 50 Berkeley Square was completely remodelled. Even the street number was changed. No further hauntings were reported after this.

Eventually the notorious structure and its neighbours were demolished to make way for a block of shops and apartment buildings.

THE GHOSTS OF LEITH HALL

**Was the staggering, blundering thing in the corridor the laird
— returning in spirit to the castle he once owned?**

Elizabeth Byrd

Two years before I saw the ghost in my bedroom we knew that
something "unnatural" lived with us in Leith Hall.

Visually, it is beautiful, set among 1,500 wooded acres in
Aberdeenshire, Scotland. Visitors to the famed flower gardens and the
Historic Wing persist in calling it a castle, although actually it's a
mansion, built in 1650 and now under the protection of the National
Trust. My husband Barrie and I were enchanted to learn that a fully
furnished, centrally-heated wing was for rent — never mind that 14
rooms seemed excessive for two people and a poodle puppy. Even so,
the rent was less than we paid for our New York apartment.

We found nothing sinister about the place when we explored
it that May day in 1966. We were both think that for once we could
have our own private studies for our writing — mine on the ground
floor, his in a turret tower on the third floor. Moreover, the Trust
assured us that we had no responsibility for the tourists — our privacy
was insured.

In July, after some painting and repapering had been done,
we moved in. I chose the master bedroom with its apricot walls, huge
canopied bed and a fireplace — but Barrie, who is bothered by my
late-night reading, chose to sleep in one of the bedrooms upstairs.
Those top-floor rooms had evidently once been a nursery.

The first evidence of anything "unnatural" came a week after
we moved in while I stood at the bottom of the spiral stone staircase
preparing to take the puppy for a walk. Satirically we had named her
"Strongheart," for unlike many of her breed she was nerveless. It was
I who was frightened when from two storeys above, I clearly heard a
child giggle. Strongheart barked. Another giggle — and the puppy
dashed joyfully upstairs, as if certain of a playmate. Then I heard her
growl and she came down shivering and whimpering. Coward that I
am, I took her out to the lily-padded loch, hoping that Barrie would
return from Aberdeen before dark.

The next afternoon Strongheart and I had another adventure. After picnicking on the loch bank we came home through the Great Hall. Behind its oak panelling there is a tiny room with a toilet and wash basin. As we passed it, there came a snarl loud as a tiger's. I screamed and Strongheart took to her heels in terror. I found her under the chaise in my study, plucked her out, held her close and — I admit — trembled with her. But I tried to think of some rational explanation. I was sure that the high window in the little room was closed — possibly, I thought, a cat had gotten in. But never had I heard a cat sound so ferocious. We stayed in the study until Barrie came home half an hour later. He found the suspect window closed.

An explanation of sorts came to us when I told a guest — an historian — about the snarling sound. "In the old days of sheep theft and clan feuds there were always fierce mastiffs chained to the corners of mansions and castles," he said, smiling. "That little room forms a corner. Perhaps you heard a guard dog."

A month later Kevin Knight, then nine years old, came with his parents to spend a weekend. He asked where the "loo" was and his mother, knowing nothing of the snarl, directed him. When he came back he said, "I'll never go in there again! I was so scared — I don't know why. ..."

No, he hadn't seen or heard anything but he felt as if something were going to attack him. Now, at 18, he still remembers his terror.

Although we never heard the snarl again Strongheart refused to go near that door. Barrie tried to lure her in with a doggy choc but she shied away and growled.

We tried to joke about a haunted toilet, about heavy doors slamming on windless summer nights and about the activity on the "nursery" floor after dark. Barrie's study was at the end of that corridor and he always kept the door closed. He often worked to music and despite thick walls I could hear the hi-fi and it disturbed my work. Several times he spoke of "something blundering along the corridor, like a big dog, then barging heavily against my door." When he investigated he always found the corridor tranquil.

This blundering sound was also heard by an American visitor, Carole Showalter, who stayed with us for about three months in 1967. She slept in one of the nursery rooms and although we had told her nothing about out "ghosts" she would say every morning at breakfast, "What goes on in that corridor? I'll be reading in bed and about midnight something big and cumbersome pads along outside — like a dog, but not Strongheart's dainty five pounds. Otherwise it's like a silent cocktail party, people moving to and fro but not a word spoken. I wouldn't open that door for the world!"

Various guests — to whom we had said nothing of our experiences — had their own. Mary Poulton, an airline hostess, used the bathroom adjoining my bedroom and later told me, "I was afraid to come back past your beautiful bed. How can you sleep in there?" Isobel Begg, an actress, unaware of Mary's reaction, said the same thing two months later: "I was scared to death when I had to pass through your bedroom. ..."

A reporter for the *Weekly Scotsman*, Iain Parr, phoned in late March 1967 to say that he had heard "from various people" that our wing of Leith Hall was haunted. We wanted no publicity but evidently word was out. He said frankly, "I'd have to treat it as a humorous piece, of course, but it wouldn't hurt your book sales."

"I'm not sure," I said. "I write historical novels, not occult stuff. Neither Barrie nor I want freak publicity."

"I promise it won't be junk," he said. So we invited Iain to spend the night of April 1 and put him in the largest and most comfortable of nursery rooms. What he wrote in the *Weekly Scotsman* for 6 April, 1967, wasn't precisely humorous:

"I've been a realist for as long as I can remember. Even as a youngster I scoffed at the idea of fairies living in our garden. I never believed in ghosts, either. Not until now. ... I was lying in bed, eyes wide open and my hands behind my head, staring up at the ceiling. ... My room seemed dark.

"For some reason I was thinking of Hernando Cortez and his conquest of the Incas when suddenly I was pulled up to a sitting position. It was quite involuntary on my part. (Then) I was allowed to flop back. I switched on the light and examined my pyjama jacket. It was not disarrayed but I assure you something had pulled me from the pillow."

A few weeks later I slept in that bed having given the master bedroom to Alanna and Alistair Knight, Kevin's parents. At dawn I was awakened by an unmistakable spank — a hard spank. I turned over prepared to scold Barrie — but the room was empty, the door closed. In what had once been nursery quarters, was some strict nanny still administering punishment?

That same night Alanna and her husband fell asleep about 1:00 am in the master bedroom, having left the draperies slightly open. She told us the next morning, "I awakened to the sound of a woman laughing — right next to me. I sat up against the pillows. The room was very dark but through the parted draperies I could see the far-off lights of Teacher's whisky distillery. All around me there was movement — swish of silk or taffeta, tinkle ol crystal, clink of china, murmured conversation of which I couldn't catch a word. I wanted to awaken Alistair to share this fantastic experience but I was afraid it would go away if I did. It lasted eight to 10 minutes and I realized that a dinner party was going on practically here on the bed! And I was like a blind woman attending it."

In that bedroom were spacious shelves where I kept my sweaters and handbags. Several of the shelves were labeled "Crown Derby," "Limoges" "Best China." These and Alanna's experience were examined when the elderly Lady Burgh came to tea and asked to look through the house. In the master bedroom she said, "Oh! But this used to be the dining room. We used to have such lovely parties here when I was a girl."

Going on past the fireplace into the hall to the bathroom she said, "The servants served from here. I think there was a sort of dumbwaiter arrangement to pull up food from the kitchen.

Back in the bedroom, Lady Burgh laughed. "The laird never dined here alone when his wife (the Honorable Henrietta Leith-Hay) was in Ireland. He had some idea that it was haunted and preferred the small dining room on the ground floor — the one you use."

Henrietta Leith-Hay gave Leith Hall to the National Trust for Scotland in 1945 but lived there, a widow, until her death 20 years later. Her portrait and those of her husband and son dominate a wall of the curving staircase. One night, looking at the portraits, I said, "We're the only tenants who've ever lived here who weren't related to them. I hope they like us."

"We're tidy," Barrie said, smiling, "but from their viewpoint, a pair of Bohemians. Old Queen Mary came here to tea but no royalty has visited us. We're just not posh, darling."

As I studied the kind-eyed serene family in the portraits I remembered what the caretaker Miss Whitt had once told me: She had said, "Mrs. Leith-Hay had over 80 rooms to wander, very few servants and in her later years as her friends and relatives died, there must have been intense loneliness. She was very fond of company."

The question of whether she "liked us" was answered about 10 days later in an extraordinary way. As I've said, Barrie and I had separate studies and they were inviolate. We never intruded on one another. Absurd as it may seem, this was the first working privacy we'd ever had and we intended to keep it. When I gathered flowers for the vase on his desk I didn't go into his turret sanctuary but gave them to him to place. When he bought carbon paper for me, he left it outside my door.

So when I entered my study one morning after breakfast I was astonished to find two plump pink and white tea cosies on my desk chair. Why had he barged in with these rather atrocious Victorian relics? I found him in the morning room and asked. "I've never seen them before," he replied.

We looked over the exhaustive inventory — it listed the most minor items, even empty jars. The list included one blue and white chintz tea cosy but not these pink and white striped ones. I took them down to the caretaker's lodge. Miss Whitt had never seen them before nor had our thrice-weekly maid Phyllis Stewart. They had appeared overnight.

The next morning Barrie found a beautiful tooled Italian leather writing case. In a corner pocket he found a tiny envelope, yellowed with age, and scrawled on it in ink were the words:

"I am in. Please ring bell. Henrietta L. H."

This valuable item did not appear on the inventory, nor had it been seen before. Surviving friends of Henrietta's had never seen, either the writing case or the tea cosies. These seemed to be gifts — one for a woman and one for a man. No intruder could have played such a prank — and anyway, intruders do not get into locked and bolted National Trust properties.

On a dour November morning Barrie asked for a shopping list and said he would go into the village. We went upstairs together and he went into his study to pick up some letters. When I heard him clattering down the stairs I started to work. Then I heard music from his study. Timidly I went up. His door was open and I saw him at his desk. "You didn't go to Kennethmont?"

"Had another letter to write," he said.

"Then you haven't been downstairs since I saw you?"

"No."

Who or what then had clattered down past my open bedroom door?

In July 1968 I was alone at Leith Hall for a week. Barrie had business in London. He worried that I might be uneasy but I lied gallantly. "Nonsense." After Barrie left I took some precautions — not for me those creepy winding stone stairs if I needed something from the study or kitchen in the middle of the night. So I had cigarettes, matches, tissues and two unscary novels. I went serenely to sleep about 11 o'clock, the draperies parted. The only sounds were the mourning of wood pigeons and the tick of my bedside clock.

In Scotland in summer light comes early. Everything in my room was clearly visible when I awoke at 4:55 am I sat up feeling refreshed and wide-awake. I would take Strongheart out to the loch for a breakfast picnic. At this early hour we'd see baby rabbits, moorhens, maybe an otter.

I had been looking toward one of the windows. Now I glanced at the dressing table — and froze in horror. Standing in front of it, facing me, was a tall massively built man with a dark brown beard, his eyes hidden by a bandage on his head. He wore a pale wide-sleeved shirt and tight dark green trousers — not modern trousers but what the Scots call "breeks." He held a short thick weapon in his left hand and stood with his legs apart in a commanding stance.

Despite my panic I felt that although he looked fierce he was not menacing. It was as if he were trying to say, "Here I am. Look at me." I shall always deplore the fact that I didn't speak, didn't ask what he wanted of me. Instead I screamed, "Go away!"

He was as solid as any human being, not transparent. He moved back a step, his glance never wavering from mine. Again I screamed, "Go away!" with what voice I had left — and after a second or two he vanished.

Now my beautiful bedroom was ruined for me. I kept my clothes there but I never slept in it again. That day I made up a room for myself on the "nursery" floor. And that day I went over to the Historic Wing to see if I find could find my night visitor's portrait. I failed. Most of the former lairds of Leith Hall had been military men but none resembled my visitor. I didn't tell the caretaker why I was interested in the lairds but she gave me a book written by Henrietta, a family history called *Trustie to the End* (Oliver and Boyd, London, 1957).

I read it looking for reference to a wounded man but Henrietta's ancestors from Culloden through Waterloo, the Crimean War, etc., seemed impervious to bullets. None had been wounded in battle. Finally I came to John Leith, an 18th-century laird. On 21 December, 1763, he rode 40 miles to Aberdeen to join a stag party at Campbell's Tavern. He and Abernethy of Mayen quarrelled. Because most of the witnesses were drunk no one can say whether John Leith was murdered by Abernethy or shot in an honorable duel. Leith died in Aberdeen three days later and a ballad immortalized the affair — and proved a bandaged head wound.

> Leith's servant bound the bleeding head
> And bore him to his bed
> And covered him with blankets warm
> And due attention paid.

Leith's widow Harriot was convinced of murder and sued Abernethy, who fled Scotland. The legal matter dragged on five years until she was finally awarded 150 pounds. But the mystery of Leith's death remains.

Ghosts are said to appear in order to "set things straight" or to tidy up their affairs or through extreme anxiety to communicate. Standing there, he may have wanted to say to me, "Listen to me. This is what really happened."

I never saw him again but for the rest of that week while Barrie was gone I heard the blundering steps lurching along the corridor — and Strongheart, who slept with me now on the top floor, growled and occasionally howled. Sleep was almost impossible.

Barrie returned and hearing my story of vacating the master bedroom he took it over. He reported peaceful nights for more than a week but then he was forced out.

"I can't describe how horrible it was," he told me. "I had just switched off the bedside light when I felt this black cloud moving toward me. No, I didn't see it. I felt it as a menace that wanted to smother me. I tried to turn over to reach the light but my body was literally paralysed. As the thing came closer it took all of my willpower — and a prayer — to activate my muscles. I got the light on. The room was tranquil. I went up and spent the rest of the night in my study on the couch."

"So you'll never sleep there again?"

"Never."

We continued to use that room for our clothes but no one slept there. During 1969 our guests continued to complain, "This house is haunted!" Alanna Knight's mother Mrs. Cleet, scornful of "silly superstition," nevertheless reported, after a night in the room next to Barrie's study, that she had heard heavy footsteps blundering along the corridor "like a military man in heavy boots but rather dragging. Then there were two sharp cracks, like pistol shots."

"That's odd," said her son-in-law "I had a nightmare about pistol shots."

Then on 8 November, 1969, about dusk Barrie went into the master bedroom for a jacket — and there was the bandaged man, this time standing next to the fireplace. "He was taller than you described and I could see an empty eye socket. He had no weapon this time."

"Did he disappear?" I asked.

"No, I did — fast," Barrie replied.

I put down my book. "This is impossible. Not just the uneasy atmosphere but we're so remote. We spend so much on travel to London and my research in Edinburgh. We should have roots in a city."

He agreed. Soon after New Year's Day 1970 we were living in Edinburgh.

Our wing of Leith Hall was vacant for nearly two years. Then we read in the paper that it had been rented by a Colonel Mitchell, a controversial member of Parliament. Newsmen phoned him to ask if he and his young family had had any strange experiences in Leith Hall. He either said, "Rubbish," or simply hung up. Then we heard that he had moved out.

Our wing was vacant again. We didn't miss it really — our Edinburgh apartment was marvelous — but tenantless old houses are pathetic and we had reason to care about this one. So we were delighted to hear that Teacher's distillery had rented it for the entertainment of VIPs. We imagined charming parties in the Great Hall and drinks before the 17th-century fireplace in the dining room.

But were guests put up overnight? I phoned to ask but received an ambiguous answer: "We don't use Leith as a hotel."

Just as well, perhaps. The old mansion lives on two levels of time perhaps, at the darkening, is best left to itself.

Author's note: in November 1977 a friend in Scotland wrote me that the Teacher's whisky people have relinquished Leith Hall.

POLTERGEIST ON A RAMPAGE

Antics in suburban London home, headlined in mass-circulation newspapers and exhaustively investigated by psychic researchers, held all of England in thrall.

Guy Lyon Playfair

It began with a bang late on the night of 31 August, 1977, in the home where divorcee Mary Harper lived with her four children. The children, Rose, 13, Jane, 11, Tom, 10, and Jimmy, seven, were all in bed, unaware that they had had their last normal night's sleep for months to come. For the Enfield Poltergeist, as it soon became known in the British press, was to become one of the most versatile and persistent in the annals of psychical research.

It was also to be the most exhaustively investigated poltergeist in history because the Society for Psychical Research (SPR) was called in within a week of its onset. And yet it caused bitter controversy among SPR members, 20 of whom eventually visited the house but only three of whom admitted witnessing inexplicable phenomena.

As for the Harpers and several of their neighbours in the formerly peaceful public housing estate near the North London suburb of Enfield, it changed their lives, perhaps forever.

The first bang — immediately followed by several more — seemed to come from the wall dividing the Harper home from that of their neighbours Frank and Betty Norton. At first Mrs. Harper thought there must be a normal explanation for the bangs. But there could be nothing normal about what happened next.

"I kept hearing this shuffling noise in the back bedroom," she said. Then, to her horror, a chest of drawers started to move on its own.

"I stood there and I pushed it back, and it moved again. It was moving out, gradually moving towards the centre of the door. By this time I was literally shaking. I was really petrified. I pushed it again because I couldn't believe my own eyes."

This was enough to send Mary Harper hurrying next door to fetch Frank and Betty. Frank, a builder by trade and a tough, cheerful man who does not scare easily, made a thorough search of the house and garden. He found nothing unusual, nothing to explain the knocking which still went on.

"It sounded as if someone was behind the wall trying to get in," Betty Norton said.

They decided to call the police.

Two constables arrived shortly after midnight and searched the house and garden again. Then, in the words of WPC Carolyn Heeps: "I heard the sound of knocking on the wall that backs onto the (Nortons') house. There were four distinct taps on the wall and then silence. About two minutes later I heard more tapping, but this time it was coming from a different wall. Again it was a distinctive peal of four taps."

Suddenly, Tom Harper pointed to one of the chairs in the living room.

"I noticed that it was wobbling slightly from side to side," WPC Heeps stated. "I then saw the chair slide across the floor towards the kitchen wall. It moved approximately three to four feet and then came to rest. At no time did it appear to leave the floor. I checked the chair but could find nothing to explain how it had moved."

Within a few hours of its arrival the Enfield poltergeist had been seen in action by a police constable.

A few days later the case made the front page of the *Daily Mirror* under the headline "The House of Strange Happenings." And strange they were. Marbles and Lego began to fly around the house with the speed of bullets. The *Mirror* photographer recalls that he became the first casualty on the case:

"I saw the Lego pieces flying around and I was hit on the head by a piece while I was attempting to photograph it in flight. I had a bump on the forehead after the incident."

The sharp-edged brick missed his eye by an inch. This was witnessed by Betty Norton and by Morris' *Mirror* colleague. Betty's arms are folded in his photo, while the reporter's hands are in his pockets. So who threw the brick?

Mirror reporter George Fallows soon decided the case was genuine. One of his colleagues saw a chair fall over in Jane's bedroom as she lay asleep beside it and they all heard the persistent knockings on the walls. It was then Fallows decided to call the SPR.

Only a few days before Maurice Grosse had asked SPR secretary Eleanor O'Keeffe to let him know of any spontaneous case in his area and so within four hours of the *Mirror*'s call, Grosse arrived in Enfield.

From that day, 5 September, the house was under almost daily surveillance by the SPR. No similar case has ever been studied so thoroughly, so soon after its inception, or for so long.

Grosse, a professional inventor with a stack of international patents to his credit, had been an SPR member only for a few months despite lifetime study and interest in the subject. For him it was a case of beginner's luck. Many veteran researchers have spent their lives hoping in vain to witness paranormal phenomena. Within a few days of his first visit to Enfield, Grosse had witnessed many strange things.

A marble slammed into a door beside his head. Hanging wall chimes swayed to and fro without apparent cause. He watched the lavatory door open and shut several times. He felt a strong cold breeze around his feet and over his head. A T-shirt jumped off the kitchen table to the floor in front of his eyes. Best of all, as he sat alone in the kitchen writing up his notes, the teapot began to rock back and forth on its stand.

This convinced Grosse that he had the case he wanted and after a week of sleepless nights spent on watch he realized he needed help.

On 8 September the SPR held its regular monthly meeting at which the subject of the lecture — arranged several months back — was poltergeists. At discussion time Grosse told fellow members about the Enfield case and appealed for help. I happened to be sitting next to him. There was nothing I needed less than a poltergeist. That very day I had handed in the manuscript of a book that had taken 14 months to write and I felt I had earned a holiday. Moreover, I had seen enough poltergeists during my years with H. G. Andrade's Brazilian Institute for Psychobiophysical (IBPP) research group in Brazil.

But I remembered Mr. Andrade's first words to me: "When a case comes up we drop everything and go after it. It will not wait for us." This was the attitude that had enabled him to build up one of the world's largest collections of original material on a wide range of inexplicable phenomena and, like him, I had come to feel that psychical research was an obligation rather than a pastime. So off I went to Enfield.

I liked Mrs. Harper at once. A typical Londoner, solid, direct and friendly, she was putting up with the poltergeist as she had put up with the bombs during World War II. It, like the war, was a nuisance but it was not going to get her down.

Grosse already had turned her into a first-rate investigator; when anything happened she immediately wrote it down. Her notes for a typical day went like this:

"Jane and I woke up. We waited a minute before we got up. We thought we heard soft footsteps. All at once the small chair by the bed jumped once, then as I got out of bed it jumped again. Time: 6:45. As I went out of bedroom, Jane followed. The big chest of drawers jumped, then went right over on its side. 6:50.

We came downstairs, all of us. Jane was in front room alone. Cushion jumps off red chair near glass cabinet, 7 Next, small TV table in corner turns over with things on top onto floor, 7:50."

And so it went day after day. Soon it was all Mrs. Harper could do to make brief notes. On 29 September, for instance, she wrote:

"4:25 Strong atmosphere front room.

4:35 Jane's chair moves (kitchen). Green chair over (front room).

4:40 Knock on window (front room).

4:45 Book shoots off table.

4:51 Fridge door moves in kitchen

4:53 Table moves out; then books shoot off.

4:55 Jane falls off kitchen chair."

Grosse and I had noted a total of 414 specific incidents by the end of October. Of these, we personally had witnessed about 30. After that we gave up counting for there was simply too much going on. The final total, if we ever get around to working it out, will certainly pass the 2000 mark.

We have, however, classified the incidents into 16 categories. These include just about everything ever reported on poltergeist activity over the past 1500 years.

The percussive sounds could be isolated bangs and thuds or rapid successions of knocks showing unmistakable signs of an intelligence behind them. On several occasions we carried on lengthy dialogues, on a basis of one knock for "no," two for "yes." Once Grosse asked the rapper how long ago it had lived in the house. In reply we both clearly heard — and recorded — a string of no fewer than 52 raps while everybody in the room was under observation. A curious detail was the way the raps faded in and out like a weak radio signal.

Despite our initial success, we learned nothing conclusive from the rapper or rappers, for at times we clearly heard two or more sequences going at once from different parts of the floor or walls. When I asked, "Do you know you are dead?" the rapping stopped and never again replied to any of my questions. When Grosse, exasperated by receiving contradictory yes/no replies to his carefully phrased questions, exclaimed, "Are you playing games with me?" a cardboard box instantly shot off the bedroom floor, travelled about eight feet and hit him squarely on the head.

This was witnessed in good light by six people and recorded on two tape recorders. I was behind the open door at the time and did not see the box leave the floor but I was in the room before it landed and am quite satisfied that nobody threw it — nobody of flesh and blood, at least. I can think of no reasonable normal explanation for it.

Our list covered the throwing of small objects, the opening and closing of doors and drawers, and the movement or overturning of chairs and tables. Each of us witnessed examples of these. In front of my eyes in good light my notebook once flew off the bed towards Mrs. Harper's head. A large armchair fell over within my full view just after Jane got up from it. A framed certificate shot off the wall behind Grosse's back when nobody else was within reach of it. The heavy sofa rose four feet in the air and landed upside down in the presence of 11 people, including Grosse.

The remaining categories, for the record, were: interference with beds and bedclothing; appearance of water and liquid or solid excretion on floors and walls; apparitions, both partial and total, of human forms; levitation of persons; physical assaults; presumed passage of solid matter through solid matter; psychological disturbances; automatic writing and drawing; automatic speech; disembodied voices of the Jürgenson type; equipment failure; outbreaks of fire.

Examples of each of the above, except for the apparitions and the passage of solid matter through solid matter, were witnessed by either Grosse or me. The most bizarre episode of the whole case, an example of the solids passing through solids, was witnessed by several persons independently. All the members of the Harper family claimed they were repeatedly pinched, slapped and even punched hard by an invisible aggressor. They also reported seeing shadows and fleeting figures around the house regularly.

The fires were certainly the most alarming events of all. Without apparent reason newspapers and dishcloths began to combust inside closed drawers or to appear, burning, on the floor. We never had to call the fire brigade because the fires would put themselves out as mysteriously as they had started. Once we even had an instance of nonfire. Rose Harper went into the kitchen and put the kettle on the gas to make tea. Two minutes later she went back to the kitchen expecting the water to be boiling. In the doorway she screamed! Under the kettle, on top of the burning gas, was a box of household tissues. They were charred but were not flaming.

I was especially intrigued by the accounts of partial apparitions. Mrs. Harper was surprised when I told her that these are reported quite often. During one of my Brazilian investigations an intelligent young medical student gave me a convincing account of the sudden appearance of a disembodied arm on the well-lit landing of his house. The fact that the Harpers and their neighbours so often reported incidents typical of similar cases suggests to me that they were speaking the truth.

This is not to say that the Harper kids did not occasionally play a few tricks on us. They did, although not often, and I guess I would have been surprised if they had not. I noticed that they tended to play their tricks only after an apparently genuine incident had taken place. It was as if it occurred to them to fake something only after a genuine incident had happened — possibly they would not have known what to fake without the genuine poltergeist to show them what they could do.

Nobody, however, could blame the children for the numerous failures and malfunctions of equipment that took place throughout the case. For example: Graham Morris' three camera flashguns all apparently were drained of power at the same time, although they all had just been charged and all worked perfectly again on the following day. The tape in a video recorder loaned to us by Pye Business Communications and operated by their chief demonstrator R. H. Denney jammed between a pin and a guide pulley as soon as it was switched on. The entire deck had to be dismantled to free it. BBC radio reporter Rosalind Morris found the tape on her Uher reel-tape recorder somehow turned itself over while it was recording — on the face of it, this is impossible. On another occasion she took her Sony TC-55 out of her bag to find the record and fast forward buttons jammed down tight. The machine had to be dismantled to free them. A photographer from the *National Enquirer* found his shutter jammed just as he was about to take a photograph inside the house.

As for our own equipment, the list of "coincidental" malfunctions is endless. Recorders switched themselves on and off. Tapes were wiped clean and — more mysteriously — partially demagnetized. My external microphone cable was wrenched from its socket right behind my back; the spring clip was bent in a way even Uri

Geller might find hard to duplicate. One night my cassette recorder disappeared altogether for about two hours, only to turn up in another room after we had made a very thorough search of the whole house.

The poltergeist even followed Grosse home. He heard footsteps in his upstairs when nobody was there and a loud bang in his garden. A ring belonging to his wife disappeared one day and reappeared several months later — on the morning after he had written to his insurance company to claim for it. The drawer in which the ring was found had been searched thoroughly several times. One day the engine of his car revved up on its own as he stood beside it.

Grosse made an original contribution to psychical research by bringing a solicitor to Enfield to cross-examine some of the principal witnesses and assess their reliability and honesty. It was his opinion that, "Any jury in the land would believe them."

From a researcher's point of view the Enfield case got better and better every day in every way. We decided to record as many data as possible hoping they might suggest a solution to the problem and thus benefit other victims. At the same time, we felt morally obliged to do what we could to stop the disturbances since it was clear they were seriously disrupting the family's everyday lives and especially the children's work at school.

But Mrs. Harper, Grosse and I were in agreement on one matter — we were not going to seek the help of an "exorcist." While our case was at its most active news came from Germany of the appalling story of young Anneliese Michel who died of starvation after no fewer than 67 "exorcisms" by Roman Catholic priests, two of whom were later tried and convicted of causing her death by negligence.

"Even if it worked," Mrs. Harper told us, "I'd never sleep at night for fear that it would come back. I want to know what this thing is and why it chose us."

So did we. Although we all believed that "this thing" could be some form of spirit or "earthbound entity" — that was certainly the impression it gave — Grosse and I both were determined to give conventional science every opportunity to explain the mysterious goings-on at Enfield.

Initially this was a frustrating and total failure. At one stage the situation became quite desperate. Eleven-year-old Jane began to fall into trances during which she screamed at the top of her voice and acted like a wholly different, quite violent person. Once four of us had to restrain her for over an hour and twice we had to call a doctor to sedate her. A total of four local doctors examined her; one diagnosed hysteria, another schizophrenia, a third decided she was quite normal and the fourth said nothing at all. Not one of the four did anything about it.

Fortunately two Brazilian Spiritist friends of mine happened to pass through London at this time. Luiz Gasparetto is well known in Brazil and Europe for his remarkable trance painting and Elsie Dubugras is a journalist and healing medium from the São Paulo State Spiritist Federation. Luiz and Elsie agreed to help and proceeded to give a most impressive demonstration of their powers. They arrived at Enfield when Jane was in one of her most violent altered states. This one had lasted nearly four days but by the time Luiz and Elsie left two hours later Jane was sleeping like a baby. She slept for 13 hours and never had another similar fit.

The Enfield case reached its climax in the middle of December 1977, just at the time when, we learned later, Jane had her first menstrual period. Although her violent trances had ceased, the furniture continued to fall over, slippers and pillows were still flung about the bedroom and one or two other incidents took place that were bizarre even by Enfield standards.

Jane was seen, by several passersby unconnected with the family, to levitate through the window of her bedroom in broad daylight. One witness, a local tradesman, took several months to get over this. He not only saw her floating around her room but also saw a large red pillow appear on the roof of the Harper house, although he was certain the window was not open at the time. On the same day Jane announced that she had "been through the wall" into the adjoining house. And a book belonging to her was found in the bedroom next door. There seemed no way it could have got there normally.

In mid-December the poltergeist began to talk to us. For some time strange whistling and barking noises had been heard coming from Jane's general direction although it was not always apparent that they came from her mouth. Grosse issued a direct challenge: "You can whistle and you can bark," he said. "So you can speak. Go on, say my name!" He repeated this order several times.

A long pause was followed by grunts and growls of a kind not normally heard from 11-year-old girls. And finally one of the most alarming sounds I have ever heard issued from her. It was a hoarse, rasping and uncannily loud sound in which the words "Maurice ... Grosse..." were distinguishable. We had made contact!

The "voice" aroused furious controversy. Two psychologists, both members of the SPR, decided Jane was "having us on." A ventriloquist brought along by the *Daily Mirror* announced before he even heard it that she was faking the voice. However, a professional speech therapist pointed out that if Jane were faking her larynx would be seriously damaged within minutes. Yet the "voice" kept up for hours on end without Jane's even clearing her throat. Finally, a laryngologist proved, after analysing one of our many tapes, that Jane's larynx was not being used at all. He stated that the sound was being made by her "false vocal folds." Grosse offered a substantial cash donation for charity if any magician could produce a child who could make the same sound for an hour. There were no takers.

The "voice" claimed to belong to not one but several dead men buried in the local graveyard, although it gave us no evidence for this that stood up to investigation. When not pronouncing a monotonous stream of obscenities, the voice gave the impression of coming from a confused "earthbound entity" unable to talk sense. For a century Spiritista have claimed this is what poltergeists are and neither Grosse nor I have a better suggestion.

When the case showed no sign of ending by mid-1978 Grosse and I insisted that Jane must leave home. After much difficulty we were able to arrange for her to enter a leading London psychiatric hospital where she spent six weeks under close observation. Here she was found to be totally normal and her general health improved considerably.

Back home in Enfield (some 30 miles away) things quieted down. However, they did not stop altogether, showing that Jane's presence as a focus was not essential. Finally Grosse managed to persuade the local authorities to rehouse the family. By now Mrs. Harper agreed she never again would be able to lead a normal life in her old home.

It remains to be seen if the Enfield poltergeist will move with them, stay at their former home, or simply go away as most poltergeists do, leaving all concerned as bewildered as they were on the day the disturbances started.

A GHOST SINGS IN IRELAND

The voice was clear, melodious and mournful — the otherworldly sound of a deeply troubled soul.

Margaret A. Blair

I was attending the 1977 Writer's Conference in the little town of Listowel in County Kerry when I first heard the strange story of the "Singing Ghost" of Monkstown. According to the story, a mysterious voice was disturbing the sleep and frightening the wits out of some half dozen or more families in this suburban section of Dublin. The press and the electronic media were giving these midnight concerts the kind of publicity any earthbound performer would envy.

I had come to Ireland primarily to collect Celtic legends, folklore and fairy tales, so of course I considered it an uncommon bit of Irish luck that a real "live" ghost had so conveniently planned his appearance to coincide with my itinerary. Since I planned to be in Dublin the following week, I thought I would arrange a meeting with those Monkstown residents who were directly involved with the disturbance.

Back in Dublin I boarded a local bus and soon found myself in Monkstown, a pleasant middle-class neighbourhood with quiet streets lined with single-family dwellings which at first glance scarcely lent themselves to anything so exotic as a haunting. In my search for witnesses I first inquired at a local pub (always a good place to gather information in Ireland) and next from a friendly woman carrying a large bag of groceries.

The woman directed me to the home of Mr. and Mrs. James Meegan in the nearby Rory O'Connor Park Subdivision. Not only had the Meegan family heard the phantom voice on numerous occasions, she told me, but their son Jimmy had made a recording of that voice.

This last bit of information fascinated me because such concrete data are rare; if genuine they represented solid scientific evidence of paranormal phenomena. Such investigators as Friederich Jurgenson and Konstantin Raudive, for example, spent years taping what they consider to be authentic voices from space.

I was doubly fortunate to find that the Meegan family were

willing to talk with me about their part in the strange happenings. After seating me comfortably in their cheerful parlour Mrs. Meegan, with true Irish hospitality, brought me a pot of hot tea and freshly-made sandwiches.

Soon their son Jimmy Meegan, a fine-looking young lad of 17 or 18 years, joined us and so did their neighbour Mrs. Alice Cunningham who also played a role in the story. I told them why I had come to Ireland and assured them my interest in their experiences was a serious one. I wanted them to know I did not consider them crackpots or liars simply because they had reported something weird and out of the ordinary. I could see that they were sensible people and as puzzled as you or I would be in similar circumstances.

I settled back in my chair to hear their story of the Singing Ghost of Monkstown.

"Several weeks ago," Mr. Meegan began, "people in the neighbourhood began to be awakened around midnight or one o'clock by the sound of a man's voice singing either 'Danny Boy' or 'Old Man River.' The singing sounds as if it comes from the treetops. It gets quite loud and then gradually fades away."

"How many people other than yourselves have heard the singing?" I asked.

"Oh, at least 20 or more, I would guess," Mrs. Meegan said.

I was impressed. "How often do you hear the voice?" I asked.

"About every other night," young Jimmy replied. "We heard it again last night but the voice was very faint. Before the singing starts, we've noticed that the dogs in the neighbourhood get restless and sometimes start to howl. And during the full moon, the voice comes every night and seems a lot stronger."

Mrs. Cunningham described her experiences with the mysterious voice.

"It was several nights ago," she said, "that my 17-year-old daughter was upstairs in her room drying her hair. Around one o'clock I heard loud singing coming from her room and called to her to turn off her radio. But the very next minute she came running downstairs terribly frightened and very nearly hysterical.

"There was no radio in her room at the time and suddenly the voice just boomed out from nowhere, it seemed. All of us were frightened and very upset and my daughter refused to sleep in her room that night. In fact, we've all been uneasy about it ever since."

The same night that the Cunninghams had their experience,

five 12-year-old boys in the neighbourhood also heard the voice. Brian Skerritt, Patrick Shorthall, Mark Cameron, David Stapleton and the Meegans' son Anthony had camped out the Skerritts' backyard hoping to experience a share of the excitement. But about 1:00 am when they too heard the strains of "Danny Boy" drifting down from the treetops directly overhead, they abandoned their campsite for the safety of their beds.

On a Monday evening some three weeks before my visit, Jimmy Meegan been inspired to try to tape the Singing Ghost. Early that evening, he told me, he put the tape recorder near an open window in the parlour and about 1:00 am the tape began to record a faint cry for help and then the familiar repertoire of the ghostly voice.

When Jimmy offered to play the tape for me the first sound I heard was the barely audible cry of "Help! Help!" Then came the distinct refrain of the opening lines of "Danny Boy," soon to be followed, by what sounded like "Old Man River." The singing stopped abruptly a few moments later to be followed by the recorded voice of Jimmy and his neighbour Ciaran who announced that both he and his mother Claire Fitzgibbon had also heard the singing. When Jimmy opened the door to Ciaran's knock, the singing had stopped suddenly as if silenced by the interruption.

The voice sounded trained. Although it was clear and melodious it had a distinctly mournful sound, like the voice of a deeply troubled soul. It also had an otherworldly quality that made it seem not quite human. To hear it suddenly ring out in the middle of the night could be a most unsettling experience.

Afterwards we discussed some possible causes for the bizarre phenomenon.

"Some of us think it has something to do with our neighbour cutting down a 'monkey puzzle' tree shortly before the singing started," Mr. Meegan said. The cutting had been done on 25 April, 1977.

"All of this property, my own house included," Mr. Meegan went on, "was at one time a part of the estate owned by Sir Valentine Grace who died about 30 years ago. After his death the estate was sold to a building company and the old home that belonged to the Grace family for several generations was torn down to make way for the Rory O'Connor Subdivision.

Mr. Meegan pointed out the window to the vacant lot across the street where the Grace family home had stood.

"You see," he said, "when the estate was sold there was an agreement that there were never to be any trees cut down on it."

I said, "You believe, then, that when your neighbour cut down the tree, this disturbed the ghost of Sir Valentine Grace, that it is his voice — or rather the voice of his ghost — that you are hearing?"

"A lot of people in the neighbourhood think there is some connection," he said.

"Our neighbor Mrs. Claire Fitzgibbon has lived in Monkstown since she was a child," Mrs. Cunningham said. "She saw Sir Grace many times and remembers hearing that his house was haunted. She also recalls that Sir Grace had the reputation of being a very good singer."

Sir Grace, a concert hall singer, had died on 3 May, 1945, at the age of 68. He was buried in a cemetery plot with his wife, who had passed on 10 years earlier, and his father and mother. His name is not listed on the headstone, supposedly because his family had disowned him.

The Meegans told me that Terry O'Sullivan, a columnist for the *Evening Press*, once had lived in Sir Grace's house and while there had had some strange and troubling experiences. Mr. Meegan generously offered to drive me to the *Evening Press* office to meet with Mr. O'Sullivan. I thanked my new friends for a fascinating afternoon and bade them all good-bye.

Mr. O'Sullivan, who has been writing a lively column for the *Evening Press* for the past quarter-century, readily agreed to tell me what he knew about Sir Grace and his family.

"Soon after Mrs. O'Sullivan and I were married," he said, "about a year before I went to work for the newspaper, we decided to rent the Sir Grace house. This was about five years after Sir Grace had died. But not long before we moved in, a friend told me he had heard the house was haunted. Although my friend was a university professor and a well-educated man who certainly was not given to superstitious fantasies, I didn't attach much importance to his warning.

"Everything about the house seemed quite normal and I had forgotten all about my friend's advice until one night several months later when my wife's father came to visit. Because it was a stormy evening we invited him to spend the night with us and around midnight my wife prepared the guest room, I banked the fires and we said good night.

"But in less than an hour my father-in-law woke us up to tell us that he had had a frightening experience. He had just dropped off to sleep when he was awakened by the sound of loud knocking. He first thought it was the wind but soon realized that the sound was coming from a location near his bed. Then the knocking stopped as suddenly as it had started and he could hear footsteps as if someone were walking across the room. Too frightened by now to wait for anything further to happen, he left the room as hastily as possible."

Nothing else out of the ordinary took place until several months later when a young gentleman friend came for a visit. Again it was a stormy evening and the O'Sullivans offered the guest room to their friend.

"But in less than an hour," said O'Sullivan, "our friend knocked at our bedroom door looking frightened and rather apologetic about making a disturbance. He too had been awakened by the sound of loud knocking in the room. But even more terrifying was the fact that he then heard someone say very distinctly, 'You can't sleep here tonight.' At that point he left the room and we all ended up spending the rest of the night by a roaring fire in the fireplace.

Mr. O'Sullivan assured me that neither his friend nor his father-in-law knew of the Grace home's reputation; therefore it seems unlikely their experiences were the result of suggestibility. By now the O'Sullivans were convinced the house really did harbour some mysterious entity or force which resented any intrusions into the guest room although they themselves had heard nothing unusual during their stay there.

O'Sullivan sought out the local parish priest the following day and learned from him that the Grace estate long had been known as a "troubled" spot. On several occasions, he learned, the clergy had been called in to sprinkle holy water on the premises when people could not sleep at night because of all the rappings and restless walking about. The local blacksmith expressed surprise that the O'Sullivans had been in the old house for almost a year, so unsavoury was its reputation.

One story Mr. O'Sullivan told me is especially interesting. It has to do with the fact, unimportant in itself, that Queen Alexandra, wife of Edward VII, had been left with a stiff knee after a severe attack of rheumatic fever. Sir Grace's grandmother, together with the other fashionable ladies of her time, had thought it stylish to affect a limp and had persisted in this absurd bit of mimicry to the end of her days. It was not long after the old lady's death, however, that occupants of the house began to report hearing the footsteps of someone walking with a limp.

Shortly after this second episode O'Sullivan changed jobs and moved to a new location. He had heard no more about the Grace family until the recent disturbance on the premises.

Not long after my interviews with the Meegans, their neighbours and O'Sullivan, I returned to the United States. Three months later, on 26 September, I received from James Meegan, Jr., the promised tape with the voice of the Singing Ghost of Monkstown. The tape also related more recent incidents involving the ghost.

According to Jimmy's account, his mother had heard a disturbance just as she was preparing for bed late one evening. She thought the sound had come from the Cunningham house. But the next day Mrs. Cunningham said she and her husband had retired early and had heard nothing out of the ordinary.

Two nights later, hearing the sounds of a loud party, she looked over to the Cunninghams' where all the lights were on and the kitchen window was open. Mr. and Mrs. Meegan both heard a beautiful male voice singing. The two of them listened for a while, then went to bed.

In the morning Alice Cunningham swore that she and her husband Tom had been away all night and the house had been locked up tight.

Jimmy related an earlier experience of his own:

"It was eight years ago — I was about 10 — and I was sleeping in the back of the house with my brother David. I was in the top bunk. One night I woke up and I felt uneasy. I sat up in bed and I could see something in the window. What the reflection looked like to me was a top hat, a cloak and a cane, and I had a terrible feeling of being stared at. I sat up all that night until the next morning. I didn't sleep in that room for about three weeks — I slept in my mother's room. That night the same thing was seen in at least seven houses around the green.

"That night — the same night — Mr. Higgins, an old man who lives down the road, was walking along when he saw a very tall man standing in the middle of the green wearing a tall hat and a long black cape and carrying a stick with a silver head. Sir Valentine was a very big man in life."

The Monkstown hauntings follow the classical pattern of ghost stories everywhere, whatever their place and time of origin. Hauntings characteristically centre on a particular location and are associated in some special way with deceased persons once linked with that place. The disturbance often expresses some characteristic trait of the deceased individual, in this instance Sir Grace's singing, or his grandmother's affected limp. Often a history of violence, possibly the desire for revenge or some other human tragedy, is connected with the haunting: murder, accidental death or great personal loss of either property or a loved one. In some unexplained manner these profound human emotions seem able to perpetuate themselves for indefinite periods of time, often for centuries.

Does some Grace family secret or now-forgotten tragedy prevent Sir Valentine and his grandmother from resting peacefully in their graves? Or is it simply that some souls, more earthbound than others, must return again and again to the place to which they were attached in life?

The Monkstown haunting also seems linked in a special way to a tradition that is as old as mankind and still widely prevalent in Ireland. This is the belief that certain trees are the dwelling places of fairies, demons or spirits. Such trees may be harmed only at the risk of great misfortune or even death, a punishment exacted by their supernatural occupants. The reader will recall that residents of Monkstown attached great importance to the felling of the "monkey puzzle" tree. Is it possible, however farfetched it may sound, that Sir Valentine's spirit has taken up residence in the trees that once surrounded his ancestral home? And is it now manifesting displeasure at the wanton destruction of one of these trees?

Perhaps serious investigators of psychic phenomena will visit Monkstown in the company of talented sensitives and find answers to some of these questions.

MERRY PRANKS IN A SCOTTISH RECTORY

Heavy-footed poltergeist, undaunted by men of the cloth, comes with the parish.

Mollie Mordle-Barnes

There was certainly no air of the supernatural about our new rectory in Tain on the shores of the Dornoch Firth in northeast Scotland. Quite the opposite, in fact. Built in the mid-19th century of local stone, it was typically square with rows of identical many-paned windows. The large bright rooms looked out on the sea and the distant headland in front and magnificent highland scenery at the back. We loved the place at first sight.

My husband Leonard, an ordained minister in the Church of England, had been rector of Holy Trinity Church in Ayr, Scotland. In the course of normal preferment in his ministry, he had been assigned to the Episcopal Church in Tain. With our three children — Angela, six, Beverley, almost four, and baby Julia — and Helen Ross, our live-in help, we moved into the rectory in the spring of 1947.

Returning from Inverness one evening about two weeks later, having left the children safely in bed with Helen in charge, we were surprised to find lights still on at the back of the house. The kitchen door had been bolted on the inside and we could not get in. Quite alarmed, we banged on the door and called out several times before Helen, shaking and white-faced, let us in. Her red eyes told us she had been crying.

"What on earth has happened?" my husband demanded.

Between sobs the terrified girl told us that soon after we had left early that evening she had distinctly heard the front door burst open, then the sound of heavy footsteps crossing the tiled hall and moving down the passage to the kitchen door, where they stopped. "And someone's been tramping up and down outside the door until a few minutes ago!" Helen concluded, bursting into fresh tears.

Completely baffled, we made a thorough search of the house. Everything was exactly as we had left it. The children were sleeping soundly upstairs; the front door was securely locked.

"Nobody could have got in," my husband said to me later. "It must have been Helen's imagination. But it looks as if we can't leave her alone in the evenings."

He seemed ready to dismiss the matter out of hand but somehow I had misgivings.

Then, only a few days later, Helen and I were preparing the evening meal when we both heard the front door open and unmistakable footsteps cross the hall. This time the footsteps proceeded steadily up the stairs. I was expecting my husband home any minute but I remember thinking it was unusual for him to come in that way and to go straight upstairs without announcing his return. Suddenly a loud commotion broke out in the bathroom overhead. We heard knocks and bangs, then a heavy thud as if someone had fallen. Fearing my husband had been taken ill, Helen and I raced upstairs — only to find the bathroom now silent and dark! Incredibly, all three children were fast asleep. Thoroughly shaken, we returned to the kitchen just in time to meet my husband coming through the back door.

"Good heavens!" he exclaimed. "Have you both seen a ghost — or something?" He was half joking but when I tried to explain he was frankly sceptical.

"Is the front door locked this time?" he inquired. And as I had expected, it was.

"The noises you heard must be due to faulty plumbing. If it happens again I'll get a plumber to sort it out. There may be air locks — or something."

I wanted to believe him but somehow I just couldn't. Glancing at Helen I saw that she was equally unconvinced. And my husband was soon to change his mind.

One morning I was sewing in an upstairs room above the front porch. Gradually I became aware of footsteps crunching along the newly gravelled drive toward the front door. A tree hid my view of the drive but I paused, expecting to hear the doorbell ring. Instead the door was opened abruptly — flung open, in fact — and again those heavy footsteps sounded clearly, crossing the hall, coming up the stairs, moving along the landing and stopping outside the door immediately behind me. Thoroughly alarmed, I leaped to the door and threw it open. Nobody was there.

At that moment my husband came out of his study into the hall.

"Who was that?" he asked.

With a sense of relief I realized that he too had heard the ghostly footsteps. Now he had to agree that there was something queer about the old house.

The next disturbance came in the middle of the night. Leonard and I we're both awakened by a terrific rumpus in the kitchen. We sat up in bed and listened. Was it our poltergeist again — or burglars?

"You must go down and find out!" I insisted. Reluctantly my husband put on his dressing gown and armed with nothing more lethal than a long-handled clothes brush he set off downstairs. I followed, my heart thumping. As we crept toward the kitchen, the uproar suddenly and inexplicably ceased. It just died away. But this time, when we switched on the kitchen light, we discovered things had been moved. Saucepans and kitchen tools, usually hanging on wall hooks or standing on shelves, were scattered all over the floor. The table and chairs had been pushed against the far wall. But — as we had come to expect — the doors and windows were securely fastened.

Now we knew for certain that we had a poltergeist on our hands. But to deal with it?

We began to make discreet inquiries in the village as to the past history of the house and its previous occupants. We received polite but noncommittal relies — even from people we had come to know quite well. We realized we weren't going to learn anything from the locals. We were stumped.

The next odd experience shortly afterwards was shared by our children. It was 15 March, 1948, Angela's birthday. My husband and I, our own children and four others were having a birthday tea in the dining room and we all heard the front door burst open and the now-familiar steps cross the hall. This time they halted outside the dining room door. Being nearest I sprang up and opened it, although I knew instinctively that nobody would be there. The older children insisted on leaving their tea and searching the house. It was a waste of time — and as usual the front door catch was securely fastened.

The next visitation occurred one evening when I was alone in the house except for the children who were asleep in their beds. As usual, the preliminaries followed the familiar pattern: front door opening, footsteps crossing the hall and proceeding to the kitchen. The commotion broke out as previously but needless to say, before I reached the kitchen the din had died away. All was quiet — but in those few moments our prankish visitor had managed to move the table and chairs and for good measure, had tossed a heavy preserving pan onto the stone hearth. Strangely, the impact had left no mark or dent on the pan!

Almost at that moment I heard Helen arriving at the back entrance. Coming into the kitchen she stared in disbelief at the disorder. This proved to be the last straw. She left us the following week for the safe haven of her sister's modern home in southern England.

The kitchen episode was repeated several times, with almost reassuring monotony. In the end I got quite accustomed to it — and I lost all fear of our poltergeist. After all, it never actually broke anything. It was evidently mischievous but not in the least malicious.

Equally puzzling was the way the strange manifestations simply stopped after about nine months. Perhaps the poltergeist tired of playing its noisy tricks. We shall never have an explanation, I suppose, for in September 1952 we reluctantly left Scotland because of another transfer. My husband became vicar of Hoton Church in Hoton, Leicestershire, England.

Some time later I went back to Tain to visit a friend and hesitantly broached the subject of the peculiar occurrences in the rectory. (My friend was Anita Carswell and we had not questioned her about the house while we lived there.)

"Yes," she admitted. "I had heard rumours about that house of yours. It seems that three local women who had been engaged to clean up the place before you took over just downed tools and refused — one after another — to work there or finish the job. Each claimed she had heard somebody come into the empty house, go upstairs or along to the kitchen but the intruder never came into the room where a woman happened to be working. So no one ever actually saw anything!"

Anita laughed. "Well, now you know that you weren't the only people given to 'hearing things.'"

THE GHOST WHO OWNED THE OFF LICENCE

Sam Marsden had died a cruel death at the hands of an evil woman and his spirit refused to leave the old haunts.

Irene Bradburn

As Kathleen Stanton entered our South London Off Licence that evening in 1951 my husband John emerged from the store room. I heard him say, "Good evening." John has sort of Errol Flynn good looks and a pleasant manner with customers.

Miss Stanton was a plain woman in her 40's, a mousey type, but earnest and friendly. I liked her. She asked John for her usual purchase and then, rather hesitantly, inquired about our dog Bill, a bullterrier. Come to think of it, he had been missing all day.

John and Kathleen stood looking at each other — for an endless time, it seemed to me — until Kathleen finally blurted out, "I saw Bill on the railway track this morning. I'm afraid he just waited for that train! As it came into the station he ran toward it and he was killed!" She hesitated, then said, "It was almost as if Bill meant to commit suicide. I'm so sorry!"

It seemed ages before John spoke. "Poor Bill. How the children will miss him. He was such a good dog for the shop. too."

John was very upset. "Miss Stanton," he said, "would you come through to the parlour? My wife is upstairs putting the children to bed and perhaps it would be better if you tell her the way it happened."

Kathleen seemed reluctant but sensing the urgency and underlying emotion in his voice, she agreed to break the news to me. As it happened, neither had to tell me, for I had overheard. I had put the children to bed early and come down the stairs, shivering as usual as I passed the small bedroom on the first landing. It would have been ideal for a nursery but somehow I had never liked that room. I walked on into the parlour and into the storeroom to enter the shop but withdrew because I felt giddy.

The shock of Bill's death on that railway track was the last straw. A series of strange happenings had occurred since we took over the management of the off licence in September 1950 and had come to live in the adjoining house. I walked back into the parlour and sat down, emotionally drained. As John brought Kathleen into the room I caught the end of their conversation. She was saying that the last time she had entered this parlor the circumstances had filled her with horror. John's eyebrows raised and then he came to me saying, "Miss Stanton has some sad news."

" I heard it," I said. The tears were running down my face. John seated Kathleen, then said, "Miss Stanton, do you believe in the occult?"

She was taken aback but answered forthrightly. "Well, I do actually. Although I myself have never seen a spirit or an apparition I have known people who have."

John continued, "Did you know the late manager of this shop. Sam Marsden and his wife? You know how the customers talk. I was told you were a friend of theirs."

She answered, "Well, I have been coming into this shop for years and would always have the usual 'courtesy conversation' with Sam Marsden. But during the last few months of his life his wife would draw me into chatting with her and now I wish she had not done so." This was the second remark that surprised us.

John was about to speak but was interrupted by the shop bell. He excused himself and I took over. "To tell you the truth, Kathleen, what John is trying to say is that we believe this off licence is haunted and we feel we must tell someone who won't scoff at the idea. We also wonder if unhappy circumstances here during Sam Marsden's lifetime would make him — silly as it sounds — want to haunt this place. Now, with Bill's 'suicide' we must investigate.

"You see, since arriving here we have not had one good night's sleep because of the strange happenings. And although there are many rooms in this house we huddle together in one room at night. I'm sorry we had to leave Bill in the shop but it was in the agreement that we would provide a dog to mind the premises at night. Bill was a marvellous dog, frightened of no man, but we believe that what Bill saw last night caused him to wait on that railway track this morning.

Last night we heard footsteps, as usual. They started quietly, then got louder, like an old man's lumbering steps, until quite near our bedroom, nearer than they'd ever come before. It was extra horrible last night. The atmosphere was so thick you could cut it with a knife and then I had a choking feeling as if my mouth was covered and I couldn't breathe.

John keeps a crowbar near the bed in case of a break-in. He grabbed it, saying, 'I can't stand this any longer!' With that he raced downstairs, looking into each room. When he reached the shop there was no one there — just poor Bill, standing in the middle of the shop, his hair standing on end and piddling. This was Bill! Frightened of no man or beast! But whatever he had seen had frightened the hell out of him."

Just then John came back into the parlour. He seemed to take up the conversation where I had left off. "Miss Stanton, so many strange things have happened — and we have not had much luck since coming into the shop. It seems things work against us. Who would have thought we would be taking over a haunted place like this? And now poor old Bill is gone." John looked exhausted.

Kathleen rose from her chair and walked toward John and me. Taking my hand she said, "I have decided to tell you all the circumstances that led to old Sam's death — how his life was virtually snuffed out. I think Sam's spirit is still wandering around here because of the hatred that was left. Mrs. Marsden was a very evil woman."

Kathleen began by saying that Sam Marsden was a tall man, very upright. No one would have believed he was 74. He wore his silvery hair in a military cut, his eyes were bright vivid blue and he sported a fine moustache. Whenever she entered the shop he would greet her jovially, she would order her small bottle of Guinness, then go back to the room she rented nearby.

One day, to her surprise, there was a woman in the shop — a woman of about fifty. Sam introduced her as Mrs. Marsden. Kathleen wondered about his marrying at his age but she was soon to learn the whole story. Mrs. Marsden, a chatty woman, revealed that the owners of the shop, a brewery company, had encouraged Sam to take a wife to help in the business.

It had been a quick courtship. Mrs. Marsden had latched onto what she termed "a good thing" but she spoke of Sam as a man of her own age. Kathleen wondered what age Sam had admitted to but dismissed the thought immediately as none of her business.

As time went on Mrs. Marsden took more and more charge of the store. She gave Kathleen daily bulletins about Sam, saying he was becoming poorly, too poorly for a man of his age. Then one day she announced they were off on a holiday. They were going camping. Kathleen was amazed. She thought camping would be a bit much for

Sam in his state of health. But she kept this to herself and wished the Marsdens a nice holiday.

Some weeks went by before the young man filling in at the shop announced that the Marsdens soon would be back from their holiday. When Kathleen called at the shop the next day, Mrs. Marsden came from the parlour into the store very quickly, almost as if she had been waiting for her.

"'Did you have a nice holiday, Mrs. Marsden?" Kathleen asked. "Sorry the weather wasn't so good for camping."

The other woman did not answer but said, "Would you come through to the parlour, Miss Stanton?"

Kathleen was a little surprised but curious about the accommodation attached to the shop. As she entered the parlour she could see the stairs rising to two landings. She thought it seemed rather a lot of room for two people.

Mrs. Marsden seated Kathleen and said, "I'm afraid Mr. Marsden is very poorly. He's upstairs in his old bedroom."

"I'm sorry to hear this," Kathleen said. "Do you think the camping was a bit much for him?"

Mrs. Marsden eyed Kathleen quizzically, then blurted out, "Did you know how old the old bastard is? I thought I was marrying a man of my own age but he's nearly 74! Have I been had!"

As she raved on, Kathleen learned the whole story, that the camping had been too much for poor old Sam and he was up there in his old bedroom dying of pneumonia. Kathleen shivered and wished she were somewhere else but she could not extricate herself from the situation. Then, as rattling sounds came from the bedroom, Mrs. Marsden walked to a chest of drawers in the corner. Taking a handkerchief from a drawer, she rolled it into a ball and screamed, "I'll stop that noise!"

She went upstairs to the bedroom on the first landing where old Sam was lying. Kathleen waited, wondering what Mrs. Marsden was doing. When Sam's wife came out of his bedroom, the noise had stopped. She muttered, "That's stopped the old bugger!" Mrs. Marsden was tight-lipped; her face showed no remorse. Kathleen thought, "Poor old Sam," and quickly made an excuse to leave.

Kathleen never saw Mrs. Marsden again. The next day she was off on holiday and when she returned Old Sam had been buried and a new family — John and I and our two children John and Jacqueline — lived in the house attached to the off licence.

That was Kathleen's story. When she finished we sat in stunned silence. Our "haunt" must be old Sam Marsden. We wondered what we could do. As if our three minds were concentrating on the thought of getting help, Kathleen said, "I have an idea. Do you know Mrs. Bart?"

John and I said, "Yes," in unison.

Kathleen continued, "Mrs. Bart is the local Spiritualist — although she admits the only spirits she ever saw came out of a gin bottle!"

That broke the tension and we all laughed. Kathleen carried on. "Perhaps we could have a séance, to clear the air and send Sam's spirit on its way."

This all seemed a little weird to us but we thanked Kathleen and promptly agreed. At last we were getting some help and at the same time I had a strange feeling that this is what Sam Marsden wanted.

Kathleen left us then and went immediately to Mrs. Bart's home. When she arrived the front door was slightly ajar. She knocked hesitantly and heard Mrs. Bart's voice saying, "Come in, dear, I have been waiting for you." Kathleen had a feeling she was taking part in a series of preordained events.

"Sit down, dear. I am sure you could do with some tea," Mrs. Bart said. Pouring a cup for Kathleen, Mrs. Bart said, "Now drink your tea, dear, and tell me why you're here."

As Kathleen related the events of the day Mrs. Bart did not interrupt even once but held Kathleen's gaze with her eyes. The psychic was "rather beautiful for her age," Kathleen told us, but her eyes were especially remarkable. They had a strange hypnotic effect. When Kathleen finished, Mrs. Bart nodded and said, "Samuel sent you." Then the psychic told her about Samuel Marsden.

He and Mrs. Bart had been friends for many years. He had come from a well-connected family and had had a distinguished military career. When his service with the army ended he received a nice pension and gratuities and with these had taken over the off licence. He had served in many fascinating foreign parts of the world and had a special fondness for New Zealand and Australia.

As Kathleen listened, she had a sneaking impression that Mrs. Bart had been more than fond of Samuel. Apparently he had not shared Mrs. Bart's belief in the supernatural, much to her regret. She sat there smiling and said, "Samuel Marsden, the unbeliever, I'll be happy to stop his wandering spirit and send him on his way."

Kathleen returned to our shop to report her meeting with Mrs. Bart and to say Mrs. Bart would hold the séance the next evening. At the appointed time Mrs. Bart, Kathleen, John and I sat in a circle in the off licence parlour. As we held hands, Mrs. Bart went into a trancelike state. I felt shivery as a thick cold atmosphere seemed to envelop us. Then Mrs. Bart started to choke and sputter; just as suddenly she stopped, cleared her throat and called to Samuel Marsden.

In the next few minutes she told Sam it was time to move on to a higher plane, to leave the off licence and let the present family get on with their lives. Then, when it was all over, face took on a resigned look. "It's a pity," she said, "that most of us have to die before we believe."

The next day when Kathleen called at the shop we were able to tell her we had had our first full night's sleep since coming to the off licence exactly a year ago to the day.

A NOISY NIGHT IN IRELAND

The house echoed with eerie sounds — voices, footsteps, crashes, roars — but our ears registered only uncanny silence.

Sheila St. Clair

At Gillhall, a country manor in County Down, Northern Ireland, two well-authenticated hauntings are separated by a span of more than two centuries. Here, in the late 17th century, the legendary Beresford Ghost appeared, and in the mid-20th century the mansion was the scene of a series of paranormal events. An investigation of the latter in June 1960, well covered by the press, assured that the mansion would become known as one of the most haunted in Ireland.

The Ulster Tape Recording Society, working with the BBC, invited me to participate in the investigation which resulted because the Society, a fortnight earlier, had obtained a tape bearing "noises" no one could explain. Sounds in the mansion ranged from muffled human voices to an odd roaring and crackling as of flames. I accepted the invitation, then decided to refresh my memory of the mansion and the story of the Beresford Ghost.

I was fortunate to be able to borrow original records from Lord Clanwilliam whose family owns the Gillhall estate. These records leave little doubt of the reality of Arabella Beresford's encounter with a ghost.

In October 1693, Lady Nicola Magill, then mistress of Gillhall, was entertaining her pregnant sister Arabella and her husband Sir Tristram Beresford. The house was new then, a fine three-storey mansion overlooking an extensive parkland and situated near the thriving market town of Dromore and the main road to Dublin.

During the Beresfords' stay at Gillhall a strange event occurred, one which cast a shadow over the remainder of Arabella's life. One night as she lay beside her sleeping husband in the guest chamber, she was astonished by the sudden appearance of her childhood friend John De Poer, Lord Tyrone. In their youth they had made an interesting pact: whoever died first would return to let the other know what religious belief was acceptable to the deity in the afterlife. Lord Tyrone's apparition reminded her of this and he said further that news of his death would come from Dublin the next day.

As if to leave proof of his visit he drew the bed curtains into a curious knot, wrote his name in a book and made a handprint on top of the bureau (now in the possession of the Clanwilliam family). As a more personal reminder Lord Tyrone laid his hand on Arabella's wrist.

He did not, however, explain the deity's preference in religious matters but he did utter several prophecies concerning Arabella herself. He said the child she carried was a boy, her husband would die soon after the child's birth, she would die in childbirth in her 47th year, and her older son would marry his (Lord Tyrone's) daughter. Having said these things the apparition vanished.

The next morning Arabella appeared at the breakfast table with her wrist bound in a black ribbon. To forestall her husband's inquiry, she said to him, "Let me conjure you never to enquire the reason why I wear this black ribbon ... If it concerned you as a husband to know, I would not for a moment conceal it ... On this I must entreat you never to urge me further ..." It is to Sir Tristram's credit that he complied with his young wife's request; the matter was not spoken of again. It is said that contemporary portraits of Arabella show the black ribbon but I have never seen one.

News of Lord Tyrone's death did in fact reach Gillhall that day and Lady Beresford accepted it with composure, to her sister's astonishment.

In due time Lord Tyrone's prophecies came to pass. The child that Arabella bore was a boy and when he was four years old Sir Tristram died. Mindful of the third prophecy, Arabella was in no hurry to remarry but when she fell in love with a handsome rake several years her junior, she went to the altar for the second time.

The marriage was not a happy one. It was marred by long separations and uneasy reconciliations but eventually Arabella found herself pregnant again. The child was due near the time of her 48th birthday. As the fateful 47th birthday had passed without incident, Arabella decided to have a small celebration. Among the guests was an elderly clergyman who had in fact christened Arabella. When the guests toasted her 48th birthday, the old man looked puzzled.

"They would make you out to be older than you are, my dear," he said. "Just this evening I looked at my diary wherein I had noted the happy event of your birth and you may believe me when I say that you are only 47."

His words had a cataclysmic effect. Arabella swooned. In the early hours of the next day she went into premature labour and by morning she and her child were dead.

Four years later, Lady Catherine De Poer, Lord Tyrone's daughter, married Arabella's son, fulfilling the last of the apparition's prophecies.

Apart from the single incident of the Beresford Ghost, there is nothing to show that Gillhall was perennially ghostridden — although in later years one room was called the "haunted bedroom." In this room a young woman was said to have set fire to her bed hangings and burned to death after an unhappy love affair. But most large houses have some similar tale.

With this information fresh in my mind I set out on 27 June, 1960, with the Ulster Tape Recording Society's sound engineers, technicians and photographers and a couple of journalists. I have a little reputation as a psychic investigator and William Scott, the Society's honorary secretary, explained that my observations might be helpful in attempting to unravel some of the baffling noises they had previously recorded and perhaps to explain the great sense of unease they had felt in the mansion.

In the words of the *Belfast Telegraph* reporter, "We arrived shortly before 10 o'clock at the gaunt, grey house, once proud but now derelict, with weeds creeping up the steps of its impressive entrance and gaping holes in its floors and ceilings ... The glass in the windows of the 50-roomed house has long since disappeared ...

Between 10 and 11:20 pm the selected locations in the house had been wired for sound and a control room, our listening post, was established on the ground floor in one of the large drawing rooms at the right of the front door. The locations selected for monitoring were those that had yielded noises on the preliminary tape: microphones were installed in the "haunted bedroom", the stairway and hall, one of the underground kitchens, the semibasement and a bedroom directly above the control room.

Only the large double doors at the main entrance were unlocked. All others were either boarded up or bolted. The windows were locked on the inside and covered with heavy wooden shutters. The semibasement had no exit door and its windows were either locked or covered with wire mesh. It was my task to sprinkle flour around paint cans and an old chair in the centre of the semibasement and finally to seal the entry with sticky tape. While doing so I noticed two large planks lying flat on the floor below a window.

The ground rules for the night's observations were simple: all monitoring and recording would be done by the sound equipment. If we moved around the house at all we moved in pairs and reported our location to the control room engineer. Other members with radio equipment patrolling the grounds outside were to report in at half-hour intervals.

When all of the arrangements were completed, we returned to the control room and called the roll. (At this point I realized there were 13 of us, one member having failed to show up.) Monitoring began at 11:45 and with thermos flasks and sandwiches unpacked, we settled down to wait.

The man from the *Belfast Telegraph* wrote, "We had not long to wait before things started happening. Ten minutes before midnight ... some members thought they saw the door of the control room, which had been blocked by a stool, move ...".

One of the double doors into the control room opened quietly about 15 inches and the stool that had been blocking it toppled over. A little later both doors opened of their own volition.

The reporter continued: "A few minutes later a metallic crash was heard from the cellar ... then another crash, again from the cellar ... Seven minutes later on the stroke of midnight a gong sounded in the room ..."

Opinions differed on the gong sound. A few of us thought it sounded like a clock striking but whatever it was, the gong was the prelude to what I privately termed "the noisiest night on record." During the next three hours we recorded a variety of sounds: muttering and humming of humanlike voices, crashes and thuds, footsteps in the hall, the sound of furniture being moved in the room overhead (where there was no furniture) and, for one awe-inspiring moment, the scratch of fingernails across the face of a microphone which we knew for a fact was 15 feet up a wall. Paradoxically, not even a rustle came from the so-called haunted bedroom!

There was no sound at all to the naked ear. The monitored rooms were visited at hourly intervals and once the control room door was opened an uncanny silence fell on the house. When everyone had returned to the control room, the pandemonium broke out afresh. Between 2 and 3 am the noise coming through the speakers reached an astounding level. The most persistent sound was the roar of a gale force wind, almost beastlike in its ferocity, accompanied by a noise that

I took to be the crackling of flames.

The outside patrols were aware of none of this until later. But they did report seeing lights passing slowly through the second floor and visible through the windows. This happened twice but the times did not correlate with inside patrols which members made with torches. When we attempted to simulate the manifestation with hand-held lamps or torches, the outside patrol said our lights bore no resemblance to the bluish light, "almost like gaslight," that they had seen.

The activity began to decline by 3:30 am and by the first streaks of dawn the house was once more undisturbed. A final inspection showed that no material changes had taken place except in the semibasement. While my seals remained unbroken and the flour undisturbed, the two planks now lay in the centre of the floor, a good eight feet from their original location,

Another mystery lay in the fact that while our treks through the house produced echoes and some distortion on the tape recording, all the crashes and bangs were "clean," as if recorded in a soundproof studio. This left the technical people completely baffled. Nor could we account for the sense of being watched and the pervading chill. On that warm June night many of us donned coats and parkas.

A decade later, in June 1970, Gillhall mysteriously caught fire. The Territorial Army had to be called in to demolish the charred and dangerous shell — a sad end to such a gracious house. Again, for a few days, Gillhall attracted the media's attention. Strange to relate, both sound and television cameras experienced mysterious malfunctions at the site and some of my fellow journalists had narrow escapes from falling slates and slamming doors.

As late as 1981 two English journalists asked me to direct them to Gillhall. I demurred until they promised to return to let me know what they found. A couple of hours later, two rueful, disheveled gentlemen of the press arrived at my door with a tale of woe. As they drove up the long avenue to the ruins, their car stalled. While they strove to restart it, out of a clear blue sky the clouds gathered and they were drenched in a sudden squall. When they tried to manhandle the car to head it downhill, one of them slipped and injured his knee.

"After that we got the message," one of them said. "All of a sudden we weren't so keen to photograph the ruins."

I could have said, "Well, I did warn you that it's a house that doesn't like to be visited." But I forebore. After all, it was pure coincidence that a summer storm blew up — wasn't it?

A SMASHING ENGLISH POLTERGEIST

This spirit's malignant antics may seem amusing but its 18-month, day-and-night harassment is no laughing matter.

Enid Anthony

When the trouble started, old Mrs. Adams had been keeping house for her 50-year-old spinster daughter Pauline for many years. They led a quiet existence occasionally highlighted by visits from friends and neighbors and especially Mrs. Adams' 17-year-old grandson Stephen Gordan. The two women were quite unprepared for the frightening occurrences that began in late 1979 and plagued them for 18 months, occurrences involving a mysterious force they could not understand and indeed, had never known to exist.

Their old two-storey house in Reading had a living room and dining room on the ground floor separated by a hall leading back to the kitchen and bathroom and a staircase up to the first-floor bedrooms.

Early every morning Pauline left to go to her full-time job with a flour company. Thereafter her mother routinely straightened up the house before making her daily shopping trip. One winter day, when she returned from shopping, she was astonished to find a couple of chairs tipped over and cabinet drawers in disarray. At first she was not unduly concerned. She is in her 80's and, foolish though it seemed, momentarily considered that she might have absentmindedly left the rooms in that condition. Fearing ridicule, she told no one except Pauline.

Then, every day for weeks, returning from her shopping excursions, Mrs. Adams found the same mindless disorder. Gradually the pattern changed. Instead of open drawers and toppled chairs, she discovered furniture moved from one room to another. More frightening still, tables, lamps, a record player and other pieces of furniture were propelled through the air by some unseen force, then dropped to the floor or shattered against a wall. Some evenings, as Pauline and her mother watched helplessly, a television set or radio floated around the room, then quivered as if shaken by powerful unseen hands before falling in pieces to the floor. Through the kindness and generosity of neighbours, television sets and radios were replaced several time but the gifts were short-lived as each was turned into debris by this malevolent force.

In the beginning the disturbances occurred in Mrs. Adams' absence but they soon began to involve the old woman and her daughter. The home invader seemed to have accumulated tremendous power and a fierce temperament. Often when the two women sat in either of the downstairs rooms they were bombarded with china and glassware — although neither was ever seriously hurt. Nevertheless, eventually almost all of the crockery they possessed had been smashed. Sitting in the living room one evening, they heard noises in the dining room across the hall. When they dared to look, they saw a sideboard smashed to pieces. As the days passed, four dining room chairs, the dining table and two armchairs got the same treatment.

Next came the power losses. When the television set or radio was plugged into a socket in one of the downstairs rooms, no power was forthcoming. If they moved the appliance into another room, it would work for a time until this circuit too lost power. Moving back to the first location, they might find the power returned. But on occasion they suffered a total loss of electricity and had to sit in the dark, helplessly waiting for lights to come back on.

Mrs. Adams appealed to the Thames Valley Electricity Board and an electrician investigated to see whether the outside mains were faulty. The garden had to be dug up — and nothing was found to be wrong. When Mrs. Adams explained that the power usually went off at night the investigator sat with them all one evening. When the power went off and he could find no reason for it, he left the house just as puzzled as the occupants.

Hardly a day was free of disturbance. Once when Mrs. Adams went to the closet where she stored her ironing board, she found it missing and had to bring out a dilapidated old one. Then, ironing completed, she took the old board to the closet to find that the new one had been returned. Looking into the closet an hour later, she found the new one still there but the old one missing. It was nowhere in the house.

Then all the clocks in the house stopped. Frequent restarts were to no avail and eventually no clock was running. Ceiling lights swung merrily around. Bottles of milk were thrown at visitors and soap powder boxes danced in midair scattering their contents all over the floor and what remained of the furniture. One day while Mrs. Adams and Pauline watched, the living room door was flung open with such force that the doorknob made a hole through the wall. Later, contents of kitchen cupboards were invisibly removed; they reappeared lined up on the hall floor.

Mrs. Adams' grandson Stephen also suffered at the hands of the invader. On occasion his bicycle, which he placed in the hall when he visited, glided around the lower rooms on its own. Once it attempted to sail up the stairs but the handlebars got jammed in the banister. On other visits the gears and other parts of the bike were damaged. Once he found the bicycle missing from the hall; it had been slung into the front garden. Mrs. Adams and Pauline were constantly cleaning up the debris, constantly living in fear. The happenings were mystifying, exasperating and costly — and worse was to come. One day Mrs. Adams was sitting by the fireside and Stephen was standing near the living room door when suddenly, with alarming speed, his clothes flew off and disappeared — shoes and socks and everything except his pants. His grandmother gave him a blanket to wrap around himself and the pair waited anxiously, hoping a visitor would call whom they could ask to collect some clothes from Stephen's home.

Then Mrs. Adams had an idea.

"Well, Stephen," she said, "if 'it' has taken your clothes, perhaps 'it' can bring them back. Let's ask."

They did just that and it worked. The clothes appeared, item by item, over the top of the door.

Said Stephen, "I had to unbutton all the shirt buttons and unlace the shoes before I could put them on. They had disappeared all buttoned and laced up, just as I was wearing them."

While he was getting dressed, a thump was heard, then another and another. Six and a half pairs of Pauline's shoes, which had been missing for months, followed the return of Stephen's clothes. The shoes fell one by one over the half-open door — left shoe first, then right. The 14th shoe is still missing — along with several other objects which had disappeared at varying intervals.

Stephen was involved in another eerie incident. A broom let itself out of the broom closet and waltzed around on its own. It entered the hall and charged at the letter box, the stick going right through the opening with such force that it shot a considerable distance down the front path and onto the pavement outside, narrowly missing a pedestrian. The head of the broom fell to the hall floor on collision with the door. Stephen dashed outside to retrieve the stick to which he fitted the head before returning the broom to its normal position in the closet.

To his astonishment the broom didn't stay there. The closet door opened; the broom emerged, waltzed around the room and again charged the front door, the stick speeding down the path toward the same pedestrian. Stephen was racing down the garden path to retrieve the stick when the man called out, "What game are you playing, young man? This is the second time you have thrown your stick at me."

The malevolent force was no laughing matter. Its activities had been restricted to the ground floor until it found Pauline's money. She had been saving for a holiday and had hidden a roll of 70 one-pound notes in her dressing table drawer. One evening as she was passing the stairs on the way to the kitchen, she saw a trail of shredded currency coming from the second floor. She gathered up the remains but only 20 serial numbers could be identified; Barclays Bank replaced only 20 of the pound notes. Stephen too lost money; 15 pound notes disappeared from his parka pocket.

Six radios and two television sets later, the local vicar from Greyfriars' Church, the Rev. Peter Downham, was called in to do an exorcism. He called more than once in October 1981 and whenever he was in the home everything was normal. After prayers in the most afflicted areas, the disturbances ceased temporarily — but inevitably resumed. It seemed no one could oust the invader.

It is not known exactly who, from among the many visitors who knew of the disturbances (the beleaguered mother and daughter finally had confided in friends and relatives), actually contacted the press. But one day reporter June Wilkinson and photographer Ian Pert from the *Reading Evening Post* turned up at the Adams home. Miss Wilkinson, who is in her 20's, admits she is a skeptic with no knowledge of psychic matters. When told there was more activity in the evening, she arranged to return. When she did, she was seated on one of the few remaining chairs drinking wine (from a mug, for no glassware or cups were left whole). She had to visit the toilet and to her alarm she saw a kettle of water pursuing her out of the living room and down the hallway. To her further horror and agitation the water spilled all over her.

Although Mr. Pert obtained some photographs and although Miss Wilkinson herself was the target of the home invader, nothing about the case was published in the newspaper — but it nevertheless became quite widely known.

Two of Mrs. Adams' friends, Harold Burton and his wife

Helen, were extremely concerned for the old woman's safety. They knew that one day while in her garden Mrs. Adams had been hit on the head by a ferociously flung medicine box. An ambulance from the Royal Berkshire Hospital had to be called and the medics treated her wound, giving her two stitches. And the Burtons had their own experience with the mysterious force.

The number of the Adams house is "121." When the Burtons called on Mrs. Adams one day, they were surprised to see that a large plastic "3" (taken from the house number next door: "123") had been added to the Adams house number; it now read "1231." Burton decided to photograph this bit of evidence and as he was focusing his camera the plastic "3" jumped from the doorpost with great force, hitting him a nasty blow on the forehead.

It was Helen Burton who took steps to obtain psychic help to rid the Adams house of this frightening activity. She first appealed to a Spiritualist organization in London, then to a member of the Society for Psychical Research who lived in Purley. The former seemed quite disinterested and the latter felt he could not afford the journey to Reading.

Not to be beaten, Helen next appealed to Mary Gordon who had been a ward sister at Cane Hill Hospital in Coulsdon. Mary is a born psychic who has practised mediumship for more than 50 years. She was eager to help and called at the Adams house in the company of the Burtons.

After hearing about the disturbances and walking through the house, Mary said she believed that the invader was an old man who had inhabited the house in his early life and who strongly objected to "new" occupants living there. Clairvoyantly she knew he had been a man of violent nature, a drinker who each evening brought his friends home from their drinking bouts where they ended up throwing furniture around.

Despite the medium's remonstrances, placing a crucifix in the house and hanging a plaque bearing a prayer (both of which disappeared within a short time), the activity continued — no worse but certainly no better than it had been earlier.

A gas leak necessitated calling the Thames Valley Gas Board. The official who responded to the call could find no reason for the sudden leakage which later apparently sealed itself off.

On another occasion Stephen's sister Julie stepped down from the kitchen to find the bathroom flooded. The Thames Valley Water

Board investigated but no reason for the flooding could be found; the roof and all piping were in good order.

The Burtons called one Saturday after they had finished their weekly shopping and after Helen had had an expensive hairdo. While they were drinking tea, unseen hands tipped over their shopping basket and flung a half-pound pack of butter at Helen. It hit her on the head and made a mess of her recent and shampoo and set.

All of this activity took its toll. Out of deep concern for Mrs. Adams, Helen tried again to obtain help. She contacted a Psychic Rescue Group who operated from the Croydon National Spiritual Church. These people, truly "rescue workers," asked only to know the names of the persons involved and the town in which they lived, then promised do what they could to help.

From that moment on, the villainous spirit lost its power. Just as suddenly as the disturbance began, so did it end.

Although bewildered by the 18 months of harassment and their sudden relief, Mrs. Adams and her daughter Pauline were once again living a quiet peaceful existence — albeit minus a lot of furnishings, 15 pounds of Stephen's savings and all but 20 pounds of Pauline's holiday cache, and one right shoe.

Author's note: The women's respite lasted only a few months. Out of desperation, when the disturbances resumed, they moved to a new flat where they have since been trouble free. I believe that neither the medium Mary Gordon nor the Psychic Rescue Group effectively removed the entity from Mrs. Adams' house — but nothing is known of the experiences of its present residents.

GHOST'S HIDDEN TREASURE

**The oddly-dressed figure stepped into my room.
What did he want, this visitor from another century?**

Frances Horner Orr

The manor house was at least 400 years old in 1941 when my parents Frank and Dorothy Horner purchased the estate on Merton Road, Bootle. They planned to operate a grocer's and tea shop. I was 16 years old and I loved the structure with its winding passages, oak-beamed ceilings and many fireplaces.

Noting my interest in the place, the stonemason told me that in ancient times a moat had surrounded the manor. Sometime during the civil war (1642-1651) Oliver Cromwell and his men had seized the manor.

My parents were busily occupied with their customers, so the renovation of the garden fell into my care. One Saturday afternoon in 1942, with the delicate English sun warming my back, I planted a border of marigolds. Suddenly my spade hit something.

Brushing the soil away with my hand, I saw what appeared to be a brooch. I showed it to Mother and we agreed it was quite old. It was made of brass and decorated with coloured chips of porcelain laid as in a mosaic and it had the shape of a musical instrument like a troubardour's mandolin.

On Saturday evening of the following week I made another discovery — this time under circumstances that can only be described as unearthly.

The first-storey bedroom in which I chose to sleep was L-shaped and the entrance door could not be seen from the alcove where I slept. I had gone to bed on Saturday night only to awake from a sound sleep at one o'clock in the morning. As if compelled to do so, I walked to the window opposite the side of my bed. I threw open the doors of the casement and leaning my arms on the windowsill looked out onto a silent, moonlit night.

Then I turned around and followed the wall toward the entrance door which I had closed from habit before retiring. I noticed the door was open.

At that moment the strangest, most incomprehensible

incident occurred. I shall remember it always as if it had happened only yesterday.

A strange man entered my room. Surprised and frightened, I froze, unable even to breathe. The intruder was attired in old-fashioned clothes but in the moonlit room I couldn't distinguish the clothes' period or colour. But in the flood of moonlight the white lace at his throat and wrists was indelibly impressed on my mind and senses, while his face made no impression on my optic nerve. In his hand he carried a candlestick but in my alarm I didn't notice (or can't remember) if the candle was burning or not.

The eerie night visitor seemed to float past me to the area of the headboard of my bed. Then like a passing shadow he turned and departed from the room.

Sensing he was gone, I took a deep breath and forced myself to move toward the door. I switched on the light and stepped onto the landing but I couldn't see anybody there. Mother and father were sound asleep and the ghost had vanished.

When I returned to bed, I kept the light on. I was too scared to sleep, so I sat up, stretched my arms and yawned. As I was stretching, my elbow hit the wall above the headboard with a loud thud. A piece of plaster chipped loose and fell onto the pillow. For some unexplainable reason, perhaps a release from the fear and astonishment of seeing the ghost, I began frantically tearing away more plaster and uncovered two small doors to a cupboard.

After opening the doors I looked inside and saw a grey stone wall. I felt down into the dark recessed space until my hand encountered a shelf. Groping inside, I brought forth the remains of an old candle. The tallow was dark brown, shrivelled with age and hard as petrified rock.

I reached down to the shelf again and found another ancient brooch and a box made of stone. Feeling much like Pandora, I raised the lid. Inside the container I discovered a string of blue glass beads, one earring made with a drop pearl (it looked as if it had been fashioned during the Tudor period), one buckle, a ring with a bezel and stone, old coins and a long chain with a filigree-worked box attached. I cannot express the delight I experienced at that moment. I placed the treasure on a chest and brushed the plaster from the bed. Exhausted, I slipped under the covers and fell asleep.

At 10 o'clock on Sunday morning Mother woke me. I had overslept and breakfast was ready. I had to explain to her about the plaster on the floor. I showed Mother the doors and interior of the cupboard and she said, "Oh yes! They used to keep a candle and Bible in there in the olden days."

I showed her the candle and box of jewels. I also told her about the frightening visitor even though I was afraid she wouldn't believe me.

I was surprised and relieved when she confided that she had also seen the apparition. It had happened unexpectedly when she was making her way to the bathroom about two months earlier. Mother said she hadn't mentioned the incident because Father would have laughed and she didn't want to alarm me.

During breakfast we discussed the ghost again and we wondered if he had been the lord of the manor at the time Oliver Cromwell's soldiers seized the house. Had Cromwell's men murdered him and plundered the manor, leaving his ghost to secure the valuables hidden in the dark recess of the cupboard? We could only speculate. But we did know that after the cupboard was uncovered and the jewels were unearthed from their plaster prison, the ghost never appeared again.

We never told Father about the ghost because he wasn't the sort of person with whom you could speak about ghosts and the supernatural. We did show him the treasure but he was only mildly interested.

In March 1943 I left for Scotland to join His Majesty's Women's Navy, did a lot of travelling and finally settled in America. Mother and Father, now deceased, travelled and moved many times after World War II. I have no idea what happened to the treasure which I'm sure was valuable. But I will never forget my encounter, that moonlit night at the old manor, with the frightening ghost.

NIGHT MUSIC

**Living alone in a 16th-century farmhouse
isolated on the edge of the moor can be a spooky
experience if one lets his imagination run wild. But as a
naturally calm person I never had any trouble with the
unusual — until one night in late February 1984.**

Margaret Willmington

A beautiful day gave way to a new moon shedding its pale light across the garden. I collected my cats and retired to bed with hot chocolate and an interesting but technical book.

At 3:30 I awoke, my scalp crawling with apprehension. The cats stood with arched backs on my large untidy bed. Loud but unmistakable music was filling the air. I immediately thought that intruders were inside the house. The music faded only to return soon afterwards. I could not identify the composer but it was the sound of Mozart or a contemporary of his.

I got out of bed to investigate. The cats refused to move. I intended to see if the television and two radios had accidently been left on. I had already discounted the idea of an intruder.

Downstairs it was quiet except for the music which continued to flow. When I turned on the light, I discovered that every picture — and I have many, both old and valuable — had been moved to right angles. I shut the light off, quite frightened. I sat on the stairs until I regained my composure.

I decided to make tea. I went around the room to put the pictures right. I found that now they had all been moved to the same degree to the left.

It was still a dark night outside, too early for the birds to be singing, and in any case the music was inside the house and all around me. Although this house has a long and interesting history, all of it is connected with peasants. In no way could this sad and beautiful music that had pervaded the air for over two hours be associated with them. I say pervaded because as I moved from room to room the sound followed me.

I sat waiting. As the dawn broke over the hills, the music gradual faded away. For the rest of the day and for several days afterwards I felt vaguely disoriented, as if the rhythm of life had been unsettled. For their part the cats — "lap" animals which rarely leave the house in the winter months, went and did not return for two whole days.

LEGION OF THE DAMNED

**We could hear the tramp of feet, the clank of arms,
the murmur of voices — the ghosts of an invisible army.**

A.C. McKerracher

I used to have doubts about the paranormal. After all, one person's psychic experience is difficult to prove or disprove. I even dismissed my own uncanny encounter as a trick of the imagination until it was unexpectedly verified in October 1984. Now I am certain I heard the ghosts of a doomed legion marching to its fate 2000 years ago.

In 1974 I moved to a new housing estate on a hill above the small country town of Dunblane in Perthshire, Scotland. Shortly after arriving I was working late one September night when I went outside for some fresh air. It was a clear and frosty night with not a sound to be heard anywhere. Most of my neighbours were in bed and down below the town was covered in mist.

As I turned to go back indoors, I suddenly heard the strangest noise coming across the fields to the south. It sounded like a large number of people on the move with faint voices rising and falling. I listened in puzzlement, then decided my imagination was playing tricks and went inside. But I couldn't get the curious matter off my mind and 30 minutes later I went outside again.

To my horror the noise was now much louder. I say to my horror because it was now passing immediately behind the houses on the other side of the street. For the first time in my life I felt the skin rise from my scalp and my hair bristle. I could now make out individual voices but couldn't understand what they were saying. But quite clearly I heard the jingle of what sounded like weapons and armour.

I stood rooted to the spot as the unearthly, unseen cavalcade passed by. The marchers must have numbered in the thousands, for the noise went on and on. Suddenly snapping out of the spell, I turned inside and went straight to bed. I was convinced I had been overworking and for this reason did not mention the episode to my family in the morning.

I put the experience from my mind until a week later when I called on an elderly couple, Major and Mrs. Chapman, who had moved in further up the street. I was telling them about our Residents' Association when their German shepherd dog rose up to stretch.

"Sit down!" its mistress commanded. "You're seeing things again."

"What things?" I asked.

"Well, the strangest thing happened last week," she replied. "We were sitting up reading at about 1 am when the cat and dog suddenly woke up. They stood bolt upright with all their hair bristling up their backs and seemed to watch something crossing the lounge for about 20 minutes. They were terrified."

When I questioned the Chapmans further, I was astonished to learn this strange episode had taken place on the same night and at precisely the same time I had heard the invisible army pass by.

Out of curiosity I began to research local history. I learned that the housing estate was built on the site of two large Roman marching camps, the first having been built in 83 A.D. when General Agricola invaded Scotland to extend the Roman Empire to the very tip of Britain. I located some old aerial photographs which clearly showed the outline of the camps. They also showed the line of the Roman road which ran north directly behind the houses on the other side of my street.

I also began to study the paranormal. I found that some modern researchers speculate that "ghosts" are nor literally spirits of the dead but are formed by a strong emotional or violent event which registers itself in the earth's magnetic field — a bit like a magnetic video recording. For some reason this can be picked up by receptive persons at particular times. This was an idea I felt I could accept. But what event had been so terrible that its occurrence on that Roman road had been recorded for eternity?

When I searched the Roman history of Britain, I learned that in 117 A.D. the Caledonian tribes in Scotland had risen in revolt and destroyed the small Roman garrisons. The Emperor Hadrian ordered the elite IX Hispana Legion, stationed at York, to march north to subdue the tribes. This unit had been known as the Unlucky Ninth ever since 60 A.D. when it had flogged Queen Boadicea of the southern English Iceni tribe and raped her daughters. Boadicea had cursed the legion to eternity and it was cut to pieces when she led all the tribes in a bloody revolt.

The IX Legion had been reformed although it never prospered. But it was still an elite unit of 4000 battle-hardened legionnaires when it marched into Scotland in the autumn of 117. It was last heard of marching along the Roman road which now lies behind the modern housing estate of Dunblane — and from there it disappeared from the face of the earth. Not a trace of the finest fighting unit in the Roman army has ever been found — not a body, not a coin, not a weapon. Four thousand soldiers simply vanished into the mist.

I never heard the noise again and I later moved to the older part of Dunblane. I had forgotten all about the incident until October 1984 when I was giving a lecture on local history to a ladies' club. Cecilia Moore,one of the members, came up afterwards to say how interested she had been.

"I never knew the Romans came as far north as this," she said. Then she astounded me by adding with a laugh, "I wonder if that was the ghost of a roman army I heard."

When I asked her what she meant, she said she had moved into a house the other side of the street from my old property.

"You won't believe this," she said, "but I was putting the cat out one night when I heard what sounded like an army passing right through my back garden. It was fascinating but when I told my family they just laughed." It turned out that she heard this at 1 am on exactly the same date in September that I had heard the sound 10 years earlier.

I am convinced that what she and I heard — and what my neighbours' animals saw — was the doomed Ninth Legion marching to its terrible unknown fate nearly 2000 years ago.

THE DEVIL'S FOOTPRINTS

**One night in 1855 something unseen walked
100 miles over freshly-fallen snow ...**

Gordon Stein

The English winter of 1855 was unusually cold. In Devon, snow was infrequent most winters. So the snow that fell during the night of 7 February was unexpected. Some reports from the period say that several inches fell, while others say that the ground was just lightly covered. Whatever the truth was, the reports all agree that something mysterious walked over that freshly fallen snow. It left tracks that remain a mystery to this day. Many people of Devon claimed that they were made by Satan himself.

The following summary has been pieced together from a number of accounts published in 1855. It contains contradictions and variations. We will examine them after we see what was being said to have occurred at the time.

Residents of Devon were astonished at what they saw when they stepped on the morning of 8 February, 1855. A trail of what appeared to be footprints ran through the front yard of virtually every resident of the towns of Totnes, Torquay, Newton and other places as far north as Topsham. The distance, on a zigzag course, was over 100 miles, although the exact beginning and end of the trail were not identified. These "footprints" were somewhat similar to those of a donkey's hoof but they were four inches in length by 2¾ inches in width and uniformly spaced 8½ inches apart.

Even more mysteriously, there was only a single line of footprints, each one directly in front of the other. No four-footed creature could have easily made these marks and it would be difficult to see how a two-footed one, walking upright, could have kept walking so precisely.

A feature that seemed to call for supernatural explanation was the way in which the footprints continued through gardens and up to walls, then right over those walls, where they resumed on the other side. One such wall was reported to be 14 feet high.

The footprints also appeared on the roofs of a number of

cottages. The footprints closely approached the front doors of various houses but then they would turn away and proceed on. When the prints reached the mouth of the River Exe, which was two miles wide at that point, they went up to the water, to reappear on the other shore.

One report has it that the footprints passed through an opening in a hedge which was one foot high by one foot wide; then they went through a drainpipe with a diameter of one foot. According to still another report, some men and dogs followed the trail to a large clump of woods in Topsham. When the dogs were sent into the woods, they emerged quickly, terror-stricken, and refused to return.

As the snow melted the footprints disappeared and were never seen again.

These are the basics of the story. Now let's see what we can make of them.

Although the size of the footprints does not seem to be in dispute, we have varying descriptions of the shape. Several witnesses wrote to report that they saw distinct claw marks and footpads in some of the prints, while others claimed that there was a distinct mark of a cloven hoof which they were certain only the devil could have made.

The famous naturalist Richard Owen wrote to point out that just because footprints appeared on one side of the River Exe and footprints of the same sort appeared on the other side of the river, it did not automatically follow that the same creature made both sets. In fact, he contended, several of the creatures may have been responsible for the 100-mile-long path. No one animal that anyone could name was capable of covering 100 miles in a period of about six hours of darkness.

No one, of course, had seen or heard anything out of the ordinary that night so there were no actual sightings of the odd creature. That, of course, did not prevent anyone from offering his favorite animal as an explanation for the tracks. Suggestions ranged from a swan to mice, rats, toads, otters, herons, badgers and kangaroos. Someone even suggested that a rope hanging from a balloon had made the marks.

Each of the animals does have one or two characteristics that make it a possible candidate, but in each case other details of the case rule it out. For example, a swan could have flown in such a way that it was able to clear the 14-foot wall and to fly over the mouth of the Exe, but its footprint looks nothing like those in question. On the other hand, a badger can make a very similar footprint but it cannot make the impressions of all four of its feet fall into a single line of tracks (it can place two feet into the impressions of the other two, however); moreover, badgers can't climb 14-foot walls. There are similar problems with every creature suggested.

The major accounts that most writers on the "Devil's Hoof Prints" have drawn on are the article in the *Times* and the series of letters from readers in the *Illustrated London News*. A careful review of these published items shows that almost all of the information we have about this creature comes from statements made in letters to the editor. In other words, the reports do not come from trained journalist investigations but from the statements of local people who claim to have heard about what happened (sometimes from eyewitnesses, sometimes not). In a few cases a writer may claim to have been an eyewitness to some of what happened.

We all know that second- and third-hand testimony is suspect. But let's examine a little more closely the source of some of the more incredible statements.

A letter in the 3 March, 1855, issue of the *Illustrated London News* is the source for the idea that the footprints went through a privet hedge with a one-foot-high opening, that there was a uniform 8½ inches between footprints and that they went up to a large haystack, then appeared on the other side of it, with the snow on the haystack itself undisturbed. This letter is signed by "G.M.M." We now know that this was the Rev. G. M. Musgrave. That letter does not say that its author is the same Reverend Musgrave who had just preached a sermon in which he warned that the devil was loose in the area and that it was a sign the people should repent and prepare for the end of the world.

The other letter that serves as a source for much of what has been written about the Devonshire footprints is signed by someone who calls himself "South Devon." In the 24 February issue of *Illustrated London News* this writer produces a somewhat inaccurate illustration of the footprints. We also learn from him that the footprints crossed a 14-foot wall, that gardens with locked gates were entered, that a two-mile-wide section of the River Exe was crossed and that the tracks extended for about 100 miles. Because we have no idea who "South Devon" was, we are unable to determine how seriously to take his or her report.

Let us go a step further. Some reports can be discarded as unsupported and contradicted by other parts of the story. When two parts of the story contradict each other, both cannot be true. We will come back to apply this test later. First, however, let us examine each explanation offered for the footprints to see what about each fits and what does not.

The first set of explanations was proposed by the famous naturalist Richard Owen, who wrote to the *Illustrated London News* to say that the prints were "obviously" those of a badger or group of badgers. While it is true that a badger (there were plenty in the region) does walk by placing the hind foot in the footprint just left by the front foot, the results would be two rows of imprints, not one.

In addition, the footprint of an animal in snow is different from that of the same animal in mud or dirt. When we look at the footprints of a badger on dirt, we can see that they are not at all like those found in Devonshire. Why would Owen (perhaps the best known naturalist of his day) say that he immediately recognized the footprints of a badger when shown the drawings of the Devonshire footprints? Perhaps badger footprints in snow are closer in appearance to the Devonshire prints. Since badgers were common in the area, we would expect a trained woodsman (as "South Devon" says he was) to recognize badger prints. We have already mentioned that badgers can't swim a river or scale a 14-foot wall.

The idea that a rope hanging from a balloon made the tracks is an appealing one. It does explain the river crossing and the 14-foot wall, as well as the rooftop imprints. But it does not fit with the drainpipe, the hedges or the report that a shed was entered, then left by a small opening in one wall, with footprints on the floor of the roofed shed.

The swan idea was suggested by one "W.W." who outlined it in a letter to the *Illustrated London News*. When the magazine refused to publish his letter, he printed a pamphlet at his own expense in which he made much of the discovery of a swan with a silver collar identifying it as the property of Prince Hohenlohe of Germany. The bird was found near the French coast five days after the excitement in Devonshire. W.W. acknowledged that a swan's footprint and the hooflike Devonshire markings look different but he claims that the latter effect was the result of "padding" of the swan's feet by the prince's staff so that it would not tear up the royal gardens.

For obvious reasons W.W.'s explanation is improbable, especially since no one has shown that the French swan had anything unusual about its feet.

The mouse and rat idea had one ingenious supporter, Thomas Fox, who argued that a leaping rat could have caused the footprint effect if it landed on its "arms" and rear feet. In fact, said Fox in a letter appearing in the *Illustrated London News*, the distance between "footprints" was exactly eight inches in the leaping rat prints he measured. He did not attempt to account for the passage through the 14-foot-high wall, the River Exe or the hayricks.

The otter had several supporters, among them an anonymous correspondent in the *Illustrated London News* of 3 March. He claimed that a number of the footprints he had observed showed a clear mark of toes and a footpad inside the horseshoe-shaped print. A friend of his recognized the prints as those of an otter. More notably, the writer added that the prints in his neighbourhood formed two distinct rows of tracks (i.e., left and right prints) and they went in several directions, not just in a single file. Some tracks were noted on a low wall.

If indeed the tracks were not in single file, we still cannot account for the high wall, hayricks or the rooftop tracks. Yet we should keep in mind that otters are small enough to get through the drain pipe and hedges and are excellent swimmers.

Other birds, such as herons, present some of the same problems that the balloon rope does, except that it is possible for a bird to go through the shed. The only problem with any bird is that there apparently is no known species whose tracks resemble those found that morning in Devonshire. But at the same time, as I noted earlier, there are few birds whose footprints in snow are well known. Of course we know that no birds have "hoofs" which would make a hooflike print but not all birds have feet with three toes forward and one behind. That is the common pattern found in the passerine or perching birds but the shorebirds or waders have different feet. Ducks have webbed feet as we all know, but does any bird have feet that might make a horseshoe shaped mark in the snow?

Although on the surface this would seem to be a simple enough question, intensive searching at one of the university libraries in the United States failed to produce any source that contains illustrations of bird footprints in snow, other than those of the crow and the duck, whose prints appear in no way similar to the Devonshire prints.

My search for good animal footprint pictures in the snow did produce some interesting information, however. Contrary to what "South Devon" says in his letter, no animal that walks on four feet leaves a trail of footprints only one print wide (as the Devonshire prints here). There are several animals which, when moving rapidly, leave only a single line of tracks. One of these has the additonal feature that its prints in the snow have a tendency not to show the footpads and claws but to take on an indistinct horseshoe shape. That animal is fox. We will consider the fox as a possibility, although of course it cannot scale 14-foot walls or leap over hayricks.

We have covered all of the likely possibilities in the animal kingdom except one. That one was suggested in a letter published in the 10 March issue of the *Illustrated London News*. The common toad, correspondent Alex Forsyth said, makes tracks exactly like the Devonshire prints. He had seen such tracks himself and had even followed them until he came to the toad, which had been crushed to death by a vehicle on a road. Fine — but since when can toads leap 14-foot walls, swim rivers, climb on roofs or jump haystacks?

In the issues of *Notes and Queries* for January 1890 correspondents discuss the possibility that a hare or rabbit was responsible. But a rabbit's tracks in the snow bear little resemblance to the horseshoe shape and of course we have the same problems related to the wall, haystacks, roofs and so on.

An entirely different solution to the mystery appears in an autobiography by Manfri Frederick Wood, *In the Life of a Romany Gypsy*. Wood, noting that the Romanies loved to play tricks, especially on their rival tribe the Didikais, recounts a bizarre story he claims to have learned from his uncle.

It seems that both tribes claimed the same piece of land in Somerset. Wood is uncertain even of the approximate date at which this event is supposed to have occurred. Nevertheless, many of the details he cites fit our 1855 Devonshire footprints case.

The story, as he tells it, is incredible. The Romanies wanted to scare the superstitious Didikais into leaving the area to them, so they planned carefully for 18 months to prepare an elaborate "manifestation" of the devil. Wood claims that seven Romany tribes made 400 sets of "measure stilts", which consisted of two pieces of wood several feet high, hinged at the top (like calipers) and bearing a "size 27" boot at the bottom. The gypsies carefully planned the route and coordination of all 400 users of the stilts and practised balancing on them. A set of stepladders was used to get up onto the stilts. When a step was taken, the free leg of the stilt was then rotated over the hinge to produce the next footprint.

Wood says that the distance between footprints produced in this manner was a uniform three yards (108 inches). Remember that the Devonshire prints have been reported as being a uniform 8½ inches apart. In addition, it seems highly unlikely that anyone could operate such stilts in the dark and snow without being seen, especially when (as the account has it) teams of hundreds of gypsies took part in the activity with each person being responsible for about ¼ mile of tracks.

When a house was encountered, the stilts were used up to the side of the house. Then the man on the stilts got off and made tracks across the roof by means of a spare set of boots (whether he wore them on his feet is not clear). When working over, on or near a public road that night, Wood alleges, each stilt-walker had to cover himself with a white sheet, which went over both him and most of the stilts, so that he would not be seen. We are asked to believe it was possible to move and balance under the sheet.

Although there is a certain crazy beauty in this explanation, there are also any number of discordant notes. First, there is the great difference in the stride lengths. To make a 108-inch stride in this way seems at least possible; to make an 8 ½-inch stride, on the other hand, seems out of the question.

Then there is the problem of the "size 27 boots." This is not a British metric shoe size because Britain has never used metric shoe sizes. The largest British shoe size is a 14, except for special orders. Rather, we seem to be dealing with a Continental metric shoe size here. A size 27 is a small child's shoe, about the equivalent of an American child's size 10, perhaps the size a five-year-old would wear. Although this does agree with the four-inch length of the Devonshire prints, it does not explain the absence of a heel print which we would expect to find if a boot were used, even a child's boot. It also does not explain the convex nature of the print, i.e., the centre of the footprint does not make a mark on the snow. Since know from the gypsy story that a great deal of weight was placed upon the stilts with each step, we would expect the imprint to be deeply impressed in the snow.

Could the British gypsies of the last century have pulled off a stunt as intricate and wild as this? I doubt it.

First of all, the working conditions under which the tracks had to be made are too difficult for any group of people to manage successfully. The likelihood of being seen was simply too great. What about all the dogs that would have barked in the night? The idea that men walked over the roofs of houses and along public roads in the dark of night on a pair of virtually unmanageable stilts, while the women and children later came by with brooms to sweep away all human tracks, seems unbelievable on the face of it. Although Wood tells us that the hoax worked and the rival gypsies left the area, no other mention of this prank can be found in any other gypsy source. Perhaps the real prank was on Wood's readers.

There have been a few other reports of similar footprints in other parts of the world. The "donkeylike" footprints reported on Kergulen Island, Antarctica, in 1840 apparently were the work of a horse which was let roam on the snow-covered island by a passing ship. There is no mention that the tracks were single file.

Reports of similar tracks in Scotland that same year likewise seem explainable as the prints of a horse. Again, these were not single file and they passed over nothing very high. There were reports of single-file footprints around a mountain in Galicia in the 1850's but this information is third-hand and uncorroborated.

When we attempt to summarize the facts and to reach a conclusion about the "Devil's footprints", we are torn in several directions. We must consider the possibility that we are dealing with exaggerated or distorted reports of the tracks of a normal known animal. There is also the possibility of a hoax perpetrated by gypsies. Or perhaps the tracks were left by an unknown animal or supernatural being. To accept any of these explanations, we are forced to reject some of the evidence.

When no explanation will exactly fit, either we need an additional explanation or else some of the "facts" may need to be discarded as weak. If we are willing to discard the wall-, roof- and haystack-climbing, then perhaps we have the tracks of a running fox. If we wish to discard the three-yard strides and the size-27 boot, we may have the results of an elaborate gypsy hoax. If we wish to discard natural explanations, we may indeed have a real but rare occurrence of the devil's taking a nocturnal stroll through the English countryside.

We simply do not have enough information to choose wisely among these explanations. And at this late date it seems quite possible we may never have a satisfactory explanation for the curious case of the Devonshire footprints.

GRANDMOTHER'S VASE
Paul Elliott

**Seven months after Grandmother Anne Kyte died,
she came back.**

That year Father, Mother and I were living in England with John W. Kyte, my mother's dad.

During her lifetime Grandmother's passion was English bone china but shortly before her death she took an intense dislike to one particular piece, a four-inch-tall, hand-painted vase. No one knew then, or has known since, why she disliked it so. Mother hid the vase in a drawer. Then after Grandmother died, Mum carried the vase upstairs and placed it on the fireside mantel in her and Father's bedroom.

In those council houses then — ours was at 337 Swindon Road, Cheltenham — all rooms were sealed by a door. Central heating was still a convenience of the future and all rooms were heated by coal fires. All doors were kept tightly shut to conserve heat.

On one frigid November night in 1937 my father Henry Elliott and I sat in front of the fireplace in my parents' bedroom relishing the warmth. Mum was directly below us downstairs, washing dishes before coming up to bed. The sounds came to us clearly — the clink of dishes and the creaks from Grandfather's wooden rocking chair as he slowly rocked. Then on the outside of our closed bedroom door the rapping began; knuckles were knocking.

"Good," Dad said. "Mum's brought up some tea. Sit, lad. I'll get the door. Just a sec', Doll." Mum's name is Dorice.

Dad opened the door, then turned to stare at me. I stared back at him and we both stared out the door. No one was there. All we could see was the unlit black stairwell. Dad shrugged, shut the door, sat back down. The rapping started again and at the same time we could clearly hear Mum and Grandfather downstairs. My back went prickly.

This time Dad sprang from his chair. "Stay away from the door, lad," he said. "I'll get it." He grabbed the doorknob. "Doll?" he called, then flung open the door. The black stairwell was empty. From the kitchen below Mum's voice came up, "Somebody call me?"

"No, Doll," Dad answered. He closed the door, then turned to me. I remember his facial expression. It was not nearly so comforting as his words, "Old houses creak, son."

When the rapping began a third time, much louder, Dad hurried me down the black stairwell and into the gaslit kitchen. I felt much better down there but still shuddery.

"... And," Dad went on after explaining to Mum, "it gave us quite a turn, it did."

"Oh, dear," Mum said. "We'd better have us some tea."

We did. But we didn't sleep in that room that night. After creeping up the stairs, Dad in front, Mum in the middle and me behind, we peered into the bedroom and saw something which we thought was impossible. The vase had moved, moved from the rear edge of the mantel to its lip, a distance of 12 inches, then fallen into the fire grate. In the white ashes the vase lay shattered.

The rapping never came again.

A SLIP IN TIME AND PLACE

They entered a landscape that did not exist, inhabited by menacing figures from a violent age long past.

Mary Rose Barrington

Personal experiences provide the case material that makes psychical research such a richly complex field of study. This report concerns a shared visual, auditory and tactile hallucination. The case was originally reported to the Society for Psychical Research in London in 1956. Because the SPR was involved in moving, no action was taken on the story. But in 1973 the couple who shared the adventure learned of my interest in psychical research and told me their story.

During the summer of 1954 Mr. and Mrs. George Benson (a pseudonym) were preoccupied with an exhibition which was taking up most of their time. They had been married for five years and were antique dealers. Being overworked and generally worn out, they decided to give themselves a day off and spend a whole Sunday walking in the Surrey hills.

But when they got up early on the scheduled morning, Mrs. Benson was afflicted by a feeling of black depression. Not wanting to spoil the day's outing, she said nothing to her husband about how she felt. After the couple returned home to London later that day, her husband admitted that he too had awakened depressed.

The Bensons originally intended to get off their country bus at the Rookery, a few miles along the main road which was between Dorking and Guildford. Although they knew the district intimately, they missed the stop and didn't get off until the next one at Wotton. Their first inclination was to make their way back to the Rookery on foot but they decided instead to spend some time at the Evelyn family church at Wotton. The church lies at the end of a minor road on the north side of the main road from Dorking.

The couple ended up spending more time at the church and in the churchyard than they had originally intended, most of the time inspecting tombs and reading their inscriptions. They noted that this was the first time they had ever found open gates to the tomb inside the church.

When they came out of the churchyard gate sometime later, they turned right and found themselves facing an overgrown path, bordered by high bushes on either side. Following the path, they climbed for a considerable time and finally came to a wide clearing where there was a wooden bench. To the left of the bench was an expanse of grass, with woodlands lying about 25 yards away behind it. To the right was a steep falling-away of the land. Mrs. Benson later said she felt sure about the height of the location because the view was consistent with a view from a hill and "down in the valley below" she could hear what sounded like wood being chopped as well as the monotonous barking of a dog. She felt uneasy but she didn't know why.

As he sat on the bench, Mr. Benson glanced at his watch and observed with surprise that it was already noon. This prompted the couple to unpack the sandwiches they had brought along but Mrs. Benson felt too depressed to eat anything, so she started crumbling bread for the birds. Suddenly all became silent and the birds seemed to stop singing. Mrs. Benson started to feel cold and was overwhelmed with fear. Then she "saw" three figures standing in the clearing.

She was aware mostly of their faces and dimly perceived that they were wearing black clerical garb. The man in the middle had a roundish, friendly sort of face but the two on either side of him radiated hatred and hostility. She felt sure that these figures somehow belonged to the past. But what she found especially frightening was that the clearing in which they stood was behind her; in other words, she could "see" these figures without turning her head! When she did try to turn around, a sense of paralysis prevented her from doing so.

An icy coldness enveloped her. She was so uncomfortable that she asked her husband if everything had gone cold. He felt her arm and remarked that she felt like a corpse. Eventually Mrs. Benson "unfroze." As soon as she did, she told her husband that they had to get out of there. Mr. Benson, well aware that his wife had undergone some sort of unpleasant experience, was more than willing to move on. They walked a little farther and began to descend from the rise. Soon they were on one of the paths that crossed a local railway line and they walked over it.

They never did take their planned walk. At this point, in true fairy-tale tradition, they lay down and went to sleep! To this day they do not remember leaving the area and cannot say whether they walked back to Dorking or returned to the road to take the bus. All they recall is that they arrived back at Dorking some hours later and took the train home to Battersea.

So far you might be thinking that this type of "haunting" experience is not unusual enough to warrant any special attention. It is odd, though, that Mr. Benson, although he never saw or even sensed the three figures, was overcome by the same subsequent fatigue and amnesia that afflicted his wife. But the truly bizarre features of this case were still to come to light.

Over the next two years Mrs. Benson never entirely recovered from the intense fear she had felt when she saw the three figures in the clearing. The experience practically obsessed her and she came to believe there was something about the experience she had to face and overcome. So almost exactly two years later Mrs. Benson set out by herself for Wotton with the intention of revisiting the church, the churchyard, the entry to the shrub-surrounded path, the hillside and the bench at the top.

By the time she arrived at the churchyard she already sensed that things were strangely different. She headed for the church, looked around inside, wandered around the tombstones and returned to the gate. She turned right after coming out of the gate, naturally expecting to come to the path leading to the hillside. But there was no path! Then was nothing even remotely resembling the hillside that she and her husband remembered climbing. Some woods lay half a mile to the west but like the rest of the land, these were low-lying. Flat field lands extended mostly around the area, while an open grass slope descended to the east.

She was so taken aback that she sought out a local resident who claimed that he knew the area well and couldn't think of anywhere that looked like the scene she described to him — with the overgrown ascending path and the woods-backed grass clearing at the top of the plateau. Nor did the man know of any wooden bench. He insisted that such a landscape was not to be found anywhere near the church.

Mrs. Benson returned home and told her husband about her remarkable visit. Unable to believe her, he vowed to investigate the situation himself. The next Sunday he visited the church arriving at around noon as the congregation was beginning to leave. He approached someone who turned out to be a woodsman on the Wotton estate. Mr. Benson described the area (the vanished landscape) he had seen during his previous visit and asked the man if he could think of any local site that filled the description. The man said he couldn't and went on to state categorically that there were no wooden seats or benches on the Wotton estate — and that, so far as he knew, never had been.

What are we to make of this extraordinary tale? It seems to be a unique case in which apparitional figures (seen by only one witness) were wafted onto a phantom landscape experienced by two persons. The expression "phantom landscape" is hardly appropriate, however, because the Bensons did not merely observe the scene. They climbed up on it, sat on a phantom bench within it and ate there too.

If the figures were contemporaneous with the landscape, we can only conclude that the Bensons spent their afternoon not only in the wrong place but in the wrong time as well. It is unfortunate that the figures were draped in black; if they had been clothed differently, we might be able to determine the historical context in which they may have existed. It seems clear though, however, that they did not belong to July 1954.

Could the Bensons have been mistaken about their experience? Could a more diligent search locate the vanished landscape? To investigate these possibilities, I decided to look into the Bensons' case personally. In 1973, together with a fellow member of the Society for Psychical Research, I spent several hours in the Wotton area looking for the Benson's ascending path, tree-packed clearing and wooden bench.

Our on-the-spot investigation confirmed the story the Bensons had reported, for we were able to see soon enough that the land around Wotton church is definitely flat. (The only exception is the grass slope at the back.) It was difficult for us to imagine that the scene might ever have looked otherwise even in the past.

We also inspected the landscapes surrounding other churches in the vicinity but concluded that this was a useless endeavour. It seems unlikely that the Bensons were mistaken about which church they had visited, especially since they had examined the Evelyn family tombs which identified the church without question. It is possible that the Bensons' mysterious landscape exists somewhere in the Surrey hills but it would take a gifted diviner or more than ordinary luck to find it.

We eventually made two further expeditions to the area without much luck. On the second visit we found an overgrown ascending path leading to a small clearing about a quarter of a mile east of the church. Later, when we took Mrs. Benson there, she declared this could not possibly be the location she had experienced in 1954. She seemed genuinely disappointed that we had not solved the mystery.

In short, there does seem good reason to assume that the Bensons experienced a psychic event. Their whole day's activities were infused with something mysterious: their early morning depression, the phantom landscape, the strange sleep into which they fell after visiting the church and the daze during which they managed to get back home.

But the most important element of the mystery may be the three figures Mrs. Benson sensed. If we can identify them, perhaps we can "solve" the enigma of the couple's apparent retrocognitive experience.

Through long experience investigating psychic phenomena, I have learned that coincidences, although not paranormal in themselves, often manifest around a paranormal event.

From talking with the Bensons I learned that it was their strong literary interests that first led them to the Evelyn church. They were interested in the life of John Evelyn, a 17th-century diarist whom they found to be a sympathetic figure. Only a few weeks after their visit, the couple received a letter from a descendant of the diarist. He was writing because of an upcoming literary festival and of course Mrs. Benson wanted to meet him to tell him about her experience at the church.

When they met, the descendant was immediately able to identify the round-faced friendly man in the clerical garb whom Mrs. Benson had seen. He was identified as a character called "Soapy Sam," more properly known as Bishop Wilberforce who died under mysterious circumstances in Deerleap woods. (This is roughly the location of the Bensons experience.) This was the first Mrs. Benson had ever heard of the bishop.

We found further clues to the nature of the Bensons' experience when we examined other cases of shared visions. The only account I know of that is similar to the story the Bensons told me appears in C. G. Jung's autobiographical *Memories, Dreams, Reflections* (1963).

Jung's experience took place on his second visit to the tomb of the Empress Galla Placidia, for whom he felt a strong sympathy, in Ravenna in Italy. (The empress was a highly cultivated woman who was

403

married off to a barbarian prince. Jung wondered how she could have endured her life with him.) His psychic encounter occurred in the baptistery, where he was surprised to find four mosaic frescoes of incredible beauty. These seemed to replace the windows he recalled from his first visit. The psychiatrist, who was accompanied on the trip by a friend, examined the frescoes for about 20 minutes and then the two visitors discussed them in some detail.

Only later, when the psychiatrist asked an acquaintance to photograph the frescoes for him, did Jung realize that he and his friend had shared a visionary experience. That realization came when he learned that the frescoes were not there, nor had they ever been there. His original memory of the four windows was the correct one after all and there was simply no trace of any mosaics at the tomb. Jung later discovered that Galla Placidia had once ordered the building of the basilica San Giovanni (also in Ravenna) which had been adorned with mosaics. But fire had destroyed the basilica sometime in the Middle Ages.

It is remarkable that Jung's experience took place in a location unalterably fixed by a tomb and that the personality of the tomb's occupant was firmly in his mind just before the paranormal event took place. Notice that this setting is precisely the one that may have triggered the Bensons' shared vision experience at the Evelyn family church. The Bensons had been particularly interested in finding the gates of the tomb open, which enabled them to study the inscriptions before setting out on their walk.

While discussing his experience in his autobiography, Jung writes that Galla Placidia's tomb "seemed to me the final legacy through which I might reach her personally. Her fate and her whole being were a vivid presence to me; with her intense nature, she was a suitable embodiment of my anima." (The feminine part of the masculine personality). The idea echoed by Jung's colleague and editor Aniela Jaffe who writes that "Jung himself explained the vision as a momentary new creation by the unconscious, arising out of his thought about archetypal intuition. The immediate cause of the concretization lay, in his opinion, in a projection of his anima upon Galla Placidia."

This hardly ranks as an explanation but nonetheless let us pursue this line of reasoning. If this sort of imaginative empathy led Jung and his companion to see some mosaics that were once part of Galla's earthly experience, might it be possible that the Bensons' sympathy for John Evelyn caused them to experience some glimpse of life as he once perceived it? Going through the six volumes of Evelyn's diaries, I read Evelyn's description of himself as "wood-born"; his earliest childhood memory was of being put out to nurse in a sweet place towards the hills, linked with wood." He tells us that Wotton, where he was born, was "situated ... upon a very great rising," though the manor house itself was situated on low ground. Evelyn loved the woods but when one of his brothers got deeply into debt, he was forced to turn most of the trees into timber. His only stipulation was that some woods close to the family house be left standing.

Perhaps in these passages are hints that the Bensons were sharing a glimpse of Evelyn's earthly experiences, not on the exact site (any more than were Galla's mosaics) but in the general Wotton area. But Evelyn could not have had a vision of Bishop Wilberforce among his memories; the bishop was born some 100 years after the diarist's death. The most significant entry in Evelyn's diaries, however, is an entry dated 15 March, 1696, in which he first notes with approval the sermon delivered that day at Wotton church by the curate. This entry is followed by another that records the execution of "three unhappy wretches, whereof one a priest," who were part of a Catholic plot to assassinate King William. Could these "unhappy wretches" have been the three Mrs. Benson saw?

I suggest that the Bensons' shared vision was of a deviant reality in which they momentarily sojourned. Such a deviant reality may differ from accepted reality by degree rather than in kind. I even suspect that such experiences take place more frequently than the occasional recorded accounts suggest.

In our usual way of looking at the world we assume that the sequence of events we experience in our day-to-day lives represents reality. If two or more persons experience events inconsistent with the mainstream, we say that they are hallucinating. But this interpretation may be simplistic. My speculation is that one day 30 years ago Mr. and Mrs. Benson deviated from their perception of "consensus" reality and were able to bend reality temporarily into a new shape. The causes for their psychic journey remain unknown but perhaps they were connected with the couple's depression, exhaustion and preoccupation with John Evelyn and his life.

But let's end this discussion with a question: If a third person had come out of the Evelyn church that afternoon, would he have walked into a flat field? Would he have been caught up in the special reality being created or experienced by the Bensons? Or would the more conventional perceptions of the vicinity have short-circuited the Bensons' experience? If such were the case perhaps it is lucky that he wasn't around. His prosaic presence would have deprived us of some fascinating grist for parapsychology's ever-operating mill.

PHANTOM JAYWALKERS

Along the A12 motorway near the village of Hopton, Suffolk, many drivers have reported seeing the ghostly figure of an old man plodding cross the road.

All over the world ghosts with no regard for traffic safety are scaring the daylights out of motorists.

Michael Goss

It was a Saturday night radio phone-in programme aimed at a potential audience of several million across London and the southeast. As suited the midnight hours and the approach of Halloween four days away, we were discussing ghost stories: more specifically, those involving that celebrated spirit of the highways, the phantom hitchhiker.

The whole point of a radio phone-in, needless to say, is that the people "out there" do phone in. It's their response or lack of it that either brings a show to life or condemns it to an embarrassingly silent death. Tonight, we hoped, listeners would be telling their own (allegedly) true experiences with the paranormal. Having spent four years researching a book about phantom hitchhikers, I guessed that the theme would stimulate a lively round of ghost stories, simply because the hitchhiker is itself a popular ghost story which encourages its audience to reciprocate with their own tales.

But I also knew it was unrealistic to expect that any of the callers would claim to have encountered a passenger who vanished from their speeding cars with the accomplished ease that characterizes the phantom hitchhiker. In my book *The Evidence for the Phantom Hitch-hiker* (1984) I argue that there may indeed be a handful of persons who could make that assertion. More typically, though, the phantom hitchhiker is not told as the narrator's personal experience but as something that befell an anonymous friend of a friend. The listeners who called in would not, I thought, add to my meagre collection of self-confessed, firsthand hitchhiker witnesses.

Nevertheless, the next hour came as a surprise to me. I heard numerous ghost stories, good, bad and indifferent. As predicted, I did not hear from any short-term chauffeurs of the hitchhiker. In fact, the listeners' professedly true-life experiences with road ghosts more or less shoved the phantom hitchhiker to one side. Nobody would or could confess to having met him, her or it. But many had been troubled by phantom jaywalkers.

First on the line was a gentleman called Clive. He said he had been driving along one night when a figure stepped abruptly off the pavement and under the wheels of his car. The young man's shock gave way to confusion when he discovered that he had somehow driven straight through this "person" — who now had vanished without leaving the hint of a physical trace behind him. "But I did, I really saw it!" Clive insisted earnestly.

Stella from Guildford told of being a "lovely young girl" in a long white gown dash in front of the car. Despite a sensation of impact there was no body to be found and — more mysterious — Stella's husband who was driving had seen nothing and nobody.

A woman named Dawn also recounted a "passenger-only" sighting. The incident began when she noticed a substantial-looking, conventionally-suited man walking along the pavement that ran beside the road up which she and her husband were driving. Dawn was concerned because he was walking on the inside, apparently neglectful of the two children who accompanied him. Not only were they dangerously near the edge of the road, but "as children do" they were jumping on and off the kerb. Indignant that the father (as she supposed he must be) would expose the kids — and motorists — to such a risk, she turned to warn her husband to anticipate that the children might do something sudden, silly and hazardous.

When she looked back, she was astonished to see that the pavement was empty. There were no side street or shop fronts to have swallowed the trio and no bushes, parked vehicles or billboards could have covered their departure. Dawn's perplexity was doubled when — just as in Stella's story — it turned out that her husband at the wheel hadn't seen the figures at all.

And so, with variations, the calls went on over the next hour. If one were to believe the callers, an alarming number of motorists in southeastern Britain were encountering apparitions with a chronic disregard for road safety: phantom jaywalkers, in other words.

Of course the environment in which I gleaned these stories may affect their credibility. For some, the temptation to get on radio — to hold an audience captive by talking about your unique ghostly adventure — is probably strong enough to persuade them to fabricate a tale which admits them to the honoured circle of storytellers.

Such an impression is hard to counter with the bare statement that the majority of my callers projected unvarnished sincerity. They didn't dramatize or talk as if hoping to create an impact. A few seemed quietly puzzled by what they were telling me and apparently reluctant to ask anyone to believe so unlikely a yarn.

Even so, the phantom-jaywalking phenomenon seems to be an experience to which even the most timid are prepared to lay claim. Some tell of a figure that walks, runs or otherwise just appears in the path of the car they are driving — and then disappears in traditionally ghostlike fashion. There are others (like the husbands of Stella and Dawn) who say that while they themselves saw no such figure, the alarm of the person beside them left no doubt that for the witness the sighting was terribly real. And the alarmed driver takes precisely those emergency procedures we would expect of someone who sees a pedestrian right in front of him; whatever the risks to or from other traffic, he slams on the brakes, skids to a halt and searches feverishly for the figure who he supposes must have been thrown clear by the collision. And although he finds no broken body, he insists on reporting the incident to the police.

This seems a good indication of the witness' seriousness. Ignoring the blatant absurdity of his story, he notifies the authorities of it, just as if he were dutifully telling them of a more mundane road accident. To all appearances, corpse or not, the driver truly believes in what he thinks he saw happen and what he is now saying.

Separating ghost stories for classification purposes by means of "motifs" — common narrative denominators like descriptive details (the Brown Lady, the Headless Horseman) — or behavioural characteristics can be misleading because many tales have a way of blending with others. Even so, the amount of material inclines me to think that phantom jaywalkers receive far less attention as a distinctive group than they deserve. Usually they are disregarded as a derivation or poor relation of the more famous phantom hitchhiker.

In fact there are some interesting differences between these two road-ghost motifs. Telling a ghost story as something that happened to you — and which consequently rests upon your responsibility or authority — is radically removed from telling a story as something that occurred to a friend of a friend who, needless to add, isn't available to confirm what the narrator says is the strict truth. In all but a few anomalous instances the hitchhiker belongs to the second school. The phantom jaywalker, on the other hand, can boast an impressive collection of convincing firsthand or eyewitness reports. In a court of law there is little doubt which of the pair would be afforded the more credibility.

Still, in the popular mind phantom hitchhikers and phantom jaywalkers are not so far apart. Express any kind of interest whatever in hitchhiker stories and chances are you will receive a number of jaywalkers — perhaps firsthand ones — at the same time. Once, after hearing of my interest in hitchhiker narratives, an acquaintance hesitantly began, "Well, something like that happened to me," and at once launched into a fine jaywalker account.

Andrew volunteered that on a dark, demanding road he had been considerably shaken when his mother leaned across from her passenger's seat beside him to make an inexplicable grab for the wheel. Subsequently she explained that it had been a sort of reflex action on her part because she was afraid he had not seen the old man in antique clothes wandering out into the road. She was right; he had not seen any old man in antique clothes. A look in the mirror at the perfectly empty road behind confirmed that there had been no such old man for him to have seen in the first place.

Looking at it solely as an artistic entity, the jaywalker tale is a poor attempt at a story. The hitchhiker tale always has a beginning, middle and end; it also has a moral. All we get in a jaywalker episode is an unidentified "something" which we take to have been a ghost. It appears and vanishes without obeying one of the chief rules of fictional ghostly yarns: namely, that the audience is always told who the ghost is (or rather, who in life it was).

But suppose we approach the issue as a possible fact — something that "really and truly" happens to drivers. Applying what little is known about apparitional behavior from the annals of psychical research, we find that — except for a very few cases — the hitchhiker is not a credible ghost. "Real" apparitions seldom do more than appear without known cause and vanish with equal lack of obvious motive. Those that engage in long conversations or who show a comprehensible reason for appearing are too close to folklore to be convincing — and in all these areas the phantom hitchhiker is suspect.

The phantom jaywalker, however, is as transient, meaningless and inconclusive a phantom as the psychical researcher could wish or expect. In this sense it is, ironically, a far more believable "true ghost story" than the vanishing hitchhiker. Finally, far from being a simple variation of the hitchhiker motif, the jaywalker may be the single convincing unit within it.

Take as an example Britain's best-known phantom hitchhiker as described in the Blue Bell Hill, Kent, stories which began about 1966. These stories concern a pathetic girl-ghost picked up by nocturnal drivers on the Hill; she gives a Maidstone address to which the shaken motorist hastens after the young lady inexplicably vanishes from the passenger's seat beside him. From the bereaved parent who answers the door, he learns that the hitchhiker was the unquiet spirit of the girl whose mother is now telling the story. She was killed in a motor accident on Blue Bell Hill some years ago and ever since then her ghost has been trying to hitch a ride to her old home.

Significantly, however, no named witnesses have ever come forward to say this startling adventure happened to them. The numerous "witnesses" invariably are anonymous. The earliest printed versions of the Blue Bell Hill saga — practically the only ones where readers can find properly-identified eyewitnesses — feature no hitchhiking phantom at all but a number of jaywalking ones.

One example appeared in the 27 February, 1969, issue of the *Kent Evening News* which reported the testimony of David Smith of Rochester. Smith claimed that sometimes, as he was driving up Blue Bell Hill, he would see a pair of pedestrians heading in the same direction — but not for long; they always vanished when he got within a few yards of them. At another time, though, the same pair promenaded down the Hill until a car sped toward them and they rushed right into its path. Smith could not understand why the car drove on as if nothing had happened. Even more baffling was the absence of two mangled pedestrian corpses on the road.

Smith's phantom pedestrians had little impact on the popular imagination compared to the more firmly-established ghostly girl hitchhiker, witnesses to whom were still strictly anonymous. Then, shortly after midnight on Saturday, 23 July, 1974, bricklayer Maurice Goodenough rushed into the Rochester Police Station to report knocking down a 10-year-old girl.

The distressed Goodenough said that a small dark-haired child in lacy white blouse and ankle-socks swam out of the night so suddenly that he could not stop the car in time. Moments after the impact, Goodenough wrapped the casualty in a blanket and laid her safely on the pavement, noting as he did so the bloody abrasions on her knees and forehead but uncertain as to how severely she was hurt otherwise.

With no motorist or telephone in sight, he drove wildly to the local police station. When the police accompanied him to the scene of the supposed road accident, they found the blanket but nothing else: no blood on the road, no dents on Goodenough's car and no small girl. Despite a search of the area, house-to-house calls, a tracking dog and massive publicity, the mystery of who she was or where she went was never resolved.

Rightly or wrongly, newspapers characterized the incident as "supernatural." Logically or illogically, they welcomed it as the latest manifestation of Blue Bell Hill's phantom hitchhiker.

One of the most intriguing British ghost stories to see print in recent years features the jaywalker as a star in his own right.

At 5:15 pm on November 23, 1980, Frank Colby of the British Transport Police was driving with his wife back to their Lowestoft home. As his car approached a recently-built stretch of road where the A12 motorway bypasses the village of Hopton, Colby spotted, about 75 yards ahead, a misty-white human-shaped figure.

Only later would Colby realize that at 75 yards he should not have been able to see anything at all. The car's lights did not reach that far. Moreover, a car travelling (as he thought) at 50mph should have covered the intervening space in seconds — too fast for him to register all that he recalled happening next.

The hunched, spiky-haired figure up ahead seemed to belong to an old man, sturdily built and around five foot six inches tall, wearing a calf-length, shapeless overcoat. He plodded across the road, fantastically large boots rising and falling in an oddly deliberate, high-stepping stride. As Colby remarked on the strange sight, he saw that the car's headlights were illuminating the central road markings — and that these were visible through the body of the figure. Colby quickly stopped the car and got out to examine the spot where the "old man" had vanished. As soon as he got back into his car, the witness drew a picture and wrote a brief account in his notebook. Once more our ghost-seer had to get along without the corroboration of his passenger:

Mrs. Colby had seen nothing!

Details of the case reached Ivan Bunn of the Borderland Science Investigation Group. Impressed by Colby's evident sincerity, Bunn published a detailed account in several issues of the BSIG's quarterly journal *Lantern*. His investigation determined that the Old Man of Hopton was by no means confined to one appearance.

Bunn uncovered reports that trace the history of the apparition back over 20 years and to several different locations in and around Hopton. A tall male figure in large boots and overcoat was seen by two drivers simultaneously as it crossed the road and vanished sometime during the early months of 1957. And at about 5:30 pm on Christmas Eve 1977, a 24-year-old nurse braked so sharply to avoid a "bent-over old man wearing a trilby hat and a heavy overcoat" that her mother, who had seen nothing, was flung against the windscreen. The driver could not shake the belief she had hit the ashen-faced, cold-looking pedestrian; but eventually she had to concede that there was no sign of any casualty and no point in staying in this haunted spot any longer.

And then on 2 November, 1981, 19-year-old Andrew Cutajar encountered an old man — the old man, presumably — in heavy boots and knee-length, capelike overcoat. As the tall and misty figure stood motionless on a road made worse by the drizzle, Cutajar braked, skidded and involuntarily shut his eyes. Then he felt as if he had passed through a cloud; seconds later the car came to a stop, its rear axle damaged. The man, typically, had disappeared. In the publicity surrounding the incident, which Cutajar reported to the police, a 66-year-old man stepped forward to say he had a similar experience on the A12. His had taken place in 1937 and he had been riding a bicycle.

Here, courtesy of Ivan Bunn, we have a highly suggestive series of incidents and an apparition generally consistent in behaviour and appearance. Bunn catalogued five spots where the old man was seen in the parish of Hopton, with the Cutajar sighting adding another.

As folk tradition has it, ghosts are spirits of the dead who are emotionally tied to a particular locality, building or room. Should the act of "passing over" have been an abrupt, tragically accidental or violent one, the chances that the rudely precipitated spirit will linger on in some form (perhaps to complete a mission left unfinished at the time of death) are much stronger.

In the case of the Old Man of Hopton, Bunn found some evidence to support this classic interpretation. In January 1899 a postman named William Balls dropped dead on his rounds in a field adjacent to what is now the A12. Balls had an admirable but ill-advised obsession with carrying out his postal duties when medical advice told him he should not have been working at all. Despite a nagging cough (left over from a bout of pneumonia) and pains in his side, he insisted that he "had to do his duty" and in the course of the same collapsed and died. Perhaps, one might speculate, Balls' devotion to duty has caused his spirit to try to complete the rounds.

Despite considerable research Bunn was unable to link Balls and the Old Man in any conclusive fashion. Elsewhere too phantom jaywalkers are seldom traceable to past accidents and to the victims of those accidents — a state of affairs that applies in general to the vast majority (although not to all) hauntings.

No single theory is likely to explain phantom jaywalkers. Every attempt at a solution only leads to more questions. To begin with, it is hard to understand why, in cases involving two persons in the vehicle, only one sees the apparitional figure. There seems no law governing whether this honour falls to the driver or to the passenger.

Of course a moving car isn't the easiest place to make reliable identifications of objects or persons glimpsed briefly in the darkness outside. Doubtless shadows, moonlight, posts, trees and columns of mist or accidental play of light in the car's headlights can and have created convincing "ghosts" on many occasions. Bunn observed that the Old Man of Hopton has been blamed on mist, bushes and even "Charlie Farnsbarn," a heron who has been visiting local fishponds for the past three years. On at least one occasion, when Charlie elected to walk across the A12 rather than use his wings, a startled lady motorist was convinced that she had solved the mystery of the Hopton phantom.

We might also speculate that phantom jaywalkers represent a type of hallucination, enhanced perhaps by the mental and physical fatigues of nighttime driving. But this concept and the optical-illusion explanation are hard to apply decisively to individual cases. Nor do they account for the fact that the "deceived" witnesses shares a curious penchant for hallucinating figures in vintage or historical dress.

One common description is of monkishly-cowled or hooded figures. Such "resident presences" have bee associated with several near-accidents on a road through Epping Forest and A253/266 junction outside Canterbury. To justify the delusion/hallucination hypothesis, critics would have to postulate that an alarming number of motorists have separately been fooled into seeing the same illusionary being; nor does this explanation find favour with the witnesses themselves. Each Christmas from 1976 through the 1978 drivers in St. Mary's Lane between the Essex towns of Hornchurch and Upminster were panicked by the vision of a whole or half-length figure which (without conferring with one another) they took to be a monk. The police investigated but were unimpressed; they believed that one witness' "ghost" had been a bearded tramp!

Maybe he was. Yet it is hard to stretch the theory to cover all the reported incidents — or to reconcile the bearded tramp with who or whatever appeared to the motorist who said, "He just walked in front of my car. I thought I had hit him, stopped and got out ... to help him. After looking all round I could see nothing. It is the weirdest thing that has happened to me."

How you feel about the viability of the delusion hypothesis depends on how you feel about the validity of the paranormal. If you accept the reality of apparitions, you will reject the delusion hypothesis. If you believe paranormal phenomena can be explained conventionally, you will discard the witnesses' insistence that they encountered ghosts.

For Antonio Gatto of Treviso, Italy, the phantom-jaywalker experience took on a very personal, intimate meaning. When he apparently hit someone in the icy fog which had cut visibility down to only three or four feet early one morning, his instinct was to get out and search gropingly through the roadside ditch for an injured person. Because he did so he was not in his car when a 30-ton truck careened into it. Gatto was convinced that he had been saved by the jaywalker who he believed was none other than the spirit of his brother Mario, killed in a crash only 50 yards away.

Could phantom jaywalkers be a warning of a less metaphysical kind? While the motorist is driving, a portion of his consciousness continues to function as a sort of defence mechanism which monitors how he is performing and in particular detects any tendency for the mind to be numbed by fatigue into a dangerous state of inattentiveness to the road. Could the apparition be a mental projection — a fabricated dramatic device solely intended to jerk the dozing mind back to being fully alert?

The idea that some part of human consciousness supplies apparitions or road ghosts could explain why sometimes it is the passenger, rather than the driver, who sees the jaywalker. Both are equally prone to night-motoring boredom and sensory deprivation. If the experience is more than a result of mental flotsam surfacing in a passenger's mind, it could perhaps signify that certain persons possess a "guardian reflex" which scrutinizes another person's driving and reacts to anticipated dangers by bringing forth a hallucinatory figure which will encourage the person behind the wheel to go more slowly.

But even if all this is feasible, it has to be said that the number of jaywalker cases on record suggests that an amazingly high number of motorists are suffering these produces of nocturnal highway hypnosis.

Aside from asking why the experience is not more widely publicized — after all, shouldn't every motorist be made aware of these dangers? — critics will find it odd that the victims are sometimes affected when travelling at different times on the same roads. Something like this must occur if all of them experience the same or similar ghostly phenomenon in that place. Are we to suppose that the Hopton stretch of the A12 or St. Mary's Lane, Upminster, has some kind of hallucinogenic quality that overshadows passing drivers after the winter sun has gone down?

More probably, the contents of the adventure — the jaywalker — could be the revived memory of a tale once heard and consciously forgotten, a memory rendered intense by conditions which increase the motorist's susceptibility to self-suggestion and hallucination. Unfortunately for this line of thinking, few of the cases contain positive proof that the witnesses were in the sensitized, susceptible fatigue-state of consciousness which is (theoretically) conducive to the proposed hallucination. Nor is there any positive proof that any of them had ever heard of the jaywalker before.

The phantom jaywalker may or may not be explicable in purely psychological terms. But one final question hovers beside this overactive road ghost and it is a chilling one.

Every year the police and medical services are called upon to attend yet another emergency — a mangled car draped across a road at some ridiculous angle, a dead man behind the wheel. As far as the accident can be reconstructed, the driver seems to have reacted suddenly and violently, putting the car into a desperate skid or swerve as if he found himself facing a terrible emergency.

Maybe he awoke from an inopportune doze after a long, hard journey. Perhaps a patch of mist or shadow tricked him into misjudging the angle of the road. Or maybe he saw something in his path, something he urgently wanted to avoid hitting. Something — or somebody?

GHOST TAKES REVENGE AT TICONDEROGA

An honourable man tricked into committing an unforgivable act rouses the wrath of the invisible world.

A. C. McKerracher

The name "Ticonderoga" may bring to mind a warship or an Indian name vaguely remembered from American history, but for an 18th century Scottish Highland chieftain, the name had a more sinister significance.

He was Duncan Campbell of Inverawe, kinsman to the powerful Duke of Argyll through his descent from one of the sons of Neil, 10th Knight of Lochawe. He is described in contemporary records as tall and well built with a dark complexion.

During the early part of the 18th century he enjoyed the simple existence of a Highland laird with his wife Jean and his children Dugald, Alexander, Duncan and Janet on his fertile wooded estate of Inverawe near Taynuilt in Argyllshire. He was renowned for his charity to all men, whatever their rank.

The laird's life passed peacefully and uneventually, unmarred by strife, until one stormy winter night in 1740 when he was sitting alone in his great hall after his family had retired. The wind was howling and shrieking around the battlements when above the noise of the storm a furious knocking sounded on the outside door.

A servant went to answer it and admitted a panic-stricken stranger whose clothes were soaked with blood. He stood panting in the entrance hall while the master was hastily summoned.

"Help me, Inverawe, help me," begged the stranger. "I have killed a man in a fight. His friends are close behind me and have sworn to kill me."

Duncan Campbell was proud of his reputation as an upholder of the traditions of Highland hospitality and without questioning the man further he agreed to shelter him from his foes. But this did not satisfy the hunted man.

"Swear it, swear it on your dirk," he gasped, casting terrified glances over his shoulder.

Although slightly hurt at the man's refusal to accept his word,

Duncan pulled out his knife and solemnized his promise before leading the fugitive to a secret recess at the rear of the castle and locking him in.

He returned to the great hall, extinguished the lights and was about to retire for the night when he heard more thunderous blows on the door. He opened it himself and saw a grim-faced band of armed men, some of whom he recognized as relatives and friends. One of them stepped forward and greeted him before telling their dreadful news.

"Inverawe, your cousin Donald has been foully murdered. We chased his killer in this direction. Have you seen him?"

Duncan was appalled to learn he was sheltering his cousin's murderer but was unable to break his oath. He denied all knowledge of the man's whereabouts. The vengeful band bade him good-night and left to carry on their fruitless search, leaving the Laird of Inverawe in an extremely troubled state. He decided to go to bed, vowing that in the morning he would ask the stranger to leave.

He lay in a disturbed sleep for two or three hours until a strange sensation made him start up, wide-awake. Standing at the foot of the bed was his cousin's ghost, bleeding from hideous wounds. The apparition stared at him sadly for a few moments before speaking.

"Inverawe, Inverawe," it wailed. "Blood has been shed. Shield not my murderer." Then it vanished from sight, leaving Duncan shaking with fear. He lay awake until dawn, then hurried to the hiding place to confront the killer.

"I cannot hide you," he cried. "I know your crime. You are my cousin's murderer. For pity's sake, go!"

The terrified man cowered before him. "But you swore, Inverawe. You swore on your dirk to protect me."

Much perturbed, Duncan wondered what to do. He decided to hide the man in a cave on the side of Ben Cruachan behind the castle. He led the wretch up the hillside to a tiny cavern which is earlier days had sheltered Robert the Bruce, Scotland's king from 1306 to 1329, and the Scottish patriot Sir William Wallace.

Duncan's heart was lighter when he returned to the castle, for at least the man was no longer under his roof and his honour was satisfied. That night he fell asleep much relieved, but he was soon awakened by a sensation of terror.

There stood the apparition again. This time its attitude was distinctly menacing as it repeated the words spoken the previous night before disappearing once more.

Duncan decided family revenge took precedence over hospitality and at daybreak he armed himself and made for the cave. But the stranger was gone — and in fact was never heard of again.

Campbell of Inverawe was now a very worried man. That night he sat in his room, unable to sleep. Would the ghost return? Sure enough, it soon materialized. This time it seemed to be sorrowful. It pointed an outstretched finger and cried, "Farewell, Inverawe, farewell, till we meet again at Ticonderoga!" Then it vanished.

In the morning Duncan told his family the whole story and wrote down the strange name the ghost had spoken. No one had ever heard of it, nor had any other person he encountered.

For some time the strange word remained in his mind. Robert Louis Stevenson put Duncan's thoughts into his verse:

It sang in his sleeping ears,
It hummed in his waking head,
The name — Ticonderoga,
The utterance of the dead.

However, as the place did not seem to exist, Duncan gradually forgot about his encounter with the spirit and his life resumed its uneventful course.

In 1744 Duncan Campbell was persuaded to join the Black Watch by Francis Grant, an old friend who held a senior position in the regiment. Duncan managed to raise a company from his local area and was given a commission as captain. He was a major by the time the regiment sailed for America in 1756 to fight the French in the Seven Years' War. His second son Alexander had also joined as an ensign and accompanied his father on the voyage.

The regiment landed in New York and set out to march to Albany. On the way, the Highland soldiers were well received by the local inhabitants, particularly by the native Americans who flocked to see them. These natives believed the Scotsmen to be of their extraction because their mode of dress and skill in woodcraft were somewhat similar.

The Black Watch remained in billets in Albany and Schenectady for two restive years. The regiment was gradually reinforced to 1300 by an influx of fresh recruits who were of the highest calibre of any of the British regiments. Many of the privates were sons of chiefs and gentlemen and were often accompanied by their servants. Due to the Disarming Act of 1746, the army offered the only opportunity for adventurous youths to carry arms and engage in warfare.

Other troops were also arriving and at the end of two years, an army of 6000 British regulars and 10,000 American fighters had been assembled.

On 5 July, 1758, 1000 vessels carried this force up Lake George to attack the French forts that lay on the disputed Canadian-American border. Among the fleet 1000 men of the Black Watch raised their voices in Gaelic songs as their brawny arms heaved on the oars. They had left 300 men behind to garrison Stamford, Conneticut. The campaign was under the joint command of the brilliant, dashing Lord Howe and the aged, failing Lord Abercrombie.

The army landed at the top of the lake on 6 July — and then tragedy occurred. A bullet from a French patrol killed Lord Howe, leaving Lord Abercrombie in sole command. He decided to attack Fort Carillon first. It stood on the main line of communication between the Canadian and American colonies and was very close to where the army had landed. Without bothering to inspect its defences, he retired to a sawmill two miles distant and set up his headquarters.

Abercrombie then dispatched his chief engineer, Lieutenant-Colonel Clark, to make a survey of the French positions and report back the best method of attack. Clark sent an incredible message: the fort could be taken by frontal attack because it was defended by only 4000 French troops. Lord Abercrombie accepted the report as fact but remained inactive.

Finally, on 7 July, he gave orders that the army was to advance on the fort the following day. An aide-de-camp brought the dispatch to Lt. Col. Francis Grant, now commander of the Black Watch, who received the news with some apprehenion. He summoned a native scout and inquired about Fort Carillon's defenses. The scout explained that the fort was situated on a point of land between Lake George and Lake Champlain and surrounded on three sides by water. Part of the narrow peninsula was marsh and the remainder was strongly fortified. The scout added, "My people call it by its Indian name — Fort Ticonderoga."

Colonel Grant was horrified to hear that name, for many years earlier he had heard Duncan Campbell's story about the ghost. His conscience troubled him, for Duncan would not have been in New York if he had not persuaded him to join the Black Watch.

He quickly summoned the other officers and instructed them to refer to the fort as Carillon whenever they were in Major Campbell's presence. Many of them also knew the story and kept Duncan in ignorance of the fort's original name while the plan of attack was being discussed that night.

In the morning the officers assembled in Colonel Grant's tent — all of them except Major Campbell. Some time passed before he arrived — a changed man, pale and haggard.

"Francis," he cried, "you have deceived me! The ghost of my cousin came to me again last night after all these years. This is Ticonderoga and I shall die today."

Many of the other officers privately feared that they too would meet death that day, for General Abercrombie's delay had allowed the French to fill the only gap in the natural defences with their own deadly fortifications. They had felled trees and set them with their branches and foliage pointing outward interspersed with stakes. Behind this was a deep trench, then a breastwork of logs nine feet high which gave the defendent a clear field of fire.

In command of the fort was the Marquis de Montcalm who was to die two years later when General Wolfe finally captured Canada from the French.

Despite their misgivings, the British Army obeyed their orders and marched on the fort. When the signal was given to advance, they attacked, only to be trapped in the branches and undergrowth. The French poured out a relentless, withering fire, and wave after wave of soldiers collapsed, dead or wounded. Most of the British-American regiments lost half their numbers long before they reached as far as the trench.

The Black Watch, still held in reserve, watched the slaughter with increasing anger. Unable to restrain themselves, they began to move slowly forward despite the shouts of their officers. Then faster — and from a thousand throats burst out the bloodcurdling scream that signaled a Highland charge.

The men raced forward shrieking their clan slogans and slashing at the branches with their claymores and axes. They leaped the trench and in a blind frenzy began to scale the breastwork. So desperate were they that many climbed on the shoulders of their comrades to get over the top. The few who managed to gain a foothold on the parapet fought with such fury that Montcalm had to bring up the French reserves to repulse them.

A short time later a general retreat was sounded but the enraged men of the Black Watch had to be ordered three times to fall back. Out of 1000 in action, the regiment lost 647 officers and men to death or wounds.

Among those who retreated safely was Major Duncan Campbell. Just as he was almost out of enemy range, a spent bullet grazed his arm and he was taken along with the wounded to Fort Edward on the Hudson for minor first aid. But infection set in and his arm had to be amputated. Brave and valiant as he was, he succumbed to depression, certain that he was going to die, and he did nine days later.

His son Alexander Campbell was wounded in the same battle and returned to Glasgow to convalesce. He was promoted to captain in the Argyllshire Fencibles but died unmarried only two years later. He was buried in the Greyfriars Churchyard in Glasgow. With his death the male line of Inverawe came to an end.

Duncan Campbell was buried in the Union Cemetery between Hudson Falls and Fort Edward. His red granite tombstone inscribed: "Here Lyes The Body of Duncan Campbell of Inversaw, Esq., Major To The old Highland Regiment. Aged 55 Years. Who died the 17th July 1758 of The Wounds He Received in The Attack on The Retrenchments of Ticonderoga or Carillon."

So ends one of the most authentic of all stories of ghostly death warnings.

The story has a curious sequel. The Misses Campbell of the Old House of Ederline in Argyllshire were walking from Kilmalieu to Inveraray on the day and at the hour when the battle was taking place thousands of miles away. They had just reached the top of the bridge over the River Aray, near Inveraray Castle, when suddenly they saw a tremendous battle taking place in the sky. They clearly recognized people they knew, including Duncan Campbell and many others who were serving in the Black Watch.

They hurried home and told what they had seen, and when the details of the actual battle were published a month or so later, they were found to coincide on every point with the women's statements.

Today Inverawe House is occupied by the North of Scotland Hydroelectric Board and used as offices for the engineers concerned with the giant Cruachan Power Scheme. Apart from having the top storey removed during recent alterations, the house looks much the same as at the time of Duncan Campbell's fateful meeting with the murderer and his cousin's ghost.

Fort Carillon was renamed Fort Ticonderoga when it was finally captured by the British some years after the battle in which Duncan Campbell was wounded. The fort has been preserved as a national shrine and museum where there is a memorial to the Black Watch. A plaque, unveiled in 1906, commemorates the members of the regiment who gave their lives on 8 July, 1758.

WASHING AWAY A GHOST

The 60-year-old murder had never been solved and the brutal killing was nearly forgotten. But a ghost remembered. ...

David Angus

One of Chaucer's *Canterbury Tales* tells the harrowing story of a murder victim's corpse which, well hidden though it is, finally cries out against the guilty party for all to hear. I had always thought it was just a tale. Now I am not so sure.

I first heard of the murder in January 1980 after I had lectured about old, unsolved crimes to a group in the Scottish town of Stirling. Audiences, of course, love to catch a speaker out and I was caught out on this occasion, for the murder, although it had occurred many years before, was committed practically on my doorstep, at Bridge of Allan near Stirling in central Scotland.

It was no use my saying I had never heard of it, that no one in the village had ever mentioned it during my 20 years' residence. My audience was elderly — very elderly in some cases — and most of them recalled the sensation from their own childhoods. That I, as "authority," should not know of it seemed incredible to them.

My particular informant — the one who spoke first and said most — was the plump, cheerful Miss Ramsay. She knew the name of the murder house — Birnock — and she knew the name of the victim — Miss Mary Traill, "a very old lady." She had forgotten the year but she remembered distinctly that the crime had taken place shortly after the end of the local Highland Games — in the small hours of the following morning, in fact.

What was most striking of all was that she claimed to know who the murderer had been, although apparently no one had ever been arrested or tried for the crime. He was, she asserted (no one else asserted this), a schoolteacher who had boarded at the house next door, at that time the annexe to a large boys' school across the road.

Miss Ramsay did not think fit to mention why the man who "was known" to have performed this dastardly deed had escaped scot-free but evidently he had. I gathered that the local police, naturally

425

enough, had suspected some doubtful character among the multitude of visitors attending the Games that long-ago August day but again, not unnaturally, they had failed to find him.

Determined not to make this faux pas a second time. I proceeded to read the contemporary accounts of the crime in the local press. The *Bridge of Allan Gazette* was a weekly paper which appeared on Thursdays, so the affair had not appeared in print locally until 11 August, 1921, although it had occurred about 1:00 am, on the previous Sunday, the seventh. Birnock was described as a "well-known boarding establishment" (no mention was made of the annexe) and the killing had taken place in a back bedroom in the second flat.

Mary Traill, 84, had been one of the permanent boarders, originally a headmaster's daughter from Aberdeen and evidently a lady of some means. Her nurse-companion Mrs. Elizabeth Sutherland, 70, had shared her bedroom.

Mrs. Sutherland, shortly before her mistress' murder, had had reason to get up and go to a small kitchen on this floor. A heavy crimson curtain hung across that little room "concealing some domestic utensils." At some point Mrs. Sutherland had grown acutely aware of feeling that she was not alone, that some unknown person lingered in concealment behind the curtain.

Some women have an infinite capacity for closing out unpleasant things from their consciousness. What Mrs. Sutherland did immediately was, of course, quite sensible. She walked quietly out of the kitchen. But by the time she reached the bedroom the process of excluding the unpleasant completed itself. She raised no alarm but went to bed beside her sleeping mistress. Nor did she even think to lock the door.

She must have slept soundly too, for what woke her was the blow that killed Miss Traill. She looked across in alarm and saw a shadowy figure bending over her employer. According to the *Gazette*, she "remonstrated," which is probably putting it mildly.

In a moment "a tall young man dressed in dark clothing (possibly blue)" was staring at her. His face was peculiarly pale and his eyes "seemed in turn through" her. When she screamed he muttered, "I'll do you in," but she screamed again.

He raised the hand holding the murder weapon and brought it down with stunning force. But, more active and alert than Miss Traill, Mrs. Sutherland quickly turned her head and the pillow bore the brunt. He struck again but by now she was struggling furiously, his aim was out and the bottle (for that is what it was) was smashed on the headboard.

And now the alarm had been raised. There were cries and movements elsewhere in the house. With a curse the intruder threw down the neck of the bottle and vanished through the open window of the bedroom. The gently sloping roof of a single-storey outhouse lay below. It was as simple for a fit young man to make his exit that way as it had been for him to enter.

Next day the police found clear traces of his hasty passage over the outhouse roof — the moss had been disturbed. Unfortunately the garden below had been chiefly under grass which bore no trace of his footprints. It was assumed that the intruder had run a few steps and jumped the low wall that gave access to Graham Street (on the opposite side from the annexe) and had escaped through the sleeping streets of the village.

It seemed clear that his object had not been murder but robbery but he had carried the empty bottle (it had once contained a pint of Guinness' stout) just in case. He had hidden behind the kitchen curtain until people went to bed and then emerged. Of course there was no evidence that he had been interested only in Miss Traill's room. From that flat there was access to every part of Birnock. It was interesting that another boarder, a Miss Inglis, had (most unusually) locked her bedroom door that very night, having experienced "an evil premonition."

The man had evidently followed Mrs. Sutherland from the kitchen, possibly to check whether she would give the alarm (at one moment she had actually felt him through the curtain!). Then, once he was satisfied all was quiet, he had entered and evidently made for Miss Traill's bedside cabinet in the midsummer gloom. But he had not been able to open it before she had been roused, which had sadly necessitated her being silenced.

The paper confirmed that the police had assumed the culprit must be one of the 20,000 visitors to the Games of the day before. Like all such public events, these attracted annually their share of pickpockets and petty crooks, and Graham Street was part of the main thoroughfare leading to the park. A sharp-eyed thief, spotting the low slopping roof and the open window, might very well, in daylight hours, have marked it as a possibility for later on.

I looked at subsequent issues of the *Gazette* but they

contained little of relevance. Police in Fife and even in Aberdeenshire had pursued suspicious characters "of no fixed abode" in this connection and caught them too, but all were equally innocent and could prove it.

No one, it seems, had dreamed of searching the annexe or of questioning anyone there. Yet only a footpath and another low wall separated the two buildings and access was as easy from there as from Graham Street. True, the school had been on holiday and the annexe was empty of boys but one or more teachers, according to Miss Ramsay, had been in residence.

Miss Traill was buried at Aberdeen in the old family lair four days after her sudden demise. For some time those who had known her or had other reason to remember her must have waited, with some impatience, for an arrest to be made but arrest there was none. When the vagrant leads all petered out, the police had nothing to fall back on, or so they thought. In the very nature of things, interest in the affair eventually languished and died. As I say, I had lived 20 years in the place without hearing one word of it, although Miss Traill had been done to death within 100 yards of my house.

But after I had read the old newspaper reports and made the necessary notes, I confess I was every bit as dilatory myself. I did not think to question Miss Ramsay further although I saw her at other lectures and I should certainly have realized she knew more than she had said. I was as much at a loss as the police of the 1920's and my interest too languished and died.

Naturally I had taken a good look at Birnock and had easily traced the path of the murderer's progress in and out. But I did not know the present occupants and saw no reason to intrude.

Of the annexe I thought even less. It was now divided into flats and I knew all the occupants, for my garage lay in a row of lock-ups to the rear of the block. Indeed, I had visited most of these flats at various times. I had never, however, been in the top or attic flat, for its sole occupant — Miss Slessor, a retired schoolteacher (and a former colleague of Miss Ramsay) — guarded her privacy with a single-minded determination that defied intrusion.

And so a year passed and then the reclusive Miss Slessor died of a heart attack. The flat was duly advertised as vacant and duly purchased and occupied by a single gentleman who soon became a friend of mine. Naturally we discussed the flat — still something of a mystery to the rest of us — and that was how I heard eventually about the remarkable finds he had made there — survivals of its days as part of the old school annexe of long ago.

The finds that my new friend Paul had made indicated that the annexe, or this part of it anyway, had once been the scene of late-night beanfeasts. Now beanfeasts had been de rigueur in all public school stories I had read but those at the annex had been dormitory revels with a difference.

I should explain that Paul had found the articles immediately under the roof and near the eaves in a corner which had been long plastered up. Miss Slessor could have known nothing about them in all her years there.

First, there was a splendid range of wine and beer bottles of various shapes and sizes. There were also one or two large wooden cigarette boxes, minus their cigarettes. And (mysteriously) there was a large number of empty envelopes addressed to a number of the boys. The postmarks all indicated the autumn term of 1904.

I remembered, vaguely, the aspersions Miss Ramsay had cast on the nameless teacher but when I told Paul the tale and asked him if any pint bottles of Guinness' stout figured in the cache, he disappointed me by saying no. In any case 1904 was far too early for the murder and so I dismissed Paul's finds from my mind.

But a month or two later, in August 1981, I was forced to think again. Chatting with him one day, I jocularly suggested that the annexe — a venerable Victorian pile — might well be haunted. Paul was an engineer whose interests were mechanical and I reflected as I asked that he of all people was unlikely to have any odd experiences to report.

To my astonishment his grizzled beard quivered and his bushy eyebrows shot up at the question. He had not seen anything but he had heard — on several occasions — certain unexplained knockings. I shall give his account in his own words as nearly as I can:

"I was working in one of the front rooms, papering it. It was very late, well after midnight, but I was determined to get that room finished. All at once I heard this tapping or rapping or knocking and I assumed someone was paying a late call. But it seemed to grow fainter, not louder, as I neared the door. When I opened it, there was no one there.

"As I closed and locked the door again, I noted that the rapping had nevertheless stopped. I shrugged, forgot it and went back to papering. But later, in bed, I heard it again, fainter but still quite distinct. Eventually I dropped off. It was still going on, I think.

"The following night I was papering another room and again I worked late. I had lost all track of the time because the pattern was difficult to match and required concentration. But when the knocking recommenced, rather louder than before, I glanced at my watch and saw it was the time I had heard it the previous night.

"I was quite certain now that the source of the sound lay somewhere within the flat. I disengaged myself from paper and paste and hunted about the room. It came loudest from one particular partition wall or rather, I sensed, from the other side. So I went through to the next room, a bedroom still unpapered.

"Here the knocking was a knocking indeed and in a moment I realized it came from a heavy, dark, old mahogany wardrobe set against the partition wall. It came from within the wardrobe which was empty and closed.

"It is, as I have said, a large and gloomy piece of Victoriana, of darkest mahogany, and now it fairly reverberated with that ghastly, ghostly inward knocking. It was exactly as if someone were trapped there, locked in and beating on the wood steadily, rhythmically and mechanically, in a hopeless effort to fight its way out.

"As I say, the thing was empty so far as I knew. I had certainly put nothing in there and there was no pet or person in the house who could possibly have got inside it. Well, I'm a phlegmatic sort of chap but there was the knocking and here was I listening to it and staring at that blasted black wardrobe door, inches from my nose.

"I swallowed very hard, turned the little key and opened it. The naked electric bulb revealed nothing but the knocking had ceased abruptly with the opening of the door. I leaned forward and gingerly peered about inside. Still nothing. So I gently swung the heavy door shut. Silence. I turned the key. Silence.

"But in bed once again I could not sleep and in a few minutes, sure enough, there came the knocking. Wild horses would not have dragged me back to that black, throbbing door! At last it stopped of its own accord or I fell asleep in spite of myself. Again, I don't know which."

This was Paul's tale in essence.

It had happened again on several occasions, he said. But when I asked if I might come up and help him in the house one night, so that I might hear it too, it transpired that the knockings were now a thing of the past. Paul had the feeling that some kind of unnoticed exorcism had occurred and the haunting spirit had now gone off for good. The flat felt quite "normal" once again and he was profoundly relieved about that.

Well, I was as piqued by the end of his story as I had been intrigued by its start and I probed further. When I asked him if he had done anything that might have contributed to this involuntary exorcism, Paul frowned suddenly and nodded.

"Do you remember those old bottles I told you about finding?"

"Wine and beer bottles? Sure."

"Didn't you say that the old lady in Birnock had been murdered with a beer bottle?"

"Stout. But. ..."

Evidently he had forgotten that the murder weapon had been smashed, for he interrupted me to say, "It's funny but the night the knocking stopped — or failed to resume — was the night I washed the bottles out for the first time."

"Well?"

"Don't you see? There could have been blood on one of them. The murder weapon. ..."

At that I had to remind him that this was impossible. Paul's face cleared at once.

"Yes, I remember your saying that, now. Oh, well, it was just a mad thought. Obviously there was no connection with the murder."

I nodded mechanically but something now nagged at me although I did not tell Paul. Why had Miss Ramsay been so certain about the guilt of Mr. X, the schoolmaster? Miss Ramsay had been vague about details, true, but there had been nothing halfhearted or unsure about her conviction regarding Mr. X. Yet how could she know?

Miss Ramsay was not within the circle of my friends or acquaintances. She lived in some neighbouring village and bred cats. I did not even have her address or telephone number. I did, however, know yet another lady who had been a teaching colleague of hers at a local girls' school and through her I soon traced Miss Ramsay and rang her up.

Miss Ramsay must have been an excellent teacher. She recalled instantly the matter in hand and told me all she knew about it without wasting a word.

She herself had been a child of six or seven at the time but her mother had been a close friend of the matron at the boys' school, had had her as a visitor on the Sunday of Miss Traill's murder and had found that excellent middle-aged lady in a state of great distress. This was not because Matron had known Miss Traill (she hadn't) but because Matron had found something that very morning. On the top of the wardrobe in Mr. X's room Matron had found (while cleaning) a pile of blood-soaked clothing. She had not, however, reported the matter. Rather, now she confided in Mrs. Ramsay and sought her advice.

Little Miss Ramsay had not, of course, been privy to those secret confabulations but she heard of them later from her mother and was astonished to hear that the ladies did not intend to take the matter further. Even as a child she had remonstrated.

But they had their reasons, however inadequate or wrongheaded. A private school must avoid scandal or parents and pupils will abandon it and the staff be left jobless. What a fury must descend on the head of the one who had unleashed the scandal, for whatever commendable reasons! And suppose there had been a quite innocent explanation. The bloodstained clothes could be those of a boy recently injured in a accident. Matron would have been out of work at once and blacklisted forever.

Next day the clothes were gone and we may be sure that Matron took care not to look any further.

So Mr. X had stayed on and the police had scratched their heads and indulged in pointless pursuits. Yet, some kind of curious poetic justice Matron (as I found out from Mr Ramsay) had been indeed instrumental at the last in having him removed from the school, and that in the most igminious circumstances.

It appeared that wristwatches and other valuables belonging to the boys had gone missing at the annexe. Finally some of the seniors had come to suspect Mr. X and one day when Matron was unlocking the door prior to cleaning they had persuaded her to go through his drawers while they stood guard outside. There, sure enough, were the purloined articles, all neatly cached away.

Matron know what to do this time. Mr. X was sacked on the spot — and stoned down the drive by the boys.

On thinking it over afterwards, I became less sure that Paul's finds had nothing to do with Mr. X. Perhaps in the 1920's they had been his finds too. The empty envelopes might well have inspired his thefts. Had he rifled the boys' mail as well as their lockers? The bottles might have inspired or even provided the murder weapon. And above all, what of that pile of blood-soaked garments. Could they have been its own?

If so, how to get rid of them? Burning? Smuggling out and hiding? Both hazardous, as many a felon has discovered, and prone to detection. Easier to wash the clothes, surely. But not in any laundry. He must do the washing himself, and in absolute privacy. A school bathroom, with desperate little boys pounding at the door, would never do.

Much wiser to carry a basin or bucket of hot water to his room in the night hours and wash the garments there, with his door locked. Dry them there too, by a heater or on a radiator or before a fire. Yes, but what of the bloody water? How to carry a basin or pail of the crimsoned liquid through a lighted corridor where any boy or colleague might see it?

How much more prudent to transfer the bloody water piecemeal in the old bottles from the attic — and not to the bathroom, where his frequent presence might be detected and where stains and splashes might be left but to the attic. It is, after all, the duty of a housemaster to patrol the corridors and stairs at night. The bottles, in their passage, would have been safely hidden in jacket or dressing gown pockets and their contents decanted from a dormer window down a nearby drainpipe, on a wet night when the rainwater would wash away all traces in a moment.

I thought of all this because I remembered Paul's knockings in the night. Had some mysterious, supernal bond tied Miss Traill's shade to her own spilt blood? Had her noumenal presence clung somehow to that lost life of hers? Had the washing out of the bottles finally served to release that aged shade or to send it elsewhere? The more I thought of it the more certain I grew.

Miss Mary Traill, whose last traces on earth had been spirited away in dribs and drabs, bottle by bottle in the night, had not been altogether spirited away. Instead she had lingered on and then chosen her own moment to go — but not without one backward look, one burning glance, one pointing finger that told (at least me) the whole gruesome story.

Miss Ramsay had voiced only suspicions. But here was proof.

One more thing: Paul had heard rappings but a friend, working with him on the flat, had glimpsed a ghost — a female figure wearing what

433

appeared to be an old-fashioned governess' uniform — disappearing through a door. I can't help wondering if this was the old matron trapped in eternal colloquy with Miss Traill's shade over justice not done. I do not know but, as I say, I can't help wondering.

MY PET GHOST

I heard the screeching and clanking of chains. Icy fingers ran down my face. My friend had come. ...

Maria Narishkin Dembicki

I first encountered the ghost that was to become my "pet" shortly after my parents Vadim and Elizabeth Narishkin, my brothers Vadim, Jr., and Theodore and I moved into a 300-year-old house in Old Headington, an ancient suburb of Oxford, in early autumn of 1931. We had been living deep in the country, in an area called Shotover Hill once occupied by a Roman legion as so much of that part of England was.

A wealthy philanthropic family named Spaulding sponsored us after we escaped from Russia in 1921. They owned a large tract of land on Shotover Hill and had built themselves a mansion with gardens and terraces, a house for their chauffeur and a little house for us, all on the same driveway.

The Spauldings had two almost-grown daughters who attended Headington Senior School for Ladies. When my mother was able to find a sponsor to pay for my schooling, I was sent to Headington Junior School, the Spauldings providing transportation for me with their daughters in their limousine.

On the day we moved to Old Headington, I was taken to school by limousine as usual but did not have to wait for a ride home. My school was on the main London to Oxford road with regular bus service. All I had to do was get on a bus, ride three stops to the High Street, then walk about a quarter of a mile down the High Street to the Church Street intersection. I had no trouble recognizing our house from the description Mother had given me. There were box trees on either side of the front door behind a little brick wall with a spiked wrought-iron fence atop it and a wrought-iron gate.

Just as I was about to turn the door-knob, the door opened and my mother stood in the doorway smiling. She drew me into the house and showed me the dining room and sitting room; then we went up the stairs. At the top she turned sharply to the right and led me to my room, saying, "This is your room."

I followed Mother into the room and tossed my hat, blazer and satchel onto my bed. Slowly I looked around the room. It had a fireplace in the wall opposite my bed. A table and chair stood near the window, my dressing table was beside my bed with a lamp on it and a bookshelf was next to the fireplace. My window faced the street and I realized that my room was directly over the dining room.

"Pick up your things," Mother said. "You can leave your books on the table where you will do your homework. You will hang your clothes in this closet," she said, going to the darkest corner of the room and opening a door. I recoiled as a blast of icy air and the smell of death enveloped me. Mother's back was toward me so she did not notice that I was swaying as if about to faint. She reached inside the closet and pulled a long string to light a bare dim bulb hanging from the ceiling. The light swung back and forth, casting strange shadows. Watching the light made me dizzy and I almost fell down.

"You will hang your things in here," Mother said and when I didn't answer, she asked, "What is the matter with you?"

"I hate it! It stinks — just like a dead mouse and it's cold and damp. I won't go in there," I answered, shaking with fear.

"Ach! What nonsense! How do you know what a dead mouse smells like?" Mother asked.

"I've smelled it lots of times before in the other house," I insisted.

"Come, I'll show you the bathroom and the boys' room," she said, ignoring my last remark.

The moment I stepped into the boys' large, bright, airy room, I exclaimed, "I want this room. It is so much prettier than mine and I can see the garden and the trees from the window. All I can see out of my window is the ugly street." I ran to the boys' closet and opened the door. It was warm and dry and did not smell. "Please, Mama, let me have this room. I hate mine!" I begged.

"You can't have this room. It is twice as big as yours and yours would be too small for two boys to share. Besides, everything is settled and you are not going to disrupt anything." So, like it or not, I was stuck in a room where I knew that something dreadful had happened.

On the night of the first full moon after we moved in, I was awakened by hair-raising screeching, moaning and chain-clanking outside my window. I lay petrified with fear until the horrible sounds began to fade. Then I became aware of another, more terrifying sound. Somebody was forcing open the dining room window. Stealthy footsteps sounded on the stairs, creeping toward my bedroom door.

Simultaneously, my closet door burst open and I heard a stifled sobbing and uneven footsteps approaching my bed. The footsteps sounded like those of a cripple — one heavy thud followed by a shuffling sound.

The "thing" came right to my bed and sat down, emitting a choking-gurgling sound, and icy fingers touched my face. I shrieked in terror and fumbled to turn on my bedside light. Immediately the footsteps outside my door hurried back down the stairs and I heard the dining room window close. I looked around my room. Not only was my closet door wide open and my bedroom door ajar but there was an imprint where a body had sat on the bed beside me. Yet I was alone in the room until my parents rushed in to see what had frightened me so. I sat shaking, unable to speak, and pointed to the open closet door and the imprint of the body on my bed. Neither of them could see the imprint and my father tried to convince me that nothing out of the ordinary had happened. He explained that the screeching was a sound cats make during mating season and the closet door had opened because the foundation of the old house had settled unevenly so that doors could pop open by themselves.

By that time I had more or less composed myself and asked why I had heard the dining room window opening and the footsteps creeping up the stairs. Father went downstairs to investigate but found everything just as he had left it before retiring. My mother blamed the whole incident on my insatiable appetite for ghost stories and forbade me to read any more of them.

Clearly my parents attributed my story to an overactive imagination. Although the ghostly manifestations continued every night when the moon was full, no one took me seriously. I soon got tired of being ridiculed and humiliated by my mother and my brothers and all the paying guests who occupied the top floor of our house. I stopped talking about the noises and muffled my frightened cries in the night. By and by I realized that the entity, whatever it was, did not harm me and I became quite used to the full moon occurrences.

To show me that he cared and half-believed me, my father made some inquiries in the village. He learned about a clever burglar who had terrorized the neighbourhood from time to time. He was so clever that nobody ever saw him — just heard a window being raised and quiet footsteps in the house — he was so swift that nobody could catch him. No matter which house he broke into, nothing of any great value was ever reported missing — except once when some silverware allegedly had disappeared from the house we lived in. The man was believed to wrap rags around his boots or to work in his stockinged feet and he became known as "Flannel Foot". I saw no relationship between this story and the incidents that continued in my room.

By the time I was 14 in the mid-1930's, I was no longer afraid and had begun to think of the entity as "my pet ghost." In fact, we had become friends. I sensed that she was a young girl, hardly older than I who had died violently, ending an unhappy life, and her spirit remained earthbound, seeking consolation.

During the summer months my mother took in au pair girls. The first of these, whom I'll call Minna, came from Estonia. My mother put a second bed in my room (having told me that it was too small for two beds) and now explained that it would be good for me to share my room with a foreign girl.

The second bed was quite close to the closet door but even so Minna put her chair with her clothes on it even closer. I did not tell Minna about my pet ghost because I didn't know how she would react, so on the night of the first full moon I purposely stayed awake waiting for the closet door to open.

Minna had been asleep about an hour when the usual screeching and other sounds started but she did not seem to be aware of anything until the closet door burst open, sending her chair flying with a crash. She screamed and sat up in bed. I flipped on the light and couldn't help laughing. Poor Minna's face was drained of colour, her frizzy hair seemed to stand straight up and she was shaking.

I apologized for laughing and quickly assured her that the ghost was completely harmless. Minna, in turn, told me she was none too sure of that because, as the door burst open, she was hit by a blast of icy air and she felt icy hands on her face.

I explained that the ghost did not expect to find another person in "our" room and that she was just trying to reach my bed but the chair was in the way. I suggested that in the future Minna should set the chair farther from the closet door. Minna complied and we never had any more trouble — although she was always a trifle nervous when the closet door opened of its own record.

By the time I turned 16, I had become really fond of my pet ghost and I decided I was mature enough to make my own inquiries about the history of our house. I decided to speak to the oldest person whom I knew and trusted in the village. I went to the proprietor of the little general store on the corner of Church and High Streets opposite our house. He told me this story:

Long ago a rich man had built three houses on an ancient Roman graveyard. He and his bride occupied the house in the middle which had little box trees on either side of the front door. Beautiful gardens were laid out behind the house where some of the Roman gravestones and gargoyles were used as decoration. The man's wife died giving birth to a grotesquely deformed girl child. The child was so ugly that the neighbours said it was his punishment for desecrating an old graveyard.

Broken-hearted at the death of his wife, the man spent most of his time travelling, providing enough money for servants to take care of the child. Physically she was deformed but she was said to have been mentally bright and normal. When the father decided the girl was old enough to be married, he offered a handsome dowry to the first man who would take her off his hands. A handsome scoundrel came forward. A betrothal was arranged and money changed hands before the father left again on one of his mysterious voyages.

One night when all the servants were asleep, the scoundrel broke into the house by forcing open the dining room window. He crept up the stairs to the girl's (my) room, strangled her and hanged her in the closet, making off with money and valuables and leaving the house by the same window, never to be seen again. Ever since then, at full moon the girl's tortured spirit came out of the closet and sat on the bed weeping. And that, Mr. Wheeler concluded, is how the legend of "Flannel Foot" began.

I felt so sorry for the poor girl that I tried to communicate with her the next time she visited me. I asked if she would like me to pray for her. She answered the only way she could, by gripping my hand tightly. Every night for a month I prayed for the release of her soul.

At the next full moon, the closet door opened as usual but instead of the choking and sobbing and the heavy limping, she skipped lightly and merrily around the room, humming a little tune. She lay down beside me as usual and put her arms around me. With a contented sigh we both fell asleep. The next morning I saw the imprint of her body which had lain next to mine.

Never again did I hear the strange sounds either outside or inside the house, nor did my closet door ever burst open again. My prayers were answered. My pet ghost was released from her 300-year ordeal, a free and happy spirit.

A FLAME THREE CENTURIES OLD

A psychic trace of a historical event from England's civil war lives on in startling photographic testimony.

Florence E. Jackson

Seldom does it happen that a tourist from overseas throws light on a little-known event in English history; yet that is what seems to have happened in the small Gloucestershire town of Painswick, set high in the Cotswold hills.

Before the Civil War began in England in 1642, between Royalists and Parliamentarians, there was great unhappiness in the country. As one historian wrote: "It was a day of wonderful searching of characters and interests, and many strange revolutions took place. Towns, villages, families, now appeared in convulsion and strife, and some felt one way, some another, not without much heartache and many tears, old friends and kindred parting asunder to meet again only to shed each others' blood."

The war lasted for years. For the most part the southern counties and mercantile places favoured Parliament; purely agricultural and remote districts favoured the King. In many areas, however, there was a fairly equal division of loyalty.

Although King Charles I had been aware that his more prudent followers were reluctant to start war, he raised his standard at Nottingham on 23 August, 1642, and battles soon raged. Every English schoolchild has heard of the Battle of Edge Hill in Warwickshire and the siege of the city of Gloucester but it is often forgotten that many minor confrontations were also taking place. For instance, between November 1643 and April 1644, fighting occurred in 13 places in Gloucestershire, and in some places more than once. While Gloucester, which had declared for Parliament, lay under siege, there were continual skirmishes in the surrounding countryside.

Many are the tales told of little known events in small towns and villages such as Painswick which had declared for the King. In March 1644 the Parliamentarians were in control there, when Sir William Vavasour, fighting for the King "having obtained two small cannons from Oxford, with proportion of powder, advanced with a strong brigade toward Painswick" and entered "with as gallant horse and foot as the King's Army did yield."

His opponent, the Parliamentarian Colonel Massey, placed a guard, under the command of a lieutenant, in a house near Painswick church. The lieutenant was ordered to hold the place against an inferior force but, in the event of an attack by a superior force, to retreat to Bruckthrop. The lieutenant underestimated the strength of the army, however, and fought with the help of the people from the neighbourhood but was forced to desert the house and barricade himself and his men in the church.

The Royalist soldiers hurled hand grenades through the windows, opened up with cannons and with blazing torches set fire to the church. Soon the whole north aisle was alight and the large Purbeck marble tomb of Sir William Kington was severely burned and partially destroyed. On the tower and east and west church walls the marks made by cannon and musket fire are still to be seen. When the southern aisle of the church was enlarged in 1890-91 a piece of moulding, evidently part of the doorway at one time, was found buried near the south door and it bore unmistakable traces of fire.

Although the men in the church were forced to surrender, the battle was not over, for Sir William Vavasour wrote to Lord Percy, General of Ordnance, "We have taken Painswick ye loss of some men and wasted of much ammunition. The Rebels have possesst themselves of many houses which will be taken by cannon. I must therefore desire your Lord to send me 20 barrels of Powdre more with some hand grenades and if you please to send a morte?? piece. ..."

There were 2000 Royalists in the little town at the time and Sir William wrote that he had lost only inferior officers, 37 common soldiers and many country men but he took 200 prisoners and killed many men.

The town was cleared in the name of King Charles I but his cause in England was waning and in 1649 he was beheaded. While the Puritans were in power Painswick's bells were silenced, her maypole felled and dancing and horse racing forbidden. But in 1660 bonfires blazed and maypoles sprouted to welcome the return of Charles II and a free Parliament.

As always after a war, however, some mourn when peace is celebrated and that night of violence and death was not easily forgotten in Painswick. No wonder, then that tales are still told and vivid stories, not to be found in the record fill in the details of how it all began. One such story persists concerning the Fiery Beacon Gallery, a house which stands opposite the churchyard.

The front of this house was extended forward sometime in the late 18th century. Prior to that the front door had opened onto what was then the village green. At this spot, according to the Painswick tale, the Royalist soldiers gathered to light their torches before storming the church. There was no proof of this but from time to time rumours arose that a strange light had been seen in the house and that one room was always icy cold. Just an old wives' tale, thought the sceptics.

In August 1984, however, a Canadian and his son-in-law, on a walking tour of the Cotswolds, paused to take pictures in Painswick. They did not have them developed until they returned to Canada. One they had taken of the Fiery Beacon Gallery was puzzling. It showed near the front door, a flame burning on the outside wall. Seeking an explanation, they wrote to the present owners Mr. and Mrs. Ward:

"We don't remember seeing anything like the flaming image seen on the right-hand side of the building. Would you please be kind enough to let us know if there is anything resembling the flame as seen in the print?"

There is no flaming image on that stone wall, so Mr. and Mrs. Ward wrote and asked if they could have the transparency. It has since been carefully examined and there is no sign of tampering. Yet the flaming orange torch is there in the picture for all to see.

Dr. Johnson's words seem particularly appropriate to the mystery of the gallery light: "We all know what light is; but it is not easy to tell what it is."

GHOST SHIP OF THE GOODWINS

When eerie legends of sea mysteries and phantom schooners are told, where does fiction end and fact begin?

Michael Goss

Eight miles or so seaward from the Kent town of Deal the Goodwin Sands sprawl in the shape of a giant lobster across one of the busiest shipping areas in the world. Pierced by clear-water channels or "swatches" varying in depth from feet to fathoms and pitted with pools known locally as "fox-falls," the Sands are desolate enough at low tide but when high tide steals in, covering even the highest (northerly) parts beneath at least eight feet of sea, they become a menace sailors have feared for centuries. In 1570 William Lambarde called this 10¼-by 4¼-mile shoal "a great gulf and ship swallower." It is perhaps the worst hazard of its kind anywhere on earth.

The Goodwins are not quicksands in the usual sense. They are clear sand resting on blue clay to depths estimated at between 15 and 90 feet and at low water many parts become dry and as hard as stone. During the last century visitors with more than their share of bravado staged picnics, cricket matches and once (on 31 August, 1855) a cycle race across this lonely vista broken only by the occasional spar or ribs of some lost vessel. Those skeletal fragments are tokens of the Goodwins' unenviable record as a devourer of ships — referred to in Shakespeare's *The Merchant of Venice* as "a very dangerous flat and fatal, where the carcase of many a tall ship lie buried."

As late as 1859 Board of Trade statistics showed that an average of a dozen British ships came to grief on the Goodwins each year. Only with the advent of a lightship system did travel become safer.

The only things more attracted to the Goodwins than hapless ships and sea gulls are legends. The best-known of them concerns a phantom ship. Few places deserve to be haunted more than this naval graveyard with its sorry catalogue of wrecked vessels and there is no shortage of candidates for the role of phantom ship, from the 13 men-of-war lost there with 1200 men on November 26, 1703, virtually up until the present. Yet the ghost ship of the Goodwins is none of these. The craft that appears on a certain day once every 50 years to celebrate the anniversary of its destruction upon the Sands is the *Lady Luvibund*.

Far more regular than the phantom craft's cyclical reappearances on the Goodwins is her recurrence in anthologies of amazing-but-true marine mysteries. The *Lady Luvibund* not only ranks alongside the *Flying Dutchman* as one of the classic ghost stories of the sea but is a tale subject to several variations in the telling. The following version is taken from *The Goodwin Sands* (1953) by George Goldsmith Carter, local historian and former light-shipman. His was definitely not the earliest printed version but it proved one of the most influential.

Tempestuous passions, love and murder are key ingredients of a traditional ghost story. The *Lady Luvibund* adventure has them aplenty but a cast of only three main players: just-married Simon Reed and his "young and beautiful bride," who are using a general cargo run to Oporto as their honeymoon trip, and the obligatory villain, John Rivers. When the ship sailed from London on 13 February, 1748, Captain Reed did not know that Rivers, best man at his wedding and now first mate on the *Lady Luvibund*, had been in love with the girl and was nursing a jealous hatred for the man who took her from him. This may never have come to light had it not been for the fact that at an inquiry sometime later Rivers' mother testified that her son had vowed to take revenge on the captain even if it cost him his life.

The vessel had cleared the Thames and was on its way past the Kentish coast. Below in the cabin laughter rang out as the bride's relatives and friends drank toasts to the happy couple. Meanwhile, on deck Rivers was being driven into a jealous rage by these festive sounds. Taking up a belaying pin, he slipped silently behind the helmsman and shattered the man's skull with one ferocious blow. Rivers seized the helm and jerked the *Lady Luvibund* deep into the treacherous Goodwins. Mast and timbers crashed down, trapping the revelers while over the din of tortured wood and pounding waves echoed "the hideous cacophony of a madman's laughter." By next morning the Sands had lived up to their reputation — every trace of the *Lady Luvibund* and those aboard her had been swallowed forever. Or so it seemed. ...

Fifty years later to the day, Capt. James Westlake of the Edenbridge was forced to swing his helm violently to avoid a three-masted schooner which bore down without warning, all sails set and sounds of "female voices and gaiety coming from below." Angered at this display of recklessness, he reported the incident when he got to shore, only to be told that a fishing vessel had seen the schooner go onto the Goodwins, where she started to break up. By the time the vessel arrived to help, the schooner had vanished without a trace. A similar phantom wreck — breaking up on the Goodwins one minute, gone the next — baffled some local boatmen and observers on an American vessel on 13 February, 1848. On 13 February, 1898, watchers ashore witnessed exactly the same phenomenon.

"So through all eternity," Carter concluded, "every 50 years and on the 13th of February, a madman's deed of violence and treachery is reenacted and the phantom schooner is doomed to wreckage on the same spot. Real ghosts are far from being the shadowy, insubstantial things of popular belief."

The remark about "real ghosts" notwithstanding, Carter's narrative resembles nothing in the records of modern parapsychology. The extreme literary flavour of the tale alone is suspicious. The plot is too neat. Can we really believe that Rivers' mother could have reconstructed the last hours of the ship (including the felling of the helmsman) so accurately? And there are too many concrete details. The allegation that the *Lady Luvibund* is available for scrutiny every 50 years, regular as clockwork, on February 13 is the sort of touch that belongs to a fiction writer.

Even so, to all surface appearances the *Lady Luvibund* has the look of a fine antique sea mystery rooted in local tradition and sanctioned by generations of storytellers. This isn't the same as saying it is authenticated, but one could argue that so many wouldn't have taken it as authentic for so long unless at least some part of it was true. Unfortunately, there is little evidence that the *Lady Luvibund* is an old story; all the signs point to a relatively modern origin.

In fact, that is what "G.H.W.," a correspondent of *Notes & Queries*, suspected when that writer saw a paragraph in the *Daily Chronicle* for 14 February, 1924, announcing that the "anniversary of the ghostly visitation of the *Lady Luvibund*, sunk in the Goodwins in 1724 [sic], was marked last night by a terrific gale. There was at least one wreck, but from enquiries ... the legendary apparition due every 50 years at midnight on 13 February was not seen."

G.H.W., who investigated, was puzzled to find no Deal resident who had heard of this purportedly famous local apparition. Just as bewildering was the fact that none of the Goodwins' many chroniclers seemed aware of it either. After checking 13 books on the history and legends of the Sands G.H.W. found no reference to a wreck in the Goodwins of a *Lady Luvibund* (or "*Lovibund*," as some writers render it), let alone to its supernatural renaissance in 1874 or any other time. "The story," G.H.W. said, "would appear to be of modern origin. Did it first appear in some work of fiction, and if so what is the title and by whom was it written? As no local historian mentions the legend, perhaps its author may be known to some ... readers." Evidently not, since none of *N & Q*'s numerous and learned correspondents appears to have replied to G.H.W.'s appeal for further information.

The questions that G.H.W. posed concerning the *Lady Luvibund* tale's origins remain unanswered today. In researching this article I trod much the same path as the *N & Q* searcher and with little more luck. Local historian Les Cozens confirmed that the tale "has been going around Deal for years" but even his extensive records of shipwrecks and other inquiries have failed to pin down its debut in print. George Goldsmith Carter told me that he couldn't remember when or where he first heard it.

G.H.W.'s source switches the year of the wreck from 1748 to 1724, necessitating a recalibration of the ghost ship's anniversary manifestations to 1774, 1824, 1874 and so on, but most recent authors follow Carter's version — including Kentish journalists who have lifted it from his book wholesale whenever a ghostly yarn is required. The wreck of the *Lady Luvibund* seemed to have been validated simply because people kept telling it. Even maritime disaster authority Richard Larn included it on a map of Goodwins wrecks in 1977, confidently assigning the site at which it took place to an east-southeast section of the Sands.

When one tracks down ghostly classics, one should always begin at the beginning: that is, to establish who first told the story and when. This was precisely what G.H.W. wanted to do and couldn't. On the face of things the *Lady Luvibund*'s dating (1724 or 1748) suggests that it must have been published sometime in the 18th century; yet surveys of notable wrecks for that period contain no reference to it. Nor does The Gentleman's Magazine, a by-the month chronicler of contemporary accidents, even the most trivial ones.

At least one of the legend-conscious authors checked by G.H.W. ought to have known of the *Lady Luvibund*, if only to poke fun at it as a silly superstition, but none knew anything about it. To the titles uncovered in G.H.W.'s literature search (covering a period of some 50 years) can be added Charles Harper's *The Kentish Coast* (1914). Because Harper was also author of Haunted Houses only seven years before, it seems hard to believe he would pass up a good phantom. T. F. Thiselton Dyer omits it in his chapter on spectral craft in *The Ghost World* (1893). So does Fletcher Bassett in his colossal *Legends and Superstitions of the Sea and of Sailors* (1885). Evidently even these aficionados of weird tales had never heard of the *Lady Luvibund* as either ship or ghost. One reasonable explanation for this may be that the story had yet to be invented.

Conceivably an oral version of the *Lady Luvibund* may have circulated during the 19th century — although, given the Victorian enthusiasm for getting folktales into print, its escape from avid collectors seems little short of miraculous. My guess is that the ghost ship of the Goodwins sailed into view between 1914 and 1924 and that the insistence on 13 February as the day of its anniversary appearance is no accident. What more appropriate time than the eve of St. Valentine's Day could there have been to bring forth a ghost story based on a tragic love affair? Or conversely, what better way of filling the need for a St. Valentine's Day story than a ghostly legend based on a tragic love affair?

It has been said that few things are harder to invent than a truly original ghost story. Whoever was responsible for the *Lady Luvibund* could hope only for a variation on a theme; yet he or she deserves credit for managing the job well by improvising with several standard motifs.

If this was to be a supernatural tale for St. Valentine's Day, the idea of a wrecked bridal party was a sound choice; perhaps the creator picked up on a hint offered by "The Last Lord of Helvellyn" from Allan Cunningham's popular *Traditional Tales of the English and Scottish Peasantry* (1822, 1874) where a wedding barge is sunk by a paranormal whirlwind to fulfill an ancient prophecy of doom on the noble hero's house. But this would have been too stagy for modern tastes; better substitute a human villain and strengthen the love interest by having him consumed with insane jealousy, then transfer the action to a place where wreck-tragedies were too familiar to sound incredible.

The note of criminal passion lent itself to the folk belief that ghosts are shades forced for all time to re-enact the crimes that bind them to the physical world. This sense of karmic justice was already part of maritime folklore. If the blasphemy of the *Flying Dutchman's*

447

skipper caused his ship to wander the seaways for eternity, the treachery of Rivers would assuredly bind the *Lady Luvibund* to the Goodwins.

It may seem unnecessarily harsh to denigrate the *Lady Luvibund* as a false ghost and fabricated phantom. After all, what does it matter if it never really existed, when its purpose was obviously to entertain? The trouble with pseudotraditions like this is that, however enjoyable they may be, they obscure the possibility that the sea holds genuine mysteries — and perhaps genuine phantom ships among them.

A close look at the hundreds of parallel stories about ghost ships reveals that many are as dubious as the *Lady Luvibund* yarn. But several other considerations emerge from this examination.

One is that ghost-ship sightings or accounts constitute a worldwide phenomenon. North America's eastern shores are especially rich in phantom craft, from Block Island's *Palatine* and the fire ship of Bay Chaleur to the *Packet Light* which rises like a ball of flame and sinks back into the Gulf of St. Lawrence or the full-rigged three-master whose fiery doom used to attract crowds of spectators to the Nova Scotia village of Merigonish each autumn equinox.

These may indicate nothing more than the universal popularity of certain folklore themes. Yet there an enough solid-sounding statement for us to believe that the witnesses truly saw something. And when looked at carefully, that "something" is consistently described as a kind of light or radiance which with little imagination — guided by folk tradition or legend — is attributed to a ship in flames.

This is not the place to review all the examples of fiery phantom ships or the many explanations put forward to account for them. But a few representative cases should suffice to raise the possibility that behind some accounts lurks what appears to be a genuine unexplained phenomenon which has been rendered unbelievable by the attachment of a prevailing "ghostly craft" legend.

For instance, it is not hard to understand the view expressed by the Rev. Samuel Livermore, historian of Block Island, who believed in the celebrated "Palatine Light" but did not believe it was the unlucky ship of that name reliving its destruction by arson in 1752 — a tale that in any case severely mangles the historical truth of the story. Dr. Aaron C. Willey describes the phenomenon as "sometimes small, resembling the light through a distant window ... at others expanding to the highness of a ship with all canvas spread" or "pyramidal or in three streamers, flickering and reappearing, but not lasting longer than three minutes." There seems no reason to doubt the occasional sightings of the light across the centuries — an effect so familiar to islanders, Willey said, that they rarely thought it worth mentioning to outsiders.

Like the Palatine phenomenon, the Bay Chaleur lights have been seen at all seasons (although usually preceding a storm). They have been compared with a 30-foot column, a mastless vessel "all glowing like a hot coal" and a big bonfire. One researcher noticed that even those who scoffed at the explanatory tale of a storm-wrecked vessel and pirate repredations "nonetheless admit that sometimes the mysterious light emits rays that ... might by a particularly well-nourished imagination be likened to the flame-lit rigging of a ship."

Likewise for the hoary *Flying Dutchman*. One of the few modern, well-attested sightings of this legendary sea wraith comes from the log of the *Bacchante* and might well have failed to attract attention but for the fact that among the mid-shipman cadets on board were Princes George and Eddy, sons of the future King Edward VII of England.

At 4 am on 11 July, 1881, close to the coast of Australia the *Bacchante* was confronted by a "strange red light as of a phantom ship all aglow, in the midst of which light the masts, spars and sails of a brig 200 yards distant stood out in clear relief as she came up on our port bow ... but on arriving there no vestige or any sign whatever of any material ship was to be seen either near or right away to the horizon." (In keeping with the tradition of bad luck attached to meeting the *Dutchman*, an ordinary seaman is said to have fallen to his death from the foremast seven hours after this episode.)

In trying to explain ghost-ship sightings, theorists have roamed freely from speculations about a "peculiar modification of electricity" and "inflammation of phlogogistous gas" to seabed petroleum deposits ignited by lightning and St. Elmo's fire. It is possible that yarns like those associated with the *Palatine* and the *Flying Dutchman* began with sightings of a peculiar light interpreted as coming from a ship; the eerie nature of the light in turn suggested a vessel not of this earth. The tale "explaining" the phenomenon followed the established traditional themes wherein hauntings are products of tragedy and unbridled passions. In some cases the tragedy linked to the (supposed) ship had something to do with arson, thus a fiery phantom.

Even if these phantasmal-vessel narratives derive from phenomena that are more meteorological than paranormal, they seem to describe a genuine anomaly — more than can be said for the *Lady Luvibund* saga.

And yet the Goodwins may have their genuine ghost ship after all. George Carter believes he saw it on 1 February, 1947, when he was serving on the North Goodwin lightship. Through a swirling blizzard he and his shipmates observed a steamer heading for the Sands, followed soon after by distress signals which prompted them to summon the Ramsgate lifeboat. Had any vessel been on the Goodwins, some sign of it would have been visible — but, as the lifeboat's coxswain tersely remarked on his return, they "couldn't find a thing".

In 1857 the Ostend-Dover packet *Violet* was lost on the Sands with all on board despite warning rockets from a lightship. Next day only a life raft with three bodies lashed to it was left. The accident occurred on an identical snow-squalling night although — disappointingly if you feel ghosts should honor anniversaries — the date was 5 January not 1 February. Carter has said he thinks he witnessed the end of the *Violet* 90 years after it took place. He concurred with my opinion that it was a more convincing story that the *Lady Luvibund*. "Yes, I told that as a legend," he said, "but I saw that other spectre".

So strange things do happen on or around the Goodwins. Les Cozens, who has examined the records of the North Deal lifeboat says he is "amazed in reading the call-outs in answer to guns being fired from light vessels and visible sightings from the shore of ships going onto the Goodwins and disappearing." He says that from 1865 to 1890 these phantom vessels-in-trouble accounted for nearly one in every four of the call-outs.

In this respect the *Lady Luvibund* story may not seem so exceptional. At all events it — and every ghost-ship story of the same ilk — is an essentially harmless, romantic response to an evocative seascape and to a sense of historical tradition. No amount of sceptical cold water can remove tales of this kind from people's hearts.

THE TRAGIC GHOST OF SANDHILL GARDENS

The thing the ghost wanted so desperately existed only in its own deluded mind.

Lorna Gulston

The phone call knocked me sideways. Betty and I had been like sisters since our schooldays. Even after Betty's marriage to American Don Morrison (a pseudonym) in 1961, our closeness had spanned the Atlantic.

Don was an executive with a big multinational corporation and his business brought him often to Ireland. That delighted him as much as it did Betty, for he was fiercely proud of his Ulster ancestry. He never tired of telling about his great-great-grandmother Sadie Gillespie who in the 1840's was a nine-year-old "half-timer," attending school in the mornings and working, up to her knees in water, in a Belfast flax mill in the afternoons. At 17 she had wed John McBride, a carrier's boy who delivered flax to the mill, and emigrated with him to seek their fortune in the United States.

Don had planned to replant his roots in Ulster soil. For his retirement he was having a bungalow built at Craigavad on the County Down coast. It would have been ready that autumn. Now he was dead, poleaxed at his desk by a massive coronary — big, kindly, vigorous Don who had looked nowhere near his 65 years. Despite an age gap Betty and he had been a devoted couple, even more so because they were childless. Betty would soon be on her way home to perform her last act of love for Don by laying his ashes to rest in Ireland.

"Can you find me a place to rent until the bungalow's finished?" she had asked me sadly. "Somewhere I can store my favourite things?"

I dashed around seeing estate agents in search of a "let." With Ulster's troubles places to rent in nonviolent areas were snapped up as soon as they fell vacant but I struck it lucky. Number 1 Sandhill Gardens was a three-bedroom, semidetached, red-brick Edwardian villa in a peaceful residential suburb of Belfast. It had been let-furnished on short leases for a number of years by an absentee

451

landlord, so the furniture and carpets were somewhat shabby. Still, it was spacious, quiet and within easy driving distance of the site of Betty's new bungalow. I felt sure she'd approve.

Betty looked tired and haggard but composed as she walked toward me in the passenger terminal at Belfast International Airport on 29 January, 1976. She was holding tightly to a blue vanity case. In it, she confided, was the casket containing Don's remains.

We buried him a few days later in a simple, poignant ceremony at Roselawn Cemetery. Roselawn, high above the city, is a beautiful place in summer, with its rolling green sward and the fragrant profusion of roses from which it takes its name. That bleak February afternoon, however, it was cloaked in mist and buffeted by a gale which tossed the rows of slender memorial saplings.

As we drove home, Betty couldn't stop shivering.

"The radiators are on full blast in the house," I comforted her. "It should be really cosy."

I was glad I had taken a week's leave from my job to be with her. I live with my elderly mother and seven cats but Mother had insisted I stay with Betty for a week at least.

"She has no family left now and the poor soul's going to feel lost without Don," she said. "It isn't right for her to be alone at the moment."

As I swung the car through the gateway and round the path to the garage, I noticed something which made me jam on the brakes in shock.

"What's wrong?" Betty asked, rubbing her elbow, which my abrupt stop had bumped against the car door.

"That bathroom window — I left it closed!"

The window, an old-fashioned sash type, was pushed up to its fullest extent, curtains flapping across the sill. Betty and I exchanged a startled glance. Burglars!

I grabbed a large wrench from the glove compartment and we crept in through the front door expecting to be pounced on. But a nerve-wracking tour of the house revealed no trace of intruders. There was just that gaping window with its billowing curtains.

"I must have forgotten to close it after all," I said doubtfully.

About 11:30 pm, as we were unwinding over a cup of coffee in the lounge, we heard a muffled noise overhead, as if someone had walked in slippers across the spare bedroom. White-faced, we set down our cups. Sticking close together, we tiptoed upstairs, armed with the poker and the fire tongs.

The spare-room window was open as far as it would go. I was certain I had closed that one too!

Again we searched every nook and cranny but could find nobody lurking. Puzzled and shaken, we gulped our cool coffee and went nervously to bed, keeping our doors ajar to hear each other yell if either of us was attacked.

The landing from which the bedrooms opened off was approximately 20 feet long, a thin corridor from the door of that extra front room to three steps down into the bathroom at the rear of the house. Just before midnight, Betty and I both heard a heavy thump. Comparing notes, we agreed that it was as if a giant fist had slammed with all its might on the landing side of Betty's bedroom wall; but when we rushed to investigate, there was nothing to account for it.

Next morning, cheered by the brightness of a wintry sun, we dismissed "The Thump" as a hiccup in the plumbing. I even convinced myself that I'd been absentminded about those windows. But that evening, at precisely the same time — a few minutes to midnight — came "The Drag." Behind the closed door of the mysterious empty bedroom, it sounded as if a heavy object were being dragged across the floor. We tumbled out of bed and inched the door open, but apart from a divan, a chair and a small walnut dressing table, the room was empty and apparently undisturbed.

Sleep was out of the question. I was glad I'd laid in a bottle of scotch. We went downstairs and made strong, hot toddy.

Suddenly Betty clutched my arm, almost spilling my drink. "Lorna," she cried, "I've been so blind and stupid. It's Don!"

"Don?"

"He's giving us signs that he's trying to get through to me."

I sipped my whisky, avoiding her gaze. I'd been a total sceptic of the paranormal until a chilling experience seven years previously, on the night my father died. Disturbed as I was by the odd goings-on in this house, I clung doggedly to the hope of a natural explanation.

Betty wrung her hands in agitation. "Have you ever done table-turning?" she asked.

I replied, "Only once, with a wineglass and the alphabet. I told you about it, remember? But never again."

Betty leaped to her feet, eyes fever-bright. "Please, we must," she implored me. "This time will be different. You won't be personally involved."

She ransacked the kitchen cupboards for a wineglass but there was none to be found. She was so distraught that, against my better judgment, I said, "If you feel that strongly about it, we'll buy one tomorrow. But don't get too built up. It mightn't work at all, especially with just two of us."

"It will. Don will talk to me now."

After tea that evening we prepared for our "séance." The whole idea depressed me. Still, I'd promised and there was no backing out now.

Almost immediately the glass sprang to life with a drive and urgency that took our breath away.

"FIND THE PAPERS," it spelled out.

"Don, is that you?" Betty asked tremulously.

The glass raced round the circle of letters so fast we could scarcely keep contact with it.

"Don, darling, I'm missing you terribly!" Betty burst out. "We didn't even have the chance to say good-bye."

"NOT DON, NOT DON. LILY."

The blood drained from Betty's face.

"Who are you, Lily?" I said hastily.

"LILY NOBLE. FIND THE PAPERS."

An inexplicable sensation of pity and distress washed over me. Betty seemed stunned but her index finger stayed on the whirling glass. It told an astonishing story. Lily Noble was a 25-year-old girl who had lived with her father in our house when it was first built. In 1924, 52 years ago, because of some lost papers, she had stabbed herself to death on the landing.

"CANNOT REST. HAVE TO FIND PAPERS," the words came. "YOU LOOK. YOU LOOK."

"Where, Lily? Where must we look?"

"LOCKED TRUNK IN COAL SHED. FIND THE PAPERS. OH, FIND THE PAPERS."

Without warning the glass went dead. We kept our fingers on its rim and Betty sobbed and begged Don to communicate. Although we persisted for a good half hour, there was not the slightest response. Betty went tearfully into the kitchen to brew coffee. When she returned, she was calmer.

"It wasn't Don after all," she sighed.

"No. I'm sorry."

"It was stupid of me. I know he's always with me anyway. You were right. We shouldn't have touched the glass. That poor girl — the kitchen knife." She shuddered. "The awful thump we heard — it could have been her body falling against the wall! Maybe we're meant to help her."

"How?"

"Well, she asked us to look in the coal shed."

Overcome with a sense of urgency, we couldn't wait for daylight. I fetched the powerful car lantern and we unbolted the rickety, creaking door of the tall brown hut next to the garage. There was no coal, just a stack of rotting wood inhabited by a creepy legion of spiders. The torchlight picked out a flat black one with windmill legs crabbing beneath something that glinted — the edge of a dusty metal trunk!

Betty and I hauled it from the mound of crumbling timber. It was padlocked but the lock was so rust-eaten that a sharp blow with the edge of a stone snapped it. Dry-mouthed with excitement, I pried open the lid.

All that lay inside were a mildewed pair of lady's strapped patent shoes, 1920's style, and a damp, warped copy of an Edgar Wallace thriller, *The Frightened Lady*.

Feeling foolish, we shoved the trunk back into its cobwebbed corner. Whatever power, occult or otherwise, had activated the wineglass, we had been the victims of a mischievous trick.

Or so we thought.

At about 11:45 pm Betty called to me from the bathroom, "What did you say, Lorna?"

"I didn't speak," I said.

"But there was a voice -"

"Probably me closing this drawer. It squeaked. I reckon we've given ourselves the heebie-jeebies."

But when my turn came for the bathroom, I could have sworn I heard a female voice, faint and whispering. Was it my imagination or had it really said, "Find the papers"?

We hid the glass at the very back of a cupboard and for three nights nothing happened. The weekend, too, passed without incident. We began to relax and tried to forget he eerie events of the previous week.

On Monday Betty was thrilled to receive an unexpected letter from a cousin of Don's inviting her to stay with the family at their farm in

County Antrim. She phoned her eager acceptance. They'd fetch her on Wednesday afternoon.

I was pleased for her. It was just the break she needed. So Tuesday would be our last night in Sandhill Gardens for at least a fortnight.

The evening passed pleasantly as I helped Betty pack. Again, it was around midnight when we made our way to bed. I'd just snuggled under the sheets when all hell broke loose. First the giant fist on the landing wall, then the dragging noise from the spare bedroom, louder than before. It lasted for perhaps 25 to 30 seconds.

Betty and I met fearfully in her doorway.

She asked, "What can we do?"

"I wish I knew. Recite the Lord's Prayer or something."

"Oh, my God, look!" she cried.

Betty pointed to the steps outside the bathroom. I saw an undulating shape, then — so clearly that I clutched the banister for support — a figure running down the stairs. At the bottom it turned and gazed up at us and we found ourselves staring into the pallid face of a young dark-haired woman wearing an expression of terrible anguish. She appeared to be crying. A gust of icy air surrounded us. Then the figure melted into nothingness.

At that moment my last vestige of scepticism died. I understood that we'd received a passionate plea for help — and we had failed.

After a sleepless night a subdued Betty was borne off to her friends' farm, while I went back home resolved to investigate Lily Noble's story. I began by sounding out the house agent but he had handled No. I only for the past eight years and knew nothing of its history prior to that. Neighbours, the richest source of local gossip, looked to be youngish people who would not have been around in the 1920's. A search through all local newspapers for 1924 yielded no information about a suicide. Where could I go from there?

I toyed with the idea of consulting the Royal Ulster Constabulary station for that area. But, apart from the fact that the Ulster police were at full strength with the grim pressures of terrorism, they'd think I was a crank if I were to say, "Excuse me, but I'm trying to trace a ghost from 50 years ago." And yet, by one of those incredible coincidences which happen only in real life, it was indeed the RUC that inadvertently supplied the key to the mystery.

On the following Friday the agent phoned. Could I please go

along to the house at once? Someone had thrown a brick through the bottom front window. A policeman would meet me there to check if anything had been stolen.

Unquiet spirits, bricks — where would it all end? I wished I had never set eyes on No. 1 Sandhill Gardens.

I was relieved to discover that the breakage had been sheer mindless vandalism. Nothing was gone.

"Pleasant here," said the constable as I signed my statement. "I live quite near myself. My kids love to play on that old railway track at the back. Not that you'd know it had ever been a railway now, except for the sleepers under the grass. And the ghost, of course."

"Ghost?" I said, nearly falling out of my chair.

The policeman, grinning, asked, "It's not been bothering you, has it?"

So I told him about Lily Noble. As it turned out, however, I'd got the wrong ghost. The one the constable meant was a male crossing-keeper mown down by a train before World War I.

"That's odd, though," he said thoughtfully. "Tell you what. I've an uncle retired from the force and living in Londonderry. He'd have been a young copper in our station about that time. I'll give him a buzz. If there was a suicide, the police should have been in on it."

The constable was as good as his word. A couple of days later he called back with some startling information.

His uncle remembered the case well. Arthur Noble, a widower, lived with his daughter Lily, an only child, in No. 1 Sandhill Gardens. He owned large portions of land in the district and he was selling the land for building. The transactions involved a lot of money but something went wrong. It came to light that the young solicitor acting for Arthur Noble was swindling him. It was a doubly cruel betrayal because the solicitor was also Lily's fiancé.

For her sake no legal action was taken and the heartless scoundrel was allowed to abandon his practice and leave the country. As a result Lily had a nervous breakdown and spent some time in a mental hospital from which she was discharged, supposedly cured. A few weeks afterwards she plunged down the landing steps with a kitchen knife in her hand.

The merciful verdict had been "accidental death" and influential friends of Arthur Noble had kept the story out of the newspapers. Lily had refused to accept her fiancé's guilt. Her delusion was that somewhere were secret papers which would clear his name.

"It's the weirdest thing I've ever heard," the constable admitted. "Whatever was in that glass certainly got its facts right."

Well, now we had the confirmation I had been seeking. I wasn't sure whether to be glad or sorry.

When Betty came back to the house, I rejoined her, half fearing, half hoping that we might regain contact with Lily and ease her tormented spirit. There was nothing. No opened windows, no thumps or drags, no soft voice calling pitifully from the landing. Even when we plucked up courage to try the wine glass again, it stayed silent and inert. The poor unhappy shade of Lily Noble had fled, leaving us with a host of unanswered questions. Where has she gone? Has she finally accepted the bitter truth or does she still wander somewhere in search of the nonexistent proof of her lover's innocence?

A decade later Betty is settled in her bungalow, with two dogs and a cat for company. She has found consolation and fresh purpose through working for handicapped children. At least one Sunday a month she spends a quiet hour with Don at Roselawn Cemetery.

Ours was the last "letting" of No. 1 Sandhill Gardens. After we left, the absentee landlord sold it. The new owner has given it a complete facelift. I drive past it often and see cars in the driveway and children playing in the garden. The once-troubled house has every appearance of being a happy family home.

Of the many casual tenants who occupied it over the years, were Betty and I the only unwitting spectators of a raw human drama which happened before we were born? Through our rash tampering with the wineglass, had we summoned poor Lily Noble back from beyond the grave to reenact her heartbreak? Was there more we could have done for our tragic ghost? If so, where did we go wrong?

We shall never know and, with lingering guilt, we shall never cease to wonder.

HOME FROM THE SEA
John Butler

One sunny afternoon in June 1953, while the narrow streets of this old mining town were lined with throngs of noisy children on their way home from school, I knocked at the door of 11 Shaw Street, Barnsley, South Yorkshire. It was a weekly call I made to collect the old widow's insurance cover for her funeral. Our arrangement was that if she was out she would leave the door unlocked and the money on the sideboard.

When there was no response to my knock, I lifted the old-fashioned lock and walked in. A bright coal fire burned in the old black range.

I collected the premium, signed the book and turned to go out again when my attention was suddenly drawn to a figure sitting in an old wooden Windsor armchair by the fire.

A young man in a sailor's uniform was staring fixedly into the flickering flames of the fire. He made no sign that he was aware of my presence.

Not wishing to intrude on his privacy, I would have left without further ado. But at that moment I caught a glimpse of his face in the sunlight. I recognized him immediately as the same young man whose large framed photograph stood so proudly on the gleaming redwood chest of drawers.

There was no denying it was the same. The prominent teeth, froglike eyes and black calf lick of hair made it instantly recognizable.

The next time I saw the old lady, Mrs. Robertshaw, I asked her if her son — I knew she had only one — had returned to his ship. As I spoke, I gestured toward the photograph.

She was upset and wanted to know how I knew he had been in the navy. I knew something was wrong the way she emphasized had. Then tearfully she told me he had been blown up and lost on *The Prince of Wales* off Singapore in 1942.

TROOPER ZOYLAND'S GHOST

**The apparition moved down the great staircase
about a foot above the treads, then vanished through
a long-gone doorway.**

Ian Paxton More

Trooper Zoyland (all names in this tale are psuedonyms) peered at his
watch: 4.30 am. Another 15 minutes and he could start his final round
of the great old building. Then his spell of guard duty would be over
and with luck he could get an hour's sleep in the guardroom before
reveille.

Despite the steady drizzle of rain outside it was a warm night
and the air in the old building felt heavy and oppressive. He looked
forward to shedding his battle dress and webbing. Still, he couldn't
complain; he might have been on sentry duty out in the rain instead of
on internal security and fire-watch in the abbey. He sighed and allowed
his mind to lapse into a comfortable state of near-vacuum, occasionally
enriched by thoughts of beer or, better still, good Somerset cider.

Rufford Abbey, some 20 miles north of the ancient city of
Nottingham, was not an abbey now, of course, although before 1537 it
had been. It was said that the monks had their sleeping quarters off the
Long Gallery at the head of the great staircase. Some time after the
Reformation the old abbey buildings had been converted into a great
rambling mansion.

If the old monks were around now, in the spring of 1942, they
would find their dormitory occupied by the officers of a British tank
regiment and the great park, where no doubt they once strolled in
meditation, dotted with Nissen huts, and the monastic stillness
disturbed by the rumble of tank engines.

Trooper Zoyland peered at his watch again in the light of a
single blue light bulb — 4:35 am. Curious how slowly time passes
when one wants it to go quickly. The sentry shivered slightly. Odd, he
thought; a few moments ago he had been looking forward to taking off
his jacket. Now suddenly he would have been glad to have his
greatcoat.

Then he saw it. ...

In a small room farther down the Long Gallery, Adjutant Adams was sleeping peacefully when suddenly he was rudely awakened. Someone was clutching wildly at his bedclothes. He dragged his sleep-numbed mind into reluctant wakefulness, grabbed his torch and shone it on his assailant.

It was not, to his relief, an invading German soldier clawing at him but Trooper Zoyland. Not the placid, rather bovine Trooper Zoyland whom he knew well but an incoherent Trooper Zoyland, eyes bulging with fright, who pointed distractedly toward the door while uttering animal sounds of terror.

The adjutant, now fully awake, got out of bed and went out into the Long Gallery. All seemed quiet. Peering over the massive banister he could make out the glow of the guardroom light off the Great Hall.

"Guard Commander!" Adams called. He heard a chair pushed back and a moment later the Sergeant emerged, buckling his belt.

"What the devil's going on?" called the Adjutant.

"I've heard nothing down here, sir," replied the Sergeant. "Trooper Zoyland is on watch inside the building and he has reported nothing amiss."

"Trooper Zoyland is either drunk or crazy," said the adjutant irritably. "Lock him in the Detention Room and I will deal with him in the morning."

Adjutant Adams was seldom in a good humour at breakfast and his mood looked blacker that morning. He helped himself to coffee and sat down next to me. I was a lieutenant in the tank regiment.

"Trooper Zoyland is in your Troop, isn't he?" he asked.

"Yes. Good chap, Zoyland," I replied.

"Well!" Adams snorted. "He's coming up on a charge before the Colonel this morning. Drunk on duty!"

"That's not like Zoyland," I said. "I'd better go and see him."

After breakfast I went along to the guardroom where the sergeant unlocked the door and admitted me to the Detention Room. Trooper Zoyland was sitting on the floor with his back to the wall and his face was absolutely green — green with fright. He was clearly in a very distressed state. I spent more than an hour with him and slowly, with much prompting, elicited from him an account of the previous night.

At about 4:30 am, he said, he had been in the Long Gallery near the head of the Great Staircase when suddenly, despite the warm

461

damp night, he felt very cold. He had then seen, quite distinctly, a hooded figure in a monk's habit emerge from the panelling. The figure was carrying a crucifix in hands clasped to its chest and from one little finger hung what was probably a rosary. Trooper Zoyland called it "a string o' beads." The figure crossed the Long Gallery and descended the stairs, but — and Trooper Zoyland was quite emphatic about this — it had appeared to walk through the air about a foot above the treads. Reaching the bottom, the figure disappeared into the wall opposite the staircase.

The apparition was so entirely outside his comprehension that he was bereft of self-control. He felt he must report this extraordinary happening to someone immediately and had rushed blindly into the adjutant's room. Once arrived there, his confusion of mind was such that he could give no coherent account of what he had seen. Clearly he had undergone a quite traumatic experience but he had certainly not been drunk.

I left the Detention Room and went to see the adjutant who was with Colonel Matson. When I told them of my talk with Zoyland, they agreed that the charge of drunkenness should be dropped and that the Medical Officer should be called in. The doctor saw Zoyland later that day, found him to be in a highly disturbed mental state and recommended that he be sent on a week's sick leave. Trooper Zoyland was given a rail pass and left for his home in Somerset that evening.

The ghost became something of a regimental joke and in the next few weeks a crop of alleged ghost sightings sprang up among sentries hoping for a spot of sick leave — but they all failed to convince the adjutant.

Some weeks later Colonel Matson had occasion to visit the agents in Nottingham who acted on behalf of the owner of Rufford Abbey.

"I mentioned Trooper Zoyland's ghost to the agent chap," said the Colonel as he stood in front of the fire in the mess that evening. "He was most intrigued and made me tell him the whole story. As you know, I was pretty skeptical at the time and not at all sure that Zoyland wasn't putting on an act. But after what I learned this afternoon I am convinced that he really did see something — quite apart from the fact that it is hard to believe he possesses sufficient imagination to think up such a story."

"And what did the agent say to make you change your mind?" asked the adjutant, who was equally convinced that Trooper Zoyland had invented the whole cock-and-bull story to relieve the boredom of guard duty.

"Three things, really," replied the Colonel. "First, you remember that Zoyland said he suddenly felt cold? It seems that a drop in ambient temperature is a common phenomenon just before a supernatural event. Zoyland would not have known that. Second, the agent told me that behind the panelling in the Long Gallery opposite the staircase is an old doorway, and at the foot of the staircase you can still make out the walled-up doorway leading into what was once the chapel. Zoyland would not have known that either. And third — and this is what clinched it for me — I learned that in 1682 a disastrous fire destroyed the great staircase and much of the Great Hall. It was rebuilt the following year and a new staircase was put it. But for some technical architectural reason, the new staircase was some 14 inches lower than the original one, Zoyland's monk, walking down the stairs about a foot above the treads, was in fact walking down the original staircase!"

A GHOST ATTENDED THE WEDDING

It was a red-letter day when my wife's niece was married — a day that banished any doubts I might have had about an afterlife.

George Frampton

I married a woman from a wealthy family who lived in a very large house called Shepherds in Bushey Heath in Hertfordshire. On 24 June, 1978, my wife's niece Clare was to be married. It was to be a big affair and the reception was to be held in the extensive grounds of Shepherds.

At that time my wife's mother Ethyl Arnot, a widow who has since died, lived in the great house with just my wife Audrey's youngest sister. There was a second sister, Beryl, between them in age, and it was her daughter who was getting married.

The run up to the wedding was an exciting time for the women. There were to be nearly 200 guests and my mother-in-law had hired outside caterers. One person who was looking forward to the wedding with great enthusiasm was Lillian Leslie, my mother-in-law's lifelong friend. Lillian, also a widow, stayed so often at Shepherds that over the years I got to know her very well. In fact, I grew quite fond of her.

In many ways Lillian was an unusual woman. She played the saxophone and she organized a small band of persons as old as she was and together they played at old people's homes — for free, of course. In addition, Lillian was a confirmed Spiritualist. Every Sunday she went to London, to Belgrave Square, which is the British headquarters of the Spiritualist movement. We often discussed the subject and once, at her insistence, I went with her to Belgrave Square. I was not impressed.

As the wedding day drew near, my mother-in-law and Lillian took themselves to London to buy new dresses for the ceremony. My wife and I were at Shepherds in the evening of that day so we watched while each lady put on her new dress for us to admire.

One week before the wedding, Lillian had a completely unexpected heart attack while staying at Shepherds and was dead when the ambulance arrived.

We were all greatly distressed, especially my mother-in-law. But of course the wedding went ahead.

As I sat in the church during the wedding ceremony, I thought of poor Lillian who had been so looking forward to the wedding. It seemed such a cruel stroke of fate that had denied her the pleasure of being there.

After the church ceremony a fleet of cars took us all back to Shepherds. A huge marquee had been erected during the days preceding the ceremony but since it was a glorious day with a bright sun shining, the caterers had placed dozens of small tables and chairs on the lawns.

I was seated at one of the tables with my wife and two daughters. The toasts were drunk and the speeches made, and when that was all over, our niece Clare and her new husband started to circulate among the guests.

I left the table and went back to the house. When I entered the bathroom, I saw — standing by the wash basin, wearing the dress she had bought for the wedding — Lillian.

I wasn't afraid, only shocked and unable to speak. She smiled at me.

"I just had to come, George," she said. "I couldn't miss it, could I?"

I cannot swear that the words were said out loud. I think perhaps they were conveyed into my mind.

I still stood speechless and as I stared at her, she faded and was gone. I leaned against the door and found my brow was wet with sweat.

When I went downstairs and back to the table, my wife and daughters remarked at once that I looked unwell.

"I've just been talking to Lillian!" I blurted out.

Of course it was hopeless. They didn't believe me and put it down to either the sun or drink. But I had had only one glass of champagne and I had not been in the sun because I prefer the shade.

Any doubts I might have had about an afterlife vanished the moment I saw Lillian.

LIGHT IN THE NIGHT
Brenda E. Payne

In May 1944 I was stationed at a Royal Air Force camp in Northwood in Middlesex. I was a Women's Auxiliary Air Force teleprinter operator and worked in a signal section which was manned 24 hours a day. My station, for safety and security reasons, was three flights of stairs beneath ground level.

During night watches, at 3:00 am the activity on the teleprinters would get very slow and we were permitted to go to another room to rest for two hours, leaving half the staff to take care of the machines.

The resting room was small and three walls were lined with three-tier bunks. Because it was below ground, the room had no natural light.

One night I lay for the longest time but sleep would not come. Everyone else was sleeping. I could hear the sounds of even breathing against the silence and darkness of the room.

Resigning myself to insomnia, I opened my eyes and stared into the darkness. I was not prepared for what I saw.

Over in the corner of the room was a white filmy "light" which became larger and brighter as I watched, moving along to one particular bunk bed. I stared in disbelief and pinched myself to make sure I was awake.

This continued for quite a few minutes. Then the door burst open and we were called back to duty. I rose from my bunk and looked to see which woman had occupied the one I had seen "visited." It was Margaret Sisson. I decided not to tell her; I did not wish to frighten her.

One evening soon afterwards I saw Margaret in tears. Her fiance, an RAF pilot, was missing and presumed killed. It happened on the night I saw the filmy visitor go to her bunk.

CURED BY A MIRACLE

A papal inquiry confirms the incredible: a 17th-century martyr saved a 20th-century man from certain death.

Trevor Holloway

Night after night Mary Fagan sat at her husband John's bedside, occasionally repeating a prayer specially written for her by their parish priest Father Thomas Reilly. John Fagan, a Glasgow dockworker, had cancer and for many weeks past the congregation of the Catholic Church of the Blessed John Ogilvie had also been praying that the Scottish martyr would intercede to bring about a miraculous cure.

For two years doctors had striven to arrest the cancerous growth which was now spreading from John Fagan's stomach to his colon. In December 1966 they said that nothing more could be done except to relieve his pain. The weeks dragged on and early in March 1967 his own doctor Dr. Macdonald predicted that the end was near.

For seven weeks John had taken no food and only for brief periods did he emerge from a comatose state. Father Reilly administered the last rites and Mary pinned a medal of the Blessed John Ogilvie to John's pyjamas.

Through the long hours of Sunday night, 5 March, 1967, Mary maintained a ceaseless vigil. It was about 6 am on Monday when she realized that her husband appeared not to be breathing and she could detect no pulse or heartbeat. There was no doubt in her mind that the long battle was over. Then, suddenly, to her utter astonishment, John whispered her name and said, "I'm hungry."

Dr. Macdonald was hurriedly summoned and when he saw that John Fagan was alive and eating a soft-boiled egg with no apparent difficulty, he was visibly shaken. He admitted to Mrs. Fagan, "I am not of your religion but if you told me right now that your husband had been to Lourdes, I would say that this was definitely a miracle."

Oddly enough, in all her excitement and bewilderment, only then did Mary Fagan realize that a miracle had in fact taken place.

From that moment John Fagan went on to make a full recovery and to enjoy years of excellent health. Frequent and systematic X-ray and fluoroscopic examinations over the years found no trace of cancer or signs of recurrence.

No one doubts that the Blessed John Ogilvie interceded in John's behalf.

Blessed John was born in Banffshire, Scotland, in 1579. At first he was a Calvinist but later showed increasing interest in the Roman Catholic Church. After serving as a novice in the Society of Jesus (the Jesuits) he was ordained a priest in Paris in 1610.

His burning desire was to return to his homeland as a missionary. He knew he would be risking his life, for the Catholic faith was banned in Scotland. He took the risk unflinchingly but his career was brief. He was betrayed in Glasgow, kept in captivity and brutally tortured but he never divulged the names of Catholics he knew in Scotland.

Eventually he was sentenced to death and hanged on 10 March, 1615, for refusing to recognize the supremacy of King James I over the Pope in spiritual matters.

Three hundred years later, after close study of his life and writings, Blessed John was beatified in 1929 by Pope Pius XI.

The Roman Catholic Church does not take miracle claims lightly. Investigation into the authenticity of the John Fagan miracle lasted nine years. A panel of top-ranking medical men was set up to disprove the miracle. Every scrap of evidence was examined and the views of numerous consultants were considered. The final verdict was clear: the cure could not have occurred naturally.

Pope Paul VI had taken a personal interest in the investigations and in the canonization cause of the Blessed John Ogilvie. He had no doubts about the Scottish martyr's role in effecting the miracle cure. So it came about that the Blessed John Ogilvie was declared a saint in St. Peter's in Rome on Sunday, 17 October, 1976.

A PLEASANT HOME FOR GHOSTS
One cannot call Springhill a haunted house because that term misinterprets the welcoming atmosphere of its sunlit rooms.

Sheila St. Clair

Near the small village of Moneymore, County Londonderry, Northern Ireland, stands a friendly, welcoming house. At the risk of sounding sentimental, I must confess to having fallen hopelessly in love with this 17th-Century family home over 20 years ago, when I first laid eyes on it. It stands amid quiet green acres and one breathes air that is heavy with the scent of honeysuckle and old roses and feels a sense of home and history lovingly interwined.

The National Trust has taken Springhill, Moneymore, into protective custody. The house and grounds have been sympathetically restored to their former glory — and it is still a home, housing the custodian appointed by the Trust. Over the past 20 years hundreds of visitors have climbed the broad flight of stone steps up to the great front door and, having entered, stepped back in time to a more gracious and leisurely age.

Originally the home of the Conynghams who came from Scotland in the reign King James VI, the house has experienced all the turmoil and strife of troubled Ireland and has emerged a little scarred here and there, to act as a perpetual reminder of the men and women who built the province of Ulster. The family later to be the Lenox-Conynghams lived in the house until 1957, when it passed into the care of the Trust.

It is an attractive white-walled house, with spreading wings over which large copper beeches stand sentinel. Close to the house are the signs of the self-sufficiency of other days, laundry, slaughterhouse and great barn. In the walled garden beyond are the famous McCartney roses named after Lord McCartney, envoy to the Imperial Court in Peking in the 18th century, and from the herb garden drift the scents of lavender and rosemary.

The interior of the house bears the stamp of family occupation over centuries: well-thumbed books in this library, a nursery full of toys, Victorian sofas and family photographs. It is precisely because it is a family house that the tapestry of the life woven within it has its light and dark patternings. One cannot call Springhill a "haunted house" because that would be to misinterpret the atmosphere of those sunlit rooms and quiet gardens, but there are those who still inhabit this house and whose unseen presence will touch you lightly on the shoulder as you linger on the staircase or turn away from a bedroom window.

Although Springhill has been a family home for over 300 years, it was not until 1832 that there were any records of hauntings within the house. The event on which most of the manifestations seem to pivot was the death in 1816 of George Lenox-Conyngham who shot himself in the Blue Bedroom. His wife Olivia's austere comment, written in the family Bible, may give some indication of the deep shock and bewilderment that this tragedy evoked:

George Lenox-Conyngham being in a melancholy state of mind for many months prior, put an end to his existence with a pistol shot. He lingered from the 20 November 1816 to the 22nd, and died, thanks to the Almighty God, a truly penitent Christian. He was in the 64th year of his age. ...

Olivia followed her husband to the grave 16 years later in 1832 and the first known paranormal events date from that time. The Hon. Andrew Stuart, the unhappy George's son-in-law, slept in the Blue Bedroom after the suicide and often found that during the night his clothes and belongings had transported themselves from one chair to another — an occurrence that did nothing for that gentleman's peace of mind!

Later, in the 1880's, a visitor to the house, a Miss Wilson, also had an unnerving experience. She had been chatting with Millie, the elder daughter of the house, in the Cedar Room, a room halfway up the main staircase and below the gallery that led to the Blue Bedroom. When it got late, the two girls separated to go to their own rooms. Millie went to her room on the upper floor, while Miss Wilson prepared to retire in the Cedar Room. As she was about to get in to bed, she realized Millie had left her diary on a chair and she decided to return it to her.

The stairs by now were lit by a brilliant moon and in the light of that moon streaming in through the landing window, Miss Wilson saw the apparition of a woman on the upper landing. The woman appeared distressed, throwing her hands up into the air and hurrying to the door of the Blue Bedroom, where to Miss Wilson's consternation she simply vanished.

This apparition has been seen on several occasions in the gallery, once it is said after the house was taken over by the National Trust. Some generations later she was seen by two small boys of the house as they lay in bed in the Blue Bedroom. They didn't seem especially concerned as they told their nurse of "the lady who stands by the fireplace" and with whom they seemed to be on conversational terms.

An even more curious manifestation took place in the Blue Bedroom in the last decade of the 19th century. A Miss Hamilton who was visiting Springhill was given the Blue Room for her guest chamber. One morning she arrived for breakfast looking decidedly pale and wan. When her hostess Charlotte Lenox-Conyngham asked what was wrong, she gave the following explanation:

"I had gone to bed in the Great Four Poster and the fire had died down and I had begun to be drowsy, when it suddenly seemed that the room was full of excited people — servants I thought — who were pushing and wrangling in whispers. I felt overcome by fear, but just then I heard a clicking sound behind me, as though a door had been opened, and then a light shone at my back, and someone seemed to come through this light and stilled the commotion, so that all fear left me, and after a while I fell asleep. ..."

Miss Hamilton had referred to a door where there was none, at the back of the bed, but her hostess looked thoughtful. "But there is a door," she said. "It is hidden by the tester of the bed and it has been papered over for quite a long time."

This door in fact was opened during the occupation of the house's last owner who found inside a small powder closet, with a bricked-up fireplace, a pair of gloves and a small bag of bullets. Could the "great commotion" have been the inevitable outcry that may have followed the shot that eventually killed George Lenox-Conyngham?

Another occasional occupant of the Blue Bedroom is a "man in a black cloak". It is interesting to note that while the female apparition arouses no dread, the children who had seen the man in black did not care for him in the slightest.

Most people believe that the female apparition is that of Olivia Lenox-Conyngham. According to reports, she haunts the nursery and her apparition has been seen too at the foot of the main stairs on one occasion. One wonders why it is the wife and not the suicide victim himself who haunts the Blue Bedroom. Recently I was given a possible explanation.

A medical friend of the present custodian, a man interested in the paranormal, suggested that when such a tragic event as suicide takes place, many people close to the victim may harbour guilty feelings about their own "sins of omission". So perhaps because of these regrets about "what might have been", those people are far more likely to haunt the scene of the tragedy than the victim himself.

But the lady who haunts the nursery is more caring than guilt-ridden. In the early 1900's, during the residence of Col. William Arbuthnot Lenox-Conyngham and his family, the children's nurse told this story. She said that she had seen — so she thought — the mistress of the house, Mrs. Conyngham, come into the nursery in the early dawn and stand at each of the children's beds. When the nurse turned up the lamp to speak to Mrs. Conyngham, however, the figure hurried away. The same event was repeated some weeks later. In fact, as Mrs. Conyngham knew well, it was not she who bent so watchfully over the sleeping children. It is known that the same Olivia who had witnessed her husband's suicide had also nursed all her children through the dreaded smallpox. Perhaps it was her spirit that came to watch over those great-great grandchildren.

I have my own story of Springhill. One afternoon as I was standing in the Cedar Room, a room that now houses the children's toys from long ago, I heard a woman's footsteps on the stairs outside. They stopped at the door of the room. Then the door swung softly back and as I watched, the heavy oak cradle at the window began to rock.

Sometime previous to this, a workman repairing the roof heard footsteps on the stairs of what he understood was an empty house. Others too have their own stories to tell of Springhill.

As for me, I prefer to think of this lovely and gracious house as a home that likes to be visited. As one wanders through the sunlit rooms, one can be forgiven for imagining that one hears the distant laughter of children at play or the sound of women going about their household tasks — and that memory, for a moment, holds the door to the past ajar.

THE PHANTOM WITNESS

The murderers thought that by killing the young woman they would ensure her silence. They were wrong.

The village miller James Grahame was working late. It was well past midnight when he was startled to glimpse a flicker of movement in the gloom of the ground floor of his mill. Having barred the door of the building earlier in the evening, Grahame decided to continue working for a few minutes and pretend he didn't know he had company. When he stopped work and calmly descended the ladder to the ground floor, he was tensed to tackle the intruder.

He was greatly relieved, however, when he saw a woman standing motionless in the shadows. He stepped forward to ask what she wanted. As his flickering candle revealed the stranger's appearance, he got the first shock in what was to be the most terrifying night of his life.

His visitor was a teenage girl in a filthy torn dress, her long hair matted with blood sluggishly dribbling from the ugly wounds in her head. Her unblinking gaze seemed to go right through him.

The miller's first reaction was to attend to her injuries, but the comforting words died on his lips and the proffered arm of assistance dropped to his side when he took another look at her ashen face. He felt the chill of horror as he realized his visitor was beyond earthly help or hope. She was a ghost.

Grahame remembered the shock of that realization to his dying day. He would also often wonder why the murdered girl had chosen him to be her instrument of vengeance.

The ghost began to speak and Grahame stood immobilized by shock and fear as she related in a quiet monotone the tragic story of her betrayal and brutal killing.

A pretty teenager, Anne Walker had come to Great Lumley to keep house for her recently widowed stepuncle whom she scarcely knew. Her Uncle Christopher quickly appreciated that his niece's good looks and shapely figure would be wasted on domestic chores. He soon made the susceptible girl his mistress.

Walker was rich and respected, an important man in the

small, close-knit community, and the village gossips were not long in sensing that his regard for Anne far exceeded that of an affectionate uncle. Rumours circulated but Walker, confident that his lover would not betray him, ignored the gossip.

He was forced to reconsider his position when Anne told him she was pregnant. He immediately packed her off to a mutual relative, an elderly widow in a nearby town, Chester-le-Street, and planned to leave her there until he decided what was to be done.

The widowed relative was not entirely persuaded by Christopher's claim that Anne's condition had resulted from an affair with a young lover. She got Walker to confess that he was the father of his niece's child, which so outraged the matron that at first she refused to house Anne, but Walker's money soon overcame her scruples.

When Walker returned home, he had time to consider what the consequences would be if his seduction of his niece became common knowledge. The wealthy man, whose actions till now had never been questioned, had been shaken by his relative's vehement reaction. He knew this was a foretaste of how a scandal could affect his reputation. Away from his lover, Walker coldly analysed his predicament.

Chester-le-Street was too close to Great Lumley for Anne to stay there when her pregnancy became obvious, so she wasn't surprised when after only a week there Walker arrived unexpectedly with a friend. He told Anne he had arrange lodgings for her in Lancashire, where she could spend her pregnancy and confinement. When the baby was born, Anne could have it fostered and then return to Great Lumley. Walker introduced his friend, Mark Sharp, a pitman who was returning home to Lancashire and who would accompany Anne on her journey.

Because Anne's landlady, fearful of scandal, was glad to be rid of her, she didn't question Anne's quick departure. Christopher Walker accompanied Sharp and his niece to the edge of Lumley Moor, a desolate tract of land which lay on the route to Lancashire.

Anne bade a loving good-bye to her seducer and unsuspectingly followed her lover's friend onto the lonely moor. What happened next has come down to us in the murder victim's own words:

"Mark Sharp slew me with a pick such as men dig coal withal and gave me these five wounds and after threw me in a coal pit nearby and hid the pick under a bank and his stockings being stained with blood he endeavoured to wash them, but seeing the blood would not forth [come off] he hid them there."

James Grahame, oblivious to his surroundings, could "see" the savage blows which forced the terrified girl to her knees. He felt her anguish as she realized there was no escape.

He was jerked back into the reality of the present when Anne Walker's ghost turned from pitiful victim into an avenging fury. The pretty features assumed a threatening expression and Grahame heard the calm voice demand that he go to the nearest magistrate and accuse Sharp and Walker of killing her. She said that he, Grahame, was the chosen instrument for her revenge and if he disobeyed her, she would haunt him into an early grave. The terrified miller promised to do as she wished.

He spent a sleepless night but with the dawn his courage and common sense returned. He knew he could not accuse the influential Walker on the word of a phantom. The magistrate would think he was drunk or mad. In any case, had he really seen a ghost?

Grahame spent the day talking himself out of any action, finally deciding not to meddle in the affairs of his rich neighbour. But he had not reckoned on the persistence of the baleful spirit of Anne Walker who, as she had promised, pursued him day and night until he broke under the strain and did her bidding.

On 21 December, 1631, James Grahame went to his local magistrate, Thomas Liddell, and recounted the weird story of his encounter with Anne Walker's ghost, concluding with an accusation of murder against Christopher Walker and Mark Sharp.

Liddell and a neighbouring magistrate subjected Grahame to a probing interrogation. Finally, convinced of his sanity and sincerity, they proceeded to investigate his allegations. They sent a search party to the spot on the moor where the murder allegedly had been committed. The party found Anne's body in the pit as well as the murder weapon and Sharp's bloodstained belongings where Grahame said the ghost had told him they would be.

On further inquiry the magistrates learned that Grahame and Anne Walker had never met, so there was no obvious motive for him to murder her. On the other hand, there had been rumours in the village of an illicit relationship between uncle and niece. Witnesses attested that Anne was last seen alive in the company of her uncle and his friend Sharp. The magistrates decided there was sufficient circumstantial evidence to charge the two men and bring them to trial.

The trial, held at Durham Assizes, lasted only one day. The two accused men protested their innocence. Popular opinion predicted that Sharp would be hanged and his wealthy friend acquitted.

But once more Anne's unquiet spirit demanded vengeance. One witness swore he saw Anne standing behind her lover. And rumour had it that she had made a more threatening appearance to the judge, Sir Humphrey Davenport.

The stories of her appearance at the trial so unnerved the jury that the scales of justice were tipped against both of the accused. Judge and jury were convinced that even without conclusive legal evidence the death penalty was justified.

Durham Assizes records were lost in the subsequent chaos of the Civil War but this trial, which aroused great interest when it occurred, was the subject of an investigation by scholars after peace had been restored. The first of these, Joseph Glanvill, was Chaplain in Ordinary to His Majesty and a Fellow of the Royal Society. He unearthed James Grahame's testimony and studied Judge Davenport's correspondence which gave a full account of the trial. He also collected testimony from several trustworthy and disinterested persons who remembered the case, including the Lord of Lumley Castle. Glanvill published the results of his investigation in his 1661 book *Witches and Apparitions*.

In the early 19th century historian Robert Surtrees reexamined the original records of the case and retold the story in Volume II of his *The History & Antiquities of the County Palatine of Durham* (1820).

The story is still remembered in local folklore. It was noted in an 1889 issue of *The Monthly Chronicle of North Country Lore & Legend*. It has even been incorporated into one verse of a local version of the folk lullaby "Rock-a-Bye Baby on the Treetop."

James Grahame apparently had no further contact with the supernatural, nor does Anne Walker's phantom appear to have walked again. But even after $3^{1}/_{2}$ centuries the strange story of their meeting has not been forgotten.

THE POLTERGEIST IN THE PUB

An old drinking establishment plays host to a new ghost and the place hasn't been the same since.

Peter A. Hough

On Easter Sunday, 8 April, 1985, Susan and Donald Flint (a pseudonym), managers of the Bull's Head in Swinton near Manchester, were planning a party. Susan invited her mother Joan and stepfather James Kilroy for the weekend. Another guest was family friend Andrew Cameron, an electronics technician in the Royal Air Force.

That night, gathered around the bar, someone brought up the subject of the pub's resident "ghost." Some of the staff claimed to have experienced strange phenomena in the building. There was much talk about "cold spots" and the sighting of an apparition in the cellar. These stories were received in a light-hearted vein and two men in particular, Kilroy and Cameron, were highly skeptical.

At the height of the discussion someone challenged the two to spend the night in the cellar. They quickly agreed. Later, when the pub was closed and quiet, they carried sleeping bags down the stone steps into the ancient cellar. They settled down on the floor opposite an alcove. Satisfied everything was in order, Susan and Donald switched off all the lights and retired upstairs to bed.

The men, still treating the affair as a joke, chatted amicably for a while, then dozed off. Not long afterwards James was awakened by the sound of Andrew's shouting. There, framed by the alcove opposite them, were several orange and red lights. They hung like a row of vertical three-foot fluorescent tubes, the light dancing, flickering. Andrew thought they resembled a row of lighted prison bars. Suddenly there was a flash like lightning and the lights were gone.

Andrew jumped to his feet screaming. In the adjacent room the sound of beer barrels rolling about, knocking into one another, could be heard. Andrew stood petrified, hearing a rapid "swishing," like someone's maniacally using a broom, all around him.

James Kilroy decided to dash for the cellar steps. Just as he was about to move, a hand gripped his left shoulder and a voice harshly whispered in his ear, "James."

The swishing stopped and Andrew felt something thrust into his hands just before the lights went on. Alerted by the bedlam, the Flints rushed down into the cellar. What they saw struck them dumb with amazement.

Andrew Cameron was crouched in a defensive position gripping the long handle of a broom like a rifle, a look of terror on his face. James Kilroy lay at the foot of the steps, blood rushing from his head and staining the cold stone floor.

James was rushed to nearby Hope Hospital where he received eight stitches for a nasty gash over his right eye. Once calmed down, he related what happened. In the darkness, he said, he got disoriented and panicked. Then he tripped over something and hit his head against a barrel.

I first heard of the case from writer Jenny Randles whose mother knows Joan Kilroy, Susan's mother. Jenny attempted without success to interview Mr. Kilroy.

"He was full of life, always telling jokes, but this experience has changed him," Joan told Randles. "All he wants to do is put it behind him, forget about it."

James was the only witness who refused to have anything to do with the subsequent investigation. Even nine months after the event, he was uncommunicative. In a letter dated 23 January, 1986, I asked him to suggest a date when we could talk or, if he preferred, to send me a written account. I heard nothing even when I informed him the case was to be published.

The Bull's Head is a building steeped in history. It was established during the 16th century but rebuilt in 1826. Opposite, across Chorley Road, stood a small chapel. But in 1869 the much grander St. Peter's Church was built. The pub is on the corner of Station Road, originally known as Burying Lane — aptly named because it led directly to the graveyard in front of the church. Down the centuries the Bull's Head has played quite a role in Swinton society, apart from providing food and ale.

To the rear was once a field where cockfighting and bull- and bear-baiting were practised. In the 19th century members of the "watchers' club" kept vigil from the pub over the graveyard against body snatchers and resurrectionists. At this time it was also a coach house, being the first stage on the Manchester-to-Lancaster route. It also served as one of the stopping points for the embryonic postal service.

In the cellar of the Bull's Head is a bricked-up archway on the south-west wall. I wondered if this was a tunnel which once led to the church or chapel. A search through old local history books in the Swinton Public Library uncovered no mention of a tunnel, however. Perhaps it is merely a blocked-off entrance to another room which had to be closed when sewers and gas pipes were laid in the road outside. I found no evidence that the public house had a historic reputation for being "haunted."

Wondering about this last point, I wrote local historian Neil Richardson, who replied, "Funnily enough I didn't come across any mention of ghosts in the course of my research, which is unusual for pubs the age of the Bull's Head."

On 20 May, 1986, Randles, I and — independently — John Fulton of the Manchester Association of Parapsychology met with Jim Wilks, then retail area manager of Tetley Walker Limited, the brewery that owns the Bull's Head. Wilks agreed to cooperate with our inquiries.

In January 1987 I was invited to appear on BBC Radio Manchester to talk generally about the paranormal. During the programme, by way of illustrating a point, I mentioned the incident in the cellar. The host, Mike Shaft, asked, "Couldn't this have been just two guys — you know — they'd been drinking, gone down to the cellar for a joke, [and] one of them decided to frighten the other; then things got out of control?"

It is a fair question. Oddly enough, the idea of a prank had been mentioned to me during the interviews I conducted with the principals. Andrew Cameron thought at first that the pub manager, Donald Flint, was the hoaxer, but Susan Flint testified he had been upstairs with her the whole time. If the two men in the cellar were having a joke at everyone else's expense, then why invent the atypical manifestation of the "bars of light"? It would have been more logical to have made up the sighting of an apparition.

A prank that went wrong? If so, then one would expect Andrew Cameron to shoulder a certain amount of guilt. James Kilroy might have been very lucky to get away with just a concussion and a head wound. But during my interview with him Cameron was relaxed and did not mind discussing the events, although like Susan's stepfather he had no desire to visit the cellar again, even in daylight.

As I told Radio Manchester listeners, the major problem with the prank hypothesis was that the incidents of Easter Sunday 1985 were not the only ones. There were other alleged happenings before and since that night.

The Flints and their two boys, ages five and six, moved into the Bull's Head during January 1985. Just a month later the first inexplicable phenomenon occurred.

The accounts office is safely situated in a room off the cellar. A small brick and stone affair, it has just one entrance and exit. After closing time on a Saturday evening it is deathly quiet down there. Susan was alone, facing the doorway as she checked some figures, when a scraping noise behind her abruptly interrupted her concentration.

When she turned around, she was astonished to see a small stool moving across the stone floor of its own volition. It moved several times a foot to the left, then back again foot to the right. It looked as if someone were pushing it, only there was no one there.

She dashed upstairs to tell her husband. Susan tried to convince herself it was caused by vibration from the road, but at that late hour traffic was light and it would have been unusual for heavy trucks to be passing by. During my own visits to the cellar, at peak rush-hour times, I detected no vibration at all, let alone enough to make a stool move along a solid stone floor.

After this first incident the couple heard from several staff members and customers that others had also experienced strange things.

All was quiet until the dramatic Easter episode. Then in August the Bull's Head held a fancy dress competition to raise money for charity. It was a successful evening.

At 12:30 am employers and employees were cleaning up the place. On the wall behind the bar hung a large white clock. Some of the money raised during the evening was piled under it. When one of the staff went around to pick it up, the clock "jumped" off its nail and smashed to pieces on the floor. Three other persons witnessed this curious event; one was Susan Flint. All were certain the clock jumped rather than fell off the wall. The nail securing the clock was still firmly embedded in the plaster.

The Flints' young sons were allowed to play in the pub after school between 4 and 5:30 pm, when the bar was closed. Not long after the fancy-dress evening, they were playing downstairs when the younger boy ran up to the flat. Susan recalled:

"The little one came running upstairs, saying, 'There's a man in the pub, Mum.' I said, 'Don't be silly; the pub's closed.' But he was insistent and I followed him downstairs where his brother was waiting. There was no one there by now but the boys were certain a man wearing a blue jumper had been sitting in a corner."

Susan also remembers just as graphically one evening when they were preparing to go to bed. The pub was locked, all the alarms were set and the couple started to go upstairs. The landing lights were always left on in case either of the boys awoke during the night and wanted to visit the bathroom. Yet as Susan and Donald made their way along the corridor, one by one the bulbs went out.

In the darkness they fumbled for the bedroom light switch but nothing happened. There was no rational explanation. If a fuse had blown, the lights would have gone out all together, not individually as if someone were turning them off. Too frightened to investigate, the couple locked the bedroom door and listened.

They could hear footsteps — clear indications that someone, or something, was moving about. But the footsteps sounded as if they were on stone instead of wooden floorboards.

In the morning every light in the building was on — including those in the pub downstairs.

Just a few weeks before the Flints were due to move to another public house, in December 1985, the final incident occurred.

It happened after their dog bit through some telephone wires on the flat roof outside and had to be destroyed. A British Telecom engineer arrived to repair the damage during the afternoon when the pub was closed. After completing his work, he asked to use the phone in the flat to call his office.

Susan and Donald thought he had a crossed line when he said, "Can you put the phone down please? I want to ring out."

He replaced the receiver, then tried again. "Will you put the phone down, please?" he asked once more.

Donald asked to whom he was speaking.

"There's someone downstairs talking on your extension," the repairman said.

Donald insisted that wasn't possible. They were the only persons in the building.

"Donald and I ran downstairs and found the phone off the hook," Susan told me. "There was no one there. The phone worked perfectly after that."

This is a perplexing case. The manifestations are what we would loosely term "poltergeist." Yet proponents of the single-witness-centred spontaneous psychokinesis hypothesis would have to think again on this one. There are reported events both before and since the Flints left the Bull's Head. Still, as I have pointed out, the pub has no historical reputation linking it to ghosts and poltergeists. It's possible, I suppose, that until the last few years paranormal events occurred with insufficient frequency to earn that sort of reputation. Perhaps only recently something triggered off the "hauntings."

I have spoken twice, in November 1986 and March 1987, with the new manager of the Bull's Head. Mrs. Hattersly, a no-nonsense woman, is no great believer in ghosts, but she did tell me of a worker who, while changing a barrel in the cellar, saw a hooded figure. Unfortunately, although I have approached him, the individual is reluctant to discuss the matter with me. Mrs. Hattersly told me she has a fierce 200-pound, five year-old German Rottweiler named Hassa who will not go down into the cellar on any account.

Meanwhile the stories continued. As I was writing this, I learned that a female member of Mrs. Hattersly's staff had a frightening experience. It happened at 2 am when the girl was at the bottom of the stairs leading from the pub to the living quarters above. She was about to ascend the stairs when she saw something gliding down them. It had the vague shape and outline of a monk. As it drew nearer, her consciousness faded and she has no memory of what happened next.

As is often the case with hauntings, the evidence in the Bull's Head affair is almost entirely anecdotal. It is enough to suggest, however, that something decidedly unusually going on at that venerable pub.

THREE MEDIEVALISTS

G.S. Vestal

In 1979 I was studying, earning a Master's degree in medieval history, at the University of St. Andrews, Scotland, in the beautiful quiet little town of that name. On a warm autumn evening I had gone to dinner at a friend's house. After a relaxed and pleasant time, I left about 11:30 to walk home.

The university playing fields lay between her house and mine, It was such a lovely night, with the moon shining and a mild breeze blowing through the tall pine trees which surrounded the fields, that I wanted to stay out a little longer to enjoy it. I strolled through the trees but stopped short when I saw people on the other side of the soccer pitch. At first I thought it must be students walking home after the pubs had closed at 11. I stood quietly among the trees. As they started to cross the field I noticed that they wore what looked like long coats and I jumped to the conclusion that they were the local police. It seemed too absurd to have to explain to them why I was in the playing fields in the middle of the night, so I continued to hide and watch.

By now I could tell that there were three figures. One of them carried a small light which I thought was a cigarette. By the time they had crossed halfway I was able to see them clearly. The sight was a shock to me; it was obvious that the long garments were monks' habits which they wore with the cowls over their heads. The one in the lead carried the strange small light and the two behind were supporting each other, as if one were hurt. The most shocking aspect, however, was that they were moving quite swiftly, yet their legs stepped slowly, as if in slow motion. It also was quite apparent that they were walking about three feet off the ground.

Time seemed to stop. There was no wind. The monks cast no shadows; yet they were as solid as the goalposts. I was frozen with disbelief. As they drew nearer I began to feel real panic. Suddenly, when they were about 10 feet away, they disappeared. I looked desperately for them, not believing what I had seen but knowing that I had seen it. I squatted down to look between the tree trunks but there was nothing. The wind suddenly picked up with a new force. Panic overwhelmed me and I ran for home.

Needless to say, I was curious to know what I had seen and why. I discovered there had been a medieval monastery in the direction from which the ghostly monks had come but, then, the town had many monasteries in its time. I guessed that the fields had been lowered and levelled for games since these three monks had lived.

St. Andrews boasts many ghosts, in many guises. I never expected to see any and I certainly did not know what my reaction would be if I did. Turning tail and running was not what I expected of myself but I am not embarrassed about it. It is one thing to talk about ghosts and another to confront them.

"WE'LL MEET AGAIN"
Maria Dembicki

I knew my brother was only pretending to be dead — until the night he came to tell me otherwise

My younger brother, Sgt. Pilot Theodore Narishkin, who was in the Royal Air Force, came home on special leave on or around 1 March, 1943, because he had volunteered to go on a secret and very dangerous assignment. He did not tell either my mother or father the real reason for the short leave but he told me, making me promise that I would not disclose his secret.

He had just completed his operational flying training as a fighter pilot and was now attached to a Hawker Hurricane Squadron. Ted informed me that the family would receive an official telegram from King George VI "regretting the death of Sgt. Theodore Narishkin." My brother told me this secret because he knew it would be perfectly safe with me. After all, I was working at the Ministry of Aircraft Production, in an office at one of the colleges of Oxford University, and I dealt with highly classified information every day.

On the last evening of his leave Ted took me out to dinner and a movie to celebrate my 23rd birthday. As we walked the four miles home from Oxford to Headington where we lived, he kept singing a popular song, "We'll Meet Again," over and over again. It went, "We'll meet again / Don't know where, don't know when / But I know we'll meet again some sunny day. ..." He stressed that I should never forget the song or its meaning. He seemed to be promising me that, no matter what, he would return and we would meet again and hinting that the contents of the telegram were not to be believed.

On 7 March, just as Ted had predicted, the dreaded telegram arrived. It said he had died in an accident during a routine practice hedgehopping flight just a few miles from our home.

My father Vadim Narishkin, a captain in the Intelligence Corp stationed at Bushey Park just outside London, was given compassionate leave to identify and bury his son's body. The body that was presented to my father as Ted's was so badly mutilated, with the head and face totally smashed, that it could not really be identified.

But in this grief my father agreed that it was his son. I was not allowed to accompany my father, perhaps because the authorities feared I might dispute the identification, although I don't know that for sure.

The plain sealed pine coffin was delivered to the small Russian Orthodox church that my mother had founded several years earlier in another Oxford suburb, Cowley, some five miles from Headington. There were specific instructions that came with the coffin: the lid was not to be opened under any circumstances, not even for religious purposes. That upset my mother because she wanted to place a small icon inside the coffin, a custom in the Russian Orthodox Church.

She was upset even more, however, that some of Ted's most prized obsessions were not returned. These included his gold and blue enamel crucifix which he wore around his neck, Great-Grandfather Prince Golitzine's silver monogramed pocket watch and Ted's U.S. Army Air Corps silver wings which he had received upon graduation from flying training in the United States. Eventually, after considerable prompting by my mother, these items and a few others were returned, appropriately "damaged." The watch crystal was broken and the outer monogrammed lid appeared to have been tapped with a hammer to make it look as if it had been damaged in the "accident." Ted's fountain pen was snapped in half.

I knew the reason why we did not receive his personal effects at that time but I could not tell anybody. I knew that Ted was alive somewhere but painfully I kept silent. But I did drop some hints to my father, thinking he would understand about the put-up job, but he insisted that he would know his own son's body even if the head and face were totally smashed. He insisted that there was no mistake.

Three young officers from my brother's squadron were sent as official pallbearers. I sensed from their strained behaviour that they were having a difficult time pretending to grieve as they buried a strange corpse while they knew Ted was alive and awaiting orders to fly off somewhere.

During the most solemn part of the requiem mass, over the loud choral singing, I heard the sound of light planes flying fast and low over the church. I knew that Ted was one of the pilots. I dashed outside in time to see the three Hawker Hurricanes disappear from my view. My heart sank because I thought I had missed seeing him. I was just about to step back inside the church when I heard the planes returning. I jumped back into the centre of the little courtyard and frantically waved my arms above my head.

He saw me! I know that he saw me. I could almost see his mischievous grin and his "thumbs-up" sign, followed by his one-finger salute, as he flew over me so low, barely missing the church roof, the slipstream from the propeller blowing my coat and almost taking my hat, which I gripped with both hands. Then he waggled his wings while banking and rising to show me that he saw me.

"That's him!" I cried. But nobody heard me. Everybody else was inside the church.

Then once again the three Hurricanes flew over in arrowhead formation, at a dignified height this time, and all three dipped their wings in turn to salute me, then flew away.

I went back inside the church smiling radiantly and whispered, "That was him. I know it was!"

Somebody standing close to me said, "Poor child, you do have a wild imagination — or is it from grief?"

After the funeral service the procession slowly moved from the little church in Cowley to the ancient cemetery in Old Headington, several miles away.

We all filed past the lowered coffin, each dropping a handful of soil and a flower onto it. At the precise moment that I was about to drop my flower and soil, the same three Hurricanes again appeared out from nowhere and circled high above the cemetery. Each dipped a wing in respect over the grave, then turned and flew off to the south.

Back at home I was passing little cress sandwiches and cups of tea to all the kind people who had come to pay their respects. The three RAF officers stood in a little group by themselves, in the bay window of the sitting room, having a jolly good laugh about something. I caught my mother's eye and knew their exuberance was upsetting her. I told them that I knew about their private little joke; I knew my brother had flown several times during the funeral. I asked them to please leave if they could not comport themselves in a proper manner. They apologized and promised to tell that I had seen him flying over the church. Then they left.

One evening, shortly after the funeral, I was sorting out negatives and snapshots of my brother when I noticed one of the negatives had a horrible distortion on it. It looked as if my brother had had his face blown off by some explosive. I began to wonder if Ted had actually been alive at the time of his "fake" funeral. And yet I remembered that he had told me not to believe the telegram or the funeral.

A girl friend, Micheline (Mickie Gifford, was spending the night with me and we got to discussing the possibility of ghostly apparitions on photographic film. I showed her the negative in question and she gasped when she saw the same thing I had seen. My mother, who was reading and listening to the our conversation, looked up and said, "Ach, what nonsense you girls ask. Give me the negative. I'm sure it's just a dirty smudge."

When I handed it to her, she tried to wipe away the "smudge" but it would not rub off. She said, "It must be something that happened to the negative while being printed." Then she resumed her reading.

The image of the shattered face remained on that one particular negative for a few months until one night I had a strange and vivid dream.

In the dream my brother was calling me urgently to meet him at once at the top of a hill, beyond a beach, in the bank of a stream.

I rushed out of the house, almost dying. Suddenly I came to rest at an familiar place. I was surrounded in the ghastly sounds, sights and smells of battle. I could hear the whistle of artillery and mortar shells and I could see them explode, spraying sand and bodies or creating water spouts which caused small landing craft filled with soldiers to rise and splash down, leaving disembered bodies floating in blood-stained water and drifting on to blood-soaked sands. The wounded and dying cried out in agony. Burning and decaying bodies lay all over the beach. But where was the peaceful, green, sunlit hill I was supposed to find?

The song lyrics that my brother had etched into my memory, "We'll meet again, don't know where, don't know when," kept running through my mind. They grew louder and louder until they nearly blanked out the sounds of battle on the beach. I was afraid that in my haste I had somehow come to the wrong place. A sudden gust of wind momentarily cleared the smoke and I glimpsed a hill beyond the beach.

I ran as fast as I could toward the hill, leaping over the dead and dying. I reached the plateau and right in front of me was the bank of a stream. But there was nobody there. Panic gripped me. I had rushed through a bloody battle, stopping here and there to check the bodies, not seeing anyone I knew. Perhaps I had tarried too long on the beach and had missed Ted. My heart sank as I sat down under a shade tree to rest and wait.

As I looked around, all I could see across the chasm which separated me from the other bank was a dazzlingly bright, almost blinding light which obscured the summit of the hill. I closed my eyes and tried to listen. But all I could hear was the echo of the song, accompanied by the rippling of the stream. Was I too late? Had he come and gone while I was searching for him on the beach? Perhaps he was not coming at all. Yet why did he summon me so urgently to this place and why was the song still echoing in my mind?

Suddenly I thought I heard a sound. I leaped up, straining my eyes to see all around, away from the dazzling light, from where I thought I heard the sound emanate — but nobody was there. I turned and sadly began descending the hill. There it was again: the sound of painful, heavy breathing and faltering steps. This time they were much closer. I wheeled around and saw Ted across the chasm.

He stopped and turned toward me without a word. I started to run to him, arms outstretched, laughing, crying and shouting all at the same time. Then I stopped dead in my tracks. I could not cross over the chasm. It was as if there were an invisible force field preventing me from moving any farther. I implored him to help me across. He spoke not a word but came to the edge of the bank on his side of the chasm, holding the right side of his face with his right hand. As he turned to face me, he slowly removed his hand from his face so that I could clearly see.

Half his face had been blown off, just as the strange smudge on the negative had shown. As I screamed in horror, he covered his face again with one hand and with the other pointed to the brilliant light at the summit of the hill.

Again, I begged him to take me with him but he just shook his head silently, hesitated an instant, then looked directly into the light. Slowly he turned back to face me, with a radiant smile spreading across his previously tortured face. He then took his hand away and I stared in amazement. There was not a sign of injury, blemish or gaping hole. His head and face were perfectly stored. He stood to attention, gave me his snappiest RAF salute, turned and briskly marched up the hill. But before being swallowed up by the brilliance, he turned once more and waved to me.

Yes, we did meet again, my brother and I, at the precise moment of his death, on a beautiful, sunny hill above the horror on the beaches of northern France. The exact location is still unknown to me.

As soon as I awoke from the strange dream, I took the negative with the "smudge" on it out of this secret drawer in my dressing table and examined it very closely. The marking was gone.

My brother's name, rank and serial number were Sgt. Theodore Narishkin, RAFVR, Serial No. 1318903. He was born 20 July, 1922. The official date of his death was 7 March, 1943. But where Ted was buried and who is in his grave in Old Headington remain a mystery. I gave up writing to the RAF Record Office years ago, because it refused to give me any information in writing, insisting that I come in person. Unfortunately, because I live in America now, that has been impossible for me to do.

THE SPIRIT OF THE GREEN LIFE
Pauline Saltzman

A glimpse of another time leads a writer into a life in two worlds. ...

The untimely death of William Sharp on 14 December, 1905, caused little stir with the general reading public. The Scottish man of letters had never intended his eclectic and intellectual output — poetry, fiction, essays, biography, literary criticism — for the mass market. His works were geared to the intelligentsia.

Paralleling Sharp's distinguished career was the mystical literary output of a reclusive young woman who by-lined her poetic prose with the name Fiona Macleod. No one knew anything about her because that was the way she wanted it. The real mystery lay in why her works held worldwide appeal. Her evocation of the Highlands' druidic past had even generated a Celtic revival.

Public indifference to Sharp's demise at the age of 50 changed dramatically when it was revealed that he and Fiona Macleod were one and the same person!

Until Sharp's death only three persons knew literature's best-kept secret: Sharp himself, his wife Elizabeth and his close friend the Duke of Bronte. The trio knew much more than the fact that "Fiona Macleod" was his by-line. She was the centre of one of the most mind-boggling psychic mysteries of all time. Her mystery and mastery rivalled the later enigma of Patience Worth.

Sharp was born in Paisley in 1885, the eldest son of Galbraith Sharp, co-owner of a prosperous mercantile firm. His mother, the daughter of a British diplomat, was partly of Celtic descent.

The Highland nanny of the Sharp children often took them on trips to her native Western Highlands. On one of these junkets Will, who was then seven, encountered a mysterious lady who would influence his life and shape his literary career.

The supersensitive child had always had an affinity for the untamed terrain of loch, legend and dense forest. Here nature had once been worshipped.

The lady had appeared as if from nowhere. She stood close to him, smiling gently. For the rest of his life he would remember this fragile and dazzling moment.

Will's parents missed him and went to look for him. They found him lying "on a carpet of wild hyacinth". He appeared dazed. When he spoke he asked his parents if they knew who the lady with "hair like buttercups" was. They had seen no one.

About this time Will met his cousin Elizabeth for the first time. The daughter of Galbraith's eldest brother, he was a year younger than he. The clear-eyed lass was fun to be with. She understood him completely when he told her about the strange Highland lady he called Star-Eyes. Elizabeth's sympathy and sensitivity cemented their relationship for all time.

Will had seen Star-Eyes only once but she haunted him. The more he matured, the more she "whispered" to his mind. The time would come when he would share her with the world.

His earliest education had been at home, followed by a term at a private school, where he was lonely and miserable. After several attempts at running away, he stowed away on a ship docked at Grangemouth. After that episode Will absconded with a band of gypsies, an adventure that lasted several weeks. All this happened before he was 12.

The family moved to Glasgow where Will was enrolled as a day student at the Glasgow Academy. Star-Eyes "accompanied" him. In 1871 Will entered the University of Glasgow, where his prodigious talent for literature was first recognized.

Always he thought of himself as a changeling who couldn't possibly belong to his conservative family. In 1874 his disapproving father placed him with a law firm, arguing discipline was what a black sheep needed. With access to libraries and theatre, Will's artistic life blossomed.

The cousins met for the second time when Will was 20. They became secretly engaged but only because the families were bitterly opposed to their marriage.

When Will was threatened with tuberculosis, his family sent him to Australia, hoping he would settle there. The silence of the bush country, together with the brilliant skies and landscapes, appealed to him. Unfortunately he was unsuited for any career available in that part of the world. Will's heart longed for the Highlands and for Elizabeth. Star-Eyes was with him, as always, appealing to his thoughts. She wanted him to return to Scotland and there create poetry about nature's deep mysteries.

His instincts were right but lack of funds kept him from making literature his life's work. He was about to enlist as a mercenary in the Turkish army when fate intervened. Through a friend's influence he obtained a clerkship at the City of Melbourne Bank in London.

Sharp wrote poetry for the *Pall Mall Gazette* and other periodicals. Sir Noel Paton introduced him to Dante Gabriel Rossetti. The pre-Raphaelite poet-painter understood the inner meanings of Will's verse. He encouraged him with advice and constructive criticism.

Sharp realized that he was not meant for the business world. He found a more gratifying post at the gallery of the Fine Arts Society. Star-Eyes never abandoned him. She continued to communicate through his mind and spirit. She inspired him to devote full time to poetry.

By 1882, at the age of 27, he had written a biography of the recently-deceased Rossetti. A collection of poems was on the bookstands. Will's *Human Inheritance* was gaining recognition. The publisher invited him to submit more poetry. Will sold a number of articles on ancient Etruscan cities to the *Glasgow Herald*, whose art critic he became.

Parental opposition to Will and Elizabeth's marriage was withdrawn. They were married in 1885.

A superbly gifted writer, Elizabeth often wondered if Star-Eyes was fashioned from poetry, imagination and her husband's emotions about Scotland's primitive and early Christian history. And why, she asked herself, did his childhood fancy — or phantom — continue to invade his thoughts?

With Elizabeth's assistance Will completed his anthology *Lyra*. He ventured successfully into fiction with *Children of Tomorrow*, *Silence Farm* and critically-acclaimed short stories. He completed biographies of Shelley, Heine and Browning, along with Greek Studies and literary essays. Without a word of complaint about his obsession with Star-Eyes, Elizabeth lifted Will's spirit with sympathy and encouragement.

In 1894 Sharp experienced the compulsion to write in the ancient Gaelic vein. The "slant" was sensitive, passionate and totally feminine. No one will ever know how the word "Fiona Macleod" entered his mind.

Fiona "wrote" through the medium of William Sharp, while

he continued to produce erudite works under his own name. In all of the documented evidence of the case there is no mention of a Ouija board or direct voice. It was as if he were controlled by some entity, perhaps an element spirit from the Highlands' dim past. The words seemed spun from shadow and fancy.

Sharp concluded that Fiona was a projection of Star-Eyes and that both he and she were incarnations, lovers, from Scottish antiquity. Did not "Fiona" mean "fair maid"?

The first work of this worldly-otherwordly "collaboration" was *Pharais: A Romance of the Isles*. The writing had begun at the Sharps' county house, Phenice Croft, where new problems were surfacing for Elizabeth.

Elizabeth began to fear their sequestered rustic home. The place seemed unnatural to her. "Uncanny" was how she expressed it in her 1910 biography of her husband. She wrote that Phenice Croft was haunted. It was hard for her to live there "unless the sun was shining." Visitors also felt uneasy about the ambience. Only when Will was away did the oppression lift.

According to the *British Dictionary of National Biography*, Sharp was writing under "the influence of mesmerism, or spiritual trance." In 1895 Macleod's *Mountain Sons* came out, followed by *The Sin-Eater, Celtic Isles* and her recreation of Celtic myth, captured in dreams." The *Washer in the Ford* and *Green Fire* drew acclaim. William Sharp's facile pen, or rather Fiona's, was busy indeed.

Fiona Macleod's popularity spread the United States. Like her British readers, who had no idea that she was a man, American fans demanded to know about her personal life. Sharp issued a statement. Fiona was a young recluse who avoided any form of publicity and human contact. She lived as a hermit somewhere in the Highlands. Nature was her only companion. William Sharp was merely acting as her literary agent — the buffer between her mystical life and the real world of publishing.

On 13 May, 1899, Fiona wrote to the *Athenaeum*, stating that she wrote only under her own name. Her readers, who ranged from the general populace to distinguished literary personalities, wrote to her. Always she answered graciously. Sharp's and her own handwriting were somewhat similar but Fiona's had some unique qualities.

At the turn of the century Thomas B. Mosher, a Portland, Maine, publisher of miniature books, requested and received Fiona's permission to reprint some of her Celtic/Gaelic/Breton lore.

Fiona was generous. *By Sundown Shores: Studies in Spiritual History* was published by Mosher in 1902. Included in this volume was *The Lynn of Dreams* (in print for the first time). A second edition of 425 copies was published in 1904.

In her foreword Fiona wrote, "You ask of me a few words the seadrift from *Sundown Shores*, to tell you are free to take up or give to others what in a sense is not mine to give."

By Sundown Shores helps the reader understand the true persona of Fiona Mcleod.

Of elemental powers: "I know one who, asked by a friend desiring more intimate knowledge as to what influences above all other influences had shaped her inward life, answered at once, with that sudden vision of insight which reveals more than the vision of thought, 'The Wind, Silence, and Love. ...'

When we consider, could any influences be deeper than these three elemental powers, for ever young, yet older than age, beautiful immortalities that whisper continually against our mortal ear. The Wind, Silence, and Love. Yes, I think of them as good comrades, nobly minstrant, priests of the hidden way.

To go into solitary places or among trees which await dusk and storm, or by a dark shore: to be a nerve there, to listen to, inwardly to hear, to be at one with, as needs shaken by, as a wave lifted before the wind: this is to know what cannot otherwise be known; to hear the intimate, dread voice; to listen to what long, long ago went away, and to which now is going and coming, coming and going, and to what august airs of sorrow prevail in that dim empire of shadow where the falling leaf rest unfallen, where Sound, of all else forgotten and forgetting, lives in the pale hyacinth, the moon-white pansy, the cloudy amaranth that gathers dew."

Fiona Macleod's views on Christianity's first inroads where nature worship had been the norm:

"Nothing is more strange than the confused survival of legends and pagan faiths and early Christian beliefs, such as may be found still in some of the isles. There's a story that Mary Magdalene lies in a cave in Iona. She roamed the world with a blind man who loved her, but they had no sin. ... It is characteristic enough to the quaint confusion that could make Mary Magdalene and St. Columba contemporary."

Fiona also tells of "an instance of a Celtic priest in Armorica and of a Celtic priest in Scotland acting identically towards an upright heathen. A large book would be necessary to relate the correspondence between the folk tales, the traditional romances, and the Christian legends of the four great branches of the Celtic race.

On the seventh day, when God rested, says a poet of the Gael, He dreamed of the lands and nations He had made, and out of that dreaming were born Ireland and Brittany. Truly, within Christian days, there were more saints, there were more lamps of the spirit lit in that grey peninsula, in that green land, in the little sand-cinctured Iona, than anywhere betwixt the Syrian desert and the meads and Glastonbury. ... The old gods have not perished but merge into the brotherhood of Christ's company."

Fiona stressed the significance of "Earth, Fire, and Water". She writes of "Old Barabal," her nanny, who could have been the old Highland companion of Sharp's childhood.

"Old Barabal has gone where the south wind blows, in blossom and flowers and green leaves, across the pastures of Death; and I ... alas can but wish that One stronger than she, for all her love, will lift me, as a child again, to the Wind, and pass me across the Fire, and set me down again upon a New Earth."

Sharp encouraged the popular conception that Fiona Macleod was endowed with "the dreamy Celtic genius." He submitted a "biographical" sketch to *Who's Who*, listing her hobbies as "boating, hill-climbing and listening." Critics agreed that the bulk of her writing reflected the influences of paganism and nature worship.

Elizabeth kept her dignified silence. She coped stoically with Phenice Croft's haunted atmosphere, feeling she was sharing her home with Will's "other woman", who was a phantom. Never did she wallow in self-pity or reproach Will for living in two worlds.

From time to time Will left Elizabeth to spend weeks on end in his enchanted Western Highlands. He wrote her in detail about "us". One letter was especially painful for her:

"There is a strange excitement in the knowledge that two people are here, for it is with me as though Fiona were asleep in another room. I catch myself listening for her step, for the sudden opening of a door. She whispers to me. I am eager to see what she will do. It seems passing strange to be here alone with her at last."

Each year Sharp observed his birthday by writing to Fiona. One letter opened with the salutation "Dearest Fiona." He went on about her "serene face and austere eyes." She wrote back how much she wanted him to go on serving her "with loyalty. ... Lovingly yours, dear Will. ..."

The ongoing play between the two personalities exacted their toll. The enormous strain proved damaging to Sharp's physical and emotional health. He travelled widely, with or without Elizabeth. The *Lynn of Dreams* attempts to explain the meld of the two diverse personas. Fiona used the character she named John O'Dreams as a stand-in for Sharp.

"What he wrote was read with eagerness," she said, "for those who turned to his books knew that they would find there not his own thought, which was deep, and his own imagination, which had a far-wandering wing, but a verbal music that was his own, a subtle use of the underplay of word-life, the colour, meaning, romance, association, suggestiveness, shadowy hints of words; the incommunicable charm.

He loved his art, and he had much to say, and above all longed to capture into rhythm and cadence the floating music that haunted him, and the wonder of life that was his continual dream."

In 1905, during a drive in the Sicilian Alcantara valley, Sharp caught a chill which escalated into a dangerous virus. He died at the Duke of Bronte's home, Castello Manicate, situated at the base of Mount Etna.

In Sharp's biography Elizabeth tells of his strangely haunted final hours:

"On the morning of the twelfth day — a day of wild storm, wind, thunder and rain — he recognized that nothing could avail. With characteristic swiftness he turned his eager mind from the life that was closing to the life of greater possibilities that he knew awaited him. About three o'clock, with his devoted friend, Alex Hood, by his side, he suddenly leant forward with shining eyes and exclaimed in a tone of joyous recognition, 'Oh, the beautiful Green Life again!' And the next moment sank back in my arms with the contented sigh, 'Ah, all is well.'"

Sharp left a letter, to be given to the Duke of Bronte, explaining his reasons for keeping his two interlocking identities secret. The Duke and Elizabeth kept that confidence faithfully.

Thirteen years after Sharp's death, the occult magazine *Light* (15 August, 1918) referred to the Fiona enigma as "one of the curiosities of modern literature."

In the author's opinion Sharp's works, written under his own name, were "curiously lacking in the wonderful elements of poetic imagination which flowed into them when he wrote his Celtic romances under the pen name of 'Fiona Macleod', a mysterious woman, the secret of whose identity was jealously preserved. ... It is as though Pope or Shelley should have produced works in the manner of Keats."

Elizabeth recalled how her husband often seemed to "enter" a place he called "The Green Life." She wrote, "I remember from early days how he would speak of the momentary curious 'dazzle in the brain,' which preceded the falling-away of all material things and precluded some inner vision of Great Beauty or Great Presence, or of some symbolic imprint. I have been beside him when he was in a trance, and I heard the room throb with heightened vibration."

Numerous theories attempting to pierce the mystery of the Sharp-Macleod relationship have been advanced: automatic writing, spirit possession, self-hypnosis, clairvoyance, split personality. The answer will never be known. But what can be stated with absolute certainty is that "Fiona Macleod" was infinitely more than a pseudonym.

PREVIEW
Brenda Shaw

My close friend Bronwyn had gone camping in France with her husband Tom and their two small children. While they were there some minor symptoms she had noted before leaving got rapidly worse and a French doctor was consulted. "Madame is very ill," he told them. "You must return to your own country at once and seek treatment."

Bronwyn was hospitalized in Ninewells Hospital, Dundee, immediately upon their return. This was late in July 1972. Within days a diagnosis of acute leukaemia was confirmed. She was too ill to see anyone except Tom. The doctors started chemotherapy, hoping to produce a remission which would keep her symptom-free for a time. Cheered and encouraged by this, Bronwyn asked to see me.

"She's feeling quite chipper now that we know it can be treated," Tom said. "Why don't you go and see her tomorrow?"

That evening I couldn't get Bronwyn out of my mind. I dreaded the impending visit. What does one say to a friend who is dying? I hadn't faced that situation before. I was making a cake in my kitchen in Dundee, where I lived at that time. As I mixed and poured the batter I ran through in my mind what I would say to Bronwyn next day. As I put the cake into the oven a sudden conviction came over me: You won't have to go tomorrow. "She's already dead."

Then a new line of thought began. I imagined hearing footsteps on our gravel path, the doorbell ringing and Tom standing there on the step, pale and shocked, saying, "She's gone — dead." I led him into the kitchen and sat him down and he told us what had happened. ·

This entire fantasy lasted perhaps 20 minutes and was interrupted by the sound of footsteps coming up our gravel path and the ringing of the doorbell. There was Tom, standing on the front step, looking pale and shocked. He said, "She's gone — dead."

THE STRANGE CRIMES OF SPRING HEELED JACK

Who was this weird being who breathed fire, bounded through the air in superhuman leaps and attacked young women?

Gordon Stein

On the night of 11 October, 1837, a mystery began. This mystery would puzzle and frighten England for the next 70 years.

At Blackheath 17-year-old Polly Adams was returning home from a local fair. As she passed the gallows that stood on a hill on Shooter's Hill Road, she saw a huge cloaked figure silhouetted against the sky. The figure, his cloak flapping around him, ran toward her with leaps that seemed hardly possible for a human being.

When she got a good look at him, Polly saw his face had eyes that glowed like coals and a mouth that seemed to spit blue flames. She could feel the warmth of the fire he spat on her face. The figure's fingers felt like iron and they scratched her, drawing blood. The man — if that's what he was — laughed in a loud, ringing way and his eyes bulged from their sockets. He reached toward her bodice and ripped it away, leaving deep scratches across her stomach. After nearly disrobing her, the figure stepped back and laughed again. He turned and fled into the night, again with what appeared to be superhuman laps.

As unlikely as Polly Adams' story seemed, it was not the first of its kind, only the most dramatic. About a month earlier, in early September, residents of Barnes Common, on the outskirts of London, spoke of a series of nocturnal attacks against pedestrians on their way across the common. At least four attacks — three against young women — supposedly had taken place. In one case the attacker had ripped a woman's clothes off, it was said. These attacks, however, were not mentioned in the newspapers.

If the attacks had stopped then, we would have no record of them today. But they were followed by a strange series of events which catapulted the weird assailant, who would become known as Spring Heeled Jack, onto the lips of nearly everybody in London.

The Lord Mayor of London, Sir John Cowan, called what would today be called a press conference on 9 January, 1838, and produced a letter which he had received from someone who signed himself only "A Resident of Peckham." The author related that some wealthy person (he had been told) had made a wager that he could visit the various villages just outside London disguised as a bear, a ghost and a devil. As a result, the writer said, seven ladies were scared half to death; two of them might never recover their sanity. The writer also claimed that, although the newspapers had been silent on the matter, there was good reason to suspect they knew who the villain was.

The mayor's listeners reacted with alarm to these revelations, although the Lord Mayor himself said he was not certain they were true. A man in the audience stood up and confirmed that he too had heard of the activities of such a character in other London suburbs.

Consequently the story of the "ghost, bear or devil" made all the London newspapers the following day. The result was a flood of new reports. The mayor promised he would try to clear the matter up and bring the perpetrator to justice.

A profile of the attacker emerged from the victims' accounts. He was described as tall and powerful. He wore a long flowing cloak and high black boots. He had "fiery" eyes, a prominent nose and ears that appeared pointed. He also possessed clawlike fingers which felt as if they were made of iron. But his most dramatic quality was his agility. Once, it was said, he caused a horse-drawn coach to be wrecked when he spooked the horses by leaping in front of the vehicle, completely clearing the wide road and a wall on the other side in a single astonishing leap.

Many of his victims were women and many of them reported having their clothes ripped off, but none complained of being raped or otherwise sexually molested. The implication seemed to be that the attacker was a voyeur.

On Friday, 13 January, Sir John Cowan announced he now had no doubts about the attacker's existence. He said he was setting up a vigilante committee consisting of magistrates, army officers and ordinary citizens. This group would try to track down the man who was now being called "The Leaping Terror," "The Suburban Ghost" or "Springald," which means jumping jack. From this last name it was only a short leap to a corruption into "Spring Heeled Jack," the name by which both his contemporaries and history have come to call the elusive villain.

On 18 February the first attacks within the city of London

were reported. One victim, 18-year-old Jane Alsop, responding to the ringing of the Alsop doorbell at 9 pm, looked through a crack in the door to see a tall figure wearing what appeared to be a top hat and a cloak. Because the ringing had been so insistent, she asked what was the matter. The figure replied, "I am a policeman. For God's sake, bring me a light, for we have caught Spring Heeled Jack here in the lane!"

The young woman hurried back into the house and brought a candle. What happened next is recorded in the court report compiled the next day from her testimony:

"She ... handed [the candle] to the person, who appeared enveloped in a large cloak, and whom she at first really believed to be a policeman. The instant she had done so, however, he threw off his outer garment, and applying the lighted candle to her breast, presented a most hideous and frightful appearance, and vomited forth a quantity of blue and white flame from his mouth and his eyes resembled red balls of fire.

From the hasty glance which her fright enabled her to get at his person, she deserved that he wore a large helmet, and his dress, which appeared to fit him very tight, seemed to her to resemble white oilskin. Without uttering a sentence, he darted at her, and catching her partly by the dress and the back part of her neck, placed her head under one of his arms, and commenced tearing her gown with his claws, which she was certain were of some metallic substance.

She screamed out as loud as she could for assistance, and by considerable exertion got away from him and ran towards the house to get in. Her assailant, however followed her, and caught her on the steps leading to the hall-door, where he again used considerable violence, tore her neck and arms with his claws, as well as a quantity of hair from her head; but she was at length rescued from his grasp by one of her sisters."

There was an intriguing new feature in this attack. As he escaped, Jack dropped his cloak, according to Jane's sister, but the cloak was picked up almost immediately by someone else. Had Spring Heeled Jack have an accomplice?

The police had no luck in catching Spring Heeled Jack. They did arrest several persons on the suspicion that they were Jack, but all were soon released.

Although there were many more reports of Jack's activities between 1838 and 1839, the incidents subsided thereafter. They resumed in 1843, when on a number of occasions a caped man wearing a mask and breathing fire reportedly jumped out and scared men, women, children and mail-coach horses. There are enough minor variations between the actions of the 1843 attack and the earlier one that it is possible that two different men were responsible for them.

In 1845 Spring Heeled Jack was accused, for the first time, of murder. On Jacob's Island, which was one of the worst slums in London (in fact, it was the setting of Fagin's hideout in Charles Dickens' *Oliver Twist*), a 13-year-old prostitute named Maria Davis was crossing a bridge over one of the muddy ditches that served as open sewers for the area when Spring Heeled Jack approached her. He had been bounding across the various wooden walkways that connected buildings in the slum.

As Maria stood transfixed, Jack bounded up to her, grabbed her by the shoulders, breathed fire into her face and threw her into the smelly muck below the bridge. Maria cried out in terror as the deep, quicksandlike mud swallowed her up. Many of the people of Jacob's Island witnessed the episode from the relative safety of their homes.

The inquest that followed ruled that Maria Davis' death was due to "misadventure," which is the official way of saying it was by unknown criminal means.

The next series of actions that seem to bear the mark of Spring Heeled Jack occurred in 1877. Almost the entire town of Caister, Norfolk, saw a strange figure leap up on the roof of a cottage, then jump from rooftop to rooftop. When the figure jumped to the ground, a man fired at him with a rifle. He missed and Jack — if that's who he was — bounded through the town. He was last seen running along the town's New Barracks walls.

According to descriptions published in the press, the figure was not entirely human. Witnesses said he had huge ears and a garment resembling a sheepskin, which gives some reason to doubt that we are dealing here with Spring Heeled Jack, at least as he was usually perceived.

Later that year, in August, at the military barracks at Aldershot's North Camp, a sentry named Private Regan heard a noise. After looking around and seeing nothing, Regan felt an icy hand touch his cheek. He shouted and another sentry came running. As the two guards stood together, a huge figure leaped over their heads and landed in front of them further down the road. The figure appeared to be a man wearing a tight-fitting oilskin suit and a "shining helmet." He was grinning malevolently.

As Regan ordered the man to identify himself and got no reply, he fired at the figure and — according to Regan's subsequent testimony — the bullet passed right through the figure with no apparent effect. The figure stepped back, then took an enormous leap into the air. As he sailed over the two soldiers, Spring Heeled Jack belched a stream of flame at them. Jack landed on top of the sentry box, let loose with his characteristic ringing laugh, then was fired upon, again without effect, by both soldiers.

At first their superiors did not believe the story about what had happened and both men were sent to the stockade. Shortly afterwards, however, Jack appeared to several other soldiers, and Regan and his companion were freed. Following other appearances at the camp, Jack again disappeared from sight.

The final series of appearances by Spring Heeled Jack, or a reasonable facsimile thereof, occurred in Liverpool in September 1904 — 67 years after the first reports in 1837.

A Mrs. Hudson of William Henry Street, Everton, noticed a large shadow cast on the wall through the curtain of her window. She pulled aside the curtain in time to observe what appeared to be the figure of a giant bat around the corner of the street.

At exactly the same time, just after nine o'clock, the next night, the form again appeared. But this time Mrs. Hudson was better prepared. She watched as the figure bounded down the street. It was a man wearing a flowing cloak and black boots. The figure leaped down the street in a series of high jumps.

The next day Mrs. Hudson learned that her neighbours had also seen the figure. One neighbour remembered the stories about Spring Heeled Jack which he had learned when he was a boy. Soon the visitor was being called Jack.

Jack terrorized two different sets of girls later that week by springing out at them, laughing and bounding away. One afternoon he appeared in broad daylight, bounding down the street, laughing and finally leaping about 25 feet up to the roof of a building. Over 100 persons watched as he leaped from rooftop to rooftop in the town. Jack finally leaped down behind a building from a roof and disappeared.

An extensive search by the police and townsfolk failed to turn up any clue to his hiding place. This marked the final report that seems to be of Spring Heeled Jack.

Who was Spring Heeled Jack? Some thought he was Henry,

the Marquis of Waterford. This Irish nobleman, who was born in 1811, would have been in his late 20's at the time of the first Jack sightings. The Marquis was a rambunctious youth, always seeking a fight. He drank to excess and loved a good practical joke.

The idea that the marquis was Spring Heeled Jack rests on slight but possibly suggestive evidence. The marquis supposedly had been overheard (where and by whom was never stated) making a bet with his drinking companions that he could do some daring deed, not specified. The marquis, in the one picture we have of him from his youth, was tall and thin with protruding eyes. He also supposedly had an unusual laugh and he was in the London suburbs during the period of the early attacks. One of the young men attacked by Jack noted that Jack's cloak wore a gold filigree letter W on it. This is similar to Waterford's crest.

Peter Haining, author of *The Legend and Bizarre Crimes of Spring Heeled Jack* (1977), thinks that Waterford had the friends and money to have a special pair of boots designed for him — boots that contained special alloy steel springs about 18 inches long. These springs would normally be concealed in the heels of the boots but would be released when Jack wanted to make his impressive leaps. But when the Germans tried to put springs into the boots of their paratroops during World War II, the scheme failed spectacularly. Instead of having their falls cushioned, they — or at least 85 per cent of them — had their ankles broken. Metallurgical engineers point out that there is no known alloy which is compressible and resilient enough both to fit into the heels of a pair of shoes and to be able to account for the leaps Jack reportedly made.

The purported last sightings of Spring Heeled Jack in 1904 were fairly similar to the initial ones nearly 70 years earlier in 1837. Obviously, the Marquis of Waterford, who died in 1859, could not have been responsible for any but the earliest attacks.

If we are to conclude that the reports of Spring Heeled Jack were caused by a human being dressed up in costume, we must also assume that witnesses to Jack's activities greatly exaggerated what they saw. We must also conclude that a number of different men impersonated Jack over the years.

Another, far more fantastic explanation (proposed, for example, by J. Vyner in *Flying Saucer Review*, May-June 1961) is that Jack was a being from another planet — a planet having greater size and gravity than earth. This would "explain" how Jack could leap so high in the earth's weaker gravity. But if this were so, no springs would be needed on his boots. Of course, we don't know why an extraterrestrial would go around England terrifying mostly young women for nearly 70 years.

The idea that some of the sightings, especially the early ones, were distorted reports of kangaroos also needs to be considered. Kangaroos were virtually unknown to the average Englishman in the 1830's. Australia had only relatively recently been discovered and its wildlife was known only to a few naturalists. Yet it does seem quite a leap of the imagination to have a kangaroo trained to spit fire and laugh, even if it were possible to train one to dress in tight oilskin and rip off women's clothes. Perhaps some of the reports were caused by a kangaroo, but probably not many.

No one explanation will account for all of the facts, real or alleged, of the case. Spring Heeled Jack has long since ceased to terrorize people, but he will probably forever remain a mystery.

RESTLESS SOULS OF MEGGERNIE CASTLE ...

A ghost missing the lower half of its body terrifies castle visitors to remind them of a brutal murder two centuries ago.

Archie McKerracher

Sinister Meggernie Castle lies in Glenlyon in the wilds of the Scottish Highlands. This is a grim and desolate place, overhung by steep hills and swirling mist. The castle was built in 1585, initially as a simple tower house, by Colin Campbell, the third Campbell laird of Glenlyon. He received the nickname "Mad Colin" after a kick on the head by a horse rendered him highly unpredictable.

Shortly after Meggernie was built, a band of cattle robbers descended on Mad Colin's lands and tried to drive away his cows. He captured 30 of the robbers and dispatched his son to the authorities in Edinburgh to seek justice. Back came the news that the judges seemed inclined only to fine the thieves. Colin promptly dragged them outside and when his son arrived home he was greeted by the sight of all 30 hanging from the trees that lined the avenue.

Mad Colin's great grandson, Robert, inherited Meggernie in 1674. He was a hard drinking wastrel whose final act of folly was to extend the castle into a miniature stately home. Having gone bankrupt, he was forced to sell Meggernie. In 1690 Robert, at 60 years of age, had no alternative but to join the array to support his family. He was ordered to billet his troops among the neighbouring MacDonalds of Glencoe.

Two weeks later on 13 February, 1692, he was given his final orders. He was to fall on his hosts and destroy every living soul for failing to take the Oath of Allegiance to King William of Orange.

The name of Robert Campbell of Meggernie and Glenlyon is still remembered with loathing today as the executioner of the infamous Massacre of Glencoe, although London politicians had selected him as the scapegoat. Every February American-Scots gather at Glencoe, Oregon, to remember the 30 who perished that day and to give thanks for the sudden blizzard that saved the rest.

Meggernie Castle passed into the ownership of the Menzies of Culdares. Robert Menzies, laird of Meggernie in the mid-18th century, falsely accused his wife of adultery. He killed her in a jealous rage, then cut her body in two and hid the parts inside a chest within a cupboard in the wall of the tower block.

Menzies left for a trip to the Continent and when he returned a few months later, he said his wife had died abroad. This explanation was accepted and on his first night home he removed the lower part of her body and buried it in the adjacent castle graveyard. He was returning for the upper part, but got no further than the tower door where he was found dead in the morning with a ghastly, terrified expression on his face. It soon became known that someone had found out his guilty secret and murdered him.

In 1862 Meggernie was rented to an English businessman called Herbet Woods who invited two friends, E.J. Simons and Beaumont Fetherstone, to join him for the deer-stalking season. They arrived late at night after a long train journey and were allocated adjoining rooms in the old tower block. Simons was intrigued to find a sealed-off door in his room. He went to confide in Fetherstone and together they examined the door which appeared to adjoin both rooms for there was also one in Fetherstone's room. Eventually the men retired to bed.

At 2 am Simons was wakened abruptly by what felt like a burning kiss on his cheek. He leaped from his bed and was horrified to see the upper part of a woman's body drifting across the room and through the sealed-off door. Lighting a candle with trembling hands, he examined his face for burns but could feel none. He sat on his bed in great distress until his candle had burned out and daylight came.

When he heard Fetherstone stirring next door, he called out, "I've had a terrible night!"

"So have I," came the reply.

"Look, don't tell me now. Let's each go separately to Herbet and see if our stories coincide."

Their apologetic host later confirmed both had had the same experience, although only Simons had received the kiss. The two guests were subsequently allocated different rooms. Simons, however, seems to have been a receptive medium because a few days later he was writing letters in the ground floor drawing room when the door suddenly flew open.

He went into the passageway and was horrified to see the faint outline of a sad, beautiful face staring in the window at him. Not surprisingly, he cut short his slay and refused to visit Meggernie again. Unbeknown to him, many of the English servants had seen the same thing and were threatening to leave.

Beaumont Fetherstone recorded the incident in his diary which survives today. "At Meggernie Castle, Perthshire, I was awakened at 2 am by a purple light and saw a female at the foot of the bed. At first I took her for a housekeeper walking in her sleep. She came along the side of the bed and bent over me. I raised myself up and she retreated and went into a small room made out of the thickness of the wall."

After following her across the room Fetherstone was mystified by her sudden disappearance. "The phantom seemed minus legs, which I am glad to say I didn't realize at the time or I should have been in a greater funk than I was."

Meggernie was purchased in 1885 by an English textile millionaire called John Bullough. He commmissioned several alterations and during the work the upper part of a female skeleton was found beneath the floor inside the recess in the wall. The bones were buried in the castle graveyard, but this did not stop the manifestations.

In the 1920's a party of five young people held a lighthearted seance in the room. One of them volunteered to be the medium. She began to talk in rambling sentences and then the others felt the room becoming colder and a smell like incense filled the air. The voice of the medium began to trail to a halt and then she suddenly collapsed with a cry of, "I can't do it!"

Norman MacKay, the local doctor for over 40 years until he retired in 1948, used to relate an experience he had at Meggernie in 1928. He had been called out late to the castle and because of the patient's condition was obliged to stay the night. He was aware of the ghost legend, having been shown the haunted room on a previous visit, and was slightly surprised to find it was to be his bedroom. He knew the castle had recently changed hands and thought the new owners might not be aware of the story.

He lay on the bed fully dressed in case of a sudden summons. Having dozed off, he was awakened some hours later by a noise at the door. He assumed it was a servant sent to fetch him and he sat up. He found the room filled with a purple light and was astounded to see the upper part of a woman's body floating round the ceiling with the face gazing down at him with a sad expression.

Possibly country doctors get used to many strange occurrences because Dr. MacKay merely muttered, "Good Lord, the Meggernie ghost," and then lay down to sleep again. In the morning he discovered that his bedroom was not in fact the haunted room but the one directly below. Interestingly, the haunted room had undergone major alterations in the early 1920's The place where the ghost had been floating about at ceiling level had originally been the floor of the room above.

Dr. MacKay recorded later, "Call it a vision if you like. Call it coincidence. If it was only a dream, then it was by far the most vivid I have ever had."

Many others have seen the dismembered woman right up to the present day and some have also seen the lower part of a woman's body sitting on a tombstone in the castle graveyard. Perhaps there is no peace for her spirit until her body is reunited but that could never happen for the burial places are now unknown.

But the ghost of Meggernie Castle is not the only mystery in this long and twisting glen.

High up in the mountains at the head of Glenlyon is the only surviving shrine in Britain to the pre-Christian Mother Goddess cult. Here is a small stone house about three feet high, the home of five oddly heavy stones shaped like dumbbells. The largest, measuring 18 inches high, is called The Cailleach or The Old Woman, and the smallest is her daughter. The little family has watched over the cattle herds here since the beginning of recorded tine. Today Bob Bissett, the local shepherd, continues the tradition by acting as their custodian. Each spring he brings them reverently outside their house and in autumn ensures they are snugly tucked away for the winter.

Strangest of all is that this desolate place is the birthplace of Pontius Pilate, said to be the love child of a Roman officer and a local tribeswoman. Certainly Caesar Augustus sent out peace envoys in 10 B.C. to all nations outside the Roman Empire.

Old chronicles relate that one such party made its way north into this wilderness to greet the local Caledonian king. They would have been given tribeswomen during their stay over the winter as was normal practice. Did one of them become pregnant and did the Roman officer take her and the child back to Italy as a slave? It is curious that Pontius derives from the name of the noble Pontii family of central Italy while Pilate comes from Pilateus, the felt cap worn by a freed shave. Did the officer make his half-barbarian son a free man?

Some say Pilate returned here to die after being dismissed as Governor of Judea and exiled. Oddly, a stone was dug up here in 1900 which bore the initials P.P. Perhaps his restless soul seeks eternal peace in this wild place.

THE BIG GREY MAN

Why do mountain climbers — both amateur and professional — run in terror off the Scottish mountain named Ben MacDhui?

Who — or what — is the figure that they see?

Dr. Karl P.N. Shuker

At a lofty height of 4296 feet, Ben MacDhui of the Cairngorms range is second only to Ben Nevis as Scotland's tallest mountain, and second to none as its most mysterious. It is usually reached by a 20-mile-long path leading away from the Glenmore Lodge and extending through the arduous Lairig Ghru pass. Ben MacDhui was once a rarely visited, lonely locale, but its towering peak with flat-topped summit began to attract increasing attention from mountain climbers when mountaineering became popular during this century's early years.

It was not long, however, before strange tales were brought back by intrepid visitors to this dark, brooding mountain — tales of ghostly music, inexplicable laughter and voices, and other uncanny phenomena. Most dramatic of all were reports concerning apparitions of colossal size, crunching footsteps that followed the climbers and, above all else, an unaccountable and uncontrollable fear that frequently drove them down and away from the mountain in a fit of blind panic.

These last three phenomena in particular seemed to share a common origin, unhesitatingly identified by the area's residents as being an entity that they firmly believed to inhabit Ben MacDhui's upper reaches, and known locally as Am Fear Liath Mor, or in English as the Big Grey Man. For many years, this mysterious matter attracted much attention in Scottish newspapers and journals, with many reports and explanations appearing. Such average culminated in 1970 with the publication of The Big Grey Man of Ben MacDhui, an indispensable book on the subject and written by Cairngorms-bred author Affleck Gray.

In more recent times, however, interest has waned. This is surprising as many of the more modern thoughts and ideas raised in relation to various other mysterious phenomena are particularly relevant to the Big Grey Man enigma. Consequently, almost 20 years after Gray's book appeared, it seemed more than timely to take the opportunity of re-analysing the subject by applying some of those concepts to it. First, however, here a few of some of the more startling encounters and experiences reported from Ben MacDhui.

THE PROFESSOR IS TERRIFIED

Probably the most famous of all such reports was that of Norman Collie, published in 1926. Until then, the subject had not attracted much serious attention. But Collie was one of the period's most experienced and respected mountaineers as well as Professor of Organic Chemistry at the University of London. He was also an austere man by nature who vehemently shunned sensationalism. Here was a witness with impeccable credentials, whose words could not be readily dismissed.

Collie was the speaker at the Annual General Meeting of Aberdeen's Cairngorm Club in December 1925. He announced that on his last visit to Ben MacDhui he had been descending from the Cairn while surrounded on all sides by dense mist. "... I began to think I heard something else than merely the noise of my own footsteps. For every few steps I took I heard a crunch, and then another crunch as if someone was walking after me but taking steps three or four times the length of my own." He attempted to laugh at himself for being fanciful, and continued walking, but the eerie sounds followed on behind him (with the mist that immersed him hiding their source from his view). Finally, he admitted that "... I was seized with terror and took to my heels, staggering blindly among the boulders for four or five miles nearly down to Rothiemurchus Forest." Not surprisingly, he vowed never to go back to that menacing mountain, and ever afterwards remained convinced that there was "... something very queer about the top of Ben MacDhui."

THE DOCTOR SEES A BIG GREY MAN

During the early 1920s, Collie was contacted by another renowned mountaineer, Dr. A.M. Kellas, who had learned of Collie's Ben MacDhui experience before it had become widely known. Dr. Fellas informed Collie that while climbing that mountain with his brother Henry, he had spied a figure that he described as "... a big grey man ..." walking from the Lairig Ghru pass up and around the 10-foot-tall

Cairn toward Ben MacDhui's summit, where it disappeared from view. Dr. Kellas affirmed that the mystery figure seemed to be at least as tall as the Cairn itself. This is a historic report, for it was responsible for providing Am Fear Liath Mor with its English appellation.

The December 1925 issue of the Aberdeen *Press and Journal* contained further news concerning this incident, based upon information given by Henry Kellas to W.G. Robertson, a friend. Apparently the Kellas brothers had awaited the Big Grey Man's reappearance at the summit, but "... fear possessed them ere it did reach the top, and they fled. They were aware it was following them, and tore down by Corrie Etchachan to escape it."

NO SAFETY UNDER SHELTER STONE
In the summer of 1940, and in the company of a friend with whom he was residing during a holiday, *More Highland Folktales* author R. MacDonald Robertson spent a night inside a famous, enormous block of stone on Ben MacDhui known as the Shelter Stone — as travellers frequently take shelter and rest beneath it. During that night, they were awakened by the growls of Robertson's pet bull terrier, and could soon discern the sound of crunching footsteps, approaching nearer and nearer along the gravel path outside. The identity of the footsteps' originator, however, was never discovered, for without warning, the sound of the steps just faded away, after which Robertson's dog relaxed once more.

In *The Big Grey Man of Ben MacDhui*, Affleck Gray reported that one evening in 1942, while in the vicinity of the Shelter Stone and gazing out toward Loch Avon (A'an), the experienced mountain climber Syd Scroggie suddenly perceived "... a tall, stately, human figure, appear out of the blackness on one side of the loch, and clearly silhouetted against the water pace with long, deliberate steps across the combined burns just where they enter the loch." The figure was not wearing a rucksack, and was soon hidden from view by the darkness on the loch's opposite side. Intrigued, Scroggie lost no time in reaching the locality of his sighting and searching it thoroughly for footprints and any other sign of the figure's movements, but he found nothing. Similarly, he called out in the hope of receiving a reply but none came. Instead, he experienced a distinct, eerie sense of unease, one that sent him on his way back with all speed to the welcome security of the Shelter Stone!

SHOOTING THE BIG GREY MAN

As far as I am aware, the month of October in 1943 has a unique claim to fame in this saga by hosting the only instance on record of someone actually shooting the Big Grey Man! Mountaineer and naturalist Alexander Tewnion had been walking along the Lairig Ghru one day that month on the lookout for some game to shoot and thereby supplement his wartime rations. He had begun to descend the track through Corrie Etchachan's deep trough, when suddenly he became aware of the sound of long, striding footsteps just behind him. As he recalled to the *Scots Magazine* in June 1958, they immediately brought to mind the strange narrative many years earlier of Professor Collie. So he peered at once through the mist in the direction of the footsteps, and was startled by a mysterious shape that loomed up menacingly, momentarily withdrew, and then charged directly at him!

Instantly, Tewnion drew out his revolver and fired three shots straight at the figure, but they had absolutely no effect — the threatening shape was still coming! Needless to say, he lost no time in turning around and fleeing precipitately downward, toward Glen Derry and safety!

These are just some of the unnerving and uncanny incidents, but how can they be accounted for?

GEOLOGICAL ARTIFACT?

The Hexham heads are a couple of small stone artifacts that were found in a garden at Hexham, in 1972, and since have been associated with a number of seemingly supernatural occurrences, including the appearance of a strange wolfman-like being, accompanied by adding footsteps. In *Tales of the Hexham Heads* (1980) by Paul Screeton, a possible solution for the wolfman entity is postulated by inorganic chemistry specialist Dr. Don Robins. The theory could be readily applied to the Big Grey Man mystery too.

Dr. Robins' theory proposes that various minerals may be capable of encoding (storing) a type of electrical energy. Under certain specific conditions a minetic image could actually be released. Among the supporting evidence that Robins provides is that of the visual similarity between modern-day three-dimensional holograph's interference patterns and the chemical nature of certain mineral compounds — a geological holograph!

Could this be the source of the Big Grey Man? Certainly one would hardly conceive of a more conducive locality for such activity than a rocky mountainous peak like Ben MacDhui. And if such mineralogical manifestations could incorporate both visual and aural components, this could then explain the crunching footsteps and huge figure reported from that mountain.

This theory does not, however, answer why Ben MacDhui should yield such a preponderance of petrological phantoms as compared with other British mountains in general. Could this anomaly be due to certain specific and crucial, but currently unrecognized, differences in geological composition, historical background, and/or other attributes?

OPTICAL ILLUSION?

Many reports of phantoms have undoubtedly resulted from optical illusions. We can all recall incidents in which we have perceived an object to be something totally different from what it first appeared to be. Such frequent occurrences are due to our brain making assumptions regarding the appearance and identity of a poorly- or briefly-seen object, and then "filling in" the missing details, so that we think we have seen it in greater detail than is really the case.

R.A. Proctor described such an illusion in an article entitled "Notes on Ghosts and Goblins" (*Cornhill Magazine*, April 1873). Very distraught after his mother's death, he awoke one night to perceive, standing at the foot of his bed in his moonlit college bedroom, a white image of his mother — he could even discern tears in her eyes. He gazed at the image for some time, then leaned forward to observe it more closely. Instantly it transformed itself into his college surplice hanging down from its hook, with the "tears" becoming the silvered buckles of a rowing belt hung over the surplice!

When he deliberately lay back in his original position in an attempt to revisualize the illusion, he found that he could not. His surplice and belt remained as such before his eyes, for now that his brain was aware of their true identity, it could not be fooled again into "filling in" the details to create the image of his mother.

One form of optical illusion involving this principle, and which is extremely pertinent to the Big Grey Man phenomenon, is termed the autokinetic effect. This illusion occurs when there is a lack of visual clues for an observer to use in determining whether or not an object is moving. The result of this is the observer's perception of apparent movement by the object when in reality the latter is completely immobile.

Climber William Hutchison Murray gave a good example of the autokinetic effect in his book *Mountaineering in Scotland* (1947). While in the Cairngorms one day, he saw what he believed to be two climbers traversing from east to west across the snowscape ahead of him. As he approached these "climbers," they paused, apparently waiting for him. Ultimately, however, when he was about 100 yards away, he discovered their true identity — they were a pair of black boulders! The autokinetic effect explains certain sightings of phantasmal figures and giant beings seemingly observed on desolate mountains.

HALLUCINATION, OR BROCKEN SPECTRE?

As a result of the very considerable publicity that followed Professor Collie's Big Grey Man account, visitors to Ben MacDhui not infrequently contemplate the legends and rumours regarding its mysterious entity while actually climbing its lonely slope. Those who do not think of it directly are generally aware of the phenomenon. Consequently, given a sudden, unexpected sound or strangely-shaped wall of mist, it could be readily envisaged how the startled minds of such climbers could "fill in the details" to create, especially if further influenced by autokinetic illusions too, a very real (to them) phantom or presence that they would sincerely believe to be the Big Grey Man.

In contrast to such psychologically-induced optical illusions, however, hallucinations — images housed within the mind of the "observer" and based not upon any external object — comprise a very different situation. Moreover, it is very difficult to believe that apparent encounters with the Big Grey Man by experienced mountaineers could be explained in this manner.

Yet another phantom form, and one that could be participating to the Big Grey Man mystery, occurs in mountainous regions under certain climatic conditions that cause a person's shadow to become greatly magnified, which in turn is sometimes thrown onto a cloudbank or patch of mist. This eerie effect is known as a Brocken specter, named after a peak in the German Harz Mountains from which the effect was first recorded. Clearly this could be responsible for various sightings of huge beings on Ben MacDhui and associated terror.

Certainly it can be an unnerving spectacle to the uninformed observer; so too can be the weird shapes sometimes produced by local condensations of water vapour. Naturally, however, neither of these could explain the aural components of Big Grey Man encounters. Various precipitation effects could, but these, conversely, could not explain the sightings, thereby failing to provide a comprehensive solution.

AN ENERGY TRACE?

Techniques such as Kirlian photography seem to reveal that living organisms release intense amounts of energy during periods of extreme emotion — energy, that can leave behind in a given locality a concentrated invisible trace even after the organism itself has moved away. The energy trace theory proposes that if a locality in which such a trace has been released experiences on some future occasion a similar emotive disturbance, the original trace may develop and actually become visible for a time, and in turn provide an explanation for reports of phantoms and ghosts. Such a process would be analogous to the original image on a photographic plate becoming visible when developed.

It can also be seen that the process could have great bearing on the Big Grey Man enigma. Some mysterious events reported on Ben MacDhui have occurred directly after the climbers concerned had been contemplating the Big Grey Man legends. Following the energy trace theory's line of argument, could their thoughts, intensified by their solitary, hitherto undisturbed travels upon the mountain, have triggered the appearance of some energy trace image originally created by earlier visitors to Ben MacDhui? The energy trace theory additionally postulates that some people release greater amounts of energy than others, thereby offering an explanation for why many climbers have not experienced anything strange on Ben MacDhui, namely that these must have followed people who did not release sufficient energy themselves to create any original invisible trace image.

ELECTROMAGNETIC PHANTOM?

Perhaps phantoms could be energy forms occupying the immediate boundaries of the visible spectrum of electromagnetic radiation, i.e., the infrared (IR) and ultraviolet (UV) regions. Ghost-like images, unseen by photographers, have been captured on film sensitive to these wavelengths.

According to one researcher, locality photographs exist that reveal ghostly heat (IR) images of people and vehicles that left the locality in question many hours before it was photographed. Heat (IR) images may explain many "photographed phantoms," especially those in contemporary attire.

Could the phantoms of the UV wavelengths conversely be the genuine article — real ghosts? According to frequent documentation in literature appertaining no paranormal phenomena, investigations of notable psychics have often revealed that their 'eyes' colour-sensitive spectrum is displaced to the right of everyone else's. That is to say, the eyes of psychics appear less sensitive than those of other people to the visible spectrum's red zone, but overtly sensitive to the violet extreme and seemingly even beyond that, into the UV zone (normally invisible to human eyes). If this is indeed true, and if psychical phantoms (whatever they may actually be) reflect UV light, this would account not only for their visibility to psychics and invisibility to everyone else, but also for many examples of mysterious photos that clearly depict forms unseen by the photographer yet which are evidently something more than mere heat images.

The Big Grey Man might be an electromagnetic phantom, an entity beyond the vision of most humans (hence the rarity of sightings in comparison with the frequent reports of footsteps) but whose presence is still sensed. Of course, this is wholly speculative at present.

"WINDOW" AREAS

In addition to Ben MacDhui, many other localities in Britain and elsewhere seem to possess mystical attributes. These appear linked not to the people who experience them but to the localities themselves. Such locations are popularly held by researchers of the paranormal to be "window" areas, portals through which visitors from other dimensions can enter our world's time and space. Applying this theory to the Big Grey Man mystery, it could be postulated that Ben MacDhui is a "window" area.

One might assume that such an inter-dimensional interface would surely be monitored and protected by some form of warden or guardian. This entity's function would be to ward off any potential intruder (deliberate or accidental), ensuring by every means available to it that everyone kept well away from the portal's vicinity. It can be seen that the above description corresponds perfectly with the reported activity and behaviour of the Big Grey Man.

A LAST WORD

Is the above scenario possible, or just science fiction? Are any of the theories discussed here the correct one? Who can say?

What can be said, and with certainty, however, is that there are many very experienced and respected mountaineers willing to testify that Ben MacDhui does possess a number of unsolved mysteries, including an entity that apparently seeks most emphatically to keep them that way.

BLACK DOGS: FACT OR FANCY?
Gordon Stein, Ph.D.

Of course black dogs exist. My neighbour even has one. So what do I mean about whether black dogs are fact or fancy? These are a very special type of black dog, namely the ones that seem to appear suddenly alongside you on a dark country road, run along with you for a while, and then vanish suddenly. Usually, they are harmless, even if scary. However, they sometimes have been reported to be quite nasty and evil.

CHURCH WORSHIPPERS ATTACKED BY BLACK DOGS

For example, on a Sunday morning in August 1577, the people at the church in the Suffolk town of Bungay had quite a shock. In the middle of the service, a severe storm arose outside. Suddenly, a large black dog appeared in the middle of the church. He ran between two members of the congregation who were kneeling in prayer. The dog evidently "wrung the necks of them bothe in one instant clene backward, insomuch that even at a moment where they kneeled, they strangely dyed."

We know enough to recognize that they really must have "died" rather than "dyed," since dyeing in church is not usually allowed. In this case, another worshipper was bitten by the dog on the back. The bite caused the man to be "presently drawen togither and shrunk up, as if [he] were a piece of lether scorched in a hot fire ..." The man "dyed not, but it is thought is yet alive."

A similar incident involving a black dog in church happened that same month (some accounts say that same day) in another church at Blythburgh, about 12 miles away. In the latter incident, the dog appeared on a beam in the church, swung down and "slew two men and a lad, and burned the hand of another person that was there among the rest of the company, of whom divers were blasted." There was supposedly a set of burn marks left on the church door by the dog as he left.

Hundreds of years later, the paint was scraped from the doors of this church by workmen, revealing the presence of what appear to be scorch marks.

Of course, this type of attack by a black dog is no longer

anything that has been reported. Yes, some of the dogs have been reported to snarl menacingly and not let you pass, but the attacks and deaths are a thing of the past. The black dog is often still thought of as a sign from the devil, but at least the devil isn't using the dogs to kill.

ARE BLACK DOGS REAL?

Some say that these black dog "sightings" are real historical events. The people who say they saw black dogs of a spectral sort really did see them, although the "dogs" were clearly of a supernatural sort.

Another school of thought says that the people who claim sightings may well believe that they saw a mysterious black dog, but whatever it was that served as the focus of the sighting — the idea or image of the black dog — was something from deep inside the viewer's mind. To this school of thought the black dog is a symbolic image of evil, something that black dogs have represented to humanity for thousands of years.

This is the old conflict between the historian and the folklorist. The historian wants to know what really happened. The folklorist simply cares what people believed. I will adopt the position of the folklorist in this article.

There is, of course, no way for us to decide at this point whether any of these incidents really happened. If someone with a movie or videotape camera were to photograph or film the supposed black dog during a sighting, the film or tape showed nothing when viewed, then perhaps the folklorist might feel vindicated for accepting what people believed. If, however, an image of a black dog appeared on the film or videotape, exactly as reported, then the first explanation might be more likely. Unfortunately, no photographic evidence exists for any black dog sighting.

There is at least one additional complication to this set of two possibilities. It is also possible that a layer of myth (perhaps in part derived from fictional treatments of the black dog theme, as in Goethe's *Faust*), is superimposed upon some actual historical cases. This happens in many other fields, such as with UFOs. There are quite a few fictional accounts of UFO encounters that have been passed off as real. Exactly how many such "real" cases remain after the probable fictitious ones are removed is an open question, both for UFOs and for black dogs.

SIGHTINGS OF BLACK DOGS

The interesting thing about the black dog is how widely it has been reported in the United Kingdom. The Germans have also reported seeing it. However, France and the United States don't seem to be among its favourite areas. There are very few reports of mysterious black dogs in the United States, but the U.S. seems to specialize in mysterious humans and humanoids.

This richness of British sightings is probably due to the fact that there is a long tradition of such sightings in Britain. Therefore, folklorists are more likely to record and investigate reports of black dogs than would other agencies (e.g., the police) in other countries. There would be little likelihood of police involvement in any case, since none of the more modern reports I can identify involves any real harm to the humans involved. Even in the United Kingdom, the types of reports and name given to the mysterious dog(s) varies.

Among the names given to this phenomenon (and hence to the dog itself) are Shuck (Black Shuck and Old Shuck as well), Skeff, Moddey Dhoo, Trash, Skriker, Padfoot, Hooter and Gwyllgi. This wide variety of names gives us the additional information that the sightings have been widespread, both geographically and in time.

What do the sightings have in common? Most of the dogs are seen at night, have glowing red eyes, vanish when you attempt to touch them, are silent, non-hostile, and leave no footprints, even in the mud. There are numerous exceptions to each one of these characteristics in many reports.

These sightings did not only take place in the past. Theo Brown, perhaps the leading British authority on the subject, identified some 39 incidents in Britain from 1829 to 1958, when her paper on this subject was published.

SCRATCHING NOISES

At the edge of Dartmoor in southern England in 1972, a farmer and his wife were awakened by scratching noises outside their bedroom door. The farmer got out of bed and looked outside the bedroom door into the hall. He could see little at first, but when he reached the top of the stairs, he saw a large shadow. It appeared to be a dog. Just as he was about to shoo it outside with the poker he was carrying for protection, the dog moved toward him. Its eyes were fiery red. The farmer struck out at it. As he hit it, there was a burst of light, the crash of breaking glass, and the dog vanished completely. Later, the farmer and his wife discovered several interesting things as they examined their home. The electricity was out in the entire house, and every window was broken. There were broken roof tiles all over the outside yard. The roofs of a number of neighbourhood houses had also been badly damaged.

The earliest incident involving a black dog of which we have a record seems to be from a French account by Bertin in the *Annales Franorum Regnum*, written in 856 A.D. About halfway through the services in a small French village church, darkness enveloped the building. A large, black dog mysteriously appeared inside the church, its eyes glowing fiercely. The animal ran around the inside of the church, as if looking for something. It then suddenly disappeared without a trace.

HARBINGER OF DEATH?

On the Isle of Man in 1927, a black dog was encountered by a man on a road near Ramsey. The dog blocked the road and refused to let the man pass. After this blockade went on for a short time, the dog moved aside and let the man pass. Shortly thereafter the father of the man died. The interpretation was that the dog had brought the message of the impending death. Black dogs have often been called harbingers of death.

Another example of this premonition of death can be seen in a 1893 Norfolk, England case. Two men driving a horse cart were forced to stop the cart suddenly due to the appearance of a black dog in the middle of the road. The driver wanted to drive straight at the dog; the passenger urged him against it. Finally, the driver's patience ran out, and he whipped the horse forward. As the cart touched the dog, there was the smell of sulphur, and the dog vanished in a ball of flame. Within a few days, the driver died unexpectedly.

PHANTOM DOGS AND THE CHURCH

Many British rural people thought that black dogs were "church grimes." These are a sort of spirit that guards churchyards from the devil. The origins of this belief may be traced to the old practice of burying a black dog (of the ordinary sort) on the north side of the church cemetery, in order to spare a human soul from having to guard the graveyard. It was thought that this duty fell to the first person buried in the churchyard. This early affiliation of churches and black dogs may help to explain why many of the early sightings were in the vicinity of churches.

Interestingly, many reports of phantom dogs state that the dog appeared unaware of the human being who saw it. The dog apparently "haunted" a section of road or an area. Sometimes the black dogs seem to be on patrol in an area. Often bridges mark the beginning or end of a phantom dog's patrol spot.

BLACK DOGS AND LEY LINES

Some writers who investigate black dogs (e.g., Janet and Colin Bord) feel that the locations of sightings can be linked with leys. Ley theory says that many ancient sites were located along straight lines from each other. These lines are called leys and represented some sort of earth current or energy flow pattern. Perhaps, the Bords state, black dog "patrols" occur along these leys. Many churches (and their churchyards) were built upon the sites of earlier pagan shrines, the location of which, in turn, was often on a ley line. The Bords even hypothesize that the appearance of black dogs themselves may be due to a "current" passing along the leys. Since the presence of such a current has never actually been demonstrated, their idea is pure speculation.

BLACK DOGS BATTLE REAL DOGS

What happens when a ghostly black dog meets a real live dog? Actually, there are several occasions when this happened, all of which indicates that there is some physical reality to ghostly black dogs. Pierre van Passen (in 1939) tells what happened when he allowed his two police dogs to meet a ghostly black dog that passed his house regularly. The dogs (who were inside) leaped for the door. They bared their fangs and snarled. They howled as if they were in pain. Although the black dog could not be seen this time by the human, the dogs reportedly snapped and bit in all directions. The battle lasted two minutes. Then one of the "real" dogs fell on the floor and died.

The appearance of black dogs has sometimes been ended by the performance of an exorcism ritual, or by the display of religious artifacts. It is difficult to know what to make of this, as there have been very few such cases.

DEVILS AND BLACK DOGS

In folklore from continental Europe, there are instances of the devil appearing in the form of a dog (often a black dog). This tradition does not seem to mean that all (or even most) black dog sightings (especially not the British sightings, where there is no such tradition), are an appearance by the devil. Although some devil appearances may be in the form of a black dog, the reverse is not true. Phantom dogs have also been said to occasionally guard treasures.

WHAT IS THE EXPLANATION FOR BLACK DOGS?

Phantom dogs are something that few people have tried to explain. Theo Brown has made a couple of attempts, but I will leave it to the reader to judge how successful they have been. She feels that one possibility is that the black dog is an aspect of a person at every stage of life, in a Jungian sense. They are projections from the unconscious, manifesting themselves visually at times of crisis. It could be viewed as a sort of "friendly double" in disguise. Going against this interpretation most strongly is the fact that black dogs have appeared to different people at the same spot. It is the location and not the person that seems to matter.

Another possible "explanation" offered by Brown is that it is probably impossible to explain the black dog in its own terms. By that she means that the more we think of the black dog as a phenomenon, the more difficult it is to explain. If, however, we could find some ancient cult or sect that had dogs as a symbol or "totem," perhaps we could compare our black dogs with them for significance. The lack of such evidence from history indicates that the symbolism aspect of black dogs is what is important.

Some aspects of dog mythology that are based upon real-dog behaviour may be of help. A dog howls at the Moon, similar to a wolf. It can be an intimate associate of humans (a possible symbol for a vampire-like creature). It protects property (i.e., it has a guardian function). It scavenges, and thus it is associated with death and graveyards. It sees "spirits," and so may serve as a link between this world and the next.

The one thing which does seem clear is that the black dog of British folklore seems to live outside of the concept of human time. It appears and disappears from human sight by its own contrivance.

CONCLUSION

What are we to make of all of this? Frankly, I don't know. We can hold all black dog stories up to the standard demanded by the historian, and then dismiss them as lacking sufficient evidence. We can also treat them (as I would prefer) as evidence of some sort of experienced perception on the part of the viewer. How we are to interpret this perception is another matter. Perhaps all black dog perceptions originate in the mind of the observer. That doesn't make the black dog phenomenon any less worthy of investigation and explanation. Right now, we are still back in the data-gathering stage. Any real explanation will have to await more data.

FAIRY DOG

A.Stewart Galwey

This happened 60 years ago in Lanarkshire, Scotland, in 1927. My widowed mother, Janet Gardner, took her young family to a new world of lonely moorland, ten miles from a station and two miles from another house. We came from a crowded city.

The isolated cottages were inhabited by shepherds and ploughmen who were deeply superstitious. Their surroundings encouraged superstitions, from the old drove roads said to have been laid down by the Roman legions to the wailing moor birds that made the supernatural expected.

The local children walked four and five miles to and from the school daily. From them we learned the country superstitions. We were a perfect audience, strangers and townies. They acknowledged a fairy presence—not dainty, winged creatures, but an invisible folk not of this world who could bring misfortune if displeased.

One of the aparitions to be feared was the Fairy Dog. These were spectral black hounds who followed travellers after nightfall. Sometimes they would bring bad luck, and at other times they were kind. We were warned never to speak to these spirits.

This was the ghostie I was most interested in, for I was seven years old at the time.

One summer afternoon I walked with the three neighbours' children from the nearest cottage to their home. They came half way, leaving me alone the last mile.

The moon rose, silvering everything. I grew aware of a black dog accompanying me at the path's edge. I was sure he was not a straying collie. He was taller than I stood, with no spot of white, and silent pawed. I remembered the story of the Fairy Dog and picked up my pace on the springy heather. Suddenly it seemed to be colder.

Then came the turn-off for home. I knew I was safe. I turned to the black dog to say good-bye in my child's way. I put out my hand to pat his head. Nothing met my fingers but emptiness and icy coldness. In a second the creature disappeared.

I ran home. I never told my story to anyone except my brother John who refused to believe me.

Soon afterwards we left for the city and a more material world with no room for Fairy Dogs.

UNINVITED VISITOR
Marjorie Phillips

Back in 1941 I was residing in England. I had been asked by my husband's boss, Kenneth Bryson, to meet him regarding the chemical formulae belonging to my research chemist husband, Cecil Alldred. The firm had moved away from London. This necessitated my travelling about 40 miles west to a small country town, Oakham, where he was living in a former vicarage of a church about 400 years old.

After a nice dinner and a pleasant evening we retired to our respective bedrooms, which were next to each other. I cannot say how long it was before I went to sleep, but I was suddenly awakened by the door being opened, and an elderly lady dressed in clothes of the early Victorian era came toward my bed. As she drew nearer I began to get a choking feeling in my throat. She appeared to glide down my bed and up the other side, then bent over me while her blue eyes stared closely at me. With difficulty I gave a shout because I felt that someone was strangling me. She suddenly disappeared and the door slammed.

The next morning my host had to unjamb the door and on doing so he said he knew that I had experienced "it."

I told him what had happened and he said that at the turn of the century the Vicar's wife had been found strangled in the basement. The murderer had never been found and since then she comes back every time there is a stranger in the house to satisfy herself that it is not her killer. The local people stay away from the Vicarage but people, particularly from America, specifically come to share the experience.

Fifty years later it's still very clear in my mind!

THE LIGHT OF SPIRIT
A Real-Life English Ghost Story

Melody Clark

It was not my first trip to England, but it was certainly my most memorable. I love England, second only to my own country, and was very happy to leave busy Gatwick airport for the soothing English countryside. We counted among a party of four a couple of psychic sensitives, but on that morning the Other Side seemed as remote to us as the crowd and bitter of our hometown, Los Angeles. We had only one goal: a memorable vacation, and nothing else mattered in the least as we drove in high spirits toward a house in Yorkshire.

Our friend Jocelyn was a ballet dancer and had gone to the Continent for a performance. She had kindly extended to us the use of her house for our week's stay in York. We were thrilled at the prospect, far preferring the convenience and comfort of a private home to yet another chain hotel. I look back on her letter of invitation now with some amusement. "See how you go around the house," she warned us. "There are some things that need fixing and don't bother at the creaks and groans at night. We're used to them. It's an old, old house."

We had surmised her warnings to be of the physical world in nature. We assumed that the "creaks" and "groans" were the work of two-century-old wood and English plumbing over anything more abstract. Certainly, Jocelyn never told us she had ghosts.

SURPRISING DISCOVERIES
We settled into the house quickly. The amiable cottage had predictably ancient lighting using dimmer switches. The antiquated plumbing featured hot water heaters we had to pummel into service. The atmosphere of dusty age prevailed and we just loved it. By the time we all shipped off to bed we were able to make our way around in the dark, entirely at home.

In the morning, I found the downstairs light on.

At first, I wasn't alarmed. Although I knew that no one had

been up before me (my bed was by the stairs) I inspected the dimmer switch and found it just slightly away from the "off" position. I decided that whoever the idiot was who shut the lights off the night before hadn't done a very good job of it. I had only myself to blame.

As soon as everyone was up for breakfast, I related the incident, only to find that the others had been smelling tobacco smoke all night long. I hadn't smelled anything — I can't sleep on planes and had barely made to nightfall with my eyes open. Apparently, the odour of pipe smoke had filled the upstairs corridor strongly enough that it leaked into each bedroom. The others were certain that it had been pipe smoke, rather than cigarettes (which we might have picked up on our clothes or luggage on the plane or at Gatwick or some other kind of smoke. Since none of us even smoked cigarettes, it was an interesting occurrence.

We shrugged all of it off, though as we prepared for a day of sight-seeing in York. We scouted the house for something unknown burning (checking the water heaters, too). I made certain that the dimmer switch was all the way off (fearing my friend Jocelyn's Scottish ire should she come back to a burned-out light switch. With the house thus firmly secured, our foursome set for the city.

We returned to the house couple of hours after dark. As my friend Marnie remembers, she knew we were in trouble the moment we drove the hired car into the drive." From the front walk we could all clearly see the living room lightly softly burning ... the one I had checked before leaving to make sure it was "off."

My first thought wasn't anything metaphysical. I decided I had best phone Jocelyn in Cherbourg and make sure she didn't have a faulty wire somewhere in the house, one that was causing the lights to go on and off and that might be burning something that smelled reasonably like pipe tobacco. A call to her produced quick assurances that she had had the house checked for wiring problems last year and there were none. In retrospect, I think had I been in her position I'd have had less confidence in my electrician and more concern about the problem ... unless I suspected the real cause to be something else.

Anyway, she cheerily wished us a great vacation, said she looked forward to seeing us soon, and rung off.

I still was feeling uncomfortable at the prospect of sleeping there, especially since Marnie was beginning to pick up feelings about the place. Marnie by profession is a schoolteacher and, contrary to what some people might believe about a person with a psychic talent, is a very practical person. I listened to her carefully as she started "scanning" the house. Within a few minutes, I was getting impressions myself — of an Englishman wearing a smoking jacket and sporting a small, manicured moustache. When it was pointed out to me that the image sounded remarkably like the late actor Leo G. Carroll (who had once played host to a couple of very trendy young ghosts in the *Topper* television series), I decided that my pattern-seeking mind was getting the best of me.

Throughout the next days, we were too busy to notice anything out of the ordinary. We took trips on British Rail to see Glastonbury, Stonehenge and other places. Each day the living room light was turned off as we left the house. Reliably, it would be burning for us when we returned home in the evening. There was never any other light involved and by the end of our week there, I wasn't sure if we were dealing with a wiring problem or a very thoughtful ghost.

On the night before we were due to leave Yorkshire for London, we had all gone off to far-flung corners of the house to rest from our day's trip or to read books scavenged from Yorkshire bookshops. I was curled up on the downstairs sofa reading a volume on standing stones when I came across a passage about Glastonbury (a place to where my friends — especially my friend Carmen — and I are very drawn). I elected to go upstairs and show the passage to her.

AN ELECTRIC-LIKE FEAR

As I reached the fifth stair, I was — as in one of those bad ghost stories — literally unable to move. I still remember very clearly what the sensation felt like. At that point on the staircase, I was shot through with what I would later describe to my friends as an "electric-like fear." Every other fear episode I've had in life was the result of objective stimuli giving me the subjective response of withdrawal or goose bumps or running shrieking in the opposite direction. But this sensation didn't originate inside me, at least in the usual sense. It wasn't a response to anything I could see or smell. A feeling I can only describe as terror just pounced on me from out of nowhere.

I had to move quickly downstairs — I definitely was not walking up them. I sat down on the sofa, trying to find a quick and dirty logical reason for what had just occurred. I soon abandoned that campaign — I just wanted to stop trembling. Images of my ghostly friend in the smoking jacket crowded in; I still don't know if the image was born of convenience or actual intuition.

At that moment, my friend Carmen came walking down the stairs, looking like she had just awakened and was rather cranky because of it. "Did you wake me up?" she said. "I felt a bad pain in the side of my head and I had a feeling I should come down and talk to you."

I told her (without mentioning the passage in the book as the reason for my trip) of the experience I had just had on the stairs. She gave me an odd look and said that the stairs "had felt just fine" to her. "But the weird part about the feeling I had about talking to you," Carmen said, "was that I felt it was connected to Glastonbury."

I showed her the passage in the book and we agreed that if it wasn't a "simple coincidence," we had either demonstrated some fairly dramatic telepathy or something bizarre was going on in that house.

NOT A SEANCE

We decided we would gather our friends together for a joint meditation/hypnosis session to unlock some intuition about what was transpiring. We often gathered together at home for such occasions — on birthdays, during problem periods, or just for fun. We're all open-minded concerning parapsychology and mysticism and enjoy engaging in such sessions. This was the only time when it felt vitally necessary to attempt one.

I should point out that we weren't trying to conduct a séance or anything of the kind. We're also all very rational, pragmatic people. Two of us (Tina and myself) are writers and the other two (Carmen and Marnie) are respectively an artist and, as mentioned before, a schoolteacher. We had seen a lot of friends of ours go overboard with such things — trance channelling, Walk-ins from Atlantis and the like. Our meditation sessions, by contrast, were always kept very firmly grounded.

The fifth participant in our meditation, the house, had been built over two centuries before. It had at one time been the servants' quarters to a large estate that had long ago burned down. A succession of very normal working class families had lived there through the years. We didn't know any other details.

We chose the living room, since our helpful "ghost" — if that was what it was — had been playing with the light there. After fussing with the current adapter, we got the tape player working and started up the hypnosis tape we always used. We all chose pieces of sofa or floor to sit in or lay down on and Carmen, who was closest to the light switch, turned it off.

I was also close to the light switch. Carmen was in the chair just across from me. I trust her implicitly, but even if I didn't, I could make out her image in the darkness (and she could see me) and we all would have easily heard footsteps on the old, noisy, wooden floors.

As we sat in the dark, the tape started with dulcimer music and the sounds of ocean waves. It occurred to me distantly that it was the perfect mood music for a haunted English house and we were probably setting ourselves tip with atmosphere. But my rational side was shut up by the beginning of the hypnotic instructions, impressed against the darkness and silence.

As the taped hypnotist initiated a relaxation exercise, the living room light abruptly came on. I looked across at Carmen and she was looking over at me and we were both blinking from the sudden attack of light. Tina and Marnie sat up quickly.

We quickly ascertained that no one had walked like a fly across the ceiling and switched the light on with a toe. We were only slightly shaken by the event, chalking it off to our old friend the "probable electrical surge," albeit a propitiously timed probable electrical surge.

Once again, the light was switched off. Carmen, not surprisingly, decided she'd rather use the opposite end of the room. So we all settled in once again and started up the tape. This time the taped hypnotist made it all the way through the relaxation exercise before the light flashed on again.

A FLASH FROM THE SPIRIT
We were now really concerned. In the six evenings we had spent in the house, we had never had the light flash on and off like this. In the last three evenings, one of us had taken to sleeping on the downstairs sofa, too. The occurrence of the incident with what we were attempting to do was just too significant.

THE LIGHT WENT OUT
"So, are you a man or a ghost?" Carmen barked back at it, really irritated. The light stayed on. "You're a ghost," she added, "turn the light out." As everyone of us in that room that night will attest at the moment after she asked this question, the light went out.

Thoughts of the nearby Holiday Inn now seemed wonderfully warm and homey. But then I could just picture four American women walking into the Holiday Inn babbling about ghosts. They have a dim enough opinion of us over there, I decided. I also tried to keep in mind that this was the home of a friend of mine and that she lived there quite happily.

So we all moved to the centre of the living room, our attention on the light. Deciding we had a electromagnetic analogue to a Ouija board, I opted to ask some questions.

"Let me verify," I said. "If you're really a ghost, turn the light on." Again, as we all will attest, the light flashed on.

We proceeded to grill "the host" for over a half hour. Whatever it was, it performed like a lamp, "answering" our inquiries with amazing consistency. We then threw it a curve, asking it to flash twice" to confirm an answer it had given us earlier. It flashed the light twice.

We went on to more complex questions using serial light flashings. It affirmed that there was a spirit world and conveyed that it was a little boy who had lived in the house a century ago. There were many other spirits in the house, it maintained.

By now I had little doubt that we were communicating with something conscious, even if it was only our own minds. There was a definite pattern to the thoughts that responded quickly to our questions. We weren't, to my kind, drawing patterns from connected electrical surges: the lamp flashed on in quick succession to all our inquiries.

By 1 a.m. we were all too tired to talk with any ghost, no matter how interesting. We bid our "visitor" good night, thanked him for the conversation, and all set off for bed. I decided I would rather take my chances with the lamp ghost than face going up those stairs once more.

The light did not flicker once during the night. I'm a very light sleeper on the best of occasions and only slept fitfully that night. I would have noticed had it come on. Throughout the next day, the lamp did not turn on by itself once.

I HOPE HE MADE IT

On our last day, we all gathered in the living room and mentally led the little poltergeist in the lamp toward the Light. We still weren't convinced it was anything other than group PK causing some interesting effects, but just in case, we certainly didn't want to leave the little fellow stranded on this plane. The guy on the stairs could find his own way back, I decided (I certainly didn't want to drum him up), but the little boy we helped. I hope he made it.

This incident is the single most memorable psychic episode I've ever had. Though it happened two years ago, it is all still very clear in my memory. Jocelyn, the owner of the home, has since verified that she has never witnessed any similar occurrence with the lamp in the house. As of this writing, there have been no other reported episodes in the house.

Tina and Marnie returned a few months ago. The stairs were silent and the lamp performed as lamps are meant to do. And Jocelyn still lives there quietly — at least that's what she claims.

MY GOD! IT'S SHUCK!
Did I meet a thousand-year-old Viking raider's dog one night many years ago on a coastal road in England? I'm not certain anymore ...

D. Tyler Hendricks

In 1952, I joined the Army and was sent to England. There I was assigned to an anti-aircraft battalion's radar site overlooking the North Sea and green Norfolk countryside. Duty was light, and I had plenty of time to move about and explore.

On one of my walks I met an man named Patrick Kearney. We became friends, and occasionally I visited him at his cottage near the beach in a village called Cley next the Sea.

Late one day, with a book under my jacket to be returned to him, I walked the few miles to my friend's home. I enjoyed our chats. He was better educated than I was then, and a little older, having served with the British army in Burma. He was an artist. Patrick didn't seem to care much what people thought, for which I both admired and envied him.

On that night we sat talking in a room lit by the fireplace's glowing coals. It was late when something prompted me to jocularly mention the frequent appearance in the English press of stories about ghosts and such. I fully expected Patrick to respond with a laugh. He did not. Instead, dead serious, he related several tales of his own of this type. Embarassed, I did not interrupt.

His final story was about an apparition reputed to have been encountered periodically for a very long time. There are variations, but Patrick's version was this:

THE LEGEND OF SHUCK
During the ninth century. the coastal area which includes Norfolk was often pillaged by Viking raiders. Their ships would suddenly appear in a defenceless sea village's harbor, and the terror began.

Among the Vikings was a leader who always brought with him his huge, vicious dog. The English called the animal "Shuck." One night, on a raid somewhere along these shores, this leader's band met unexpected resistance, and in their retreat, the dog was left behind.

On following nights, Shuck ran up and down the coast looking for his master and the ship. Not finding them, he has continued his search ever since.

At least, that is what people around there believe. Over the years, many in those parts have reported meeting Shuck, most often on moonlit nights, sometimes with unhappy results.

I am the son of a doctor who had little tolerance for such myths. Overall, my attitude on this subject was (and remains) similar to his. That night I was Patrick's guest. I did not scoff, but I had learned he possessed a nutty side. As soon as I could, I left.

I'm not sure what the hour was; I remember the lights were out in the pub not far from Patrick's house. Familiar with the road, accustomed to returning alone to my barracks in the dark, I had never been afraid in rural Norfolk This night was no different.

A TRIP THROUGH THE DARK

From Patrick's door (where one could hear the sea), I walked down the curved main street through Cley, past an old windmill, and began the gentle ascent toward Blakeney, the second of three villages I would go through. Once in a while the moon came out from behind clouds to aid my seeing the road.

I may have thought about Patrick's words as I walked, I'm not sure. It seems likely my attention was mostly occupied with making certain my feet correctly found the macadam in the dark. No auto passed.

The moon came out as I reached the church at the top of the hill at Blakeney's outskirts, then went under again as I started down the other side.

When I arrived at the base of the hill, Blakeney was behind me. On my right there was marsh between the road and the sea, on the left a hedgerow and an empty field behind it. I was on the road to Morston, the last village before my barracks. The night remained quiet and ordinary.

When it entered my consciousness, the noise was indistinct. It came from somewhere in back of me. I glanced over my shoulder, and saw nothing in the moonless gloom. The sound continued, growing more discrete, nudging the edge of memory, calling up uneasy feelings. I kept turning my head to listen better.

Suddenly I knew! It was the sound made by a dog's nails on pavement, in this case a running dog soon to overtake me! I stopped, turned, and faced the sound, still in control, my heart ready to spring to my throat. At that moment I didn't think of Shuck, only of keeping peace with the stranger I was about to meet.

"Good boy," I called softly, holding out my hand in the dark, hoping my voice didn't betray me. He kept coming. "Nice boy, here boy," I said. On he came, making his loud, then louder "scratch! scratch!" sound in the dark. With my heart racing now, I kept up a low, propitiatory incanting of "Good boy, good boy."

Without pausing, he ran past me, a presence felt but not seen against dark hedgerow. Then the noise receded, and with it my fear.

"MY GOD! IT'S SHUCK!"
Moments later the moon came out. Ahead I saw a dog, all right, lopping up a rise in the road, an agile, calf-sized canine. "My God!" I thought, "It's Shuck!" Then I dismissed the thought.

I left England soon afterward. Thereafter the incident came to mind from time to time. I made it one of the stories I told my children, though always recited wearing a half smile of disbelief.

In 1972, I returned to England, and visited a now more prosperous, married Patrick. For the first time I related to him what I had not told before.

PSYCHOLOGY OR ...?
Patrick was certain I'd seen Shuck. But aloud to him, I strongly expressed disbelief. And who would not? Today virtually any adult is amateur psychologist enough to recognize my experience as no more than a midnight concoction of equal parts suggestion, coincidence and fear.

But to tell the truth, that perfectly good explanation has never seemed good enough. For some reason Patrick's view feels right, and I wonder why. Is it possible my equal mix of Viking and English peasant genes carry vague memories of ancient places and ideas?

Sometimes late at night, when my body is nearing sleep, scenes return from that brief encounter on a Norfolk road, and I hear my voice in the dark saying to no one, "My God! It's Shuck!"

THE HYLTON CASTLE GHOST
A LEGEND CONTINUES

Matthew P. Hutton

Situated between Gateshead and Monkwearmouth stands the tall, dark tower of Hylton Castle. Built in the early years of the 15th century by Sir William Hylton, who died in 1457, it was home to one of the oldest, richest and most powerful families in England's history. It also has the reputation of being one of the most haunted homes in the North.

The ghost at Hylton, known as the "Cauld Lad," is said to be the spirit of a servant who had been found guilty of disobedience and brutally murdered by an impatient and cruel master. The facts recorded at a coroner's inquest on 3 July, 1609, show that the body of Roger Skelton, a young stable boy employed by Sir Robert Hylton, Esq., was discovered in a pond near the castle. The youth was killed with the point of a scythe, and Robert Hylton was named as his murderer.

The inquest was told that Robert Hylton ordered his horse to be ready on a particular occasion. He grew impatient and proceeded to the stable, where he found the boy, Roger Skelton, fast asleep and the horse unsaddled. Hylton tried to rouse him with a hayfork and accidentally stabbed the boy to death. Fearful of the consequences, the laird dumped the corpse in a pond.

On 6 September, 1609, Robert Hylton obtained a free pardon for the manslaughter of Roger Skelton, but from then on the home of the Hyltons seemed to have a life of its own. Doors opened and closed at will, kitchen utensils and furniture began to move unaided, but what frightened the household most was the disembodied, childlike voice whose mournful, midnight cries of "I'm cold, I'm cold," struck terror into the hearts of all who heard it.

The ghost remained at Hylton Castle even after the death of the last of the Hyltons, and has made his presence known to the subsequent occupants. At the turn of this century the castle was abandoned, but in more recent times it was placed in the keeping of English Heritage, which has opened the monument to the public. With hundreds of visitors a year it's not surprising that many people now claim to have experienced strange happenings at Hylton Castle.

One of the most remarkable stories I have ever heard about the castle, was told by Eric Little, custodian. The story is about a group of students who stayed at the monument to help raise money for a local charity.

"It was 31 October, 1987," he told me. "The group of students were linked by phone to a local radio programme as a sort of Halloween special. At around 11:30 over the radio came a scream, then the telephone link to the castle went dead. After 15 minutes the radio company still could not make contact with the students locked inside Hylton Castle."

The custodian explained, "At first I thought it was some sort of joke, but having heard some of the stories about the place, I thought I had better check on them just on the off chance that something had gone wrong. When I got there, I opened the door and the four students ran like mad from out of the castle, jumped into their car and away they went. I wanted to know what could have frightened them, so I went into the castle, but found nothing. However, when I went into the topmost room on the fourth floor, I found they had left behind their sleeping bags, cups and torches. You could even see where one of them had thrown a cup of tea across the room. I don't know what it was," the custodian concluded, "but something scared them. They didn't even contact me about getting their stuff back."

IN SEARCH OF THE CAULD LAD

In was on 19 October, 1989 when I found myself being locked into Hylton Castle for the night. Unlike my predecessors, I armed myself with an array of sophisticated equipment and a good team of psychic investigators in the form of Mark Ross, Paul Armstrong and my brother Jonathan Hutton, who are fellow colleagues from the Gateshead Technical College, Chris Storey, a much-respected local reporter from the *Sunderland Echo* and the very gifted medium Tony McQueen.

Everything that was said at the castle was recorded by my colleagues immediately upon entering the premises, and our vigil started at 9:45 p.m. with the team making our way to the top-most room, a narrow chamber with a large stone fireplace and arched wooden roof.

We didn't have long to wait before Tony McQueen announced that there were at least two spirit presences in the room, a middle-aged man and a young teenager of no more than 14 years old;

the latter we presumed to be the "Cauld Lad," or Roger Skelton. As I stood listening to Tony's description of our spectral companions, I suddenly, and for no apparent reason, began to feel physically sick, and to my surprise so did Jonathan and Mark, who were standing close by. Tony told us that the boy had moved toward us and that what we were experiencing was the boy's condition, just before he died!

Over at the other side of the room, the reporter and Paul complained that the temperature had dropped to an unbearable level, and so it went on. For the following 30 minutes we were subjected to a variety of different emotions and ailments and I was only too pleased when the whole experiment ended and we moved down to the third floor. As we reassembled in the small, dark room on the third floor, Tony told us he felt that the presence was strongest in here.

He was right. Within minutes we heard music, then the umistakable sound of a crying child, He next told us that he felt something was coming from the room above. As we turned to face the doorway we saw what seemed to be a fog or mist starting to form. Tony said he could see people in it, and described a young boy cartwheeling through the room and people marching down the stairs. One, he said, peeped in to the room at us and gave a crafty smile as if he were planning to play a trick on us. We saw none of this, only a misty glow in the darkness. As it began to fade, the reporter walked toward it and we were treated to a remarkable sight, a man silhouetted by a psychic mist.

THE COMIC SPIRIT

As we climbed the stairs to the fourth floor to try to get some sleep, Tony told us he could see a clock face that registered 3:05 or 3:15. He felt it could have something to do with the spirit he saw peeping in at us from out of the mist. We all waited for the "trick" to occur but nothing happened and so we tried to get some sleep.

Fifteen minutes later the alarms on the cars outside the castle started to sound. I ran down the stairs followed by Paul, Jonathan and the reporter, but as soon as we pulled open the castle door, the sound stopped. Not only was there no one in sight, but the doors to the castle, which should have been locked, were now open. The large padlock which had kept them tightly closed was gone. So it would seem that the trick had been played on us by the comic spirit after all.

The next day when Paul and Jonathan played back the cassette that had been recording all night, they discovered that the tapes had recorded perfectly up to the point when we had made our way down to the lower floor to the room with the psychic mist.

Everything recorded in that room sounded slow and drawn out, not because the batteries had run down, but because it must have been recorded at high speed.

A week later, when the photographs were developed, out of over 200 pictures only one had developed — a group photo taken on the ground floor.

THE ROSE COURT GHOST

London's Rose Court Hotel, at the corner of Great Cumberland and Berkeley Streets, hardly seemed the place to see a ghost. Its lounge faced Great Cumberland Street, with French windows and a wrought iron fence between the hotel and the pavement. Anyone coming from the Oxford Street area had to pass those windows to reach the Berkeley Street entrance.

In July 1958, I met three fellow Americans — Judy Hudson, Carroll Lynn Busse, and Carroll Lynn's mother, Margot. They had come from Paris to spend a few days in London before returning to the states. Carroll Lynn's fiancé, Bill McElroy, a U.S. airman stationed in Scotland, had promised to drive down to give her a ride in his new car, a white Jaguar with a blue interior. Coincidentally, Bill was the nephew of then U.S. Secretary of Defense Neil McElroy, back in 1958.

That morning, Judy, Carroll Lynn and I were playing chess near the French doors. Both girls and Mrs. Busse, sitting across the room, had a clear view of the street. Carroll Lynn and her mother, suddenly leapt to their feet, saying, "There's Bill, he just went by the window."

"Oh, was that Bill?" Judy asked.

I turned, but he was gone. Mrs. Busse went out to the lobby, but returned a few moments later, alone.

"I'm worried," she said. "I'm calling the base." When she returned the second time, her face was pale. "People are so rude. The desk sergeant said, 'All right lady, I'll check his bunk.' Then he came back and said, 'I guess he won't be using that bunk anymore. We're holding funeral services for him right now.' Bill has been killed in an accident."

Although I had never met him, I know that on that summer morning, in the middle of London in broad daylight, Bill McElroy's spirit passed by.

THE MYSTERIES OF GHOSTLY FRAGRANCE

Joyce Rushen

Perfume, with its indefinable allure and strange alchemy, has long been regarded as a mysterious and magical substance. It has the power to captivate the senses in subtle fashion, almost akin to witchcraft, according to old beliefs. Even after the source of the perfume has gone, its fragrance lingers. An elusive scent in a bowl of potpourri will long continue to fill a room, despite its floral contents having been gathered from the garden months before. A pressed flower found between the closed pages of a seldom-opened book still has traces of its scent remaining.

The skills of the perfumers of ancient Egypt are well known. When the tomb of the high priest Ra Ouer was discovered, among its treasures was a container filled with a substance likened to the delicious scent of flowers. Amazingly, the fragrance remained, even after of 4000 years. When the tomb of Tutenkhamun was opened, his golden face was garlanded with flowers wonderfully preserved, their scent still lingering.

Equally mystifying is the unaccountable fragrance detected in old houses from time to time. This has given rise to a number of tales about how an unseen presence from the past makes itself known by emitting the scent of what was its favourite perfume in life.

John Aubrey, a 17th-century English antiquarian, once recorded how, when questioned, a spirit that appeared before a gathering promptly vanished, leaving behind a curious perfume.

Exotic perfumes were not unknown in earlier times, but floral types, such as lavender, were among those most widely used. Lily and rose were the most common of these. The great Queen Elizabeth I favoured rose and made lavish use of it.

At Bramshill House, a rambling old mansion in southern England (now a police college), the old-fashioned perfume of lilies of the valley is said to waft through the corridors and the long gallery. Bramshill has long had the reputation of being haunted.

It is reputed to have been the scene of the well-known legend of the Bride in the Chest. The story holds that abride became trapped in an old oak chest on her wedding day, only to be discovered many years later by her husband, now old and gray. All that was left was a skeleton still clad in wedding finery.

THE WHITE LADY

Known as the White Lady, she is said to wander about the house accompanied by the lingering scent of lilies of the valley — perhaps her wedding bouquet contained these blooms. More than one person, including police officers, has encountered this fragrance, and their accounts are well documented.

Another common ghostly fragrance is the smell of lavender. It is one of the oldest English perfumes, and was first mentioned by the Abbess Hildegard in the 12th century.

A lavender-scented ghost is reputed to comfort the ailing in a Norfolk rectory. The ghost is said to be an elderly woman wearing a cap. She supposedly appears when people, particularly children, are suffering and cannot sleep. Her scented presence is always accompanied by a feeling of warmth.

A famous coaching inn in East Anglia has an upstairs room that constantly smells of lavender. The smell is so distinct the chamber is called the "Lavender Room."

The source of this smell cannot be determined. But all manner of legends are woven into the history of the ancient inn. Some people claim to sense a presence and a feeling of tragedy and despair in the room. Others are merely conscious of the sharp, clean smell.

People living and working in an old manor house at Bury St. Edmunds, have spoken of the beautiful scent that suddenly greets them in the passages. The unidentified fragrance is of a ghostly nature. Its presence has given rise to the saying "There goes the Scented Lady again."

There are also accounts of families living in very old cottages who, at times, smell an ancient perfume that none of the women in the house use. They can only conclude that it has something to do with the past.

Equally odd and inexplicable is the powerful whiff of an herbal fragrance experienced by a number of visitors at Cotehele, an early medieval manor house in Cornwall. It is now a National Trust property and open to the public.

Peter Underwood, in his book *Ghosts of Cornwall*, relates a story told to him by a recent visitor to the manor. The witness, while exploring the oldest part of the building, experienced an overwhelming odour of herbal fragrance and heard plaintive music. Instilled with a timeless quality in its remote setting, Cotehele certainly lends itself to legend and matters of a ghostly nature.

A SCENT OF INCENSE

The smell of incense in what were formerly religious houses is also a common experience. An incense-like fragrance has been noticed at lovely Beaulieu Abbey in Hampshire. For several centuries, until the dissolution of the monasteries in 1538, the abbey was the home of the Cistercian Monks.

Fragrances can linger in the atmosphere almost beyond the scope of time. The ancient Egyptians, who knew all about the magic of perfume, recognized the power of scents in evoking feeling of continuity. Perhaps this is why the smell of perfume is common to many haunted locations.

MEDIEVAL MURDER IN A WELSH CASTLE

**The Grey Lady had already killed one rival with an axe.
Would she consider my beloved Ginger a threat and attempt
to get rid of her as well?**

In retrospect, it may have been paranoid to fear for my wife's safety, because the Grey Lady is a ghost and the murder she committed occurred hundreds of years ago. But Ginger and I were staying at the scene of the crime, Ruthin Castle in north Wales, and I suspect that I was a part of that medieval tragic triangle. It was a feeling that had gradually grown on me from the moment I entered Ruthin Castle. The place felt familiar, even homely. Later, when we toured the castle and the grounds, it felt like homecoming.

Then we came upon the grave of the Grey Lady. Looking at the unadorned pile of rocks that covered the grave filled me with sadness.

According to legend, the Grey Lady was the wife of the commander when the castle was a fortress garrisoned by the armies of Edward I. She is the resident ghost and is called the Grey Lady because she is always seen dressed from head to foot in grey. She discovered that her husband was having an affair with a local lady, so, to end it, she murdered her husband's lover with an axe. I wonder why she committed this act. In those days there was no women's lib and it was common for a husband to have an affair, many affairs, or a mistress. The Grey Lady must have been extremely jealous or passionately in love with her husband.

When her dastardly deed was discovered she was sentenced to death. Because of her crime she could not be buried in the consecrated ground of a churchyard, so she was buried just outside the castle walls. For these many centuries the Grey Lady has roamed the battlements, the castle grounds, and the former chapel. Does she feel she can't get to heaven because she was not buried in consecrated ground? Is she seeking something? Forgiveness? Absolution? Her lost love?

In retrospect our entire vacation seemed to prepare us and lead us to this encounter with the Grey Lady at Ruthin Castle. When Ginger and I had decided to take a month-long motor tour through the

United Kingdom we did not dream that we would stir up old hosts or open a window to the past.

THE JOURNEY TO RUTHIN CASTLE

Had I been more aware I might have expected it because of my abnormal fascination with castles. I stopped wherever there was a castle to examine — and there are a lot of castles in the U.K. In our trip through England, Wales, Ireland, and Scotland, we toured or clambered over more than a score.

We explored remodelled castles like Warwick; museum castles, like the ostentatious Cardiff, where everything that looked like gold was; empty hulks like Blarney in Ireland, where I kissed the famous Blarney Stone; and many throughout the U.K. that were in ruins. It was these that intrigued me. Invariably they were on high ground with a view of the surrounding area. This enabled the occupants to see the approach of hostile forces and also meant that the enemy had to fight uphill. Why had they been abandoned? Were they destroyed in battle?

Standing on a remaining tower or rampart, I could almost hear the shouts of the invaders and the clang of steel on steel. I played a sort of game with myself trying to imagine how I would have attacked the castle or how I would have defended it. Ginger couldn't understand how I could spend so much time "just looking at the scenery." Later the reason for my obsession became more clear.

Since we had no set itinerary or schedule, we had made no reservations for our overnight stays. We did, however, plan to spend at least one night in a castle that accommodated guests.

While there are many castles, only a few have been remodelled to include hotel facilities. We selected the magnificent Ashford Castle, which dates back to the thirteenth century and is rated as the finest hotel in Ireland. The Connemara countryside around the castle was the locale for the John Wayne movie *The Quiet Man*. Unfortunately, or as it turned out, fortunately, Ashford Castle was hosting a convention and there was "no room at the inn." So it was not to be Ireland where we stayed in a genuine castle.

For no reason we were aware of except that it was in the general direction of our rambling route, we then chose Ruthin Castle in the north of Wales. I did not realize it at the time but I was about to have a homecoming.

This area of Wales abounds with names that sound like

something from *The Lord of the Rings*. Towns like Rhufoniog, Tegeingl, Dyffryn Clwyd, and Dolwyddelan dot the countryside. Numerous uprisings, revolts, and wars with England have occurred there through the ages. After a war with England in which Welsh resistance was crushed, Edward I awarded the Lordship of Ruthin to Reginald de Grey, Baron of Wilton, in 1282.

Around 1283, de Grey erected a wall around the town of Ruthin and employed the best military architects to enlarge and strengthen the castle. The finished product was in romanesque style with seven towers and massive, 100-foot-high red walls, seven to nine feet thick, rising above a protective moat. The castle withstood many attacks and sieges due, in part, to a secret tunnel into the town, through which fresh supplies were brought to the garrison.

While the castle was a self-sufficient entity, the lordship of Ruthin included not only the castle but the region of Dyffryn. In this area the lord was the law of the land. Therefore, the castle had facilities for dealing with lawbreakers. For minor infractions there was the pillory. For more flagrant offences there was the whipping pit where wrongdoers were flogged according to the degree of their crime. For long-term offenses and torture there were the dungeons, where often the only way out was horizontally.

Instead of the gibbet or beheading, capital punishment was administered in the drowning pit. This was a walled-in and covered extension of the moat. A trap door was opened, the condemned were tossed in and the door closed. The victims had two options. They could sink into the water and drown immediately, or they could struggle to keep their heads in the shallow air space above the water until exhaustion forced them to sink to their death in the murky depths.

Through its long history Ruthin Castle has had its share of deception, intrigue, skulduggery, treachery and treason, Machiavellian plots, wars, war casualties and murder, so it is not unusual that a lot of psychic energy has become anchored or trapped there.

THE TWO KNIGHTS

While we were touring the castle I spotted the figure of a knight in full black armour guarding the landing to the upper floors from the inner hall. Knights in shining armour are legendary, but black armour is not common. I was drawn to this standing suit of armour like a magnet. As was the norm in that time, the original occupant of the armor was only about five feet six inches tall. One arm was extended, so I asked Ginger to take a picture of me shaking hands. I put one arm on the suit's back to steady it, and I grasped the outstretched gauntlet. As I did, I suddenly had the strange sensation that I was shaking hands with myself.

Ginger, who is somewhat of a sensitive, had a strange experience at the same time. As she looked through the camera viewer, she saw, not me in mufti shaking hands with the black knight, but two knights shaking hands. At first she thought there was some distortion in the viewer, but when she looked past the camera she saw the same thing.

At that instant she got a quick flash of me in a different life in ancient Wales. "This should be interesting," she thought as she snapped the picture. But, of course, when the photo was developed, what she had seen psychically did nor appear on the photograph.

The odd thing was that in Ginger's vision, she did not see me at my present height of six feet but at the same height as the black knight, around five feet six inches. In that quick flash she did not get any details of my life or who I was, but she said that I had been an expert swordsman, in fact, the best. Perhaps I have a past life as a knight to thank for the fact that I have accumulated championships and over 200 medals and trophies in foil, epée, and sabre and was ranked eighth nationally in sabre.

All the feelings I had been having seemed to be confirmed by Ginger's vision. I felt I had an insight into a former existence, and this sharpened my interest in the castle as we toured the grounds. The battlements and defensive features took on added meaning. I now understood why I was so engrossed with the hypothetical defence of the previous castles we visited. At one time I may have been involved with the responsibility of defending Ruthin Castle.

I became more convinced of my connection to Ruthin Castle that evening when we stopped for an after dinner drink in the former library, now a bar. We were seated at a table, enjoying our drinks, when I became aware of an enchanting, haunting fragrance. It smelled like jasmine. I knew Ginger wasn't wearing it, so I looked around for the source. Aside from the bartender and two men seated at the bar about 10 feet away, no one else was in the room. I didn't think anything of it at first but when it persisted I got curious. The two men at the bar left and the bartender was not around, so I asked Ginger if she smelled it.

"Smell what?" she asked.

"That fragrance."

"What fragrance?" was her reply.

Ginger has a nose like a bloodhound, so it seemed odd that she couldn't smell the aroma. I asked her to come near me. She did and she sniffed but detected nothing. The fact that I could smell the fragrance but Ginger could not seemed significant. Was it meant for me alone? I wondered if it was the drink or the fragrance or a combination of the two that was causing me to feel mellow, or was there a third cause, a loving presence?

By now I was convinced that I had spent time at Ruthin Castle. Had I been the errant commander and the Grey Lady was still in love with me? Was that her fragrance? Was she here now? There was no other evidence but I was certain she was. That thought intrigued me and then worried me. Would she be jealous of Ginger and try to hack her to death as she had her medieval rival? When we returned to our room I kept sniffing to see if the fragrance had followed me, but it had not. If it had, I planned to sit up all night to keep an eye on Ginger. Maybe that was irrational but when dealing with the unknown, especially the paranormal, I tend to function on an emotional level, and logic takes flight.

Although I had felt a loving presence with the jasmine smell, I was still dealing with an entity who had murdered a rival, and I did not want to take any chances on Ginger's safety.

My mood turned from mellow to sad. I felt sorry that the Grey Lady was condemned to remain earthbound. I wondered whether she felt doomed to remain here forever. I wanted to tell her, as Jesus told the afflicted, "Your sins are forgiven." Before I drifted off to sleep I said a prayer for her.

It did not end there. I felt compelled to pray for her every night. Maybe owed it to her. Since it was not by chance that I returned to Ruthin Castle, perhaps it was for the purpose of helping her. Several centuries of penance seem enough. If I was the cause of her death, then it is just that I make amends. Someday I will return to Ruthin Castle and ask when the Grey Lady was last seen. Somehow I have the feeling that the answer will be "Not in recent years."

PENFOUND MANOR

A lovelorn ghost haunts one of Britain's oldest manors.

Kenneth Nickel

My first peek at Penfound Manor was through the leaf-patterned, wrought-iron gate. An older man and woman were clearing verdant overgrowth from the courtyard, and they did not see me for a moment.

In Los Angeles, I had boarded a British Airways 747 with the idea of finding little-known Penfound Manor. But now that I was here, I wondered how I might get to see the inside, since local people had told me that strangers were not welcomed.

Then the lady saw me and advanced, smiling. So far, so good.

Why did I want to see Penfound? I was curious about a place that his been situated in the same spot for close to 1000 years, little changed in the last 500 or so. It is fascinating to imagine how many people have lived in this continuously occupied house, on this plot of land. It is a place almost unique in all of Britain.

In October of 1066, Duke William of Normandy and King Harold Godwinson of England had their famous tiff near Hastings. Penfound Manor probably already existed at that time, so it is older than the Tower of London or even the present Westminster Abbey.

Today, Penfound is called the best-hidden country house in England. You can be close enough to hit it with a rock and not see it or even "see the chimney pots," as a nearby resident told me. The present owners are delighted with that inconspicuousness.

I first became aware of Penfound Manor while reading a somewhat obscure book about English ghost lore. The idea of a house — not a stone castle with walls eight feet thick, but a house — standing on the same plot of land for nearly a millennium invades the imagination. Needless to say, Penfound became a must-see on my English trip, with or without the ghosts.

The book in which I had read about Penfound contained no pictures and gave little information about the manor's location. But later I found a very approximate location on an old map and it was all I needed.

Well, okay, I also needed the directions given to me by the barman of a pub in a nearby village. When I asked, his directions were prompt and exact. But he also confided that I would be cordially refused admittance.

Nevertheless, I had white-knuckled it out from London in my rented car. If the house's current residents peremptorily told me to get lost, I would cheerfully do so, for I would have at least seen the exterior of Penfound.

Located in one of the most storied and legend-crammed areas of western England, Penfound Manor carries many legends of its own, including a Romeo-and-Juliet type of story and rumours of a haunting by a young female ghost.

THE MANOR'S EARLY HISTORY
The exact age of Penfound is not known, but when Duke William of Normandy achieved victory at Hastings and changed his name to William the Conqueror, he gave the house to his half-brother, Robert, Count of Mortain. Penfound is mentioned in the *Domesday Book*, a roster of William's newly acquired real estate in Britain, which reads in part, "Briend holds Penfou' of the Count of Mortain ... There is one plough with one serf and two bordars. In times past, it was worth 20 shillings and so now." Maybe Mortain could not envision himself residing in a mere 20-shilling house while his brother was busily ensconcing himself in his new White Tower on the Thames, because he allowed Briend the Saxon to stay on at Penfound Manor.

The nonmathematical mind goes limp when it considers the numbers of people who must have continuously inhabited this relatively small plot of land over the centuries since it was built. But possibly the descendants of Briend the Saxon became the original Penfounds, the family that took its surname from its house.

Penfound means "head of a stream," which seems fitting, because the family was an ambitious, prosperous bunch, hurling themselves into various businesses. The present owners of the manor point out what they call a possible "smuggler's hole" in the courtyard as evidence that some of these enterprises may not have been legal.

In the time of Briend, Penfound was a huge, lofty single room with a cooking fire in the middle of the floor and a hole in the roof to let out the smoke. This room is now the Great Hall — though a few improvements have been added. The hall's present floor, for example. For the past 300 years, it has laid over the original floor, which is made from trampled-down sheep knucklebones.

Another improvement is the darkly polished yet rough and

irregular Armada Staircase, built from wreckage that floated ashore from that Drake-dogged clutch of Spanish ships. A Penfound built this staircase purposefully irregular to lessen the chances of his being surprised in his bed at night — possibly a necessity because of those illegal businesses.

But one of the very first additions to Briend's high single room was the second storey bedroom, the Norman Solar, a newfangled idea that gave privacy to the lord and/or lady of the manor. The Norman Solar, with a descending, narrow staircase, was the bedroom of the teenager, Kate Penfound.

Legend has it that Kate was in love with John Trebarfoote of Trebarfoote Manor, three or four miles away. Everything would have been rosy except the English civil war was going on and the Trebarfootes had declared for the insurrectionist, Oliver Cromwell. Kate's father, Arthur Penfound, a hot-tempered Royalist, supported the incumbent monarch, King Charles I. This was bloody time in England, and the enmity between these groups left no place for a marriage for John and Kate.

STAR CROSSED LOVERS
But the young lovers cared nothing for the political predilections of their progenitors. They decided to elope. On the night of 26 April, in a year not precisely known, Kate climbed out the Solar window while John waited with horses in the courtyard below.

Wily Art Penfound then appeared and caught them. The stories differ at this point, but the one most widely accepted has it that in the swordplay that followed, Kate was killed trying to intervene, and John Trebarfoote was also killed. It is known that Art survived to die naturally much later.

Penfounds have not lived in the manor since 1759, when it was confiscated by the Crown because the Penfounds were Stuart supporters. Sadly, the last of the direct line, Henry Penfound, died in a poorhouse in 1847.

AN ANNUAL GHOSTLY APPEARANCE
Today, villagers are said to shun Penfound Manor on 26 April, when the duel in the courtyard between Art Penfound and John Trebarfoote is said to phantomly reenact itself annually. Past residents of the manor have also seen Kate descend the staircase from the Solar, cross the Great Hall, and ascend the Armada Staircase in the newer part of the house as she had often done in life.

It was a perfect September day when I first saw Penfound Manor. As I watched the owners working there, I could see that the manor sprawled across the cobbled stones, the rightmost side lost to view among the foliage. "In a dip in the land, at the source of a little stream, snuggled into the fold of the down, bedded into foliage, open to the sun, hummed about by butterflies ..." was how this idyllic old English home was described by Sabine Baring-Gould, novelist and cleric, in 1898. This was the scene I saw, and I can describe it no better than Baring-Gould did.

The owners I saw were a handsome retired couple who valued their house, privacy, and anonymity. Ostensibly, I do not even know their names, and I am still not sure why, when I appeared at their gate, they gave consent, after many questions and conferences, not only for a tour but also for a story with pictures. But the reader may already have noticed that I give no real clue about the location — except one unavoidable one.

If it is possible for a space-time continuum to exist in microcosm, Penfound Manor must be it. The barely recorded past is still manifest here, along with the present and future.

In geologic time, Briend and his Saxons were here only moments ago standing in the Great Hall. It feels as though if you turn your head fast enough, you could glimpse them watching benignly from the darker recesses of the room. Indeed, Briend's well was the main water supply for Arthur Penfound and for the present owners as well.

Arthur Penfound's cobblestone courtyard still passes through the middle of the house and to the front entrance as a pathway to this well. In the past, a dairy was part of the house, and the dairy workers wiped their feet in a perfectly circular depression filled with wet rushes before entering the living quarters. This depression is preserved, thickly carpeted in red, and it still gets damp in wet weather from springs that feed it. Behind one wall, now sealed over, the lady of the house pointed out, there used to be a minstrel's gallery.

The tour was nearing a close and no mention had been made of the ghosts, even in Kate's old bedroom, so I asked. The lady could not verify the annual replay of the courtyard scene, but she certainly has heard Kate, even above the television.

The Solar is now thickly carpeted but Kate is still heard walking the bare boards of her old bedroom above the Great Hall. Both the lady and her husband have heard this sound on at least two occasions. It gave me goosebumps to hear a calm, rational confirmation of the ghost story when I had expected an amused, if not derisive, denial.

FOOTSTEPS IN THE BEDROOM

I asked the lady if it bothered her to live in the same house with the ghostly Kate. She replied, "Certainly not." In fact, she wishes she could see Kate sometime, as others allegedly have in the past.

A famous ghost chaser and sensitive had once visited Penfound and could not detect anything paranormal, other sensitives have characterized Kate as an innocuous and spritely wraith who quietly goes about her own business with no malicious intent — in short, possibly the least troublesome kind of house guest.

Too soon, it was time to leave. I had found Penfound and it was much as I had imagined it would be. The present owners had graciously given me a tour of their polished, tasteful home, but it was time to clear out.

I looked back at Penfound as I closed the leafy gate. The house was an earth-coloured extension of the Earth itself, an eternal symbiosis. The scene was utterly tranquil, utterly timeless, and quintessentially English. Mr. Baring-Gould would love it still.

But other adventures awaited me. I left the manor to the latest of its uncounted and uncountable residents. ... and to Kate, who, some people say, has never left.

TRUE MYSTIC EXPERIENCES
**Personal accounts of strange and mystical experiences
by our readers**

SACHA

My daughter Elizabeth was born ten weeks prematurely with little hope of survival. That night I went to my parent's home to report on her progress. Sacha, my mother's cat, was in the garden. I carried her into the house. Later Sacha got out and was run over. I was the last person to handle her or see her alive.

Every evening after visiting the hospital I phoned both my parents and my wife's parents to keep them up to date. My mother said that everything was going to be fine because the cat had appeared to her. Elizabeth was allowed home a few days later.

I continued to phone, though less often. One night my mother asked me to keep an eye on Elizabeth because she had dreamed about Sacha. She was sure that Sacha and Elizabeth were connected. The following day at work I received a message that Elizabeth had been taken to the hospital with a hernia.

From March 1978 until my mother's death in 1986, Mother often phoned me to say that the cat had appeared to her. This always happened just before Elizabeth came down with some minor childhood illness.

One night shortly before Elizabeth was due to go onto solid foods, my mother called to say that the cat had appeared for quite a while, making Mother wonder if something serious was going to happen.

Elizabeth had to be hospitalized again. A paediatric nurse was needed to help her cope with the change from milk to solid foods. Everyone was worried, but then the cat reappeared briefly. Elizabeth began to improve. She kept her food down, and she was discharged more quickly than we had expected.

Sacha appeared to warn us of every crisis in Elizabeth's life. The more serious it was, the longer the appearance. In the most serious cases Sacha always appeared to reassure us just before the climax of a crisis. My family now believes in spiritual guardians, although previously we were sceptical.

GHOSTLY FOOTSTEPS

During World War II, I served in the Auxiliary Territorial Service (ATS), the woman's section of the army, in the Royal Army Pay Corps. I was stationed in York. We had various offices scattered around the city in buildings that had been requisitioned by the army for wartime use. My office was the non-effective section, which meant that we dealt with the pay accounts of soldiers who were no longer in active service. That could mean one of three things: they were dead, they were missing, or they were prisoners of war. It was depressing work, but it was work that had to be done — sorting out the affairs of army men stated to be missing in action because no one knew what had become of them.

Even worse was closing the accounts of those killed in action and returning their effects, if any, to their next of kin. It was not unusual to come across a blood-splattered AB 64, the soldier's ID booklet and pay record. I even saw one with a bullet hole through it that must have penetrated the man's heart, since AB 64s were kept in the left breast pocket.

We worked long, regular office hours. Saturday lunchtime to Monday morning was our time off, but we still had to do picket duty to guard our premises over the weekend. The male pay clerks worked the evenings, and the women covered Saturday afternoon and Sunday morning or afternoon.

My office was in an area known as Lady Peckett's Yard. I entered it through a narrow passageway from one of the city's main streets, and I came our into a rectangular open space surrounded by tall buildings. This yard was always uncannily quiet, considering how close it was to a busy thoroughfare. I had to walk to a far corner to reach my place of work, which was located on the top floor of the farthest building.

Despite our gruesome tasks, we were a friendly bunch, with lots of teasing between the men and women. So when the men tried to frighten us by telling us about heavy, unexplained footsteps on the floor above at 2:15 a.m. each night, we didn't believe them. We thought they were just trying to scare us before we did our weekend stint. The ATS women would have been on picket duty at that time. All we had to do was be there in case of incendiary bombs, so we sat in the ground floor office. We relaxed, wrote letters, and read books.

One Sunday afternoon, my colleague Gladys and I were on duty. Our mutual friend Mary would come to sit with us, and, when we finished at 6, we would trot off to the Methodist church canteen for tea before going into the chapel for the 6:30 service. We had not thought about the footsteps because we knew they were impossible. The large room above us was divided into two sections that were separated by a glass partition. No one could walk across it diagonally.

We were sitting quietly when we heard the first heavy footfalls. I looked at my watch: it was exactly 2:15 p.m. Gladys and I looked at each other in terror as the footsteps continued diagonally across the room above us. We jumped up and fled into the farthest corner of our room, clinging to each other as we huddled in the corner.

"Whatever is the matter with the two of you?" Mary asked in surprise. We couldn't speak and just stared at the ceiling, mesmerized by the regular sound of what seemed to be army boots. Obviously Mary was not hearing anything.

Gladys and I couldn't stay there. We grabbed chairs and sat in the doorway of Lady Peckett's Yard, praying for 6 and our relief guards. The yard was, as usual, uncannily quiet, frightening us even more. We sat as far as we could from the bottom of the stairs leading to the haunted office we had just left. Mary, who thought our imaginations had got the better of us, stayed in the office, quite impervious to our panic.

It was freezing cold and dark long before six o'clock. With the darkness and blacked out conditions, our terror deepened. We cast fearful looks at the bottom of the stairs, now shrouded by nightfall. At last our soldier colleagues arrived to take over. We blurted out what we had heard, but they showed no surprise. "We'll go upstairs and check. Come with us Jean, and then you will know that there is nothing there to harm you," one of them said.

My curiosity overcame my fear, and although nothing would have persuaded me to climb those stairs by myself, I was quite brave with a familiar figure at either each side of me. I couldn't believe that a glass partition went across the office. I thought that it must have had a door in the middle, which it did, but the door was locked. The men tried it to make sure. No explanation for those footsteps was ever found.

Years later, while reading a guidebook to York, I learned that it was one of the most haunted cities in the United Kingdom. The book even mentioned the "ghost of Lady Peckett's Yard," but it gave no details.

THE GHOST THAT COULD NOT BE FORGIVEN

Tarona Gail Hawkins

This ghostbuster encountered one of the most frightening cases of her career in a quiet English village.

From the outside there was nothing extraordinary about the house. It was an ordinary residence in a quiet village. As I knocked loudly on the door, however, I thought about the letter that had brought me here this cold morning. The contents of this letter had informed me that my present surroundings could hide a dark and sinister presence.

The door was opened by a woman in her late twenties. She was casually but smartly dressed in slacks and a sweater. I introduced myself and was at once invited in.

I always protect my client's identities by not using their real names, so I will call this woman "Jane." Jane led me through the house to the lounge. Here she introduced me to her husband, Paul, a handsome man who looked tired and worried.

We began discussing the letter they had sent me. I asked Jane to tell me from the beginning exactly what had happened to cause her to ask me for help. Jane glanced at her husband and then, hesitantly at first, began to tell me the story:

"I suppose it all started when we moved into this house about eight months ago. My grandfather had died and left me a little money, and we had always wanted to move to an older village house with character. Finding this house on the market for such a low price prompted us to buy it. It was within the first fortnight after we had moved in that we started to notice the stench. It was such a bad smell that we thought a dead animal must be under the floorboards. We tore up all the carpets, inspected the floorboards to see if any were loose, scrubbed the house from top to bottom, and went through gallons of disinfectant. We even had the drains inspected. But nothing made any difference. The smell would come and go without warning. It became embarrassing when anyone came to visit us. Often we would see friends inspecting the bottom of their shoes.

"Next came the touching. I could be washing up at the kitchen sink or dusting a room when I would feel a hand touching me in intimate places. At first I laughed and told Paul to get off, but Paul would be nowhere in sight. I was completely alone.

Because Paul's job took him all over the country, he would occasionally spend the night away from home. We had been in the house about three months when Paul telephoned one evening to say he would not be coming home that night. He had been asked to stay in Oxford an extra day.

"I was determined to cope alone, so I reassured Paul that all was well, and we ended our conversation. It must have been pretty close to 10:30 when I went to bed. I had had a couple of glasses of wine and felt tired. I must have fallen asleep as soon as my head hit the pillow.

"When I woke up in the morning, I could feel Paul's body snuggled against mine, just like every morning. I turned over to ask him what time he had arrived back home last night. I was met by an invisible force lying next to me.

"A grey mist hung over me and it started to grope my body. I must have leaped ten feet out of bed. I ran out of the room, down the stairs, and into the front garden. My next-door neighbour was just fetching his milk when he noticed me standing barefoot in my my pyjamas.

The lady next door made me tea that I drank with shaking hands. Her husband inspected my house in the hope of finding this mystery man in my bed.

He returned and reported, 'It looks like you've been dreaming, luv, there's nothing and no one in your house.' I knew it was best to leave things at that, so I thanked them and returned home.

Paul did not believe that the invisible force was anything more than a dream. He said it must have been the wine. Nothing happened for the next month, and just when things seemed to be trouble free, my sister rang to ask if I could go to Leeds for a couple of days to look after Sam, her 13-year-old, while she went to London with her husband to celebrate her birthday.

I went, and the second day I was there, I could tell as soon as I called home that something was bothering Paul. He seemed to be less cheerful than normal. When I asked him if something was bothering him, he told me that nothing was wrong.

I returned home on a Thursday evening and was met by a worried-looking Paul. It took him a week to tell me that he had experienced the same invisible entity lying next to him in bed. He had also felt the spirit touching him and he had smelled the bad odor.

I said, 'Thank goodness it happened to you. Now that proves I'm not going around the bend.'

We decided then and there to put the house on the market and move on. If only things could be that simple. Every time someone came to view the house, the smell would start.

Every room in the house felt cold and unfriendly. People's expressions gave them away; we could see that they couldn't wait to get out of the house.

Please help us," Jane begged me. We have had so many people in from churches, all of them promising to get rid of it, but up to now nothing has helped."

THE INVESTIGATION

I told Jane and Paul that I would do my best, but I made it quite clear that I couldn't make any promises. My next task was to walk around the house and see if I could tune in to the ghost.

Jane led the way upstairs. Then, I caught a glimpse of it. It was a grey mist that started to walk behind Jane. This ghost had attached itself to her. It could go anywhere with her if it wished, or it could stay in the house alone. The question was, why Jane?

Jane was the one who needed help, not the house. If this spirit were not removed, it would follow her to her new residence. My experience with ghosts and hauntings had taught me to be crafty about never letting the spirit know what I intended to do next.

After touring the house we returned to the lounge. I asked Jane to sit down while I did a little healing with her. Paul stood on one side and I placed my hands over Jane. The second time I made a pass over her, something sent me sprawling across the room. Thankfully, Paul managed to catch me before I fell to the ground. This was a powerful ghost and I was a little afraid.

Suddenly, the grey fog seemed to engulf Jane. It started to take on the shape of an old man. He seemed to superimpose himself over Jane. He had gaunt features and a vile smell that almost made me vomit.

My last hope was to talk to the ghost — to plead with it and tell it of a better place, a world of peace.

"What do you want from Jane and Paul?" I asked.

"Forgiveness," it replied.

"For what?" I asked.

"For touching her," it said.

"But you also touched Paul. Do you want his forgiveness?"

"That was to show him I existed," came the reply. "Tell Jane her grandfather wants to be forgiven. I can't move on until she can honestly forgive me."

Jane's face registered every kind of emotion from horror to shame when I told her who it was. "I will never forgive him," she said. "My flesh still crawls when I think of all the dirty things he did to me. He knows I'll never forgive him."

After Jane said this, the grey mist disappeared.

Jane's grandfather had molested her when she was a child. She was only nine when he first started touching her. He was an evil man who was continuing beyond the grave his habit of molesting her. His ghost was still abusing her.

Jane was not able to forgive this spirit, Her grandfather's ghost feeds off her hate and he welcomes it. If she were able to send out forgiveness and love, the energy would be too powerful for him to break through. But it was impossible for me to move him as long as he had Jane's hate to feed him.

So his ghost is not gone. Jane knows that when she lets go, I will be there to help her.

JACK'S BACK
Andy Ellis

In autumn 1888, a madman struck terror into the hearts of the people of London's East End. Between August and November, five female prostitutes were brutally murdered — four of them were literally ripped to pieces. The world came to know the killer as Jack The Ripper.

Today, the dimly lit alleys and small, quiet side streets are all but gone, a distant memory of a time that is perhaps best forgotten. There are, however, a few historic buildings left that Jack would recognize.

The best known of these is the Ten Bells public house, resting in the heart of Ripperland on Dorset Street. Over the years, the pub has had its name changed twice. It was known as The Jack the Ripper for ten years in the seventies.

The pub is literally a shrine to the anonymous murderer. It has elaborately decorated walls awash with original newspaper cuttings and hand painted tiles depicting the scenes of horror. Such is the fascination with the crimes that the pub now has a preservation order attached to it, which means its interior decor can never be altered.

There is a side to the legend that has seemingly escaped the intense interest that other parts of the Jack the Ripper story attract. The pub has sudden mysterious cold spots, lights that go on by themselves, small trinkets — including plates and ornaments — that disappear for weeks on end, and taps, knocks, and occasional moans that seem to originate in the attic, now mainly used for storage.

THE RIPPER'S GHOST?
So few identifiable buildings remain from Jack's time that Yvonne Ostrowski, the landlady for the Ten Bells, believes that Jack's ghost now walks the pub rooms. So far, no one has actually seen the ghost, but Yvonne says, "The pub has a completely happy history. No one has ever died here or even been hurt. Most of the pub's landlords and landladies have only stayed a few years. There is no special attachment to the pub by anyone — other than Jack — so who else could it be?"

It is almost certain that Jack would have known the pub well, probably drinking there himself. Three of his victims, Mary Ann

Nichols, Annie Chapman, and Elizabeth Stride, were all found murdered within half a mile of the pub, and all but one of the ladies, Mary Jane Kelly, was known to drink at the Ten Bells.

With regard to the actual haunting, Yvonne says, "There have been many times when I have been woken in the middle of the night by footsteps in the attic, which is unused. The first time it happened I thought that perhaps we were being burgled and went downstairs to have a look. When I arrived in the bar area, all the lights were on and several decorative glasses were missing. I knew I had turned the lights off, and I always wash up before I retire to bed."

About three weeks later I was again woken up by noises. The lights were back on and the glasses had been returned, except they weren't hanging up in the normal place, but were neatly stacked on the bar."

A short walk from the pub is Miller's Court, one of the few remaining Victorian streets to survive modernization in the East End. Miller's Court was where Mary Jane Kelly was butchered. In the late seventies, one side of the street was improved. The other side was scheduled for demolition.

A MYSTERIOUS FIGURE

Late one September evening, as the sun began to sink in the sky casting long gloomy shadows over the area, Joseph Ogrowski was looking out of his bedroom window. This is what he says he saw: "The entire street was quiet when suddenly this figure appeared. It walked slowly down the street and it really caught my attention because of the way it was dressed. It had on some type of felt cap and a long brown coat that covered its body from tip to toe. Even the collar was turned up, so that none of his — or maybe her — features could be seen. It was carrying a small parcel under one arm. When it drew close to number 13, it stopped, looked around, and walked straight through the hoardings that blocked the entrance."

Joseph, like everyone else in the area, had heard of Jack the Ripper, but wasn't well versed enough to know that number 13 was where the Ripper's final victim, Mary Jane Kelly, had been murdered. Joseph continued his story: "At first I thought I must be seeing things, or perhaps the shadows had been playing tricks on me. I went outside, crossed the road, and peered through a crack in the boards. It was too dark inside to see anything, but the boards were nailed firmly to the building and I decided that I must be mistaken. But the incident bothered me, so I decided to watch again the following night.

"Nothing happened for a week. Then, exactly one week later, the same figure, dressed exactly the same way, walked down the street and again disappeared through the hoardings. This time I was sure of what I had seen. Two days later, work began on knocking down the old houses and I have never seen the figure since."

GHOST MATCHES OLD ACCOUNTS

The most striking point about Joseph's description is that it matches almost exactly the description given by a witness almost a century earlier of a man seen with Kelly on the night of her murder. Even the parcel being carried tallies exactly with the old account.

It is odd, too, that something strange has happened in the last two buildings that Jack would be able to recognize from his time, and when one of those places was irreversibly altered, the sightings ceased.

Ghosts are most closely associated with scenes of violence, the theory being that the victims died so suddenly that they cannot accept their death and so do not pass over to the other side. If the most popular theory regarding Jack the Ripper is to be believed, then Jack did indeed suffer a violent death. Overcome by insanity from his terrible deeds, he is said to have thrown himself into the Thames and drowned.

The body of the person with the strongest claim to being Jack is Montague John Druitt, and his body was fished out of the Thames on 31 December, 1888. He was a failed barrister and part-time teacher who lived in King's Bench Walk, just across the river and whose cousin, Lionel, had a medical practice in the Minories, just two minutes walk away from The Ten Bells and five minutes from Millers Court.

Who knows, perhaps one day Jack's ghost will decide to reveal his identity and tell us exactly why he committed the murders. In the meantime, it seems fitting that while he escaped human justice, he has not escaped a higher justice that keeps his spirit earthbound in everlasting torment, forced forever to visit the places where he dispatched his victims to an early grave.

GHOST OF THE FERRY BOAT INN

Joyce Rushen

A number of old inns in Britain are reputedly haunted, often by ghostly Tudor ladies, handsome cavaliers, fugitive priests, smugglers, highwaymen like the famous Dick Turpin, and in one instance, an ostler whistling in long disused stables. After all, old inns have sheltered a vastly changing population of travellers over the centuries, and many tragic, illicit, or lurid events may have transpired within their walls. Generally, hauntings originated within the confines of an individual inn at some point after it was built.

There is, however, one inn that is reputedly haunted by a ghost that belongs to a time long before the inn was built.

The story begins in the fenlands, then a vast, watery waste of marshlands and dikes. In time the tale came to be associated with the Ferry Boat Inn, an ancient thatched inn on the banks of the River Ouse at Holywell in Cambridgeshire.

In 1050, a young girl named Juliet Tewsley, who lived in the village of Holywell, fell deeply in love with a handsome reed cutter named Tom Zouls. He was a rough fellow, and preferred the company in low-down taverns in the area. Tired of Juliet's charms, he spurned her for another.

On one of those brooding, melancholy days of low-lying mists peculiar to the fen country, heartbroken Juliet hanged herself from a willow tree on the riverbank. Because she was a suicide, it was forbidden to bury her in the sanctified ground of the parish churchyard.

Instead, according to custom, the village folk buried her, still clothed in her pink gown, at a crossroads — in this case, close to where she hanged herself. The site was also where the ferry made its daily crossings over the river, linking road to road. People crossed themselves when they passed by the grave and avoided it altogether after dusk.

Sometime later, probably in early medieval times, the Ferry Boat Inn was built close to the ferry crossing at Holywell. The building foundation surrounded Juliet's tombstone, which was incorporated into the bar parlour of the inn. Just when whispers arose that Juliet's ghost had taken to haunting the inn cannot be ascertained, but according to legend, her restless spirit has returned to it again and again over the centuries. The stone slab remains a part of the flooring to this day, and it has been trod upon by countless generations of customers.

From all accounts, the pink-clad wraith of a young girl is seen to materialize above the stone slab and then drift away in the direction of the river running by outside. The most significant day for this spectral materialization is 17 March each year, the date Juliet is believed to have committed suicide.

Old oral tradition is a strong factor in the community life of East Anglia and the fens. So, despite a lack of proof for the story of Juliet's life, the presence of the gravestone in the floor of the heavily beamed bar parlour of the Ferry Boat Inn have long aroused interest among people far and wide. For many years now people have gathered at the inn — especially on "Juliet's Night," as 17 March is called locally — to watch for the wraith's appearance at midnight.

In 1952 the landlord went so far as to obtain a late extension permit. Two years later, in 1954, hundreds of curious people invaded Holywell on Juliet's Night. So great was the crowd that police from the nearby town of St. Ives had to be drafted to cope with it. People jostled for space in the packed inn as the tension increased by the hour.

Sometime later, intrigued by the sensation caused by the haunting, the Cambridge Psychical Research Society sent a team of investigators to the inn, but no ghostly figure materialized. Clairvoyants have also visited the inn and have tried to contact Juliet.

All manner of odd happenings have taken place at the inn. Strange sounds have been heard, and patrons have claimed that doors left shut have opened in mysterious fashion. Old-fashioned music, rather like a dirge, is occasionally heard, seemingly coming from nowhere. Described as haunting and strangely beautiful, the music can only be heard by women in the bar parlour. Dogs do not like being in this room. Some will growl and bristle with fear if guided too close to the gravestone slab.

There would most certainly seem to be something supernatural centred around this room in the inn. It is not a place to be in alone after dark. Local women are reluctant to go near the inn on the night Juliet is said to rise up from the floor and head for the river. They are fearful lest they encounter the unknown. The ghost of a lovelorn girl who cannot rest has become part of the history and the haunting of the Ferry Boat Inn at Holywell.

THE LANDMARK OF HORROR
Stephen L. Marchant

A Roman road to the south and east of the ancient village of Elsdon climbs steeply out of Elsdon Vale. A more modern road detours along a gentler gradient than its Roman predecessor, but at the crest of the hill, the current road turns sharply left and rejoins the ancient track.

At this point a strange sight appears on the skyline, and as travellers approach, they are brought face-to-face with one of the oddest scenes in Britain: The gallows of William Wynter, hanged for murder in 1791, where it still stands today.

In 1791, the sound of a howling dog brought people to a horrendous scene. An elderly woman living on the outskirts of Elsdon was found dead. It was obvious she had been savagely attacked. The only clue to the assailant's identity was an impression of the hobnails left by the boots of some recent visitor clearly visible in the mud close by the victim.

Not long after, a shepherd with his young son was relaxing in one of the cottages on a nearby hillside before moving on to another pasture. The shepherd took little notice of the travelling man resting against the east wall, sheltering from the chilly northwest wind, but his little son did.

Later in the day, the boy told his father of the strange pattern made by the nails in the man's boots. His father had heard the news from Elsdon, so he made his way down the village to raise the alarm.

The villagers set out after the traveller, who turned out to be William Wynter. When Wynter was caught, he pled his innocence, but the nails of his boots matched the cast taken from the scene of the old woman's murder.

Wynter was taken to the victim's cottage, where the dog sealed his fate, for it was not the old lady's dog, but Wynter's own. In a tragically vain gesture the dog had remained cuddled with Wynter's victim. The dog snarled at his former master, and, had he not been restrained, would certainly have attacked him. From that moment on, William Wynter was doomed.

The trial took place in the city of Newcastle upon Tyne in the late spring of 1791. Only three years earlier Wynter's father and brother had been hanged in the town of Morpeth, only 14 miles north of Newcastle. They had been arrested and tried for burglary. Wynter was following a family tradition, a fact not lost on his jurors.

The judge had only one recourse under the law — Wynter was sentenced to be hanged. The judge made a special provision in his judgment, however, which is why visitors are confronted with the strange sight on the skyline of Elsdon Vale to this day. Following the execution, Wynter's body was to be returned to a spot overlooking the place of his crime, there to be hung in chains on a gibbet. It would remain as a perpetual warning to evildoers "until the end of time." Wynter's gibbet still stands on the ancient crossroads known as Steng Cross, where originally two Roman roads crossed.

Since Wynter had no formal burial (the words "to hang until the end of time" were taken literally), his shade is said to be seen often, on an endless search for a final resting place.

A few minutes after midnight three years ago, when I travelled by the spot where the gallows hangs, all but one of the fuses in my lorry blew. This was a curious thing to happen and probably coincidence, but also on that dark November night, others distinctly heard the sound of a dog whining, even though no physical trace of a dog was found. Authorities have received a number of calls from other drivers who have made journeys in this lonely area. They, too, have reported that they heard a phantom dog. Perhaps the main witness against Wynter still snarls at his former master's heels.

DERWENTWATER'S LIGHTS

The gloomy ruins of England Dilston Castle conceal its secret political history. James Radcliffe, Earl of Derwentwater, was a cousin of the old pretender James Stewart, son of James II. During 1715 he deliberated about whether or not to rise against the Hanoverian kings in support of his kinsman. His wife taunted him, offering him her fan and a place with her ladies if he did not rebel. He rode out of Dilston with his brother and joined the rebels under Thomas Forster.

They marched south and were surrounded by the government forces in the midlands. Compelled to surrender, many of the common folk were killed or transported to Virginia and slavery. The leaders were condemned to death. Forster was saved by his sister Dorothy, but Radcliffe was executed on Tower Hill in 1716. The aurora borealis gave such a magnificent display on the eve of his death that people in the area called it Lord Derwentwater's Lights. It carries this name in parts of Northumberland to this day.

At the time of Radcliffe's execution, there was a terrible storm. A contemporary account says that the castle gutters ran with a red liquid resembling blood. Other reports claim that thousands of adders were seen swimming in the River Tyne. Local people thought that each was the soul of one of Radcliffe's followers.

Radcliffe's body was embalmed and brought home to Dilston for interment in the chapel. His ghost was often seen carrying its severed head, wandering through the woods above the nearby Devil's Water. (This stream's name has nothing to do with Satan. Instead, it is named after the early Norman family of d'Eivill.) A flickering light seen shining from the ruined keep is believed to be a spectral beacon to guide Radcliffe's soul home.

Eight miles south of Dilston lies the hamlet of Blanchland. The town square follows the lines of an abandoned monastery, and the hotel was formerly the monastary's guest house. All this belonged to a prince and the Bishop of Durham, Lord Nathien Crewe. He was the guardian of Thomas and Dorothy Forster, who lived there. Dorothy's spirit is often seen sitting in a hotel room allegedly waiting for Radcliffe's return. This is unlikely, as there would have been a great gulf between a Catholic lord and a protestant commoner in eighteenth-century England.

IRELAND'S HELLFIRE CLUB
Harry Warren

Sitting at the foothills of the Dublin mountains in Ireland is one of the country's most mysterious and haunted places. At the summit of Montpelier Hill, part of what is now a state forest, stands the well-preserved remains of the Hellfire Club. The hill and the surrounding area have a history of paranormal phenomena dating from the eighteenth century and possibly even farther back into the distant past. Reports of apparitions, ghostly black cats, and active poltergeists abound in this area.

The Hellfire Club was built from stones taken from a megalithic burial chamber or cairn. It is of a similar construction — on a smaller scale — to what may be the earliest building ever built, the great megalithic passage tomb of Newgrange in County Meath.

The cairns and standing stone circles in Ireland pre-date the more well-known site of standing stones at Stonehenge in England by at least several thousand years. The original burial cairn on the summit of Montpelier hill was used both as a place of ancient worship by its builders and as a burial chamber for the leader of the ancient Irish clan who had it built. Such sites, which are scattered about Ireland, were built by a powerful culture whose existence is only told of in Irish myths and sagas.

ASTRONOMICAL ALIGNMENT AND FAIRY FORTS
The pre-druidic, ancient Irish people who built these burial chambers chose their sites very carefully. Recent observations have shown the chambers to have important astronomical significance. Their entrances are usually aligned with the mid-winter sunrise and other astronomical phenomena.

Dowsers have tracked energy fields around Montpelier Hill of such strength that their rods or dowsing pendulums have been torn from their hands! Psychically gifted people have detected strange paranormal energy currents circulating around these sites and most especially at the Hellfire Club, where Earth energy pathways appear to crisscross the hill.

Nearby hills have their own megalithic constructions that seem to place Montpelier Hill at the centre of the energy network. It is likely that Montpelier Hill was deliberately chosen and used as a gateway to altered states of consciousness by the wizard priests or shamans of the people who built the cairns, to enhance their psychic powers and to enable them to contact the spirit world.

Megalithic sites in Irish mythology are popularly known as "fairy forts" and the standing stone circles are known as "fairy rings." Extreme bad luck is said to befall anyone who disturbs them. They are supposed to be gateways to the underworld where the race of the Tuatha De Dánann, a fairy folk, reside. Even today farmers and construction firms avoid disturbing the cairns.

Folk tales abound about the harm that has befallen the transgressors who did not show the respect the "fairy folk" required. Many myths tell of abductions to the fairy world that have striking comparisons to present-day UFO reports — the victims are whisked away to a mystical land and upon returning realise they have suffered inexplicable lost time.

Recognizing the immense historical importance of megalithic sites, the Irish government has placed them under state protection. Only archaeologists may examine them under licence, but there is free and open access to the public as long as the sites are treated with respect.

DRINKING WITH THE DEVIL

The building we are discussing was originally known as Montpelier House. It was erected in 1720 as a hunting and shooting lodge by Mr. Connolly, the Speaker of the Irish House of Commons. The house was constructed from grey stone blocks and mortar. The builders, ignoring the warnings of locals who said harm would befall anyone disturbing an ancient burial chamber, tore stones from a nearby cairn and used them for constructing Montpelier House. The locals spoke ominously of the fairy folk and said they would soon have their revenge for the desecration of the cairn. Shortly afterward the roof of the building was ripped off in a storm.

In 1735 the painter James Worsdale and his friend Richard Parsons, the first earl of Rosse, bought the building and renamed it the Hellfire Club of Ireland. Hellfire Clubs were started in the eighteenth century by "young rakes" of the gentry who dedicated themselves to lives of blasphemy and debauchery. Drinking, dueling and gambling were carried out with wild abandon. The Montpelier Hill club soon attracted a following, with many members of the upper classes joining in search of excitement beyond mere Bohemianism.

To prove oneself a worthy member, certain tasks had to be performed. One rule of membership required a member to consume 10 glasses of whiskey before dinner, one quart after dinner, and then find his own way home unaided! Anyone breaking the rule suffered a heavy penalty — least of all being instantly dismissed from the club.

Soon rumours spread of more nefarious activities at club meetings. Members were reputed to pledge themselves to the Devil before a night of gambling and debauchery began.

A tavern worker at the club who intruded upon something he wasn't supposed to see was overpowered, seized, and thrown into the blazing fireplace of the central hall to be burned alive. His ghost is said to haunt the place today. Mysterious screams in the night have been heard on the anniversary of his murder. Psychics have found a cold spot in the room where the murder occurred.

Other murders reputedly happened, but were kept secret by the club and its members — the victims' bodies were secretly buried on Montpelier Hill. Night after night the hills echoed with the sound of roars and screams coming from the club. Rumours spread of Hellfire Club members participating in black magic rituals with the Devil presiding.

One such story is set on a stormy winter's night. A young clergyman, newly arrived in the parish, was returning from tending a sick parishioner. On his way home, he was caught in a blinding snowstorm. As the weather closed in he lost his way. He saw a light at the top of the hill shining from the window of the club and ascended the hill seeking shelter from the storm.

As he neared the Hellfire Club, the young clergyman became disturbed by the sound of moaning that echoed from within. He knocked at the entrance and the sounds stopped. Thinking one of their cohort was seeking entrance, a club member opened the door. When club members saw who it was, the clergyman was struck, dragged into a dining hall, and held captive. A satanic meeting of the Hellfire Club was taking place. The clergyman was astounded to see a large group of cloaked and masked men standing in a circle around a large black cat at the centre of the room.

The animal sat upon a velvet cushion placed on top of a table. Before the clergyman disturbed them, the Hellfire Club members had been carrying out some black magic ritual that involved chanting and venerating the cat.

The cat, representing the devil, was reverently offered a drink of red liquid from a skull. With club members' attention upon the animal, the clergyman momentarily broke free and grabbed the skull and threw it against a picture of Satan that adorned the dining room wall. The picture crashed to the floor. After recovering from their shock, the members grabbed the clergyman and rained heavy blows upon him, beating him within an inch of his life.

They forced the clergyman into a chair and held a mock trial with 13 jurors. They found him guilty of attacking their master, and they sentenced him to death. They mocked the clergyman and forced him to kneel in front of the animal. They taunted the man with cries of "So where is your God now when you need him?" A knife was held to the clergyman's throat and he was ordered to claim Satan as his lord and master and beg Satan for a quick death. Instead, the clergyman bravely recited the Rite of Exorcism. The cat arched its back and snarled. Its hideous red eyes blazed menacingly as it dug its extended claws into the cushion.

The clergyman's captors, shocked by the hissing cat's fearsome reaction, momentarily loosened their grip and the clergyman broke free from their hold. With a tremendous effort he managed to seize the cat from the table. He then flung it across the room into the blazing fireplace, scattering sparks and ash from the fire about the floor.

An unearthly scream came from the animal as it metamorphosed into the devil. Powerless to attack the clergyman, who continued the exorcism, Satan writhed in the flames of the fireplace. The exorcism completed, the devil burst into a huge ball of flame and set the club on fire as he smashed his way through the roof and disappeared into the night. The members ran from the club, some on fire.

The survivors, chastened and repentant, were freed from the grip of Satan by the power of God. They begged the clergyman for his forgiveness and left that place never to return. The Hellfire Club had closed its doors.

PHANTOM CATS AND FRIGHTENED DOGS

But what of today? The well-preserved ruins stand alone on top of the hill beside the outline of the desecrated burial cairn. Supernatural activity continues. There are many reported sightings of an unnaturally large black cat said to haunt Montpelier Hill and the surrounding woods.

A typical phantom cat sighting happens at twilight. The cat is commonly described as having blazing eyes. It soon disappears into the woods or vanishes into the Hellfire Club.

Today the Hellfire Club is a forlorn building, an eerie place where updrafts howl through the windows of the building. Its reputation still attracts curious onlookers and it is still occasionally used for magic rituals. It is not unknown to find pentagrams drawn upon the floor with the symbols of black magic practitioners daubed on the walls.

My attention was first drawn to the house when my dog, a large German shepherd, refused to take shelter in the old doorway during a downpour. No amount of coaxing would bring him over to me and he sat whimpering in front of the building until I left.

He eventually became more accustomed to the house as I researched the premises. The dog, normally a brave and playful animal, warily enters the building, but refuses to go near the master fireplace. On occasion he has detected a presence in the Hellfire Club and comes to my side growling at something only he has sensed in the room.

His whole demeanour changes when we leave. Perhaps animal instinct helps the dog sense the shadows of the past and know best to leave well enough alone.

THE GHOST IN GRANDMA'S BATHROOM
Dennis Chambers

Sometimes a longstanding mystery can be solved with a little help from the most unexpected of sources. That's how it was for Jackie and Neil Johnson, who had puzzled for months as to why their son, Ben, always behaved hysterically in the bathroom at his grandmother's house.

Learning of my interest in unusual experiences, Neil approached me with a brief account of their story. What I heard was intriguing enough for me to accept an invitation to the Johnson home in Gillingham in Kent, to hear the story in full.

In March 1993, Neil and Jackie had attended an "open evening" at Ben's school to find out how their four-and-a-half-year-old son was progressing. "We were delighted when his teacher, Miss McGill, gave him a glowing report," Jackie told me. "But we were puzzled when she said she wanted to tell us about something Ben had said." Miss McGill told them that a few days earlier the class had watched an educational programme on TV dealing with the subject of fear in young children. It had cited the types of things that tended to cause them upset — spiders, the dark, large dogs, bigger children, and other scary things.

When the programme was over, she had asked her pupils what frightened them. The responses were much as she had expected, more or less a repetition of the things featured on the programme — until she heard Ben's answer. His reply was both novel and specific: "I don't like having a bath at my Gran's house," he said.

Miss McGill told Jackie and Neil that she had then passed out sheets of paper, already headed with the title "I am frightened," and invited the children to illustrate the things which frightened them. "This is what Ben drew," she said, handing over a sheet of paper.

Neil gave me Ben's drawing to examine. The drawing had four primary elements. First, there was a series of vertical lines that Ben had told Miss McGill was the bath at his Gran's. Second, there was a circle containing two smaller circles at its top and below them a curving stroke. Together these represented a smiling face. "That's me," Ben had said. On the far right of the page was a square filled in with heavy pencil strokes except for a small gap through which peeped another face. This was the moon shining through the bathroom window. The last item in the line-up was the most interesting. According to Neil, "It looks just like a banana standing upright with two dots at the top, like eyes. When Miss McGill had asked Ben what it was, he had announced, "That's the ghost I see."

"What does it do ?" she asked.

"Nothing. It's not horrible," Ben had replied.

Miss McGill told the Johnsons that she had been so intrigued with Ben's picture and his explanations that she had called a fellow teacher into the classroom to see the drawing and hear what else Ben had to say. It seemed that whenever he had taken a bath at his grandmother's house, the ghost of a man appeared at the end of the bath. Miss McGill felt she had to tell Neil and Jackie about it.

The revelation was of greater significance than she could ever have imagined. Between them, Neil and Jackie mapped out for me the history of events. Ben was born on 8 June, 1988, and spent the first two years of his life in Osnabruck, Germany, where Neil, then in the army, was stationed. When Neil left the army in September 1990 the family returned to England and moved in with Jackie's parents in their house in Gillingham while they looked for a house of their own. It was only when they took up residence with his grandparents that Ben's bath times became a problem. Soon, every bath became an ordeal, with Ben screaming, kicking, and fighting to get away.

It was a mystery why Ben became so distressed as soon as he was moved toward the bath. Experiment had satisfied them that it wasn't the room itself that caused his reactions. He would be quite content to stand at the washbasin while his hands and face were washed. His aversion appeared to be directly related to the bath itself, but why that should be was beyond them. To avoid the inevitable upset, they would often bathe him in the kitchen sink where he was quite happy to splash around. This pattern of behaviour continued until December 1991, when the Johnsons moved into their own home. In their new house, Ben's bath times instantly reverted back to the happy events they used to be.

Until Miss McGill brought Ben's claims to their attention, the reason behind Ben's behavior in the bath at his grandparents' had been an unsolved mystery. Had Miss McGill unwittingly discovered the answer?

A ghost in her parent's bathroom? Jackie wondered how this could be possible. Then suddenly things began to click into place. She recalled that a few years before, her mother had told her something about the house's history which she had purposely withheld when Jackie was a child.

In 1956 — eight years before Jackie's parents had bought the house, it had been occupied by an elderly widower — a stocky man with white, wavy hair, who was known to have had a girlfriend of whom he was deeply fond. One day the police were called in to investigate a strong smell of gas that neighbours had pinpointed as coming from the house. On breaking in, the police discovered the man lying dead in the bath. A gas ring was lying on his chest with the long rubber tube feeding it connected to a nearby gas tap, which was fully open.

Draped across the top of the bath was a tarpaulin, which had apparently been tugged over the bath by the man once he had climbed inside, effectively creating an improvised gas chamber. It was concluded that he had killed himself when his girlfriend had rejected his proposal of marriage.

Knowing the house had been the scene of a suicide had not deterred the Barrys from buying the house. It was a nice, well-maintained house in an area where they wanted to live. No one else had ever noticed any strangeness while using the bathroom.

"How about the rest of the house ?" I asked. Jackie recalled how when she was a young child she had felt a distinct sense of unease in her own bedroom. "At one period these feelings became so intense that I was allowed to remain downstairs until I fell asleep, and then Dad would carry me up to bed."

Despite sensing a strange, oppressive presence in her room, Jackie never experienced anything to give substance to her inner feelings.

From what Jackie was told by her mother, it appears that the people who had lived in the house immediately after the suicide had replaced the bath. There is nothing to indicate that this was done to clear the memory of that tragic event. Maybe the bath's condition had made its replacement desirable. In any case, the bath in which Ben was sitting whenever he saw his ghost was not the same bath in which the man had ended his life. However, it did occupy exactly the same position in the bathroom.

Ben's assurance to Miss McGill that the ghost didn't do anything might well have been nothing more than a show of bravado in the knowledge that it no longer presented a threat to him. He didn't have to climb into that bath again. That he introduced this ghost when being asked about what frightened him suggests that he was far from happy about its presence.

Neil, Jackie, and her mother, Myra Barry, tell me that this tragic event in the house's history has rarely been discussed, and when it has been mentioned it has never been in Ben's presence. As far as they are concerned, Ben's revelations to Miss McGill came from his personal experiences.

I talking to Miss McGill about the facts concerning her involvement in Neil and Jackie's story. She told me that she is totally convinced that Ben believes he saw what he told her he saw. "He was very definite about these appearances," she said. "His story rang so true it gave me goose pimples."

Jackie's father died in 1990. Her mother lives on in the house as its sole occupant. "I do believe in these things," Myra told me, "but I am quite satisfied that I have the house to myself now."

584

MEG O'MELDON

A legendary ghost learned that you can't take it with you.

Stephen L. Marchant

People in Northumberland have been passing down stories, legends, and myths for generations. In the days before radio and television, the spoken word was a vehicle for news, gossip, and the telling of tales. Storytellers related old tales of the curious and macabre, and whether they spun their yarns in a medieval hall or in a Victorian kitchen, their stories can make the hair on one's neck stand on end even today.

The spirit of Meg Of Meldon, or Meg O'Meldon as she is known locally, haunted the parish of Meldon for some three hundred years. Her tale is comparatively unusual in that many details of her life have survived in historical documents.

The Fenwick family, like many in the country, was divided during the English Civil War. Often, a family deliberately chose to divide its forces between the two sides, thus ensuring that not only would the family name continue but the family might retain its wealth almost intact. One of the most adept at sustaining her family fortune through the turbulent years of commonwealth and restoration was Lady Margaret Fenwick, who took her responsibilities to family wealth a step beyond the usual.

During the period when Margaret "Meg" Selby married Sir William Fenwick, it was not unusual to find marriages that matched the wealth of one party to the title of another. In this case, the wealthy Selby married the titled Fenwick. Margaret was a shrewd operator. She inherited her business sense from her father, a successful merchant, and she soon set the Fenwick fortune on the right path.

Margaret and William's son, knighted in 1616 by James I, slowly built a fine estate in Northumberland with Sir William, while his mother planned to increase the family estate in a less direct way.

Another land-owning family, the Herons, had mortgaged their estate to Meg in difficult times. She knew full well that the Herons' situation wasn't getting any easier, and she knew she could use her hold over them to add their estate to her own family's; all she needed was an excuse to foreclose the mortgage. The first delay in payment gave her the opportunity to snatch the Heron's estate, and she did just that.

She may have been a lady by title, but Meg's manners hardly lived up to that name. She had a penchant for money lending, and she made sure the security for the loan was iron-clad.

FRIGHTENING THE LOCALS

When Meg lost her husband, her obsession with making money was the only drive left in her life. She was reluctant to spend even a penny of her fortune. As she aged, her old clothes became more and more tattered. It seemed that the once-elegant Margaret was slowly turning into a genuine old crone, and as she did so, the local people became more and more frightened of her.

Politics managed to loosen Meg's tight fist, however, when the Lord Protector Cromwell extracted payment from her as a fine for being a Royalist, and King Charles I fined her for supporting Cromwell! On both counts she was forced to turn over a substantial sum, and everyone thought she would surely go bankrupt. In truth, since she still held the bulk of her estate in land, her fortune continued to increase.

As her wealth grew, so did her paranoia. She buried gold and jewels everywhere. She hid money in the walls of her houses and down wells, but she still dressed in rags and ate the most frugal of diets. Meg was in love with wealth itself — what her fortune might accomplish didn't enter her mind. Meg never considered that she might live longer, for instance, by spending some of her fortune to eat better.

She spent much of her time scurrying around her hiding places, checking that they were secure. As she grew weaker, her rushing grew more frantic. The estate servants began to call her "Mad Meg" or "Meggie Meldon", and soon, amid the frantic counting of her fortune, she died.

Meg was not prepared to leave her money behind, however. For many years when anyone approached one of her hiding places, they were confronted by her shade menacingly warning them off.

For years Meg of Meldon was seen emerging from wells and walls, or sitting in or on horse troughs. She was often seen by the roadside counting paces from a milestone on the old coach road. Over the years many of her treasures came to light, but just how much of the total sum was found may never be known. Some people handed over their finds to the authorities, and some presumably didn't, but Meg's specter still roamed Meldon.

One of her properties had been the village school, and it was here in late Victorian times that a small boy sat at a desk placed against a slightly damp and bulging patch of plastered wall. As the teacher droned, the boy picked and prodded at the plaster. Unexpectedly, it collapsed and, amid the cries from the teacher, the children heard a crash as part of Meg's fortune fell out of the wall. Gold coins, jewelery, and even one of her account books tumbled down.

The book clearly showed that she had held every land-owning family in Northumberland in her debt. Her death released many titled people from a difficult situation. The list of landowners included a cross-section of Royalists and Parliamentarians, and this made it clear how Meg ensured her family's survival. Mad Meg's scheme required a clever head and a tenacious spirit, but since the discovery of the schoolroom hoard, Meg's shade, as far as we know, has never been seen again.

MY DAD'S LAST VISIT

In 1979 in London, my father had a slight stroke while out getting the Sunday paper. My mother was worried because he had been gone so long and, after nearly an hour, he came around the corner all bloodied on the face and legs from the fall caused by his stroke. A police officer and an ambulance driver escorted him home. He was lucid enough, at that time, to refuse to go to the hospital.

Although his speech was not slurred at all, his memory certainly was. He never again uttered an intelligible sentence. He thought he was making sense and we had to pretend we knew what he was talking about, which was very hard. This was a man who had been a well-respected police officer in London and the champion boxer of the police force.

Months passed and he grew worse. Eventually, he had to go to the hospital. Doctors said there was nothing wrong with him physically, but his mind was practically gone (oxygen didn't get to his brain while he was unconscious). Sometimes he would remember who we were — and then nothing!

After that, they transferred him to a psychiatric hospital. I went with my mother, son, and then-husband to visit him on Christmas Eve 1979. It was a very sad occasion. I did not know then that it would be the last time I would ever see him on this side.

A couple of weeks after Christmas, just before my Dad's birthday in January, I called the hospital to tell them that we would be out with his birthday cake. They informed me that they had just been going to call me to tell me my father had disappeared a few hours earlier. He had walked out of the hospital into the cold January night. They had search parties out looking for him and had informed the police.

Three years later, we finally learned what had happened to him. After walking nearly 10 miles to try to get back home again, he had collapsed and was taken to a hospital. There he was classified as a "unknown" — he had cut all the name tags off his clothing before leaving the hospital so that there was no identification at all. The police had posters everywhere, but there was no response.

On 14 March, 1980, at 8 p.m., I was sitting in the kitchen knitting by myself. I was going through a divorce at that time, and preparing to go to the United States. I suddenly felt very peaceful, and I felt the pressure of a familiar hand on my shoulder. I heard Dad's voice, as perfectly normal as it used to be. "I've gone over, sweetheart," he said, "I'm all right and don't worry: You're doing the right thing with your life." The experience left me very sad but feeling peaceful.

In 1983 the police realized through computer records that the "unknown" who had been taken to Charing Cross Hospital was, indeed, my father. They told me exactly when he had passed away: 8 p.m. on 14 March, 1980.

GRANDMOTHER'S WARNING

Everyone in my family has seen ghosts. My brother, Paul, saw the ghost of a young girl dressed in Victorian clothes walking through his house. My mother, Frances, saw blue lights darting around her bedroom, and my dad, Terry, once saw the ghost of an elderly Chinese man when he was staying at his grandparents'. Those stories pale, however, in comparison to a ghost that appeared to both me and my father in April, 1981 — and saved our lives.

I was 18 and living with my parents on a barge moored on London's Regent's Canal. One night I was asleep in my small cabin, situated at the front of the barge. Around 2 a.m. I awoke with a start. I distinctly heard my Grandmother Irene.

"It's my birthday today," she said. It was indeed her birthday, but she had died the year before.

I looked around the darkened cabin. Everything was quiet and I could barely hear my parents at the other end of the barge, laughing at something on television. Because it all seemed so natural and because I had loved my grandmother, I wasn't frightened.

Instead, I was curious. I had no doubt that the voice I'd heard had belonged to my grandmother, but there was no one there. So where was she?

Feeling brave, I said, "Granny, if you are here, show yourself." As I said this, a white misty shape appeared on the wall opposite my bunk. It shimmered and pulsated, and then turned into an image of Irene. She was smiling and wearing a white silk dress with a corsage of wonderful orange lilies pinned to her right shoulder. She looked like an angel.

I watched her image for about ten seconds when I was overcome by an incredible fatigue. As my head hit the pillow, I thought that some unseen force had caused my sleepiness.

Two hours later I awoke with a start, remembering what had happened. I was horrified — in real life I'm a scaredy cat where ghosts are concerned.

I jumped out of bed and ran screaming to my parents. They asked me what was wrong. I stuttered that Grandmother Irene had appeared in my cabin, and I vowed never to sleep there again.

At first my parents pooh-poohed my experience and told me I must have been dreaming. This only made me more adamant. I knew what I'd seen! Sensing that I wouldn't be so easily calmed, my mother looked at my father and said, "Terry, you'd better tell Sharon what you just told me."

He admitted that two hours before, he'd been watching television when he heard Grandmother Irene's voice telling him to check the mooring ropes.

At first my father hadn't wanted to leave the cosy warmth of the cabin, but when he got outside he was glad he did. During the night the heavy rain had eased. As a result, the canal's water level had dropped considerably, leaving our ropes tangled around the mooring poles and our barge half-suspended in the air. If Grandmother Irene hadn't appeared with her warning, our barge would have snapped its mooring ropes, capsized, and left us trapped beneath the murky depths of the canal.

There is no doubt in my mind that Irene's ghost appeared that night to warn my father. She saved me and my family from a cold and watery death. That she appeared to me as well makes this guardian angel story all the more special to me.

THE VAMPIRE PRIORESS AT ROBIN'S HOOD'S GRAVE

Craig Miller

A secret, haunted grave. Gun-toting gamekeepers. A murdering prioress. A vampire-hunting bishop. Animal mutilation. Wailing ghosts. Not many people link Robin Hood with these dark images. Most associate him with noble vigilanteism in medieval Sherwood Forest and Nottingham.

Yet in the neighbouring county of Yorkshire, deep in the woods on the Kirklees Hall Estate, lies the reputed grave of Robin Hood. It is situated at the crossing of ley lines on the desecrated grounds of an ancient Cistercian priory, an order founded by reformist Benedictines in France in 1098. According to legend, it was here that Robin Hood was bled to death by his kinswoman, the prioress Elizabeth de Staynton, and her lover, Red Roger of Doncaster.

While some hold that the Prioress was (or is) a vampire, folklore has it that Robin sought her out for a bloodletting, a medieval cure for a variety of ailments. The prioress drained Robin Hood's blood in the priory gatehouse. He was buried a few hundred yards away.

The grounds at Kirklees teem with rabbits and peacocks. A narrow path through the woods leads to the grave. A nineteenth-century stone marker, a replacement for earlier tombstones ravaged by time, bears an epitaph proclaiming the site as Robin Hood's final resting place.

The estate and grounds are imbued with an ominous character. *Land of Lost Content, The Luddite Revolt* (1812) describes it: "There was a mystery about it which local people only reluctantly tried to penetrate. The mystery was helped physically by the thick shroud of trees that surrounded the place, and was sustained by local tales of the ghosts of prioresses and nuns and of the death of Robin Hood whose grave is so imperturbably marked as lying within Kirklees' grounds, in spite of any facts history might suggest to the contrary."

According to Richard Gough's *Sepulchral Monuments of Great Britain* (1786), Sir Samuel Armytage, who owned the estate some two centuries ago, went to the grave and "caused the ground under it to be dug a yard deep, and found it had never been disturbed."

No one knows why he tried to exhume Robin Hood's body. It may have been mere curiosity. Armytage may also have suspected a vampire infestation.

UNANNOUNCED VISITORS

Lady Margerete Armytage, a descendant of Sir Samuel, now owns the estate. Her desire to limit access to the grave is well documented.

"Cameras are forbidden from the site where Robin Hood is reputedly buried, so secret is its exact location," wrote Andrew Robinson in an April 1996 issue of the *Bradford & Pennine News*. "Many people living only an arrow's flight from busy roads running near the grave would be hard pushed to find it. If they did, what they would discover in the grounds of Kirklees Hall at Clifton, near Brighouse, is little more than a heap of ruins."

Lady Armytage selectively grants a privileged few permission to visit the grave. Those she refuses often seem to fall under the heading "people on a mission." She has turned down, for instance, proposals from Anglican priests who would perform a blessing at the site.

"I'm afraid I don't have a clue about Lady Armytage's motives for keeping such a close guard over the grave and the priory ruins," said Reggie Naus, a Netherlands-based vampirologist and correspondent for the Vampire Research Society (VRS), in Highgate, London. "Could it be that she suspects there's evil there, and wants to avoid the publicity? Maybe she is actually trying to protect people by making them stay away from the grave?" Later in Robinson's article, he reveals Lady Armytage's stated motives for keeping the grave private: "Vandals and trespassers have plagued the grave site and damaged the metal railings protecting it.

'People come with hacksaws and take everything they can get hold of,' says Lady Armytage. 'Urban people do not understand this place, they don't know the difference between grass and barley. ... It has nothing to do with snobbery. It is just not practical.'"

UNEASY SPIRITS

However, recent events indicate that Lady Armytage may indeed keep potential visitors from the grave for their own good. Ruthwen Glenarvon edits the VRS research journal. In 1987, he inspected the earth above Robin Hood's tomb and found a number of finger-width perforations.

Such holes sometimes suggest the exit by which the undead will escape as mist, according to ancient lore. There have also been reports of mutilated and drained animals in the vicinity, as well as terrified people in nearby villages.

Bishop Anselm Genders of the Community of the Resurrection in Mirfield and former Bishop of Bermuda said that exorcizing Kirklees would be an even more hazardous undertaking than the Bermuda Triangle, which he exorcized some years ago.

Six years ago, the Yorkshire Robin Hood Society asked Reverend John Flack of Brighouse, Yorkshire, to hold a blessing over the grave. After the Bishop of Wakefield, the Right Reverend David Hope, received an angry complaint from Lady Armytage, however, he denied Flack permission for the blessing.

Barbara Green, president of the society, said, "You would think we were asking to hold a Black Mass at the graveside the way things have developed. We are, in fact, acting in accordance with Christian tradition."

Green said she had a supernatural experience while on a clandestine midnight visit to the gravesite. There she not only saw the ghost of Robin Hood, but the Wicked Prioress and Red Roger as well.

Evelyn Friend, a psychic investigator who also has visited the grave, experienced such overwhelming vibrations of evil all around the area that she suspected that the site was used as a place for occult activities.

Roger Williams of Bradley in Kirklees saw the ghost of the wicked prioress and drew a sketch of the apparition from memory. He stated, "Wild horses would not drag me to that place again. I wouldn't go up there again for a million pounds."

After numerous reports of spiritual encounters, Brother Keith McClean, a hermit monk from Berkshire, strongly urged any ghostbusters to keep away from the grave — for their own safety.

"BEHOLD THE LIGHT!"

One of the most notable figures to visit the haunted site under cover of darkness was Bishop Sean Manchester, whom Green has called one of Britain's foremost vampire hunters and exorcists. Manchester approached Lady Armytage "for permission to hold a vigil and carry out a number of experiments near the tomb," he said. "Unfortunately, this was not granted."

Undaunted, Manchester sneaked onto the grounds for an unofficial vampire hunt on the evening of 22 April, 1990.

"I was to be accompanied by two assistants," Manchester recounts in *The Unexplained* (Orbis Publishing, Ltd.), a magazine of the paranormal, "but once we reached the edge of the wood, one of them became extremely agitated and returned to the vehicle. I continued with just one helper.

"First, we inspected the crumbling priory gatehouse — the sinister setting of that gruesome murder. We then made the discovery of occult symbols etched into the priory wall. These ancient signs were another indication of diabolism all those centuries ago.

"We approached the grave, which has for centuries lain forgotten beneath a shroud of ivy and vineweed. Behind us, in the fields where our companion had retreated, lay the dismembered body of a goat, totally drained of blood."

Manchester and his assistant had more unusual sights in store: "Then we came upon the great tomb. I unfastened my large bag of accoutrements and removed an armoury of crucifixes, holy water, garlic, candles and all known vampire repellents before continuing.

"Nothing happened for almost three hours. Then we heard it. First of all, it wafted faintly on the night air, like the discordant sound sometimes made by the wind in trees. But then it grew louder — and closer — and we recognized it to be more akin to a dreadful wailing. Something was approaching.

"I quickly lit a candelabrum stuffed with five candles, grabbed the largest crucifix available, and stepped into the path of the unearthly groaning. 'Behold the light!' I shouted.

"This brief exorcism caused the wailing to cease abruptly. But it was replaced by a very human noise — my assistant yelling in discomfort. When I returned, I found him caught up in brambles which had severely cut his hands and face. He said that shortly before its termination, the source of the wailing had manifested in the form of a darkly clad woman who it first appeared serene — then rapidly altered into a hag with red, staring eyes. He insisted that she had been real.

"No more was seen or heard that night. Holy water was poured into the holes still remaining in the tomb, and [we planted] garlic — hateful to vampires. The Kirklees vampire had evaded [us] on this occasion, but I vowed to return to exorcize the pollution."

A TORMENTED SOUL?

In her book *The Outlaw Robin Hood, His Yorkshire Legend* (1991), Barbara Green asks, "What will be the future of Robin Hood's grave ... should [it] be left in its present state of neglect, hidden away from public eyes? The church has sought, and been denied, permission to bless the grave — in spite of the fact that Robin ... was gruesomely murdered and buried outside the consecrated ground of the nunnery."

Green believes the grave site cries out for spiritual rescue and physical restoration, so that the grave can at last take its rightful place in England's heritage and Robin's soul can rest in peace.

Under Lady Armytage's stewardship, however, the gravesite is protected from trespassers by gamekeepers and a high iron fence that was erected during the construction of the nearby Lancashire and Yorkshire Railway in the 19th century. The workers constructing the line were fond of visiting the grave and chipping off bits of stone as mementoes or cures for toothaches.

Barbara Green and other locals see a crumbling historic site that could generate tourist dollars. Lady Armytage wants nothing to do with tourists, saying she has a farm to run. For the present, Robin Hood stirs up as much controversy dead as he did alive.

WHO'S BURIED IN ROBIN HOOD'S GRAVE?

The authenticity of claims concerning Robin Hood's grave is thoroughly examined in James C. Holt's *Robin Hood* (revised edition 1989, Thames and Hudson, New York). Holt, a professor of medieval history at the University of Cambridge, reveals the difficulty in pinpointing Robin's resting place. For instance, a drawing of the grave at Kirklees made in 1665 shows the inscription "Here lie Roberd Hude, William Goldburgh, Thomas," though the latter two names never figure in the Robin Hood legend.

Holt notes that Thomas Gale, dean of York from 1697 to 1702, wrote about an epitaph allegedly inscribed on the grave giving 1247 as Robin's date of death. Martin Parker's 1632 *The True Tales of Robin Hood* provides another epitaph placing his death on 4 December, 1198.

"An inscription based on Gale's epitaph [below] was erected in the nineteenth century when the slab was enclosed by iron railings," Holt writes, stating that the epitaph is "couched in pseudo-antique English which betrays its spurious character."

"Hear underneath dis lairt Stean,
Laz robert earl of Huntingtun
Ne'er arcir ver as hie sa geud,
An pipl kauld 'im robin heud.
Sik utlawz as hie an iz men
Vil england nivr si agen."

While early versions of Robin's tale portray him as a mere yeoman, sixteenth-century playwright Anthony Munday dubbed him Robert, earl of Huntington — the title used in both epitaphs and in retellings to this day.

Confusion surrounding the grave springs from the greater confusion surrounding Robin Hood's life. "He cannot be identified," Holt writes in the prologue to his book. "There is a quiverful of possible Robin Hoods. Even the likeliest is little better than a shot in the gloaming."

For now the historical mystery beneath the Kirklees grave remains as impenetrable as its above-ground hauntings.

THE GHOST OF ST. MARY'S
Steve McGrail

Old churches have a reputation for supernatural activity. But some people might expect the average ecclesiastical spirit to depart once the building is vacated or turned over for other, nonreligious uses.

That doesn't seem to have happened at the one-time Roman Catholic church of St. Mary's in Stirling, Scotland. The church is located in the oldest part of the town, below the shadow of ancient Stirling Castle. Although in secular use for many years, the building appears to have retained at least one of its inhabitants from those distant days of cassock, thurible, and pew: the ghost of a young girl, to be precise.

For the last 10 years, St. Mary's has been the base for various tourism-related projects and small businesses. Currently, Stirling's Heritage Events company (which performs street theatre plays) is located there, as well as a potter, a silversmith, a printer, a costumer, and other community merchants.

The original church was opened in 1838, with a school attached, to cater to Stirling's growing Catholic population, generated by the Highland Clearances, with Highlanders, frequently Catholics, driven from their ancestral glens, making for the Lowlands and the promise of work. Later, the numbers were swelled by the Irish poor fleeing the Great Hunger in their land. Eventually, neither the church nor the school were big enough to support the congregation, and a new church and school were built on another site.

There have long been tales about St. Mary's. Odd things have happened to phones and computers in the building, while lights have gone on upstairs for no apparent reason. A presence has been seen there, too.

One person who has encountered the presence is Tony Stewart, a street theatre actor. Although he worked in the building, he knew nothing of its history, he hadn't heard the stories, and he didn't believe in ghosts. Admittedly, from time to time he'd seen somebody near the stage where the altar had once been, and he'd heard a child's footsteps. He supposed he'd imagined it.

One day he had to go upstairs to the former schoolroom. On

the landing he came across a girl of about nine or ten. Pretty, with a sort of half-smile on her pale, grubby face, she was singing to herself. Her coarse brown dress reached down to her calves and her flaming red hair was tangled and filthy. He passed her and went over to the fire door. She was still singing, and he heard the patter of her bare feet behind him. He turned around to hold the heavy door open for her, but she had vanished.

"I was puzzled," he says, "but I made nothing of it at the time. When I went downstairs, I asked if any kids were in. Staff members' kids were often around, but I'd not seen this particular one before. The reply was 'no' and my heart instantly turned to ice. I was absolutely positive about what I'd seen. I was scared, really scared."

Other people also have experienced peculiar things in the building, according to John McGuire, who was once on the committee that ran it. "I've never seen anybody myself," he explains, "but when I've been at evening meetings I've often heard voices upstairs, even though I knew there was nobody there. In the 1970s, our rock band regularly rehearsed downstairs. Our guitarist Marie Ross said she'd often seen the wee girl. She didn't seem frightened by her, though."

The girl, with her flaming red hair and rough clothes, has the sound of a child from a poor Highland or Irish family. The pale face is an interesting detail. Despite images of healthy, sturdy Highlanders, tuberculosis was rife in the north, as it was in Irish villages, too. The hospitals of Scotland's big cities overflowed with sickness brought down from the Highlands and from across the Irish Sea. But there's no real evidence to support tuberculosis in this case, and no record of any tragedy taking place on the site.

Who could the girl have been? Without evidence, there's no telling.

I subjected the manor to a barrage of high-tech detection and surveillance activity. The equipment I used included night-vision cameras, magnetic and electrostatic field monitors, event detectors, radiation counters, sophisticated video and audio surveillance sets, infrared intrusion detectors, and a thermal imaging camera.

Psychic Maureen Conway immediately picked up on strong paranormal activity throughout the house, which she said radiated sadness. Reverend Willis told me he sensed a definite negative presence throughout the house and was concerned about the safety of those within.

David Furlong's detailed research and fieldwork indicated that the manor house rests at the intersection of five different ley lines. Ley lines are invisible alignments said to have complex powers and seeming to provide links between many sacred places and natural magical sites. Their convergence at Little Dean Hall may have altered the area's energy fields, thereby causing or contributing to the supernatural events in the area. Furlong said that the ancient Celts were somehow aware of or sensitive to the energy fields in the little Dean area and established their temple site at what they interpreted as a magical location.

Unfortunately, whatever walks unseen though the corridors of Little Dean avoided interacting with my detection equipment during the investigation. Whether the forces were dormant or just skilled at dodging our spectre-detectors, I did not record any unusual energy manifestations or fluctuations, with one exception:

Nick Rose and I did detect an unusual, tightly defined band of electrical interference, apparently suspended in space, that traversed two ground-floor rooms at a height of about six feet. The field was isolated and did not seem to emanate from any structural surface. Checks of all surrounding walls, ceilings, and floors disclosed no power conduits or wiring in the area. Just to be sure, we cut off the main power supply to the house, but the anomaly persisted. We were intrigued but cautiously sceptical, not wanting to jump to any premature conclusions of paranormal activity.

On our last day at Little Dean, Reverend Willis approached Donald Macer-Wright and his wife, Janet. Concerned about the oppressive presence he felt, he requested and obtained permission to perform a clearing ritual to exorcize whatever forces were present. I was in the house doing some final monitoring and noted that the unexplained band of interference was still present.

In the early morning mist, the clergyman completed the ritual as I left the house. Everyone — including a sceptical film crew on hand to document the investigation — reported an immediate, almost palpable, change in atmosphere, like a smothering veil had been lifted away from the house.

As the Reverend walked away from Little Dean Hall, I went back into the house to check my instruments one last time. The band of electrical interference was gone.

FIVE SPECTRES ON A ROMAN ROAD
Sixteenth-century revellers still visit an old English restaurant.

Kenneth Nickel

You may disagree if you wish, but I think it is totally intolerable that nobody has ever asked me for the name of a good 800-year-old haunted restaurant.

Well okay, maybe not totally intolerable, since Castle Dairy in Cumbria near the Scottish border is possibly the only 800-year-old haunted restaurant I can think of. At least the only one that accepts American Express.

And it's more than a little ironic that while imposing Kendal Castle is in scattered ruins on a hill nearby, its little service outbuilding, Castle Dairy, is still intact and thriving in its original capacity — the food business. This is probably because border wars with the Scots are no longer fun or fashionable, while genteel dining has never fallen completely out of favour, despite the intrusion of Wendy's and Burger King into the previously unsullied British countryside.

On a noisy side street in Kendal, Castle Dairy is cheek-by-jowl with and elbowed in by larger modern building around it. And it's not generally known, but if you sit at a certain table you may see five Elizabethan dandies drinking ale in the corner. Now look down at the floor; looks like cobblestone doesn't it? It's a real Roman road, almost 2000 years old.

A blue plaque on the outside of Castle Dairy says it was once a dower house, built in the 14th century. But inside, owner Elaine Wright disagrees emphatically. "I know how old it is ... a twelfth-century exterior over a Roman road from about A.D. 210, and a Tudor interior, about 1558," she says.

Elaine Wright has a ready laugh, but is anything but lighthearted on the subject of Castle Dairy's history. "All the bits of plaques outside that say 14th century are rubbish!"

And the part about the dower house: "Two-foot-thick walls weren't built to keep widows and orphans in — built to keep Scots out! This is a mini-fortress! Dairy is an old word for larder or meat store, and this was built at the same time as the castle — to service it with meat — and had to be defended from the marauding Scots!"

Wright has been running Castle Dairy as a posh restaurant for a select clientele for 27 years. Her candlelit dinners, bathed in 16th century ambiance, run seven courses or more with wild duck, venison, pigeon, guinea fowl, duckling, sorbet, truffles, and French wines. Yes, you've guessed it, mate — you can drop a few quid here.

About the spectral quintet, Wright says, "We've had two lots of people who've seen five men around a fireplace that doesn't exist anymore — in the 27 years I've been here, two lots of people. One lot was from Coventry or Birmingham, another lot was from Morecambe."

"One of them asked if the men were going to a fancy dress party. I thought they'd had one or two jars too many," she laughed. "When it happened again about three or four years after, well. ... She indicates the nearby table and chairs. "The people sat at this table, and said, 'They are really enjoying themselves in that corner!' There was nobody there!"

Wright says that both parties that saw the men sat at the same table. Of one party of six and one group of four, only two in each saw anything. But both pairs specifically said they saw five men. She can't recall the times of year it happened, but says it might have been on Saturdays because it was busy both times.

THE STRANGENESS MOUNTS

Colin Wilson, a well-known writer on the paranormal, told me that it sounded like a "tape-recording" type phenomenon, in which a certain event is imprinted on the environment like magnetic tape and plays back under ideal circumstances. And some investigators say that stone is a good recording medium. Castle Dairy is made of nothing but thick stone that all but completely shuts out the steady traffic noise only yards away.

Wright has not seen anything at Castle Dairy herself. "Oh yes, I've felt them — I have, I have — nothing frightening, but a definite chill." But more than 30 years ago, she did have a full-blown paranormal experience when she saw green smoke waft through her fingers, in total darkness, at the Old Trafford Cricket Ground building; she remembers it felt like ice. That building, oddly enough, is a modern chrome and glass structure, now part of greater Manchester, but it was built on the site of Trafford Old Hall, a medieval manor house.

And she says, extrapolating from her own experience, that she does not doubt the local stories of Roman soldiers seen marching on their knees over High Street, a range of hills just to the north of Kendal in the Lake District.

The Roman pavement grips me more than the remote possibility of seeing five spooky lager-louts, and it's definitely more tangible, consisting of two-foot-long slabs of slate turned end-up, laid as wide as the building. "These are not little chippings," Wright says, nor are they cobblestones. It is like a stone wall turned on end. The construction was discovered when a corner of it was excavated in 1923 "and put back not quite as well," Wright says with a chuckle. "The Romans built things to last."

This part of Castle Dairy with the Roman floor was not always roofed. But it was always enclosed, and that probably preserved the Roman road for 20th century tourists. It was originally a walled compound where 12th century soldiers were on guard to "keep their eye on the nosh next door," Wright says. Four hundred years later, the room gained not only a roof and fireplaces, but possibly also Elizabethan revenants whom Wright wishes very much she could see.

Wright does not advertise her ghosts much. For one thing, she's never seen them herself, and besides, she wants her guests to expect good food, not tipsy phantoms. Otherwise, "They're not gonna sit and enjoy the food and the chat," she says. "They're gonna sit and wait for something that might never happen!"

LIQUID LIABILITY
Peter Hough

The inhabitants of a soggy English bungalow wanted to know - Did they have a poltergeist or a plumbing problem?

The spade bit into the soft topsoil, and I didn't know whether to laugh or cry. Here I was, with several fellow investigators, turning over someone's garden when my own was in dire need of a major overhaul. We were acting on information received from a psychic during a vigil at a haunted house. "I'm getting an impression," she said, "of a box, a small box, buried in the garden, behind the shed."

Now we were digging it up, searching for a box about the size and shape of a small coffin. The neighbours looked on and took it all in stride. They didn't ask too many embarrassing questions and they supplied us with beer and coffee.

Unlike on The X-Files, real-life paranormal investigators usually arrive weeks, months, or years after an incident. When I was asked to lead an investigation into a poltergeist case, I never expected to be in the thick of it.

It began when members of the Northern Anomalies Research Organization (NARO) spotted an item in a local newspaper. The story described a family in Rochdale, who were plagued with water dripping from the ceiling of their prefab bungalow. The complaint had been investigated by the council, which was unable to discover the cause.

Investigator Alicia Leigh arranged an interview with the Gardener family. She consulted me, as chairman of NARO, and, with investigator Stephen Mera, we went to the house in Hill Top Close on 31 August, 1995.

Jim Gardener, Vera's second husband, explained what had been happening. "It started about ten months ago when we noticed a damp patch on the wall of the back bedroom." This was occupied by Vera's 33-year-old daughter, Jeanette. "It began to seep water, and we called the housing department. They examined the attic but couldn't find any leaks. We left it, and at first it stopped — then it began on the ceiling."

The Gardeners wondered if the moisture was caused by condensation. They were later astounded when water flashed across the ceiling. "It would start dripping in one place then shoot from corner to corner," Jim said.

The phenomenon ceased in the bedroom and moved to the kitchen. Men from the town council, who rented the bungalow to the Gardeners, re-examined the attic. An electrician dismantled the light fittings while Mr. Gardener watched, sheltering beneath his umbrella. "It was coming down just like rain!"

Because there were no leaking pipes in the attic, the council decided that the explanation was either condensation or fraud.

"Two council officials accused us of turning a hose pipe on the ceiling, so they would move us out," Vera Gardener said. "That's ridiculous! I've lived here 14 years and was perfectly settled until this started. Now I can't wait to leave."

The housing department installed an extraction fan in the kitchen, and then one in the bathroom, because water had begun dripping there, too.

The phenomenon moved back into Jeanette's bedroom for four or five months. The bedding and carpet were regularly wet and had to be dried out. The continual dripping was becoming too much for the family.

They moved Jeanette into the front bedroom. No sooner was this done than it started dripping there. After they complained again to the council, a hygrometer was left overnight to measure the water-vapour content of the air. Officials claimed the results indicated condensation, but Jim disagreed.

"I told them you don't get condensation in the middle of summer,' he said. "Even during the heat wave it's been dripping, and we've been mopping up almost every day!"

Suddenly it stopped, and for a whole week nothing happened. Jeanette moved back into her bedroom. Jim put the carpet back down. Within ten minutes water started dripping from the ceiling.

There were other strange happenings. One evening Jim and Vera watched the handle of the door leading to the hallway turn slowly. When the door swung open no one was there.

The smell of cigarette smoke often pervaded their bedroom, with a distinct aroma of licorice. Jim smoked a pipe, but Vera's first husband, Geoffrey, had smoked cigarettes rolled in licorice papers.

"Last Friday night," Jim related, "we went to bed as normal. There was no one else in the house. We hadn't been in bed ten minutes when we heard a coughing in the corner. I got up and checked through the house, but we couldn't explain it."

At this point the interview was interrupted. Jeanette, who had gone to use the bathroom, reappeared. Her shoulders and hair were wet. We rushed out into the hallway, and saw water dripping from the ceiling near a light fitting.

There was an irregular damp patch some six inches across from where droplets were forming and falling to the carpet. Eighteen inches away was a trap door leading into the attic.

The air in the attic was hot and dry. Dust pirouetted in the yellow beam of the torch as it probed the darkness. The attic was well insulated, but the fiberglass layers were disturbed where council officials had searched for leaking pipes. They had done a thorough job. I removed the insulation from over the place where water was now falling. The attic floor was bone dry. I pulled up some of the surrounding layers but there was no evidence of moisture.

How was it I was standing here, in broad daylight, on a warm summer's day, watching water form and drip from a dry plasterboard ceiling?

But this was only the beginning. Alicia's shoulders had become wet even though she had not been standing under the water dripping from the ceiling. Her body temperature fell suddenly. She complained of a pressure on her chest and became nauseated. After a few minutes she began to recover.

We attempted to resume the interview but Jim called us into the kitchen. "It's started in here now!"

A large area of the ceiling was dripping. Were the Gardeners throwing water about when our backs were turned? Alicia stared incredulously at the open door.

"I saw that the bottom of the door was wet," she said. "As I was about to alert the others, thousands of tiny droplets suddenly, and instantaneously, covered the entire door."

We began to search the house. Water was dripping from the ceiling of the back bedroom and had collected on the walls and door frame.

Once again we continued our interview with the Gardeners, but Stephen who was standing in the doorway behind the living room and the hall suddenly called out to us.

Water had flashed across the ceiling in the hallway, just as Jim Gardener had described. The evidence was there for all to see. In front of the original wet patch was a boomerang-shaped area of moisture which began to drip.

"It was as if the ceiling was the floor, and someone had thrown a cup full of water across it," he said. The phenomenon had defied gravity!

Jeanette called us into the living room where she had been sitting alone. On the wall were several painted masks strung on nails. One of them had apparently fallen off the wall onto a wooden unit, although no one had heard anything. It rested face up, with the nail neatly beside it. Suspicion was cast on Jeanette. Had she pulled the nail out of the wall?

I picked up the nail and found the hole. The plaster around the edges was not cracked as one would expect if the nail had become loose or someone had deliberately waggled it free. In fact, the hole made a tight fit. It would not receive the nail without the aid of a small hammer.

Photographs were taken and samples of the suspect water were collected along with a control sample of tap water. Arrangements were made for a team of investigators to carry out a night-time vigil on the property the following week. The family agreed to leave the premises for the evening.

ANALYSIS AND SPECULATIONS

I made arrangements with North West Water to carry out some tests on the samples. Rather than risk losing them in the post, I drove to the laboratory complex in Cheshire. The results came back a few days later.

In his report, Kevin Platt of North West Water's Customer Support Team said, "While the results for the tap sample are typical for those determinants listed, the suspect sample results are higher except for magnesium. We can only conclude from this that the high results are due to leaching of components from the plaster into the water."

This was a rational conclusion, but one which was not borne out by my own observations. The water was not soaking through the plaster ceiling, but forming on its under surface, on the emulsioned woodchip paper. More research was required.

Alicia contacted British Gypsum to inquire about the contents of plaster. They told her that the main ingredient was calcium sulphate with an insignificant amount of sodium chloride. Crown Wallcoverings told her there were no chemicals in woodchip paper. Dulux, a paint manufacturer, said that emulsion paint contained none of the chemical compounds found by North West Water.

If the water was leaching chemicals from the plasterboard, why did North West Water fail to find traces of sulphate? The indicators were that the phenomenon was not a product of tap water thrown on to the ceiling.

In poltergeist cases there is usually a focus or catalyst. Jeanette was the obvious candidate. From our observations she seemed to have a mental age much younger than her 33 years. The phenomena had begun only ten months before, when Jeanette had moved into the bungalow. We learned that she was at the centre of huge family problems. These had their roots in the past, creating a rift between Jeanette and her late father which had never healed.

There are two explanations commonly accepted for poltergeist activity — one mundane, the other paranormal. In the mundane scenario the subject deliberately creates phenomena in order to attract attention. Many, although not all, of the events we had observed at the Gardener home would have required the aid of other family members.

What would the motive have been? Jim Gardener wanted to move, but until recently Vera and Jeanette had been perfectly happy living in Hill Top Close. We interviewed several neighbours who had witnessed the Gardeners' distress and had examined the attic. They thought the hoax scenario unlikely. Our observations backed up that view. However, later evidence forced us to modify our conclusions slightly.

In the paranormal scenario, phenomena are produced as a direct consequence of negative emotional energy unwittingly created by the focus. Some parapsychologists think that such energy projects from the mind, causing things to happen. Others say that the energy attracts entities which then feed on it. This allows the entity to manifest itself in our world. Could Jeanette's negative state of mind have created a bridge that connected the household with her deceased father?

HELL BREAKS LOOSE

I assembled a team of six investigators for the vigil on 5 September. Alicia, Stephen, and I were joined by fellow NARO investigators Vic Sleigh and Carole Morse, and psychic Valerie Field.

Our team was greeted by Jim and Vera. Jim's son, David, Jeanette's 14-year-old daughter, Ann, and Ann's friend, Susan, were also present. Ann related an incident which had occurred in the front bedroom a few days before our initial interview.

"Me and my friend were looking at some new shoes," Ann said. "She was lying on the floor when a hair dryer left the dressing table, flew around the room, then smacked her on the head!"

Susan confirmed this. We learned of a number of things that had happened since our first visit. The previous Saturday night Jeanette had entered the house and made for the bathroom. As she walked past the open doorway of the back bedroom a picture had shot across the room and had hit the wall.

Vera claimed that objects had levitated. "I went in the kitchen and a pair of scissors floated off the table, over my head, and fell into the sink," she said. "Some knives and forks near the microwave rose and fell onto the floor. Jeanette was so frightened she screamed and wouldn't come back into the house."

Vera, Jim, and David reported being hit by objects and told us of a strong smell of "licorice tobacco" in the front bedroom where Ann was sleeping. Vera also described seeing the lampshade in the hallway swinging like a pendulum. Something kept interfering with a radio alarm clock, plugging and unplugging it when their backs were turned.

The taps in the bathroom turned on of their own accord, and the soap tray shot upward and struck Ann. This was witnessed by Susan's brother, Andrew. The last thing to happen, just hours before our arrival, was the appearance of a key in the centre of the bed in the back room — and the lampshade had started swinging again.

WINGS OF JUSTICE

The family left and we were alone in the building. Armed with tape recorders, two video recorders, still cameras, note pad, and a thermometer, we paired off, each couple positioning themselves in one of the primary areas of the bungalow. While we were setting up the equipment, Stephen made a video record of the position of objects around the house.

At 9:45 p.m. the vigil began. Alicia and Stephen were in the living room. From there they could see into the kitchen and out into the hallway. Vic and Carole were in the back bedroom, allowing them to view the hall, and Valerie and I were in the front bedroom, facing the open doorway. Audio and video recorders were running, and still cameras were at the ready.

Just after 10 p.m. we heard Alicia cry out, "How did that get there? Where did that come from?" The four of us rushed into the living room. Stephen was standing near the video camera looking bemused. Alicia was sitting in an armchair near the kitchen doorway, pointing at a bronze statuette on the carpet.

"I was looking into the kitchen," she gasped. "As I turned my head to make a comment to Steve, I saw the statuette standing on the floor near the television set. I swear it wasn't there moments before!"

"Great!" I said. "It must be on film."

Stephen shook his head and looked embarrassed.

"I was fiddling with the camera, and unfortunately it was pointing toward the hallway at the time," he said.

Sceptics scoff at moments like this, but I know too well that it is typical for equipment to malfunction at vital moments. The fact that the statuette appeared the instant the camera was turned away was not surprising, but it was frustrating.

I picked up the small bronze figure and examined it. It depicted a robed woman with her left arm raised, the other holding a sword. "Themis" was inscribed on the base. In Greek mythology, she was the daughter of Uranus and Gaia, and the wife of Zeus. Themis was the goddess of law and justice. What justice was being meted out in this troubled house? The raised left arm should have held a pair of scales, but they were missing.

Where had she come from? Valerie and Alicia were sure they had seen the figure on top of the television on their arrival at the house. Indeed, there was a space where the goddess would fit, yet the icon obviously had not fallen off the set. We resumed our stations.

The next incident occurred just after 11:30 p.m. Valerie and I were in the back bedroom. Stephen was standing in the doorway talking to us when suddenly his expression changed and he looked alarmed. He had heard Alicia speak his name, as if she had been right behind him. But Alicia had not moved from the front bedroom.

Exactly an hour later, Carole was in the hallway. We all clearly heard her shout to Vic, who, like Alicia earlier, was in the front bedroom.

"I heard a man's voice over my right shoulder," she told us. "It sounded as if it was coming over a police radio, so I couldn't make out what he was saying." She had thought she was hearing Vic tuning in a radio.

The hallway was a focus for activity. The three women and I detected the fragrant smell of hyacinths there. Later Carole, Valerie,

Alicia, and Stephen experienced the sensation of fine rain on their exposed hands and faces.

The final incident occurred at 3 a.m. Stephen went into the back bedroom to talk to Carole and Valerie. He sat on the end of the bed beside Valerie, who suggested they switch off the light and sit quietly in the subdued illumination from the hallway.

Stephen and Carole heard someone wheezing and leaned forward to confer. The sound had come from the top of the bed as if someone were lying there. Ironically, Valerie heard nothing.

Moments later Stephen arched his back and complained something had "flicked" him. He left hurriedly for the living room, where Alicia and I examined a red blotch above his waist, which faded after ten minutes.

During the night Valerie reported a number of impressions and images that had entered her mind. She reported in detail a violent incident that had befallen Jeanette, and she accurately pinpointed a number of emotional pressure points in the family. It was also then that she told us about the possibility of a box buried in the garden behind the house.

When Vera and Jim returned the following morning, we were able to make sense of some of the incidents that had occurred during the night.

Stephen and Carole had heard laboured breathing, and it turned out that Vera's first husband, Geoffrey, had been a chronic asthmatic.

When Carole heard a man's voice over a radio, she assumed it was connected with the police, but the revelation that Geoffrey had been a taxi driver put this in a new light.

Geoffrey had collapsed and died in the hallway after a massive heart attack. Was this why so much activity was centred there?

Vera told us the statuette of Themis had been a present from Geoffrey. She said it was normally displayed on a stand to one side of the television. When I told her that Valerie and Alicia thought they had seen it on top of the television, Vera said they must have been mistaken. She added that it had been displayed there when Geoffrey was alive, but had been moved to its new position three weeks before our arrival.

So how had Themis materialized on the carpet? Not by falling, surely. The statuette was too far from the television, and the investigators would have heard something. The goddess was standing upright, facing Alicia, her cold, empty fist clenched.

We studied Stephen's video record. His initial sweep through the house would surely show whether the statuette had been on the television or beside it. Imagine our surprise when we found that the tape showed no trace of the statuette at all! Where on Earth — or beyond — had it been?

All indications were that Jeanette's arrival at the bungalow ten months earlier had aroused the wrath of her deceased father. Certainly many of the phenomena pointed strongly in this direction.

Were the strange happenings in the house Geoffrey's attempts at communication? Water is a purifying symbol. Themis is the goddess of law and justice. Was Geoffrey telling the family to sort out their problems and purge themselves of the past? Or was he just hell bent on making life miserable? According to Vera, he had not been the nicest of men.

FAKERY UNCOVERED

Not long after our vigil, the council agreed to move the family to another part of Rochdale. We kept in touch with Jim and Vera and they assured us that they were happy in their new home and that nothing odd had happened. Then Vera told us that things had started flying across the room when Jeanette was present. Had Geoffrey followed them across town?

The team went to the new address and carried out another vigil. But we found no funny smells, disembodied voices, materialization of objects, or mysterious dripping water.

Things seemed only to happen at the new address when Jeanette was present. Vera and Jim agreed to let the team set up their video cameras in the house while the family went about their normal day-to-day routine.

The team began to suspect that Jeanette was directly responsible when Alicia saw her deliberately knock a picture off the wall leading upstairs. What happened later stunned everyone. Jeanette and Vera were in the kitchen preparing a meal when Vera screamed. At the same time a smashing sound was heard. Jim and the investigators ran into the room and found Jeanette standing there nonplussed, while Vera was gasping and in shock. The broken remains of several pot ornaments which had stood on the window sill lay broken around the trembling woman.

According to Vera, while she was bent down looking in the

refrigerator, her back to the window, the pots had come flying across the room at her. Fortunately there was a video camera pointing through the open doorway of the kitchen at the time. The team eagerly left the house looking forward to viewing the film.

Whether Jeanette thought the camera was not operating because it was unmanned, or whether she just did not care, no one knows. But the evidence was captured on film. She had waited for her moment, then swept her hand over the sill, sending its contents across the room. We had no choice but to let Vera and Jim view the evidence.

Does this invalidate the entire case? Of course not. Like Rochdale there are other cases on file, like the famous Enfield poltergeist, where people were caught cheating. But like Enfield, phenomena were recorded and experienced at Rochdale which could not have been trickery. Sometimes, especially where adolescents are involved, the focus enjoys the attention of investigators and manufactures phenomena in order to maintain their interest. However, this should not detract from the overall case, and certainly in Rochdale things occurred which defy a mundane explanation.

With any investigation there are always pieces that do not fit. We never did find that box buried in the garden. Then again, perhaps we should have dug deeper.

LORD DOWDING'S RETURN

A departed British war hero who believed in life after death is still doing his best to prove it.

J.J. Snyder

In the summer of 1940, the British Royal Air Force Fighter Command won the Battle of Britain. Fighting overwhelming odds, they saved their country from Nazi domination by defeating the German Luftwaffe in a series of hard-fought air engagements over the threatened islands.

The head of Fighter Command during those desperate times was Air Chief Marshal Hugh Dowding, a long-time pilot and and brilliant air combat strategist. One of Britain's earliest airmen, Dowding began flying in 1913 and had been wounded on a combat mission during World War I.

That spring, Dowding had faced down Winston Churchill and, after a heated argument, persuaded the prime minister not to send the few remaining fighter aircraft of the RAF to France in what would have been a fruitless attempt to reinforce the British Expeditionary Force. Even though Dowding's strategy eventually led to England's victory in the Battle of Britain, Churchill still held bitter feelings toward him. Soon after the Nazi air blitz faltered, the prime minister, with the help of Dowding's detractors, saw to it that the Air Chief Marshal was removed from his post.

Dowding was disappointed that political animosity had removed any further opportunity of serving his country, but he bore Churchill and the others no ill will. In retirement, he turned to exploring and writing on a subject that had long been of interest to him.

This less-known but highly meaningful aspect of Dowding's life was his dedication to communicating with the dead. He was especially drawn to making contact with "his boys" — RAF pilots and air crew who had made the supreme sacrifice for king and country.

Dowding's two books, *Many Mansions* and *Lychgate*, which present hard evidence for the continuity of all life, are classics of survival literature. During and after the war, he travelled throughout the country, speaking about his many contacts with those in the astral realms. In these appearances, he offered what he considered irrefutable proof of existence beyond the physical life.

Dowding cautioned his audiences not to accept his evidence solely on the basis of his fame. He told them instead to employ their own reason and intellect when examining the possibility of life beyond physical death. He thought that any rational, unbiased person would come to see the truth on the strength of the verifiable facts.

In 1970, after a long and distinguished mortal life, Lord Dowding departed for the etheric world he knew so well. Since his passing, he has communicated several times with the physical level he left behind. His most recent contact, on 15 September, 1996, is perhaps the most compelling.

AN ANNIVERSARY APPEARANCE
The date is important, for it marked the culmination of the 1940 Nazi air assault against Britain. It was on this day that the forces of Fighter Command were stretched to their thinnest. 15 September — Battle of Britain Day — is celebrated throughout the United Kingdom. It is surely no coincidence that Dowding chose to appear on that date 56 years later at a session conducted by the Noah's Ark Society.

The NAS is a British organization dedicated to promoting and developing physical mediumship as a means of proving the survival of personality beyond death. To this end the Society has sponsored numerous events to initiate and verify communication between the physical and etheric planes. Lord Dowding's materialization at the NAS seminar in Cardiff, was one of the best documented in the history of these events. Dowding made his appearance through Colin Fry, a gifted psychic medium. Although the proceedings were held in total darkness (a condition mediums feel is more conducive to materializations than a lighted room), Dowding reportedly was seen, touched, and spoken to by many people.

Although hearing voices and making visual contact with inhabitants of etheric regions are rather common, full physical materialization, during which mortals are able to touch and feel the etherians, is relatively rare. Even so, it has been studied extensively and verified by a number of respected scientists, including Sir William Crookes, Professor Charles Richet, and Sir John Logie Baird. Modern researchers are also conducting experiments to learn more about this phenomenon.

Reports submitted by scientists who have investigated these events indicate that full materialization is usually accomplished through a specially talented medium — one who can enable the finer subatomic structure and higher frequencies of the discarnates to coalesce into the coarser vibrations of this mortal plane. When this occurs, the etherian becomes visible and may be touched and communicated with by those present. Spontaneous materializations — occurring with no medium present — have also been recorded, usually involving people who were close to each other on the physical plane.

At his own request, Colin Fry was securely tied and strapped to his chair, which was located in a cabinet constructed of black cloth. Tying and strapping the medium is a common practice in materialization experiments, which can be open to charges of fraud and deceit, especially when conducted in total darkness. Binding the medium tightly and noting and photographing the position and type of knots and straps before and after the session provide evidence that the medium has not moved while the lights are out.

A recording of the session was made by the NAS. At the beginning, Dowding can be heard uttering the words "jolly nice" a number of times. Although he was in his late eighties when he transitioned, his voice has the timbre of a middle-aged man.

LORD DOWDING APPEARS

After touching several of the participants, Dowding tapped and rattled the two microphones placed on either side of the room. Then, in an imitation of Lord HawHaw, the notorious English traitor whose propaganda broadcasts were transmitted to Britain during the war, he said "Germany calling, Germany calling" several times. These were the opening words of Haw Haw's broadcasts. Those in the audience were unaware the personality which had just materialized was Lord Dowding. He at first refused to reveal his identity. Urged to make himself known, he finally stated, probably some of you know of me ... Dowding." He continued shaking hands. When told that he might write a page on a piece of paper that had been placed on the floor, he declared the last time he wrote on the floor was at the age of three, when he drew pictures of birds in flight. Then, seemingly to express regret for his part in a terrible war, he said that "to learn to soar in the skies, to be free like a bird, is an honorable thing. But the only things that birds drop on us don't blow people to pieces ... and that is my shame."

Dowding was then questioned as to whether those who caused him to be removed from his post, many of whom were now presumably discarnate, had become aware of what they had done.

"They probably are," he said, "but it doesn't make a damn bit of difference to them Offended sensibilities are in the end only bloody arrogance. If you can behave better toward those who are at odds it makes you a better person, doesn't Above all else have honour. If you behave honourably toward other people, it really doesn't matter how they behave toward you."

He continued moving through the crowd, touching those present and shaking hands. He recognized one woman and noted that he had spoken with her many times before.

Having known Dowding during the war, the woman confirmed the apparition's identity. She said that he displayed his keen sense of humour, of which she had firsthand knowledge.

Her statement is important, since only those who were close to Dowding are aware of this facet of his personality. Although his public image was that of a stiff, correct military officer — his RAF nickname was "Stuffy" — his friends knew and appreciated his quick, dry wit. Upon parting with the lady, Dowding kissed her hand, a sound clearly audible to the gathering.

In his closing words, Dowding once again voiced deep regret for the tragedy of World War II.

"Don't look to past victories," he said. "Pain, suffering, and unnecessary bloodshed, even one drop of blood or one life lost to our side is no victory — just awful, hideous defeat. I'm sorry I couldn't touch you all, but I hope that I can touch you with my heart."

In answer to a "God bless you" from a member of the audience, he replied, "No, God bless you, my friends. You are the ones still in the battle. I would have rather played a more valuable role in a more honourable game." He then said goodbye and left.

One of the many present who shook hands with Lord Dowding was NAS committee member Geoff Hughes, who noted that the etheric Air Marshal shook his hand "quite hard." Dowding also walked behind the back row and patted people on the shoulder as he passed.

The large number of witnesses who observed this remarkable event, and the similarity of their accounts of what occurred, as well as the audio recording, seem to make it one of the most convincing materializations on record. It is hoped that Lord Dowding will see fit to return to this mortal level and perhaps allow himself to be photographed by infrared camera and videotape, which should be compatible with the total-darkness requirement for materialization. If this happens, and the tapes and photos match witnesses' testimony, it will be a telling refutation of those who deny the continuity of life.